THE HISTORY OF
THE ALBIGENSIAN CRUSADE

THE HISTORY OF
THE ALBIGENSIAN CRUSADE

Peter of les Vaux-de-Cernay's
Historia Albigensis

Translated by
W. A. and M. D. Sibly

THE BOYDELL PRESS

First published 1998
The Boydell Press, Woodbridge

ISBN 0 85115 658 4

The Boydell Press is an imprint of Boydell and Brewer Ltd
PO Box 9, Woodbridge, Suffolk IP12 3DF, UK
and of Boydell and Brewer Inc.
PO Box 41026, Rochester, NY 14604–4126, USA

A catalogue record for this book is available
from the British Library

Library of Congress Cataloging-in-Publication Data
Petrus, Sarnensis, d. 1218.
    [Historia Albigensis. English]
    The history of the Albigensian Crusade / Peter of les Vaux-de-Cernay ;
    translated by W.A. and M.D. Sibly.
        p.   cm.
    Includes bibliographical references and index.
    ISBN 0–85115–658–4 (alk. paper)
    1. Albigenses – Source. 2. Theology – Early works to 1800.
    3. Heresies, Christian – France – Languedoc – History – Middle Ages,
    600–1500 – Sources. 4. France – Church history – 987–1515 – Sources.
    I. Title.
    BX4890.P3813   1998
    272'.3 – dc21   97–49978

This publication is printed on acid-free paper

Printed in Great Britain by
St Edmundsbury Press Ltd, Bury St Edmunds, Suffolk

CONTENTS

PREFACE

Whilst a few isolated passages of the *Historia Albigensis* of Peter of les Vaux-de-Cernay have appeared in English,[1] there has never been a translation of the full text. Our primary purpose in preparing this edition of the *Historia* has thus been to provide a readable but accurate translation of the work into modern English.

Through our footnotes, we have also sought to provide detailed references to other sources, both narrative and documentary, and to some of the main secondary works which consider the events covered in the *Historia*. Our aims have been to amplify Peter's account where possible; to draw attention to and discuss events not covered by Peter; and to clarify the order of events when Peter's chronology is confused. In addition, we have included in the appendices translations of some ancillary documents so as to make available to English readers important material which complements Peter's narrative.

Like anyone approaching Peter's history, we are immensely indebted to the edition of the *Historia* prepared by Pascal Guébin and Ernest Lyon, which provides a definitive Latin text with full *apparatus criticus*, and copious general notes. We are grateful to Malcolm Barber of the University of Reading for his interest in this work. Charles Coulson commented on a draft of Appendix A. Janet Barlow kindly gave advice on certain passages in the *Chanson*, although her translation of it appeared too late for us in general to use it. Gloria Mundy typed most of the first draft of the translation, and Jane Watkinson likewise some of the appendices. Christine Elliott gave us expert help with wordprocessing, and prepared the family trees. Lesley Collett of the Oxford Archaeological Unit drew the maps. Caroline Palmer and Pru Harrison at Boydell & Brewer have also offered valued advice. We are grateful to these and others who have helped us, but are of course ourselves responsible for any errors which remain.

Finally, we would like to thank Mary Sibly for her forebearance over the long period during which this translation has been in preparation; Barbara Fawcett for her help; Anne Sibly for her support throughout this and all else, and also for reading the whole of the book in typescript and proof; and Lydia and William Sibly for putting up with 'daddy and grandad's book'. Elizabeth Sibly was born shortly after the arrival of the proofs.

---

[1] See Wakefield and Evans, pp. 235–41; E. Hallam, *Chronicles of the Crusades* (London, 1989), pp. 228–9, 234–6; and W. E. Wakefield, *Heresy Crusade and Inquisition in Southern France 1100–1250* (London, 1974), Appendix 2, pp. 200–204 (which unfortunately contains three significant errors).

ABBREVIATIONS

Belperron	P. Belperron, *La Croisade contre les Albigeois et l'union de Languedoc à la France (1209–1249)* (Paris, 1942)
Cahiers de Fanjeaux	Vol. 1: *Saint Dominique en Languedoc* (Toulouse, 1966)
	Vol. 2: *Vaudois languedociens et Pauvres Catholiques* (Toulouse, 1967)
	Vol. 3: *Cathares en Languedoc* (Toulouse, 1968)
	Vol. 4: *Paix de Dieu et guerre sainte en Languedoc au XIIIème siècle* (Toulouse, 1969)
	Vol. 21: *Les Cisterciens en Languedoc* (Toulouse, 1986)
CAML	Centre d'Archéologie Médiévale du Languedoc
Catel	Guillaume de Catel, *Histoire des comtes de Toulouse* (Toulouse, 1623)
Chanson	*La Chanson de la croisade albigeoise*, trans. and ed. E. Martin-Chabot, 3 vols. (Paris 1931, 1957, 1961) (cited by volume, laisse number and page number)
G&L	*Petri Vallium Sarnaii monachi Hystoria albigensis*, eds. Pascal Guébin and Ernest Lyon, 3 vols. (Paris, 1926, 1930, 1939) (the Latin text of the *Historia*)
G&M	*Histoire albigeoise*, trans. Pascal Guébin and Henri Maisonneuve (Paris, 1951) (translation into French of the *Historia*)
Glossarium	*Glossarium Mediae et Infimae Latinitatis*, eds. Du Cange et al. (Niort and London, 1884)
Griffe, *Croisade*	E. Griffe, *Le Languedoc cathare au temps de la Croisade* (Paris, 1973)
Griffe, *Débuts*	E. Griffe, *Les débuts de l'aventure cathare en Languedoc (1140–1190)* (Paris, 1969)
Griffe, *LC*	E. Griffe, *Le Languedoc cathare de 1190 à 1210* (Paris, 1971)
HGL	*Histoire générale de Languedoc*, eds. Claude Devic and J. Vaissète, vols. V, VI, VII, and VIII, Edition Privat in 16 vols. (Toulouse, 1872 onwards) (cited by volume and column number unless otherwise indicated)
Itinerario	J. Miret y Sans, *Itinerario del Rey Pedro I de Cataluna, II en Aragon*, in *Boletin de la Real Academia de Buenas Letras de Barcelona*, vol. IV (Barcelona, 1907–1908)
Lambert	M. Lambert, *Medieval Heresy: Popular Movements from the Gregorian Reform to the Reformation* (Oxford, 1992)
Layettes	*Layettes du Trésor des Chartres*, ed. A. Teulet (Paris, 1863–66) (cited by volume and column number)

Lexicon	*Lexicon Manuale ad Scriptores Mediae et Infimae Latinitatis*, ed. W.-H. Maigne d'Arnis (Paris, 1890)
Llibre dels feyts	*The Chronicle of James I, King of Aragon, surnamed the Conqueror (written by himself)*, trans. J. Forster (London, 1883)
Mansi	*Sacrorum conciliorum nova et amplissima collectio*, ed. J. D. Mansi (Florence, Venice and Paris, 1799 onwards)
Molinier	*Catalogue des actes de Simon et Amaury de Montfort*, ed. A. Molinier, Bibliothèque de l'Ecole des Chartres (Paris, 1873)
Niermayer	*Mediae Latinitatis Lexicon Minus*, ed. J. F. Niermeyer (Leiden, 1976)
PL	*Patrologiae . . . Latina (Patrologiae cursus completus . . . ab aevo apostolico ad tempora Innocentii III, anno 1216 . . . series Latina)*, ed. J.-P. Migne et al., 221 vols. (Paris, 1844–64) (quoted by volume and column numbers)
Potthast	*Regesta pontificorum romanorum*, ed. A. Potthast, 2 vols. (Berlin, 1875)
Pressutti	*Regesta Honorii papae III*, ed. P. Pressutti, 2 vols. (Rome, 1888–95)
Rhein	*Les actes des seigneurs de Montfort*, in *La Seigneurie de Montfort en Iveline*, ed. A. Rhein, Mémoires de la Société archéologique de Rambouillet, vol. XXV (Versailles, 1910)
RHGF	*Recueil des Historiens des Gaules et de la France*, ed. Dom Bouquet et al. (1871 onwards)
Roquebert I	M. Roquebert, *L'epopée cathare 1198–1212: l'Invasion* (Toulouse, 1970)
Roquebert II	M. Roquebert, *L'epopée cathare 1213–1216: Muret ou la dépossession* (Toulouse, 1977)
Roquebert III	M. Roquebert, *L'epopée cathare 1216–1229: Le lys et la croix* (Toulouse, 1986)
Roquebert IV	M. Roquebert, *L'epopée cathare: Mourir à Montségur* (Toulouse, 1989)
Vicaire	M.-H. Vicaire, *Saint Dominic and his Times*, trans. K. Pond (London, 1964) (English translation of *Histoire de Saint Dominique*, 2 vols. (Paris, 1957))
Wakefield and Evans	*Heresies of the High Middle Ages*, eds. W. E. Wakefield and A. P. Evans (New York, 1969, 1991)
William of Puylaurens	*Chronica Magistri Guillelmi de Podio Laurentii*, ed. and trans. into French by J. Duvernoy (Paris, 1976) (earlier writers quote by reference to page numbers in the edition by J. Beyssier in *Troisièmes mélanges d'histoire du moyen âge*, ed. A. Luchaire (Paris, 1904); this uses chapter heading XVII twice)
William of Tudela	author of the first part of the *Chanson*, see above

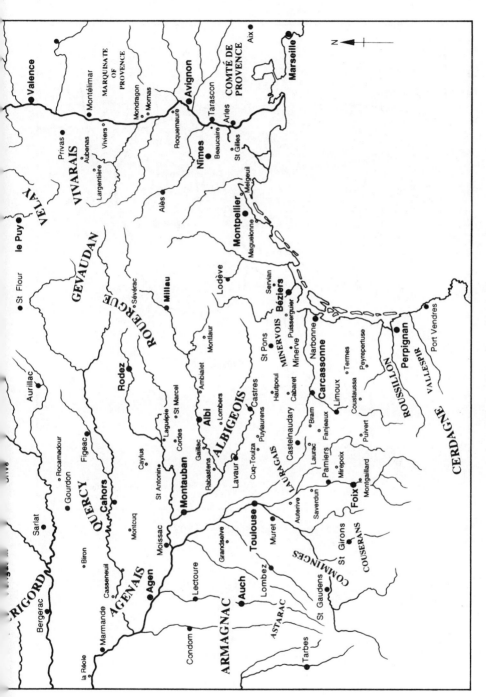

Map 1. The Midi in the early 13th century

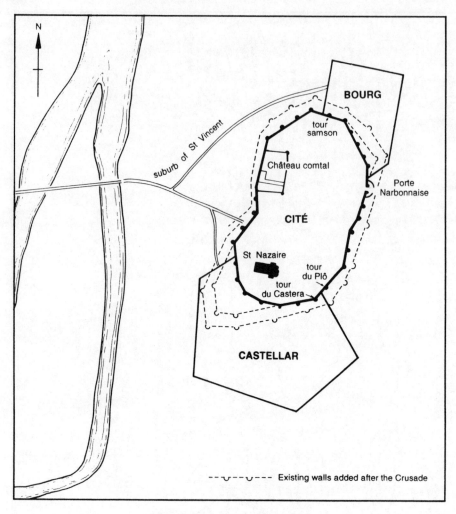

N

BOURG

tour
samson

Château comtal

Porte
Narbonnaise

CITÉ

suburb of St Vincent

St Nazaire

tour
du Plô

tour
du Castera

CASTELLAR

– – ᴖ – – ᴖ – – – Existing walls added after the Crusade

Map 2. Carcassonne in 1209

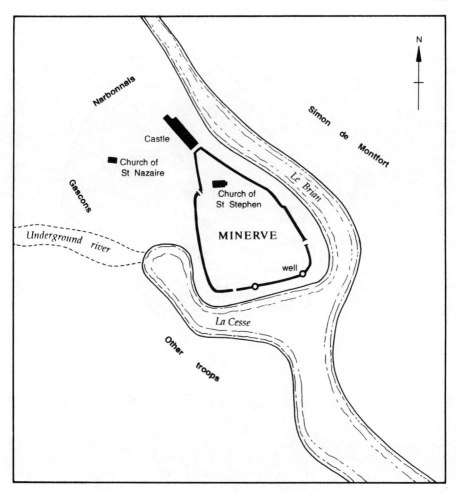

Map 3. Minerve in 1210

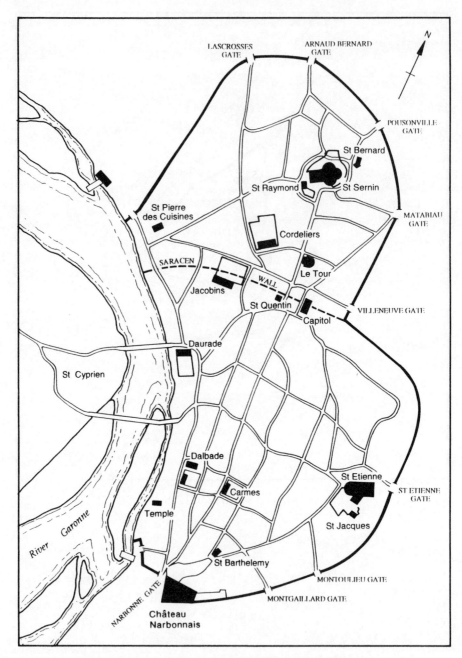

Map 4. Toulouse in the early 13th century

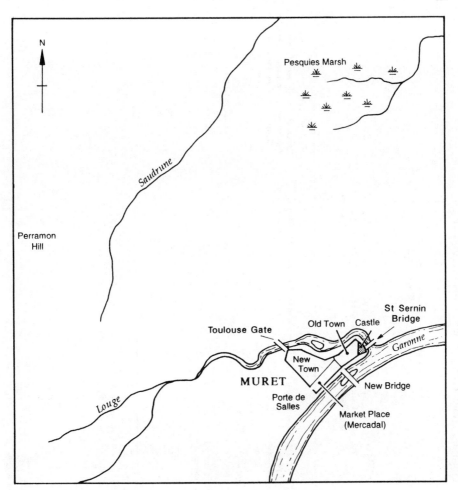

Map 5. Muret at the time of the Crusade

Outline Family Tree 1: The Counts of Toulouse

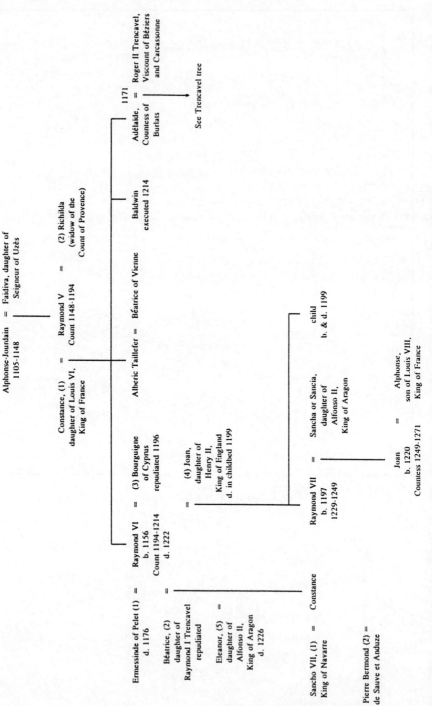

Note: for the wives of Raymond VI, see §38 and notes. He had several illegitimate children, including the daughter who married Hugh d'Alfaro (n. 72 to §319).

Outline Family Tree 2: The family of Simon de Montfort

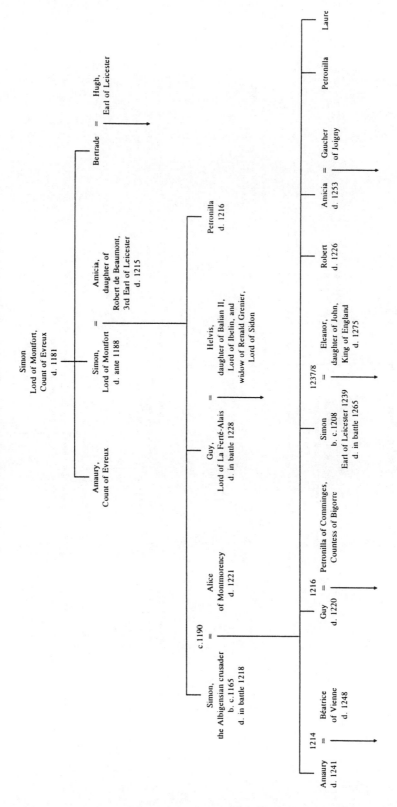

Simon
Lord of Montfort,
Count of Evreux
d. 1181

Amaury,
Count of Evreux

Simon,
Lord of Montfort
d. ante 1188
=
Amicia,
daughter of
Robert de Beaumont,
3rd Earl of Leicester
d. 1215

Bertrade = Hugh,
Earl of Leicester

Simon,
the Albigensian crusader
b. c. 1165
d. in battle 1218
= c.1190
Alice
of Montmorency
d. 1221

Guy,
Lord of La Ferté-Alais
d. in battle 1228
=
Helvis,
daughter of Balian II,
Lord of Ibelin, and
widow of Renald Grenier,
Lord of Sidon

Petronilla
d. 1216

Amaury
d. 1241
= 1214
Béatrice
of Vienne
d. 1248

Guy
d. 1220
= 1216
Petronilla of Comminges,
Countess of Bigorre

Simon
b. c. 1208
Earl of Leicester 1239
d. in battle 1265
= 1237/8
Eleanor,
daughter of John,
King of England
d. 1275

Robert
d. 1226

Amicia
d. 1253
= Gaucher
of Joigny

Petronilla

Laure

Outline Family Tree 3: The Trencavels

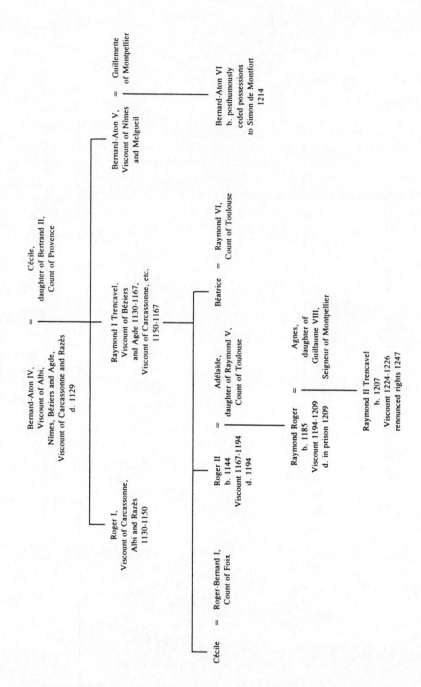

INTRODUCTION

The general background

Peter of les Vaux-de-Cernay's *Historia Albigensis* is one of the principal sources of evidence for the origins and first ten years of the Albigensian Crusade. It was written in stages between about 1212 and 1218, and is thus largely contemporary with the events which it covers. It begins with an account of the preaching campaign in the south of France[1] against the Cathar and Waldensian heresies which was organised by Pope Innocent III during the years 1203–08, and includes a description of the main features of Catharism. It then provides a detailed narrative of the Crusade launched in 1208–09 by Innocent against the heretics and those amongst the aristocracy of the South who were seen as their protectors. The narrative continues in varying degrees of detail until, shortly after an account of the death in June 1218 of Simon de Montfort (until then the leader of the Crusade), the *Historia* ends abruptly with a brief account of events in the winter of 1218–19.

The author of the *Historia* was a young monk at the Cistercian abbey of les Vaux-de-Cernay, about 35km to the south-west of Paris, where his uncle Guy had been Abbot since at least 1181. Guy was one of those Cistercian abbots who took part in the preaching mission against heresy in the South in 1207. He later played an important part in the Crusade, and in 1212 became Bishop of Carcassonne. Peter accompanied his uncle to the South in 1212–13, and again in later years (see below). As a result he was not only brought into personal contact with those involved in the events he narrates, but himself witnessed many of them.

The abbey of les Vaux-de-Cernay had close connections with the family of Simon de Montfort, whose family seat was nearby. De Montfort was chosen to lead the Crusade after the fall of Carcassonne to the crusaders in August 1209. Peter knew him well, and his admiration for him permeates his writing. Because of this, and because Peter's main sources of information about the history of these years came from the crusaders and their allies, the *Historia* is written very much from the point of view of the crusaders in general and of Simon de Montfort in particular. Peter's hero de Montfort is '*comes noster*', 'our Count', '*athleta Christi*', the 'athlete of Christ' (§§509, 541, 579), the '*miles (Jhesu) Christi*', 'knight of Jesus Christ' (§§454, 463, 610/2), while the crusaders are '*nostri*', 'our men'. Those who oppose the Crusade are portrayed in the worst possible light, usually branded as heretics or supporters of heresy, acting from base motives. Peter especially loathed Raymond VI, Count of Toulouse (who became the main target of the Crusade), and Count Raymond-Roger of Foix, and

---

[1] Hereafter referred to as 'the South' or 'the Midi' or 'Languedoc'; see Appendix A on '*Provincia*'.

the *Historia* abounds with denunciations of them and with details of their alleged iniquities. They are the agents of Satan in what is portrayed as an almost Manichean struggle between good and evil – which may now seem ironic, given the dualist beliefs of the Cathars whom Peter so detested.

These features of the *Historia* contribute both to its strengths and its shortcomings. Its strengths derive from Peter's personal involvement, and its shortcomings from his prejudices and the one-sidedness of his approach. His account of many episodes is detailed and, where it can be checked against other sources, is usually found to be accurate. It is also vivid, reflecting its author's first-hand knowledge of many of the people and places involved. But Peter was also thoroughly partisan, and because events are recounted solely from the point of view of the crusaders, we gain little if any insight into the motives and attitudes of those against whom the Crusade was directed, and some aspects – notably diplomatic developments – are only partly covered. Overall, however, while Peter of les Vaux-de-Cernay writes very much from the perspective of one side he is not deliberately untruthful, and he provides a lively narrative of events which is an invaluable source for the period he covers.

The remainder of this Introduction sets out the approach taken to preparing this edition; considers the author's life and the style and composition of the *Historia*; discusses in more detail the value of the *Historia* as a source; and offers a brief account of the historical background to the Crusade.

The text and the translation

This translation is based on the Latin text of the *Historia* given in the threevolume edition prepared by Pascal Guébin and Ernest Lyon (hereafter G&L).[2] The first two volumes of this edition contain the Latin text. The third discusses Peter's life, his approach to writing the *Historia*, and the manuscripts and their history; it also considers previous French editions and translations, and contains some ancillary documents, or *pièces annexes*. G&L's edition is accompanied by a full *apparatus criticus* and copious general notes. At no point have we felt it necessary to follow an alternative reading of the manuscripts, although occasionally we have drawn attention in our footnotes to variants. We have also consulted the French translation by Guébin and Henri Maisonneuve, published in 1951 (hereafter G&M), and have relied on this work especially for the rendering of Latin place names into their French equivalents. G&M's translation includes some short passages in §§592–7 which appear only in some of the manuscripts and which are not given by G&L in the main body of their Latin text. We have included translations of these passages in square brackets in our text, although it seems to us on stylistic grounds that they are unlikely to have been written by Peter.

---

2 For full bibliographical references to this and other works cited in this Introduction see the list of Abbreviations, above.

In his introduction (§4) Peter says that he has divided his work into parts to help the reader (*'per varias distinctiones digestum est opus istud'*). It is not entirely clear what he meant by '*distinctiones*', but he may simply be referring back to §3, where he writes of three main divisions of the work, concerning the heretics (§§5–19), the preachers (§§20–54) and the Crusade (§§55 to the end). G&L's edition prints headings at the beginning of these three divisions, in square brackets but without further comment (*'Pars prima: de hereticis'*, *'Pars secunda: de predicatoribus'*, and *'Pars tertia: de crucesignatis'*).

The division of the *Historia* into what we have called sections (§§1–620) was introduced by G&L. These 620 sections have become established as the standard basis for reference purposes, and are used as such in cross-referencing throughout this edition. The manuscripts give rubrics at the beginnings of many of these sections (printed in italics in this translation), but they occur in widely different forms in different manuscripts, and are thus clearly not part of Peter's original work. We have also ourselves, for the reader's convenience, divided the translation into eighteen parts (numbered I–XVIII) of varying length, each headed with a short summary of the main topics covered (given in square brackets) and each with its own set of numbered footnotes.[3]

As indicated in our Preface, we have set out to produce a version of the *Historia* in readable modern English which although not literal seeks accurately to convey the sense of the original. The following additional points may be noted.

Peter and his sources draw frequently on the Bible (sometimes there are whole sentences, sometimes mere echoes) and here we have generally followed the words of the Authorised (King James) Version. We have drawn attention to many but by no means all of these biblical references in our footnotes; full references are given in both G&L and G&M.

For personal names we have usually used French forms except (somewhat arbitrarily) where an English form seemed more natural. There is a variety of practices followed by both French and English writers in rendering certain names: thus the Abbot of Cîteaux, whose name in Latin is Arnaldus Amalricus, is given by us as Arnold Amalric; by the French as Arnaud-Amaury; and by some English writers as Arnold Aimery. We have sometimes given female names as ending in 'a', whereas the modern French form usually ends in 'e' (thus Petronilla rather than Pétronille), and have tended to give contemporary personal names in a form closer to their original rather than the modern French form (thus Giraud rather than Guiraud). For place names we have normally used the modern French form.

Peter usually dates events by reference to Feast Days, in so far as he is precise, and we have translated these as they stand, giving the modern date in a footnote. Like his contemporaries, he regarded the New Year as beginning in the spring, usually on 25 March (Lady Day), not on 1 January. We have modernised Peter's

---

[3] To provide a convenient synopsis of the content of the *Historia* as a whole these summaries are reproduced on pp. 2–4.

dates in this regard and indicated in a footnote where we have done so. Occasionally Peter dates events by the Roman Calendar (see n. 45 to §65); we have indicated such cases but translated using a modern date. Letters emanating from the Papal Chancery always use the Roman system of dating (where a date is given), and we have modernised these.

As regards coinage and money, the units usually referred to in the *Historia* are in Latin *librae, solidi*, and *denarii*. We have given these in their French forms as *livres, sous* and *deniers*.

The notes and appendices

The footnotes and appendices to this translation draw attention to the gaps in Peter's account, and to the other sources which can be used to fill them, and refer to a limited range of modern secondary literature which discusses the events narrated by Peter with close reference to the sources.

Other contemporary or near-contemporary narrative sources which are especially relevant to the period covered by the *Historia* are the *Chronica* (Chronicle) of William of Puylaurens, also written in Latin, and the *Chanson de la croisade albigeoise*, written in a form of Provençal.

There is no English edition of William of Puylaurens, and citations are made by reference to the 1976 edition (which includes a parallel French translation) of Jean Duvernoy. We have at times quoted from it in translation, and have included in Appendix I a full translation of its account of the battle of Muret. For the *Chanson*, we have used the three-volume edition of E. Martin-Chabot, which likewise has a parallel translation into modern French, together with full and very helpful notes. Volume I contains the first part of the *Chanson*, written by William of Tudela, and covering the years 1204 to mid-1213. Volumes II and III contain the continuation by an anonymous poet, probably a Toulousain, covering mid-1213 to mid-1219. We have frequently drawn attention to the evidence of the *Chanson* in our notes, but as there is now an English translation by Janet Barlow[4] we have generally been more sparing in quoting extracts, except notably in Appendix B on the massacre at Béziers and in our notes on Peter's account of the battle of Muret in §§446 ff. For the main events from the Fourth Lateran Council onwards the *Chanson*'s account is much more detailed than Peter's and it is the principal narrative source. We have therefore referred the reader to the *Chanson* rather than attempting to fill out Peter's condensed account in detailed notes.

A third narrative of relevance is the *Llibre dels feyts*, or Book of Deeds, of King James of Aragon, son of King Peter II. Although James was only an infant at the time of the Crusade he included an account of the battle of Muret in 1213 in which his father died, and gives other information which is of interest.

---

4   Translated as ed. Janet Shirley, *The Song of the Cathar Wars* (Aldershot, Scolar Press, 1996).

The other main contemporary sources on which we have drawn are the records of letters exchanged between Pope Innocent III (and after his death in July 1216 Pope Honorius III) and their main correspondents, i.e. the papal legates, Count Raymond VI and the consuls of Toulouse, King Philip Augustus of France and King Peter of Aragon. Also important are documents such as the oaths sworn at Saint-Gilles in June 1209 by Raymond VI and others (see §§75–7), and those sworn in 1214 (§§504–507 and notes). This material is to be found in various collections, most notably Migne's *Patrologiae . . . Latina*, the *Histoire générale de Languedoc*, the *Recueil des Historiens des Gaules et de la France*, and the collections in A. Teulet's *Layettes du Trésor des Chartres*. We have quoted extracts from some of the more important of these documents in our notes and have also provided full translations or extended extracts of some papal correspondence in Appendix F. The dating of many episodes relies on charter evidence, which also provides other valuable information, and the catalogues of acts of Simon de Montfort prepared by Molinier and Rhein are especially useful. For minor sources covering lesser points we have relied particularly on the thorough documentation in the notes by G&L to the Latin text. Volumes V–VIII of the 19th century edition of the *Histoire générale de Languedoc* contain not only material by the original 17th century editors Devic and Vaissète but much supplementary material by the 19th century editors (Molinier and others), and they remain fundamental in providing a wealth of detailed information. Again, full details of all these works are in the list of Abbreviations, above.

In addition to the papal correspondence already mentioned, the Appendices deal with matters which could not easily be accommodated in footnotes; we have also included a translation of the Statutes of Pamiers of December 1212, since we have not been able to trace a previous published English version.

The author's life and the composition of the *Historia*

The only reliable information we have about the author of the *Historia* comes from the *Historia* itself. In the opening paragraph of his work he describes himself as '*frater P., qualiscunque Vallium Sarnaii monachus*', 'Brother Peter, a monk of Vaux-de-Cernay'. The *Historia* says nothing about his early upbringing, but it seems certain that as the nephew and protégé of his uncle, Abbot Guy of les Vaux-de-Cernay, he would have been educated in the abbey from an early age. The abbey had been founded early in the twelfth century by the de Neauphle family, and it received donations of land from the de Montforts and other local aristocratic families. Members of some of these families were to accompany Simon de Montfort on the Fourth Crusade in 1202–1203 (see §106) and later on the Albigensian Crusade. The monks of the abbey enjoyed a network of links with the seigneurial society of the neighbouring area, and Peter would thus have grown up with a good knowledge of this society and its members. Indeed he refers (§51) to his uncle as being 'of noble birth', '*nobilis genere*', and presumably he himself came from a privileged background.

xxiv   *Introduction*

We do not know when he was born. He was a monk in 1212 (§300), and would thus have been at least eighteen years old by then. More precise estimates depend very much on how we regard his description of himself as '*puer elementarius*' in the dedication of his work to Pope Innocent III (§2), probably written in 1213. The phrase seems literally to mean simply 'a schoolboy': *elementarius* is a rare post-Augustan word meaning 'to do with the elements of learning', and thus '*senex elementarius*' in Seneca means 'an elderly schoolmaster' (Seneca, *Epistles*, 36). Although *puer* by itself often means 'a young man', in so describing himself Peter is clearly indulging in rhetorical exaggeration; the question is how far this is so.

G&L (III, p. I) seem to take the phrase at face value and suggest that Peter will have been born in 1194 or a little before ('*ou peu avant*'). However, if he was born as late as 1194 he would have been only eight or nine years old in 1202 when he accompanied his uncle and Simon de Montfort to Venice to join the Fourth Crusade, and when on his own testimony he was able not just to read but to comprehend a papal bull (see §106) – perhaps not impossible for an eight-year-old, but surely unlikely.

At the other extreme Yves Dossat (*Cahiers de Fanjeaux*, vol. 4, p. 223) argues that Peter must have been a monk by the time he went to Venice in 1202, which would make him about thirty in 1213. Dossat's assumption would involve stretching the meaning of *puer* to an extreme. Whilst there can be no certainty the answer may lie between these views, and we might therefore assume that Peter was born in 1190 or a little earlier, making him twelve years old or a little more in 1202 and thus in his early twenties in 1213.

Peter tells us (§299) that his uncle Guy had long been a close friend ('*familiarissimus*') of Simon de Montfort, and Peter may thus already have been personally acquainted with Simon before he went to Venice with his uncle in 1202. At that time he probably met other knights who were with de Montfort and who were later to take part in the Albigensian Crusade. They included Simon's brother Guy, Robert Mauvoisin, Enguerrand de Boves and Simon de Neauphle (see §106 and notes).

Peter's uncle went to join the reinvigorated Cistercian preaching campaign against heresy in 1207 (n. 26 to §25) and thus began his involvement in the affairs of the Midi. In March 1212 Guy took his nephew Peter (who was by now a monk) with him to the Midi to join Simon de Montfort and the crusaders, and 'to support him in his journey to foreign lands' (§300). Guy had been elected Bishop of Carcassonne, and was consecrated in the office in May 1212 (see n. 24 to §299). From this point onwards Peter witnessed and took part in some of the events he describes, and apart from a three-week visit to Narbonne remained with the crusaders until the Council of Lavaur in January 1213 (see §§40 and 368). His account of events during this period is clearly influenced by his personal knowledge, and for example he describes how at the siege of Moissac in late summer 1212 he himself narrowly escaped being killed by a bolt from a crossbow (§347). After the Council of Lavaur Abbot Guy went to northern France to rally support for the Crusade, and Peter evidently went with him.

Indeed, it is likely that he accompanied Guy on his preaching campaign in the north during 1213 (see §508) and was with him in Paris in April (§418).

Peter was still with his uncle when the latter returned to the South in April 1214 (§508), and remained with the crusaders until at least the end of June that year. We find him in the South again in 1216 (§§577–581) and he also seems to have been present at some stages at the second siege of Toulouse in 1218 (§§606C, 607).

Peter's presence with the crusaders during these periods is attested by frequent use of the verb in the first person singular or plural.[5] His uncle Guy played an important role in the leadership of the Crusade, especially after Arnold Amalric went to Spain to join the campaign against the Almohades in May 1212, and thereafter became increasingly preoccupied with his see at Narbonne. There are numerous references in the *Historia* to Guy's role, and in §§324 and 520 we find him acting as vice-legate. As his privileged nephew Peter must have become increasingly familiar with the leaders of the Crusade, as well as with the principal churchmen involved in it. His vivid portrait of Simon de Montfort in §§104–107 is clear testimony of this familiarity, as is his apparent awareness of the thinking of the leaders of the Crusade when describing their campaigns. His uncle will undoubtedly have participated in their meetings, and Peter himself may have been in attendance at some of those meetings, an assumption perhaps confirmed by his statement in §452 that he heard Simon discussing the preparation for the battle of Muret, and his statement in §40 that he was present at the Council of Lavaur in January 1213.

It seems almost beyond doubt that Peter must have died soon after the last events he recorded, which took place in December 1218. This is suggested particularly by the fact that he clearly left his work in an incomplete state. G&L, to an extent following earlier scholars, point out (III, pp. XVIII–XXIII) that the *Historia* seems to fall into three sections, of which only the first (to §398) is fully fleshed out; the other two, §§399–601 and 602–620, which they describe as the first and second continuations, are less detailed and would, they believe, have been expanded and refined had Peter lived. They argue that the prefatory letter dedicated to Innocent III was almost certainly written in 1213 at the Council of Lavaur, and that the main part of the work, §§5–398, was composed by that time, probably during the preceding twelve months. They believe that the second section was probably started in 1213 and added to in succeeding years but not properly revised, and point out that the final section, §602 to the end, which covers the death of Simon de Montfort and events of the second half of 1218, is clearly in a less than complete state.

These conclusions seem reasonable. For instance the prefatory dedication to Pope Innocent, §§1–4, must obviously have been written before the Pope's death in July 1216; perhaps even, as G&L argue (III, p. XIX), before Innocent suspended the Crusade in January 1213. As to §§5–399, the most important evidence that these were completed by 1213 arises from Peter's much favoured practice of

5   Listed in detail in G&L III, pp. VIII–IX.

looking forward in his narrative to events that were to occur in later years. In the first 316 sections there are a score of such references to events due to occur in 1210–12, but not a single reference to events after January 1213. G&L point to other minor indications which support their view that it was at this time that these sections were finalised. An incidental point is that Peter twice refers to Simon de Montfort in the present tense (§107 and §193), suggesting that he had no chance to revise the early sections after Simon's death in June 1218.

Peter writes fluently and he has an assured command of Latin.[6] Despite differences in detail, his Latin is not far distant from the Latin of the classical period, but it seems that he may not have been directly influenced during his formative years by studying the established authors of that period. There are records of the contents of the library at the monastery of les Vaux-de-Cernay[7] at about Peter's time which suggest that they consisted exclusively of texts by Church writers (including a large number of tracts against heresy), and no works by classical writers are listed. We find a few quotations from classical authors in the *Historia* (two each from Ovid and Horace, and one each from Juvenal and Plautus), but even these may have been culled from other Church writers or sources such as the treatises on the art of composition which were in wide use.

Following well-established convention Peter claims in his introduction that his aim is not 'to decorate the text with superfluous and meaningless rhetoric, but to tell the plain truth in plain fashion'. The claim seems to have been forgotten when he is indulging himself in attacks on the heretics and their supporters (where his full command of his medium is especially demonstrated), but it is true that his writing is generally straightforward (especially as compared with the papal letters) and his meaning is rarely obscure. His narrative passages are direct and to the point, and he paints vivid pictures of the towns and the country round them, and frequently gives copious details of military activities. The various stylistic devices he uses (many of which cannot comfortably be accommodated in translation) are part of the traditional stock in trade of medieval writers. We may especially note his fondness for puns: his favourite, which occurs several times, is '*Tolosa dolosa*', 'treacherous Toulouse'.[8] Other examples of his use of word play are given in the notes.

---

[6] The ability to write fluently and accurately in Latin was widespread, as is well illustrated by the letters exchanged between the prelates and King Peter of Aragon at the time of the Council of Lavaur (reproduced by Peter in §§370–388), and the letter of King Philip Augustus translated in Appendix F(ii). From the translator's viewpoint the most notable feature of the style of the period is the use of long, complex sentences. Letters emanating from the Curia at this time (of which the three reproduced by Peter – see p. xxvii below – are good examples) take this practice to extremes, and show remarkable virtuosity in this respect. The standard of Latin in other documents to which we refer varies greatly and the style is sometimes very laboured.

[7] Examined in detail by G&L (III, pp. II–VI).

[8] This pun appears to have been generally current, since we find it, for instance, in a letter to the Pope from various prelates at Orange in February 1213, *PL* 216, 836, '*dolosissimae civitatis Tolosanae*'.

The value of the *Historia*

The general value of the *Historia* as a source stems from several factors which have already been mentioned above. Peter of les Vaux-de-Cernay was an eye-witness to many of the events he recounts; he personally knew many of the leading actors involved on the crusader side, including not only his uncle Guy and Simon de Montfort, but the legates, many of the crusaders, and even St Dominic (§54). He also had access to official documents, some of which he inserts in his text. Examples are three letters from Pope Innocent III (§§56–65, 401–11, 554–9); the requests of King Peter of Aragon to the Council of Lavaur, the prelates' reply and a further letter to the King (§§370–6, 377–84, 387–8); the prelates' report to the Pope on the results of the Council (§§392–7); and the prelates' account of the battle of Muret (§§468–83). There are also numerous references to other documents (mainly papal correspondence) which are listed in G&L III, pp. XVI–XVII: see especially §§106 and 196, where Peter specifically mentions having read certain documents. He himself defends his veracity at the end of §2 in his dedicatory epistle to Innocent III: '. . . all I have written is true, and I have set down nothing which I did not either witness personally or learn from entirely authoritative and reliable persons', and in addition to the numer-ous indications of his own presence[9] there are frequent references in the narra-tive to other eye-witnesses.[10]

Some significant details are, however, omitted, even in the first 400 sections where Peter's account is most complete. Thus, for example, the establishment of the 'Black' and 'White' confraternities in 1211 in Toulouse which is described in William of Puylaurens' *Chronica* (see above) is not mentioned directly in the *Historia*, and some of the diplomatic developments of the years 1210–16 are either ignored by Peter or mentioned only very briefly. As indicated in the footnotes to this edition, these gaps have to be filled from other sources. More generally, Peter seems to have had no understanding of the aristocratic society of the Midi, whose culture and values were very different from those of north-ern France. Usually, however, Peter's value as a source is questioned not on the grounds of defects such as these: doubts about his reliability have focused mainly on the fact that his account is highly partisan, sometimes (to modern eyes) almost ludicrously so. Certainly his approach to writing the *Historia* re-flected his background and education, his close involvement with the leaders of the Crusade, and his inability to understand or even record the attitudes of the Crusade's opponents. His detestation of heresy and those he believed supported it was deeply ingrained. For him there was no grey area between good and evil, so that any opponent of the crusaders was *ipso facto* a heretic or a supporter of heretics. It was beyond him to think that the southern lords and King Peter of

[9] See n. 4 above.
[10] §§40, 54, 127, 160, 201, 248, 273, 298, 360, 361, 452.

Aragon might have had a legitimate point of view. His prejudice is so great and so manifest that at times it is tempting to think of him as a mere propagandist, perhaps even a cynical propagandist. Roquebert, for example, appears to take this view: see his comment on §508, referred to in our note to that section.

However, close acquaintance with the *Historia* suggests a different conclusion: that Peter was a rather naive young man, quite intelligent, but unsophisticated, a zealous believer in orthodox dogma (he himself would no doubt have said simply that he was steadfastly faithful), and glad to accept what his superiors told him without question.[11] This is not especially surprising. He belonged to the eccesiastical aristocracy of the north, and his values and prejudices were those of that society. His writing simply reflects this.

This view is borne out when we consider the reliability of the *Historia* as a source. While Peter is thoroughly partisan his basic honesty and indeed his naivety made it difficult for him to dissemble. Despite his complete lack of detachment we have a clear impression of a man striving to give a full and as he would see it true account of events. We have already noted his use of documentary evidence, and that he records both his own presence at certain events and specific cases of his use of other eye-witnesses. He certainly presents the crusaders' actions in the best light and their opponents' in the worst. Atrocities committed by the heretics are condemned, but while those by the crusaders are excused they are nonetheless recorded. Moreover he does not entirely ignore developments which were highly awkward from the crusader perspective. For instance, he describes (albeit briefly) Innocent III's acceptance of Peter of Aragon's representations early in 1213 (see §399), which led Innocent temporarily to suspend the Crusade, and also mentions the quarrel which broke out after 1212 between Simon de Montfort and Arnold Amalric (Abbot of Cîteaux and chief papal legate in the early stages of the Crusade) over the title of Duke of Narbonne, which they both claimed after Raymond VI was dispossessed (see §561).

Nor does Peter fail to reveal divisions amongst the crusaders or to criticise the mighty, for example the Count of Nevers (§108), Count Robert of Dreux, the Bishop of Beauvais and the Count of Ponthieu (§181), the Count of Bar (§242), and Alard de Strépy (§423). In dealing with reverses suffered by his hero Simon de Montfort at Saint-Marcel (§297) and at Beaucaire (§584) he glosses over what happened but he does not suppress it: his basic honesty prevents him from presenting a reverse as a victory, but in each case he tells us that Simon gained honour and credit from his conduct.

In general, where his version of events can be checked against other sources (which include numerous minor documents as well as the narrative sources and

---

[11] The most extreme example of naivety is to be found in §546. We may contrast the attitude of William of Puylaurens, a sincere Catholic, who when writing of the situation after the Fourth Lateran Council (and with the benefit of hindsight) says (XXIV) that the crusaders brought the wrath of God down on themselves; he says that after Simon de Montfort – a man admirable in every respect – had conquered the territory and divided it amongst the potentates and knights, they lost sight of the original purpose of the Crusade and became slaves to their own greed.

principal documentary sources we have mentioned) it is usually found to be reliable and there is no reason to doubt his general accuracy.

Turning to particular examples of the worth of the *Historia*, it provides a great deal of information about military aspects of the Crusade, and is especially valuable in this respect. Pitched battles were rare; apart from the battle of Muret in 1213 (§§446–83) only the encounter at Castelnaudary (Saint-Martin) in the autumn of 1211 (§§251–76) might qualify for that description. Skirmishes and raids by both sides were more common, and Simon de Montfort frequently used the tactic of destroying crops and vines and laying waste to an area, as a means of undermining the ability of opponents to support themselves. Examples are found in §§144, 147, 245, 327, 423 and 434. Another practice, adopted especially by the southerners, was the capture for ransom of crusader knights such as Bouchard de Marly, Lambert de Thury and Walter Langton (§248), or Dreux de Compans (§284). Atrocities were committed by both sides: the most infamous was the mutilation of the defenders of Bram carried out by de Montfort, in retaliation for a similar atrocity perpetrated by the southerners (§§142, 127).

However, the warfare of the Crusade was dominated by the siege of fortresses or fortified settlements which are usually described as *castra* or *castella*, terms which are discussed in more detail in Appendix A. Control of an area depended on the possession of these strongholds, and Peter himself makes this point (§321) when he writes of 'Penne d'Agenais . . . which was in effect the principal place in the whole of the Agenais and the key to controlling it'. Throughout his narrative Peter records changes in the control of *castra*, usually naming all the important ones. As well as providing the basis for military and political control of an area, possession of these strongholds gave control over its economic resources. When Raymond VI of Toulouse lost control of most of the *castra* around Toulouse in 1212, the crusaders were able to ravage the hinterland of Toulouse and destroy crops, and the desire to prevent such damage was an important factor in their decision to attack Muret (cf. §447).[12] Equally significant was control of communications. For example, de Montfort's occupation of Pamiers and Saverdun in 1209 gave him control of the Ariège valley, and such control brought with it the ability to exact profits from trade and tolls.

The crusaders' first aim was to win control of *castra* by persuasion, or by the threat of force. Fear of attack by the crusaders was an important factor in the surrender of many places. This was especially so after the fall of Béziers and Carcassonne in 1209, but other examples abound (see for instance §§326, 339 and 596). There are frequent instances of seigneurs of *castra* seeking to avoid combat by switching allegiance as the fortunes of war changed. Simon de Montfort did attempt to win the loyalty of some southern lords by accepting their surrender, sometimes granting other lands and sometimes allowing them to

---

[12] We may note also the claim in the letter of July 1211 from the consuls of Toulouse to King Peter of Aragon (see n. 42(i) to §137 etc.) referring to the first siege of the city in June of that year: '. . . the legate and the Bishop and the crusaders attacked us violently, and killed the men, women and children working in the fields, destroying our vines, fruit trees, crops and possessions and some farms . . .'.

retain their existing or equivalent fiefs: examples were Stephen of Servian, Giraud de Pépieux (§125–7), William of Minerve (§157), Aimeric of Montréal (§167), Peter-Roger of Cabaret (§214), William Cat (§266) and William of Aura (§288). In general, however, this policy was unsuccessful: all of those mentioned rebelled sooner or later, with the exception of Stephen of Servian.

If an attack was needed to gain control of a place this usually involved a siege, and the *Historia* provides much detail on some of these, in particular Minerve in 1210 (§§151–7), Termes later that year (§§168–90), Lavaur in 1211 (§§215–27), Penne d'Agenais in 1212 (§§321–34), Moissac, also in 1212 (§§340–53) and Casseneuil in 1214 (§§519–27). On many occasions the crusaders lacked the manpower to lay siege to a *castrum* by encircling it completely, and had to attack it from one or two sides only: examples are at Termes in 1210, Moissac in 1212, Puycelsi (§427) in 1213, and the first siege of Toulouse in 1211; writing of the siege of Minerve in 1210 Peter specifically makes the point that the crusaders were able to lay siege to the town from all sides.

There are many references to the use of siege-engines, especially by the crusaders, who seem to have been adept at siege warfare. Skilled teams of engineers (*artifices*), working under a master (*magister*), and usually paid in cash, were responsible for the building of these engines: examples occur at the sieges of Termes and Casseneuil. Siege-engines were sometimes built beforehand and transported to the scene of a siege (as at Minerve and Termes in 1210), but they might also be constructed on site. Particularly important were machines for throwing stones at the walls of places under attack. These are variously described as petraries, mangonels, and trebuchets. In §610 *machafundae*, sling-staffs, are mentioned as being used by the defenders of Toulouse in 1218 to hurl stones at the crusaders, and Simon de Montfort was killed by a blow from a stone hurled in this way. Other machines (called 'cats') were used in the sapping of walls or for filling in defensive ditches. Peter does not usually describe their construction but was clearly impressed by the work of engineers in building a bridge and a siege-tower at Casseneuil. The high costs of building and maintaining these engines is also clear. The most skilled exponent of engine building was a cleric, William the Archdeacon of Paris (on whom see in particular §175). The southerners are sometimes described as using siege-engines, as at Castelnaudary in 1211 (§261) or at Foix also in 1211 (§288), but their use was apparently unsuccessful.

Once captured, *castra* would usually be garrisoned by troops left behind for the purpose by the crusaders, and might be handed as a fief to one of Simon de Montfort's knights. Alternatively they might be destroyed, so as to remove the possibility of their rebelling and falling into enemy hands again. This latter policy was followed notably by de Montfort in his campaign in the Agenais in 1214 (see §§517); it is also reflected in his abortive proposal to do this at an earlier stage in the Crusade, after the defeat of the southern forces at Castelnaudary (§280).

Some information about the costs of campaigning can be gleaned from the *Historia*. The crusading army, which fluctuated considerably in size from one period to another, was partly made up of those who had taken crusading vows and come south for a period. However it is clear from the *Historia* that de

Montfort also employed soldiers for wages,[13] including the skilled engineers who built his siege-engines, and he also had to find the means to provision his forces. The war was thus expensive, and at one time at least it was said to have reduced Simon de Montfort himself to penury (§180). We know from other sources that de Montfort borrowed money from a banker of Cahors called Raymond de Salvanhac or Salvagnac (see n. 40 to §226). In §329 the Archbishop of Rouen is praised for his contribution. In §152 we have a specific reference to the cost of running siege-engines – twenty-one livres a day. The rank and file had to buy their own bread; it was cheap at Carcassonne (§97) but dear in 1211 at the first siege of Toulouse (§242), which we are told was abandoned largely on grounds of cost (§243). The problem would probably have diminished, especially after 1213, as de Montfort and his vassals established themselves more firmly as lords of the occupied territories, able to exploit their economic resources.

The *Historia* also provides information about the composition of the crusading forces, and their geographical origins. To take just two examples, at the siege of Minerve in 1210 we are told of the presence of Gascons (§152), and later that year at the siege of Termes, Bretons, Germans, Lotharingians and (northern) French crusaders are all mentioned (§§168, 173 and 188). The crusaders who came south were usually in groups led by both lay and ecclesiastical lords: in §216, for example, a force arrived at the siege of Lavaur led by the bishops of Lisieux and Bayeux, and the Count of Auxerre. These and other groups were recruited in part through preaching campaigns in the north, some of which are mentioned in the *Historia*: examples are in §§285 (preaching by Jacques de Vitry), 418 and 439 (preaching by Guy of les Vaux-de-Cernay).

In general Peter's information about the different categories of combatants on either side is sketchy – he would doubtless have expected his readers to be sufficiently informed on this and similar matters. It is, however, clear throughout that the knights and their attendant mounted sergeants (see n. 53 to §98) were predominant. Although the presence of footsoldiers (*pedites*) on both sides is mentioned quite frequently, their role was usually subordinate and we may note, for example, that Simon de Montfort is said to have forbidden the few foot-soldiers he had available at the battle of Muret to join the fighting (§460). The vulnerability of footsoldiers to attack in the open by armoured cavalry is very clearly demonstrated by the slaughter of the Toulousains, despite their vastly superior numbers, after that battle. On the crusader side, there is a reference in §581 to footsoldiers recruited from the local population, but the footsoldiers in the crusading army would seem to have consisted mainly of individuals or groups who had taken the cross; see for example the references to '*pedites peri-grini*', 'crusaders on foot', at Termes in §188, at Puycelsi in §426 and at Muret in §357, where they are also called 'crusaders of the poorer sort' ('*pauperes pere-grini*'). Indeed, as well as knights, sergeants, and footsoldiers, the crusading forces at times clearly included many poor people, in effect camp- followers, who were apparently unarmed. They were critical to the crusaders' success at Béziers in

---

[13] See also Appendix D on mercenaries.

1209 (see Appendix B in particular), and are also mentioned at the siege of Saint-Antonin in 1212 (see §315).

For de Montfort the most severe problem was that crusaders from the north came to perform the forty days' service required for papal indulgences and then went home, unless they could be persuaded to stay on for a time. In consequence he was frequently left with inadequate support; see for example §§115, 184–7, 248, 329, 428–9, 442, 489. Often the result was that many of the *castra* he had captured or persuaded to support him were retaken by the southerners or defected.

Peter frequently tells us that the southern forces were reluctant to engage the crusaders, even when they had the advantage of superiority in strength; see for example §§140, 257, 259–62, 279, 283, 293, 297, 300, 309, 359, 490, 581. Even if we allow for prejudiced reporting this suggests that the southerners were well aware of the general superiority of the northern crusaders in all forms of warfare, which is apparent throughout the narrative. This was one reason for the military success of the crusaders, which by 1215 seemed almost complete, but the examples cited also illustrate the marked and vitally important contrast between the cohesive leadership of the crusaders and the fragmented, hesitant and often timid southern opposition, especially in the period to 1216. Raymond VI in particular was very cautious. In contrast, Simon de Montfort, whilst regularly taking advice and discussing tactics with his leading knights and with the prelates (see for example §§168, 214, 254, 317 and 340), is portrayed as a courageous leader. Even after discounting Peter's prejudices, what most stands out from his narrative is the decisive and able leadership of de Montfort and his sheer determination, without which the Crusade might not have been sustained beyond the period of its initial success in the summer of 1209.

To summarise, while Peter of les Vaux-de-Cernay may have been extremely biased he avoids the charge of being deliberately untruthful; he does not wholly suppress episodes which are uncomfortable to his point of view; and his interest in accuracy is reflected in his practice of citing the source of his accounts of particular episodes, and from time to time quoting important documents. Whatever its shortcomings the value of the *Historia* is undoubted. Together with the Chanson, it is the prime account of the preaching campaign of 1203–08 and of the Crusade from 1209–18, and indeed for many episodes it is the only source. It provides a lively and detailed narrative as well as much information about the conduct of the campaigns, about the practice of siege warfare, and other matters.

The historical background[14]

The subject of the *Historia Albigensis* is the origins and first ten years of the Albigensian Crusade, which was fought against alleged supporters of the Cathar or Albigensian heresy which flourished in the south of France in the later 12th and 13th centuries. The Crusade began in 1209 and was to last until a final settlement was made by the treaty of Meaux/Paris in 1229. It was initiated by Pope Innocent III (1198–1216) and was fought with the aim of eradicating heresy in the South and restoring an orderly Christian society there. Its immediate targets were the leaders of the local aristocracy (and in particular Raymond VI, Count of Toulouse) who, in Innocent's eyes, had failed to protect orthodox religion, failed to support the Church in suppressing heresy, and had fostered disruption of the peace and undermined the good government of Christian society.

Heresy in the Midi

There were two heretical movements active in the Midi in the early 13th century. The first, which posed by far the most serious challenge to the Catholic Church, was Catharism. This was a dualist heresy: its adherents believed in the existence of two wholly antagonistic principles of good and evil, personified as God and Satan (or the Devil). The earth and all material or corporeal things were the creation of the Devil. God had created all spiritual things, including men's souls, but His realm was a heavenly and spiritual one quite separate from this earth. Men's bodies, being physical entities, were the Devil's work. Some Cathars, known as 'mitigated' dualists, accepted that in origin the Devil was a fallen angel, but others ('absolute' dualists) considered that Satan was co-eternal with the good God.

Most evidence about the Cathars comes from their detractors, so that it is not always possible to develop a clear or coherent view of their beliefs or the organisation of their church; moreover, their religion included a wide range of myths to explain the world, not all of which are consistent. Broadly speaking, however, they believed that the souls of men, created by the good God, were imprisoned in bodies of flesh in a physical world created by the evil god. Unless they achieved salvation through the Cathar church, men's souls were doomed to an eternal round of reincarnation in this earthly prison, and at least some Cathars believed that the same was true of all warm-blooded creatures, who had souls of equal dignity with those of men and shared in the process of reincarnation with them.

Christ was God's son, but only took on the appearance of corporeal form: he was never in reality incarnate, since that would have involved his soul entering a physical body which was Satan's creation. When Christ came to earth, he founded a church of which the Cathars were the true representatives. He taught

---

[14] More detailed accounts of, and evidence for, the brief outline which follows may be found in the text of the translation and in our notes; in Appendices D (on mercenaries) and G (on the policies of Innocent III); and in the general works cited in the bibliographical note at the end of this Introduction.

its adherents how to achieve salvation through receipt of the one sacrament of the Cathars, namely baptism in the spirit by the laying on of hands, known as the *consolamentum*, a ritual in two parts (see §§13 and 19).

The *consolamentum* was given only to fully instructed and prepared adults, or to the dying. Only those who had received the *consolamentum* were full members of the Cathar church, able to look forward to the release of their souls to Heaven. Once they had received the *consolamentum*, they had to prepare for this release by, as far as possible, denying all earthly things and living a strictly ascetic life; if they relapsed, then so too did the efficacy of the *consolamentum*. Because of the practical difficulty of this requirement, most Cathar believers postponed receipt of the *consolamentum* and full entry into the church until they were close to death; before this they were known simply as *credentes*, or believers. Those who did receive the *consolamentum* earlier in life were relatively few. They were in effect the Cathar priesthood, and were known as 'perfects', Latin *perfecti* (in the case of men) or *perfectae* (women). They renounced all property; undertook never to take the life of any man or warm-blooded beast, no matter what the circumstances; consumed no animal products, such as meat, cheese, eggs or milk; and promised never to tell any lie or swear any oath. They were to abstain completely from sex, which, since it was the means whereby physical procreation took place, was intrinsically evil.

Catharism probably had its immediate origins in the Balkans and spread to western Europe during the 12th century, becoming especially well-established in southern France and northern Italy. The first clear evidence of dualist or Cathar heresy in the south of France comes from the 1140s (see n. 23 to §9), and it seems to have spread rapidly in the succeeding decades. A debate between Cathars and Catholics took place at Lombers near Albi in 1165, attended by Bishop William of Albi, the Archbishop of Narbonne, the Trencavel Viscount of Carcassonne, and Constance, wife of Raymond V Count of Toulouse. Shortly afterwards, in the late 1160s or early 1170s, a Cathar priest called Niquinta or Nicetas from the absolute dualist Bogomil Church of Drugunthia at Constantinople came to the west and apparently sought to convert the Italian and French Cathars from the mitigated dualism they had hitherto mainly upheld to the tenets of his own church (see §10, n. 4). He seems to have met leading Cathars in the Midi at a Council at Saint-Félix de Caraman in the Lauragais, held probably in 1167 or 1172. The outcome was a reorganisation of the Cathar church in the Midi, with the establishment of new Cathar dioceses based on Toulouse, Carcassonne and (probably) Agen, to supplement the diocese which already existed based on Albi.

The growing strength of Catharism at this time is revealed by the letter written in 1177 by Count Raymond V of Toulouse to the General Chapter of Cîteaux (see §7, n. 10). He complained that his vassals were supporting the spread of Catharism, and that the Catholic Church was in danger. The outcome of this appeal was a legatine mission to Toulouse in 1178, which was not well received there. In the next year measures against heresy were set out in Canon 27 of the Third Lateran Council, which in particular urged the use of force by the secular authorities against heresy. Further missions to the Midi followed in 1179–82, and in 1181 Henry de Marcy Abbot of Clairvaux led a small army to besiege Lavaur, which lay within the domains of Roger Trencavel II of Béziers and Carcassonne, and was allegedly a nest of heretics.

However these initiatives had little impact, and Catharism continued to gain in popularity. Its strength lay above all in the support it enjoyed amongst the middling and lesser aristocracy of the South, and especially those of the counties of Toulouse and Foix, and the Trencavel lands. The most significant lord whose family included active Cathars was the Count of Foix, Raymond-Roger, 1188–1223. His wife Philippa was a well known Cathar sympathiser and was later accused of having presided over a Cathar house for women. Raymond-Roger's sister Esclarmonde of Foix received the *consolamentum* at a ceremony held at Fanjeaux in 1204. This was a grand social occasion, presided over by the Cathar deacon Guilabert de Castres and attended by representatives of many seigneurial families. By the early 13th century places such as Lavaur, Puylaurens, Laurac, Fanjeaux, Montréal and Mirepoix, strongholds of local seigneurial families, were also centres of Catharism, with houses of Cathars established in many of them, which formed the basis for Cathar preaching and ministry. Later Inquisition records (such as those preserved in the Doat collection[15]) provide a wealth of detail about the involvement of local seigneurial families in such places with heresy. These have been much used by historians, including E. Griffe in his four-volume study of Catharism in Languedoc, mentioned in the bibliographical note below. For some examples of the information which can be provided by such records see n. 5 to §6, n. 94 to §110, n. 108 to §116 and n. 119 to §192. How far Catharism enjoyed significant support within the lower ranks of rural society or in urban communities is less clear: for example, while the heresy seems to have gained some adherents in urban centres such as Toulouse, Carcassonne and Béziers (see notes to the text, especially §§4–9, 24 and 92), these places were not its main sources of support.

As well as Catharism, another quite distinct heresy had also gained some strength in the Midi by the early 13th century: this was Waldensianism. In terms of their doctrinal beliefs the Waldensians differed little, at least initially, from Catholic teaching. The issue which turned the Waldensians into schismatic heretics was not theology or belief but their refusal to obey Catholic discipline; the main theological points at issue between them and Catholics concerned matters such as the validity of sacraments performed by unworthy priests. They were always very hostile to the Cathars. The Waldensians were never as numerous in Languedoc as the Cathars. They are mentioned only three times in the *Historia* (see §§18, 48 and 513).

---

[15] In the Bibliothèque nationale in Paris: the collection comprises 17th century copies of documents, taken mainly from the archives of the Inquisition, and including testimony from witnesses covering events dating back to the early 13th century.

The Counts of Toulouse, the Trencavels, and the feudal society of the Midi
The Church expected secular powers to co-operate in extirpating heresy by pun-
ishing those identified by ecclesiastical authority as heretical, who were to be
handed over to secular authority for punishment. The view that it was the duty of
the secular authority to co-operate with ecclesiastical or spiritual authority in this
way had been set out in Canon 27 of the Third Lateran Council of 1177 (as noted
above), and was reasserted in the decretal *Ad Abolendam* issued by Lucius III in
1184 at Verona. Initially the Church was vague about the penalties which should
be imposed on heretics by secular authority, and did not formally condone
burning. Innocent III himself expressed his own views on the question in his
decretal *Vergentis in senium*, issued at Viterbo on 25 March 1199. This set out the
argument that since heresy was an attack on peace and civil order, as well as on
religious order, it must be dealt with by removing heretics and their supporters
from society, in particular by confiscating their lands and goods.

The most important member of the southern aristocracy, on whom the
Church might have expected principally to rely in the suppression of heresy, was
Count Raymond VI of Toulouse. He was the head of the ancient and distinguished family of Saint-Gilles. Amongst his predecessors, Count Raymond IV of
Toulouse (d. 1105) had been one of the leading figures in the First Crusade, and
may well also have fought the Moors in Spain. It was Raymond IV who by
marriage acquired for his family the marquisate of Provence east of the Rhône,
while his crusading exploits in the Holy Land brought him the title of Count of
Tripoli. On his death his elder son Bertrand succeeded to the titles of both Count
of Toulouse and Tripoli, but when Bertrand died in 1112 on crusade in the east
the inheritance was divided, and Bertrand's brother Alphonse Jourdain inherited
Toulouse, while another brother, Pons, became Count of Tripoli.

In the next generation, Raymond IV's grandson, Raymond V (1148–94), married
Constance, sister of King Louis VII of France. This alliance was designed as a counterweight to the marriage of Henry II of England to Eleanor of Aquitaine, which
gave Henry control over the duchy of Aquitaine and also claims over the county of
Toulouse itself. Raymond VI later reversed alliances and in 1196 took as his third
wife the sister of King Richard I of England, Joan, who brought the Agenais, a region to the north-west of Toulouse held by the English kings, as a dowry. She died
in 1199, and in 1204 Raymond married again, this time taking as his wife Eleanor,
sister of King Peter of Aragon. But although over several generations their dynastic
alliances may have shifted, the continuing importance of the counts of Toulouse as
a leading family in western Christendom was clear.

Despite this illustrious pedigree, Raymond VI nonetheless found himself the
principal target of the Albigensian Crusade, and was charged by the Church with
many crimes, including heresy. Raymond himself was certainly not a Cathar, nor
an active supporter of Cathars, and during his lifetime he continued to make
donations of lands and rights to abbeys, while even during the Albigensian
Crusade he supported the rebuilding of the nave of the cathedral of Saint-
Etienne in Toulouse. However, his relations with the Church were often unhappy,
and he was involved in many disputes with it over jurisdiction and property

matters. In 1196 he was threatened with excommunication by Celestine III for one such conflict with the abbey of Saint-Gilles, a sentence which appears to have been carried out, since in April 1198 he was absolved by Innocent III.

Raymond VI never showed any real interest in suppressing heresy, and was apparently willing to tolerate its supporters and adherents, many of whom were his vassals. Such an attitude was common within the society in which Raymond moved, and tolerance of or active support for heresy was an acceptable feature of the life of many families of the middling and lesser aristocracy of the Midi at this time. Such families often had at least some members who were active believers (*credentes*) and who provided support for the Cathar church, and many of them became *perfecti* and *perfectae*. Some families were divided: Bernard-Raymond of Roquefort was Bishop of Carcassonne when the Crusade began, but his mother and brothers were Cathar supporters who resisted the Crusade at the siege of Termes in 1210. Southern society also extended a relatively high degree of tolerance to the significant Jewish communities in cities such as Béziers, Narbonne and Toulouse; for example, Raymond VI used Jews in his service. Such tolerance of religious pluralism was an attitude which Peter of les Vaux-de-Cernay, coming from a quite different social and cultural background, found incomprehensible. He regarded Raymond's failure actively to persecute heretics as incontrovertible proof that Raymond himself must have been a heretic.

However, even if Raymond VI had, like his father before him, shown an active interest in combating heresy it is doubtful that he would have had the means to do so. One of the features of 12th and early 13th century Languedoc was the fragmentation of political authority in the region, and the weak control exercised over their vassals by great lords such as the counts of Toulouse. In the first place, the feudal geography of the region was complex and shifting. Based on the county of Toulouse, Raymond's domains comprised a scattered collection of fiefs extending from the Agenais in the west to the marquisate of Provence in the east, and from Castelnaudary in the south to the Dordogne river in the north. Territorially they were not compact, and interspersed amongst them were areas held by other lords not subject to him. The most notable of these was the bloc of lands held by the Trencavel family, based on the viscounties of Carcassonne and Béziers, and including the Razès and the southern Albigeois. During the 12th century the Trencavels had escaped the overlordship of the counts of Toulouse and established ties with the counts of Barcelona, who had become kings of Aragon in 1137 through marriage. Raymond-Roger Trencavel, who was Viscount when the Crusade began, had inherited his domains on the death of his father Roger II Trencavel in 1194, but was only a minor, aged nine, at the time. His guardian, Bertrand de Saissac, was sympathetic to Catharism and the young Viscount exercised little independent authority (see §88).

The interest which the kings of Aragon had acquired over the Trencavel domains was not their only one north of the Pyrenees. In the early 13th century King Peter of Aragon also held the counties of the Gevaudan and Millau, the lordship of Montpellier, and the county of Provence to the east of the Rhône, as well as Roussillon and the Cerdagne which formed part of Catalonia north of the

Pyrenees. He also exercised suzerainty over the counties of Foix, Comminges and Couserans, and the viscounty of Béarn, all of which lay on the northern side of the Pyrenees. Other major powers with an interest in the region included Raymond VI's principal overlord King Philip Augustus of France. The kings of France had for centuries exercised no effective influence in the area, and their suzerainty was nominal; nonetheless, while Philip Augustus showed little interest in the Midi prior to the Albigensian Crusade, he had certainly not abandoned his claims, nor had they ceased to be recognised in the South.[16] The kings of England, as dukes of Aquitaine, also had interests: Raymond VI held the Agenais as a fief of King John of England, having acquired it in 1196 when he had married Joan of England and retained it after Joan's death in 1199. Finally, we may note that in the east Raymond held the marquisate of Provence as a vassal of the Holy Roman Emperor.

The political fragmentation which characterised the Midi at this time discouraged the formation of strong consolidated lordships, and weakened the ability of the leading seigneurs to command the loyalty and military resources of their vassals. These characteristics were strongly reinforced by other features of the region. In particular formal feudal ties were much looser than they were in northern France. The middling and lesser nobility in the South were bound only by loose ties to their nominal overlords, the counts of Toulouse and the viscounts of Béziers and Carcassonne. The counts of Toulouse were moving towards establishing a more effective administration in their own courts, with the appointment of seneschals to represent them in their territories, and officials called *viguiers* to represent them in the towns, but this development had not yet had a wider impact on their relations with their vassals. One consequence was that petty warfare was endemic in the Midi, and disputes between local lords amongst themselves and between them and ecclesiastical lords were common. Another consequence was that Raymond VI and other lords tended to have to employ mercenaries, because they could not usually rely on their vassals to provide them with the necessary support. (The charge of employing mercenaries was regularly laid against Raymond and others by the Church, and is discussed in more detail in Appendix D.)

The fragmentation of authority was also encouraged by the inheritance customs adopted by many of the lesser southern nobility. Partible inheritance was widespread. In other cases, practices of free bequest rather than primogeniture prevailed, so that a lord could divide his estate amongst several heirs, including women if he wished. The leading nobility had abandoned these practices but they remained widespread amongst the lesser aristocracy, and as a result there were numerous multiple lordships in the South, which inevitably discouraged the development of close feudal ties between an overlord and his vassals. Multiple

---

[16] Cf. C. Higounet, 'Problèmes du Midi au temps de Philippe Auguste', in *La France de Philippe Auguste* (Paris, 1982), pp. 311–21; see also n. 65 to §72 and the letter from the King to Innocent III translated in Appendix F(ii).

co-seigneurs of a single place were by no means uncommon: at one time there were thirty-five at Mirepoix.

Finally, the rise of self-government in many southern towns had also restricted the powers of the counts of Toulouse and the Trencavels, and, even when lordship over a town was shared with a bishop or abbot, considerable independence had often been acquired by communal authorities. A high degree of self-government was especially characteristic of Toulouse at this time,[17] but was also present in varying degrees in other places such as Saint-Gilles, Béziers and Carcassonne. One reason for the resistance of such places to Simon de Montfort was the desire to preserve such self-government.

In this society Raymond VI could not command his vassals to relinquish support for heresy, nor could he compel them to do so; and when Innocent III called upon Raymond to suppress heresy and dispossess those who protected its followers, there were severe limitations on what Raymond could in practice do, unless he was to alienate his vassals completely and undermine his own position.

The southern church

If Raymond was unable or unwilling to act against heresy, neither were many members of the local episcopate in a position to do so. One problem was that political fragmentation was paralleled by the fragmentation of ecclesiastical authority, so that the Church in the region lacked coherent leadership. The archiepiscopal see of Narbonne included the bishoprics of Toulouse, Carcassonne, Elne, Béziers, Nîmes, Lodève, Uzès, Agde and Maguelonne, but the see of Agen was subject to Bordeaux, and those of Albi, Cahors and Rodez were subject to the Archbishop of Bourges. The sees of Comminges and Couserans were under the jurisdiction of the Archbishop of Auch.

Another difficulty was the poverty of many sees, where lack of resources apparently hampered effective administration. William of Puylaurens (VI) describes how at the beginning of the 13th century the Bishop of Toulouse, Fulcrand, received little revenue: 'he received no tithes, which belonged to the knights or the monasteries, and the parish priests took the first fruits'. At Carcassonne, the aged Bishop Otto resigned his see in 1198 in part because of his discouragement at the advances made by the Cathars and Waldensians in his diocese.

Furthermore, few of the southern bishops at this time were committed to the ideas of the reformed papacy as espoused by Innocent III, and a number of them showed little active interest in combating heresy. At Béziers, Bishop William de Roquessels refused to co-operate with Innocent's legates Peter of Castelnau and Ralph of Fontfroide in 1203, and was shortly afterwards suspended. Archbishop Berengar of Narbonne also resented what he saw as interference by papal legates in his affairs; he was a member of the royal house of Aragon, the illegitimate son of Raymond-Berengar, and was criticised by Innocent from the beginning of his

[17] See in particular J. H. Mundy, *Liberty and Political Power in Toulouse 1050–1230* (New York, 1954).

pontificate for his failings, which included paying insufficient attention to his pastoral duties, and for pluralism (he continued to hold the abbacy of Mont-Aragon in Catalonia after he became Archbishop of Narbonne in 1191). At Toulouse, Bishop Raymond of Rabastens was accused of having obtained the see by simony, and was deposed by Innocent in 1205. There were exceptions: Bishop Navarre of Couserans became closely associated with the legates and was a steadfast supporter of the Crusade, and Bishop William Peyre retained his see at Albi throughout the period, but in other cases Innocent found it necessary to replace existing incumbents with new appointees more committed to his ideals.[18]

Innocent III

When Innocent III ascended the papal throne in 1198, he regarded action against heresy in the Midi as one of his priorities. He signalled his interest in April 1198 in a letter to the Archbishop of Auch, which mentioned the need to invoke the temporal sword to combat heresy, and also through his early appointment of the legate Rainier to act on his behalf in the Midi. In the ensuing years he sought to achieve his aims through further appeals to secular authority to help; through attempts at reinvigoration of the southern episcopate; and through the establishment of a preaching campaign against heresy in the Midi. Innocent's principal chosen agents were a series of legates who were appointed to represent him in the South. The full extent and scope of Innocent's programme in the Midi was very wide. Whilst heresy itself was the prime target, his objectives were broader. Fundamental to the fight against heresy was the restoration of peace and orderly Christian government, and the failure of Raymond VI to co-operate with the Church in dealing with heresy was but one aspect of his general failings as a ruler. Others included his use of mercenaries, which created insecurity and disorder; his imposition of unjust tolls and taxes; his disregard for ecclesiastical jurisdiction and disrespect for the property rights of the Church; and his employment of Jews in his administration. Peaceful Christian order had to be restored before heresy could be effectively pursued. This programme, and subsequently the Crusade itself, are often referred to by both Peter of les Vaux-de-Cernay and by Innocent in his correspondence as the 'business of peace and of the faith' (Latin *negotium pacis et fidei*), or similar phrases. The implications of the phrase and the general development of Innocent III's policies towards the Midi are considered in more detail in Appendix G.

As the *negotium* was pursued by Innocent in the years 1198–1207, attention increasingly focused on Raymond VI of Toulouse. The legates regarded Raymond as a serious obstacle to the furtherance of their aims, condemning him for his alleged protection of heresy within his domains, and for his failure to uphold Christian peace and protect the Church. The culmination was Raymond's excommunication in April 1207 by Peter of Castelnau, and the renewed call to

---

[18] On the general question of the southern clergy at this time see Yves Dossat, 'Le clergé méridional à la veille de la Croisade Albigeoise', in *Revue historique et littéraire du Languedoc* I (1944), pp. 263–78, reprinted in Dossat, *Eglise et hérésie en France au XIIIe siècle* (London, 1982).

Philip Augustus to intervene militarily against Raymond in November 1207, which was coupled with an appeal to others to intervene and dispossess Raymond. As on earlier occasions Philip paid little heed to this plea, and how far Innocent would have continued to press it must remain uncertain. Innocent excommunicated other leading princes of Christendom, and Raymond probably thought he could see out this setback and gain reconciliation, just as he had in the case of his first excommunication by Celestine III in 1196, and as King John of England was to do when excommunicated by Innocent III in 1209. Raymond probably also judged that Philip Augustus, who was preoccupied by his conflicts with the Emperor Otto and King John of England, was unlikely to take any notice of Innocent's calls for armed intervention against him. However on 8 January 1208 the legate Peter of Castelnau was murdered crossing the Rhône, and this gave a new impetus to calls for a crusade. It was alleged, but never proved, that Raymond was implicated in the murder, and on hearing the news in March 1208 Innocent renewed his call for a crusade against Raymond. This time the appeal bore fruit.

The Albigensian Crusade

Practical arrangements for the launch of the new crusade were completed by the spring of 1209, Philip Augustus in particular having given permission to some of his leading vassals (such as the Duke of Burgundy and the counts of Nevers and Saint-Pol) to take part. The crusaders seem at this stage to have been drawn mainly from northern France, Burgundy and the Rhineland. In June 1209 the army assembled under the overall command of Innocent's legate Arnold Amalric, Abbot of Cîteaux. By this stage the preaching campaign against heresy had largely been abandoned, with the exception of the work of St Dominic, based at this stage at Fanjeaux and Prouille, and later, from about 1215, at Toulouse.

As the crusaders marched south down the Rhône valley from Lyon Raymond VI was busily negotiating with the legates appointed by Innocent, and in particular with Milo, Innocent's notary. The outcome must have seemed from his point of view a great success: he was reconciled to the Church in a formal ceremony at Saint-Gilles in June 1209 in return for detailed undertakings to maintain the peace and co-operate in combating heresy. While the ceremony humbled Raymond, he had removed the immediate threat of military intervention against him, and shortly afterwards he himself took the cross and joined the crusaders, ensuring that his lands would be protected.

These developments placed the crusaders in a potentially very difficult position. The Crusade had been launched against Raymond VI, but he had suddenly ceased to be the target. The discussions which followed are unknown to us, but a decision must rapidly have been taken by Arnold Amalric and the other leaders of the crusading force that it should instead attack Viscount Raymond-Roger Trencavel. As far as we know he had received no warning and had been given no opportunity to answer any charges against him, but in July 1209 the crusading army advanced past Montpellier towards his principal strongholds, Béziers and Carcassonne.

Thus began the Albigensian Crusade. The warfare which followed can be divided into several phases. The first was the period from the beginning of the Crusade in July 1209 until the middle of 1211, during which the crusaders conquered all the former Trencavel lands, despite considerable resistance. After the fall of Béziers in July 1209 and then Carcassonne a few weeks later, the crusaders chose Simon de Montfort to succeed the young Viscount Raymond-Roger Trencavel, who was imprisoned in the vicecomital palace at Carcassonne and died there on 10 November 1209. Simon de Montfort assumed all the Trencavel titles, and Raymond-Roger's widow later ceded all her rights to him, as did his son in 1210. In the immediate aftermath of the fall of Béziers and Carcassonne many other *castra* in the Trencavel viscounties were deserted, and the lesser nobles who lived in them became *faidits*, outlawed and dispossessed opponents of the crusaders. During the autumn of 1209 de Montfort traversed his newly acquired lands, and also occupied Pamiers, Saverdun and Preixan, which were fiefs of Count Raymond-Roger of Foix.

De Montfort's main problem was a shortage of troops: most crusaders who had come south in the summer of 1209 had returned home having completed the forty days' service required to fulfil crusading vows (this was to be a recurring problem for de Montfort – see p. xxxii above). In the last months of 1209 he suffered major reversals and most of the places which had submitted to him now defected again (see §§121–36). The situation turned in the spring of 1210 when de Montfort's wife Alice arrived with reinforcements. Most of the places lost over the winter were retaken, but the three stongest *castra* in the former Trencavel lands, Minerve, Cabaret and Termes, remained defiant. With characteristic determination de Montfort now moved against them. Minerve fell in July, after which a mass burning of Cathars took place; fresh reinforcements arrived later in 1210 and after a prolonged and difficult siege the great fortress of Termes fell in November. The fall of Termes had a considerable impact and much resistance crumbled over the winter of 1210–11. In the spring of 1211 Cabaret surrendered and Lavaur, on the edge of the Trencavel lands on the border with the county of Toulouse, was besieged and fell on 3 May. Thus Simon de Montfort now had in his control all the former Trencavel holdings.

A second phase of the Crusade then began when de Montfort openly attacked Raymond VI's domains for the first time. Notwithstanding his successful reconciliation at Saint-Gilles in June 1209, Raymond had suffered a renewed excommunication at the hands of the legates at a Council held at Avignon in early September 1209. In response, Raymond went to Rome and engaged in considerable diplomatic activity over the winter of 1209–10, and the result was a further attempt at his reconciliation. However, the legates were determined to avoid this, and the culmination of the negotiations was a further excommunication of Raymond at another Council, held at Saint-Gilles in September 1210. Raymond made yet further efforts over the winter of 1210–11 to negotiate a settlement with the legates, and this time the discussions involved King Peter of Aragon. He was concerned at the way in which de Montfort had established himself in the Trencavel territories without reference to him, their overlord, and initially he refused to accept Simon de Montfort's homage for the conquered lands. However, at the time he was also keen to see a stable situation north of the Pyrenees, in part to enable him to concentrate on campaigns against the Moslems in Spain. Two sets of negotiations took place early in 1211, at Narbonne and Montpellier, at which King Peter sought to negotiate with the legates and de Montfort on behalf of Raymond VI and Raymond-Roger of Foix. King Peter eventually agreed to accept de Montfort's homage for the Trencavel lands, but the attempt to reconcile Raymond VI failed, and on 5 February 1211 Raymond was again excommunicated and his lands declared liable to seizure.

This paved the way for the open attack on Raymond's territories which began after the fall of Lavaur. In June 1211 de Montfort campaigned in the northern Albigeois, and then began the first siege of Toulouse. This was a typically audacious move by de Montfort, but he did not have the resources to mount a full scale siege of the city. The siege had to be abandoned, but de Montfort thereafter occupied Quercy. Raymond VI and Raymond-Roger of Foix then joined together to campaign against de Montfort, and in September 1211 their combined forces besieged the crusaders inside Castelnaudary, but de Montfort seized the initiative and attacked and routed the southern forces (many of whom were mercenaries). Even so, rumours spread that de Montfort had lost the encounter, and many places earlier taken by de Montfort defected again. Reinforcements arrived to bolster the crusaders in December 1211, and Simon de Montfort's brother Guy joined him. In 1212 de Montfort campaigned widely over Raymond's domains, capturing many places; a number of sieges took place, including at Hautpoul, Saint-Antonin, Penne d'Agenais and Moissac. De Montfort also campaigned in the county of Foix, in Comminges and in Gascony. By the end of the year he had occupied almost all of Raymond's territory, and in December 1212 he held a meeting of his knights at Pamiers, where he promulgated a series of laws or customs for the government of his territories, known as the Statutes of Pamiers.

The following year, 1213, saw renewed intervention by King Peter of Aragon. Now freed from preoccupations in Spain after the Christian victory at the battle of Las Navas de Tolosa the previous year, he was seriously alarmed at the sweeping gains made by de Montfort. The King's envoys in Rome successfully persuaded Innocent III that de Montfort and the legates were treating Raymond VI and his allies unjustly, and were pursuing the Crusade solely for their own ends. Innocent's interests were turning towards his plans for a new crusade to the Holy Land, and he ordered the suspension of the Albigensian Crusade and called for the restoration of Raymond's rights and those of his allies. At the Council of Lavaur early in 1213 the legates, as yet unaware of Innocent's decision, refused King Peter's demands for a cessation of hostilities and a reconciliation of Raymond and other southern lords, and as a result the King formally took under his protection the counties of Toulouse, Foix and Comminges, and the city of Toulouse, and repudiated de Montfort. The legates and de Montfort meanwhile lobbied Innocent intensively and eventually, in May 1213, he revoked his earlier acceptance of Peter of Aragon's case. King Peter ignored this and confronted de Montfort at Muret, south-west of Toulouse, in September 1213; despite the superiority in numbers of the combined forces of Aragon, Toulouse and Foix, de Montfort again took the initiative, attacked the Aragonese head on, and King Peter was killed in the battle. He left an infant son (James) as his heir. Aragonese intervention was at an end.

However, Muret did not by any means see the end of resistance to the crusaders, and indeed de Montfort was unable to occupy Toulouse because he had too few troops to mount a successful siege. Over the next two years therefore campaigning continued, in Provence, Quercy, the Agenais, and the Rouergue. Innocent III's reaction to the battle of Muret is unknown, but he was almost certainly not pleased with the death of King Peter there: for all his opposition to Simon de Montfort and the legates, the King was a loyal Catholic, a personal vassal of the Pope's, and a hero in the fight against the Moslems in Spain. In 1214 Innocent appointed a new legate, Peter of Benevento, to make a settlement in Languedoc and secure the return of the infant King James of Aragon (who was in de Montfort's custody) to Spain. This took place, and Raymond VI was absolved and his lands placed in the charge of the Church. However de Montfort was allowed to administer them and he continued to act aggressively, despite Peter of Benevento's settlement. By 1215 he was de facto in possession of Toulouse and all of Raymond's lands, and his conquests culminated in the confirmation of his assumption of most of Raymond VI's lands and titles at the Fourth Lateran Council in November 1215. In the following spring King Philip Augustus of France formally invested de Montfort with them.

However, as we have seen, his successes in the previous six years had frequently been interrupted, not least because the southerners seem never to have accepted that their cause was lost. Their continued determination was to surface again during the third phase of the Crusade which began early in 1216, soon after the Lateran Council. The southern forces, under both Raymond VI and his son Raymond the younger (later Raymond VII), now started to stage a successful fight back. This began in Provence, and particularly important was the siege of Beaucaire in 1216, when the southern forces under Raymond the younger occupied the town and captured its castle from the crusader garrison after a long siege. De Montfort was again seriously hampered by a lack of troops, while the southerners benefited from the capable leadership of the younger Raymond. In September 1217 Raymond VI, who had spent most of the preceding eighteen months in Aragon, was able to enter Toulouse, with only the comital fortress in the city (the Château Narbonnais) remaining in the crusaders' hands. As soon as he heard of this de Montfort, who had been campaigning in the Rhône valley, rushed to Toulouse, joining his wife Alice in the Château Narbonnais, and the crusaders embarked on a prolonged siege of the rest of the city. Simon de Montfort was killed by a stone hurled from the city walls on 25 June, and the siege was abandoned a month later.

Amaury de Montfort, Simon's son, succeeded him but he lacked the determination and skills of his father. (At which point, as noted earlier, Peter of les Vaux-de-Cernay's account comes to an end.) Even though in 1219 Prince Louis of France, son of King Philip Augustus, came south with a large force to support

Amaury, the southerners continued to enjoy success, and recruiting additional crusaders to support de Montfort was increasingly difficult, especially because of the rival attractions of the Fifth Crusade to Egypt. By 1222 Raymond VI had recovered all his possessions and Roger Trencavel, son of the disposessed Raymond-Roger, recovered all his father's lands. Amaury de Montfort left the South, and ceded all his claims to the area to the new French King Louis VIII.

This was not, however, to be the end of the Crusade. Honorius III urged fresh intervention and, preaching a new Crusade, he persuaded Louis VIII to intervene. Louis came south in 1226, and although his army was delayed for several months when he was refused entry by the citizens of Avignon, he was able to pass through much of the South unopposed. Most southern lords submitted, although Raymond VII did not. Louis died later that year, leaving his widow Blanche of Castile to rule in the name of his young son Louis (St Louis), but the royal intervention which he had begun was to prove decisive. Fresh campaigns took place in 1227 and 1228, led by Humbert de Beaujeu, cousin of Louis VIII, and were bolstered by the royal seneschals and bailiffs who had been installed in those areas which had submitted or been conquered. Raymond VII was increasingly isolated. Recognising that he was no longer fighting a fluctuating group of crusaders but facing the increasingly well organised might of the French Crown, Raymond sued for peace.

In January 1229, at a council held at Meaux, a peace agreement was reached. This was ratified on 12 April at Paris, when Count Raymond VII underwent public penance in the cathedral of Nôtre Dame. He undertook to prosecute heretics and dismiss mercenaries; to restore the property and enforce the privileges of the Church; to destroy the new fortifications he had built up in Toulouse; to crusade in the Holy Land for five years; and to give to the French Crown or the papacy all the lands which he held in Provence. This treaty of Meaux/Paris marked the end of the Albigensian Crusade. However, despite the military and the diplomatic victory of the kings of France, Raymond VII of Toulouse retained a substantial part of his lands, and subsequently regained the marquisate of Provence. Moreover the Cathar heresy was still well entrenched in Languedoc in 1229. The history of the next fifty years was one of sporadic military resistance by Cathar lords against the forces of the Crown; and of the growing power of the papal Inquisition in its efforts to root out heretics and their lay protectors. Raymond Trencavel rebelled unsuccessfully in 1240, as did Raymond VII in 1242 in an attempt to get a revision of the treaty of 1229. In 1249 Raymond VII died, and since he had no male heir the county of Toulouse passed to his daughter Jeanne and her husband, Alphonse of Poitiers, brother of the King of France. On the death of Alphonse and Jeanne the county of Toulouse and its dependent lands finally passed directly to the French Crown. Catharism finally died out in the Midi in the early part of the fourteenth century.

Bibliographical note

Detailed references to secondary works relevant to Catharism and the Crusade are given in the footnotes to this translation. Of general works, the best introductions to the subject in English are W. E. Wakefield, *Heresy, Crusade and Inquisition in Southern France 1100–1250* (London, 1974), and B. Hamilton, *The Albigensian Crusade*, Historical Association Pamphlet G.85 (London, 1974), reprinted in the same author's *Monastic Reform, Catharism and the Crusades 900–1300* (London, 1979). Both contain helpful bibliographies. Other accounts include J. Sumption, *The Albigensian Crusade* (London, 1978), and M. Costen, *The Cathars and the Albigensian Crusade* (Manchester, 1997). Good introductions to Catharism and Waldensians, with extensive further references, are to be found in M. Lambert, *Medieval Heresy: Popular Movements from the Gregorian Reform to the Reformation* (Oxford, Blackwell, 1992). The standard work on St Dominic, which includes a detailed analysis of the preaching campaigns prior to the Crusade, is M.-H. Vicaire, *Saint Dominic and his Times*, English translation by K. Pond (London, 1964).

Inevitably, perhaps, most of the writing on these subjects is in French. The first three volumes of M. Roquebert's *L'epopée cathare* (Toulouse, 1969, 1971, 1978) provide the best detailed account of the origins and course of the Crusade, and are especially helpful because of their close reference to the sources. An older 'standard' account is P. Belperron, *La Croisade contre les Albigeois et l'union du Languedoc à la France 1209–1247* (Paris, 1942), but this is now dated and is vitiated by its author's strong bias in favour of the crusaders and by his failure to give any detailed references to sources. A better account, which is strongly sympathetic to the southerners, is Zoe Oldenbourg, *Le Bûcher de Montségur* (Paris 1959), which is also available in English as *Massacre at Montségur*, translated by P. Green (London, 1961). The development of Catharism in Languedoc throughout this period is particularly well treated in E. Griffe's four books: *Les Débuts de l'aventure cathare en Languedoc (1140–1190)* (Paris, 1969); *Le Languedoc cathare de 1190 à 1210* (Paris, 1971); *Le Languedoc cathare au temps de la croisade (1209–1229)* (Paris, 1973); and *Le Languedoc cathare et l'Inquisition (1229–1329)* (Paris, 1980).

Historia Albigensis

SUMMARY OF THE TEXT

I. §§1–4: Letter of dedication to Pope Innocent III.

II. §§5–19: Spread of heresy in the South – Peter of Castelnau and Brother Ralph appointed in 1203 as legates to combat heresy, of which Toulouse the main centre – description of the beliefs of the Cathar heretics – the Waldensians a less obnoxious heretical sect – the Cathar *consolamentum*.

III. §§20–54, 1206–07: The preaching campaign of 1206–07 – Bishop Diego of Osma and his companion [St Dominic] – their meeting with the legates Arnold Amalric, Abbot of Cîteaux, Peter of Castelnau and Ralph at Montpellier, June 1206 – debates with heretics at Servian, Béziers and Carcassonne (autumn 1206) – debate at Montréal (April 1207) – Peter of Castelnau goes to Provence – excommunication of Count Raymond VI of Toulouse (April 1207) – account of the unbelief of Raymond VI – arrival of twelve Cistercian abbots to join the preaching campaign – debate at Pamiers (September 1207) – Bishop Diego returns to Osma – Guy, Abbot of les Vaux-de-Cernay, appointed chief preacher – miracle at Montréal recounted by Dominic.

IV. §§55–81, January 1208 – June 1209: Murder of Peter of Castelnau – Pope Innocent's letter of 10 March 1208 describing the murder and renewing calls for the Crusade against Raymond VI – Bishops Fulk of Toulouse and Navarre of Couserans go to Rome – Raymond VI sends a mission to Rome to argue his innocence – Innocent III appoints Master Milo (March 1209) as an additional legate, assisted by Master Thedisius – Milo in Provence – reconciliation of Count Raymond at Saint-Gilles, June 1209.

V. §§82–120, summer/early autumn 1209: Arrival of the crusaders in the South – Raymond VI joins the crusaders – the crusaders march against Raymond-Roger Trencavel – massacre at Béziers, 22 July 1209 – siege and fall of Carcassonne, August 1209 – Simon de Montfort chosen to succeed Raymond-Roger Trencavel as Viscount of Béziers and Carcassonne – portrait of Simon de Montfort – departure of main crusading army – initial campaigns in the viscounties of Béziers and Carcassonne – Duke of Burgundy then returns home, de Montfort left largely alone – further campaigns in the former Trencavel lands.

VI. §§121–140, autumn 1209 – spring 1210: Intervention of King Peter of Aragon – reverses for the crusaders – Bouchard de Marly taken prisoner – Giraud de Pépieux defects – murder of the Abbot of Eaunes – defections of Castres and Lombers – Raymond-Roger of Foix breaks with the crusaders – loss of Montréal and further losses by Christmas 1209 – the Count of Toulouse in France and Rome, winter 1209–10.

VII. §§141–192, spring–autumn 1210: The crusaders, now reinforced, resume their conquest – atrocity at Bram – siege of Alaric – attack on Foix – further involvement of King Peter of Aragon – failed negotiations between King Peter and the lords of Cabaret, Termes and Montréal – siege of Minerve (June–July

1210) – Council of Saint-Gilles and renewed excommunication of Count Raymond VI of Toulouse (July 1210) – siege of Termes (August–November 1210).

VIII. §§193–212, winter 1210 – spring 1211: Simon de Montfort in the Albigeois, reoccupies many *castra* – meeting of the King of Aragon, de Montfort, Count Raymond VI of Toulouse and the papal legates at Narbonne, January 1211 – discussion of the position of Raymond VI and of Raymond-Roger of Foix – iniquities of the Count of Foix – Peter of Aragon accepts de Montfort's homage – further meeting at Montpellier to discuss the position of Raymond VI.

IX. §§213–230, spring 1211: Arrival of new crusaders (March 1211) – surrender of Cabaret and release of Bouchard de Marly – siege of Lavaur by de Montfort – attack on crusaders by the Count of Foix – Raymond VI gives covert help to the defenders of Lavaur – Bishop Fulk leaves Toulouse (2 April 1211) – Lavaur falls (3 May 1211) – Roger of Comminges submits to de Montfort – Puylaurens occupied by the crusaders.

X. §§231–250, summer 1211: Opening of hostilities with the Count of Toulouse – siege of Les Cassés – the Catholic clergy leave Toulouse – siege of Montferrand – Count Baldwin of Toulouse joins the crusaders – Simon de Montfort occupies the northern Albigeois – arrival of the Count of Bar – first siege of Toulouse, June 1211 – departure of the Count of Bar – abandonment of the siege – raid on the county of Foix – de Montfort in Quercy – submission of the Bishop of Cahors and lords of Quercy – capture of Lambert de Thury and Walter Langton by the Count of Foix – de Montfort returns to Pamiers.

XI. §§251–285, autumn 1211: Puylaurens defects from the crusaders – gathering of southern forces under Raymond VI, Raymond-Roger of Foix and Gaston de Béarn – siege of Castelnaudary by Raymond VI and his allies – defections from de Montfort – battle of Castelnaudary/Saint-Martin – the crusaders victorious but the southerners claim victory – further defections from the crusaders – Simon de Montfort at Pamiers and Fanjeaux – recruiting campaign of William, Archdeacon of Paris and Jacques de Vitry in northern France and Germany.

XII. §§286–366, December 1211 – December 1212: Arrival of Robert Mauvoisin with reinforcements for the crusaders – campaign in the Toulousain – Guy de Montfort joins his brother at Christmas 1211 – sieges of Les Touelles, Cahuzac, Saint-Marcel, January–March 1212 – arrival of Guy of les Vaux-de-Cernay, accompanied by his nephew Peter – siege of Hautpoul, April 1212 – consecrations of Guy as Bishop of Carcassonne and Arnold Amalric as Archbishop of Narbonne – recapture of Puylaurens – arrival of more crusaders – campaigns in the Albigeois – siege of Saint-Antonin, May 1212 – campaigns in the Agenais – Simon de Montfort assumes lordship of many places – siege of Penne d'Agenais, June–July 1212 – campaigns in the county of Foix under Guy de Montfort – more crusaders continue to arrive – Martin Algai captured and hanged at Biron – invasion of Quercy and siege of Moissac – Simon de Montfort goes south and reoccupies Saverdun – campaigns in the county of Comminges and in Gascony – Toulouse virtually surrounded – Council and Statutes of Pamiers, December 1212.

XIII. §§367–398, January 1213: King Peter of Aragon goes to Toulouse – Council of Lavaur – exchange of letters between the King and the legates – the legates reject the King's demands – the King takes the Counts of Toulouse, Foix and Comminges and Gaston de Béarn under his protection – report of the legates to Innocent III.

XIV. §§399–445, January–August 1213: Innocent III orders the suspension of the Crusade (letters of January 1213) – envoys from the legates go to Rome – Innocent III's volte-face – he withdraws his support for King Peter (letter of 21 May) – King Peter repudiates his ties of allegiance with de Montfort – Prince Louis of France takes the cross – King Peter sends envoys to Paris – the crusaders are reinforced – campaigns near Toulouse – siege of Puycelsi by Guy de Montfort – Amaury de Montfort knighted – Simon de Montfort in Gascony – recapitulation of earlier events.

XV. §§446–486, August–September 1213: Campaign and battle of Muret – Peter's account (§§446–466) – the prelates' account (§§468–483) – negotiations with the Toulousains after the battle.

XVI. §§487–549, September 1213 – January 1215: Simon de Montfort in Provence – Count Baldwin hanged (February 1214) – breach between Narbonne and the crusaders – Peter of Benevento, the Pope's new legate, reconciles the Narbonnese, the Counts of Comminges and Foix and the Count and consuls of Toulouse (April 1214) – marriage of Amaury de Montfort – reinforcements join the crusaders, including the legate Robert de Courçon (April 1214) – activity in Quercy and the Agenais – siege of Casseneuil (June–August 1214) and campaigns in the Périgord and Rouergue (autumn 1214) – the Council of Montpellier (January 1215) recommends to the Pope that Simon de Montfort should be declared Count of Toulouse.

XVII. §§550–573, April 1215 – April 1216: Prince Louis joins the crusaders – the Pope confirms de Montfort's provisional tenure of the county of Toulouse and other conquered territories – breach between Arnold Amalric and de Montfort – activity of Prince Louis – Fourth Lateran Council, resulting in de Montfort taking over the county of Toulouse – de Montfort does homage in Paris to King Philip Augustus.

XVIII. §§574–620, April 1216 – December 1218: Major uprising of the southerners – siege of Beaucaire, summer 1216 – partial sack of Toulouse by de Montfort, September 1216 – marriage of de Montfort's second son, Guy, to the Countess of Bigorre – siege of Montgrenier in the county of Foix, February–March 1217 – campaign of Simon de Montfort in the Rhône area, summer 1217 – Count Raymond returns to Toulouse, September 1217 – prolonged siege of Toulouse, autumn 1217 – summer 1218 – death of Simon de Montfort, 25 June 1218 – his son Amaury takes his place as leader of the Crusade – Prince Louis and others join the Crusade, winter 1218 – military activity in the areas of Foix and Comminges.

[Introduction]

[I. §§1–4: *Letter of dedication to Pope Innocent III.*]

[1] *Letter to the lord Pope which forms the preface to this work.* To the most holy father and blessed lord Innocent,[1] by God's grace Sovereign Pontiff of the Universal Church. May his humble and unworthy servant, Brother Peter, a monk of the abbey of les Vaux-de-Cernay,[2] kiss not only his feet but his very footprints.

[2] Blessed be the Lord God of Hosts! His Church in the South,[3] assailed by the storms of heresy, was almost driven to shipwreck; but recently, most holy father, during your pontificate and with your zealous help and the support of His servants, He has mercifully snatched Her from the mouths of lions and saved Her from the claws of beasts. I believe that such a marvellous achievement should not be forgotten by generations to come, but rather that the Lord's mighty acts[4] should be made known amongst the nations;[5] and I have therefore set down – however inadequately – this account of what was done, which I now dedicate to your majesty. I humbly pray that a schoolboy[6] will not be accused of presumption for turning his hand to so great a task, and attempting to shoulder a burden which is beyond his powers. My intention in this history, my sole purpose in writing it, is to ensure that the nations will be aware of God's marvellous works. The approach I have followed in writing my history will make this clear; my aim has been not to decorate the text with superfluous and misleading rhetoric but to tell the plain truth in plain fashion. Good father, your holiness may be quite satisfied that, even if I have not been able to cover in detail everything that happened, at least all I have written is true, and I have set down nothing that I did not either witness personally or learn from entirely authoritative and reliable persons.[7]

---

1   Innocent III, Pope 1198–1216. Innocent died on 16 July 1216, so the dedication must have been written before then. G&L III, pp. XVIII–XX, argue that it was probably written as early as 1213. See also Introduction, p. xxv.

2   The abbey lay in the valley of the Cernay, about 25km south-west of Paris. It was founded by Simon de Neauphle, probably in 1118, but possibly in 1128, and soon became part of the Cistercian Order. It was suppressed at the Revolution; its ruins remain. See G&L III, pp. IX–XII, and G&M, p. ix, n. 1. Cf. M. Aubert, *L'Abbaye des Vaux-de-Cernay* (Paris, 1931). Montfort l'Amaury, seat of Simon de Montfort, the future lay leader of the Crusade, lies about 10km north-west of the abbey.

3   Latin '*provincia*', here and frequently elsewhere denoting broadly the area of southern France from the Alps in the east to Aquitaine in the west, and translated by G&M (passim) as *Le Midi*. The term is in contrast to *Francia* or *Gallia*, which meant northern France. For this and other meanings of *provincia* see Appendix A(i).

4   Psalm 145, v. 12.

5   Latin '*gentes*'; usually so translated in the King James Bible (see e.g. Matthew 25, v. 32, and Acts 14, v. 16).

6   Latin '*puer elementarius*', literally 'a schoolboy', and almost certainly a rhetorical exaggeration here. See Introduction, p. xxiv, for a comment on the implications of the phrase for Peter's age.

7   Peter was himself an eyewitness to many of the events he describes in the years 1212–18, and would have gained information about the preceding years and about events he did not witness directly from those involved, whom he met when he came south with his uncle Guy in 1212. He had personally known Simon de Montfort since at least 1202 when he and his uncle, Abbot Guy of les Vaux-de-Cernay, accompanied

[3] In the first section of this work I will touch briefly on the heretical sects,[8] and describe how the inhabitants of the South were infected by the leprosy of heresy for many years past. Next, I will tell how these heretics of the South were urged by preachers of the word of God, and your holiness's ministers, to take their evil ways to heart – not once, but many times; then I will relate in order, to the best of my ability, the coming of the crusaders, the capture of cities and towns and other matters relating to the advancement of the business of the faith.[9]

[4] Readers should note that the general term 'Albigensians'[10] is used frequently in this history to refer to the heretics of Toulouse and other cities and towns, and their defenders,[11] since this is the name which came to be used by outsiders to refer to all the heretics of the South. Also, to help the reader find his way through the book, it has been divided into sections to correspond with the succession of events which took place as the business of the faith progressed.

him on the Fourth Crusade (§106). See Introduction, pp. xxiii–vi, for Peter's life, his approach to writing his history and his use of documents and other souces, and the value of the *Historia* itself as a source.

[8]   I.e. the Cathars and the Waldensians. See §§10–19 below, and the Bibliographical Note.

[9]   Latin '*negotium fidei*'. This phrase, its sister expression *negotium pacis*, and the composite *negotium pacis et fidei* ('the business of peace and the faith'), are used to describe the attempts to combat heresy in the Midi, firstly by the preaching campaign and then by the Albigensian Crusade. (In contrast, the term '*terrae sancte negotium*' in §439 means 'crusade to the Holy Land'.) The phrases occur quite frequently in Innocent III's letters (see e.g. §557 of the *Historia*; *PL* 216, 175; *Layettes* V, 1113 and 1115; and *RHGF* XVIII, 598). His use of the term may also be seen very clearly in the letter setting out the decisions of the Fourth Lateran Council translated in Appendix F(v). The French usually translate the composite phrase as *l'affaire de la paix et de la foi*. In the *Historia*, Peter uses the complete phrase *negotium pacis et fidei* only occasionally (e.g. §§67, 74, 138 and 596), but the shorter variants *negotium fidei* and *negotium (Jesu) Christi* occur very frequently. They also occur in papal correspondence and have essentially the same connotation as the full phrase. In practice Peter employs them virtually as synonyms for 'the Crusade'; we have usually translated as 'the business of the faith' etc., but in some contexts, such as '*negotium fidei contra hereticos*', we have translated simply as 'the Crusade' rather than 'the business of the faith against the heretics'. *Negotium fidei et pacis* is another variant found e.g. in William of Puylaurens (XVII), and later writers or documents (including a document referring to St Dominic as '*amicus negotii fidei et pacis*'); for these and an extended discussion see M.-H. Vicaire in *Cahiers de Fanjeaux*, vol. 4, *Paix de Dieu et guerre sainte en Languedoc*, pp. 102–127; and for further discussion of the ideas behind the phrases see Appendix G.

[10] Latin '*Albigenses*', from the city of Albi, on the River Tarn, and about 70km north-east of Toulouse. The term normally denotes the Cathars and not the Waldensians, and Peter seems to be using it in that sense here by specifying that it refers to the 'heretics of Toulouse'. '*Terra Albigensis*' or '*partes Albigenses*' is then the whole territory where heresy was considered to be prevalent and which was subject to attack by the crusaders (cf. the Latin title of the present work, *Historia Albigensis*, literally 'The Albigensian History'). When referring to the limited area of the Albigeois, or the ecclesiastical diocese of Albi, Peter uses the adjective *Albiensis*. For discussion of these terms see *HGL* VII, Note XIII, pp. 33–7; Wakefield and Evans, p. 720 n. 1; and the further references given there. The Albigeois had a Cathar bishop by the 1160s, since Sicard Cellerier seemed already to be acting as Cathar bishop of the Albigeois (possibly based at Lombers) at the Cathar Council held at Saint-Félix de Caraman, perhaps in 1167 or 1172, when three new Cathar bishoprics were set up; these were based at Toulouse, Carcassonne, and probably Agen. For this see B. Hamilton, 'The Cathar Council of Saint-Félix Reconsidered', *Archivum Fratrum Praedicatorum*, XLVIII (1978), esp. pp. 34–6, reprinted in B. Hamilton, *Monastic Reform, Catharism and the Crusades (900–1300)* (London, 1979); and see also William of Puylaurens IV, where Sicard is also mentioned. However, by the early 13th century the Albigeois was not a stronghold of Catharism, whose heartlands in the Midi lay in particular in the Toulousain, the Lauragais, the Carcassès, and the Razès (see e.g. Griffe, *LC*, pp. 61–9).

[11] See n. 26 to §10 on this and related terms.

[Part 1 – The Heretics]

[II. §§5–19: *Spread of heresy in the South – Peter of Castelnau and Brother Ralph appointed in 1203 as legates to combat heresy, of which Toulouse the main centre – description of the beliefs of the Cathar heretics – the Waldensians a less obnoxious heretical sect – the Cathar* consolamentum.**]**

[5] *In the name of our Lord Jesus Christ, and to his glory and honour, here begins the Albigensian History.* In the province of Narbonne,[1] where once the true faith had flourished, the enemy of the faith began to sow tares.[2] The people lost their senses and profaned the sacraments of Christ – the very essence and wisdom[3] of God; they deserted true religion and in their folly wandered at random in the pathless wastes of error, in the wilderness where there is no way.[4]

[6][5] Two Cistercian[6] monks, Brother Peter of Castelnau[7] and Brother

---

[1]   I.e. the ecclesiastical province – see Appendix A(i) on *provincia*. In the early 13th century the Archdiocese included the bishoprics of Carcassonne, Toulouse, Elne, Béziers, Agde, Lodève, Maguelonne, Nîmes and Uzès. However, other sees in the area were not subject to Narbonne: thus the bishoprics of Albi and Rodez were in the archiepiscopal province of Bourges, while that of Couserans was subject to Auch. Further east the sees of Avignon and Orange were subject to Arles, and Viviers to Vienne. For a discussion of the ecclesiastical geography of the Midi, see E. Griffe, 'Géographie ecclésiastique de la province de Narbonnaise au moyen âge', in *Annales du Midi*, XLVIII (1938), pp. 363–82.

[2]   Latin '*zizania*', meaning here the seeds of unbelief. Cf. Matthew 13, v. 25: 'the enemy . . . sowed tares amongst the wheat . . .'.

[3]   Latin '*sapor et sapientia*', literally 'taste and wisdom'. This is one of Peter's many alliterative puns and word-plays, not all of which can easily be reflected in translation. Cf. '*Tolosa dolosa*', §8 below, and other examples noted later.

[4]   Cf. Psalm 107, v. 40.

[5]   Peter's account of the preaching mission against heresy under Innocent III begins with events in 1203. He makes no mention of the earlier legatine mission by the Cistercians Rainier and Guy, who were appointed by Innocent in 1198 almost as soon as he had become Pope. A mission was also undertaken by the Cardinal of Santa Prisca (John of St Paul) to Montpellier in November 1200, but little is known of this. For these early initiatives see *PL* 214, 81ff, and ibid. 142, 457–8 and 675–6; *HGL* VI, pp. 222–6; Griffe, *LC*, pp. 206–13; Roquebert I, ch. 9; C. Thouzellier, *Catharisme et Valdéisme en Languedoc à la fin du XIIe et au début du XIIIe siècles, politique pontificale – Controverses*, 2nd edn (Paris, 1969), pp. 139–43 and 154–8; H. Maisonneuve, *Etudes sur les Origines de l'Inquisition*, 2nd edn (Paris, 1960), pp. 179–81; and Appendix G where Innocent's approach to combating heresy in the years 1198–1208 is discussed.

[6]   The Cistercians had been in the forefront of preaching efforts against the heretics in the South since these began in the mid-12th century. Cf. the missions to Toulouse in 1145 and 1178–82 discussed below in n. 24 to §9. The Cistercian order was the main source of preachers during the period 1203–1208, especially so after the appointment of Arnold Amalric, the Abbot of Cîteaux, as legate in the Midi in 1204 (see §20 below). William of Tudela, *Chanson* I, 2, p. 9, refers to 'the Order of Cîteaux, which was put at the head of this [preaching] mission'. See also William of Puylaurens VII–VIII. For the legation of Peter of Castelnau and Ralph of Fontfroide see *HGL* VI, pp. 229–30, and Thouzellier, op. cit., pp. 184–93. On the Cistercians' role in general in the Midi in this period see *Cahiers de Fanjeaux*, vol. 21, *Les Cisterciens en Languedoc*.

[7]   Peter, a native of Castelnau-le-Lez, near Montpellier, had been a canon (1182) and later (1197) archdeacon of the church of Maguelonne. He was a monk of the Cistercian abbey of Fontfroide, just south of Narbonne. Innocent III had known him before he became Pope, having as cardinal been involved in assessing Peter's case in a dispute over the validity of his election as archdeacon of Maguelonne (*PL* 214, 223–5). In 1199 he had been appointed by Innocent to assist the legate Rainier in resolving a case concerning the monastery of Saint-Guilhem-du-Desert (*PL* 214, 1053–7). He became a monk of Fontfroide in 1202. See A. Villemagne, *Bullaire du bienheureux Pierre de Castelnau* (Montpellier 1917), and cf.

Ralph[8] – men fired with zeal for the true faith – were appointed legates by the authority of the Supreme Pontiff to fight against the plague of faithlessness. Determined to perform their mission with dedication and enthusiasm, they went to the city of Toulouse,[9] the chief source of the poison of faithlessness which had infested the people and deflected them from the knowledge of Christ and His pure splendour and divine glory.[10] The root of bitterness springing up[11] was now so strongly and deeply embedded in the hearts of men that it could no longer be easily dug out. Time and again the citizens had been strongly urged to renounce heresy and drive out the heretics, urged by men following the ways of the Apostles,[12] but with little success; their listeners had abandoned life and were determined to cling to death. Infected and diseased[13] with a worthless animal cunning, earthly and devilish in its nature, they knew nothing of the true wisdom which comes from above and is easy to be entreated and in harmony with virtue.[14]

[7] But now at last these two olive trees, these two candlesticks shining before the Lord,[15] were able to inject a servile fear into their servile audience. By threat-

---

Griffe, *LC*, pp. 214–16. The appointment of Peter and Ralph as legates took place in 1203, probably in the autumn, but the exact date is uncertain because the papal letters confirming the appointments do not survive.

8 Brother Ralph (Latin *Radulphus*, in French *Raoul* or *Razouls*) was also a Cistercian monk of Fontfroide. He is described by William of Puylaurens (VII) as '*magister Radulfus, persona litterata multum et honesta*' (Master Ralph, a very learned and honoured man). He died in July 1207 (see §50 below).

9 For the early history of heresy at Toulouse in general see Griffe, *Débuts*, esp. pp. 33–40; Griffe, *LC*, pp. 70–6; Maisonneuve, *Etudes sur les Origines de l'Inquisition*, pp. 121–37; and Roquebert I, chs. 1–5. The city had long been regarded as the centre of heresy in the South. As early as 1022 the Chronicle of Adhémar of Chabannes refers to 'Manicheans' in Toulouse (translated in R. I. Moore, *The Birth of Popular Heresy* (London, 1975), pp. 8–10, and in Wakefield and Evans, pp. 74–6) although they were probably not dualists; see discussion in R. I. Moore, *The Origins of European Dissent* (London, 1978), p. 30. In appealing to the General Chapter of Cîteaux for help to combat the spread of heresy in his domains in 1177 (*RHGF* XIII, p. 140), Count Raymond V of Toulouse complained that heresy was causing discord within families and had even corrupted members of the clergy, and that he was powerless to prevent its spread. Henry de Marcy, Abbot of Clairvaux, described Toulouse as '*mater haeresis et caput erroris*' (*PL* 204, 236) when writing about his mission to Toulouse in 1178–82, on which see n. 24 below. Peter of les Vaux-de-Cernay always regarded Toulouse and its citizens as the incorrigible enemies of the Crusade and of the Catholic Church, and thus by definition favourable to heresy; cf. the more extended attack on Toulouse in §§8–9 below. However, Peter exaggerates the strength of heresy in the city and the proportion of its population which actively supported it; indeed in their letter of July 1211 to King Peter of Aragon (*HGL* VIII, 612–19, for which see n. 42(i) to §137 and elsewhere), the then consuls of Toulouse, protesting their orthodoxy, said that a long time previously it had been decreed by the former Count (Raymond V) in agreement with the citizens 'that if any heretic were found in Toulouse . . . he would be handed over for punishment, together with his receiver [see n. 26 to §9] and the possessions of both confiscated, after which we burnt many [heretics; Latin '*unde multos combussimus*'] and have not ceased to do this when we have discovered [any]'. On the other hand there is no confirmation of this claim and, in general, the city authorities remained unwilling to take action against heresy.

10 Cf. II Corinthians 4, v. 6.

11 Hebrews 12, v. 15.

12 Latin '*viri apostolici*', apostolic men. See also §26, '*viri apostolici, scilicet predicatores nostri*'. The phrase alludes to the concept of the *vita apostolica*, whereby preachers against heresy would live simply like the Apostles, which was so important a guiding force in the renewed preaching mission after 1206, on which see below, §§20–2. Peter's allusion in the context of the 1203 mission is somewhat anticipatory.

13 Word-play: '*affecti et infecti*'.

14 Cf. James 3, vv. 15–17.

15 Cf. Revelations 11, v. 4.

ening them with the loss of their possessions and calling down on them the wrath of kings and princes, they persuaded them to agree to forswear heresy and expel the heretics.[16] However, this rejection of sin was not prompted by love of goodness but – as the poet[17] says – by fear of retribution; the proof was that they at once went back on their promises, suffered the renewal of their wretchedness and gave concealment to the heretics who preached in their meeting places under the protection of darkness. How hard it is to break with evil habits![18]

[8] It is said that since its first foundation, treacherous Toulouse[19] has rarely if ever been free of this detestable plague, the sin of heresy.[20] The poison of super-stitious unbelief was passed from father to son one after another. Indeed, there is a tradition that on a previous occasion long ago the city suffered avenging hands in expiation of this great sin, and deservedly endured the destruction of her people, to the extent that the ploughed fields extended to the very centre of the city.[21] Moreover, one of the famous kings who ruled the city in those times, believed to be called Alaric, suffered the supreme dishonour of being hanged from a gibbet at the city gates.

[16] Here Peter refers to events of December 1203, on which see *HGL* VI, pp. 229–30, and Thouzellier, *Catharisme et Valdéisme en Languedoc,* pp. 184–5. The two legates arrived in Toulouse early that month. On 13 December, in the presence of the Bishop of Toulouse and the Abbot of Saint-Sernin, the consuls and assembled citizens swore a solemn oath to expel heretics and uphold orthodoxy. The legates are said to have confirmed the liberties of Toulouse before the oath-swearing, and this was no doubt an important factor in the consuls' readiness to co-operate. The presence of the legates is also mentioned in William of Puylaurens, VII, who suggests that Raymond VI also swore an oath to them (see n. 37 to §27 below). Dates for these events come from an act of the consuls of Toulouse of March 1204, reported by Guillaume de Catel, *Histoire des Comtes de Toulouse,* p. 236, and the consuls' oath is also mentioned in their letter of 1211 to Peter of Aragon in *HGL* VIII, 612–19 (see n. 9 to §6 above); see also Griffe, *LC,* pp. 217–18, and Roquebert I, pp. 159–61. The consuls of Toulouse seem to have co-operated with the legates both quickly and without external pressure. Peter is exaggerating the role of the secular overlords of the region in supporting the legates; only King Peter of Aragon took an active part, convoking the debate at Carcassonne held in 1204, on which see Vicaire, pp. 87–8; *HGL* VI, p. 231; and the account in the *Chanson* I, 2, pp. 8–10. From Toulouse the legates went early in 1204 to Carcassonne and Béziers.
[17] Horace, *Epistles* I, xvi, lines 52–3: '*Oderunt peccare boni virtutis amore./ Tu nihil admittes in te formidine poenae.*' ('Good men hate to sin because they love virtue. You however will stay clear of wrong-doing because you fear punishment.')
[18] The consuls seem to have taken few if any active steps to expel heretics from Toulouse after the oath of 1203, and its practical results were minimal. It did, however, enable the legates to claim some immediate success, while later the consuls would cite it as evidence of their orthodoxy and willingness to co-operate (again see their letter of 1211 to King Peter of Aragon). From his account of the oath of December 1203 Peter launches into an attack on Toulouse (§§8–9), and then gives a description of the Cathars and Waldensians in the Midi; his chronology is very compressed here, and he makes no reference to events in 1204–1205, resuming his narrative in §20 with an account of events in 1206. For the continuing activities of the legates in 1204 and 1205 see, for example, Griffe, *LC,* pp. 218–45.
[19] A pun, '*Tolosa dolosa*'; cf. '*Tolosanus dolosanus*' in §68. (*Dolosus* is from *dolus,* guile or deceit, not *dolor,* grief.) The same pun occurs frequently in later sections.
[20] Latin '*heretice pravitatis*', literally 'heretical wickedness'. '*Heretica pravitas*' recurs constantly in the *Historia* and in the papal correspondence, effectively as an equivalent to *heresis,* and we have usually translated simply as 'heresy'.
[21] This tradition is mentioned by Bertrand, Bishop of Béziers, writing to the Pope in 1213 (*PL* 216, 844). He says: 'this city, which is and has from of old been a nest of heretics, with the result (it is said) that it was for a similar reason utterly destroyed and ploughed up (*eversa funditus et exarata*)'. G&L suggest (I, p. 8 n. 2) that the following reference to Alaric may arise from a misunderstood reading of a text relating to King Alaric I of the Goths.

[9] So infected with this ancient filth were the people of Toulouse – the generation[22] of vipers – that even in our own times they could not be torn from their deep-rooted wickedness; indeed even after their inborn disposition to embrace heresy has been driven out by an avenging pitchfork,[23] they are always ready to allow its return – such is their thirst to follow the ways of their fathers and their reluctance to abandon their traditions.[24] Just as a bunch of grapes can take on a sickly colour merely from the sight of its neighbour, and in the fields the scab of a single sheep or the mange of one pig can destroy a whole herd,[25] so, following the example of Toulouse, the neighbouring cities and towns where the heresiarchs had taken root were caught up in the shoots put out by that city's unbelief, and became infected with the dreadful plague, miserably and to an amazing degree. The barons of the South almost all became defenders and receivers[26] of the heretics, welcomed them to their hearts and defended them against God and the Church.

[10] *On the sects of heretics.*[27] This is an appropriate place for me to describe

---

[22] See Matthew 23, v. 33. Latin '*genimen*', translated in the Authorised Version as 'generation' in the sense of 'progeny'. '*Genimen viperarum*' occurs in the letter of Bishop Bertrand referred to in the previous note.

[23] A reflection of Horace, *Epistles* I, x, line 24: '*Naturam expelles furca, tamen usque recurret.*' ('Although you may drive out Nature with a pitch fork, she will always hurry back.')

[24] Peter may here be alluding to several earlier missions against heresy in Toulouse. St Bernard of Clairvaux undertook a preaching mission against heresy in the city in 1145. His efforts were directed against the radical preacher Henry the Monk, who was certainly not a Cathar, but St Bernard may also have encountered other less numerous heretics (referred to as '*Ariani*'), who were dualists. For contemporary accounts of this mission in translation see Wakefield and Evans, pp. 122–6 (translation of *PL* 182, 434–6, and 185, 312–13), and Moore, *Birth of Popular Heresy*, pp. 41–6 (translation of *PL* 185, 410–16). For discussion see Griffe, *Débuts*, pp. 33–7; Roquebert I, pp. 50–61; and the general discussion of early Catharism in Lambert, pp. 55–61. A subsequent mission was headed by Peter of Pavia, Cardinal-priest of St Chrysogonus, in 1178, accompanied amongst others by Henry de Marcy, Abbot of Clairvaux, who continued the preaching until 1181–82. For Peter of Pavia's account see *PL* 199, 1119–24, and for Henry de Marcy's see *PL* 204, 234–42; both are translated by Moore, *Birth of Popular Heresy*, pp. 113–22. Another version of Peter of Pavia's account is translated in Wakefield and Evans, pp. 194–200. See also Griffe, *Débuts*, pp. 90–99 and 123–38, and *HGL* VI, pp. 78–85 and VII, pp. 11–14.

[25] From Juvenal, *Satire* II, 79–81: '*sicut grex totus in agris/ Unius scabie cadit et porrigine porci,/ Uvaque conspecta livorem ducit ab uva.*' ('Just as, in the fields, the scab of a single sheep or the mange of a single pig can destroy a whole herd, and a bunch of grapes takes on a sickly colour from the sight of another.')

[26] Latin '*defensores et receptatores*'. 'Defenders' of heretics were those who knowingly defended them in word or deed, and 'receivers' those who knowingly welcomed them to their houses (cf. Wakefield and Evans, p. 721). There was a well established canonical tradition that those who gave help, counsel or favour to heretics shared in their sin, and this had been reasserted at the Third Lateran Council in 1179. The terms *defensores . . . et receptores* had been used in Canon 27 of that Council (on which see for instance Griffe, *Débuts*, pp. 115–19) and were commonly employed to cover those who supported, sympathised with, or tolerated heretics. Examples of the use of these terms can be found in §§381, 382, 388, 409 and 453. A related term was *fautor*, protector of heretics, which occurs for example in §§382, 394 and n. 91 to §523 below: the term is also found, for example, coupled with *receptatores* by the legate Milo in the Processus of June 1209 (*PL* 216, 92, and see §77 below).

[27] What follows, save for §18 on the Waldensians, concerns the Cathars only. Peter's comments are (as he acknowledges) brief, and they are highly partisan, written so as to make the Cathars seem ridiculous or outrageous. They are, however, also clear, and once allowance is made for the value judgments incorporated within his description, it does not in general conflict with our knowledge of Catharism from other sources. G&L (I, pp. 9–20) provide copious notes on these chapters which we have not attempted to summarise. For general comment on the organisation and beliefs of the Cathar church, and its history in Languedoc before and after the period covered by the *Historia*, see: Lambert, ch. 7; translated texts with notes in Wakefield and Evans, esp. sections 28–38; Moore, *The Origins of European Dissent*, chs. VI–VIII;

briefly but clearly the various heresies and heretical sects. First it should be understood that the heretics maintained[28] the existence of two creators, one of things invisible whom they called the 'benign' God and one of the things visible whom they named the 'malign' God. They attributed the New Testament to the benign God and the Old Testament to the malign God, and rejected the whole of the latter except for certain passages quoted in the New Testament. These they considered acceptable because of their respect for the New Testament. They maintained that the author of the Old Testament was a 'liar'; he said to our first ancestors[29] 'on the day that ye eat of the tree of the knowledge of good and evil, ye shall surely die'; but they did not die after eating the fruit as he had predicted (although, of course, the real truth is that as soon as they had tasted the forbidden fruit they became subject to the misery of death). They also called him 'murderer' because he exterminated the inhabitants of Sodom and Gomorrah by fire and destroyed the world by the waters of the flood; and because he drowned Pharaoh and the Egyptians in the sea. They declared that all the patriarchs of the Old Testament were damned; they asserted that St John the Baptist was one of the chief devils.[30]

[11] Further, in their secret meetings they said that the Christ who was born in the earthly and visible Bethlehem and crucified at Jerusalem was 'evil', and that Mary Magdalene was his concubine – and that she was the woman taken in adultery who is referred to in the Scriptures;[31] the 'good' Christ, they said, neither ate nor drank nor assumed the true flesh and was never in this world, except spiritually in the body of Paul. I have used the term 'the earthly and visible Bethlehem' because the heretics believed there is a different and invisible earth in which – according to some of them – the 'good' Christ was born and crucified. Again, they said that the good God had two wives, Oolla and Ooliba,[32] on whom he begat sons and daughters. There were other heretics who said that there was only one Creator, but that he had two sons, Christ and the Devil; they said moreover that all created beings had once been good, but that everything had been corrupted by the vials referred to in the Book of Revelations.[33]

[12] All these people, the limbs of the Antichrist, the first-born of Satan, the

---

and J. Duvernoy, *Le Catharisme: La Religion des Cathares* (Toulouse, 1976), esp. ch. VI (2) on Cathar rituals. Griffe, in *Débuts* and *LC*, provides a full and well documented account of the spread of Catharism in the South from its beginnings. See also *Cahiers de Fanjeaux* vol. 3, *Cathares en Languedoc*, and Y. Dossat, 'Cathares et Vaudois à la veille de la croisade albigeoise', *Revue historique et littéraire du Languedoc* III, repr. in Dossat, *Eglise et hérésie en France au XIIIème siècle* (London, 1982). On the Waldensians see §18 below.

[28] Wakefield and Evans, in translating §§5–19 (pp. 235–41), comment in their notes (p. 721) on Peter's use of the past tense in §§10–18, and ask: 'Did the author presume that when he wrote heresy had been eradicated by the Crusade? Or is this due to his reliance on some source?'

[29] Genesis 2, v. 17.

[30] The Cathars held that John the Baptist was an agent of Satan, quoting as evidence passages such as Matthew 11, v. 11, where Jesus says: 'he that is least in the Kingdom of Heaven is greater than he [John the Baptist]'. The Cathars believed that John's baptism with water, which used an element of the physical world, was designed to obscure Jesus's baptism in the spirit – the Cathar *consolamentum*. Cf. J. Duvernoy, *Le Catharisme: La Religion des Cathares*, p. 87.

[31] John 8, v. 3.

[32] Cf. Ezekiel 23, v. 4: 'Aholah and Aholibah'.

[33] Revelations 16, v. 1.

seed of evildoers, children that are corrupters,[34] speaking lies in hypocrisy,[35] the seducers of simple hearts,[36] had infected almost the whole of the province of Narbonne with the poison of their perfidy. They said that the Roman Church was a den of thieves, and the harlot spoken of in the Book of Revelations.[37] They ridiculed the sacraments of the Church, arguing publicly that the holy water of baptism was no better than river water, that the consecrated host of the holy body of Christ was no different from common bread; instilling into the ears of simple folk the blasphemy that the body of Christ, even if it had been large enough to contain the whole Alps, would by now be wholly consumed and reduced to nothing by those eating of it. They considered that confirmation, extreme unction and confession were trivial and empty ceremonies; they preached that holy matrimony was mere harlotry, and that no one could find salvation in it by begetting sons and daughters. They denied the resurrection of the body, and invented new myths, claiming that our souls are really those angelic spirits who were driven from heaven through their rebellious pride and then left their glorified bodies in the ether; and that these souls after successively inhabiting any seven earthly bodies will then return to their original bodies, as though they had then completed their long penance.[38]

[13] It should be understood that some of the heretics were called 'perfected' heretics or 'good men', others 'believers of the heretics'.[39] The 'perfected' heretics wore a black robe, claimed (falsely) to practice chastity, and renounced meat, eggs and cheese. They wished it to appear that they were not liars although they lied, especially about God, almost unceasingly! They also said that no one should take

---

[34] Isaiah 1, v. 4.
[35] I Timothy 4, v. 2.
[36] Cf. Romans 16, v. 18.
[37] Revelations 17.
[38] For a succinct discussion of Cathar myths see Lambert, pp. 121–5.
[39] A 'perfected heretic' (male *perfectus*, female *perfecta*; plurals *perfecti* and *perfectae*) was one who had been fully received into the Cathar church through receipt of the Cathar equivalent of baptism, a ritual known as the *consolamentum*. This meant that on death the recipient's soul would gain release from its earthly imprisonment and be reunited with its heavenly body and spirit, ascending once again to heaven. The receipt of the *consolamentum* by those not close to death usually required an arduous preparation to prove the ability of the individual concerned to live the life of a *perfectus*. The ritual was administered by other *perfecti* and involved the laying on of hands and the making of declarations. *Perfecti* and *perfectae* lived a harsh ascetic life, renouncing the things of this world as far as possible. Local communities of *perfecti* usually met (monthly) in a ceremony known as the *apparallamentum*, which involved a mutual confession of venial sins. The majority of those who supported Catharism were not, however, 'perfected', and did not receive the *consolamentum* until near to death. Close adherents of Catharism were called 'believers' (*credentes*, singular *credens*) who showed their respect for the *perfecti* through a ritual known as the *melioramentum*, a formal greeting which was often called an 'adoration' by members of the Catholic Church. *Credentes* were not bound by any of the strict rules of conduct required of a *perfectus* or *perfecta*, and for this reason were often accused by their opponents (on a priori grounds) of licentiousness, as in the passage which follows. The *credens* would, however, expect to receive the *consolamentum* and thus become a full member of the Cathar church before death, gaining release for his or her soul. The distinction between *perfecti* and *credentes* was sometimes (as in §14 below) compared to that between clergy and ordinary believers in the Catholic Church. There were also those who appear to have been classed as mere 'sympathisers', but the distinction between their status and that of the *credentes* is not wholly clear. These and other points are developed in the next few sections; and see, for example, Lambert, pp. 106–11, for a fuller discussion.

oaths for any reason. The term 'believers' was applied to those who lived a secular existence and did not try to copy the way of life of the 'perfected', but hoped that by following their faith they would attain salvation; they were separated in the way they lived, but united in their beliefs – or rather unbelief! Those called 'believers' were dedicated to usury, robbery, murder and illicit love, and to all kinds of perjury and perversity; indeed they felt they could sin in safety and without restraint, because they believed they could be saved without restitution of what they had stolen and without confession and penitence, so long as they were able to recite the Lord's prayer and ensure a 'laying-on of hands' by their masters, in the final moments of their lives.

[14] To explain further, they selected from the 'perfected' heretics officials[40] whom they called 'deacons' and 'bishops', and the 'believers' held that no one of them could attain salvation without the laying-on of hands by these clergy just before death; indeed, they considered that however sinful a man might have been, then provided he had undergone this laying-on of hands on his deathbed, and so long as he was able to recite the Lord's prayer, he would gain salvation and (to use their own expression) 'consolation'; to the extent that he would immediately fly up to heaven without making any amends or reparations for wrongs he had committed.

[15] Here I would like to tell an amusing story I have heard relating to this subject. A certain heretical believer, at the point of death, received 'consolation' from his master by the laying-on of hands, but could not recite the Lord's prayer, and died. His 'consoler' did not know what to say about the man; he seemed to have been saved through having received the laying-on of hands, but damned because he had not recited the Lord's prayer. So, the heretics consulted a certain knight, Bertrand de Saissac,[41] a heretic, as to what decision they should make. His advice was: 'as to this man, I will support the position and declare him to be saved. However, my judgment is that all others who shall have failed to recite the Lord's Prayer in their final moments are damned.'

[16] Another amusing story concerns a believer who willed three hundred sous to the heretics and instructed his son to pass that sum to them. When he died they asked his son for the legacy, and he said to them 'First, please tell me in what state is my father.' They replied: 'You may be entirely satisfied that he is

---

[40] Latin '*magistratus*'. For descriptions of the structure of the Cathar churches and their officials see the general accounts cited in the notes above and Roquebert I, pp. 99–101.

[41] Saissac was a *castrum* in the Montagne Noire region to the north of Carcassonne, and its seigneur Bertrand was one of the most important lesser lords of the Carcassès. He was a trusted vassal of Roger II, Viscount of Béziers, and when Roger died in 1194 Bertrand became protector of the young Viscount Raymond-Roger, who was only nine at the time (*HGL* VIII, 429–31). Bertrand was well known for his heretical sympathies and was almost certainly a Cathar 'believer' (*credens*). The presence of Cathar *perfecti* at Saissac is discussed in Griffe, *LC*, pp. 165–68, and Roquebert I, pp. 142–3. Bertrand was also well known for his disrespectful attitude to the Church, but was not atypical of southern lords in this. In 1194 he swore an oath to Bishop Geoffrey of Béziers to protect the Church and drive out Cathars and Waldensians, but despite this he continued to tolerate them freely. In 1197 he intervened with force in the election to the abbacy of Alet, south of Carcassonne, when he overthrew the monks' election of a new abbot in order to secure the installation of his own candidate, Bozon, who later obtained the approval of Archbishop Berengar of Narbonne by offering a money payment; see *HGL* VI, p. 158.

saved and has already joined the heavenly spirits.' Smiling, he rejoined: 'Thanks be to God and to you! Truly, since my father is now in glory his soul has no need of alms, and I know you are too kind to call him back from glory. Know therefore that you will get no money from me.'

[17] Other points I must report are as follows. Some of the heretics declared that no one could sin from the navel downwards; they characterised images in churches as idolatry; they maintained that church bells were the trumpets of devils; and they said that it was no greater sin for a man to sleep with his mother or his sister than with any other woman. One of their most absurd heresies was to say that if any of the perfected heretics committed a mortal sin (for example by eating even the smallest amount of meat or cheese or eggs or anything else forbidden), then all who had received 'consolation' from him lost the Holy Spirit and must receive consolation again; and even that those already saved would have fallen from heaven because of the 'consoler's' sin.[42]

[18] There was another sect of heretics who received the name 'Valdenses'[43] from Valdius a citizen of Lyon. They were evil men, but very much less perverted than other heretics; they agreed with us in many matters, and differed in some. Ignoring many lesser heresies, their error arose in four major points. They wore sandals in imitation of the Apostles;[44] they condemned the swearing of oaths or the taking of life in any circumstances; and they maintained that in cases of need, it was in order for anyone to administer holy communion even though he had not received holy orders from a bishop, so long as he was wearing sandals.

This brief commentary on the heretical sects will, I think, be sufficient.

[19] *The form of conversion (or rather perversion) used by the heretics.*[45] When anyone wishes to join the heretics, the person receiving him says: 'Friend, if you wish to join us you must renounce all beliefs of the Roman Church.' He replies: 'I so renounce.' 'Therefore receive the Holy Spirit from the good men,' and he breathes seven times into the convert's mouth. Then he says: 'Do you renounce

---

[42] In other words the efficacy of the *consolamentum* depended on the continuing observance of its conditions not only by the recipient but also by the *perfectus* administering it. The implications of this point are considered by Lambert, p. 108.

[43] The Waldensians, or Poor of Lyon, were the other heretical sect active in the Midi in the early 13th century. Their movement was founded in 1173 by one Waldes (or Waldo or Valdes), a merchant of Lyon who gave up his worldly wealth and devoted himself to evangelical preaching and vernacular Bible reading. Waldes and his followers soon fell foul of the Archbishop of Lyon, and appealed to Rome. They were examined at the Third Lateran Council in 1179 and found to be theologically sound, but were to be allowed to continue their preaching only if licensed by local ecclesiastical authority. When such permission was inevitably refused, they ignored the prohibitions placed on them and in 1182 were excommunicated. Their condemnation was repeated and strengthened in the decretal *Ad Abolendam*, issued by Lucius III at Verona in 1184. The Waldensians were thus very different from the Cathars, and the issue which turned them into schismatic heretics was not theological belief but refusal to submit to Catholic discipline. Although in subsequent years they did come to disagree with aspects of official dogma, they always remained very hostile to the Cathars. The movement spread into northern Italy, Languedoc and northern Spain. See Lambert, ch. 5, for an account and further references; *Cahiers de Fanjeaux*, vol. 2, *Vaudois languedociens et Pauvres Catholiques*; and Thouzellier, *Catharisme et Valdéisme en Languedoc*, pp. 16–18 and 24–38. The Waldensians are mentioned again in the *Historia*, in §§48 and 513.

[44] Note how Peter mentions that the Waldensians sought to imitate the *vita apostolica*, on which cf. n. 8 to §21 below.

[45] I.e. the *consolamentum*, on which see n. 39 to §13 above.

the sign of the cross which the priest who baptised you made with oil and unguent on your chest, shoulders and head?' The convert replies: 'I so renounce.' 'Do you believe that the water of baptism helps to gain salvation for you?' He replies: 'I do not so believe.' 'Do you renounce the veil which the priest placed on your head after baptism?'. He replies: 'I so renounce.' In this way he receives the baptism of the heretics and rejects the baptism of the Church. Then all present place their hands on his head and kiss him and clothe him in a black robe; from that time he is counted as one of them.

[Part II – The Preachers]

[III. §§20–54, 1206–07: *The preaching campaign of 1206–1207 – Bishop Diego of Osma and his companion [St Dominic] – their meeting with the legates Arnold Amalric, Abbot of Cîteaux, Peter of Castelnau and Ralph at Montpellier (June 1206) – debates with heretics at Servian, Béziers and Carcassonne (autumn 1206) – debate at Montréal (April 1207) – Peter of Castelnau goes to Provence – excommunication of Count Raymond VI of Toulouse (April 1207) – account of the unbelief of Raymond VI – arrival of twelve Cistercian abbots to join the preaching campaign – debate at Pamiers (September 1207) – Bishop Diego returns to Osma – Guy, Abbot of les Vaux-de-Cernay, appointed chief preacher – miracle at Montréal recounted by Dominic.*]

[20] *Here begins the account of the coming of the preachers to the Albigensian area.* In the year 1206 of the Incarnation of the Word, Diego, Bishop of Osma[1] (a great man, greatly to be praised) went to the Curia at Rome. His ardent wish was to resign his bishopric so that he could more easily devote himself to preaching the gospel of Christ to the pagans.[2] However, Pope Innocent was unwilling to grant this holy man's request, and instead instructed him to return to his see. On his way back from the Curia he stopped at Montpellier[3] and there met the three legates of the Holy See, Arnold the venerable Abbot of Cîteaux[4] and the two

---

[1]   Diego de Acebes, Bishop of Osma in Old Castile, from 1201 to his death in December 1207.
[2]   Probably amongst the Cumans in eastern Europe, but conceivably the Moslems in Spain (see the translation of Jordan of Saxony and associated sources by M.-H. Vicaire, *Saint Dominique et ses Frères: Evangile ou Croisade?* (Paris, 1967), p. 57 and n. 4). According to Jordan of Saxony, Diego had visited Denmark in 1203 and again in 1205, to act on behalf of King Alfonso of Castile who was seeking to arrange a marriage between his son Ferdinand and the daughter of a Danish nobleman. Dominic accompanied him on both journeys. When he returned on his second visit in 1205 it was found that the young woman had died, and he then decided to visit Rome on his return journey, probably in 1206, in order to ask Innocent to allow him to give up his bishopric and preach. Jordan of Saxony confirms that Innocent refused. See also Vicaire ch. 4 and Roquebert I, pp. 183–8.
[3]   Vicaire dates this meeting at Montpellier to June 1206 (see p. 80 and n. 1 to ch. VI) and in ch. VI discusses the meeting in detail. According to Jordan of Saxony, Diego, Dominic and the rest of Diego's company had, after leaving Rome, gone first to visit Cîteaux, on which see Vicaire ch. IV. Given that Innocent III had in July 1206 written to the Cistercian General Chapter appealing for help (*PL* 215, 940–1), it may be that Diego's visit to Cîteaux was connected with this. Vicaire (see esp. pp. 91–3) considers the possibility that the meeting was not accidental but arose because Diego had discussed plans for changing the approach to the preaching campaign against heresy in the Midi with Innocent himself while in Rome, and gone to Cîteaux to further the arrangements. See also discussions in Thouzellier, *Catharisme et Valdéisme*, pp. 193–5, and Maisonneuve, *Etudes sur les Origines de l'Inquisition*, pp. 181–2.
[4]   The first mention of Arnold Amalric, Abbot of Cîteaux, who was to play so important a part in the leadership of the early stages of the Crusade. We do not know his origins, but he was Abbot of the Cistercian monastery of Poblet near Tarragona in Catalonia from 1196 until 1198. In 1198 he was installed as Abbot of Grandselve, about 40km north of Toulouse, which was the wealthy mother house of Poblet and other Cistercian abbeys in the Midi, including Fontfroide. He remained there until his election as Abbot of Cîteaux itself and head of the Cistercian Order in 1201. See G&L III, pp. XIV–XV, and *Chanson* I, p. 13 n. 1. He had been appointed as a third, and in effect senior, legate in the Midi by Innocent III in May 1204, in an effort to bolster the work of Peter of Castelnau and Ralph: see letter of 31 May 1204, *PL* 215, 358–60. He was effectively in overall charge of the Crusade in its first few years: see e.g. §71, §101 (where he is

Cistercian monks, Brother Peter of Castelnau and Brother Ralph. The legates were weary of the task entrusted to them by the Pope and wished to abandon it, since they had achieved little or nothing in preaching to the heretics. Whenever they tried to preach to them, the heretics countered by pointing to the disgraceful behaviour of the clergy and argued that if the legates wanted to reform the life style of the clergy, they would have to give up their preaching campaign.[5]

[21] To calm the concerns of the legates the Bishop gave this salutary advice: leaving everything else aside, they should concentrate more vigorously on their preaching; and they should counter the criticisms of the ill-disposed by display- ing humility in all their conduct; by following the example of the Divine Master in deed and word; by going about on foot and without gold or silver ornaments;[6] and by generally imitating the ways of the Apostles in all respects.[7] However, the legates did not themselves wish to take responsibility for such an initiative; instead they promised that if some acceptable authority were to set an example, they would most willingly follow it.[8] What more? At once the Bishop, that dedi- cated servant of God, put himself forward to show the way; he sent his household and waggons back to Osma and, content with a single companion[9] left

described as '*hujus sacri negotii pater et magister*', ('father and master of this sacred business'), and §154 for his intervention at Minerve in 1210. He was elected Archbishop of Narbonne in 1212 (see §299), but was still prominent in the leadership of the Crusade at the Council of Lavaur in January 1213 (§§367ff), and at the time of the battle of Muret (§§446ff). Subsequently he became less and less involved in the Crusade, more especially since his claim to the Duchy of Narbonne led to a bitter quarrel with Simon de Montfort (see §561 and n. 29).

[5] Peter of Castelnau and his fellow legates Arnold Amalric and Ralph had become increasingly discour- aged in 1204 and 1205 by the failure of their preaching effort, by the continuing weakness of the Church in the Midi, and by the obduracy of their opponents and the willingness of the local aristocracy to protect them. Cf. Innocent's letter to Peter of Castelnau in *PL* 215, 525–6, 26 January 1205; Innocent's renewed appeals to Philip Augustus at this time in *PL* 215, 526–8, 7 February 1205; and the comment by William of Tudela in the *Chanson* I, 3, p. 12: 'the more he [Arnold Amalric] preached to them [the heretics], the more they held him up to ridicule . . .'. The meeting with Diego, described in the next section, marked an important turning point and led to a reinvigoration of the preaching campaign.

[6] Cf. Matthew 10, v. 9.

[7] I.e. following the *vita apostolica*, living on alms and going about on foot dressed simply: see n. 12 to §6 above.

[8] That the legates were reluctant to take up Diego's proposals may partly have stemmed from the Cistercians' traditional dislike of mendicancy, on which see Vicaire, p. 89 and n. 66 to ch. VI. Their reaction does not suggest that Diego presented his ideas as ones he had discussed with Innocent, who did, however, later give his formal authority to the new style of preaching in a letter of 17 November 1206, addressed to the legate Ralph (*PL* 215, 1024–5) instructing him to appoint preachers in the Midi who might recall the heretics from error by imitating the poverty of Christ and setting a good example in the way they carried out their duty of preaching ('*paupertatem Christi pauperis imitando . . . per exemplum operis et docu- mentum sermonis*'), not hesitating to deal humbly with humble folk. See also Appendix G on the develop- ment of the preaching campaign.

[9] This was the sub-prior of the cathedral at Osma, Dominic Guzman, a native of Caleruega in Old Castile, the future St Dominic and founder of the Order of Friars Preacher named after him; see Vicaire passim, and *Cahiers de Fanjeaux* vol. 1, *Saint Dominique en Languedoc*. He was to continue his preaching, based first at Fanjeaux and then at Toulouse, after the main preaching effort ceased following the murder of Peter of Castelnau in January 1208. Dominic is mentioned by name by Peter in §54 below. At the time Peter was writing, Dominic had not yet assumed his later importance; compare the account of William of Puylaurens, writing (probably) in the 1250s, who gives Dominic more prominence in the events of these years. He became well known to Simon de Montfort and to other crusaders, and received material support from them for his work; cf. Appendix C.

Montpellier together with Peter of Castelnau and Ralph. The Abbot[10] returned to Cîteaux, because the Chapter General of the Cistercian Order was due to be held shortly,[11] and also because after the Chapter he wished to take with him certain abbots of the Order to assist him in conducting the preaching campaign which had been entrusted to him.[12]

[22] After leaving Montpellier the Bishop of Osma and the monks arrived at a *castrum* named Servian,[13] where they came across an heresiarch named Baldwin and a certain Theodoric[14] – a son of perdition, the fuel of eternal hell-fire. This person originated in France,[15] of noble descent, and had been a canon of Nevers; later, however, after a certain knight who was his uncle and a heretic of the worst sort[16] had been condemned for heresy at a council in Paris in the presence of Cardinal Octavian, a legate of the Holy See, Theodoric realised that he could no longer rely on concealment and moved to the Narbonne area. There he was much admired and esteemed by the heretics – partly because he seemed a little cleverer than the others, partly because they took great pride in the fact that a man from France (recognised as the principal source of knowledge and of the Christian religion) had come amongst them as the ally of their faith and defender of their iniquity. I should add that he had chosen to be called Theodoric, although previously he was known as William.

[23] After engaging in debate with these two for eight days, our preachers succeeded, by their salutary counsels, in turning the whole population of Servian to hatred of the heretics. Indeed the townsfolk would most willingly have driven them out, but the lord of the place[17] – infected with the poison of heresy – had made them his familiars and friends. It would take too long to describe this debate in all its details, but I think it is worth recording just one point: when the venerable Bishop had brought Theodoric to the end of the argument, the latter

[10] I.e. Arnold Amalric.
[11] On 13 September 1206: see G&L I, p. 24 n. 1.
[12] Cf. n. 3 to §20, Innocent III's appeal to the Cistercian General Chapter of July 1206.
[13] Servian was a small *castrum* north of Béziers which was to be invested by the crusaders as they made their way southwards in July 1209 (see n. 16 to §83). It was well known as a Cathar centre: cf. n. 17 below on its seigneur Stephen, and Roquebert I, pp. 246–7. The debate at Servian was probably held in July 1206; for accounts largely based on what follows, see Griffe, *LC*, p. 252, and Vicaire, pp. 93–4.
[14] Theodoric (Thierry in French) was also known as William of Châteauneuf. He is probably to be identified with a former canon of Nevers in Burgundy, who belonged to an important family in the Nevers/Auxerre region and is known to have been accused of heresy in 1190: see G&M, p. 13 n. 1. He reappears in §52 below. Little else is known of Baldwin. The presence of both men at Servian is attested by Stephen of Servian's abjuration given in February 1210 (see n. 17 to §23 below).
[15] Latin '*Gallia*', i.e. what is now northern France; the same meaning is conveyed a few lines below by '*Francia*'. See Appendix A(ii) for these terms.
[16] Theodoric's uncle was Evrard de Châteauneuf, a knight from Burgundy, who had been accused of heresy along with his nephew in 1190, and was finally condemned in 1200 after being accused of heresy at the council of Paris by the Bishop of Auxerre. He was handed over to the Count of Nevers and burnt in 1201.
[17] Stephen of Servian, an important seigneur of the Biterrois, and a well known heretical sympathiser. Stephen of Servian was reconciled to the Church in February 1210 and received back some of the lands which Simon de Montfort had taken from him in the campaign of 1209: for his abjuration see *HGL* VIII, 584–9.

said 'I know of whose spirit you are; you have come in the spirit of Elias.'[18] The
Bishop replied: 'If I have come in the spirit of Elias, you have come in the spirit of
the Antichrist.' At the end of the eight days the people followed the venerable
preachers for almost a league as they left Servian. [24] They then[19] proceeded by
a direct route to the city of Béziers where during fifteen days of preaching and
debate[20] they confirmed in the faith the few Catholics in the city, and confounded
the heretics.[21] The Bishop of Osma and Brother Ralph then advised Brother Peter
to leave them, since they feared that because the heretics detested him above
everyone else he might be murdered. He therefore left them for a period.[22]
Leaving Béziers they went quickly to Carcassonne where they engaged in preaching and debate for eight days.[23]

[25] *A miracle.* At this time a miracle occurred near Carcassonne, which I
must not pass over. Some heretics were harvesting their crops on the day of the
nativity of St John the Baptist[24] – whom they said was not a prophet but a most
evil man.[25] One of them looked at his hand and saw that the bundle of corn he
was holding was all bloody. He thought he must have cut his hand, but then saw
that his hand was in fact unhurt and called out to his companions, each of whom
then examined the bundles they were holding and found that they were covered
with blood – but that their hands were unharmed. Guy the venerable Abbot of les

---

18 Luke 1, v. 17.
19 Probably in the second half of July 1206.
20 Cf. the same phrase in §26 and elsewhere. Peter does not seem to have in mind any sharp distinction
between formal debates such as those at Montréal or Servian and the general preaching undertaken by the
legates and their helpers: they went on together. For this debate at Béziers see Vicaire pp. 94–5.
21 Peter is almost certainly exaggerating the number of heretics in Béziers – for comment see nn. to §§83
and 89 below. Part of Peter's animosity towards Béziers may result from the refusal of its consuls to
co-operate with the legatine mission 1203–1208. Early in 1204 Peter of Castelnau and Ralph had gone to
Béziers after the oath-swearing at Toulouse, but had met strong opposition both from the consuls and
Bishop William of Roquessels, whom the legates promptly suspended for his failure to recognise their
authority. This was later confirmed by Innocent III in a letter of 18 February 1204 (*PL* 215, 272–3). He was
then replaced by Bishop Renaud of Montpeyroux (wrongly called 'of Montpellier' by Peter in §89 below).
22 Peter of Castelnau left the other legates, perhaps towards the end of July 1206, to begin a period of
diplomatic activity against Raymond VI. He had also received instructions from Innocent III to investigate
the position of King Peter of Aragon's marriage to Maria of Montpellier (see Vicaire p. 470 n. 103).
Henceforth, apart from his appearance at the debate at Montréal in April 1207 (see §26 below), he does not
appear to have taken any part in the preaching mission. This was in part because, as Peter says here, he was
hated so much, but his temperament and skills were no doubt more suited to diplomacy. Peter of Castelnau went east and we hear of him again at Villeneuve-lès-Maguelonne (just outside Montpellier) in
October (see G&L I, p. 27 n. 2), where he was apparently involved in brokering a peace between King Peter
II of Aragon, lord of Montpellier, and the city authorities; this was confirmed by Innocent III in April 1207
(*PL* 215, 1338). He then seems to have gone to Provence, east of the Rhône, seeking to extend this initial
peace to cover the marquisate and county of Provence: see the account in *Cahiers de Fanjeaux*, vol. 4, pp.
111–15. For the significance of this initiative, and its outcome, see n. 33 to §27 below.
23 This was probably in September or October 1206 but firm information is lacking. William of Tudela
also refers to a disputation at Carcassonne in the context of the 1206 Diegan mission, but this was almost
certainly a disputation chaired by King Peter of Aragon which took place there in 1204 (see *Chanson* I, p.
10 n. 2, and Roquebert I, pp. 169–70).
24 24 June 1207.
25 See n. 30 to §10 above on Cathar attitudes to John the Baptist.

Vaux-de-Cernay,[26] who was in the area at this time, himself saw the bloodied bundle of corn and told me the story.

[26] It would take too long to describe in detail the progress of these followers of the Apostles,[27] our preachers, as they went through the towns[28] preaching the gospel and debating everywhere;[29] let us instead turn to the most important events. One day all the heresiarchs met at a *castrum* in the diocese of Carcassonne named Montréal,[30] with the objective of joining together in argument against the preachers. Brother Peter of Castelnau (who as mentioned[31] had left his two colleagues at Béziers) returned to join in the meeting. Judges, chosen from the heretical believers, were appointed to preside over the debate which continued for a full fifteen days. The various arguments were set down in writing by each side and handed to the judges so that they could deliver a definitive judgment. However, since they could see that the heretics had very clearly lost the contest, the judges refused to give a verdict. Since they did not want the arguments recorded by our side to be made public they refused even to return the record to us but instead handed it over to the heretics.

[27] Next Brother Peter left his fellow-preachers for Provence,[32] where he laboured to make peace amongst the nobles of that country.[33] He hoped that

---

[26] The first of many references to the author's uncle, on whom see the article by M. Zerner-Chardavoine, 'L'abbé Gui des Vaux-de-Cernay prédicateur de croisade', in *Cahiers de Fanjeaux*, vol. 21, pp. 183–204. Guy first came south to join the preaching effort in April 1207.

[27] See n. 12 to §6.

[28] '*Castella*'; see Appendix A(viii) for this term.

[29] Luke 9, v. 6. Peter gives no details of the progress of the preaching campaign between the legates' visit to Carcassonne in about September 1206 and the spring of 1207, when his account resumes with the meeting at Montréal in April 1207. However, William of Puylaurens (VIII) reports on a disputation at Verfeil which he says was one of the earliest, and which (since Verfeil lies west of Carcassonne, towards Toulouse) presumably took place in the autumn of 1206, after they had left Carcassonne, and certainly before April 1207.

[30] Montréal, to the south of Carcassonne, near Fanjeaux, and a renowned centre of heresy in the Lauragais: see Griffe, *LC*, pp. 160–5. William of Puylaurens, IX, names the Cathar representatives as Arnaud Othon (or Oth), Guilabert of Castres, Benedict of Termes and Pons Jourdain ('and many others'); and the judges as Bernard of Villeneuve, Bernard of Arzens, Raymond Got and Arnaud Rivière. The debate is dated to April 1207. See also discussions in Griffe, *LC*, pp. 254–7; Vicaire pp. 100–106; and Roquebert I, pp. 197–200 and 295–8; and see n. 37 to §135 below on the lordship of Montréal.

[31] See §24 above.

[32] Here Peter uses '*provincia*' to mean the Rhône valley and the area to the east of the Rhône, the latter approximating to Provence in the modern sense; see Appendix A(i).

[33] Peter of Castelnau left Montréal in April 1207 and seems to have returned to Provence and the Rhône area where he had spent at least part of the winter of 1206–1207. The reference in this section is to the outcome of his diplomatic initiative amongst Raymond VI's vassals in the marquisate of Provence, referred to in n. 22 to §24, and by Peter in this section. In the early 13th century Provence was divided between the marquisate (broadly to the north of the river Durance), which was held by Raymond and whose nominal overlord was the Holy Roman Emperor; and the county (to the south of the Durance) whose overlord was King Peter II of Aragon and which was held by his brother as Count at this time. Raymond's authority as Marquis over his Provencal vassals was weak, and he was frequently engaged in disputes and petty warfare with them, as well as against the Church. Peter of Castelnau's objective was to advance the *pax* element of the *negotium pacis et fidei* (on which see n. 9 to §3) and establish a more effective peace amongst the aristocracy of the area. This was to be achieved by persuading Raymond's eastern vassals to swear oaths to uphold the peace and the faith and support a 'league of peace' against heretics and mercenaries. It was very unlikely that Raymond VI would be prepared to join (cf. the phrase 'enemy of peace' a few lines below), but failure to do so risked not only the condemnation of the Church but also his isolation from his vassals. By

with the help of those who agreed to swear to keep the peace he would be able to uproot the heretics from the province of Narbonne. Raymond, Count of Toulouse,[34] was the enemy of peace and unwilling to accede to Peter's proposals. However, he was at length compelled to join in swearing the oath of peace by a combination of military action taken against him by the nobles of Provence at the instigation of Peter, that man of God, and the pronouncement of a sentence of excommunication[35] by Peter against him. But the Count, who had renounced the faith, and was worse than any infidel,[36] put no store by oaths; he gave his solemn word often enough but perjured himself just as often.[37] That most holy man, Peter, challenged him with great courage. He saw that this tyrant richly deserved censure, and indeed condemnation, and so could approach him and confront him without fear. His firmness of purpose and clear knowledge of right and wrong enabled him to confound the Count in argument, to the extent of

the early spring of 1207 Peter of Castelnau had managed to involve most of Raymond's eastern vassals in his 'league', which in effect constituted an alliance of his vassals against Raymond. At Beaucaire in March 1207, Raymond refused to join in the oath-swearing, but his position was made even more difficult when, in April, King Peter of Aragon, as suzerain of the county of Provence, swore the oath (referred to in Innocent's letter to Raymond, *PL* 215, 1166–8, see n. 35 below). As a result Raymond was now isolated, and forced into a position where he was seen to be refusing to co-operate in upholding the peace, so that the way was open for his excommunication in April 1207. As noted by Roquebert (I, pp. 201–4) it is possible to argue that Peter of Castelnau had never expected Raymond to join the league, and that the whole affair was designed to enable his excommunication. See also discussion in *Cahiers de Fanjeaux*, vol. 4, pp. 111–15, and Griffe, *LC*, pp. 273ff.

34   The first mention of Raymond VI, who was about fifty years old at this time and had been Count since 1194. See William of Puylaurens V for details of his ancestry and birth, and *HGL* VII, pp. 5–8, and family tree on p. xvi.

35   This took place in April 1207 and was confirmed by Innocent III in a letter of 29 May addressed to Count Raymond, in which he denounces the Count vehemently and at length (*PL* 215, 1166–8, see Appendix F(i) for extracts in translation). The reason for Raymond's excommunication was not only his alleged protection of heretics but also his failure to swear to Peter of Castelnau's oath and to uphold the peace generally (the letter cites the main charges; on heresy, it falls just short of accusing Raymond of being a heretic but says that his association with heretics has led to his being personally suspected of heresy – for further comment see n. 38 below). Cf. William of Tudela, *Chanson* I, 4, p. 14, who says that Peter 'had excommunicated the Count of Toulouse because he retained mercenaries who continually pillaged the country' (on mercenaries see Appendix D). As the letter sets out, the particular significance of the excommunication was that it implied the possibility that other Christians would be free to attack Raymond and his lands with impunity, reflecting the doctrine that the lands of heretics and their supporters were liable to seizure (*exposition en proie* in French, for which see §62 and n. 34, and Appendix G). This idea was developed more fully later the same year in Innocent's letters of 17 November 1207 to King Philip and the barons of France calling for a crusade against Raymond VI (*PL* 215, 1246–8) which similarly threaten the lands of heretics with confiscation, and on which see also n. 79 to §51. However, while in principle a serious penalty, excommunication was not uncommon and Innocent used it against other princes: Philip Augustus was excommunicated in 1200 because of his repudiation of his wife Ingeborg of Denmark, and King John of England received the same penalty in March 1209. It should also be noted that at the same time as proceeding against Raymond VI, Peter of Castelnau had also moved against Archbishop Berengar of Narbonne, and had obtained Papal authority to depose him (*PL* 215, 1164–5); cf. also Griffe, *LC*, pp. 273–80, and Roquebert I, pp. 201–4.

36   Cf. I Timothy 5, v. 8.

37   Peter may be referring to Raymond's oaths at Saint-Gilles and the requirements set out in the *Processus*, on which see n. 75 to §77. William of Puylaurens, VII, also says that Raymond had been required to swear an oath to Peter of Castelnau and Ralph at the time of the oath sworn by the consuls of Toulouse in late 1203 (see n. 16 to §7 above), and if this is correct Peter may have known of it and be referring to it here.

upbraiding him for being in all things a deceiver and perjurer – as was indeed the truth.

[28] *Account of the unbelief of Count Raymond.*[38] I will take this opportunity to give a short account of the unbelief of the Count. First it must be said that almost from the cradle he always loved and cherished heretics, kept them in his domains and honoured them in whatever manner he could. Indeed, it is said that even today, wherever he goes he takes with him heretics dressed as ordinary people so that when the time comes he may die in their hands; since he believes that, however great a sinner he may have been, he will be saved even without repentance so long as he can ensure the laying-on of their hands at the point of death.[39] He also ensures that a copy of the New Testament is always with him so that if the need arises, it can be available when the ceremony of the laying-on of hands is performed. The heretics detest the Old Testament and say that the God who laid down the Old Law is 'evil', calling him a 'betrayer' because of the plagues which beset Egypt and 'murderer' because of the Flood and the drowning of the Hebrews.[40] They also say that Moses, Joshua and David were mercenaries and servants of this evil God.

[29] One day the Count told the heretics (we have it for certain) that he wished his son[41] to be brought up at Toulouse amongst the heretics, so that he could learn their beliefs (or rather unbelief). [30] Again, one day he said that he would give a hundred silver marks to ensure the conversion to the heretical faith of a certain knight of his whom he had frequently urged to embrace the faith, having made sure that it should frequently be preached to him.

[31] Also, whenever the heretics sent him gifts of provisions, he received them most gratefully, saw that they were kept safely and allowed no one except himself and his immediate household to eat them. Also, we know for certain that time and again he reverenced the heretics on bended knee, asked for their blessing and embraced them. [32] One day the Count was awaiting the arrival of some men who were due to meet him; when they failed to come, he said: 'It is clear that the

---

[38] The following sections constitute a diatribe against Raymond VI, but despite Peter's assertions and attempts to prove Raymond's personal heresy, there is ultimately no direct evidence of this; see also Introduction p. xxxvi. Pope Innocent's own reservations about the accusation, revealed in his letter of April 1207, were maintained until the Fourth Lateran Council in December 1215; see for example his letter of 25 January 1210 translated in Appendix F(iii) and discussed in n. 49 to §137, and his letter of May 1212 (see n. 5 to §368). It is implausible to suggest that Raymond himself was ever a Cathar or an active sympathiser, but his opponents found it easier to maintain the charge that he tolerated heresy (and could thus be regarded as a *receptator et defensor* of heretics, on which see n. 26 to §9); and indeed the terms of his eventual condemnation at the Fourth Lateran Council refer to his failure to expel heretics, not to his being a heretic – see §572 and Appendix F(v). See also the review of Innocent's dealings with Raymond VI in Appendix G.

[39] For the significance of this ceremony, the *consolamentum*, see §14 above.

[40] '*Hebreorum*', the reading of the manuscript usually preferred by G&L, who say the reading is justified by the context '*propter diluvium*', 'because of the flood', and that other manuscripts which read '*Egiptiorum*' appear to have been altered to conform with the reference in §10 above. However, G&M in their translation follow the reading *Egiptiorum*.

[41] Raymond, b. 1197, later Count Raymond VII, 1222–49 (again see William of Puylaurens V for details, and also *HGL* VII, Note X, pp. 24–8).

Devil[42] made the world, since nothing I wish for comes about.' [33] The Count also told Fulk, the Bishop of Toulouse,[43] that the Cistercian monks could not attain salvation because they kept sheep which indulged in wantonness – I heard this from the Bishop himself; what an unheard of heresy! [34] He also invited the Bishop to come to his palace at night to hear the heretics preaching; from which it may be deduced that he himself often listened to their preaching at night.

[35] One day the Count was in a church where mass was being celebrated. He had with him a clown who, in the way of such jesters, was poking fun at people by imitating their expressions. When the priest who was celebrating the mass turned to the congregation reciting the 'Lord be with you', the Count told his clown to mimic the priest and make fun of him.

[36] The Count once said that he would rather be like a certain heretic, a very evil man living at Castres[44] in the Diocese of Albi, who had lost his limbs and lived in wretchedness, than be a king or emperor.

[37] The most convincing proof that he always cherished heretics is that none of the papal legates could ever persuade him to drive the heretics from his domain,[45] even though the legates did very often compel him to denounce them. [38] Moreover he attached such little weight to the sacrament of marriage that whenever his own wife displeased him he sent her away and married another – indeed he had four wives[46] of whom three are still living. He first married the sister of the Viscount of Béziers, Béatrice;[47] after repudiating her, he married the

---

[42] I.e. the 'evil' God described in §10; the 'world' is the material world.

[43] Bishop 1205–1231. Fulk (or Foulques or Folquet) had been appointed as successor to Raymond of Rabastens in July 1205 (see n. 52 to §68). Fulk was a native of Genoa, and as a younger man he had been a distinguished troubadour, known as Folquet of Marseille. He became a Cistercian monk at the abbey of Thoronet in Provence in about 1195, and was abbot there by 1199. His election was an important step in placing as Bishop of Toulouse a man who could be relied upon by the legates and the papacy, and in succeeding years he played an important part in many of the events of the Crusade. William of Puylaurens spent his early years in Fulk's household, and gives details about him (VII and VIII of his chronicle). He gives 5 February 1206 as the date of Fulk's formal installation at Toulouse; and see *HGL* VI, pp. 243–5 for Fulk and his election. See also S. Stronski, *Le Troubadour Folquet de Marseille* (Cracow, 1910); and P. Cabau, 'Foulque, marchand et troubadour de Marseille, moine et abbé du Thoronet, évêque de Toulouse', in *Cahiers de Fanjeaux*, vol. 21, pp. 151–79.

[44] About 40km south of Albi, on the river Agout and to the north-east of the Lauragais. It was the site of an important Benedictine abbey, but was also a well known centre of Catharism. Cf. below, §§112–13, and Griffe, *LC*, pp. 63–5. There is little direct information about heresy at Castres, although two well known Cathars are named as from the *castrum*: Guilabert de Castres, future Cathar Bishop of Toulouse, and Isarn de Castres, a Cathar deacon. Simon de Montfort spent Christmas 1211 at Castres: see §290. It was granted to Guy de Montfort and remained in the family's possession for many years: see *HGL* VII, pp. 124–8.

[45] Raymond VI may have been unwilling to combat heresy, but he was also largely powerless to do so because of his limited control over his vassals. For the similar problems faced by his father, Raymond V, see n. 9 to §6; the same point is made in relation to Raymond-Roger Trencavel by William of Tudela in the *Chanson* I, 15, pp. 44–6. Innocent III and his colleagues do not seem to have acknowledged this point: see discussion in Appendix G.

[46] Raymond VI in fact had five wives. The first was Ermessinde of Pelet, Countess of Melgueil, whom he married in 1172 and who brought Melgueil as a dowry; she died in 1176. Béatrice of Béziers was his second wife. See *HGL* VII, pp. 24–8, on Raymond VI's wives.

[47] Sister of Roger II Viscount of Béziers, whom he married before 1193.

daughter of the Duke of Cyprus;[48] after divorcing her, he married the sister of Richard, King of England, who was a blood relative of his in the third degree;[49] on her death he took to wife the sister of the King of Aragon, although she also was related to him in the third and fourth degrees.[50] [39] It is also to be recorded that he repeatedly urged one of his wives to enter religious orders. Knowing well what he intended, she first asked him purposefully whether he wanted her to become a nun in the Cistercian Order; he said no. Then she asked whether he wished her to become a nun in the Order of Fontevrault; he said he did not wish it. The she asked him what he did want; and he replied that if she was willing to become a heretic, he would take care of all her needs; and this is how it turned out.[51] [40] There was a particularly depraved heretic at Toulouse named Hugo Faber. One day he fell into such depths of madness that he emptied his bowels beside the altar in a church and by way of showing his contempt for God wiped himself with the altar cloth – an unheard of crime! The same heretic said that when a priest was receiving the sacrament during the Mass, he was taking an evil spirit into his body. When the Abbot of Cîteaux, who was at that time Abbot of Grandselve in the territory of Toulouse,[52] told the Count of Toulouse about this monstrous crime and urged him to punish its perpetrator, the Count replied that in no way was he prepared to punish one of his subjects on such a matter. The Abbot of Cîteaux, who had by then become Archbishop of Narbonne, described these abominations to the bishops – about twenty in number – attending the Council of Lavaur,[53] where I was present.

[41] Moreover the Count was a vicious and lecherous man to the extent that – we can take it as an established fact – he abused his own sister as a way of showing contempt for the Christian religion. Again, from early youth he lost no opportunity to seek out his father's[54] concubines and felt no compunction about bedding them – indeed none of them could please him unless he knew his father had previously slept with her. So it came about that his father frequently threatened to disinherit him, for this enormity as much as for his heresy.

[42] The Count always had a remarkable liking for mercenaries,[55] whom he

---

48 Bourguigne, daughter of Amaury of Lusignan, and Raymond VI's wife between 1193 and 1196.
49 Joan, who married Raymond in 1196 and died in 1199. The common ancestor giving rise to the 'third degree' relationship was Pons, Count of Toulouse, with the lines: William IV of Toulouse (first son of Pons) – Phillipa – William X of Aquitaine – Eleonore of Aquitaine – Joan; and Raymond IV (Pons' second son) – Alphonse Jourdain – Raymond V – Raymond VI. Marriages within this degree of kinship were by no means unusual in this period amongst the aristocracy.
50 Eleanor. The common ancestor in the 'third degree' was King Alfonso VI of Castile, who had two daughters giving lines of descent: Urraca – Alfonso VII – Sancia of Castile – Eleanor; and Elvira, who married Raymond IV of Toulouse, great grandfather of Raymond VI. Eleanor was also descended from William IV of Toulouse in the line Philippa – Agnes of Poitiers – Petronilla of Aragon – Alfonso II of Aragon – Eleanor, giving rise to the 'fourth degree' relationship.
51 See G&L I, p. 37 n. 1, for other anecdotes to this effect; the wife who was said to be a heretic was Béatrice of Béziers.
52 Arnold Amalric was abbot of Grandselve 1198–1201 (see n. 4 to §20).
53 In 1213; see §368 below.
54 Raymond V, 1148–94.
55 Latin 'ruptarii', French routiers. Throughout the *Historia* Peter frequently draws attention to the

employed to rob the churches, destroy the monasteries and, wherever he could, deprive his neighbours of their possessions.[56] Always he acted as a limb of the Devil; a son of perdition, an enemy of the cross, a persecutor of the Church, the defender of heretics, the oppressor of the Catholic faithful, the servant of treachery, forswearer of his word, replete with crime, a veritable treasury of all sins.

[43] One day the Count was playing chess with his chaplain and said to him: 'The God of Moses, in whom you believe, will not be able to help you to prevent me winning this game,' and added: 'Never let that God come to my aid.' [44] On another occasion, when the Count was about to leave the territory of Toulouse to fight some of his enemies in Provence, he got up in the middle of the night, went to a house in which the heretics of Toulouse were meeting and said to them: 'Masters and brothers. The fortunes of war are mixed. If anything should happen to me I commend my body and soul into your hands.' Whereupon he took with him two of the abundant number of heretics, dressed in ordinary clothes, so that if he were to meet with death he could die in their hands.

[45] At one time this cursed Count fell ill in Aragon and when the illness worsened he had a litter made and had himself carried back to Toulouse on the litter which was borne by horses. When someone asked him one day why he returned in such haste when he was so ill, the wretch replied: 'There are no Good Men in that country, in whose hands I could meet my death.' (The heretics were of course called 'Good Men' by their supporters.)[57] [46] An even clearer admission that he was a heretic is to be found in this statement: 'I know that I will suffer disinheritance[58] for the sake of these Good Men; but I am ready to suffer not just disinheritance for them, but even execution.' I have now said enough about the unbelief and wickedness of this wretch.

[47] *Return to the main narrative.*[59] Let us now return to my main theme. After the conclusion of the debate at Montréal[60] our preachers remained there,

---

employment of mercenaries by Raymond VI and other opponents of the Crusade. The suppression of mercenaries was a fundamental part of the *pax* element of the *negotium pacis et fidei*, and employing mercenaries was one of the main charges laid against Raymond VI when he was excommunicated in 1207. The diplomacy of Peter of Castelnau in 1207, and Milo in Provence in 1209, was to a considerable extent concerned with trying to persuade local lords not to employ mercenaries. For a fuller discussion of the use of mercenaries both by the southern lords and by the crusaders, and of the Church's view of the close links between the suppression of heresy and the suppression of mercenaries, see Appendix D.

56 These charges echo those which led to Raymond's excommunication in April 1207, on which see above, §27. His earlier excommunication by Celestine III in 1196 had also been connected with his disputes with, and attacks on property of, the abbey of Saint-Gilles (see n. 7 to §58 below). G&L (I, p. 39 n. 1) give extensive detail on Raymond's alleged depredations, citing multiple sources. For examples see also §340 (Raymond's disputes with the abbey of Moissac), and §394 (his dispute with the Abbot of Montauban).

57 See above, §13.

58 As happened; see §359. Peter is here perhaps indulging in prophetic hindsight.

59 §§47–55 cover the period from the debate at Montréal in April 1207 to the death of Peter of Castelnau in January 1208. There is limited information about the exact dates of events in this period. G&L I, p. 42 n. 6, argue that the Cistercian Abbot Henry of Mont-Sainte-Marie (from eastern Burgundy) was in Pamiers (presumably preaching) in September 1207 (see also §201); and ibid. p. 45, n. 1, quote a Spanish source to date Diego's return to Osma to October 1207, which implies that the debate at Pamiers (§48) was a little earlier.

60 See §26 above.

preaching the faith and the way of salvation everywhere, and begging their daily bread from door to door. Here they were joined by Arnold, the venerable Abbot of Cîteaux, who came from France bringing with him twelve abbots,[61] men of complete faith, consummate learning and incomparable sanctity; twelve in number to reflect the most holy number of the twelve Apostles, thirteen with their leader Abbot Arnold. They were ready always to give an account of the faith and hope that was in them to any man that wished to dispute with them.[62] They and the numerous monks whom they had brought with them went about on foot displaying humility in all they did according to the example shown to them on the Mount,[63] as they had been urged to do by the Bishop of Osma.[64] They were immediately dispersed far and wide by the Abbot and each assigned to a particular area in which they were instructed to pursue their preaching campaign and involve themselves in debate.[65]

[48] The Bishop of Osma had decided to return to his see, since he wished to attend to the affairs of his own household and also to make provision from his revenues for the material needs of the preachers of the word of God in the province of Narbonne.[66] As he was on his way to Spain he arrived at

---

[61] He left Cîteaux in March 1207: see G&L I, p. 42 n. 1, citing Robert of Auxerre. This initiative seems to have been at least in part a response to Innocent III's appeal to the General Chapter of Cîteaux for help in the preaching against heresy in the south issued in July 1206 (*PL* 215, 940–1), on which see also n. 3 to §20. The identity of most of the twelve abbots (probably all Cistercian) is not known, but Guy of les Vaux-de-Cernay was one, and §201 below suggests that Henry of Mont-Sainte-Marie was another. Vicaire, pp. 107–8, makes some further suggestions. The arrival of Arnold Amalric with these abbots and 'numerous' (see later this section) companion monks to join Diego, Ralph and Dominic represented a substantial strengthening of the preaching effort. There may also have been Cistercian monks from local southern abbeys, such as Fontfroide, working with them. §48 below also mentions Bishops Navarre of Couserans and Fulk of Toulouse (himself a Cistercian) as being involved. The total size of the preaching force is a matter of conjecture.

[62] Cf. I Peter 3, v. 15.

[63] Cf. Exodus 25, v. 40.

[64] See §21 above.

[65] The additional manpower available now made it possible to divide up the area of the preaching mission into sectors. Peter's uncle, Abbot Guy, was allotted the Carcassès and was there by late June (G&L I, p. 27 n. 3). Dominic was given Montréal and Fanjeaux, having already in March 1207 established a convent and brotherhood of preachers at Prouille, just outside Fanjeaux. It is possible that Ralph was allotted Saint-Gilles, but he died soon after, in early July (see §50). Abbot Henry of Mont-Sainte-Marie seems to have been allotted Pamiers, but otherwise details are not known. For a discussion of these arrangements see Vicaire, pp. 108–9. With Arnold Amalric absent and Peter of Castelnau having withdrawn to focus on diplomatic activity, Diego and Ralph must have been the effective leaders of the mission in the early summer of 1207: cf. Peter's statement to this effect in §67 below, and see Roquebert I, p. 201.

[66] The practical arrangements for the support of the enlarged preaching mission are also mentioned by Robert of Auxerre who states that Diego was able to use revenues from his see of Osma to provide local centres, the most successful of which was that at Prouille run by Dominic: his evidence is discussed in Vicaire, pp. 111–12. In the period before Diego arrived, the legates had sought financial support from the local episcopate, but many sees including Carcassonne, Toulouse and Narbonne were poor and had serious financial problems. Archbishop Berengar of Narbonne had refused to provide horses and lodging for the legates in part because he had not the resources to do so, while William of Puylaurens (VII) reports that Bishop Fulk complained that when he came to Toulouse in 1205–1206 the income of his see was only 96 sous a year. A major reason for such poverty was the confiscation of property and the expropriation of tithes by local seigneurs, and one of the aims of the *negotium pacis et fidei* was to stop this and ensure restoration of and respect for the economic rights of the Church on the part of lay lords. Failure to respect

Pamiers[67] in the territory of Toulouse where Fulk, Bishop of Toulouse,[68] and Navarre, Bishop of Couserans,[69] and several abbots came to meet him. Here a debate was held with the Waldenses, who were plainly worsted and confounded.[70] The people of Pamiers – especially the poorer classes[71] – nearly all took our side, and the man appointed to act as judge in the debate (a notable of the place)[72] who had previously been well disposed to the Waldenses, renounced heresy and offered himself and his possessions to the Bishop of Osma. From that day forward he courageously opposed the followers of the superstition of heresy.

One of the participants in this debate was that most evil traitor the Count of Foix,[73] the most cruel persecutor of the Church, the enemy of Christ. He had a wife who was an acknowledged heretic and a member of the Waldensian sect, and two sisters of whom one followed the Waldensian sect whilst the other professed the general errors of the other heretics.[74] The debate I have referred to took place in the Count's palace; the Count himself gave attention on alternate

such rights was an important aspect of the charges against Raymond VI in 1207–1209, and is reflected in the *Processus* (*PL* 216, 89–98, see §77). The relative poverty of the Church in the South was one of the reasons for its difficulties in combating heresy; it meant that prelates like Berengar of Narbonne spent much time on the financial administration of their sees, which in turn provoked accusations of worldliness and neglect of pastoral duties. See also Appendix G for Innocent's efforts to reinvigorate the southern episcopacy.

67   Pamiers, a fortified town on an important line of north-south communication in the Ariège valley. It had a castle and an abbey of St Anthony, and was jointly ruled by the regular canons of the abbey and by the Count of Foix (although there were frequent disputes). For details of Pamiers in the early 13th century see the note on 'Pamiers au début du XIIIème siècle', by G.-M. Llobet in *Cahiers de Fanjeaux*, vol. 2, pp. 195–204; and see below, §116, for subsequent developments.

68   Pamiers lay within Fulk's diocese.

69   The Couserans was a region to the west of Foix, the seat of whose bishopric was at Saint-Lizier. Its bishop at this time, Navarre, was a reliable supporter of the legatine mission. In May 1207 he had been instructed jointly with Arnold Amalric to help in the disciplining of Archbishop Berengar of Narbonne (*PL* 215, 1164–5), and cf. n. 35 to §27 above. See also §§63, 67, 205, 358, and 363 for Navarre of Couserans.

70   For the debate at Pamiers, see William of Puylaurens, VIII; Vicaire pp. 132–5; M.-H. Vicaire, 'Rencontre à Pamiers des courants vaudois et dominicain (1207)', in *Cahiers de Fanjeaux* vol. 2, esp. pp. 163–73; and Maisonneuve, *Etudes sur les Origines de l'Inquisition*, pp. 182–6. The debate was primarily between the Catholics and representatives of the Waldensians, led by Durand of Huesca. Many of the Waldensians at the debate, including Durand, were won over by their opponents, and were received back into the Catholic Church. Durand of Huesca went on to found the *Pauperes Catholici*, Poor Catholics, an order of friars who preached against heresy. He had always strongly opposed the Cathars and later (1222–23) published his *Liber Contra Manicheos*, an important source of knowledge about the Cathars.

71   Peter's comment here reflects the lack of sympathy for the preachers amongst the local aristocracy, underlining that the strength of support for heresy amongst the seigneurs of the Midi was one of the main sources of its strength.

72   William of Puylaurens, VIII, names him as Arnold of Crampagna, who he says was 'then a secular clerk' ('*tunc clerico seculari*') who was chosen by both sides. No mention is made of any Waldensian leanings. See Roquebert I, pp. 209–10, for a summary of his later history. He appears as late as 1247 before the Inquisition as a witness against heretics.

73   Raymond-Roger, 1188–1223, who was to play a major role in the Crusade. For Peter's 'portrait' of the Count see §§197–209.

74   Raymond-Roger's wife, the Countess Phillipa, was a Cathar sympathiser and later Inquisition records in the Doat collection refer to her; see Griffe, *LC*, pp. 154–5. Phillipa's Catharism was later confirmed in a deposition made by her son Roger-Bernard, who gave details of the presence of Cathars with his mother during his infancy (see *HGL* VIII, 1034–7, deposition of 12 March 1241). As Peter says, one of Raymond-Roger's sisters (Cecilia) was known as a Waldensian sympathiser; another sister, Esclarmonde of Foix, was a widow who had become a Cathar *perfecta* in a ceremony administered by the Cathar Guilabert de Castres

days first to the Waldenses and then to our preachers. What hypocritical courtesy!

[49] After this the Bishop of Osma arrived at his see, firmly intending to return as soon as possible to the province of Narbonne to further the business of the faith, but after staying there a few days, and whilst he was preparing to leave, death suddenly overtook him and his long and saintly life came to a peaceful end.[75] [50] Before he died Brother Ralph (whom I have often mentioned and whose memory we cherish) departed this life at the Cistercian abbey of Franqueveaux near Saint-Gilles.[76]

[51] After the loss of these two luminaries, Guy, Abbot of les Vaux-de-Cernay[77] in the diocese of Paris (a man of noble birth but nobler far in learning and character), who had come to the province of Narbonne with certain other abbots to join the preaching campaign, and was later to become the Bishop of Carcassonne, was appointed chief and leader of the preachers, since at that time the Abbot of Cîteaux was elsewhere,[78] engaged on other matters of great importance. The blessed preachers then went about and engaged in debate with the heretics. They clearly won the argument, but could not convert opponents who were so firmly attached to their false beliefs. Accordingly after some considerable time, since they could achieve little or nothing by preaching and debate, they returned to France.[79]

---

at Fanjeaux in 1204 (see Roquebert I, pp. 113–15). Cf. also §§198–9 below for one of Raymond-Roger's aunts at Pamiers, also a heretic, and §373 and §381 for charges of heresy against Raymond-Roger himself.

[75] Diego died on 30 December 1207: see Vicaire, p. 135, and for full details M.-H. Vicaire, 'Saint Dominique en 1207', in *Archivum Fratrum Praedicatorum*, XXIII (1953), pp. 335–45.

[76] Ralph had died in July 1207, possibly on 7 or 8 (G&L I, p. 45 nn. 2–3; and Vicaire, p. 113).

[77] See §25 n. 26 and Introduction, pp. xxiii–xxv, for Guy.

[78] At Marseille (G&L I, p. 46 n. 1).

[79] As Peter here suggests (and restates in §67 below), by the end of 1207 the preaching mission had almost come to a halt, and the future of the Cistercian mission must have been in doubt. Cf. William of Puy-laurens, X, who says that 'after this work had continued for two years and more, the blessed warriors of God ('*benedicti Dei pugiles*') had not succeeded by this means [i.e. preaching] in quenching the fire that had been ignited; they realised that the matter needed counsel from a higher quarter and were driven to call on the Apostolic See'. William of Tudela also remarks upon the impossibility of converting heretics (*Chanson* I, 2, p. 10). However, as Peter notes in the previous section, Diego intended to continue preaching: on his and Dominic's plans, with especial reference to Prouille, see Vicaire, pp. 113–14. Overall, however, despite the success against the Waldensians at Pamiers, there had apparently been no inroads into support for Catharism by the end of 1207. Both Diego and Ralph were dead, Arnold Amalric was spending most of his time at Cîteaux, Peter of Castelnau was in Provence, and the abbots brought to the Midi by Arnold had mostly returned home. Whether the Cistercian preaching would have been renewed on any scale in 1208, even had Peter of Castelnau not been murdered, is a moot point. As it was, military intervention in the form of a crusade against Raymond VI was already being envisaged in November 1207 (on which cf. Appendix G). The excommunication of Raymond in April 1207 had not achieved any concrete results and on 17 November Innocent III wrote to Philip Augustus and separately to the barons of the north (*PL* 215, 1246–8) effectively recognising the failure of the preaching and calling for armed intervention. These letters, which refer specifically to heresy '*in partibus Tolosanis*' ('in the area of Toulouse') and of which Peter makes no mention, were sent not just to Philip Augustus but also generally to 'the counts, barons, knights, and all the Christian faithful in the kingdom of France', as well as separately to many of the greater lords such as the Duke of Burgundy. They offered crusading indulgences to those who fought, and in other respects clearly show that the idea of a crusade against Raymond was well developed by late 1207; see also n. 34 to §62. It was in this tense atmosphere that Raymond decided to seek reconciliation with Peter of Castelnau in January 1208.

[52] An incident[80] which is well worth recording was as follows: the Abbot of les Vaux-de-Cernay engaged frequently in debate with Theodoric, mentioned above,[81] and another leading heresiarch, Bernard of Simorre,[82] who was regarded as the chief heretic in the diocese of Carcassonne. Always he overcame them in discussion, and one day Theodoric, unable to answer the argument, said to the Abbot: 'The harlot has kept me long enough, she shall keep me no longer.' By 'harlot' of course he meant the Church of Rome.[83]

[53] Nor should I pass over another incident which occurred when one day the Abbot entered a fortress known as Laure[84] near Carcassonne in order to preach. At the gates he made the sign of the cross; seeing which a certain heretical knight who was in the *castrum* said to the Abbot: 'May the sign of the cross never come to my aid.'

[54] *A Miracle.* At this time a miracle occurred which I think is worth recording at this point. One day certain of our preachers, men of deep religious faith, were engaged in debate against the heretics. One of our men, Dominic[85] by name, a man of consummate piety, and a companion of the Bishop of Osma, put down in writing the authorities he had produced and handed the paper to a certain heretic so that they could discuss its contents. That night when the heretics were gathered in a private house, sitting by the fire, the heretic to whom the man of God had given the paper produced it. His companions suggested that he should throw it into the fire saying that if it burned it would prove that the faith of the heretics (he should have said 'faithlessness!') was true; if it remained untouched by the fire, they would admit that the faith preached by our men was true. What more? All agreed and the paper was thrown into the fire. After staying in the middle of the fire for a little time it jumped out, totally untouched by the flames. The watchers were astounded but one of them – made of harder stuff than the rest – said: 'Throw it in again so that we may make a more thorough test of the truth.' It was thrown in again – but again it jumped out, untouched by the fire. Seeing this the hardened heretic, slow of heart to believe,[86] said: 'Throw it in a

---

80 The following incident, and those in §52 and §53 below, seem to relate to the debate at Montréal (§26 above, in April 1207), and may therefore have occurred at about that time.

81 See §22.

82 Bernard of Simorre was the second Cathar Bishop of Carcassonne, and one of the most forceful Cathar leaders at this time. He took part in the colloquy of 1204 at Carcassonne presided over by King Peter of Aragon; see also Griffe, *LC*, pp. 157–8. Simorre is in the diocese of Auch, west of Toulouse.

83 Cf. §12 above; this was a common charge and alludes to the harlot of the Apocalypse (Revelations 17, esp. v. 5).

84 For heresy in Laure (in the Minervois north-east of Carcassonne) see Griffe, *LC*, pp. 180–81, who notes that the presence of at least two Cathar houses in the village in the early 13th century is confirmed by a deposition made many years later to the Inquisition by a knight, Raymond Huc, who came from a neighbouring village.

85 Dominic Guzman of Caleruega (St Dominic), here mentioned by name; see also n. 9 to §21 above. St Dominic's biographer, Jordan of Saxony, writing in the 1230s, also tells this story, but places it at Fanjeaux. Since our author says specifically that he heard his version directly from Dominic in person, his statement that it took place at the debate at Montréal is usually accepted. See discussion in Vicaire, pp. 104–5, and n. 57 to his ch. VII. William of Puylaurens, IX, who gives a description of the debate at Montréal, does not mention this incident but does refer to the use of written testimony at the debate.

86 Luke 24, v. 25.

third time, then we shall know the end of the matter beyond doubt.' It was thrown in for the third time, but even then refused to burn, but jumped from the fire entire and unharmed. Despite having witnessed these signs the heretics were still unwilling to be converted to the true faith but persisted in their obstinate belief and very strictly enjoined each other to make sure that the miracle should never come to the knowledge of our side through anyone reporting it. However, a knight who was present and had some sympathy with our faith did not wish to hide what he had seen and told a great many people about it. This happened at Montréal; I heard of it from that most pious man who passed the paper to the heretics.

[Part III – The Crusaders]

[IV. §§55–81, January 1208 – June 1209: *Murder of Peter of Castelnau – Pope Innocent's letter of 10 March 1208 describing the murder and renewing calls for the Crusade against Raymond VI – Bishops Fulk of Toulouse and Navarre of Couserans go to Rome – Raymond VI sends a mission to Rome to argue his innocence – Innocent III appoints Master Milo (March 1209) as an additional legate, assisted by Master Thedisius – Milo in Provence – reconciliation of Count Raymond at Saint-Gilles, June 1209*].

[55] *Martyrdom of Brother Peter of Castelnau.*[1] After this short introductory account of the activities of the preachers of the word of God, let us turn, with the Lord's help, to the martyrdom of that venerable man and most courageous champion, Brother Peter of Castelnau. I can give no better or more authentic account of this than by inserting in my narrative the letter which the lord Pope sent to the faithful followers of Christ and which gives full details of the martyrdom. The letter[2] reads as follows.

[56] 'Innocent, servant of the servants of God, sends greetings and his apostolic blessing to his beloved children, the noble counts and barons and all the people of the provinces[3] of Narbonne, Arles, Embrun, Aix and Vienne.

[57] 'News has reached us[4] of a cruel deed which must surely bring grief on the whole Church. Brother Peter of Castelnau of blessed memory, monk and priest, a man surely renowned amongst righteous men for the conduct of his life, his learning and his high reputation, was sent by us with others to the South to preach peace and support the faith. He had performed the tasks entrusted to him in distinguished fashion, and was indeed still doing so, since all that he taught he had learnt in the school of Christ, and by holding fast to arguments which were

---

[1]   The murder is said to have taken place on 14 January 1208 (*HGL* V, 36, and G&L I, p. 51 n. 1). See Roquebert I, pp. 211–19, for a discussion of the various accounts of the murder of Peter of Castelnau, which is recounted briefly by William of Puylaurens, IX, and William of Tudela, *Chanson* I, 4, pp. 12–16.
[2]   The letter is highly rhetorical in style and is masterfully composed in long and elaborate periods; in this it is typical of letters emanating from the Papal Curia. The letter is quoted verbatim by Peter without further comment; it is also printed in *PL* 215, 1354–8, and *Layettes* I, 841. It was accompanied by virtually identical ones issued at the same time by Innocent III to the province of Lyon (*PL* 215, 1358), and to Philip Augustus (ibid., cols. 1358–9).
[3]   I.e. the ecclesiastical provinces.
[4]   How Innocent heard the news, and the circumstances of the composition of the letter, are not certain. According to William of Tudela (*Chanson* I, 5–7, pp. 16–22) Arnold Amalric was in Rome at the time. He says that after the ceremony of anathematisation, there was a meeting at which Arnold Amalric and Milo were present and it was they who argued that a crusade should forthwith be launched against Raymond VI and all heretics in the Midi. William of Tudela cites as his source an envoy of the King of Navarre named Pons de Mela, who was at Rome at the time (see *Chanson* I, p. 19 n. 3), and his account also mentions the presence of a number of other southern prelates (ibid., p. 23). Peter does not mention any of this. It is just possible that the visit of Bishops Fulk and Navarre to Rome, described below, §67, also took place at this same time, i.e. February/early March 1208, and that they also were involved in the discussions with Innocent which resulted in this letter, but the context of Peter's account suggests that their visit took place early in 1209; see n. 49 to §67.

faithful to the true doctrine he could both encourage his hearers with wholesome teaching and confute objectors.[5] He was always ready to give an answer to every man who questioned him,[6] as a man Catholic in faith, experienced in the law and eloquent in speech. Against him the Devil roused his minister, the Count of Toulouse. This man had often incurred the censure of the Church for the many grave outrages he had committed against her,[7] and often – as might be expected of a person who was crafty and cunning, slippery and unreliable – had received absolution under the guise of feigned penitence. At last he could not hold back the hatred he had conceived against Peter – since indeed in Peter's mouth the word of God was not restrained from executing vengeance upon the nations and punishments upon the people;[8] hatred the stronger because the Count himself was so richly deserving of punishment for his great crimes. He then summoned Peter and his fellow papal legate[9] to the town of Saint-Gilles,[10] promising to give complete satisfaction on every heading under which he was accused. [58] When they came to the town the Count at one moment seemed truthful and compliant and promised to carry out all the salutary instructions given to him; at the next he became deceitful and obdurate and absolutely refused to do so, with the result that the legates at last decided to quit the town. Thereupon the Count publicly threatened them with death, vowing to keep a close watch on their departure whether they went by land or water. He immediately matched his words with actions and dispatched his accomplices to lay a carefully chosen ambush. His insane fury could not be calmed either by the prayers of our beloved son, the Abbot of Saint-Gilles,[11] or by the remonstrances of the consuls and townsmen; so the latter escorted the legates – against the Count's wishes and indeed to his great annoyance – under the protection of an armed guard to the banks of the Rhône. As night fell the legates settled down to rest, unaware that encamped with them[12]

---

5   Cf. Titus 1, v. 9.
6   Cf. I Peter 3, v. 15.
7   Probably a reference to Raymond's previous excommunications. In March 1196, he had been threatened with excommunication by Celestine III for having despoiled or destroyed churches and for building a fortress on lands claimed by the abbey of Saint-Gilles, with which he was often in dispute (1 March 1196, *HGL* VIII, 436; and *PL* 206, 1155–6). The threat seems to have been carried out since in November 1198 Innocent III gave Raymond a pardon, his penance being a pilgrimage to the Holy Land which could, however, be carried out by proxy (4 November 1198, *PL* 214, 374–5; see also Roquebert I, pp. 139 and 156). Raymond's second excommunication in 1207 is referred to in §27 above.
8   Psalm 149, v. 7.
9   Bishop Navarre of Couserans, legate since May 1207, on whom cf. above, §48, and below, §63.
10 The town ('*villa*') of Saint-Gilles lies on the plain about 15km west of Arles, and 20km south of Nîmes. It had long been in the possession of the family of the Counts of Toulouse, who took the family name 'of Saint-Gilles'. It was a prosperous trading centre, and had an important abbey church housing the relics of Saint-Gilles (Aegidius), and the shrine was visited by pilgrims including those on their way to Santiago de Compostela. Lordship over the town was shared between the abbey and the Counts of Toulouse, and there was a consulate; tension between the secular and monastic authorities was common. For details see Roquebert II, pp. 322–3, and III, pp. 75–6, and see also §§586 and 592 below for the support given by the inhabitants of Saint-Gilles to the revolt by the younger Raymond of Toulouse in 1216.
11 Abbot Pons (G&L I, p. 54 n. 3).
12 '*Ejusdem comitis satellitibus (ipsis prorsus ignotis) hospitantibus cum eisdem*'; the basic meaning of *hospitor* is 'to be a guest', but the order of words implies that the legate's party did not know of the presence of the Count's followers (rather than that they were unaware of their hostile intentions).

were some of the Count's attendants who, as events proved, intended to seek their blood.

[59] 'Early the next morning, after Mass had been celebrated in the customary manner, as the innocent soldiers of Christ were preparing to cross the river, one of those attendants of Satan, brandishing his lance, wounded Peter from behind between the ribs – Peter who stood with immovable firmness on the Rock of Christ,[13] unguarded against such treachery. Then – good confronting evil – Peter faced his attacker and, following as did St Stephen[14] the example of Christ his teacher, said to him: "May God forgive you, even as I forgive you", repeating these words of pious forbearance again and again. Then injured though he was, the hope of heavenly things allowed him to forget the bitterness of the wound he had suffered, and even though the moment of his precious death[15] was now approaching, he continued discussing with his fellow priests what needed to be done to further the cause of the faith and peace; until at last after many prayers he went happily to rest in Christ.

[60] 'So he shed his blood in the cause of the faith and peace – surely no more praiseworthy cause for martyrdom can be imagined. His death would, we are sure, have shone with glorious miracles but for the existence of unbelievers like those of whom it is said in St Matthew's gospel[16] "and Jesus did not many mighty works there because of their unbelief". For[17] although it is true that tongues are for a sign not to them that believe, but to them that believe not,[18] nevertheless when the Saviour was brought before Herod (who, as St Luke says,[19] "was exceedingly glad to see him, for he hoped to see some miracle done by him"), he scorned to make a sign or reply to questions, because He knew that what delighted Herod in the performance of miracles was not that it led him to belief, but rather that he admired empty vanity. Now, this evil and corrupt generation which seeks after a sign[20] is not worthy to receive that sign (so soon as perhaps it hoped) from the man it has itself made a martyr; nevertheless we believe it is expedient that one man should die for it rather than that it should all perish;[21] for it is indeed so contaminated by the contagion of heresy that it may well be recalled from error more readily by the voice of the blood of its victim[22] than by anything he could have done had he gone on living. For such is the ancient cunning of Jesus Christ, the marvellous genius of our Saviour, that just when He seems to have been defeated in the persons of His followers, it is then that He

---

[13] I Corinthians 10, v. 4
[14] Acts 7, vv. 59–60.
[15] Latin '*pretiosus*' – cf. in the Prayer Book, the Litany, 'by thine agony . . . by thy precious Death and Burial'.
[16] Matthew 13, v. 58.
[17] The laboured thinking and language of the following passage seem to arise from an attempt to draw comparisons between Peter and Christ without going too far.
[18] I Corinthians 14, v. 22.
[19] Luke 23, vv. 8–9.
[20] Cf. Matthew 12, v. 39.
[21] Cf. John 11, v. 50.
[22] Cf. Genesis 4, v. 10.

wins in them His greatest victory; and by that same goodness by which in dying He overcame death, He brings it about that His defeated followers win victory over those who defeated them. Now, except a grain of wheat fall into the ground, it abideth alone; but if it die, it bringeth forth much fruit.[23] [61] We may therefore hope that from the death of this most fertile grain, much fruit will be forthcoming for the Church of Christ, since surely any man must be obstinately culpable and culpably obstinate if his heart is not pierced by the sword[24] which killed Peter. Nor must we entirely lose hope that some purpose will be served by his death, in that God will grant our wishes and ensure even greater success for the holy preaching campaign in the South which Peter initiated and for which he himself descended into corruption.

'With all this in mind we have thought it right to issue to our venerable brothers the Archbishops of Narbonne, Arles, Embrun, Aix and Vienne and their suffragans the following instructions (which we strongly urge them to carry out, and indeed enjoin them to do so through the Holy Spirit and by virtue of their duty of strict obedience):[25]

> that the word of peace and the faith sown by Peter should be watered by their preaching and so made to take root, and that they toil with unwearying zeal to expunge heresy and strengthen the Catholic faith, and eradicate vices and encourage virtues;

> that throughout their dioceses, in the name of God the Father, the Son and the Holy Spirit and by the authority of St Peter and St Paul, His apostles, and of ourselves, they denounce as excommunicated and anathematised[26] the murderer of the Lord's servant and all those who by whatever means may have helped, advised or encouraged him to commit such a crime, and likewise all those who may become his receivers or defenders;[27]

> that they put under a formal interdict[28] (which they should personally

---

23 John 12, vv. 24–5.
24 Cf. Luke 2, v. 35.
25 Innocent III (as also other popes of this era) routinely used a string of words and phrases to indicate his wishes. Here we have '*monendos duximus et hortandos, per Spiritum Sanctum . . . mandantes*'. In §64 we find '*monemus . . . exhortamur . . . injungimus et in remissionem peccaminum indulgemus quatinus*'. Other words used include '*postulamus*', '*obsecramus*', '*rogamus*', '*commonemus*', '*praecipimus*', '*exoramus*'. '*Mandamus*', especially '*per apostolica scripta mandamus*' is very common; such 'mandates' would usually be binding for subordinates, but for others perhaps only so long as it suited them; see Appendix F(ii) for a letter where King Philip Augustus politely rejects a mandate from Innocent, but appears to accept his right in general to issue mandates.
26 Anathematisation, 'cursing', was a formal process more severe than excommunication. The main difference was one of degree, in that anathematisation was used against those guilty of particularly serious crimes, such as murder or sacrilege, and as a further penalty against those like Raymond VI who had already been excommunicated. The procedure for administering anathematisation involved a bishop and twelve other clergy, who held candles; once the bishop had solemnly pronounced the sentence, the clergy would throw the candles to the ground and crush them under foot. William of Tudela, *Chanson* I, 5, pp. 16–18, refers to this procedure in describing Raymond VI's anathematisation. See also G&M, p. 28 n. 6.
27 Cf. n. 26 to §9.
28 Latin '*interdictio*'. To put an interdict on a place meant that the clergy could no longer minister to

attend to pronounce) all places to which the murderer or any of his abetters may resort;

that this sentence of condemnation be solemnly renewed, to the accompaniment of bells and lighted candles, every Sunday and feast day until the guilty men proceed to the Holy See and win pardon by giving appropriate satisfaction.

'Let us turn now to those who, fired with zeal for the true faith, are ready to gird themselves to avenge this righteous blood (which will not cease to cry from earth to heaven[29] until the Lord of Vengeance descends from heaven to earth to confound the corrupt and their corrupters); and to resist those villains who are attacking peace and truth. To these, let the archbishops and bishops give a firm promise that they will be granted remission of sins by God and His vicar, so that their labour in such a cause will provide adequate satisfaction at least for offences for which they offer heartfelt repentance and true confession to the true God. Let us emphasise that those villains are striving not merely to snatch our possessions but to take our lives; they are not merely sharpening their tongues to attack our souls, they are raising their hands to attack our bodies; they have become corrupters of souls and despoilers of lives.

[62] 'The Count of Toulouse has already been struck with the sword of anathema for many great crimes which it would take too long to list.[30] Now, there are sure indications that he must be presumed guilty of the death of that holy man;[31] not only did he threaten him with death publicly and lay an ambush for him, but also, it is maintained, he has accepted the murderer into close intimacy

---

people living there. It was thus an indiscriminate weapon and affected everyone. Interdicts were threatened many times during the 12th century and sometimes enforced, but the precise implications were not always well defined. Innocent had laid interdicts on Laon in 1198, France in 1199, and Normandy in 1203, but it had been necessary for local clergy to seek clarification from him about what they should do as a result. In March 1208, at almost exactly the same time as he was using the interdict against Raymond VI, Innocent was also issuing one against King John of England: see W. L. Warren, *King John*, 2nd edn (London, 1978), pp. 163–8. See also E. B. Krehbiel, *The Interdict: Its History and Operation with Especial Attention to the Time of Pope Innocent III* (Washington, 1909); and G&M, p. 28 n. 7.

[29] Cf. Genesis 4, v. 10.

[30] Another reference to Raymond's earlier excommunications in 1196 and 1207, on which see §27 and n. 7 to §57.

[31] It is impossible to be certain about exactly who was responsible for the murder of Peter of Castelnau. However, the charge of responsibility or at least complicity was to hang over Raymond's head indefinitely; see e.g. Innocent's letters of 25 January 1210 (Appendix F(iii) and n. 49 to §137) and May 1212 (n. 5 to §368) and §360 where Peter restates the charge. In fact there is no clear evidence of Raymond VI's involvement, and he was never formally arraigned on the charge. Such details as we have come from sources deeply hostile to Raymond (e.g. the letter quoted here, and reports from the legate Milo to Innocent, *PL* 216, 124–6). William of Puylaurens (IX) simply says that suspicion attached to Raymond ('*suspicione non caruit*'), while William of Tudela blames one of Raymond's knights who, he alleges, murdered Peter to curry favour with Raymond (*Chanson* I, 4, p. 14). The strongest evidence advanced against Raymond was that he received the murderer afterwards, as Innocent now says; in the oath he swore at Saint-Gilles in June 1209 (see §77) Raymond admits to this, but says in regard to the actual murder merely that he was held suspect, mainly because of his close association with Peter's murderer ('*de interfectione . . . Petri de Castronovo suspectus habeor, pro eo maxime quod interfectorem ipsius in magnam familiaritatem recepi*'). The arguments are fully discussed in Roquebert I, ch. 14.

and rewarded him most generously – to say nothing of other outrageous actions which have become known to us.[32] For this reason, the archbishops and bishops must publicly declare him to be anathematised. Since moreover the canons of the holy fathers provide that men need not keep faith with a man who does not keep faith in God and has therefore been excluded from communion with the faithful (and is to be treated as one to be shunned rather than cherished), they should pronounce that all those who are tied to the Count by any kind of oath, whether of fealty or alliance or treaty, are now released from that oath by our apostolic authority;[33] moreover, that it will be permitted to any Catholic person – provided the rights of the superior lord are respected – not only to proceed against the Count in person, but also to occupy and possess his lands,[34] in the expectation that the right thinking of the new occupier may purge those lands of the heresy which has hitherto so foully defiled them in consequence of the Count's villainy. Indeed, since his hand is now raised against all men, it is fitting that all men's hands should oppose him.

'If this vexation fails to lead him to understanding,[35] we shall make it our business to step up our action against him. However, if he at any time promises to give satisfaction, then for sure he will have to give clear proofs of his repentance; he must expel the followers of heresy from the whole of his dominions, and he must devote himself to the cause of reconciliation and fraternal peace. It was chiefly because of the faults he is known to have committed in these two respects that the Church's condemnation was pronounced against him – although if the

---

[32] Presumably from Arnold Amalric and Milo, who according to William of Tudela were at Rome when Innocent anathematised Raymond: see n. 4 to §57.

[33] The doctrine that vassals were released from oaths of fealty to excommunicate lords, and that in general sworn obligations to wrongdoers were void, were based on writings of the canon lawyer Gratian, and had been developed in particular by Gregorian reformers in the later 11th century. The doctrine was enshrined in canon 27 of the Third Lateran Council of 1179, and Lucius III's decretal *Ad Abolendum* issued at Verona in 1184 also referred to it. Cf. also Innocent's letter *Vergentis in senium* of 1198, in *PL* 214, 537–9. See G&M, p. 30 n. 1, and the extensive discussion in Maisonneuve, *Etudes sur les Origines de l'Inquisition*, esp. chs. 3–4.

[34] Innocent is here setting out an important doctrine which had been developed to deal with Raymond VI; it is first encountered in his letter of 29 May 1207 (*PL* 215, 1165–8; see n. 35 to §27 and Appendix F(i), and summary discussion in Appendix G). There were few precedents for it. Established tradition was that the Church should call upon a superior lord to dispossess an excommunicate vassal, and this was reflected for example in King Philip Augustus's comment in his letter to Innocent of April 1209 referred to below. Innocent had repeatedly sought to persuade Philip Augustus, as Raymond's principal overlord, to intervene: see his letters of 28 May 1204 (*PL* 215, 361), 16 January 1205 (*PL* 215, 501–3) and 7 February 1205 (*PL* 215, 526–8). However, Philip Augustus had failed to intervene; neither had he responded positively to Innocent's further appeal in 1207 (see n. 65 to §72). Thus in 1208, in the present letter, Innocent finally takes the initiative and, as foreshadowed in his letters of 1207, he now declares that Raymond's lands are open to seizure by any good Christian, although with the vitally important proviso that the rights of the ultimate feudal overlord must be respected ('*salvo jure domini principalis*'). This idea of 'liability to seizure' (*exposition en proie* in French) was to provide the justification for the actions of the crusaders against Raymond and the other southern lords. The development of these ideas is discussed in Appendix G, with further references. In referring to the rights of superior lords Innocent will have had particularly in mind the need to assure Philip Augustus that this call to dispossess Raymond VI did not threaten the king's own rights as ultimate suzerain, and he will also have been thinking of the rights of the German Emperor from whom Raymond held the marquisate of Provence. Philip Augustus was not happy with Innocent's approach; for his reaction see again §72, n. 65, and his letter of April 1208 in Appendix F(ii).

[35] Cf. Isaiah 28, v. 19

Lord were to mark all his iniquities,[36] he would be hard put to it to give suitable satisfaction whether for himself or for the host of others he has brought to the net of damnation.[37]

[63] 'If we follow true belief, we should fear not them which kill the body, but him which is able to send both body and soul to Hell.[38] Let us therefore trust in Him who, in order to free His believers from the fear of death, Himself died and rose again on the third day; and hope that our venerable brother the Bishop of Couserans[39] and our beloved son the Abbot of Cîteaux, legates of the Apostolic See, and other followers of the true faith, will find no cause for fear in the death of Peter, man of God, but that on the contrary it will set fire to their ardour, so that they will be ready to follow the example of one who gladly exchanged a temporal death for eternal life, and will not shrink from laying down their lives for Christ in so glorious a struggle, if needs must. Accordingly we enjoin and instruct the archbishops and bishops (reinforcing our prayers with commands and our commands with prayers) to give most careful heed to the advice and directions of the legates and help them like true comrades in arms to carry out whatever instructions they issue for the success of our enterprise. Let them understand that we have laid it down that any sentence pronounced by the legates against those who stand against us or those who stand idly by are to be held valid and strictly observed.

[64] 'Forward then soldiers of Christ! Forward, brave recruits to the Christian army! Let the universal cry of grief of the Holy Church arouse you, let pious zeal inspire you to avenge this monstrous crime against your God! Remember that your Creator had no need of you when He created you; but now, although He does not truly need your support, nevertheless – acting as if through your help He were less wearied in achieving His will, and His Omnipotence were in fact the less through needing your obedience – He has at this time given you an opportunity of serving Him in a way that is acceptable to Him. After the murder of that just man the Church in the South sits without a comforter in sadness and grief.[40] We are told that faith has vanished, peace has perished, that the plague of heresy and the madness of our enemies have gone from strength to strength, and it is clear that potent help must be provided for the ship of the Church in that area in this unprecedented storm if she is not to founder almost totally. We therefore advise and urge you all most strongly (confidently enjoining you at this most critical time in the name of Christ, and supporting our request with our promise of remission of sins): do not delay in opposing these great evils. In the name of the God of peace and love, apply yourselves vigorously to pacifying those nations. Work to root out perfidious heresy in whatever way God reveals to you. Attack the followers of heresy more fearlessly even than the Saracens – since they are

---

36 Cf. Psalm 130, v. 3.
37 Cf. Psalm 66, v. 11.
38 As in Matthew 10, v. 28.
39 See §48.
40 Cf. Isaiah 3, v. 26.

more evil – with a strong hand and a stretched out arm.[41] As to the Count of Toulouse who, like one who has made a covenant with Death, gives no thought to his own death[42] – if his punishment starts to turn him to understanding, if his face, filled with shame, begins to seek the name of the Lord,[43] continue by the added weight of your threats to drive him to give satisfaction to ourselves and the Church and indeed God; expelling him and his supporters from the towns[44] of the Lord and seizing their lands, where Catholic inhabitants will take over from the displaced heretics and will serve before God in holiness and righteousness according to the tenets of the true faith which you follow.

[65] 'Given at the Lateran on 10 March 1208[45] in the eleventh year of our papacy.'

[66] After this account of the death of this most holy man, let us return to my narrative.

[67] *Resumption of the main narrative.*[46] Faced with the death of these blessed men – the Bishop of Osma, Brother Peter of Castelnau and Brother Ralph, the leaders and masters of the preaching campaign in the South,[47] – the prelates of the province of Narbonne and others concerned with the business of peace and the faith realised that the campaign had now almost reached the end of its course, with little result; indeed the outcome they had looked for had almost entirely failed to materialise.[48] They therefore thought it desirable to send a mission to the Supreme Pontiff. The venerable Fulk, Bishop of Toulouse, and Navarre,

---

[41] Cf. Psalm 136, v. 12, and Deuteronomy 5, v. 15.

[42] Cf. Isaiah 28, v. 15.

[43] Psalm 83, v. 16.

[44] Latin '*castra*', on which see Appendix A(v), but here in a rhetorical context most appropriately translated as 'towns' in the sense of places, including fortified places, in which people dwelt. A similar usage is found in §3 above.

[45] Latin '*[Ante diem] VI Idus Martii*', literally 'six [days before] the Ides of March', following the classical Roman system of dating. Papal and other letters are usually dated in this way; for examples see §§384 and 411 below. Peter, however, usually gives dates by reference to Feast Days in the Christian Calendar but occasionally also follows the Roman system (e.g. §§448, 527, 602).

[46] §§67–77 cover the period between the murder of Peter of Castelnau in January 1208 and the reconciliation of Raymond VI at Saint-Gilles in June 1209. The events of this period are difficult to reconstruct since evidence is patchy and the sequence of events is uncertain. Peter's narrative is important in that it provides information which other sources do not; on the other hand his chronology is not wholly clear, and other sources (notably the *Chanson*) give details which he does not mention. The main features of the period are: preparations for the Crusade, under the leadership of Arnold Amalric; the appointment of Milo and Thedisius as new legates; continued and persistent efforts by Innocent to involve Philip Augustus, which are unsuccessful although Philip did sanction the involvement of two of his leading vassals, the Duke of Burgundy and the Count of Nevers; and important diplomatic efforts by Raymond VI on several fronts. According to the *Chanson* (I, 9, p. 26), Raymond made an approach to Arnold Amalric at Aubenas, perhaps early in 1209, but was rebuffed, and he also discussed the possibility of joint resistance with Raymond-Roger Trencavel. Peter mentions only Raymond's embassy to Rome in the first months of 1209. The period ends with the advance of the crusading army down the Rhône valley in June and July 1209. Further details are given in subsequent notes.

[47] Cf. also nn. 65 and 66 to §47 above.

[48] Cf. §51, n. 79, above. Note that Peter describes the crisis in the conduct of the *negotium pacis et fidei*, and the call for help to Rome, as being the result of the deaths of Diego, Ralph and Peter of Castelnau, rather than just the last of these three, implying that the Crusade was in part a result of the general failure of the preaching mission.

Bishop of Couserans, made their preparations and hurried to Rome,[49] to beg the
Pope to give a helping hand to the Church, now in peril and almost foundering in
the province of Narbonne and parts of the provinces of Bourges and Bordeaux.[50]
Pope Innocent, applying all his powers to the defence of the Catholic faith, placed
a healing hand on the Church's grave affliction by issuing general letters in
France as will be explained below.

[68] When he heard that two such eminent Bishops had gone to the Curia, the
Count of Toulouse – or should we say, 'the Count of cunning'[51] – began to fear
that he would receive his just deserts. Realizing that his acts could not go unpunished, he feigned penitence and in the hope of safeguarding his future sent a
succession of emissaries to Rome, ending with two detestable and ill-disposed
men, the Archbishop of Auch and Raymond of Rabastens, a former Bishop of
Toulouse who had been deservedly deposed.[52] Through these emissaries he laid
complaints to the Pope against the Abbot of Cîteaux (who was charged as papal
legate with responsibility for the business of the faith), alleging that the latter was
treating him with undue harshness and unjustly.[53] The Count promised that if

---

[49] The date of this mission, for which Peter is our only source, is not certain. Peter places it immediately
after the deaths of Diego and Ralph and the murder of Peter of Castelnau, which suggests early 1208, and
this is accepted by Roquebert (I, p. 222). However, we have no other evidence that Fulk and Navarre were
in Rome at so early a date. Moreover, although we have no firm date for the mission sent by Raymond to
Rome it probably did not arrive before January 1209, since the appointment of Milo as legate which was a
result of that embassy took place on 1 March 1209 (see n. 55 to §69); and since also Peter says that
Raymond's emissaries were sent when he heard of this mission by the two bishops, it is possible that the
bishops' journey was late in 1208 or even early in 1209, rather than early in 1208. This general uncertainty
means that there is also uncertainty as to which letters Peter is referring to at the end of this section, and in
§72 and §73. During this period Innocent issued three sets of letters dealing with arrangements for the
Crusade and appealing for support: (i) the letters of 10 March 1208 reporting the death of Peter of
Castelnau, i.e. the letter reproduced in §§56–65 and the similar letters referred to in the note to §55; (ii)
letters of 8, 9 and 11 October 1208, *PL* 215, 1469–71, also with a wide circulation and including one to
Philip Augustus; and (iii) a general letter of 3 February 1209 and a letter to Philip Augustus of the same
date, *PL* 215, 1545–6. Depending on the date assumed for the mission of Fulk and Navarre the letters
referred to at the end of this section, which Innocent is said to have issued in response to the mission, could
be any of the three sets. The letters referred to in §72 and §73 would most probably be those of February
1209, notwithstanding that Peter places them after the assembly at Villeneuve (§72) which took place on 1
May 1209. We have here a good example of Peter's often vague approach to chronology; it is also possible
that he might have referred more than once to the same letters, without explanation – for similar repeti-
tions see e.g. notes to §83 and §162.
[50] I.e. the ecclesiastical provinces. William of Puylaurens, in his Introduction, refers to heresy having
spread to the dioceses of Albi, Rodez and Cahors in the province of Bourges, and Agen in the province of
Bordeaux.
[51] A pun on '*Tolosanus dolosanus*' (cf. §8).
[52] The *Chanson* (I, 10, p. 30) also mentions the embassy sent to Rome involving these two prelates, which
probably took place in the winter of 1208–1209 (see n. 49 to §67 above). The Archbishop of Auch was
Bernard de Montaut, who had held office since 1201; he was to be asked by Innocent III to demit his office
in 1211 (*PL* 216, 408), and had been deposed by 1214 (*Chanson* I, p. 30 n. 1). Raymond of Rabastens was
Bishop of Toulouse 1201–1205. He had been deposed because his election was alleged to have been
simoniacal; however, Innocent allowed him, while deposed, to exercise his liturgical functions on holy days
at the invitation of the local clergy. He also received an income so that he would not be reduced to poverty.
See *PL* 215, 682–3, and above, §33 n. 43, on Raymond of Rabastens' successor Fulk. The *Chanson* (loc. cit.)
mentions two other members of this embassy, Peter Barreau, who was Prior of the Hospital in Toulouse,
and the Abbot of Condom.
[53] Raymond evidently found it impossible to deal with Arnold Amalric; relations between the two seem

the Pope would send a legate *a latere*,[54] he would follow his wishes in all things – a promise made not with any intention of changing his ways but in the belief that he was subtle and clever enough to get round any of the Pope's cardinals that might be sent to him.

[69] But the Almighty, who searches the hearts of men and knows their secrets, did not wish the integrity of the Holy See to be subverted, nor the Count's evil nature to be hidden any further. So, in His justice and mercy the Just Judge brought it about that the Pope satisfied the Count's request (just as if he were a deserving petitioner) but at the same time ensured that his ill-will would not be concealed. The Pope sent to the South one of his personal priests, Master Milo,[55] a man distinguished for his honourable way of life, his knowledge and his eloquence who – to describe his uprightness of character in a few words – could neither be daunted by fear nor won over by bribery. The Count was highly delighted to hear of his coming, believing that Milo would follow his wishes in all matters. He went about his domain boasting: 'It has turned out well for me, I have a papal legate after my own heart. In fact, I shall be legate myself.' But in the event, everything turned out contrary to his prayers, as I will report later.[56]

[70] A priest named Master Thedisius,[57] a canon of the cathedral of Genoa, was sent to accompany Milo and help him in furthering the business of the faith. He was a man of great learning, remarkable steadfastness and outstanding virtue. The course of events, and my account of them, will show in detail how well he conducted himself in Christ's business, and the many grievous dangers and tribulations he endured.

[71] The Pope had instructed Milo to consult the Abbot of Cîteaux in all matters relating to the business of the faith,[58] and especially in anything concerning the Count of Toulouse, since the Abbot would be aware of the state of that business and have a thorough appreciation of the twists and turns of Count

already to have broken down and never recovered (see e.g. the events related in §162, §195 and §212). The *Chanson* (I, 9, p. 26) refers to an attempt by Raymond to seek a reconciliation by going to meet Arnold at Aubenas in the Vivarais where Raymond is said to have tried to make a submission to the legate 'on his knees'; the latter refused, however, arguing that he did not have the powers to absolve him. This was probably late in 1208 or early in 1209. Arnold Amalric was clearly one of Raymond's most implacable opponents; when the legate Peter of Benevento dealt with Raymond in 1215 (see §503) his attitude was markedly different.

54 I.e. a plenipotentiary legate.

55 Milo was Innocent's notary; he was appointed legate on 1 March 1209 (*PL* 216, 187), which means that the embassy from Raymond VI was before that date. See also *Chanson* I, 11, p. 32, for his appointment as legate. For his later involvement see §74, §81 and §138, and for his death in December 1209 see §165. His eloquence is attested in the *Chanson* (I, 5, p. 18), where he is described as '*maestre Milos, qui en lati favela*', 'Master Milo who spoke Latin so well'.

56 §75.

57 He was a canon of the cathedral church of Genoa by 1203, and is said in §440, below, to have been a native of Pisa. He worked as legate firstly with Milo, and later with Hugh of Riez (see §137). He came with Arnold Amalric to the siege of Minerve in July 1210 (§154), was closely involved in the Council of Saint-Gilles (§162–4), and appears again in §398. He became Bishop of Agde in 1215 but continued to be involved with the Crusade and was present at the Fourth Lateran Council and reportedly present at the second siege of Toulouse. For full details and further references see G&L I, p. 69 n. 2.

58 Reflecting Arnold Amalric's leadership of the Crusade, which had been set out in Innocent's letter of 28 March 1208 (*Layettes* I, 843).

Raymond's mind. Indeed, for this reason the Pope had expressly instructed Milo: 'The Abbot will do everything, you will be his instrument.[59] The Count is suspicious of him, you he will not suspect.' Arriving in France, Milo and Thedisius found the Abbot at Auxerre,[60] and Milo consulted him on a number of specific points concerning the business of the faith. The Abbot gave his advice in writing and under seal, giving him detailed instructions on all points. In addition, he recommended that before Milo approached the Count of Toulouse he should call together the archbishops and bishops and any other prelates whose presence he judged would be useful and question them and seek their advice; naming individually some of the prelates whose advice he thought Milo should especially adhere to.

[72] The Abbot of Cîteaux and Milo now went to see the King of France,[61] who was holding a formal assembly of many of his barons at Villeneuve in the territory of the Senonnais.[62] Among them were Odo, Duke of Burgundy, the Counts of Nevers and Saint-Pol and numerous other powerful nobles.[63] The Pope wrote a personal letter to the King,[64] urging and praying him to help the Church in its hour of need, beset by dangers in the province of Narbonne; preferably in person or failing that through his son Louis. The King replied to the Pope's messenger that he was beset on his flanks by two great and dangerous lions,[65]

---

[59] The Latin word '*organum*', 'instrument', was also used by Innocent III in a letter of 23 January 1210 to Arnold Amalric, writing about the role of the legate Thedisius, who was not to act on his own initiative but was to take instructions from Arnold Amalric in all things, and act as his '*organum et . . . instrumentum*' (*PL* 216, 174–6); see also n. 49 to §137.

[60] Probably around the end of March 1209 (cf. Roquebert I, p. 230).

[61] Philip II 'Augustus', b. 1165, King 1180–1223.

[62] This took place on 1 May 1209 (see G&L I, p. 72 n. 3).

[63] See notes to §82 for details of these nobles.

[64] Latin '*litterae speciales*', a confidential letter or one with a single addressee as opposed to the letters with a wide circulation referred to in §73, which are *litterae generales*. As suggested in our note to §67, Peter is probably referring to Innocent's letter to Philip Augustus of 3 February 1209, *PL* 215, 1545. That letter particularly requests the King to appoint an energetic, wise and loyal man ('*virum strenuum, providum ac fidelem*') to lead the crusaders.

[65] Philip Augustus had twice previously cited hostilities with England as a reason for giving very limited support to the Crusade, in response to appeals from Innocent of 17 November 1207 (*PL* 215, 1264–7) and 10 March 1208 (*PL* 215, 1358–9, following the death of Peter of Castelnau); the King's replies, of December 1207 and April 1208, are in *HGL* VIII, 557–9. In fact the King's lukewarm attitude to the Crusade arose at least in part from a belief that it was an inappropriate interference in the affairs of one of his vassals, Raymond VI, and potentially an instrument for extending papal influence in the South. The letter of April 1208, of which a translation is given in Appendix F(ii), gives a clear indication of this; the King has no inclination to support Raymond, but firmly reminds the Pope that the Count is his vassal (even though in practice, as the letter implies, the tie had been a weak one), and that any declaration exposing his lands to seizure should come from him, not the Pope; see discussion in Roquebert I, pp. 223–6. The King maintained his distance from the Crusade for several years. In February 1213 he allowed his son Prince Louis to take the cross, but in the event prevented him from joining the Crusade, again advancing involvement with King John as a reason for limiting his support (see §§417–21; apparently his decision to allow Louis to take the cross was not a reaction to Raymond VI's decision in January to transfer his allegiance to King Peter of Aragon – see n. 34 to §417). He seems to have begun to show greater interest when in spring 1215 he sent Prince Louis to the South (see §§550ff and n. 10 to §552); this worried the crusaders who feared he might be intending to involve himself in the Midi to their detriment, but Louis behaved diplomatically and the King's objective seems to have been the limited one of registering his interest. An important development occurred in April 1216 when Simon de Montfort, after being formally recognised as Count of Toulouse at

Otto,[66] self-proclaimed Emperor and John, King of England, who – one from each side of France – were devoting all their powers to overturning his kingdom, so that in no way could he leave France himself or send his son; he felt it would be enough for the present if he allowed his barons to go to the province of Narbonne to confront those who were confounding peace and the faith in that province.[67]

[73] However, the Supreme Pontiff wished to hasten the involvement of the faithful in the struggle to root out the scourge of heresy, and sent general letters[68] to all prelates, counts and barons and all the inhabitants of the Kingdom of France, forcefully urging them to hurry to avenge the wrong done to the crucifix in the province of Narbonne, in the knowledge that all those who, inspired by zeal for the true faith, took up arms for this task of piety would receive indulgence for all their sins from God and His vicar, so long as they were penitent and made confession. No more need be said. The promise of indulgence was published in France; a great multitude of the faithful took up arms under the sign of the cross.

[74] *Milo arrives in Provence.* After the meeting at Villeneuve, Master Milo with his colleague Master Thedisius set out for Provence. Arriving at a *castrum* called Montélimar[69] he called together a large number of archbishops and bishops. When they had arrived he carefully sought their advice as to what steps should now be taken in regard to the business of peace and the faith, especially in connection with the Count of Toulouse; indeed he wished each prelate individually to give him, in writing and under seal, their views on the specific points laid down by the Abbot of Cîteaux. His wishes were carried out and – incredibly – the recommendations of the Abbot and the prelates were in agreement on all points without exception. Surely this was the Lord's doing!

the Fourth Lateran Council in December 1215, did homage for the county to Philip Augustus, apparently with Innocent's full approval (see §573), and in 1217 the King sent a hundred knights to help de Montfort (§598). However – and despite the fact that ultimately it was the French crown which benefited most from the Crusade and its aftermath – it was only at the end of the period covered by the *Historia*, in 1219, that the King mounted a serious intervention (see §619).

[66] Otto IV of Brunswick, the Guelf claimant to the title of Holy Roman Emperor during a long dispute in which Innocent III, who claimed to be the ultimate suzerain of the Empire, was much involved. From 1198 the main rival claimant was Philip of Swabia, the Staufen candidate, who was supported by Philip Augustus (aside from a short period when he favoured Otto). Philip of Swabia was assassinated in 1208 and at the time of which Peter is now writing, spring 1209, Philip Augustus was supporting Henry of Brabant, and Otto and King John were in alliance against Philip Augustus and Henry. Otto had been supported by Innocent and was still enjoying his support; indeed Innocent crowned him Emperor at Rome later that year, in October. However, the two fell out when Otto invaded southern Italy in 1210, so that by the time the *Historia* was being composed Otto was out of favour with Innocent – hence Peter's hostile reference. For later developments see n. 32 to §383 and for a brief general account W. Ullmann, *A Short History of the Medieval Papacy*, pp. 208–13.

[67] In May 1208, as a partial response to Innocent's appeal of 10 March, the King had authorised the Duke of Burgundy and the Count of Nevers to take part in the Crusade, fixing at five hundred the maximum number of knights they could take with them; see *HGL* VIII, 563–4. This is probably what Peter has in mind.

[68] See n. 49 to §67.

[69] Montélimar, south of Valence in the Rhône valley, lay in the county of the Valentinois whose Count was nominally a vassal of Raymond VI. See also §597 below.

[75] Milo then sent to the Count of Toulouse instructing him to attend a meeting with him on a named date at the city of Valence.[70] The Count arrived on the day arranged. This deceitful, cruel, tortuous and perjured man then promised to follow the legate's wishes in all matters, but in bad faith. However, the legate was a cautious and prudent man. On the advice of the prelates, he required the Count to hand over as security seven *castra* from the territory which he held in Provence.[71] He also demanded that the consuls of the cities of Avignon, Nîmes and the town of Saint-Gilles should swear on oath that if the Count were to presume to go against his orders, then they would not be bound to the Count by any ties of homage or fealty;[72] also the county of Melgueil[73] would then be handed over to the Holy Roman Church.[74] The Count was driven by necessity, albeit very sadly and unwillingly, to give his word to carry out all the legate's instructions. So it came about that the man who had complained that the Abbot of Cîteaux was hard now declared that the legate was by far harder. We may believe that under God's guiding hand a just outcome was achieved; a tyrant who had hoped for a remedy for his troubles, found instead a whip to punish him.

[76] Immediately Master Thedisius, a man of total honesty, went on the legate's orders to Provence to take over the seven *castra* referred to earlier and fortify them in the name of the Holy Roman Church.

---

[70] In the Rhône valley, about mid-way between Lyon and Avignon. Here Raymond gave preliminary undertakings referred to later by the legate Milo in the *Processus* of June 1209, on which see nn. 72 and 75 below.

[71] The *castra* were: Oppède, Mornas, and Beaumes de Venise on the east side of the Rhône valley; Roquemaure and Fourques, on the west bank of the Rhône itself; Montferrand in the county of Melgueil; and Largentière, which lies about 30km west of Montélimar in the county of Vivarais. See also the *Chanson* I, 11, p. 32, where the agreement to hand over castles is also mentioned. Details are again in the *Processus*.

[72] Oaths were sworn at this time by Raymond VI, numerous of his Provençal vassals and the consuls of Saint-Gilles, Nîmes, Avignon, Orange, Valence, Montpellier and other cities. They and the associated documents are recorded in *PL* 216, 89–98 as the *Processus* (see n. 75 to §77) and in *PL* 216, 127–38 as *Forma iuramenti baronum, civitatum, aliorumque locorum, Domino Papae dandae* in an annexe to the letter of September 1209 from Milo to Innocent, for details of which see n. 80 to §81. Most (including those mentioned here by Peter) were dealt with at Saint-Gilles between 18 and 22 June; those handled by Milo during his subsequent journey described in his letter are later, the last being 10 September. The documents are long and wordy, and their general effect is to bind those concerned to obey the Church, to keep the peace and help in combating heretics. In their oaths the consuls promise to put pressure on Raymond to abide by his undertakings and, as Peter says here, declare that their ties of fealty to Raymond will be nullified if he should fail to do so; they promise to follow the Church's orders in regard to tolls and other exactions, to respect the rights of the Church and its officers, to pursue heretics and finally 'to ensure that our successors will swear to all this . . . If anyone refuses so to swear we will treat him as a manifest heretic . . .'. For further comment and the oath of Raymond in particular again see n. 75 to §77.

[73] The county of Melgueil (now Mauguio) was a small area based immediately to the north and west of Montpellier. It had been acquired by Raymond VI, whose first wife Ermessinde de Pelet brought it with her as a dowry when she married him in 1172 (cf. *HGL* VI, p. 45). Raymond held it as a fief of the Holy See. In his letter of 29 May 1207, confirming Raymond's excommunication (n. 35 to §27 and Appendix F(i)), Innocent had expressly stated that those lands which Raymond held of the Roman Church would be liable to be recovered by the Church, and the county of Melgueil was no doubt particularly in his mind. In April 1211, after Raymond's renewed excommunication at the council of Montpellier (see §212), Innocent finally wrote to Bishop Raymond of Uzès and Arnold Amalric ordering them to take over the county (*PL* 216, 410).

[74] The meaning is that Raymond was required to agree to the confiscation of the county, should he renege on his oath. Raymond registered his acceptance of this in section II of the *Processus* (see next note).

[77] *Reconciliation of the Count of Toulouse.*[75] The legate then went to Saint-Gilles to arrange the reconciliation of the Count of Toulouse. The form of the ceremony of reconciliation and absolution was as follows.

The Count was led naked[76] to the doors of the church of Saint-Gilles. There, in the presence of the legate, and the archbishops and bishops (of whom more than twenty[77] had gathered for the ceremony) he swore on the Body of Christ and on numerous relics of the saints which priests were displaying with great reverence in front of the church gates, that he would obey the commands of the Holy Roman Church in all matters. Then the legate had a robe placed round the Count's neck. Holding him by the robe, he gave him absolution by scourging him and led him into the church. [78] It should be mentioned that after the Count was scourged and led into the church, as just described, God disposed that because of the crowd of spectators he was quite unable to leave the church by the way he had entered. Instead, he had to go down through the crypt and pass,

---

[75] This took place on 18 June 1209, on which day Raymond also swore his oath. The undertakings imposed on him are recorded in the *Processus negotii Raymundi Comitis Tolosani*, in *PL* 216, 89–98. The document is in fourteen sections. The first records the preliminary undertaking, *prima obligatio*, given by the Count at Valence (n. 70 to §75) which deals chiefly with his undertaking to hand over the seven *castra* mentioned there (Raymond was to continue to pay for their upkeep and provide soldiers to man them). In the oath itself, section II, Raymond swears to stand by the Church's requirements ('*mandata*') on all the issues referred to him by the Pope himself or Milo or other legates, which were given as reasons for his excommunication in 1207. There is then a list of fifteen items, most of which reflect or copy the wording of Innocent's letter of 29 May 1207 confirming the excommunication (see n. 35 to §27 and Appendix F(i)). On many of the charges Raymond merely acknowledges that he has been accused (e.g. '*pacem aliis juriantibus dicor noluisse jurare*', 'I am said to have been unwilling to swear to [keep the] peace when others swore to it', or '*de fide suspectus habeor*', 'I am held suspect in the matter of the faith'). On others he appears to admit the charge (e.g.'*ruptarios sive mainadas tenui*', 'I have maintained mercenaries'); see also n. 31 to §62, above, on the question of Raymond's involvement in the murder of Peter of Castelnau. Raymond then agrees that if he reneges on his undertakings he will forfeit the seven *castra* and the county of Melgueil and be excommunicated and forfeit also his claims on his vassals, and in the final item promises to keep the public roads safe. Sections III and IV of the *processus* record *mandata* imposed by Milo on Raymond before absolution (five items) and after absolution (fifteen items). The remaining ten sections record in detail undertakings given by Raymond and his Provençal vassals and the consuls of Avignon, Nîmes and Saint-Gilles and others, and tie in with those given in the *Forma juramenti baronum*, in *PL* 216, 127–38. Inter alia, on 18 June oaths were sworn also by William of Baux, Prince of Orange, who handed over three *castra* (and on whom see below, §593), and by five other seigneurs who handed over *castra*. The effect of the process of oath-taking was to remove the threat of military action against Raymond's territories. We cannot be sure of Raymond's thinking at this time; he was by nature cautious (compare his conduct at the first siege of Toulouse in 1211 (§241 n. 32) and at the battles of Castelnaudary in 1211 (§268 n. 43) and at Muret in 1213 (§462 n. 40)), and most probably he was reacting to the legates' pressure in the belief that appeasement, and indeed collaboration to the extent of taking the cross (§80), would be more likely to protect his position for the immediate future than armed resistance. In any event at this stage he and his vassals and the various consuls could reasonably hope that if they were co-operative the threat from the crusaders would soon go away (we may compare the belief of the Biterrois, n. 18 to §84, that the Crusade would not last for even fifteen days), or at least that they would be immune from attack. Belperron, pp. 156–7, sees a more sinister motive, viz. an expectation on Raymond's part that he would be able to take advantage of the situation to enrich himself at the expense of Viscount Raymond-Roger Trencavel (cf. §111 below). For a discussion see Roquebert I, pp. 235–9, and Maisonneuve, *Etudes sur les Origines de l'Inquisition*, pp. 210–16.

[76] '*Nudus*'. Peter applies the term to Raymond again in the next section, perhaps (in his keenness to score a point) having overlooked the point that in the meantime the Count had donned a robe ('*stolam*').

[77] For their names see *PL* 216, 94. In fact three archbishops are named (Michael of Arles, Guy of Aix and Bernard of Auch), and nineteen bishops.

naked, by the tomb of the blessed martyr Brother Peter of Castelnau whose death he had caused. How just a judgment of God! The Count was compelled to show reverence to the dead body of the man he had used so spitefully whilst he lived.

[79] *A miracle.* I must also note that when the martyr's body, which was at first entombed in the monks' cloister at Saint-Gilles, was after a long period transferred to the church proper, it was found to be as whole and unimpaired as it if had been buried that very day. A marvellous perfume arose from his body and clothing.

[80] *The Count of Toulouse takes up the Cross.* After all these events, the Count, displaying his usual cunning and fearful of the arrival of the crusaders[78] who were now well on their way from France to the area of Narbonne where they intended to expel the heretics and their supporters, asked the legate to bestow the cross on him as a means of protecting his territory against invasion by the crusaders. The legate agreed and bestowed the cross on the Count and just two of his knights.[79] I declare the Count a false and faithless crusader; he took the cross not to avenge the wrong done to the Crucifix, but to conceal and cover his wickedness for a period.

[81] After this, Master Milo and Master Thedisius returned towards Lyon, to meet the crusaders who were now approaching the city ready to attack the heretics in the South.[80] The indulgence which the Pope had promised to anyone proceeding against the heretics had been published throughout France, with the result that huge numbers of nobles and commoners had taken up arms, ready with the sign of the cross on their breasts to confront the enemies of the cross.[81]

With so many thousands of the faithful in France already taking up the cross to avenge the wrong done to our God, and others yet to join the Crusade, nothing remained but for the Lord God of Hosts to dispatch his armies to destroy the

---

[78] Latin 'crucesignati', Peter's preferred word for the crusaders, but he also frequently uses *signati* and *peregrini* (which also means pilgrims and indicates the close connection between the ideas of crusade and pilgrimage), without any distinction. For examples of *peregrini* see §105 n. 70, and for a further comment n. 56 to §313 on *burdonarius*.

[79] This took place on 22 June 1209: see *PL* 216, 95. Innocent reacted to the news of Raymond's reconciliation in a letter of 27 July, *PL* 216, 100, written in warm terms and suggesting that he expected no further difficulties in relations between the Church and the Count.

[80] The crusaders probably arrived in Lyon early in July 1209; see n. 2 to §82. Milo himself arrived at Lyon at some point in July 1209, possibly before 7 or 8 July since that is when the crusaders are likely to have left. Milo describes his actions in the succeeding weeks in a letter of September 1209 to Pope Innocent (*PL* 216, 124–6). He says that after accompanying the crusaders from Lyon to Montpellier he was instructed by Arnold Amalric and the leaders of the Crusade 'to return to the territories of the Counts of Provence and Fourcalquier partly to arrange an agreement between them and partly to make a collection from the local churches to help the Crusade' ('*pro collecta facienda ad opus et subsidium exercitus Jesu Christi*'). He continued the work begun in June in imposing oaths of peace on local seigneurs and obtaining the surrender of castles as guarantees. See again the discussion by M.-H. Vicaire in *Cahiers de Fanjeaux* vol. 4, pp. 116–23, for details. Copies of the documents (the *Forma juramenti baronum*, discussed in n. 72 to §75) were submitted to Innocent for inclusion, if the Pope wished, in the Vatican's official records ('*ponendam, si vestrae sanctitatae videbitur, in Regestis*'). Innocent III then, on 27 July, instructed Milo to continue with his legatine duties – *PL* 216, 100.

[81] Wearing the cross as a sign of being a Crusader was introduced by Urban II in 1095 at the time of the First Crusade.

cruel murderers – God who with His customary goodness and inborn love had shown compassion to his enemies, the heretics and their supporters, and sent his preachers to them – not one, but many, not once, but often; but they persisted in their perversity and were obstinate in their wickedness; some of the preachers they heaped with abuse, others they even killed.

[V. §§82–120, summer/early autumn 1209: *Arrival of the crusaders in the South – Raymond VI joins the crusaders – the crusaders march against Raymond-Roger Trencavel – massacre at Béziers, 22 July 1209 – siege and fall of Carcassonne, August 1209 – Simon de Montfort chosen to succeed Raymond-Roger Trencavel as Viscount of Béziers and Carcassonne – portrait of Simon de Montfort – departure of main crusading army – initial campaigns in the viscounties of Béziers and Carcassonne – Duke of Burgundy then returns home, de Montfort left largely alone – further campaigns in the former Trencavel lands.*]

[82] *Arrival of the crusaders.*[1] In the year 1209 of the Incarnation of our Lord, in the twelfth year of the papacy of Innocent III, in the reign of Philip, King of France, about the time of the feast of St John the Baptist,[2] all the crusaders who had been making their way from various parts of France converged on Lyon, the ancient capital city of Gaul,[3] in accordance with a common prearranged plan.[4] Most important of those who came were the Archbishop of Sens, the Bishops of Autun, Clermont and Nevers,[5] the Duke of Burgundy,[6] the Count of Nevers,[7] the Count of Saint-Pol,[8] the Count of Montfort,[9] the Count of Bar-sur-Seine, Guichard of Beaujeu, William des Roches the Seneschal of Anjou, and Gaucher de Joigny.[10] There were many other noble and powerful men, too numerous to list.[11]

---

1 In this section Peter, without explaining why, recounts events already covered in §81.
2 I.e. 24 June 1209; as often when Peter gives dates by reference to the Church calendar this is a very approximate date (cf. for example comments in Appendix E and nn. to §137 and §367). G&L I, p. 81 n. 2, quote E. Petit, *Histoire des ducs de Boulogne*, III, 167, as saying that an examination of acts of some crusaders shows that 'les troupes bourguignonnes ne purent passer à Lyon que dans les premiers jours de juillet'.
3 Latin '*urbem Gallie*'. Peter does not usually refer to places as *urbs*; we follow G&M who translate as '*ancienne capitale de la Gaule*'. See also Appendix A(iv).
4 Peter is here presumably referring to the the plans made by Innocent III and the legates over the preceding months, which are described in §§72–81 above, and reflected in Innocent's letters of 1208–1209, which are discussed (for instance) in Roquebert I, chs. 15 and 16, and W. L. Wakefield, *Heresy, Crusade and Inquisition in Southern France 1100–1250* (London, 1974), pp. 91–7.
5 Peter of Sens, 1200–1222; Gautier of Autun, 1190–1223; Robert of Clermont, 1195–1227 (brother of Count Guy of Clermont and the Auvergne); and William of Nevers, 1201–21. See G&L I, notes on pp. 81–2.
6 Odo (Eudes) III, who was the most important layman taking part. He had been amongst those barons urged directly by Innocent III to take up arms against heresy in the south from late 1207 (see e.g. *PL* 215, 1246–8), and his participation in July 1209 had been explicitly sanctioned by Philip Augustus (*HGL* VIII, 563–4). Cf. §72 above. He took part in the Crusade again in late 1213: see §491.
7 Hervé IV. Also specifically authorised by Philip Augustus to join the Crusade; cf. §72 above.
8 Gaucher de Châtillon; cf. above §72, and below §550 (when in 1215 he again came south to join the Crusade).
9 Simon lord of Montfort, to the west of Paris in the Ile de France. The first reference to the future lay leader of the Crusade. The title 'count' which was regularly given to him by contemporaries derives from his having inherited the rights to the English earldom of Leicester through his mother. For this and a note on his background and family see Appendix C, and for Peter's appreciation of him see §§104–7 below.
10 Milo IV, Count of Bar-sur-Seine; Guichard IV of Beaujeu (who rejoined the Crusade in 1215: §550); William des Roches, seneschal of Anjou 1199–1222; Gaucher de Joigny, lord of Châteaurenard in the Gâtinais region of north-west Burgundy: see G&L I, p. 83 nn. 1–4.
11 G&L (I, p. 84 n. a) note that some MSS add the names of Guy de Lévis (see §185), Lambert de Thury

[83] *The Count of Toulouse goes to meet the crusaders.*[12] When Raymond, Count of Toulouse, heard of the arrival of the host of crusaders he became afraid that they would invade his territory, since his conscience was troubled by the recollection of the villainies he had perpetrated. He therefore went out to meet them, almost as far as the city of Valence,[13] but they had gone out with a high hand.[14] Accordingly he joined them near the city, pretended that he wanted peace and gave a false pledge of compliance and a firm promise to subject himself to the orders of the Holy Roman Church and even to the will of the crusaders. As his security for keeping to these undertakings he handed over certain fortresses[15] to the barons and even indicated his willingness to offer his son or himself as a hostage. What more? The enemy of Christ allied himself to the soldiers of Christ; they joined together and proceeded directly to Béziers.[16]

[84] *Siege and destruction of Béziers.*[17] Béziers was a most notable city, but entirely infected with the poison of heresy.[18] Its citizens were not only heretics,

---

(see §248), and Philippe Goloin, each of whom was to play an important part in supporting de Montfort in the south in the years to come. The *Chanson*, I, 12–13, pp. 34–40 also gives further details, and reports another contingent of crusaders who entered the Agenais and Quercy, further west. Peter makes no mention of them, nor of the campaign in Quercy undertaken by them at about the same time as the attack on Béziers and Carcassonne, which is described only by the *Chanson*, ibid. See also Roquebert, I, pp. 239–43, for an account of this '*croisade Quercynoise*'.

[12] Peter here, again without explaining why, recapitulates events already described in more detail in §§74–80 above.

[13] Valence lay on the east bank of the Rhône, at the northern edge of the county of Valence and Die (the Valentinois and Diois). Its Count Adhémar was a vassal of Raymond VI of Toulouse by virtue of the latter's lordship over the marquisate of Provence and according to the *Chanson* (I, 12, p. 36) he was with the crusading army at this stage, but later opposed them (below, §490). See also §598.

[14] Cf. Exodus 14, v. 8.

[15] See note to §75.

[16] As is very clear from Innocent's letter establishing the Crusade, §§56–65 above, intervention against Raymond VI had always been the prime objective of the Crusade. His reconciliation had removed this threat from him and his lands, so that in a sense it left the Crusaders without a clear target. Thus a decision was taken, details about which are unknown, to attack the lands of Raymond-Roger Trencavel instead; for the possibility that Raymond may have encouraged this see n. 75 to §77 and n. 98 to §111. William of Tudela simply says (*Chanson* I, 13, p. 38) that Toulouse having made its peace the crusaders said they would take Carcassonne and the Albigeois, Trencavel possessions. Raymond VI is also said by the *Chanson* (I, 14, p. 44) to have guided the crusaders from Montpellier (which they left on 20 July) to Béziers, where they arrived on the evening of 21 July. Peter does not mention that on their way the crusaders occupied the *castrum* of Servian, north of Béziers, which had apparently been deserted by its inhabitants and its seigneur, Stephen. This took place on 20/21 July (date derived from the from the legates' letter to Innocent III, see following note, and see *HGL* VIII 584 for Stephen of Servian's abjuration in February 1210).

[17] See Appendix B for a discussion of the attack on Béziers, and the accounts of other sources, principally the *Chanson* I, 15–22, pp. 44–60; William of Puylaurens XIII; and a letter sent to Pope Innocent in late August by the legates Arnold Amalric and Milo, *PL* 216, 137–41. (This letter is a major source for the early stages of the Crusade; see various references in succeeding notes.)

[18] It is by no means clear that Béziers was as significant a centre of heresy as Peter claims. He is almost certainly exaggerating because of his identification of all opponents of the Crusade as heretics. When Bertrand of Saissac was made guardian of the young Viscount Raymond-Roger in 1194, he was made to swear to tolerate '*nec hereticos nec Valdenses*' in the city (*HGL* VIII, 430), which suggests that heresy was present, but is not in itself evidence of any great strength of heresy in the city. For discussion of the question see Roquebert I, pp. 248–50, and Griffe, *LC*, pp. 184–7, and also n. 30 to §89 below, on the list of alleged heretics in Béziers drawn up at the time of the siege. Whatever the case, there was certainly a strong history of anticlericalism in Béziers (examples follow in the next section). To judge from the account of William of Tudela (*Chanson* I, 17, p. 50) the principal reasons for the inhabitants' resistance to the

they were robbers, lawbreakers, adulterers and thieves of the worst sort, brimful of every kind of sin. I hope it will not weary the reader if I give some examples of the evil ways of these people.

[85] *An example of brutality.* One night just at daybreak a priest of the city was going to his church to celebrate the divine mysteries, carrying a chalice. Some of the citizens laid an ambush, seized him and beat him violently, breaking his arm and seriously wounding him. They took the chalice, disrobed him and urinated on him to show contempt for the body and blood of Jesus Christ.

[86] *Another example.* On another occasion, in the church of St Mary Magdalene in the city,[19] the citizens in an act of dreadful treason killed their lord Raymond Trencavel Viscount of Béziers,[20] and broke the teeth of their Bishop when he tried to defend the Viscount from their attack.

[87] *A miracle.* One day a certain canon was leaving the great church[21] of Béziers, after the celebration of Mass. Hearing the noise of men working on the city's defences[22] he asked what it was. Bystanders replied: 'The noise comes from men working on the ditches – we are fortifying the city against the French who are coming here'; (this happened just when the arrival of the crusaders was imminent). While this exchange was taking place, there appeared an old man of venerable years who said to them: 'You are defending the city against the crusaders, but who will be able to defend you from above?' By this he meant that the Lord would be attacking them from Heaven. Hearing this, they were extremely disturbed, but when they tried to attack the old man, he disappeared and was nowhere to be found.

[88] To return to our main theme; before the crusaders arrived at Béziers,[23] the Viscount of Béziers, Roger (of noble birth and a nephew of the Count of Toulouse,[24] who was following his uncle's evil example and was doing nothing to restrain the heretics),[25] had promised the citizens of Béziers that he would not

crusaders were their confidence in the strength of the city's defences, their belief that the crusading army would be unable to sustain a long campaign and their unwillingness to allow any loss of civic autonomy or any increase in the influence of the Bishop over their affairs. William says: 'the majority of the inhabitants . . . would grant nothing to the crusaders, not a penny, which would lead to any change in the government of their town. They did not believe the army could maintain itself; they were convinced that in less than fifteen days it would disperse . . .' He goes on to describe their belief that the defences would allow them to resist a siege even for a whole month.

19   The church lies about 500m north of the Cathedral of Saint-Nazaire.
20   Raymond Trencavel I, Viscount of Béziers 1130–67. The Bishop was Bernard IV, 1167–84: G&L I, p. 88 n. 3. G&L I, p. 87 n. 2 cite several sources which refer to this incident, dated to 15 October, 1167. The legates' letter of August 1209, col. 139, also notes it, as does William of Puylaurens, XIII; see also *HGL* V, 30 and 36.
21   Presumably the Cathedral of Saint-Nazaire, at the western edge of the city, overlooking the river Orb.
22   The cathedral lies on the western edge of Béziers, very close to its ramparts, and the ground immediately to the south and west of the cathedral descends very steeply to the river Orb below. Both the *Chanson* (I, 17, p. 50) and legates' letter of August 1209, col. 139, note how well-fortified Béziers was in July 1209.
23   According to William of Tudela (*Chanson* I, 11, p. 32) Raymond-Roger Trencavel attempted to negotiate a settlement with the crusaders as they approached, but was rebuffed. Peter makes no mention of this.
24   His mother was Adelaide, daughter of Raymond V of Toulouse, and hence Count Raymond's sister. She married Roger II Trencavel (1144–94) in the early 1180s, and Raymond-Roger Trencavel was b. 1185. He married Agnes daughter of William VIII of Montpellier.
25   Because of his youth and his weak control over his vassals he lacked the ability to do so, even had he so

under any circumstances desert them, but would stand firmly by them to the death and would stay in the city to await the coming of Christ's soldiers. However, when he heard that our armies were approaching, he forgot his promises and undertakings, broke faith and fled to Carcassonne,[26] another important city in his domains, taking with him a number of heretics[27] from Béziers.

[89] When our men reached Béziers,[28] the Bishop of the city, Master Renaud of Montpellier[29] (a man deserving respect for his age, the conduct of his life, and his learning) had come out to meet them, and they sent him back into the city. Through him they said that they had come to destroy the heretics, and they ordered any Catholics amongst the citizens to hand over the heretics, whose names the venerable Bishop would give, since he knew them well and had even listed them in writing;[30] if they could not do this, they should quit the city and leave the heretics behind, so as to avoid perishing with them. When the Bishop had delivered this message from our side to the citizens, they refused to listen to it. Instead they set themselves up against God and the Church, made a covenant with death[31] and chose to die as heretics rather than live as Christians; indeed even before our side made any attack on them, some of them came out of the city and began to assail our men with arrows.[32]

[90]Seeing this the servants of the army (who in the common tongue are called *ribauds*) became extremely angry. They approached the city walls, and – without the knowledge of the chiefs of the army and quite without consulting them – mounted an attack. Astonishingly, they captured the city inside an hour. What more? They entered it immediately, killed almost all the inhabitants from the youngest to the oldest, and set fire to the city.

---

wished. Cf. the *Chanson* I, 15, p. 44: his vassals 'had no respect or fear for him, and treated him like an equal'.

[26] In the valley of the Aude, some 60km inland from Béziers. Peter's portrayal of the retreat to Carcassonne as an unseemly flight is at variance with the account of William of Tudela in the *Chanson*, I, 15–16, pp. 46–8, where it is portrayed as strategic, and the Viscount is said to be in good heart ('*gran cor*').

[27] He also took many of the Jews of Béziers; cf. *Chanson*, I, 16, p. 48.

[28] On 21 July 1209 (see the legates' letter). They camped on the plain on the west bank of the river Orb, beneath the city walls and the Cathedral which lay on the high ground on the opposite bank; cf. *Chanson* I, 18, p. 52.

[29] *Recte* of Montpeyroux; Renaud II, Bishop 1209–11.

[30] A list of names survives which may very well be the list here mentioned (printed by L. Domarion, in 'Rôle des hérétiques de la ville de Béziers à l'époque du désastre de 1209', *Cabinet Historique* (1863), pp. 95–103). It refers to over 220 persons of whom 210 are named. Commentators have sought to use this list to estimate the number of heretics in Béziers (out of a total population taken as around 20,000) but there can be no certainty. If as e.g. Roquebert (I, pp. 248–50) argues, the list consists mainly of the names of Cathar *perfecti* then the number of *credentes* must have been many times greater. Against this Griffe (*LC*, pp. 184–7) argues that by no means all were *perfecti*, and that the list includes both *credentes* and mere sympathisers. Perhaps the list was an ad hoc concoction of Bishop Renaud, noting those he knew to be *perfecti* and adding prominent believers and sympathisers and other enemies of the Bishop in a city with a long history of anti-clericalism. See also in particular H. Vidal, *Episcopatus et pouvoir épiscopal à Béziers à la veille de la Croisade albigeoise* (Montpellier, 1951), pp. 75–90.

[31] Isaiah 28, v. 15.

[32] See Appendix B. (The *Chanson* I, 18–19, pp. 52–4, gives more details, saying that a French soldier was killed in this skirmish.)

[91] The city was taken on the feast day of the Blessed Mary Magdalene.[33] What a splendid example of divine Justice and Providence! As I wrote earlier in this book,[34] the heretics said that Mary Magdalene was Christ's concubine; moreover, as I mentioned above, it was in her church in the city that the citizens of Béziers killed their lord, and broke the teeth of their Bishop. So it was right that these shameless dogs should be captured and destroyed on the feast day of the woman they had so insulted and whose church they had defiled with the blood of their lord, the Viscount, and their Bishop. In the very church in which the citizens of Béziers had killed their lord, up to seven thousand[35] of them were killed on the day of the city's capture. It is especially worth noting that just as the city of Jerusalem was destroyed by Titus and Vespasian forty-two years after the Passion of Our Lord, so the city of Béziers was devastated by the French forty-two years after the murder of the lord of the city. Nor should I omit the point that the city, which was destroyed several times[36] for the same reasons, on each occasion met its fate on the feast of the blessed Mary Magdalene, in whose church so enormous a crime had been committed, and so suffered a punishment worthy of its crime.

[92] *Siege of Carcassonne.* After the capture and destruction of Béziers, our army decided to march straight[37] to Carcassonne, whose citizens were heretics[38] of the worst sort and sinners before the Lord exceedingly.[39] The people living in the *castra* between Béziers and Carcassonne fled in fear of the army, leaving their homes deserted, although a few who were not marked down for heresy surrendered to us.[40]

[93] When the Viscount heard that our soldiers were moving towards Carcassonne to lay it under siege, he gathered together as many knights as he could, withdrew with them into the city and made preparations to defend it against our

---

[33] 22 July, 1209. The date is confirmed by the legates' letter, col. 139, and by William of Puylaurens, XIII.

[34] §11.

[35] See Appendix B, where it is pointed out that the church of La Madeleine could not have contained so great a number, and that the figure of 7000 may relate to the cathedral church of Saint-Nazaire.

[36] G&L I, p. 93 n. 2, cite a 13th century tradition that there were three such occasions.

[37] The crusaders remained encamped below Béziers for three days, and then began to march inland along the valley of the Aude. Peter omits to mention that Archbishop Berengar of Narbonne, Viscount Aimeric of Narbonne, and a deputation of local nobility and representatives of the citizens of Narbonne came to meet the crusaders (probably near Capestang) and submitted to them, offering money and support in return for immunity from any attack. For details see the legates' letter, and Roquebert I, p. 265.

[38] Support for Catharism was widespread in Carcassonne and the Carcassès. One of the Cathar bishoprics established after the Cathar Council at Saint-Félix (probably) in the 1170s was based on Carcassonne, and its first bishop was one Giraud Mercier. By the early 13th century he had been succeeded by Bernard of Simorre, already mentioned by Peter above, §52. Carcassonne was also the site of a disputation held in February 1204 between Bernard of Simorre and the legates Ralph and Peter of Castelnau; this was convened by Peter of Aragon, and is mentioned in the *Chanson*, I, 2, pp. 8–10 (and see also Vicaire, pp. 87–8). Peter will have heard about the diocese of Carcassonne from his uncle Abbot Guy, who had preached there against the Cathars in the summer of 1207; cf. §25 above. For details of the Council of Saint-Félix (esp. on its date) see Hamilton, 'The Cathar Council of Saint-Félix reconsidered', cited in n. 10 to §4 above. For Catharism in the Carcassès and neighbouring Lauragais see Griffe, *LC*, pp. 156–76, and E. Griffe, 'Le Catharisme dans le diocèse de Carcassonne et le Lauragais au XII siècle', *Cahiers de Fanjeaux*, vol. 3, pp. 215–36.

[39] Genesis 13, v. 13.

[40] For details see the legates' letter, *PL* 216, 139; *Chanson*, I, 21, p. 58; and Appendix B.

army. I must not omit to record that the evil and faithless citizens of Carcassonne destroyed the refectory and cellar of the cathedral canons (who were canons regular), and – even more execrable – the stalls in the church itself, as a source of material to fortify the walls.[41] What a sacrilegious design, what a useless protection, built by violating and destroying the holy sanctuary of the house of God, and therefore deserving to be destroyed! The houses of peasants are left intact, the houses of the servants of God are pulled down!

[94] When our soldiers reached the city,[42] they pitched their tents in a circle all round it, thus strengthening the siege. With their troops so disposed they undertook no action for that day and the next. Carcassonne, which is built on the summit of a hill, was flanked by suburbs on two sides, each of which was fortified with walls and ditches.[43]

[95] The first suburb was less strongly fortified than the second one,[44] and on the third day our soldiers, thinking to capture it by an assault without using siege-engines,[45] made a concerted attack on it. The bishops and abbots and all the clergy joined together and chanted the '*Veni Sancte Spiritus*' with great devotion, confidently expecting that Divine help would soon arrive. Immediately the outer suburb was deserted by the enemy and taken by force. I should add that Simon, the noble Count of Montfort, courageously advanced into the ditch ahead of all the others – indeed he was the only knight to do so – and thus played an

[41] The cathedral of Saint-Nazaire lies at the south-west corner of the Cité of Carcassonne. The canons' cloister lay between the cathedral and the walls (cf. G&L I, p. 95 n. 1).

[42] The legates' letter, col. 139, gives the date as the Feast of St Peter, 1 August 1209. Thus 'the third day' in §95 is 3 August, 'the following day' in §96 is 4 August and the events in §96 took place on 4–8 August, with the entry into the second suburb ('on the following morning') on 8 August, '*octavo die*' in the legates' letter, col. 140.

[43] The *cité* of Carcassonne lies on a hill on the east bank of the river Aude. Fortified since Gallo-Roman times, in the early 13th century it had a single ring of ramparts, incorporating a series of (about 30) towers, with ditches below. The walls were topped by wooden covered walkways from which the defenders could view any assailants in safety. The *Chanson*, I, 23, p. 62, describes Viscount Raymond-Roger watching the arrival of the crusaders from one of these. At the foot of the walls were two suburbs known as the Bourg, to the north, and the Castellar, to the south. Both were also fortified, but much less strongly than the *cité* above. Another (unfortified) suburb, called Saint-Vincent, lay at the eastern end of the bridge over the Aude. See also *HGL* VII, pp. 455–7.

[44] The first suburb was the Bourg, the second the Castellar.

[45] Peter refers to stone-hurling engines as *petrariae* (petraries) or *mangonellae* (mangonels), or sometimes simply as *machinae*. For a discussion of medieval siege-engines, see P. Contamine, *War in the Middle Ages*, trans. M. Jones (Oxford: Blackwell, 1984), pp. 102–6, and J. Bradbury, *The Medieval Siege* (Woodbridge, 1992), ch. 9. Bradbury notes (pp. 250–9) that mangonels are usually described as engines which possessed a long arm, or beam, with a fixed cup at one end. The beam was drawn backwards and held in place; it was attached to twisted ropes, so that on release, the torsion caused the arm to revolve upwards until it smacked against a cross beam. The stone or missile was placed in the cup, and when the arm hit the bar, it would be released at the target. There are some indications that petraries threw larger stones, but Bradbury points out that up to about the twelfth century direct evidence about siege-engines is in short supply and that medieval chroniclers give little detail and use descriptions in a loose way; there is thus usually uncertainty about exactly what type of engine is meant – and indeed some uncertainty as to whether engines in use in Peter's time even used torsion ropes. The only references in Peter to 'trebuchets', which in their fully developed form were engines with a sling and counterweight, occur in §606C and §610 (second siege of Toulouse), but the *Chanson* refers to an engine at Castelnaudary as a trebuchet which Peter calls *machina* – see §261.

outstanding part in capturing this suburb. Once captured it was razed to the ground and the ditches filled in.

[96] Seeing how easily they had taken the first suburb, our men thought they might be able to capture the second suburb, which was much more strongly fortified, by a similar assault. Accordingly on the following day they advanced to the wall, but as they started to press their attack, the Viscount and his followers defended themselves so fiercely that our men were compelled by a very heavy bombardment of stones to retire from the ditch they had occupied. In this encounter it happened that one of our knights stayed in the ditch because his leg was broken. No one dared approach to bring him out because of the incessant bombardment of stones, until that man of consummate virtue, the Count of Montfort, went into the ditch, and with only a single squire to help him succeeded in rescuing the victim at enormous risk to his own life. After this, our men quickly built siege-engines of the type known as petraries to knock down the wall of the suburb. After the top of the wall had been somewhat weakened by bombardment from the petraries, our engineers[46] succeeded with great difficulty in bringing a four-wheeled wagon,[47] covered in oxhides, close to the wall, from which they set to work to sap the wall. By throwing down fire, wood and stones in vast quantity the enemy quickly broke up the wagon, but the sappers were able to take cover in the hollow in the wall which they had already dug out, so the enemy could not prevent them from continuing their digging. What more? On the following morning at daybreak the wall, now undermined, fell down. Our men at once rushed in with a great shout, and the enemy retreated to the higher parts of the city.[48] Later however, seeing that our men had left the suburb and returned to their tents, they emerged from the city, chased off any of our men they found still in the suburb, slaughtered many who could not escape, set fire to the entire suburb and finally went back to the higher parts of the city.

[97] *A miracle.* There was a particular feature of this siege which should not be passed over, and which must indeed be regarded as a great miracle. It was said that the number of men in the army was as great as five hundred thousand.[49] However, our enemies had destroyed all the mills around the city, so that our men were unable to obtain bread except from a few of the neighbouring *castra*; and yet there was such an abundance of bread that it was still being sold for a very modest price.[50] For this reason the heretics said that the Abbot of Cîteaux

---

[46] The first mention of engineers (*artifices*), who played so important a part in conducting siege warfare. The most often-cited by Peter is one William, Archdeacon of Paris, on whom see §175 below.

[47] A 'cat', a kind of covered wagon, mounted on wheels or rollers, which could be dragged up to the walls of a besieged town or fortress and provide cover for besieging troops engaged in filling up a moat or ditch, or undermining a wall. The use of these at Carcassonne is also noted by the *Chanson*, I, 30, pp. 74–6. See also Bradbury, *The Medieval Siege*, pp. 270–4 for comments. For other 'cats' see §190 (at Termes), §224 (Lavaur), §348 (Moissac), and also n. 120 to §607 (Toulouse).

[48] I.e. the *cité* proper, as opposed to the suburbs.

[49] Clearly a very inflated figure. However, Peter (and his contemporaries) tended to use such figures in effect to mean 'a very large number'.

[50] The *Chanson* (I, 25, p. 68) also testifies to the plentiful availability of bread, and mentions a price of 'thirty loaves to the denier [penny]'.

was a wizard[51] and had brought in demons in the shape of men, because it seemed to them that our men were not eating.

[98] *Surrender of Carcassonne.*[52] After these events, our army took counsel as to how they should capture the city, bearing in mind that if matters turned out as they had at Béziers, the city would be destroyed. All the goods in it would be ruined and whoever was put in charge of the territory would have no means of maintaining the knights and sergeants[53] needed to garrison it.[54] On the advice of the barons the basis of a peace was determined as follows:[55] it was ruled that all the inhabitants should come out of the city naked and should then be allowed to go free; the Viscount would be imprisoned[56] and all the contents of the city would be kept for the designated future lord of the territory, for the purpose outlined above. And it was so. All the inhabitants came naked[57] out of the city, bearing nothing but their sins.

[99] Thus was borne out the prediction of the venerable Berengar, a former Bishop of Carcassonne.[58] One day he was preaching to the citizens and, as was his habit, denouncing heresy, but they would not listen. So he said to them: 'You will not hear me? Believe me, I will utter against you such a mighty roar[59] that men shall come from the ends of the earth to destroy this city. Know you for sure that even if the walls of the city were built of iron and very high, yet you would not be able to avoid receiving from the most Just Judge a worthy punishment for your unbelief and wickedness.' For this and similar pronouncements which this most

---

51 Latin '*magus*'.

52 The *Chanson* (I, 26–30, pp. 68–76) describes at length how at this stage King Peter of Aragon arrived 'with a hundred knights' hoping to mediate. However, the terms demanded by Arnold Amalric were too harsh for Viscount Raymond-Roger to accept and the King departed 'unhappy and with a heavy heart'. Neither Peter nor William of Puylaurens mentions this.

53 Latin '*servientes*', literally attendants or servants, also with the sense of those owing (feudal) service. (French *sergent* and – via the French – English 'sergeant' are derived from *serviens*, and the word is conventionally so translated when used in the military sense.) They were ranked immediately below knights, and Contamine, *War in the Middle Ages*, p. 69, mentions various types of 'sergeants'; from the contexts, it appears that the *servientes* encountered in the *Historia* on both sides were usually mounted men. In any grouping they tended to outnumber knights considerably: for example at Puissiguier (§126) there were only two knights but up to fifty sergeants; at Castres (§132) one of Simon's knights is captured along with 'numerous' sergeants; and in §179 there was a force of 300 sergeants and five knights; see also n. 38 to §460 on the make-up of the forces engaged at the battle of Muret.

54 See Appendix B on this change of policy, especially the reference to the legates' letter, col. 140. This shows that the crusaders were well aware of the need to provide for their subsequent occupation of any conquered territory, and the difficulties which would be involved. The next phrase suggests that the barons rather than the ecclesiastical leaders of the army were especially alive to such logistical problems.

55 The surrender took place on 15 August 1209. The legates' letter, *PL* 216, 140, states that it was the besieged inside Carcassonne, not the crusaders, who took the initiative in negotiating a surrender. William of Puylaurens (XIV) says that Viscount Raymond-Roger was terrified into submission, and hence accepted a surrender. The *Chanson*, I, 30, p. 76, gives more detail, and states that conditions inside the *cité* had become insufferable because of the crowds of refugees inside, the heat of the summer and shortage of water.

56 For his death in November 1209, see §124 and n. 16.

57 The *Chanson* (I, 33, p. 80) says '*en queisas et en bragas*', and William of Puylaurens (XIV) says '*in camisiis et braccis*' indicating the same: 'in shifts and breeches'.

58 Berengar, who succeeded Bishop Otto, who had resigned the see in 1198. Berengar died on 23 October 1208; see Griffe, *LC*, pp. 40 and 269–70.

59 Cf. Jeremiah 25, 30–31.

steadfast man made to them the citizens at one time expelled him from the city, and issued a formal directive, through the public herald, that no one should venture to have dealings with him or his associates, either for buying or selling, on pain of suffering a most severe punishment.

[100] Let us now resume my narrative. After the surrender of the city and the departure of all the inhabitants, knights were chosen from the army to guard the contents of the city faithfully.[60]

[101] *The Count of Montfort is chosen.*[61] After this process was duly completed, the barons took counsel together as to whom they should put in charge of the conquered territory.[62] First the lordship was offered to the Count of Nevers, and then to the Duke of Burgundy, but they refused it. Then two bishops and four knights were selected from the whole army, and these, together with the Abbot of Cîteaux, the legate of the Apostolic See, were given the task of choosing a lord for the territory. They gave a firm promise to choose the man they knew would best serve the interests of God and man. These seven,[63] with the help of the grace of the sevenfold Holy Spirit and its merciful concern for the territory, chose a man true to the Catholic faith, honourable in his way of life and strong in battle – Simon, Count of Montfort.[64] At once the Abbot of Cîteaux, legate of the Apostolic See and the father and master of this sacred business, together with the Duke of Burgundy and the Count of Nevers, went to Simon de Montfort and urged and begged him to accept what was both a burden and an honour. However, this most singular man firmly refused, declaring that he was inadequate for the task and unworthy of it. The Abbot and the Duke threw themselves at his feet, redoubling their entreaties, but as the Count continued to resist the Abbot made use of his authority as papal legate and firmly instructed him by virtue of his duty of obedience to do as they asked.

[102] *The Count takes charge of the whole territory.* So this noble man took charge of the government of the territory for the glory of God, the honour of the Church and the suppression of heresy.[65]

---

[60] Carcassonne henceforth became the main base for the crusaders. The knights chosen to guard the contents of the city were excommunicated three months later for misappropriating booty to the value of 5000 livres: Innocent III writing to the Bishop of Auxerre and others, for which see G&L I, p. 100 n. 2, and for the text of the letter, G&L III, pp. 193–5.

[61] See the *Chanson*, I, 34–6, pp. 84–8, for a fuller account, which mentions in particular that the Count of Saint-Pol was also offerred the lands but refused. The *Chanson* states that all concerned thought it would be dishonourable to accept lands despoiled of another. Belperron, however, dismisses this as poetic dramatisation, and argues (p. 175) that the offers to the Duke and Counts were a matter only of courtesy. For a full discussion, including de Montfort's motives and the role of Arnold Amalric, see Roquebert I, ch. 19.

[62] I.e. the lands of Raymond-Roger Trencavel, which the crusaders now claimed. These were the viscounties of Carcassonne, Béziers, and the lordships of the Albigeois and the Razès. Outside Béziers and Carcassonne themselves, Trencavel lordship was weak, and local seigneurs had developed a high degree of autonomy, while much of the Albigeois north of the Tarn was controlled by the Counts of Toulouse (see, for instance, §118 below). Thus the crusaders were dealing with a territory whose local aristocracy were unused to strong overlordship.

[63] The *Chanson* (I, 35, pp. 86–8) speaks merely of an assembly of crusaders which chose de Montfort of a common accord; the legates' letter to Innocent III, *PL* 216, 140, uses the term '*communi consilio*'.

[64] See Appendix C on Simon de Montfort.

[65] Simon de Montfort thus became Viscount of Béziers and Carcassonne. The election took place before

[103] *A remarkable occurrence.* Here I must turn to an event, well worth recording, which occurred a little earlier[66] in France in relation to the Count of Montfort. One day the venerable Abbot of les Vaux-de-Cernay, Guy (whom I have referred to earlier[67] and who was doing everything in his power to advance the business of the faith in the struggle against heresy) came to the Count from the Duke of Burgundy with a letter from the Duke in which he begged Simon to take up arms with him in the army of Jesus Christ against the heretics and to become his ally. His request was accompanied by substantial gifts and more were promised if Simon would agree. It happened that when the Abbot came from the Duke he found the Count in the church of Rochefort,[68] a *castrum* in his domains, engaged on certain business. The Abbot called him aside to show him the Duke's letter; and as the Count was crossing the chancel, by some divine inspiration he picked up a psaltery which he found on a desk and opened it. Placing his finger on the first line he said to the Abbot: 'Explain this text to me.' The passage was: 'For he shall give his angels charge over thee, to keep thee in all thy ways. They shall bear thee up in their hands, lest thou dash thy foot against a stone.' Subsequent events demonstrated most clearly that this occurrence resulted from the intervention of Divine Providence.[69]

[104] *The many qualities of the Count of Montfort described.* As the opportunity now arises – as indeed my approach to writing this history requires – I propose to set down here what I know personally about the noble Count of Montfort. First, he was of illustrious birth and of outstanding courage, and extremely experienced in warfare. Moreover – to turn to his physical appearance – he was tall, with a splendid head of hair and fine features; of handsome appearance, broad-shouldered with muscular arms, of excellent physique generally, agile and nimble of hand and foot, quick and active; indeed there was not the smallest fault that even an enemy or envious person could point to. To go on to his more important qualities, he was eloquent of speech, eminently approachable, a most congenial comrade-in-arms, of impeccable chastity, outstanding in humility, wise, firm of purpose, prudent in counsel, fair in giving judgment, diligent in the pursuit of military duties, circumspect in his actions, eager to set about a task, tireless in completing it, and totally dedicated to the service of God.

the end of August 1209, since the decision was communicated to Innocent III in the legates' letter written that month (*PL* 216, 137–41; see n. 17 to §84 etc.). Simon wrote to the Pope at the same time (*PL* 216, 141–2) to obtain Innocent's confirmation of his election, and Innocent replied in two letters of 11 and 12 November (ibid., 151–3). Although Simon de Montfort now in effect became lay leader of the Crusade, Arnold Amalric remained in overall charge, and continued his involvement with the military operations – see n. 4 to §20. By no means all the local Trencavel vassals were as yet willing to submit, as Peter himself points out below in §108. §§110–20 record de Montfort's campaign of autumn 1209 to assert control of his territories.

66 Presumably in 1208, when preparations for the Crusade were being made.

67 §26 and §51; the following comment no doubt refers to Guy's involvement in the preaching campaign of 1207 described in §51.

68 Rochefort-en-Yvelines, on the southern edge of the Forest of Rambouillet, and about 25km south of Montfort-l'Amaury.

69 The text is from Psalm 91, 11–12. See especially §§147, 190, 191 and 604 for occasions when Simon narrowly escaped death.

[105] How wise the choice of the army's leaders, how sensible the acclamation of the crusaders![70] To have picked a man of such great faith as defender of the true faith; to have elected a man so in tune with the whole Christian world to take charge of the sacred business of Jesus Christ in the fight against the infection of heresy! How fitting it was that the host of the Lord of Hosts should be led by such a man, adorned, as I have said, with nobility of birth, integrity of character and distinction in war; how fruitful that such a man should be raised up for the defence of the Church in her peril, whose skilful protection would ensure that Christian innocence should survive unharmed and that the heretics, for all their presumptuous audacity, should not expect their hateful error to go unpunished; and how splendid that one sprung from 'the Strong Mountain' (and indeed of so strong a mind)[71] should be sent by Christ, a veritable mountain, to stand by the foundering Church and defend her from the persecution of the heretics. I must record that although individuals might perhaps be found who were his equal in some particular quality, I venture to say that rarely if ever would a man be discovered in whom such a rich endowment of gifts – whether naturally present or provided by God's grace – came together all at once. Such an abundance of God-given advantages might have produced in him excessive pride; but God prevented this by saddling him with the torment of incessant anxiety, the consequence of most pressing poverty. On the one hand the Lord did great things for him,[72] in the capture of fortresses and the destruction of his enemies; but this he countered by burdening him with such cares and such a weight of poverty that he had no chance to be at peace and become vain.

[106] The excellence of this most distinguished man will become more evident – and I hope it will not weary the reader – if I relate certain actions of his, of which I was a witness, from an earlier period. At one time[73] the Count and Guy, Abbot of les Vaux-de-Cernay (who was later[74] Bishop of Carcassonne and whom I have often mentioned) were on their way to Outremer[75] with certain French barons. The French nobles met at that very rich city, Venice, having previously agreed that this was where they would need to take ship in order to cross the sea.

---

[70] *'Peregrini'*, see n. 78 to §80. It is notable that Peter uses the word five times in referring to the crusaders on the Fourth Crusade in the following section.

[71] Word play on *monte*, mountain, and *mente*, mind. In writing to Simon de Montfort in November 1209 (*PL* 216, 151) Innocent III similarly refers to him as 'like a mountain (*mons*) and strong (*fortis*) in the Lord's battle'.

[72] Cf. Psalm 126, 2–3. For de Montfort's poverty see also §180.

[73] Probably in September 1202, as the participants in the Fourth Crusade gathered at Venice before beginning to make their way east. The main other contemporary source for what follows is Geoffrey de Villehardouin, *La Conquête de Constantinople*, 2 vols., ed. J. Faral (Paris, 1938–9), and also translated by M. R. B. Shaw, *Joinville and Villehardouin: Chronicles of the Crusades* (Harmondsworth: Penguin Classics, 1963). For accounts of the Fourth Crusade, including events at Zara which Peter now relates, see also D. E. Queller, *The Fourth Crusade* (Leicester, 1978), and J. Godfrey, *1204: The Unholy Crusade* (Oxford, 1980).

[74] He became Bishop in April 1212; see §299 below.

[75] Latin *'ultra mare'*. This seems in effect to be a translation of French *Outremer*, the name given collectively to the crusader states established in the Levant after the First Crusade. The phrase recurs later in this section and in §290, where in addition within the space of a few lines Peter uses *'a partibus transmarinis'* to mean 'from overseas' and *'in partibus ultramarinis'* apparently to mean 'in the region of Outremer'. (G&M translate as *'outremer'* or *'les pays d'outremer'*.)

Here they hired the ships they needed at a very high price. Among those present were nobles from all over France, including Baldwin,[76] Count of Flanders, and his brother Henry; Louis, Count of Blois;[77] the Count of Montfort and many others too numerous to mention.[78] The Venetians, a cunning and ill-disposed people, saw that our crusaders had used up all their funds – a consequence of the excessive cost of hiring the ships – and that with almost no resources remaining to them they were in fact unable to pay most of the charge; thus the crusaders were under an obligation to them and in their power. Seizing the opportunity thus created, the Venetians induced the crusaders to join in attacking a Christian city which belonged to the King of Hungary, named Zara.[79] When the crusaders reached the city,[80] they pitched camp near the walls, following the normal practice of a besieging force. However, the Count of Montfort and the Abbot of les Vaux-de-Cernay refused to follow the multitude to do evil[81] and join in the siege, but camped some distance from the city. Meanwhile the Pope sent a letter[82] to all the crusaders ordering them – under threat of withdrawal of the indulgence of sins which he had granted them and on pain of severe excommunication – not to do any harm to the city of Zara. On a certain day[83] the Abbot of les Vaux-de-Cernay was reading this letter to the assembled nobles of the army, and the Venetians wished to kill him. The Count of Montfort got up and went to the centre of the gathering, confronted the Venetians and prevented them from murdering the Abbot. The noble Count then addressed the citizens of Zara (who had come to the meeting to seek peace) in the presence of all the barons, to the following effect: 'I have not come here to destroy Christians. I will do you no wrong, and whatever others may do, I will ensure that you suffer no harm from

---

76 Baldwin (Baudouin) IX, Count of Flanders, who left his county in 1202 and in 1204 became Latin Emperor of Constantinople.

77 Count of Blois since 1191 and a benefactor of the abbey of les Vaux-de-Cernay (G&L I, p. 107 n. 5).

78 According to Villehardouin (trans. M. R. B. Shaw, p. 54), they included several knights who were later to join Simon de Montfort on the Albigensian Crusade, such as Simon de Neauphle (see §241), Robert Mauvoisin (§129) and Enguerrand de Boves (§326).

79 Zara or Zadar, a port on the Dalmatian coast. Like most of that coast it had fallen under Venetian control in the 11th century, but rebelled in 1111 and again in 1186, after which King Bela III of Hungary had assumed overlordship. The Venetians had been trying to retake it since then, but it remained under the control of Bela's successor, King Emeric of Hungary, who had himself taken crusading vows.

80 10 November 1202 (G&L I, p. 108 n. 4).

81 Exodus 23, v. 2.

82 The letter warning the crusaders not to attack Zara was carried to the crusaders there by the Cistercian Abbot Peter of Lucedio, who arrived about 12 November 1202. It does not survive but is referred to in a later letter (PL 214, 1178–9) in which Innocent says that although his legate, Cardinal Peter of St Marcellus, had explained Innocent's warning ('prohibitio') to some of them and his letter had been read out to them ('publice presentatae'), they paid no heed and went on to compel the inhabitants of Zara to surrender. Innocent procedes to threaten the crusaders with excommunication if they do further harm to Zara. In a subsequent letter, PL 214, 1179–82, Innocent accepts a plea of mitigation from the Bishop of Soissons and others, that they had attacked the city not because they wished to do so, but because they were driven by circumstances ('non inducti propria voluntate, sed quasi quadam necessitate coacti'), but orders the crusaders to do penance for their actions to date. Letters in PL 215, 105–110, apparently all from the following April-June, deal with this penance. These events show how Innocent was capable of swift changes of mind, a characteristic which was to be revealed in his dealings with Raymond VI and King Peter of Aragon during the Albigensian Crusade. See also Appendix G.

83 12 November, 1202 (G&L I, p. 109 n. 1).

me or mine.' So spoke this valiant man, and withdrew himself and his followers from the meeting place. Let me delay no longer – the barons of the army chose not to heed the Pope's instruction, but seized and destroyed the city;[84] the wretches were comprehensively excommunicated in a second papal letter.[85] I myself was present at these events and can therefore vouch for the truth of this account; indeed I actually saw and read the Pope's letter dealing with the excommunication. The noble Count refused to follow the opinions of the majority and turn from the way of truth; leaving the company of sinners, he set out on a difficult and costly journey through a deserted land where no roads led, until after many hardships and unbelievable labours he came to Barletta, a notable town in Apulia. There he hired fresh ships, went aboard and enjoyed a trouble-free passage to Outremer.[86] He stayed there for a year or more and achieved numerous successes against the pagans. Whilst the French barons he had left at Zara had to endure many dangers and nearly all perished,[87] he himself returned safe and well and with honour to his own country. It was then that he started on the tasks which he finally completed so triumphantly, and first gained his honourable reputation, which was to be further enhanced in later years when he turned to the suppression of heresy.

[107] I must add that gifted and great as the Count was, the Lord provided him with a helpmate like himself – his wife, who was, in short, pious, wise and caring. Her piety adorned her wisdom and her concern for others, her wisdom shaped her piety and concern, her concern stimulated her piety and wisdom. To add to all this, the Lord blessed the Countess in her offspring; she gave the Count numerous fine children.[88]

After this short commendation of the Count, let us return to our main theme.

[108] *The Count of Nevers returns to France.* After the election of the Count of Montfort by the process described above, the Abbot of Cîteaux and the Count approached the Duke of Burgundy and the Count of Nevers, begging them to prolong their stay with the crusaders in the service of Jesus Christ. They pointed out that there were a great many strong fortresses occupied by the heretics still to be captured; in particular, there were three heavily defended *castra* around

---

[84] Zara surrendered after a siege of five days on 24 November 1202. The Venetians and Franks then occupied the city and wintered there.

[85] See n. 82 above.

[86] Simon de Montfort, his brother Guy, and Abbot Guy of les Vaux-de-Cernay left Zara about Easter 1203, and travelled first through the mountainous country behind the Dalmatian coast before reaching Italy and eventually the Apulian port of Barletta. Simon went on to the Holy Land and returned in 1206 (G&L I, p. 111 n. 2). His brother Guy stayed on and became seigneur of Sidon by virtue of his marriage to Helvis, widow of the former seigneur; for details of this and Guy's return to join Simon at Christmas 1211 see §290 below.

[87] Amongst those who had remained, Matthew of Montmorency-Marly died of illness in 1203, as did Hugh of Saint-Pol in 1205; Louis of Blois was killed in 1205: Villehardouin, cited by G&L I, p. 111 n. 1.

[88] Simon de Montfort's wife was Alice of Montmorency, on whom see M. Zerner, 'L'épouse de Simon de Montfort et la croisade albigeoise', in *Femmes – Mariages – Lignages, XII–XIV Siècles. Mélanges offerts à Georges Duby*, ed. J. Dufournet, A. Joris, and P. Toubert (Brussels, 1992), pp. 449–70. She subsequently played an active part in Simon's campaigns in the South, having joined her husband there in March 1210 (§141 below). See Appendix C for further details of de Montfort's marriage and children.

Carcassonne, in which the principal enemies of our faith were living at the time – on one side Minerve, on another Termes and another Cabaret.[89] The Duke of Burgundy, as was to be expected of a man of exemplary good will, cheerfully acceded to these requests and undertook to stay with our Count for some time. However, the Count of Nevers would not listen to any pleas and returned home forthwith. In fact he and the Duke did not get on well together, but also that enemy of peace, the Devil, aroused such mutual hostility between them that every day there was concern that they might kill each other; and it was believed by our people that there was a lack of good will on the part of the Count of Nevers towards the Count of Montfort because the latter was on good terms with the Duke of Burgundy and had come with him from France.

[109] What inveterate hatred of the Inveterate Enemy, who saw with invidious eyes the success of the business of Jesus Christ and made it his purpose to impede what he grieved to see succeed! The army of crusaders present at the siege of Carcassonne was so large and strong that had they wished to go further and work together to attack the enemies of the true faith, they would have met with no resistance and could quickly have taken possession of the whole territory; but (so far as human reasoning can understand matters) Heavenly Providence decreed otherwise, and, looking to the salvation of the human race, wished the conquest of the territory to be reserved for sinners. The Lord in His compassion did not wish this most holy war to be ended quickly, but rather to afford the opportunity for sinners to win pardon and for the righteous to attain a higher state of grace; I affirm that He wished His enemies to be subdued gradually and progressively, so that as sinners gradually and progressively took up arms to avenge the wrong done to Jesus Christ, the prolongation of the war would prolong the opportunity for them to gain pardon.[90]

[110] *The Count leaves Carcassonne.*[91] After staying a few days at Carcassonne,

---

[89] William of Tudela (*Chanson* I, 49, p. 116) also singles out Minerve, Cabaret and Termes as being especially impregnable, and William of Puylaurens XIV calls them '*castra fortia*'. Minerve lies about 40km north-east of Carcassonne in rugged hilly country, on a site which is naturally strong; for further details and the fall of Minerve in July 1210, see §§154–6 below. Termes lies about 35km south-east of Carcassonne, in mountainous, wooded and impenetrable country; for further details and its fall in November 1210, see §§168–9 below. For Cabaret, in the Montagne Noire, about 15km north of Carcassonne, see n. 103 to §114, and for its surrender in 1211, see below, §214. See also the article by M. Barber, 'Catharism and the Occitan Nobility: the lordships of Cabaret, Minerve and Termes', in *The Ideals and Practice of Medieval Knighthood, III: Papers from the Fourth Strawberry Hill Conference, 1988* (Woodbridge, 1990), pp. 1–19.

[90] G&L I, p. 114 n. 2, and G&M p. 50 n. 1, note that Innocent III developed a similar theme in a letter of 12 November 1209, written to the Archbishops of Arles and others (*PL* 215, 1547, and *Layettes* I, 899).

[91] §§110–36 narrate events which occurred between the last weeks of August and Christmas 1209. There were two main phases: (a) in late August and September Simon traversed as much as he could of his newly acquired domains (§§110–20); and (b) from, probably, late September onwards renewed resistance began to occur, and by Christmas Simon had lost control of much of the former Trencavel territory (§§121–36). Peter's account is the principal source, and is therefore invaluable, but the detailed chronology is very uncertain. He gives hardly any firm dates, using '*in ipso tempore*' ('at this time'), or similar phrases, in most places. Problems arise especially in relation to the timing of the recovery of Preixan by the Count of Foix and his attack on Fanjeaux described in §134. There are also uncertainties for example about the dating of de Montfort's earlier occupation of Preixan (§120), its relationship to his occupation of Mirepoix, Pamiers and Saverdun (§116), and the timing of his visit to Limoux (§119). These and the general chronology are

the noble Count of Montfort left the city with the Duke and a large section of the army, hoping with God's help to advance further; most of the crusaders had returned home with the Count of Nevers.[92] Accordingly, on the day they left Carcassonne they pitched camp by a town known as Alzonne.[93] The next day, the Duke advised the Count to go to the *castrum* known as Fanjeaux.[94] This place had been deserted by its knights and other inhabitants for fear of our army, and had then been occupied and fortified by some knights from Aragon[95] who were followers of our Count. (In fact most of the most notable and strongest fortresses in the area had been left empty through fear of the crusaders.)[96] The Count took a few knights with him, leaving the Duke with the army. He went to the *castrum*, took charge of it and set his own people to defend it.[97]

[111] I must record that the Count of Toulouse, who had been at the seige of Carcassonne and was envious of our successes, urged our Count to arrange for the destruction of some *castra* which were close to his own domains. He himself – wearing the mask of virtue and with the approval of our Count – had pulled

discussed in Appendix E. But whatever the precise chronology, §§110–20 show that, after leaving Carcassonne, Simon de Montfort's strategy in late August and September was now to traverse as much of the Trencavel domains south, west, and north of Carcassonne as he could, in order to receive the formal submission of those towns and *castra* willing to recognise him, and to secure his possession of the Carcassès, the Razès and the Albigeois. Usually he left at least some troops to occupy places which submitted or were taken, and for example he also sent Lambert de Thury to Limoux, Bouchard de Marly to Saissac, and William of Contres to Béziers: this was the beginning of his allocation of fiefs to his own followers. For the effect of the ruthlessness of the attack on Béziers (which would have been compounded by the subsequent swift success against Carcassonne) in encouraging other places to submit or their inhabitants to flee see Peter's comment later in this section and Appendix B.

92 See below, n. 105 to §115, for details.

93 Alzonne, about 20km west of Carcassonne, in the valley of the Aude; see also below, §142.

94 Fanjeaux lies about 30km west of Carcassonne, occupying a hilltop site overlooking the plain of the Lauragais and the Carcassès to its north. It was strategically important, dominating the surrounding area and being at the crossroads of several important lines of communication. De Montfort was to make it one of his strongholds in the coming years. Before the Crusade, it had been home to various lesser noble families, and was renowned (along with nearby Laurac) as one of the most important centres of Catharism in the Midi, with numerous Cathar houses. Most detailed knowledge of this comes from later Inquisition records in the Doat collection. For discussions of heresy at Fanjeaux in the early 13th century see Griffe, *LC*, pp. 108–121, and Roquebert, I, pp. 112–15. Fanjeaux, and nearby Prouille at the foot of the hill, were also where Dominic Guzman of Caleruega established himself during the preaching mission of 1206–07, and where he was based until moving to Toulouse in 1215, on all of which see Vicaire, chs. VIII–IX, and *Cahiers de Fanjeaux*, vol. 1.

95 The *Chanson*, I, 34, p. 84 mentions Fanjeaux and Montréal as having been occupied by one Peter of Aragon, who was '*un mainader ardit*', a bold leader of a '*mainada*', or band of mercenaries, 'who gained from them [the occupied *castra*], it is said, much money' (cf. Griffe, *Croisade*, p. 18 n. 13). He was almost certainly the same Petrus Aragonensis who was a witness to a donation made by de Montfort to the Bishop of Béziers in July 1210 (*HGL* VIII, 601). His identity, and the apparent presence of Aragonese mercenaries fighting with the crusaders, is discussed by Roquebert, I, pp. 298–300, who also notes that a later Inquisition witness stated that Fanjeaux had been burned at the time of its occupation, and suggests that this was more probably undertaken by the fleeing inhabitants than the mercenaries. Peter does not here refer to the occupation of nearby Montréal, which occurred at about the same time, but mentions it in §135.

96 For instance Montréal, Saissac and Alzonne. The *Chanson*, I, 34, p. 84 also says that all the inhabitants had fled the area.

97 It was probably at this time (late August) that, as well as occupying Fanjeaux and Montréal, de Montfort sent Lambert de Thury (or Crécy) to occupy Limoux to the south in the Razès (see *Chanson* I, 37, pp. 92–4; and n. 48 to §248 on Lambert). See also Appendix E.

down and burnt several fortresses, on the pretext that this would prevent attacks on our men. However – faithless and unjust as he was – his real purpose was to ensure that the country should be ruined and no one should be in a position to resist him.[98]

[112] *The townsmen of Castres offer their town to the Count.* Whilst these events were taking place, the townsmen of a notable *castrum* named Castres[99] in the Albigeois came to the Count, offering to receive him as their lord and to obey his will. The Duke advised the Count to go and take possession of Castres, on the grounds that it was virtually the principal place in the whole Albigeois. The Count therefore set off with a small force, leaving the Duke with the army. Whilst he was at Castres and the townsmen were paying homage to him and handing over the *castrum*, knights from Lombers,[100] a notable *castrum* near Albi, came to him prepared to make the same offer to the Count as the men of Castres. However, the Count was anxious to return to the army and unwilling to go with them; nevertheless he took Lombers under his protection until he could find the time to visit it.

[113] *A miracle.* A miracle occurred at this place in the Count's presence which I do not wish to pass over. Two heretics were brought before the Count, one a 'perfected' heretic and the other a sort of 'novice' and a disciple of the first one.[101] After taking counsel the Count decided that they should be burnt.[102] The second heretic – the disciple – was seized with heartfelt grief; he began to show

98   As usual, Peter puts the worst possible interpretation on Raymond's motives and intentions, but despite this, these actions by Raymond VI are consistent with the view that he was hoping to use the Crusade to his benefit by ensuring that it was directed against Trencavel lands (cf. n. 75 to §77). The destruction of these *castra* was also almost certainly an indication of goodwill between Raymond and Simon de Montfort, consistent with the position of Raymond as a local lord who had been reconciled to the Church, and who had taken the cross himself. There was also discussion of the possibility of a marriage alliance between Raymond's daughter and Simon's son, on which see also §139 below. If the two were on such good terms, the position was to change in the winter of 1209–10: see §§137–9 below.
99   See n. 44 to §36 on Castres. It was to remain a possession of the de Montfort family through several generations; see *HGL* VII, n. 44, p. 127.
100   About 25km north of Castres, en route to Albi. Simon occupied it shortly afterwards: see §117 below. Lombers was well known as a centre of Catharism in the 12th century, and was the location of a debate between Cathars and Catholics which took place in 1165; see Griffe, *Débuts*, pp. 59–67, and Moore, *The Origins of European Dissent*, pp. 200–3.
101   Those who were candidates to receive the *consolamentum* and become *perfecti* usually had to live closely with an existing *perfectus* for a year, living the rigorous life of the *perfecti* under a kind of probation; see Lambert, p. 107.
102   This is the first instance of the burning of heretics mentioned by Peter, although the *Chanson* (I, 14, pp. 42–4) says that many heretics were convicted and burnt during the separate expedition in Quercy earlier in the year. The development of ecclesiastical and secular penalties against heresy is discussed in particular by Maisonneuve, *Etudes sur les Origines de l'Inquisition*. The Church's position had been set out in the decretal *Ad abolendam*, issued by Lucius III at Verona in 1184. In essence this provided that heretics, once found guilty by the Church, would be subject to ecclesiastical penalties of excommunication, anathema, and *infamia*, and their lands were to revert to their overlords or (if allodial) were to be placed under interdict (on which see also n. 34 to §62 above). In addition, convicted heretics were to be handed over to the relevant secular authority for 'fitting' (but unspecified) punishment. The use of burning as the penalty to be carried out by secular authority against heretics thus convicted had gradually developed in the 11th and 12th centuries, primarily in northern Europe. The Church refused formally to condone burning but as the events of the Crusade show, the legates were zealous to see its use by Simon de Montfort (as at Minerve in 1210, on which see §§151–159 below). In this case at Castres there does not seem to have been a prior

contrition and promised that he would freely forswear heresy and obey the Holy Roman Church in all things. A heated discussion arose amongst our people when they heard this; some said that now that he was prepared to do what we had told him to do, he ought not to be condemned to die, others maintained that on the contrary he deserved death, arguing that it was plain that he had been a heretic and that the promises he was now making owed more to his fear of impending death than to his desire to follow the Christian religion. What more? The Count agreed that he should be burnt, taking the view that if his contrition was genuine, the fire would serve to expiate his sins; if he was lying, he would receive a just reward for his perfidy. Both heretics were then tied with strong chains round their legs, middle and neck, and their hands were fastened behind them. The man who appeared to be repenting was then asked in what faith he wished to meet his death. He said: 'I forswear the evil of heresy. I wish to die in the faith of the Holy Roman Church, and I pray that this fire will serve for me instead of purgatory.' A fire was lit round the stake, and burned vigorously. The 'perfected' heretic was consumed by the flames instantly; but the other quickly broke the strong chains that bound him and escaped from the fire so unharmed that he showed no sign of injury from the flames except that the tips of his fingers were slightly scorched.

[114] *The Count returns from Castres.* The Count then returned from Castres to the army which he had left in the neighbourhood of Carcassonne. The Duke of Burgundy and the knights of the army now recommended an approach to Cabaret,[103] with a view to harassing its defenders and if possible mounting an attack to compel them to surrender. Our soldiers therefore moved their camp, marched to within half a league of Cabaret and pitched their tents there. Next morning the knights and a large part of the army took up their arms and marched to Cabaret with a view to capturing it. An assault was made but they were able to achieve very little and returned to their tents.

[115] *The Duke of Burgundy returns to France.* Next day[104] the Duke and the entire strength of the army made their preparations to depart and on the third day left our Count to go back to their homes. So, the Count was left alone and

trial, or indeed any involvement at all, by ecclesiastical authority. Peter quotes no authority for his account (contrast e.g. the miracles described in §54, §160 and §298).

[103] Cabaret, in the Montagne Noire north of Carcassonne, was one of the strongest *castra* in the region and its ruling family were important members of the aristocracy of the Trencavel domains (cf. n. 89 to §108 and the article by M. Barber cited there). The castle of Cabaret itself was the largest of three on the site, a craggy ridge above the valley of the Orbeil; there were two other castles on the site, called Surdespine and Quertinheux. A fourth, Tour Régine, was built later. Their ruins now overlook the village of Lastours in the Orbeil valley below. The lordship of Cabaret extended over much of the eastern Cabardès, and into part of the Minervois where in particular it included the *castrum* of Laure. The two most notable members of the family of Cabaret at this time were Peter-Roger of Cabaret (on whom see §123) and Jordan of Cabaret, who may have been brothers, and both were to play an important part in resistance to de Montfort. The mining of gold, silver, iron and copper were important activities in the surrounding area. Cabaret was a well known centre for Cathars, and later Inquisition depositions make it clear that at the time of the assault in 1209 there were Cathars present. For discussion see Griffe, *LC*, pp. 170–6, and Roquebert, I, pp. 313–18 (and his n. 14 to ch. 21 on the genealogy of the lords of Cabaret). A convenient summary of the history and archaeology of Cabaret is in the booklet by M.-E. Gardel in the CAML series, *Les Châteaux de Lastours* (Revue Annuelle du CAML, Supplément au tome 1, 1981).

[104] Probably early in September 1209.

almost unsupported.[105] He was left with a very few knights – about thirty – who had come from France with the other crusaders and were more devoted to the service of Christ and to the Count than the others.

[116] After the army had gone, the Count went to Fanjeaux. When he arrived there, the Venerable Abbot of Saint-Antonin de Pamiers[106] in the territory of Toulouse sent to him asking him to go to the Abbot who would then personally hand over to him the notable *castrum* of Pamiers.[107] Whilst on his way to Pamiers, the Count came to the *castrum* known as Mirepoix[108] and immediately captured it. This place was a centre for heretics and mercenaries and was under the lordship of the Count of Foix. After this success the Count went straight to

---

[105] Latin '*solus et quasi desolatus*'; a similar phrase is used again in §§187 and 442. In a letter written about this time to Innocent III (*PL* 216, 141–2) Simon de Montfort says that after the departure of the bulk of the crusaders he had been left almost alone ('*me fere solum inter inimicos Christi . . . cum non multo milite reliquerunt*'). William of Tudela in the *Chanson*, I, 41, p. 100, says much the same (referring to his having '*N'ot gaire companhos*', 'scarcely any companions'). Those knights who remained included Guy de Lévis, de Montfort's Marshal (see §185); Bouchard de Marly (§123); Robert Mauvoisin (§129); Lambert de Crécy (or Thury: see §110, n. 97, and §248), and Amaury, William and Robert de Poissy (§122). William of Tudela (*Chanson* I, 36, pp. 88–90) mentions several of these and adds more names including Robert de Picquigny, and William of Contres (see also below, §168, n. 70). Those remaining with de Montfort are discussed in Belperron pp. 186–90 (who terms them de Montfort's '*équipe*' or 'team'), and in Roquebert I, pp. 288–90. As well as these and other knights will have been sergeants, but the numbers cannot have been large, and clearly de Montfort's forces were now very stretched and he was not to receive reinforcements until the following March (see §141). His forces also included soldiers working for pay, *soldarii*, since in the letter quoted above he complains that 'I am having to hire the *soldarios* who have remained with me for a greater price than in other wars. I can hardly keep any of them unless they are paid twice the usual amount.' (*Soldarii* presumably implies men recruited individually, possibly including some brought from the north, as opposed to the *ruptarii* who were anathema to the Church: see n. 55 to §42, and Appendix D.)
[106] Abbot Vital, 1206–11 (G&L I, p. 120 n. 1). For Pamiers at this time, where lordship was shared between the abbey and the Count of Foix, see nn. to §48 above. The Abbot and Count Raymond-Roger of Foix had been at loggerheads for some time, and Vital was clearly intent on substituting Simon de Montfort as co-seigneur, and guaranteeing the rights of his abbey. For examples of disputes between Raymond-Roger of Foix and Abbot Vital, see §§197–209 below.
[107] The crusaders' invasion of Raymond-Roger of Foix's domains and assumption of control of Pamiers (and Preixan if this happened first: see Appendix E) was apparently undertaken without warning and must have been highly provocative to Raymond-Roger, and to his overlord King Peter of Aragon. Although Raymond-Roger of Foix was widely reputed to be sympathetic to heresy, and members of his family were closely involved with both Catharism and Waldensianism (cf. the debate at Pamiers in 1207 in §48, and Peter's detailed charges against the Count in §§197–209 below), he had at this stage not been subject to any formal charges. Nonetheless de Montfort was presumably regarding the Count's lands as *exposées en proie*, and thus open to seizure, but if this was the legalistic justification for the attack the main motive was probably a mixture of opportunism and shrewd awareness of the strategic importance of the Ariège valley, which Pamiers and Saverdun commanded.
[108] Mirepoix lies about 50km south-west of Carcassonne. It was subject to Trencavel lordship during the 11th century but by the early years of the 12th century it had become a fief of the counts of Foix. Immediate lordship was shared at the time of the Crusade by no fewer than 35 co-seigneurs, of whom the most important was Peter-Roger of Mirepoix (see G&L I, p. 120 n. 2). He and his family were strong supporters of Catharism, part of a network of such families in the area, and encouraged Cathar houses for both men and women at Mirepoix, about which much is known from later Inquisition testimony in the Doat collection. As far as is known Mirepoix was occupied without resistance, and the inhabitants, including the co-seigneurs, *perfecti* and Cathar *credentes* perhaps fled southwards towards Montségur and the mountains of the Pays d'Olmes for refuge. Mirepoix was given as a fief by Simon de Montfort to Guy de Lévis (see §185), one of his knights and his Marshal, whose family retained possession for several generations. For details of heresy at Mirepoix and the local families, see Griffe, *LC*, ch. 8; and Roquebert I, pp. 318–20, and n. 10 to his ch. 25.

Pamiers. The Abbot welcomed him with honour and transferred Pamiers to his control.[109] The Count accepted and did homage to the Abbot, as was correct since the *castrum* properly belonged to the lordship of the Abbot and canons of Saint-Antonin (who were canons regular) and there were no rights to possession of it unless granted by the Abbot. However, that base man the Count of Foix, whose tenure of Pamiers was really subject to the Abbot's overlordship, was maliciously plotting to appropriate the overlordship to himself, as I shall describe below.[110] From Pamiers our Count went to Saverdun,[111] where the townsmen surrendered to him without opposition. This *castrum* was controlled by the Count of Foix and in his demesne. [117] *The Count returns to Lombers.* The Count then returned to Fanjeaux and then proposed to go to Lombers (mentioned above)[112] to take possession of it. There were more than fifty knights present there. On his arrival, the Count was received with honour, and the knights promised that they would submit to him on the following day. Next morning, the knights started to discuss the idea of betraying the Count; the debate went on until the ninth hour[113] when the Count became aware of what was going on. On some pretext or other he immediately left the *castrum*. Seeing this the knights followed him; they became afraid of what might happen, did what the Count wanted and handed the place over to him. They did homage to him and swore on oath of allegiance.

[118] From there the Count went to Albi.[114] This city had been under the lordship of the Viscount of Béziers. However, William, Bishop of Albi,[115] who was the principal lord of the city received the Count gladly and handed the city over

---

[109] The deed dated to September 1209 recording this is in *HGL* VIII, 577–9.

[110] §206.

[111] Saverdun is in the Ariège valley, about 15km north of Pamiers, and was strategically placed close to the boundary between the county of Toulouse and the county of Foix. See *HGL* VI, pp. 193–4 for disputes between Raymond VI and the counts of Foix over Saverdun.

[112] See §112, and n. 100.

[113] Three o'clock in the afternoon.

[114] As noted in Appendix E, the date of this is uncertain, but de Montfort's visits to Albi and to Limoux (§119) probably took place during the second half of September or early in October. Albi lies on the south bank of the Tarn, on high ground overlooking the river. It was here that Trencavel lordship in effect reached its northernmost point, since the counts of Toulouse largely controlled the Albigeois to the north of the Tarn (on which see §237 below). By reaching Albi Simon now entered into possession of the last of the four Trencavel viscounties, that of the Albigeois. Ultimately, the suzerain of the Albigeois was Peter II of Aragon, from whom it had been held by the Trencavels. Lordship over the city had gradually been assumed by the local bishops, and any direct Trencavel authority was minimal by the early 13th century; in 1194 the bishops' rights had been confirmed after a conflict between the counts of Toulouse and the Trencavels (G&L I, p. 122 n. 2). See also n. to §4 above and Appendix A(iii) on the term Albigensian to denote the heretics of the Midi, and other details of Albi at this time.

[115] William Peyre (Guilhem or Guillaume in French) was Bishop from 1185 to 1227. A member of a local landed family, he had been a canon in the church of Saint-Salvi in Albi. He welcomed de Montfort and remained in office throughout the Crusade, slowly building up the resources of his see and apparently successfully keeping heresy out of the city. On William Peyre and the church at Albi, see L. de Lacger, 'L'Albigeois pendant le crise de L'Albigéisme', in *Revue d'histoire ecclésiastique*, 1933, pp. 272–315, 586–633, and 849–904, and the article by M. Becamel, *Cahiers de Fanjeaux*, vol. 3, pp. 237–43, 'Le Catharisme dans le diocèse d'Albi'.

to him.[116] What more? The Count then took control of the whole diocese of Albi, except for certain *castra* held by the Count of Toulouse,[117] which the latter had taken from the Viscount of Béziers. After this, our Count returned to Carcassonne.

[119] A few days later the Count went to the *castrum* known as Limoux, in the territory known as the Razès, intending to fortify it.[118] This place offered itself to the Count immediately after Carcassonne had been captured. Arriving there he captured some fortresses which were opposing the Holy Church, and hanged some of the inhabitants from gibbets, as they richly deserved.[119]

[120] *The Count takes Preixan.*[120] Returning from Limoux, the Count went to a fortress named Preixan, which was near Carcassonne and belonged to the Count of Foix, and laid siege to it. Whilst the siege was still going on the Count of Foix came to the Count and swore to stand by the orders of the Church in all things and gave his son to the Count as a hostage; in addition he handed over the *castrum* under siege.[121] After this, the Count returned to Carcassonne.

---

[116] Simon de Montfort now called himself '*dominus Albiensis*' 'lord of the Albigeois', and this title was confirmed by Innocent III (*PL* 216, 282).

[117] The strongholds controlled by Raymond VI and referred to here included Montégut, Gaillac, Cahuzac, Saint-Marcel and Saint-Martin-Laguépie, all to the north of the River Tarn and all taken by the crusaders in 1211 (§§237ff below).

[118] On the timing of de Montfort's visit to Limoux see Appendix E. Limoux lies about 25km south of Carcassonne, on the River Aude, and was the principal *castrum* of the Razès. Simon de Montfort had despatched Lambert de Thury (or Crécy) to occupy Limoux for him in late August: see n. 91 to §110.

[119] Roquebert, I, p. 309, suggests that the other fortified places taken by Simon may have included Mazerolles-du-Razès, Alaigne, Cailhavel, Cailhau, Brugairolles, Lauraguel and Paulaigne. Simon now took the title '*dominus Reddensis*', 'lord of the Razès' (cf. G&M, p. 53 n. 5).

[120] For the timing of this episode see Appendix E. Preixan lies between Carcassonne and Limoux, on the west bank of the Aude, and was a possession of the Counts of Foix in territory otherwise subject to the Trencavels.

[121] This submission by Count Raymond-Roger of Foix is also reported in the *Chanson*, I, 41, p. 100, where it is specified that it was the Count's youngest son Aimeric who was given as a hostage. For Raymond-Roger's recapture of Preixan, see §134 below.

[VI. §§121–140, autumn 1209 – spring 1210: *Intervention of King Peter of Aragon – reverses for the crusaders – Bouchard de Marly taken prisoner – Giraud de Pépieux defects – murder of the Abbot of Eaunes – defection of Castres and Lombers – Raymond-Roger of Foix breaks with the crusaders – loss of Montréal and further losses by Christmas 1209 – the Count of Toulouse in France and Rome, winter 1209–10.*]

[121][1] *Hostility of the King of Aragon.* Peter, King of Aragon,[2] under whose lordship the city of Carcassonne fell, was wholly unwilling to receive homage from our Count, but wished to hold the city himself.[3] One day, when he wanted to go to Montpellier[4] but was afraid to make the journey, he sent to the Count with an instruction to meet him at Narbonne.[5] The pair duly met and went on

---

1   If we assume that Peter's ordering of events is approximately correct (see discussion in Appendix E) the events related in §§121–3 will have taken place in October 1209, perhaps towards the end of the month. If not then they will have been earlier.

2   Peter II, King of Aragon and Count of Barcelona, 1196–1213.

3   Carcassonne was originally a dependency of the county of Barcelona, which was united with the Kingdom of Aragon in 1137. In November 1179 the Trencavel Viscount Roger II had done homage for his lands to Peter's father Alphonse II, and Peter of Aragon thus inherited overlordship of the viscounty, and Raymond-Roger Trencavel was his vassal: cf. T. N. Bisson, *The Medieval Crown of Aragon* (Oxford, 1986), ch. 2. Whilst in practice this overlordship usually meant little, Peter II of Aragon did have personal and perhaps dynastic ambitions in the area (witness his marriage to Maria of Montpellier in 1204 – see next note and §419 and n. 39). His interest is reflected in his presiding over the colloquium at Carcassonne in 1204 (see n. 23 to §24), and in his intervention at the siege of Carcassonne in August 1209 (*Chanson* I, 26–30, pp. 68–76). Simon de Montfort had taken the Trencavel territories by force and without reference to their overlord King Peter, and he had become Viscount of Béziers and Carcassonne by virtue of Innocent III's doctrine of *exposition en proie* discussed in n. 34 to §62. This nonetheless required that the rights of the superior lord of any territory seized must be respected, so that in order properly to legitimise his assumption of the Trencavel lordships, it was necessary for Simon to do homage for the former Trencavel lands to King Peter, and he thus sought to persuade him to receive this homage and acknowledge him as Viscount of Béziers and Carcassonne. King Peter's position was therefore a strong one in that de Montfort required his consent before he could legitimately claim the Trencavel domains. The position might have been complicated by the fact that King Peter himself had pledged fealty to Innocent when he was crowned by him in 1204; de Montfort's assumption of the Trencavel viscounties had been instigated by Innocent and at about this same time confirmed by him (cf. his letters of 10 and 11 November 1209, *PL* 216, 151–3), and so King Peter might have felt some obligation to accept de Montfort's homage. However, in practice King Peter's personal fealty to Innocent probably weighed very little if at all in his thinking. Much more important was his likely concern that Simon de Montfort was already a vassal of the King of France and that to recognise him might encourage the ambitions of the French Kings in the southern territories. Although at this stage King Peter elected to maintain his refusal to acknowledge Simon, he was pressed into changing his mind after the Conference of Narbonne in January 1211 (see §210).

4   King Peter was lord of Montpellier as a vassal of the Bishop of nearby Maguelonne, as a result of his marriage in 1204 to Maria of Montpellier, daughter of William VIII, the previous lord (*HGL* VI, pp. 213–14; see also n. 39 to §419 for Maria). The crusaders had passed it in July 1209 on their way to Béziers, but on Innocent III's orders it had not been attacked (letter of 1 March 1209 to the legates, *PL* 216, 187). Its consuls had joined in the swearing of oaths to combat heresy in the summer of 1209 (*PL* 216, 133–4, 24 July).

5   Perhaps King Peter thought it risky to cross the lands between Narbonne and Montpellier now controlled by the crusaders without Simon's personal protection, or perhaps he was making a political point in summoning Simon and traversing the territory with him. Immediate lordship over Narbonne was shared by its Viscount Aimeric and the Archbishop Berengar, but the Counts of Toulouse claimed ultimate suzerainty in virtue of their title of Dukes of Narbonne. For details see esp. §299 and note.

together to Montpellier.[6] Here they stayed for fifteen days, but the King still could not bring himself to accept homage from the Count. It is said moreover that the King sent secret orders to the nobles throughout the viscounties of Béziers and Carcassonne who were still opposing the Holy Church and our Count, telling them not to come to terms with the Count and promising that he would join them in attacking him.

[122] Indeed it so happened that whilst the Count was on his way back from Montpellier,[7] it was reported to him that a large number of knights in the dioceses of Béziers, Carcassonne and Albi, and the fortresses they controlled, had gone back on the oaths of fealty they had made to him. The reports were true; indeed two of the Count's knights, Amaury and William of Poissy,[8] had been besieged by some traitors in the keep of a *castrum*[9] near Carcassonne. Hearing of this the Count hurried to reach the *castrum* before his knights could be taken, but he could not cross the River Aude because of floods, and had to go to Carcassonne since there was no other way of crossing the river. When he got there he heard that his knights had been captured.

[123] *Bouchard de Marly taken prisoner.*[10] One day whilst the Count was at Montpellier, Bouchard de Marly[11] and Gaubert d'Essigny[12] and some other knights based at Saissac[13] (a very strong *castrum* in the diocese of Carcassonne which the Count had handed over to Bouchard), set out to harry the enemy as far as Cabaret.[14] This was a strongly fortified *castrum* near Carcassonne, almost impregnable and defended by a large group of knights. It was outstanding in its opposition to Christianity and the Count, a veritable fountain of heresy. The lord

---

6   Simon de Montfort and Aimeric of Narbonne were both in Montpellier on 24 November 1209 since in a deed they witnessed on that day (*HGL* VIII, 579–82) Raymond-Roger Trencavel's widow Agnes ceded her rights over Pézenas and Tourbes (her dowry) to de Montfort and his heirs, in return for an annual pension. Since in the next sentence Peter says that de Montfort and King Peter remained at Montpellier for fifteen days, the journey from Narbonne probably took place in the second or third week of November, and Aimeric of Narbonne may have accompanied them (cf. G&M, p. 54 n. 3).

7   Probably in the last week of November 1209; see Appendix E.

8   See G&L I, p. 125 n. 3. Amaury de Poissy is mentioned in charters of the monasteries of Abbecourt and les Vaux-de-Cernay; William was his brother. Another brother, Robert, and a cousin Simon were both involved in the Crusade of 1209 (*HGL* VIII 578 refers to '*Simone et Roberto de Pisiaco militibus francigenis*'; and 580 refers to Simon). These men were knights from the Ile de France who were closely associated with the de Montforts and formed part of the small group who had remained with him in the Midi in the autumn of 1209, on whom see n. 105 to §115 above.

9   Latin '*turrem castri*'; see Appendix A. Roquebert (I, p. 329) suggests this may have been the castle of Alaric, whose ruins today are called Miramont.

10   This episode is one of the few from the autumn of 1209 also related in the *Chanson* (I, 41–2, pp. 102–4).

11   Bouchard, lord of Marly in the Ile de France west of Paris, 1204–26. He was granted Saissac by de Montfort: see §268 and *Chanson* I, 41, pp. 102–4, and p. 103 n. 5. For his release from captivity at Cabaret in 1211 see §214 below. Simon de Montfort's wife Alice was his cousin. He is mentioned again taking part at the battle of Castelnaudary in 1211 (§270) and came south with Alice de Montfort at the end of 1218 (§618). His mother, brother Matthew and cousin Matthew of Montmorency also took part in the Crusade (see §156, §264 and §550). His son Thibaud later became Abbot of les Vaux-de-Cernay. For sources see G&L I, p. 126 n. 3.

12   North of Paris, in the Ile de France, and just south of Saint-Quentin.

13   For Saissac see n. 41 to §15.

14   See above, n. 103 to §114 for details of Cabaret.

of Cabaret, Peter-Roger (an old man rich in years of evil-doing), was a heretic and an open enemy of the Church. It happened that as Bouchard and his companions approached Cabaret the knights from the *castrum* who were waiting in ambush attacked and surrounded them and captured Bouchard. However, Gaubert refused to surrender and was killed. Bouchard was taken to Cabaret and imprisoned in the keep where he was held in chains for sixteen months.[15]

[124] At about the same time[16] – before the Count had returned from Montpellier – Roger, Viscount of Béziers, who was being held in the palace[17] at Carcassonne, was suddenly taken ill and died.[18] Now to return to our main narrative.

[125] *Giraud de Pépieux defects from the Count.* After the Count's return from Montpellier to Carcassonne, Giraud de Pépieux,[19] a knight of the viscounty of Béziers, whom the Count had treated most kindly and as a close friend, and had entrusted with the duty of guarding certain *castra* of his near Minerve, became a despicable traitor and a cruel enemy of the faith. Denying God, forswearing his given word and unmindful of the favours he had received and the affection shown to him, he rejected the Count's friendship and the promises of fealty he had given. Even if he no longer had God and His faith in mind, he should surely have been turned from such cruelty by the kindness the Count had shown him. Giraud went with some other knights, enemies of the faith, to Puisserguier,[20] a *castrum* belonging to the Count in the territory of Béziers, where they captured two of the Count's knights left to guard it and numerous sergeants. They promised under oath that they would not kill them but would conduct them unharmed with all their possessions as far as Narbonne. Hearing of this the Count went as fast as he could to the Puisserguier. Giraud and his fellow knights were

---

[15] November 1209 to March 1211 (see §214)

[16] The necrology or death-roll of Carcassonne, given in *HGL* V, 36, gives 10 November 1209 ('*IV idus novemb. anno MCCVIIII*') as the date of the death of Raymond-Roger Trencavel (see also Appendix E).

[17] Latin '*palatium*', meaning the heavily fortifed vicecomital castle built against the western wall of the cité, which had been the Trencavels' stronghold within Carcassonne and which was now Simon's headquarters. Cf. §549 where Peter describes the Château Narbonnais at Toulouse as '*munitio et palatium*'.

[18] The *Chanson* (I, 37, p. 94) says he died of dysentery. However, the death of the young Viscount occurred at a time when resistance to de Montfort was beginning to mount, and it was undoubtedly very convenient for him, since the deposed Viscount Trencavel could have provided a rallying point for opposition. Hence reports soon began to circulate that he had been assassinated. They were vigorously denied by William of Tudela in the *Chanson* (loc. cit.) and by William of Puylaurens (XIV), but Innocent III was later prepared to believe them since in writing to Arnold Amalric and others in 1213 (*PL* 216, 739) he refers to the Viscount as '*miserabiliter interfectus*', 'wretchedly slain' (although when he wrote this Innocent was heavily influenced by recent representations made to him by the envoys of King Peter of Aragon: see §399 and notes and Appendix G).

[19] Giraud had held Pépieux, a small fief to the south of Minerve, of the Trencavels. In July 1209 he had declared allegiance to the crusaders and had been rewarded by de Montfort accordingly. The *Chanson* (1, 41, p. 102) states that he defected because his uncle was murdered by a (northern) French nobleman; Simon of Montfort had the murderer buried alive but this did not seem to Giraud to be sufficient revenge. §291 below relates the capture of his father by the crusaders. Giraud himself continued to resist the crusaders and the Inquisition until his death in 1240.

[20] About 15km west of Béziers, north of Capestang. Berengar of Puisserguier was the brother-in-law of William of Minerve and features with Giraud de Pépieux as a witness of various acts; he was also dispossessed by the crusaders (G&L I, p. 129, n. 2).

still there, and the Count wanted to lay them under siege, but Aimeric the lord of Narbonne (who was with the Count)[21] and the men of Narbonne did not wish to join in the siege and forthwith returned to Narbonne. Realizing that he had been left almost alone the Count retired for the night to a *castrum* nearby known as Capestang intending to return next day at first light.

[126] There occurred, however, a miracle at Puisserguier which I must not omit from my narrative. After Giraud had come to the place and captured it, he made little of his promise to conduct his prisoners unharmed to Narbonne but imprisoned the Count's sergeants he had captured – up to fifty in number – in the keep. However, on the night the Count left the *castrum* Giraud became afraid that the Count would return next morning to besiege it and fled in the middle of the night. Since he was in too great a hurry to take with him the men he had imprisoned, he put them into the ditch surrounding the keep and had straw, fire, stones and anything else that came to hand thrown on top of them, until he believed they must be dead. Then he left taking with him the Count's two knights whom he had captured, and went to Minerve. What appalling treason! At daybreak the Count returned to the place, found it empty, and destroyed it. The men imprisoned in the ditch by Giraud, who had starved for three days, were found to be unhurt and unaffected by the fire, and the Count had them pulled out. What a great miracle, what an unprecedented event.

[127] Leaving Puisserguier the Count razed to the ground numerous *castra* belonging to Giraud and after a few days returned to Carcassonne. But the traitor Giraud, after taking the Count's knights to Minerve, made light of the promise he had made and gave no regard to his oath; certainly he did not kill them, but, more cruelly, he put out their eyes; more than that, he cut off their ears and noses and upper lips and sent them off naked to find their way back to the Count. He threw them out at night, exposed naked to the wind and cold (the weather was very severe), and one of them (the story cannot be heard without tears) died in a dung pit. The other, as I heard from his own mouth, was taken by a poor man to Carcassonne. A wicked crime, unheard of cruelty! This was the beginning of sorrows.[22]

[128] *The Abbot of les Vaux-de-Cernay travels to Carcassonne.* At this time[23] Guy, the venerable Abbot of les Vaux-de-Cernay,[24] a wise and good man, who had embraced the business of Jesus Christ with great enthusiasm and was doing more to advance it than anyone save the Abbot of Cîteaux, came from France to Carcassonne to give comfort to our men, who were at that time in a state of great depression. His devotion to Christ's business was, as I have said, very strong, to

---

[21] Presumably he was still with Simon following the meeting at Montpellier with Peter of Aragon (§121).

[22] Matthew 24, v. 8. The crusaders were to inflict reciprocal punishment of this kind on the defenders of Bram when they captured it the following spring: see §142 below.

[23] This section and §132 and §133 refer to events which probably took place in late November or December 1209 – see Appendix E.

[24] For Guy's part in the preaching mission of 1207, see §51 above. A letter of 9 November from Innocent to Guy (*PL* 216, 157) refers to 'instructions' ('*mandata*') to join the Crusade given to Guy by Arnold Amalric, and urges him not to delay.

the extent that from the beginning of the conflict with the heretics he was always to be found either in the province of Narbonne or travelling in France, preaching for the cause. Our people in Carcassonne were in such confusion and fear that they had almost abandoned hope and could think only of flight; indeed they were surrounded on all sides by innumerable powerful enemies. But this man of virtue, trusting in Him who, whilst allowing temptation, provides a way to escape from it,[25] soothed their fears and anxieties by salutary counsel given to them each day.

[129] *Robert Mauvoisin returns from Rome.* At this time there arrived on the scene Robert Mauvoisin,[26] who had been sent by the Count to Rome; a most noble knight of Christ, a man of marvellous probity, accomplished in learning and of incomparable virtue, who for many years had given himself and all he owned to the service of Christ and was outstanding in pursuing His business most keenly and effectively. It was through him more than anyone, save God Himself, that the army of Christ renewed its strength, as I shall show later.

[130] *Death of a certain Abbot.* At this time[27] the Count of Foix had sent the Abbot of Eaunes,[28] a Cistercian monastery between Toulouse and Foix, to Saint-Gilles to transact certain business on his behalf with the papal legates. On his return he passed through Carcassonne accompanied by two monks and a lay brother. They left Carcassonne and were about a mile on their way when a great enemy of Christ, a most ferocious persecutor of the Church, William of Roque-fort,[29] brother of the then Bishop of Carcassonne,[30] suddenly attacked them – he

---

[25] Cf. I Corinthians 10, v. 13.

[26] A prominent crusader, who had earlier taken part in the Fourth Crusade with Simon de Montfort and had left Zara with him (see §106 above). He was a vassal of the Count of Champagne and was a close associate of de Montfort's, and had remained with him in the South after the fall of Carcassonne (cf. n. 105 to §115). He had been to Rome to deliver the letter from de Montfort, written in late August, which sought Innocent's confirmation of his assumption of the Trencavel viscounties (*PL* 216, 141–2). He is referred to below in §154, §286, and §336. He was one of those crusaders who made a grant of land to Dominic's house at Prouille, and his wife was a benefactrice of les Vaux-de-Cernay. He died in November 1214. For detailed references see G&L I, p. 133 n. 1, and also Vicaire, p. 126 on Prouille.

[27] The incident now related probably took place in the second half of November 1209, since the legate Milo was in Saint-Gilles on 6 November (G&L I, p. 134 n. 1), and the abbot probably met him there at about that time before beginning his return journey. See Appendix E for a fuller discussion of the chronology of this period.

[28] The Abbot was Stephen of Eaunes, a Cistercian house south of Toulouse and close to Muret (cf. *Cahiers de Fanjeaux*, vol. 21, p. 28). For the purpose of his visit, see n. 35 to §134.

[29] Roquefort was a *castrum* on the western edge of the Montagne Noire north of Carcassonne, and the family of Roquefort held it as a fief from the Trencavels. In the early 13th century the family also held many other fiefs in the Carcassès, and was one of the most important seigneurial families in the area. Like many others, they were also deeply involved with Catharism. Later Inquisition depositions reveal that William of Roquefort's mother was probably a *perfecta*, several other brothers were *perfecti*, and a sister Romenga kept a house for *perfectae* at Puylaurens. William's brother in law, Peter Isarn, was Cathar Bishop of the Carcassès. William himself was also a strong Cathar supporter, and after the fall of Carcassonne he initially took refuge at Roquefort, and became one of the most well known of the *faidits*, outlawed opponents of the crusaders (on which term see Introduction p. xlii). He later took refuge in Termes with others of his family (see §185 below), and subsequently at Toulouse where he was killed during the first siege of the city in 1211 (see §240). For discussions of the Roquefort family, and detailed source references, see Griffe, *LC*, pp. 102–6, and Roquebert I, pp. 148–9.

[30] Bernard-Raymond de Roquefort, who became Bishop of Carcassonne in 1208–1209, and resigned the

armed, they unarmed, a cruel man against men of peace, a man without feeling against innocents. For no reason except that they were Cistercians this most cruel man inflicted thirty-six wounds on the Abbot and twenty-four on the lay brother, killing them on the spot. He left one of the monks half dead, with sixteen wounds. The other monk escaped alive, because he was known to this tyrant's companions and they were to some extent friendly towards him. What a shameful act of warfare, what an inglorious victory!

[131] When our Count (who was at Carcassonne) heard what had happened, he ordered the bodies to be conveyed to Carcassonne for honourable burial – the act of a man of the Church, a leader true to the faith. He saw to it that the monk who had been left half-dead was given proper medical treatment and sent him back to his monastery when he had recovered. The Count of Foix, who had sent off the Abbot and his companions to transact business on his behalf, shortly afterwards received their murderer into intimacy and friendship; he kept the executioner by his side; moreover the Abbot's horses, which the murderer had seized, were soon afterwards seen in the entourage of the Count of Foix. Oh most evil man (I mean the Count of Foix), Oh most base traitor! Nor must I fail to record that the murderer himself – smitten with divine retribution by God the just Judge, as the voice of the blood of his victims cried out to God from earth against him[31] – soon afterwards received the just reward for his cruelty. He who had inflicted so many blows on men of the Church, soon afterwards himself suffered innumerable wounds and met a well-deserved death at the hands of the soldiers of Christ at the gates of Toulouse.[32] A just judgment indeed! A fair measure of Divine retribution! 'For there is no law more just than that those who contrive the death of others should die by the means they themselves devised.'[33]

[132] *The inhabitants of Castres desert the Count.* At this time the inhabitants of Castres rejected their friendship with the Count and his overlordship and captured a knight whom he had appointed to guard the place, and numerous sergeants. They dared not do them any harm because some of the most important inhabitants of Castres were being held hostage in Carcassonne.

[133] *The Count loses the* castrum *of Lombers.* On almost the same day the knights of Lombers deserted God and the Count, captured some sergeants of the Count who were in the *castrum* and dispatched them to Castres to be imprisoned in chains. The townsmen of Castres placed them in a tower[34] (along with the Count's knight and the sergeants whom they had captured, as described above).

---

see in 1211, to be succeeded by Guy of les Vaux-de-Cernay (see §299 below). Although his family were amongst those supporting Raymond-Roger Trenvcavel in 1209, he did himself not oppose the crusaders, and was with them at the siege of Termes in 1210 (see §185 below). See also Griffe, *LC*, pp. 269–71, who defends his orthodoxy. He was reinstated as Bishop on Guy's death in 1224 (*HGL* VI, 575).

31 Cf. Genesis 4, v. 10.
32 See §240, below.
33 From Ovid, *Ars Amatoria* 1, 655–6: '*nec enim lex justior ulla/ Quam necis artifices arte perire sua*'.
34 '*Turris*', which is normally rendered as keep; here the Tour-Caudière on the west bank of the River Agout (G&L, p. 137 n. 4)

However, one night the prisoners made a sort of rope out of their clothes and, with God's help, escaped through a window.

[134] *The Count of Foix deserts our Count.* At this time[35] the Count of Foix who had as previously narrated made a pact of friendship with our Count, in an act of treachery took over the *castrum* of Preixan which he had previously handed over to him. He abandoned his alliance with our Count and began to attack him vigorously. A little later, on the feast of St Michael, this traitor came by night to the *castrum* called Fanjeaux and arranged for ladders to be erected against the walls. Enemy soldiers scaled the walls and began to run through the *castrum*. Our men inside – very few in number[36] – saw what was happening and counter-attacked. They compelled the enemy to make a shameful withdrawal and tumble into the ditch round the walls; several they killed.

[135] *The Count loses Montréal.* Near Carcassonne was another notable *castrum*, Montréal.[37] The lord of the place was a knight named Aimeric, the most powerful and noble man in the whole area except for the Counts. At the time of the siege of Carcassonne Aimeric, fearful of our soldiers, left Montréal empty; later he came to our Count and for a little time was friendly with him, but after a few days, he became a foul traitor and deserted God and the Count. The Count then occupied Montréal and entrusted it to a French clerk to guard, but this man, corrupted by the Devil's influence and worse than any infidel, soon afterwards in an act of cruel treachery handed it over to Aimeric and stayed for a time with our enemies. However, the Divine judgment of God, the righteous Judge, intervened, and shortly afterwards[38] our Count took a *castrum* near Montréal called Bram and there captured the clerk together with other adversaries of the faith. The Count then arranged for him to be degraded by the Bishop of Carcassonne, and

35 See Appendix E for the issues arising from the date of the Feast of St Michael, 29 September, given a few lines below for the attack on Fanjeaux. If, as seems more likely, that date is wrong but Peter's ordering of events correct, then the attack on Preixan now related will have taken place in mid-November. If so then it is possible that Count Raymond-Roger of Foix, who would have been irked by de Montfort's accord with the abbot of Pamiers (§116), decided at this time to reject his accord with de Montfort (for which see §120) because of the crusaders' weakness (see §128 et seq.), which must by now have become increasingly obvious. The purpose of the visit to Saint-Gilles early in November on behalf of the Count of Foix by the Abbot of Eaunes (§130 above) might then perhaps have been to try to reach some agreement with the legates before he took any action. This must remain conjecture.
36 The garrison was clearly small; it may have comprised the Aragonese mercenaries who had initially occupied it (see §110).
37 Montréal lies about 20km west of Carcassonne, on a hill overlooking the Aude valley and the Lauragais. For its occupation by the crusaders, probably in late August 1209, see n. 95 to §110. In the later 12th century Sicard de Laurac was one of the most important co-seigneurs of Montréal; he was head of a powerful local family from Laurac, some 20km further west. His wife was Blanche de Laurac, and at about the time of Sicard's death c. 1200 she became a *perfecta* (Griffe, *LC*, pp. 109–10). They had a number of children, including Aimeric of Montréal (below, next sentence), and Giraude who married the lord of Lavaur (see §215). William of Tudela (*Chanson* I, 68, p. 164) refers to Aimeric as the richest and most noble knight in the county of Toulouse and a supporter of the Waldenses, and in 1200 he called himself lord of Montréal and Laurac: cf. Griffe, *LC*, pp. 160–1. Montréal was, like neighbouring Fanjeaux, one of those *castra* in which Catharism was most firmly established: see n. 30 to §26 above for details of heresy at Montréal. Aimeric and Giraude were besieged at Lavaur in 1211 (§§215–27), and for their deaths after the siege see §227.
38 In March 1210: see below, §142.

had him dragged by a horse through the city of Carcassonne and hanged – a fitting penalty for his crime.

[136] I need delay no longer. Almost all the local people became affected with the same ill-will and deserted our Count. In a short space of time[39] he lost more than forty fortresses and he was left with only Carcassonne,[40] Fanjeaux, Saissac, the *castra* of Limoux (although he had little hope of retaining that place), Pamiers, and Saverdun, and the city of Albi together with a single *castrum*, Ambialet.[41] I must also record that most of those whom the Count had left to guard the *castra* in the area were either killed or mutilated by the local traitors. What was the Count of Christ to do? Any other man would surely have given up the struggle in the face of such adversity, and yielded to despair in such a crisis – but the Count, putting all his faith in God, was not to be borne down by misfortune, just as he did not become overweening in success. All this took place about the time of the feast of Christ's Nativity.

[137] *The Count of Toulouse goes to France.*[42] Whilst these events were taking place the Count of Toulouse went to the King of France to see if he could by some

---

[39] During late November and December 1209; see Appendix E.
[40] As well as Carcassonne and the other places now mentioned, de Montfort also retained possession of Béziers.
[41] On the River Tarn, about 20km east of Albi.
[42] In §§137–139 Peter's vague chronology becomes especially confusing, partly because in §137 he records events which occurred after, and largely as a consequence of, the Council of Avignon which he records in §138, and partly because he fails to record events preceding the Council. It may therefore be useful to summarize diplomatic developments during the period covered by these three sections, i.e. September 1209 to spring 1210. (Some further details will be found in later notes.)
   (i) After leaving Carcassonne, apparently on good terms with de Montfort, Raymond VI had returned to Toulouse towards the end of August 1209; see n. 98 to §111 above. Early in September Arnold Amalric and Simon de Montfort sent a delegation to Toulouse. This delegation is not mentioned by Peter, but is referred to by William of Tudela (*Chanson* I, 39, pp. 96–8), and details are given in a letter from the Toulousains to King Peter of Aragon of July 1211 (*HGL* VIII, 612–19, for which see especially n. 11 to §234). The delegation demanded that suspected heretics (named on a list probably furnished by Bishop Fulk of Toulouse) be handed over for judgment, and that Raymond fulfil all the undertakings he had made at Saint-Gilles in June 1209. If not, Raymond would again be excommunicated, and Toulouse put under interdict. Raymond and the consuls of Toulouse refused to fall in with these demands. Instead, they determined to appeal over the legates' heads directly to Innocent III, and Raymond also decided to approach his two liege lords, Philip Augustus and the Emperor Otto.
   (ii) Meanwhile, during the first weeks of September 1209, the legate Milo was presiding over a Council at Avignon. The business of Raymond and the Toulousains was brought before it, and the outcome included a second (but suspended) excommunication of Raymond; for details see §138 below. Milo reported the results to Pope Innocent in a letter (*PL* 216, 126–8) which also vehemently attacks Raymond and warns the Pope of Raymond's intention to visit the Curia (as well as Philip Augustus and Otto).
   (iii) Raymond then sent a delegation to Rome (which included the former Bishop of Toulouse, Raymond of Rabastens) to prepare the way for his own visit: see *Chanson* I, 39, p. 98. The *Chanson* (I, 40, p. 98) also says that Arnold Amalric sought to dissuade Raymond himself from going to Rome, but unsuccessfully. Raymond then set off first for Paris to meet Philip Augustus (as recorded by Peter in §137), shortly after making a will on 20 September (*HGL* VIII, 573–77). He is then recorded as passing through Saint-Gilles on 6 November (see G&L I, pp. 140–1 n. 4), presumably on his way to meet Innocent in Rome, where he arrived either late in November or during December 1209. The outcome is described later in §137 and subsequently in §§162–4.
   (iv) A delegation of the consuls of Toulouse also visited the Pope (*Chanson* I, 42, pp. 104–6) apparently at the same time as Raymond. This is not recorded by Peter. Innocent seemed to accept their representations since in a letter of 19 January 1210 (recorded in the Toulousains' letter to King Peter, *HGL* VIII, loc. cit.), he

means obtain the King's help and authority for the re-imposition of tolls, which he had had to abandon on the orders of the papal legates. He had previously increased the tolls in his territories quite excessively, and had frequently been excommunicated on this account.[43] However, having had no success with the King on the matter of imposing tolls,[44] he left him and went to the lord Pope, to see if he could win the Supreme Pontiff's help in recovering his lands (which the papal legates had occupied as a guarantee, as described above,[45] and were still holding). This most deceitful man then put on a show of the utmost humility and obedience, promising to follow faithfully all the Pope's instructions. However, the Pope heaped on him such a quantity of rebukes and reproaches that the Count became quite desperate and did not know what to do. The Pope accused him of being 'an unbeliever, a persecutor of the cross, an enemy of the faith' – and rightly so.[46] However, the Pope, reflecting that the Church in the province of Narbonne was now defenceless as an orphan, thought it possible that if he became desperate the Count might start to attack her more intensely and more openly. He therefore told him that he must purify himself of the two crimes of which he was principally accused – the murder of the papal legate, Brother Peter of Castelnau, and the offence of heresy. The Pope sent a letter on this issue to the

instructed the legates to reconcile the Toulousains to the Church. Peter refers to these instructions later, in §162.

(v) After staying in Rome for some time Raymond met the Emperor Otto in January or February 1210 in Tuscany. He then made the second journey to Paris recorded by Peter in §139. He probably returned to Toulouse in March or April but at the latest in time to attend the meeting at Pamiers (§146), which probably took place in early May 1210: see n. 15 to §145.

Peter's account of diplomatic developments during the ensuing year or so, spring 1210 to February 1211, is also confusing; see the further summary in n. 17 to §146.

[43] The suppression of what were seen by the Church as unjust tolls and other exactions was part of Innocent III's overall aim of securing a justly ordered Christian society, and was thus part of the *negotium pacis et fidei* (on which see Introduction). The levying of tolls by local lords was ostensibly for the upkeep of bridges and roads, but in practice it was often largely a means of raising taxes and was an important source of revenue. Hence the significance of this issue to Raymond VI, for whom this was an important source of revenue. The tolls here referred to were being exacted by Raymond in the Toulousain, the Agenais and in Provence: see for instance *HGL* VIII, 527–30, which gives details of an inquiry made in 1205 by the consuls of Toulouse about tolls levied in the Toulousain, and G&M p. 59 n. 5. Raymond's first excommunication in 1207 had in part been because he had allegedly increased tolls (*PL* 215, 1166–8, see n. 35 to §27 and Appendix F(i)), whilst at Saint-Gilles in June 1209 Milo had been given an undertaking by Raymond that he would raise no tolls '*nisi quas regum vel imperatorum concessione probaveris te habere*', i.e. 'except those for which you have the permission of the King and the Emperor'. When Milo wrote to Innocent after the Council of Avignon (*PL* 216, 126–8) Raymond's failure to abolish tolls and other unjust taxes was also one of the six charges laid against him.

[44] William of Tudela (*Chanson* I, 42, p. 106) says that Raymond was well received at Philip Augustus' court, and for instance met Blanche of Navarre, Countess of Champagne, and the Duke of Burgundy and the Count of Nevers. For the King's attitude to the Crusade see n. 65 to §72.

[45] See §§75–7 above, and notes for details of the seven *castra* Raymond was required to hand over as a guarantee.

[46] Contrary to Peter's version of this meeting, the *Chanson* (I, 43, p. 106) says that Raymond was made very welcome by the Pope; that he was given valuable gifts (and even shown the relic known as the cloth of St Veronica, with which she was said to have wiped Christ's brow); and that the two became close friends. Whilst there may be some poetic exaggeration in William of Tudela's account, there is probably also an element of truth in it. For instance, the letters issued by Innocent between 19 and 25 January, including the one mentioned by Peter at the end of this section, show that Innocent was at least willing to listen to Raymond's representations and still wished to see him properly reconciled: see following notes for details.

Bishop of Riez,[47] in Provence, and to Master Thedisius,[48] instructing them that if the Count was able, in their presence, to offer adequate purification in regard to these two crimes, they should accept it.[49]

[138] Meanwhile Master Milo (who as related above had been carrying out his duties as legate for the business of peace and the faith in the area of Provence[50]) summoned a council of prelates at Avignon.[51] The main business was to excommunicate the citizens of Toulouse and declare their lands liable to seizure,[52] because of their refusal to carry out their promises to the legate and the crusaders to expel the heretics. At the meeting a conditional sentence of excommunication was also pronounced against the Count of Toulouse, to take effect if he attempted to reimpose the tolls he had renounced.[53]

---

[47] Hugh, Bishop of Riez in eastern Provence, 1202–23. He had been appointed as a legate to help Arnold Amalric in March 1208 (see Innocent III's letter of 28 March 1208, *Layettes* I, 843). For his role at the time of the Council of Saint-Gilles in 1210 see §§163–4; and at the time of the Council of Lavaur in 1213, see §379.

[48] See §70 above.

[49] As well as this letter to Hugh and Thedisius, Innocent wrote to the Archbishops of Narbonne and Arles: the letters, issued on 25 January, 1210, are in *PL* 216, 171–3, and are identical in content for most of their length. Their contents are important in following the diplomatic manoeuvres between Raymond VI and the legates in the period to the Council of Lavaur in January 1213: extracts in translation of the letter to the legates, *Veniens in praesentiam*, are given in Appendix F(iii). In effect Innocent went a long way towards accepting Raymond's complaints of unfair treatment by the legates, and instructed them 'within three months of receiving this letter' to arrange a council to hear complaints against Raymond and allow him the opportunity to purify himself, with special reference to his alleged lack of true Catholic faith and complicity in the murder of Peter of Castelnau; in the meantime he lays down immunity for Raymond's lands from the attacks of the crusaders. The legates were to report back to Innocent on the results of this process – he indicates very clearly his intention to remain in control of the situation, since he says 'whichever way things turn out the oracle of a response from the Apostolic See should be awaited' ('*in utroque casu apostolicae oraculum expectetur*'). Innocent was to maintain his insistence that Raymond should be given a proper hearing up to and including the Fourth Lateran Council (see Appendix G). Three other important letters had also been issued by Innocent just before these: (a) the letter of 19 January instructing the legates to lift the interdict on Toulouse (see above, n. 42(iv) to this section); (b) a letter of 23 January to Raymond referring to the procedures and terms for his reconciliation (*PL* 216, 173–4); (c) a letter of 23 January to Arnold Amalric (*PL* 216, 174–6) assuring the Abbot that Raymond had genuinely sought reconciliation and would fulfil all undertakings, and importantly also stating that following Milo's death in December 1209 (on which cf. §165 below), Thedisius was to act wholly under Arnold Amalric's orders, as his '*organum*', or agent (on which word cf. §71 above). For the subsequent reaction of the legates to these letters and later developments, and their determination not to reconcile Raymond despite Innocent's instructions, see §§162–4 and notes.

[50] Peter is referring to Milo's diplomatic activity in the summer of 1209; see §§74 et seq. and n. 72, and n. 80 to §81. See also G&L I, p. 143 n. 2, and G&M pp. 60–1 n. 4 for other details.

[51] The Council took place in the first weeks of September 1209. Its main purpose (notwithstanding Peter's statement in the next sentence) was the reform of ecclesiastical discipline, and its 21 canons repeated much of the legislation issued at the Third Lateran Council in 1179. Attending the Council were the Archbishops of Vienne, Arles, Embrun and Aix, along with 20 bishops (including Hugh of Riez) and a number of abbots, including Arnold Amalric: see G&L I, p. 143 n. 3. Arnold Amalric seems to have raised the issue of Raymond VI and the Toulousains once the failure of his delegation to Toulouse early in September became known (see above, n. 42(i) to §137).

[52] Peter says simply '*fuerunt . . . expositi cives Tolosani*', but is referring to the process known in French as *exposition en proie*, for which see §62.

[53] The details of these sentences are set out in the letter written in September 1209 to Innocent by Hugh of Riez and Milo, in *PL* 216, 126–8. Raymond was conditionally excommunicated, and given until All Saints' Day (1 November) to do as the Church required, at which time, if he failed to give satisfaction, the sentence would come into effect: '*alioquin tam ipse quam terra ipsius, ut supra diximus, et excommunicationis*'

[139] *The Count of Toulouse returns from Rome.* On his way back from the Roman Court the Count of Toulouse went to Otto, the so-called Emperor,[54] intending to gain his support and beg his help against the Count of Montfort.[55] He then went on to see the King of France, hoping that by painting a false picture he could deceive him and win his favours. However, the King, who was a discerning and intelligent man, treated him with the contempt he deserved.[56] When the Count of Montfort heard that the Count of Toulouse was going to France he ordered his vassals in that area to put their lands and possessions at the latter's disposal. At this time there was no open hostility between them – indeed the Count of Toulouse had promised under oath that his son would marry the Count of Montfort's daughter.[57] Afterwards he went back on his oath and, deceitful and unreliable man that he was, refused to carry out this undertaking. Realising that he could make no progress with the King, the Count of Toulouse returned home in confusion.[58] Let us now return to our main narrative.

[140] That winter[59] the noble Count of Montfort, surrounded by enemies on every side, kept himself to himself and concentrated on guarding the small amount of territory he still controlled, whilst frequently harassing his enemies.[60] I must record that although his supporters were very few and his enemies numberless, they never dared attack him in open warfare.

---

et interdicti sententia teneatur' – 'otherwise he himself and his territories will be subjected to the sentence of excommunication and interdict'.

54 Raymond held the marquisate of Provence as a vassal of the Holy Roman Emperor. For Otto's position at this time see n. 66 to §72.

55 See n. 42(v) to §137. Otto is known to have been in Tuscany in January and February 1210, when Raymond presumably met him: see G&L I, p. 144 n. 3.

56 William of Tudela states (I, 42, p. 106) that Philip Augustus was displeased by Raymond's having visited Otto, no doubt because this implied recognition of him as Emperor (see n. 66 to §72). Raymond needed to seek the help of both his liege lords, but since they were enemies an approach to one risked alienating the other.

57 The daughter will have been Amicia, on whom see Appendix C. See also §111 above for the apparently good relations between Raymond and Simon in the autumn of 1209, which continued into the spring of 1210: cf. *Chanson* I, 44, p. 108 which speaks of the amity between them at that time.

58 Probably in March or April 1210: cf. n. 42(v) to §137 and §150 and §162 below, which give further details of dealings during the spring between Arnold Amalric, Raymond VI, and the consuls of Toulouse, and also see the *Chanson* I, 44–7, pp. 108–112. *Confusio*, here translated as 'confusion', occurs frequently in the *Historia*; it can also mean 'shame' and it is often difficult to know which meaning is predominant in the author's mind.

59 I.e. winter 1209–10.

60 Cf. above, §136.

[VII. §§141–192, spring – autumn 1210: *The crusaders, now reinforced, resume their conquest – atrocity at Bram – siege of Alaric – attack on Foix – further involvement of King Peter of Aragon – failed negotiations between King Peter and the lords of Cabaret, Termes and Montréal – siege of Minerve (June–July 1210) – Council of Saint-Gilles and renewed excommunication of Count Raymond VI of Toulouse (July 1210) – siege of Termes (August– November 1210).*]

[141] *Arrival of the Countess of Montfort.* At the beginning of Lent,[1] news reached the Count that his Countess (whom he had summoned from France) was on her way accompanied by numerous knights.[2] He then went to a *castrum* known as Pézenas in the territory of Agde[3] to meet her, found her there and returned towards Carcassonne with great joy. However, when he reached a *castrum* called Capendu[4] it was reported to him that the inhabitants of a *castrum* named Montlaur, near the monastery of Lagrasse,[5] had betrayed him and started to besiege his sergeants who were in the keep. At once the Countess was committed to the safety of a certain *castrum*[6] and the Count and his knights went to Montlaur. There they found that the reports were true. They captured many of the traitors and hanged them – the rest had fled at the sight of our soldiers. The Count and his companions then went to Carcassonne.

[142] From there they went to the town of Alzonne[7] which they found deserted. Going on, they came to a *castrum* known as Bram.[8] Finding it defended against them, they besieged it and captured it within three days, by direct assault

---

[1] Lent in 1210 began on 2 March.
[2] The arrival of Simon de Montfort's wife Alice with additional troops enabled him to go on the offensive again after the reversals at the end of 1209, and the apparent inaction of the first few months of 1210. Even so, they cannot have been a large contingent since Simon's ability to attack difficult targets remained limited. In these circumstances the crusaders resorted to destroying crops in the hinterlands of enemy strongholds (e.g. §144 and §147 below), and were apparently unable to attack Montréal directly in May, when Peter states that their numbers were few (§148 below). More knights seem to have arrived in June before the attack on Minerve (see *Chanson,* I, 49, p. 116), but even then the support of the Narbonnais was important in enabling the siege to be mounted (see §151). Large numbers of troops do not appear to have arrived until late July and August 1210, at the beginning of the siege of Termes, and even then the crusaders' vulnerability was displayed by the attack on their siege engines near Carcassonne: see §§168–70 and 173–4. On Alice de Montfort see §107 above, and Appendix C.
[3] Pézenas lies inland from Agde, about 25km north-east of Béziers.
[4] Capendu is about 15km east of Carcassonne. Its lord was Bernard-Raymond, a Trencavel vassal, who was dispossessed by the crusaders in 1209 and became a *faidit.* His sister Alice married another *faidit,* William of Peyrepertuse. See G&L I, pp. 146–7 n. 4, and on Peyrepertuse, §591 below.
[5] Montlaur lies between Capendu (to its north) and Lagrasse (to its south-east), in the northern Corbières. The seigneur of Montlaur, Raymond-Ermengaud, had been in dispute with the Benedictine Abbey of Lagrasse, and he and his brother are known to have been *faidits* at the time of the Crusade ('*faiditus tempore comitis Montis Fortis*'): see G&L, p. 147 n. 1.
[6] Presumably Capendu. The *Chanson* (I, 50, p. 118) comments that the Count instructed her to join him at Pennautier after the capture of Minerve, which took place towards the end of July (see §166). Thus she may have remained at Capendu throughout this period.
[7] Occupied in August 1209; cf. §110 above.
[8] Cf. §135 above. Bram lies between Carcassonne and Castelnaudary in the Lauragais plain, and had no natural defences.

and without using siege-engines. They put out the eyes of the defenders, over a hundred in number, and cut off their noses. One man was spared one eye so that, as a demonstration of our contempt for our enemies, he could lead the others to Cabaret. The Count had this punishment carried out not because such mutilation gave him any pleasure but because his opponents had been the first to indulge in atrocities[9] and, cruel executioners that they were, were given to butchering any of our men they might capture by dismembering them. It was right that they should fall into the pit they had dug themselves[10] and drink from time to time of the cup they so often administered to others. The Count never took delight in cruelty or in the torture of his enemies. He was the kindest of men and the saying of the poet fitted him most aptly: 'a prince slow to punish, and quick to reward, who grieved when driven to be hard'.[11]

[143] Then the Lord, who seemed perhaps to have been asleep,[12] rose up to help His servants and could now be seen more clearly to do great things for us.[13] In a short space of time we gained the whole region of Minerve save Minerve itself and a *castrum* known as Ventajou.[14]

[144] *A glorious miracle.* One day a miracle occurred near Cabaret, which I must not pass over. The crusaders from France uprooted the vineyards of Cabaret, on the Count's orders. One of our adversaries shot at one of our men with a cross-bow, and hit him in the chest, just where the sign of the cross was fixed. Everyone thought he must be dead, since he wore no armour; but he was found to be quite unhurt – the bolt had failed even to penetrate his clothing, but had rebounded as if it had struck the hardest stone. Such is the wonderful power of God, his immense strength.

[145] *Siege of Alaric.* About Easter-time[15] the Count and his followers set out

---

9   This atrocity was a reprisal for the similar one carried out by Giraud de Pépieux, recorded in §127 above. A similar atrocity was perpetrated some years earlier by Richard the Lionheart at Château Gaillard in Normandy, when 15 French prisoners were blinded and sent back to King Philip Augustus, led by a one-eyed man: see J. Bradbury, *The Medieval Siege*, p. 132.

10   Cf. Proverbs 26, v. 27.

11   Ovid, *Ex Ponto* I, 2, lines 123–4: '*Hic piger ad poenas princeps, ad praemia velox,/ Quique dolet, quotiens cogitur esse ferox.*'

12   Cf. Psalm 44, v. 23.

13   Cf. Psalm 126, vv. 2–3.

14   Ventajou was near Félines, about 15km west of Minerve. There are no other details of Simon de Montfort's recovery of control of the Minervois, but in February 1210 Stephen of Servian, a *castrum* north of Béziers occupied in July 1209 (see n. 16 to §83 above), had abjured and was reconciled, along with a number of his vassals: this abjuration is in *HGL* VIII, 584–9.

15   Easter Day in 1210 fell on 18 April. To date events described in §§145–150 we have to rely on approximate dates given by Peter: '*circa Pascha*', 'about Easter', for the start of the siege of Alaric (§145), which lasted for about fifteen days; and '*circa festum beati Johannis Baptistae*', 'about the feast of St John the Baptist', i.e. 24 June (§151) for the start of the siege of Minerve, which may have been earlier in June since in §158 and §166 we are told that the siege lasted for almost seven weeks ('*ferme per VII ebdomadas*'), and ended '*circa festum beate Marie Magdalene*', 'about the feast of St Mary Magdalene', 22 July. This latter date is roughly confirmed by William of Tudela (see *Chanson* I, 49, p. 116, and n. d) who says that Minerve fell 'before the grain harvest'. Thus the meeting at Pamiers, §146, probably took place in the first half of May; the attack on Foix, §147, and the events described in §§148–150 probably occurred in the second half of May. Both E. Martin-Chabot (*Chanson* I, pp. 110–11 n. 2), and G&M (p. 64 n. 2) discuss the detailed chronology of events at this time, citing King Peter's itinerary as given by Miret y Sans in *Itinerario*, and show that G&L's proposed reconstruction (G&L I, pp. 153–4 n. 2) is untenable.

to lay siege to a *castrum* named Alaric[16] between Carcassonne and Narbonne, which was in a mountainous region and surrounded by snow. The siege presented our men with great problems because of the severe weather, but after a fortnight our enemies in the *castrum* fled during the night and we captured it. A great many of the defenders, unable to escape our pursuit, were killed.

[146][17] Our men returned to Carcassonne and a little later went to Pamiers.[18] The King of Aragon, the Count of Toulouse and the Count of Foix had met near this place, hoping to arrange peace between our Count and the Count of Foix. Finding they could not do so, the King and the Count of Toulouse went back to Toulouse.

[147] The Count of Montfort then marched against Foix,[19] and there displayed astounding courage. He set on the defenders, who were positioned in front

---

[16] The Montagne d'Alaric is at the northern edge of the Corbières overlooking the Aude valley to the east of Carcassonne. The ruined castle is known as Miramont. Evidently Simon de Montfort had enough troops to mount this siege, notwithstanding the limitations noted above in n. 2 to §141.

[17] §§146–212 take the narrative of military and diplomatic events up to early February 1211. On the military front, the period was dominated by the great sieges of Minerve and Termes, on which Peter writes at length (see §§151–9 and 168–91 below). As regards diplomatic developments, Peter's account omits some important episodes and alludes only briefly to others. There were several concurrent sets of developments of which the following is a summary.

(i) The intervention by King Peter of Aragon, beginning with the conference at Pamiers involving the Count of Foix (§146), and continuing with the negotiations with the lords of Minerve, Termes and Cabaret described in §148. (King Peter continued to refuse to accept Simon de Montfort's homage – see §121 – throughout the year, eventually agreeing only at Narbonne in January 1211: see §210.) Throughout the period King Peter was also keen to ensure peace between his vassal the Count of Foix and the crusaders (see following note).

(ii) Developments flowing from the Toulousains' delegation to Rome over the winter of 1209–10 and Innocent's letter of 19 January (n. 42(iv) to §137). The business of implementing Innocent's instructions that the city should be reconciled was initially taken up by Arnold Amalric, and after some wrangling the Toulousains were formally reconciled by Bishop Fulk in late March. For these developments see §162 and note.

(iii) Developments following Innocent's letters of 23 and 25 January regarding the position of Raymond VI. After Raymond's visit to Rome over the winter, Innocent had set out the procedures to be followed which would enable Raymond to purge himself of the charges of heresy and complicity in the murder of Peter of Castelnau (see §137). However (see §§162–4 below), despite Innocent's instructions, the legates were determined to find a way of avoiding a reconciliation with Raymond VI, and arranged his renewed excommunication at a council held at Saint-Gilles in July. Events culminated in the conferences at Narbonne and Montpellier in January 1211, on which see §§194–6 and 210–12 below.

Further details are given in the notes to the relevant sections, which also discuss the uncertain dating of some events during this period.

[18] See §48 and §116 above on Pamiers. The meeting now described will have taken place in the first half of May 1210. King Peter's intervention to try and secure the position of one of his vassals, the Count of Foix, indicates his desire to prevent any further incursions by Simon de Montfort into his vassals' fiefs. A reconciliation was finally arrived at in late May or early June (§150 below). The *Chanson*, I, 44–5, pp. 108–10, mentions what seem to be two other meetings around this time. The first was between Raymond VI, Simon de Montfort, and Arnold Amalric, '*pres d'una abadia*', 'near an abbey'; G&L (I, pp. 153–4 n. 1) assume this to be a reference to the meeting at Pamiers but since William of Tudela does not mention the presence of King Peter this seems implausible. The second was at Portet (between Muret and Toulouse), perhaps in mid-May, between King Peter and Arnold Amalric. Both meetings were inconclusive.

[19] This immediate attack suggests that at this point de Montfort was determined to continue pressure on the Count of Foix. His position rapidly changed when the threat emerged of a direct alliance between King Peter and the lords of Termes, Cabaret and Minerve (§148), and a peace with Raymond-Roger of Foix was then quickly agreed (§150).

of the gates, with only a single knight supporting him, and – astonishingly – forced them all to retreat inside. He would have followed them, had they not closed the gates in his face. When the Count retired the knight who had followed him was overwhelmed by stones hurled down from the walls by the defenders – the passage was narrow and walled on either side. After destroying the crops, vines and trees round Foix the Count returned to Carcassonne.

[148] *The Albigensian knights appeal to the King of Aragon.* At this time[20] Peter-Roger, lord of Cabaret, Raymond, lord of Termes, Aimeric, lord of Montréal and other knights opposed to the Church and our Count, asked the King of Aragon, who was then in the area, to come to them; they would then recognise him as their lord and hand the whole territory over to him.[21] Hearing this our Count discussed his course of action with his knights. After diverse views were expressed, agreement was reached on a proposal to besiege a castle near Montréal, since it was at Montréal that the heretical knights were gathered to await the King's arrival. The Count's objective was to show his enemies that he was not afraid of them, although he had with him only a few knights. Accordingly our men set off to besiege the castle, which was named Bellegarde.[22]

[149] Next day the King arrived near Montréal. The knights who had called in the King, and who had already spent several days building up a copious supply of provisions, left Montréal and approached the King, asking him to enter Montréal so that they could do homage to him as they had requested; their idea was that by so doing they could drive the Count of Montfort from the territory. However, as soon as they reached him the King demanded that they hand over to him the castle of the *castrum* of Cabaret.[23] He added that he would accept them as vassals on condition that they should hand over to him all their castles, whenever he asked them to do so. The knights took counsel together and again asked the King to enter Montréal, when they would carry out their previous undertakings. However, the King still refused to do so unless they agreed to his terms. Since they refused, everyone left the meeting-place in confusion.

[150] Whilst the Count of Montfort was besieging Bellegarde, the King sent a

---

[20] This was during the second half of May 1210; cf. n. 15 to §145 above for the dating of events at this time.
[21] On these three lordships see n. 89 to §108. The three lords had held their fiefs as vassals of the Trencavel Viscounts of Béziers and Carcassonne, who were in turn vassals of the King of Aragon. While Simon de Montfort had taken over the Trencavel viscounties, he was recognised neither by their overlord King Peter, nor by the three vassals in question. Thus the three were attempting to establish direct fealty to the King, bypassing de Montfort's position in the feudal hierarchy, and gaining the King's protection against the crusaders (cf. note to §121 above). This would have been very advantageous to both parties, and it is perhaps surprising that, as narrated in the next section, they failed to agree terms. Roquebert (I, pp. 351–2) suggests that the three lords were anxious to avoid exposing the heretics who had taken refuge in their strongholds to the danger of expulsion or worse by the King if he gained complete control, and certainly they were themselves heretical sympathisers and had friends and relatives who were *perfecti* or *perfectae*. Peter-Roger later reached an accord with de Montfort: see §214. For the fate of Raymond of Termes see §189; and of Aimeric of Montréal, §227.
[22] Bellegarde du Razès, south-west of Montréal; described in this section and those following as a *munitio*, on which term see Appendix A.
[23] See n. 103 to §114.

request to him to make a truce with the Count of Foix, to last until Easter.[24] This was duly arranged. Bellegarde was captured soon afterwards,[25] whereupon a number of other castles were evacuated by the enemy, in fear of our Count, and even more surrendered to him. The Count then returned to Carcassonne.[26]

[151] *Siege of Minerve.*[27] In the year 1210 of the Incarnation, about the time of the feast of John the Baptist,[28] the citizens of Narbonne urged the Count to lay siege to Minerve; they would do everything in their power to help him.[29] They did this because the people of Minerve were a constant source of trouble to them, but they were moved more by a wish to further their own interests than by zeal for the Christian faith.[30] The Count told Aimeric, the lord of Narbonne, that he would lay siege to Minerve provided they genuinely intended to give him more support than they had done previously and would maintain this support until Minerve was captured. This they promised to do, and the Count at once set out with his knights to initiate the siege.

[152] When they reached Minerve, the Count pitched camp on the eastern side; one of his knights, Guy de Lucy,[31] together with some Gascons who were present,[32] encamped to the west, Aimeric of Narbonne and his fellow citizens to the north and other crusaders[33] to the south.[34] In the whole army, only the Count

---

[24] I.e. the next Easter, 1211, not Easter 1210 as G&L I, p. 153 n. 4 incorrectly assumed (see n. 15 to §145). See also §196 for attempts to extend this truce at the conference of Narbonne in January 1211, and §373 for the King's efforts to gain reconciliation for the Count of Foix at the time of the Council of Lavaur in January 1213.

[25] It was given as a fief to Guy de Lévis (who had earlier received Mirepoix): *HGL* VIII, 677–80.

[26] Presumably about the middle of June 1210.

[27] Cf. the shorter account of the siege in the *Chanson*, I, 48–9, pp. 114–18.

[28] 24 June. See n. 15 to §145 for the chronology. Peter continues his narrative of the siege without interruption, but then reverts to events which took place before or during the siege: see n. 53 to §162.

[29] Contrast the attitude of Aimeric of Narbonne at the time of the attack on Puisserguier in the autumn of 1209 (§125 above). The support of the Narbonnais would have been important both in providing additional troops at the siege and also in providing supply trains.

[30] See §488 below for later hostility of the Narbonnais to de Montfort.

[31] Guy de Lucy, a knight from Saint-Martin-sur-Ocre, near Gien east of Orléans. For his presence at the siege see n. 44 to §155 below. He remained with de Montfort in 1211, and was with him at the siege of Lavaur (see *HGL* VIII, 608–9); he received Puylaurens from de Montfort (see §230), and in 1212 went to Spain to fight in the Las Navas de Tolosa campaign: cf. also §§230, 251, and 255 below.

[32] Innocent III had on 12 November 1209 written to the Archbishop of Auch asking him to organise the recruitment of crusaders in Gascony (*Layettes* I, 899).

[33] William of Tudela (Chanson, I, 49, p. 116) mentions Frenchmen from the Ile de France and crusaders from Champagne, also Manceaux, Angevins, Bretons, Lorrains, Frisians, and Germans.

[34] Minerve is sited on a sloping plateau of rock lying between the course of two rivers flowing down from the north (the Cesse on the west side and the Brian on the east) whose confluence forms Minerve's southern limit. The rivers have cut deep gorges into the rock, so that the town is virtually surrounded by ravines and is connected to the neighbouring countryside only by a narrow isthmus at its northern end. On the western side of Minerve the Cesse flows underground for part of its course, and for much of the year the bottom of the ravine is a dry bed of pebbles and sand. The Brian is narrower, but some flow of water usually remains in the summer. For a summary of the history of Minerve and a description of its site, and further bibliography, see the booklet by J.-P. Sarret, *La Cité de Minerve*, in the CAML series (Revue Annuelle du CAML, Supplément au tome 3, 1985). Simon de Montfort would thus have encamped on the east bank of the Brian, Guy de Lucy to the west overlooking the ravine formed by the Cesse, Aimeric of Narbonne to the north of the isthmus which was defended by the castle, and the others to the south. See map 3 on p. xiii.

and Aimeric were in a position of command. The fortifications of Minerve were incredibly strong. It was surrounded by deep, natural ravines, so that none of the besieging forces would be able to bring help to each other if the need arose without great risk. On the west side the Gascons now erected a siege-engine called a 'mangonel', on which they worked unceasingly day and night. Siege-engines were built, similarly, to the north and south. Finally, on the east, in the Count's sector, a huge and most effective petrary[35] was constructed; each day twenty-one livres were spent on the pay of those employed in keeping it supplied.[36]

[153] Our men struggled for some time to bring about the capture of Minerve, until one Sunday night the defenders came out and went to the place where the petrary had been constructed. They filled baskets with oakum, dry wood, rubbish and fat and attached them with hooks to the back of the petrary. The baskets were set on fire and the flames soon rose high. It was summer and very warm, about the time of the feast of John the Baptist, as I mentioned previously. However, by God's will it happened that one of the men supplying the petrary retired just at that moment to satisfy a call of nature. He saw the fire and shouted; one of the enemy engaged in setting the fire threw a spear, and wounded him severely. The alarm was then raised in the camp and a crowd rushed to defend the petrary, so successfully and with such miraculous speed that it was out of action no longer than the time taken to fire two shots.

[154] After some days,[37] the siege-engines had seriously weakened the *castrum*. The defenders were also short of provisions,[38] so that they no longer had the will to resist. The enemy now sought peace. The lord of the place, William of Minerve, came out to parley with the Count, but even whilst they were discussing terms the Abbot of Cîteaux and Master Thedisius, whom I mentioned previously, arrived on the scene suddenly and quite unexpectedly.[39] Our Count, ever discreet

---

[35] Given the name 'Malevoisine' ('*Mala Vezina*') by William of Tudela (*Chanson* I, 48, p. 114). He describes it as '*dona e reina*', 'dame and queen', of de Montfort's petraries.

[36] We take this to be the meaning of the Latin '*trahentibus ad machinam*', 'those hauling to the engine'. Isolating Minerve from outside supplies and bombardment with heavy stones in order gradually to break down the morale of the defenders and the strength of their fortifications was the only serious tactic open to the crusaders, since the defences of Minerve largely ruled out a direct assault. On siege engines in general in the *Historia*, see n. 45 to §95 above. If Peter is accurate, the sums being expended on those employed to build and attend to the machine were very large. In §180 below Peter says that during the siege of Termes Simon de Montfort was almost bankrupt, underlining the high cost of these operations; while in September 1209 de Montfort had mentioned the expenses of hiring soldiers in a letter to Innocent (see n. 105 to §115).

[37] This will have been in the second half of July: see n. 15 to §145.

[38] As well as shortages of supplies, lack of water was almost certainly a problem for the defenders. It seems clear that the steps leading down to a well at the southern edge of the town, the only source of water, had been destroyed by the bombardment. On the other hand the crusaders will have had access to the Brian for water; cf. §158 below.

[39] On Thedisius see §70 above. It is possible that Arnold Amalric had come from Toulouse. Thedisius had been in Toulouse in the second half of June but was at Saint-Gilles on 10 July (cf. §164 below), so presumably came to Minerve from there. Roquebert (I, p. 357) suggests that both men were en route to Saint-Gilles from Toulouse to attend the council at which the position of Raymond VI was to be dealt with, but this is hard to reconcile with Thedisius' presence at Saint-Gilles as early as 10 July.

and reliant on good counsel, declared that he would take no action in regard to accepting the surrender of the *castrum* unless it had the approval of the Abbot, the appointed leader of the whole of Christ's business. Hearing this, the Abbot was greatly troubled; he wanted the enemies of Christ to die but as a monk and priest, he did not dare condemn them to death. He therefore looked for some means of inducing either the Count or William (who had offered to submit to arbitration by the Abbot on the question of surrendering) to go back on the agreement they had made to submit to arbitration, and instructed each of them to put into writing their terms for the proposed surrender; hoping that when the conditions were set down on paper one or other of them would find the proposals unacceptable and revoke his agreement to accept arbitration. When the proposals were read out in the Count's presence, he refused to accept them, and told William to go back to his *castrum* and defend it as best he could. William refused, and offered to submit completely to the Count's wishes. However, the Count still wanted to ensure that matters would turn out as the Abbot intended. The Abbot therefore ordered that William and all the inhabitants of Minerve, including the heretical believers,[40] should be allowed to live, provided they agreed to be reconciled and obey the orders of the Church; Minerve itself was to remain in the Count's hands; the perfected heretics (of whom there was a great number) would also be spared if they agreed to be converted to the Catholic faith. Robert Mauvoisin,[41] a noble and dedicated Catholic, was present. When he heard what was happening, with the implication that heretics might be freed, whereas the crusaders had come for the very purpose of destroying them, he became very concerned that once they were captured fear would lead them to promise to do whatever our side demanded. He therefore opposed the Abbot, to his face, declaring that our soldiers would not tolerate such an outcome. The Abbot replied: 'Forget your concern, I believe very few of them will accept conversion.'

[155] Then, with the holy cross leading and the Count's standard next, our soldiers entered Minerve singing the '*Te Deum*', and went into the church. After purifying the church,[42] they placed the cross of our Lord on top of the tower, and the Count's standard elsewhere. Christ had captured the place, and it was fitting that His emblem should lead the way in and be set in a position of great eminence to bear witness to a Christian victory. The Count himself did not go in at this stage.[43] After this, the venerable Abbot of les Vaux-de-Cernay, who had joined the Count in the siege and had embraced Christ's business with the

---

[40] '*Credentes hereticorum*', meaning those followers of the Cathars who had not yet received the *consolamentum*, in contrast to the *perfecti hereticorum*, mentioned a few lines below, who had. (See Peter's own account in §13.)

[41] See note to §129 above.

[42] The small church of St Stephen, built in the 11th and 12th centuries, which still stands.

[43] The proceedings seem to have followed the formal practice laid down by the Church as discussed in n. 102 to §113. The first stage was an attempt by the churchmen present to convert the heretics. Only if they failed would the heretics be handed over to the secular authority, Simon de Montfort, for punishment. Presumably therefore de Montfort remained outside Minerve until the heretics were to be handed over to him.

utmost zeal,[44] heard that a large group of heretics had gathered in a certain house and went to them. He tried to convert them to better things by offering words of peace and counsels of salvation, but they interrupted him and said with one accord: 'Why do you preach to us? We will have none of your faith. We renounce the Roman faith. You labour in vain. Neither death nor life can separate us from the beliefs we hold.'[45] Hearing this the venerable Abbot left the house and went to another house where the heretics' womenfolk were gathered, intending to preach to them, but he found the women heretics even more obstinate and determined than the men.[46]

[156] Our Count now entered Minerve and went to the place where the heretics were gathered. As a true Catholic he wished them all to win salvation and come to know the way of truth, and he began to urge them to be converted to the Catholic faith. When he could make no progress, he had them taken out of the *castrum*. There were at least a hundred and forty perfected heretics.[47] A huge pyre was made ready, and all were thrown on it – indeed there was no need for our soldiers to throw them on, since they were so hardened in their wickedness that they rushed into the fire of their own accord. Three women only were rescued, whom the noble lady the mother[48] of Bouchard de Marly snatched from the flames and reconciled to the Holy Church. So the heretics were burnt; all the other inhabitants renounced heresy and were reconciled to the Church. [157] The noble Count granted William, who had been the lord of Minerve, the revenues of certain other lands near Béziers, but a little later William renounced the allegiance he had sworn to God and the Count, abandoned them and allied himself with the enemies of the faith.[49]

[158] *Two miracles.* I must not pass over two miracles which occurred at the

---

[44] Guy's presence is also attested by a document recording the surrender to Simon de Montfort of his rights by Raymond Trencavel, the young son of Raymond-Roger. Drawn up in June 1211, this records that the complete cession of his rights was publicly made by the Trencavel heir the previous year, '*in obsidione castri de Minerba*', 'at the siege of Minerve', adding that it was in the presence of Arnold Amalric, Archbishop Berengar of Narbonne, Bishop Fulk of Toulouse, Bishop Raymond of Uzès, Thedisius '*et aliorum multorum*', 'and many others' (*HGL* VIII, 609–11). This cession must therefore have taken place towards the end of the siege after Arnold Amalric and Thedisius had arrived. Abbot Guy returned north to his abbey after the siege: see G&L I, p. 160 n. 1.

[45] Cf. Romans 8, vv. 38–9.

[46] The attractiveness of the Cathar church to women has often been remarked on; see for example the various discussions in A. Brenon, *Le Vrai Visage du Catharisme* (Portet-sur-Garonne, 2nd ed. 1994), chs. XIV–XV; *Cahiers de Fanjeaux*, vol. 24, *La femme dans la vie religieuse du Languedoc*; L. Julien, 'Le Catharisme et la femme', *Cahiers d'études Cathares* 27 (1976), pp. 29–37; R. Abels and E. Harrison, 'The Participation of Women in Languedocian Catharism', *Mediaeval Studies* 41 (1979), pp. 215–51; and J. H. Mundy, *Men and Women at Toulouse in the Age of the Cathars* (Toronto, 1990).

[47] Many of these will have been from elsewhere in the region, who had taken refuge in Minerve.

[48] Mathilde de Garlande (G&L I, p. 161 n. 2).

[49] De Montfort was prepared to allow William to continue as one of his vassals, albeit in possession of lands near Béziers. This policy of allowing the reconciliation of local lords had been followed unsuccessfully in 1209 in the case of Giraud de Pépieux (see §§125–7), and apparently more successfully with Stephen of Servian in February 1210 (see n. 14 to §143). As recorded below in §167, Aimeric of Montréal was also reconciled for a time shortly after the fall of Minerve. William of Minerve himself joined the Knights Hospitaller, but in 1216 he joined the Southern forces at the siege of Beaucaire and in 1218 fought in the defence of Toulouse against de Montfort: see *Chanson*, II, 167, p. 176, 169, p. 190, and III, 214, p. 304, and Roquebert I, pp. 358–9.

siege of Minerve. When the army first arrived to start the siege, there was a spring nearby which produced only a little water; but when our men came, Divine compassion ensured that it flowed in such abundance that it provided enough for men and horses throughout the siege, which lasted for almost seven weeks. When the army left, the flow was reduced to a very small amount as before. Such are the mighty works of God, so large the Redeemer's bounty!

[159] *The second miracle.* When the Count left Minerve, the footsoldiers set fire to all the huts which the crusaders had made out of branches and leaves. They were very dry, and caught fire at once, so that the whole valley was filled with flames as if a great city was burning. There was, however, one hut, made of leaves like the others, in which a priest had worshipped during the siege, shut in by the other huts. This was miraculously saved from the flames: indeed it showed not a trace of having been burnt. As I have heard from venerable churchmen who were there, when our men rushed to see the miracle, they found that the huts that had been consumed were separated from the hut which survived by only half a foot. Such is the immense power of the Lord!

[160] *An unparalleled miracle.* Here I will include an account of a miracle which occurred at Toulouse whilst the Count was besieging Minerve. There is in the city, near the palace of the Count of Toulouse, a church consecrated to the Blessed Virgin Mary, whose walls had recently been whitewashed.[50] One day, towards evening, crosses began to appear in great numbers on the walls of the church on all sides, which were seen as silvery, brighter than the walls themselves. They were constantly in motion, appearing suddenly then quickly vanishing. Many people saw them but could not point them out to others; a cross that someone tried to point to would disappear before he could lift his finger. These crosses appeared as flashes of all sizes, large, middling and small. This sight lasted for almost fifteen days, each evening, until almost everyone in Toulouse had seen it. To encourage the reader to give credence to this account, he should know that Fulk Bishop of Toulouse and Raymond Bishop of Uzès,[51] not to mention the Abbot of Cîteaux, legate of the Apostolic See, and Master Thedisius, all of whom were in Toulouse at the time,[52] saw the miracle and gave me a detailed account.

[161] It happened that the chaplain of the church could not see the crosses, so one day he went into the church and gave himself over to prayer, asking the Lord to deign to show him what almost everyone else could see. Suddenly he saw

---

50   The church is known as *Sancta Maria Dealbata*, or Nôtre Dame de la Dalbade, so called from its whitewashed walls (Latin *dealbare*, to whitewash), which had always distinguished it. It lies about 500 metres north-west of the site of the Château Narbonnais. It had been completely rebuilt in 1164–72, but was destroyed in a fire in February 1442, and replaced by a new church consecrated in 1455 which in turn was replaced by the present church, finished in 1544–45.

51   Raymond III, Bishop of Uzès to the west of Avignon, 1208–12. He had come with Arnold Amalric and Thedisius to Minerve (see n. 44 to §155). He became a legate and was certainly acting as such by April 1211 when he was asked by Innocent III to take over the county of Melgueil (*PL* 216, 410). He was present at the conference of Narbonne early in 1211, when Peter refers to him as a legate (see §195 et seq. below), and acted as legate on various business in 1211 (G&M p. 80 n. 7). See also §285 (organising preaching in favour of the Crusade in the winter of 1211–12), §317 (on campaign with de Montfort in the Agenais), and §458 (present at Muret in 1213).

52   They were in Toulouse dealing with the question of Raymond VI's purification; see §§162–3 below.

innumerable crosses – not on the walls, but in the air about him, one of them larger and more prominent than the rest. Soon the large cross moved out of the church; the others followed and began to move straight towards the city gate. The priest, utterly dumbfounded, followed the crosses, and as they were moving out of the city, there appeared to him, coming towards the city, someone of awe-inspiring and noble aspect, holding an unsheathed sword. Helped by the crosses and just at the entrance to the gates, this figure then slew a huge man who was emerging from the city. The priest, almost fainting with astonishment, ran to the Bishop of Uzès, threw himself at his feet and told him the whole story.

[162] *The Count of Toulouse returns from Rome.* About this time the Count of Toulouse had returned from the Curia;[53] as I mentioned above,[54] he had gone there to see the Pope. As I described, the Pope instructed the Bishop of Riez and Master Thedisius to compel the Count to be purified, chiefly in respect of two crimes, the death of Peter of Castelnau, the papal legate, and the crime of heresy.[55] As I mentioned above in my account of the miracle at Toulouse, Master Thedisius had entered the city whilst our soldiers were besieging Minerve;[56] his purpose was to take advice from the Abbot of Cîteaux (who was in the area) on the matter of granting purification to the Count for his crimes; and also to carry out the Pope's order to grant absolution to the citizens of Toulouse according to the proper procedure of the Church, by putting them under an oath to abide by the Church's orders.[57] However, the Bishop of Toulouse had already given them

---

[53] I.e. a reference back to §139 where the Count's return was recorded. Peter now reverts to events which occurred before the end of the siege of Minerve. Peter's comment is perhaps confusing in that he has already dealt with one relevant and important event, the meeting at Pamiers (§146) which took place (in May) after Raymond's return; the phrase 'about this time', '*circa idem temporis*', is typically vague (cf. Appendix E), and Peter is simply using it as a means of reintroducing the subject of dealings with the Count. This section covers events in Toulouse between Raymond's return in March or April 1210, to Thedisius' arrival there in June.

[54] For Raymond VI's visit to Rome see §§137–9 and notes, and §146 and note.

[55] See n. 59 to §163 on the importance of these two charges.

[56] Thus Thedisius cannot have reached Toulouse until around the middle of June 1210 at the earliest (see n. 15 to §145). This also has implications for the dating of the Council of Saint-Gilles: see §164 below. The events involving King Peter, narrated above in §§146–9, occurred between the reconciliation of the city by Bishop Fulk about 25 March, and Thedisius' arrival at Minerve, probably in the latter part of that period.

[57] See §§137–9 and 146 and notes. Arnold Amalric had gone to Toulouse, probably during March 1210, after receiving Innocent's letters of 19 January 1210, inserted into the consuls' letter of July 1211 to King Peter of Aragon, (*HGL* VIII, 612–19, see n. 42(i) to §137, n. 26 to §221 and especially n. 11 to §234), and 23 January (*PL* 216, 174–6, n. 49 to §137), concerning the reconciliation of the citizens of Toulouse and Raymond VI. He was almost certainly accompanied by Bishop Raymond of Uzès, who appears to have been with him throughout the coming months. His entry into Toulouse is described by William of Tudela, *Chanson* I, 44–5, p. 108, who says that Raymond agreed to hand over to Arnold and Bishop Fulk the Château Narbonnais. The political situation in Toulouse at this time was tense, because of divisions between the 'White' and 'Black' confraternities ('*confratria candida*' and '*confratria nigra*'), groups of citizens based in the cité and the bourg respectively; these divisions are not mentioned by Peter but are referred to by William of Tudela (*Chanson* I, 47. p. 112) and by William of Puylaurens (XV) who says Bishop Fulk set up the White confraternity with the help of Arnold Amalric and that it included 'the whole city except for a few people, and some from the bourg'; dissension then arose between the *cives* (inhabitants of the cité) and the *burgenses* (inhabitants of the bourg), who set up the Black confraternity as a counter-organisation (see also §§217, 220 and notes, and for a discussion see Roquebert, I, pp. 348–9). The negotiations between the Toulousains and the legates are described in the consuls' letter. Arnold Amalric sought to negotiate the absolution of the city, but the consuls refused his initial terms and argued that only

absolution in the proper fashion and in addition had taken ten of the more important citizens as hostages and as a guarantee.[58]

[163] Once in Toulouse, Thedisius held a secret meeting with the Abbot on the question of granting purification to the Count. He was a prudent, careful man, most concerned to protect the business of the faith, and was therefore anxious to find legitimate reasons for refusing to allow the Count to be purified; he saw that if he granted purification, and the Count was able by lying and deceit to achieve it, then the Church in the area would be destroyed and the faith and Christian worship would perish. As he pondered anxiously over these problems, the Lord opened up the way for him and suggested a means of denying purification to the Count. He recalled the letter from the Pope, which included the remark: 'It is our wish that in the meantime the Count of Toulouse should carry out all our instructions.' A great many instructions had been given to the Count, to expel heretics from his lands and to refrain from imposing new road tolls, and so on, all of which he had refused to obey. However, it was necessary to avoid giving the impression that he wished to be unfair to the Count or do him any wrong, so Master Thedisius and his colleague, the Bishop of Riez, arranged a day for the Count to be offered purification at Saint-Gilles.[59]

[164] Accordingly Thedisius and the Bishop summoned the archbishops, bishops and numerous other prelates of the Church to Saint-Gilles.[60] The Count

---

Thedisius had Innocent's authority to deal with them. Eventually the consuls agreed terms, involving paying Arnold Amalric and the crusaders 1,000 livres. After 500 were paid over, further disputes broke out, but finally Bishop Fulk formally reconciled the citizens, as Peter notes in the next sentence. (The reconciliation did not last beyond the siege of Lavaur in the following spring.) William of Tudela also refers to a further preaching campaign at this time, undertaken by Fulk and Arnold Amalric, which was not successful (*Chanson*, I, 46, pp. 110–12). For the legates' actions vis-à-vis Raymond see §163 and n. 59.

[58] The ceremony of reconciliation took place towards the end of March 1210; the ten hostages were taken to Pamiers, and were released in August: again see the consuls' letter to King Peter, *HGL* VIII, 619.

[59] Peter here (it would appear naively rather than cynically) lays bare the determination of the leading prelates to ensure that, come what might, there would be no accommodation between Raymond VI and the Church. In this they were going against Pope Innocent's wishes, as revealed in the letter of 25 January 1210 to Bishop Raymond of Uzès and Thedisius (*PL* 216, 173, see n. 49 to §137 and the translation in Appendix F(iii)), containing his instructions for Raymond's case to be heard by a council following specified procedures. Innocent clearly intended to indicate that purgation would depend essentially on Raymond's ability to defend himself against the two major acusations of being a heretic, and complicity in the murder of Peter of Castelnau (the two charges noted by Peter in the preceding section and again in the next section). He does refer incidentally to his mandates to the Count on other issues ('*quem interim ea quae injuncta sibi sunt praecipimus adimplere*', 'whom [Count Raymond] in the meantime we order to fulfil the instructions given to him', expressed by Peter as '*Volumus quod comes Tolosanus interim impleat mandata nostra*', 'It is our wish that in the meantime the Count should carry out our instructions'); however, it is clear that he regards such matters as of secondary importance. By converting this incidental request into a *sine qua non* the Bishop and Thedisius created a pretext for denying Raymond a proper hearing. Hence at Saint-Gilles (§164) in August 1210 the legates maintained that Raymond's purgation on the two serious charges was inadmissable on the grounds that, having failed to carry out earlier promises on lesser matters, his purgation on the two serious charges would be worthless. For a detailed discussion see Roquebert I, pp. 367–70.

[60] The exact period during which the council met is unclear. G&L (I, p. 167 n. 2) state that it was summoned in June, and it was sitting by 10 July 1210, since an act of that date (*Layettes* I, 930) records the regulation of a dispute between Raymond VI and the Abbot of Saint-Gilles, '*in concilio apud Sanctum Aegidium*', 'at the council at Saint-Gilles'. As well as Raymond and the Abbot, Thedisius and Hugh of Riez were then present, together with 19 other bishops, including Fulk of Toulouse, Raymond of Uzès, and

of Toulouse was also present to try to purify himself by whatever means of the murder of the papal legate and the crime of heresy. On the advice of the prelates, Thedisius told the Count that purification would be denied to him because he had failed to carry out the instructions previously given to him (based on the instructions of the Pope), even though he had frequently sworn to do so. He added that it was probable, indeed quite obvious, that since the Count had failed to abide by his oath in regard to less important matters, he would find it easy, indeed he would be only too willing, to perjure himself and his accomplices in seeking purification for the enormous crimes of the murder of the legate and heresy; the Count would therefore be refused purification on these charges until he had carried out the instructions previously given to him on lesser matters. Thereupon the Count, displaying his evil nature, began to weep. Thedisius knew that his tears were not tears of piety and penitence, but of evil and grief, and said to him: 'In the floods of great waters thou shalt not come nigh unto God.'[61] At once and on the spot, by the advice and common consent of the prelates, and for many justifiable reasons, the Count was again excommunicated along with all his supporters and helpers.[62]

[165] I also wish to add that before these events took place, in the preceding

---

Renaud of Béziers, and seven abbots. The act also confirms the presence of Guy Cap-de-Porc, one of the leading members of Raymond's chancery and described by William of Tudela as 'the best jurist in Christendom' (I, 58, p. 142), whom Raymond had evidently brought to help in the negotiations.

[61] Psalm 32, v. 6.

[62] The date at which this sentence was pronounced on Raymond is uncertain. The act in *Layettes* I, 930 noted above shows that the Council was in session by 10 July 1210, and it is often assumed therefore that sentence was pronounced against Raymond at about this time. However, Peter places it clearly after the siege of Minerve, which ended about 22 July, and there are reasons for thinking that the judgment may not have taken place until about a month after that. Roquebert I, pp. 370–1, reconstructs Raymond's movements in July and the first half of August, showing that he spent the period in intensive activity which involved reaching agreements with a series of lay and ecclesiastical lords with whom he had been in dispute; the agreement of 10 July with the Abbot of Saint-Gilles would have been part of this. (Some of the sources for this reconstruction are cited by G&L I, p. 169 n. 3.) The most obvious explanation of this activity would be that Raymond was seeking to deal with the lesser charges against him, perhaps because he suspected or knew that the legates were intending to raise the matter. If this was so, then the judgment against him may not have been pronounced until after the middle of August, since on 17 August Raymond was still settling disputes, in this case with the Bishop of Viviers. Peter's account of the Council is also printed in Mansi, XXII, 811. Thedisius' own account of the Council (*PL* 216, 833), written at the time of the Council of Lavaur early in 1213 (see §§367ff), is skilfully designed to put his case in the best light but agrees closely with Peter's account. How far Innocent accepted what the legates did at Saint-Gilles in 1210 is unclear: he later wrote to Raymond on 17 December 1210 (*PL* 216, 356) pointing out that the consequences of failing to fulfil his promises to the Church and to expel heretics would be severe (see n. 6 to §195), but no mention is made of the sentence of excommunication pronounced at Saint-Gilles. (Innocent was to show his scepticism of the legates' position later when he wrote to Philip Augustus in August 1211 (*PL* 216, 524) acknowledging that Raymond failed to justify himself but commenting 'we do not know if it was his fault', '*utrum per ipsum steterit ignoramus*'.) In any case, as indicated in our n. 49 to §137 above, in his instructions to Hugh and Thedisius, Innocent had reserved to himself the right to impose any final sentence on Raymond. Thus the outcome of the council at Saint-Gilles was probably still inconclusive, and matters were not further resolved until the meetings at Narbonne and Montpellier in early 1211, on which see §195 and §§211–12. The council of Saint-Gilles in 1210 is also described by William of Tudela (*Chanson*, I, 58, pp. 140–4), who wrongly dates it to after the fall of Termes on 23 November, but whose account may also suggest that matters were not settled conclusively.

winter, Master Milo, legate of the Apostolic See, died at Montpellier.[63] We shall now return to our main narrative.

[166] *Ventajou submits to the Count.* After Minerve had been taken – this was about the time of the feast of the Blessed Mary Magdalene[64] – and provided with a garrison, a certain knight, the lord of Ventajou, came to our Count and handed his *castrum* over to him.[65] However, in view of the many troubles suffered by Christians because of this place, the Count went to it and pulled down the keep.

[167] *The Count recovers Montréal.* When Aimeric, lord of Montréal, and men of the *castrum* heard that Minerve had been taken, they began to fear for their own safety and sent to the Count seeking peace on these terms: Aimeric would hand Montréal over to the Count, on condition that the Count provided him with equivalent territory, to be on level ground and unfortified.[66] The Count agreed and acceded to Aimeric's request; but afterwards[67] Aimeric, a traitor of the worst sort, broke his agreement, seceded from God and the Count, and joined the enemies of the cross.

[168] *The Count proposes to besiege Termes.* At this time a crusader of noble rank, William of Cayeux,[68] arrived from France, with some other crusaders. The Count was told that a large force of Bretons was on its way.[69] After taking counsel with his followers,[70] and trusting in God's help, the Count led his forces to besiege Termes.

[169] Whilst he was on his way, the knights in Carcassonne had some siege-engines that were in the city hauled out and placed outside the walls, ready to follow behind the Count who was pressing on to start the siege. When our enemies at Cabaret heard that the siege-engines were now lying unprotected outside Carcassonne, they sent a large force of armed men during the night with the intention of disabling them by attacking them with axes. When they arrived, our men came out from the city, and though few in number bravely attacked them and put them to flight, and pursued the fugitives for a long way in all

---

63 Milo died in December 1209; his place as legate was taken up by Thedisius, whose subordinate role to Arnold Amalric was set out in Innocent's letter of 23 January 1210 to Arnold (*PL* 216, 174–6, referred to in n. 49 to §137 and n. 57 to §162).

64 22 July, 1210.

65 On Ventajou, cf. 143 above. Its lord was Peter-Roger, who was one of the *faidits* who had retaken Montréal the previous autumn: *HGL* VII, Enquêteurs 335.

66 This was a similar arrangement to that agreed for William of Minerve (§157). The Latin translated as 'on level ground' is *planam*, which might be reflected in French *en plaine*, 'in flat open country'; the implication is presumably that such a place would be harder to defend against the crusaders than a site on a hilly ground, if Aimeric were to renege – as indeed he did.

67 See §215.

68 Cayeux is near Saint-Valery, at the mouth of the Somme: cf. G&L I, p. 170 n. 5.

69 William of Tudela mentions Bretons as being present at Termes (*Chanson*, I, 56, pp. 132–4).

70 William of Tudela, *Chanson*, I, 50–2, pp. 118–22, states that this discussion took place at Pennautier, where de Montfort was joined for three days by his wife. Robert Mauvoisin, Guy de Lévis, William of Contres, Lambert de Thury (or Crécy), and Régnier de Chauderon are mentioned as being present. The main point of discussion was who should be left in charge of Carcassonne whilst Termes was besieged, and in the end William of Contres was chosen. That it was necessary for one of de Montfort's most able and loyal followers to guard Carcassonne shows that he was not confident that it would be free from attack: see next section.

directions. Even so the fury of our adversaries continued unabated; they came back that same night, as dawn appeared, still hoping to disable the engines. Seeing this, our men came out and pursued them, even further and more energetically than before. They captured Peter-Roger, the lord of Cabaret, two or three times; but fearing for his safety he joined our men in shouting 'Montfort! Montfort!' as if he were on our side. So he escaped and fled into the hills, returning to Cabaret only after two days had elapsed.[71]

[170] The Bretons whom I mentioned above reached Castelnaudary[72] on their way to join the Count. This place was in the territory of Toulouse and still controlled by the Count of Toulouse. The townsmen refused to allow them into the town, but compelled them to pass the night in the fields and gardens; indeed the Count of Toulouse continued surreptitiously to hinder Christ's business as much as he could. When the Bretons reached Carcassonne they followed our Count on his way to besiege Termes, taking the siege-engines with them.

[171] *Description of Termes.* The *castrum* of Termes was in the territory of Narbonne,[73] five leagues from Carcassonne. It was marvellously, indeed unbelievably, strong and in human estimation appeared to be quite impregnable.[74] It was situated on the summit of a very high peak, overlooking a huge natural cliff, and surrounded on all sides by very deep and inaccessible ravines, with water flowing through them, surrounding the whole *castrum*.[75] In turn the ravines were surrounded by huge crags, so difficult to climb down from that anyone wishing to approach the walls would need first to throw himself into a ravine and then as it were 'crawl back towards heaven'. Moreover, a stone's throw from Termes itself, there was a crag on whose summit there was a small but very strong fortified tower known as 'Termenet'. So situated Termes could be approached from one side only,[76] where the rocks were lower and less inaccessible.

---

71 This episode is recounted in detail by William of Tudela, *Chanson* I, 53–5, pp. 124–30, who stresses the role of William of Contres in defending the siege engines. He adds that the raiding party from Cabaret contained over 300 men, including (as well as Peter-Roger) William Cat and Raymond Mir; and that they attempted to set the engines on fire.

72 In the plain of the Lauragais, roughly mid-way between Carcassonne and Toulouse. It was taken by the crusaders in May the following year, after being burnt by Raymond VI (see §§233–7 below), and was to be the scene of a major conflict in autumn 1211, see §§253–277.

73 This phrase, '*in territorio Narbonensi*', must mean simply in the area of, or not very far from, Narbonne since the lords of Termes rendered homage to the Trencavels both during the 12th century and at the time of the Crusade (as Peter says below), and in 1179 Alfonso II of Aragon had confirmed Termes as a fief of Roger Trencavel (*HGL* VI, 90–1). As Peter also notes below, they enjoyed a very high degree of independence.

74 Termes lies about 30km south-east of Carcassonne, in a mountainous area known as the Termenès, on the western edge of the Corbières. It was one of the most inaccessible places besieged by the crusaders; William of Tudela called it '*un castel meravilhos*', 'a wondrous castle', and it clearly impressed Peter, who will have had first hand accounts of the siege. As well as the outlying tower (Termenet, 200 m. north-west of the castle), there were dwellings crowded onto on the terraces on the southern side of the castle. For a summary of its history, description of the site, and bibliography see Lucien Bayrou, *Le Château de Termes*, Revue Annuelle du CAML, Supplément au tome 6, 1988; and M. Roquebert, *Citadelles du Vertige* (Toulouse, 1966), pp. 63–78.

75 To the east and north, the River Sou; to the west, a brook – the Caulière.

76 The south.

[172] The lord of this place was a knight named Raymond who as an old man had become given over to a reprobate mind;[77] a manifest heretic who (to describe his evil in a few words) feared not God neither regarded man.[78] So confident was he in the strength of his *castrum* that from time to time he was prepared to take up arms against the King of Aragon, the Count of Toulouse or his overlord the Viscount of Béziers. When this tyrant heard that our Count planned to besiege Termes he gathered together as many knights[79] as he could, filled the *castrum* with large stores of food and whatever else he needed for its defence and prepared to withstand the siege.

[173] *Siege of Termes.* Arriving at Termes, our Count started the siege with a modest force and was able to occupy a small part of the *castrum*. The defenders, numerous and well protected, showed no fear of our modest army; they were able to come and go freely to obtain water and whatever else they needed whilst our men watched, too weak to oppose them. Whilst this and similar events were taking place small groups of French crusaders were arriving each day to join the army. Seeing them arrive our adversaries climbed the walls and poured down abuse on our men, because the newcomers were so few and poorly armed, calling derisively: 'Fly from the sight of the army, fly from the sight of the army!' Soon afterwards crusaders began to come in large groups from France and Germany,[80] whereupon the enemy began to be afraid, stopped heaping insults on us and became less bold and confident. Meanwhile the men of Cabaret, the chief and most cruel enemies of the Christian religion at that time, patrolled the public roads near Termes night and day and whenever they came across any of our men either condemned them to a shameful death or, to show their contempt for God and our side, most cruelly put out their eyes and cut off their noses and other members, and sent them back to the army.[81]

[174] *Arrival of the Bishops of Chartres and Beauvais and many other nobles.* So matters stood when a number of noble and powerful men arrived from France; Renaud, Bishop of Chartres, Philip, Bishop of Beauvais, Count Robert of Dreux

---

77 Romans 1, v. 28.
78 Luke 18, v. 2. The family of the lords of Termes was allied by marriage to that of Minerve, and appears to have had close links with the Cathar church. Benedict of Termes, who may have been Raymond's brother, was in the Cathar party which took part in the colloquium at Montréal in 1207 (see §26 above), and he later became Cathar bishop of the Razès, and took refuge at Quéribus in 1229 (Roquebert IV, p. 176). The family had a history of disputes with the Abbey of Lagrasse. Many Cathars seem to have taken refuge in Termes at the time of the siege, including William of Roquefort, brother of the Bishop of Carcassonne, and their mother (cf. §185 below).
79 From Aragon, Catalonia and Roussillon, according to the *Chanson* I, 56–7, pp. 132–40.
80 William of Tudela mentions Germans, Bavarians, Saxons, Frisians, Manceaux, Angevins, Normans, Bretons, Longobards (i.e. southern Italians), Lombards, Gascons and Provençales (*Chanson*, I, 56, pp. 132–4).
81 Cf. the mutilations carried out by Giraud de Pépieux (§127 above) and by Simon de Montfort at Bram (§142). The ability of those based at Cabaret to harry the crusaders and their supply lines underlines again the difficulty of de Montfort's position: the assault on Termes had required him to devote most of his available forces to it, and left the rest of his conquests exposed. Even then the successful pursuit of the siege of Termes was heavily reliant on a continuing flow of fresh crusaders from the north to replace those who left, often after fulfilling only the minimum forty days' service required to obtain the appropriate indulgences: cf. §§181, 184. and 187 below.

and also the Count of Ponthieu.[82] They were accompanied by a substantial force of crusaders whose arrival greatly cheered the Count of Montfort and the whole army. It was hoped that strong action would result from the arrival of these powerful men, and that they would grind down the enemies of the Christian faith with a strong hand and a stretched out arm.[83] But He who puts down the mighty and gives grace to the humble, through some secret design known only to Himself, wished nothing great or glorious to be achieved by their hand. As far as human reasoning can determine, the Just Judge so acted either because they were not worthy to be the instrument for the great and worshipful God to do great and wonderful things; or because if great men were to perform any great deed it would be ascribed entirely to human power, and not Divine. So, the Heavenly Disposer thought it better to keep that victory for the humble, so that by winning through them a glorious triumph He might give glory to His own great name.[84] Meanwhile our Count had siege-engines erected of the kind known as petraries. These bombarded the outer wall of Termes,[85] whilst our men laboured day by day on the siege.

[175] *The Archdeacon of Paris.* Present in the army was a venerable man of high honour, William the Archdeacon of Paris. Inspired by zeal for the Christian faith, he had dedicated himself totally and devotedly to the service of Christ. He preached every day, organised collections to contribute to the cost of maintaining the siege-engines and carried out other similar and necessary duties with great enthusiasm. He frequently led large groups of crusaders to a wood and had them gather large quantities of timber for the engines. One day our men were trying to erect an engine near the walls but were prevented by a deep ravine. This man of steadfast purpose and incomparable zeal, in the spirit of wisdom and courage[86] found the solution needed to overcome this obstacle; he led the crusaders to the wood, instructed them to take back a huge quantity of timber, and had them fill the ravine with wood, earth and stones thus providing a level place for our men to erect the engine. Since I cannot describe in full all the planning, care and effort the Archdeacon devoted to the siege, or the burden of work he undertook, suffice it to say that to him more than anyone, save God alone, must be ascribed the unceasing and dedicated enthusiasm brought to the siege and the victorious outcome. He was a man outstanding in piety, wise in counsel, and of a courageous heart. Whilst the siege was in progress God granted him such grace that he was found to be most expert in all things needed for its success; he taught the smiths, he instructed the carpenters, he excelled every craftsman in showing what

---

[82] Renaud, Bishop of Chartres 1182–1217; Philip, Bishop of Beauvais 1175–1217; Robert, Count of Dreux 1184–1218 and brother of the Bishop of Beauvais; and William, Count of Ponthieu, 1192–1221. See G&L I, notes on pp. 176–7. Bishops Philip of Beauvais and William of Ponthieu came south on crusade again in 1215: see §550.

[83] Psalm 136, v. 12.

[84] Cf. Psalm 96, v. 8.

[85] The castle of Termes had an inner and outer ring of walls, but in this case Peter is probably referring to the walls of the outlying bourg, on the southern side of the castle, i.e. the '*burgum castri*' referred to in §176 below.

[86] Cf. Isaiah 11, v. 2.

had to be done to further the siege.[87] As already described, he arranged for the ravines to be filled and again when it was necessary, had the high hills made level with the deep valleys.[88]

[176] *Attack on the outer bourg.*[89] So the siege-engines were set up close to the *castrum* and employed for some days in hurling missiles against the wall. As soon as our men saw that the outer wall had been weakened by the continuous bombardment of stones, they armed themselves with the intention of taking the outer bourg by a frontal attack. Our opponents observed this and as our men drew near to the wall, set fire to the outer bourg and withdrew to a higher bourg. However, as soon as our men entered the outer bourg the enemy came out to meet them and quickly drove them out in flight.

[177] Such was the state of affairs when our men realised that their attempts to capture the *castrum* were being severely impeded by the tower of Termenet which I described above, and which was defended by a body of knights, and they began to consider how they might capture it. They therefore set guards at the base of the tower (which, as I mentioned, was built on the summit of a high crag), so as to prevent the men in the tower having access to Termes itself or those in the *castrum* providing help to the tower if need arose. After a few days our men succeeded, with great difficulty and at great risk, in erecting a siege-engine of the type known as a 'mangonel'[90] in an inaccessible place between Termes and the tower. The defenders in their turn erected a mangonel and bombarded our engine with huge stones, but could not knock it down. Thus our mangonel was able to continue bombarding the tower. The defenders now realised that they were besieged and could expect no help from their comrades in Termes, and one night in fear for their safety they sought protection in flight, leaving the tower empty. The guard at the base of the tower was being mounted by the sergeants of the Bishop of Chartres; they occupied the tower as soon as they saw what had happened, and erected the Bishop's standard on the roof.

[178] Whilst this was going on, our petraries on another side of the *castrum* kept up a continuous bombardment of the walls. When our adversaries – who were admittedly courageous and astute – saw that the engines were weakening any part of the walls, they at once built a barrier of wood and stones inside at the weak point. The outcome was that whenever our men were able to force their way inside the walls at any place, the barrier built by the enemy prevented them from going any further. As space does not permit me to describe every detail of the siege, I shall simply say that every time the defenders lost any part of their wall they built another wall inside in the manner I have described.

---

87 William took part in the Crusade from 1210–1214. His role at the siege of Termes (on which see also §180) was clearly vital. He appears frequently in the *Historia*; he was an expert in siege warfare and assisted at various sieges (see §§326, 330, 342, 351), and helped in recruiting crusaders in Northern France (§§285, 306, 310, 508). In 1212 after the siege of Moissac Simon de Montfort described him as a vice-legate: see n. 109 to §342. In §366 he is reported to have refused the bishopric of Béziers, and he was one of the envoys to the Pope after the Council of Lavaur (§398).

88 Cf. Isaiah 40, v. 4.

89 '*Primum burgum*', which we give as 'outer bourg'.

90 See n. 45 to §95 above.

[179] Meanwhile our men erected a mangonel in an inaccessible place at the foot of a crag near the wall, which inflicted no slight damage on our enemies when it was put to use. Our Count sent a force of three hundred sergeants and five knights to defend the mangonel; there was great concern for its safety, because our men knew that our opponents would spare no effort to destroy an engine that was causing them so much trouble, and also because the difficulty of access to the mangonel would make it impossible for the main army to help those guarding it in a emergency. One day a force of enemy soldiers, up to eighty in number, protected by shields, rushed out to destroy the mangonel, followed by a huge number of other men carrying wood, fire and other materials for setting light to the mangonel. When they saw the enemy coming the three hundred sergeants guarding the mangonel were seized with panic and fled, leaving only the five knights to maintain the defence. What more? When the enemy drew near all the knights fled save one, William of Ecureuil.[91] This knight, seeing the enemy approaching, began with great difficulty to climb over the crag to meet them; they made a concerted rush against him, and he defended himself vigorously. They saw that they could not capture him, and instead thrust him with their spears onto the mangonel, and threw dry wood and fire after him. This courageous man at once rose up and dispersed the fire, so that the mangonel was unharmed. Once again he started to climb up to face the enemy; once again they thrust him back and threw fire on him. Again he rose up and went for the enemy; four times in all they hurled him onto the mangonel. Finally our men realised that since no one from our side could reach our knight to help him, he would be unable to escape; they therefore went to another part of the wall and made as if to mount an attack, whereupon the enemy soldiers harassing William retired into the *castrum*. William, albeit exhausted, escaped alive. His incomparable courage had ensured that the mangonel was unharmed.

[180] At this time the noble Count of Montfort was beset by extreme poverty,[92] to the extent that he was very often even short of bread, and had nothing to eat. Frequently – I have it on sure authority – when a meal-time was at hand he would deliberately absent himself, ashamed to return to his tent, since it was the time to eat and he did not even have bread. The Venerable Archdeacon William organised fraternities and made collections,[93] as I mentioned above. Everything he collected he spent conscientiously on the siege-engines and whatever else was

---

[91] See also §427 below for this knight, who was again amongst the crusaders in 1214.

[92] Here Peter refers to the high costs of mounting a campaign of this sort and the drain on Simon de Montfort's resources which it created. The point is reflected by William of Tudela in the *Chanson*, I, 50, p. 118, who says of Termes that '*despendra el seti mot marc e mant tornes*', 'many marks and many deniers would be spent during the siege'. De Montfort was by now presumably raising at least some revenues from his new domains, and Peter states a few lines below that he was drawing on local sources of supply. Even so the costs of hiring men, building the siege engines, and maintaining supplies evidently outweighed his income. Cf. the costs of the siege of Minerve, §152 above, and de Montfort's complaint to the Pope about the cost of hiring soldiers, n. 105 to §115.

[93] These fraternities seem to have been specially organised groups whose purpose was to provide food and supplies for the crusaders; cf. G&M, p. 75 n. 3.

needed to further the siege: truly an admirable tax-gatherer, a virtuous plunderer!

[181] So matters stood when our opponents ran out of water, for our soldiers had cut off the approaches to the *castrum* and they could not get out to draw water.[94] Lack of water produced lack of courage and of the will to resist.[95] What more? They started to parley with us, and sought to negotiate peace on these terms: Raymond, the lord of Termes, promised to hand it over to the Count provided the Count allowed him to retain all his other possessions; also the Count was to return Termes to him after Easter.[96] Whilst discussions on these proposals were going on, the Bishops of Chartres and Beauvais, Count Robert of Dreux and the Count of Ponthieu proposed to leave the army.[97] The Count begged them to stay a little longer to carry on the siege, and everyone else added their pleas; but as they could not be diverted from their purpose, the noble Countess of Montfort[98] threw herself at their feet and begged them passionately not to turn their backs on the Lord's business in the hour of such great need, and to give help at this time of crisis to the Count of Jesus Christ, who every day was exposing himself to mortal danger on behalf of the Catholic Church. The Bishop of Beauvais, Count Robert and the Count of Ponthieu were unmoved by the Countess's prayers, but said that they would leave the next morning and were quite against staying even for one more day. The Bishop of Chartres, however, promised to remain with the Count for a short time longer.

[182] *The Count accepts proposals for a truce.* The Count realised that with the departure of these three leaders he would be left virtually alone, and was driven by plain necessity, however unwillingly, to consent to the terms for an agreement offered by our adversaries. What else is there to say? Talks were reopened with the enemy and the agreement was confirmed.[99] The Count at once instructed Raymond to leave his *castrum* and surrender it; the latter refused to leave that day, but gave a firm undertaking to hand the place over early next morning. That Divine justice willed and foresaw this delay is most clearly demonstrated by subsequent events; for God, the most just Judge, did not wish that the man who had so grossly wronged His Holy Church (and was ready to do still worse, if he could) should escape immune and unpunished after a life so dedicated to cruelty, since – to say nothing of his other crimes – thirty years and more had now passed

---

94 This was probably in the first half of October 1210. The siege began early in August, and the Bishops of Chartres and Beauvais seem to have arrived a little later (§174). Assuming that they remained at Termes for about six weeks (although it may have been somewhat less: see §184), it was probably about the beginning of October that they were proposing to leave, and Peter says below that this was during the negotiations with Raymond of Termes.

95 I.e. Easter (3 April) 1211.

96 I.e. Easter (3 April) 1211.

97 This would presumably have been because they regarded their proper period of service, forty days and nights, as having been fulfilled, although Peter says below, §184, that in fact they had not even served for this length of time.

98 See §107 for Countess Alice. According to William of Tudela (*Chanson* I, 50–1, pp. 118–22) she had been present at the discussions at which it had been decided to attack Termes: cf n. 70 to §168 above.

99 The negotiations may have been conducted by Guy de Lévis, Simon's Marshal, who is identified in §185 below as Simon's spokesman.

(as I have heard from trustworthy witnesses) during which the Holy sacraments were never celebrated in the church at Termes.[100]

[183] The following night, there was a sudden intense rainstorm, as if the sky had broken apart and the floodgates of heaven had opened.[101] So great was the downpour that our enemies, who had long suffered from an extreme shortage of water, and had for this reason proposed to surrender to us, now found themselves with an abundant supply. Our harp is turned to mourning, the grief of our enemies is changed to joy![102] They at once became arrogant and recovered their courage and the will to resist. Their cruelty, their eagerness to oppose us, increased, the more so because they dared to think the storm was a sign that some Divine aid had come to them in their hour of need. What a vain and unjust presumption, to boast of help from Him whose worship they despised, whose faith they had rejected! They said indeed that God did not wish them to surrender; all this, they asserted, had been done for their benefit – but in truth Divine justice had arranged it for their downfall.

[184] *Departure of the nobles.* So matters stood when the Bishop of Beauvais, Count Robert and the Count of Ponthieu left the army and returned home, leaving Christ's business unfinished and indeed in a most critical and dangerous position. If I may be allowed to record what they allowed themselves to do[103] they left without completing their forty days' service. Indeed the papal legates, aware that most of the crusaders were somewhat lukewarm in their enthusiasm for the campaign and perpetually anxious to go home, had laid it down that the indulgence promised to the crusaders by the Pope would not be granted to anyone who failed to complete at least one full period of forty days in the service of Jesus Christ.

[185] At first light the Count sent to Raymond, the lord of the *castrum*, ordering him to hand it over as he had promised on the previous day. Raymond, however, who now had water in plenty instead of the shortage which had produced his willingness to surrender and who also saw that almost the whole strength of the army was leaving, changed his mind and wormed his way out of his undertaking. However, two knights in Termes who had on the previous day given firm promises of surrender to the Count's Marshal[104] did come out and give themselves up to the Count. When the Marshal, who had been instructed by the Count to go in person to parley with Raymond, returned and reported what the latter had said, the Bishop of Chartres (who wanted to leave next day) urged that the Marshal should be sent again to Raymond and offer a truce on whatever

---

100   There was a chapel within the castle of Termes, and a church in the outer bourg: an act from December 1163 (*HGL* V, 1277–9), which records the division of lordship over Termes in the form of an agreement between Raymond V of Toulouse and Raymond Trencavel, mentions the building of a new church outside the castle in a lower bourg ('*ecclesiam novam in barrio de Terminio*') to replace the chapel ('*locus ecclesie veteris de castro*'). Peter may be referring to either or both.

101   Genesis 7, v. 11.

102   Cf. Job 30, v. 31 and Jeremiah 31, v. 13.

103   Apparently Peter is reluctant to criticize such eminent personages but feels he must.

104   Guy de Lévis, who may well have been with de Montfort since 1209 (see §82, n. 11); he had received Mirepoix as a fief in 1209 (§116, n. 108; see also §357).

terms were acceptable to him, so long as he agreed to hand over the *castrum*. In the hope that it would help in persuading Raymond to agree, the Bishop further advised that the Marshal should take with him the Bishop of Carcassonne,[105] who was with the army, because he was a native of the area and was known to the murderous lord of Termes; moreover the Bishop's mother – a heretic of the worst sort – was in the *castrum* as was his brother William of Roquefort whom I have already mentioned.[106] William was a most cruel man, who strove to excel others in hostility to the Church. The Bishop and the Marshal again approached Raymond. Arguments were succeeded by prayers, prayers by threats, as they strove energetically to persuade the tyrant to accept their advice and surrender himself to our Count, and indeed to God, on the basis I described above. Previously the Marshal had found Raymond obstinate and determined in his hostility; now the Bishop and the Marshal found him even more obstinate. He refused even to allow the Bishop to speak privately with his brother. With nothing achieved, the two returned to the Count. As yet, our people did not clearly see that (as I have already said)[107] Divine goodness had ordained matters in this way, the better to forward the interests of His Church. [186] *Departure of the Bishop of Chartres.* At first light next day the Bishop of Chartres left. The Count left the army and went with him, intending to follow him for a short distance. When he was some little way from the army, a large armed band of our enemies came out of Termes intending to demolish one of our mangonels. The shouts of our army induced the Count to return. He reached the enemy soldiers who were pulling down the mangonel and, quite alone, compelled them willy-nilly to return to the *castrum*. He pursued them with great courage, and put them to flight not without peril to his own life – the act of a courageous leader and a valiant man.

[187] The Count saw that with the departure of these nobles, that is the Bishops and the Counts, he was virtually alone and almost deserted.[108] He was now extremely anxious and concerned, and did not know what to do. He did not want to abandon the siege, but could not stay where he was any longer; he had many well-armed opponents, but few allies of whom most were ill-equipped, since, as I have said, the whole strength of the army had gone with the Bishops and the Counts. Besides, Termes was still very strong and it was felt that it could be taken only by a strong and numerous force. Moreover, winter was approaching and was usually very severe in that region; Termes was situated in a mountainous area (as I have already described),[109] and consequently, what with heavy rainfall, violent winds and an abundance of snow, it was an unusually cold and almost uninhabitable place.

[188] Whilst the Count was thus troubled and distressed and at a loss what to

---

[105] Bernard-Raymond of Roquefort, Bishop 1208–11; see nn. 29–30 to §130 for details of him and his family.
[106] He had murdered the Abbot of Eaunes in the previous year: see §130 above.
[107] §182.
[108] Cf. the similar phrase used in §115 about the position in the autumn of the previous year; and see also §442 where it is used again.
[109] §171.

do, one day a contingent of crusaders on foot came on the scene from Lorraine.[110] The Count was delighted by their arrival and strengthened the siege. With the industrious help of Archdeacon William, our men regained their spirits and began to work hard on everything concerned with the siege. At once the siege-engines, which had previously had little success, were brought nearer the walls. Our men worked on them continuously and did no little damage to the walls. In some strange way, by the incomprehensible dispensation of God, a marvellous thing happened; the engines, which had achieved little or nothing whilst the nobles and bishops were with the army, began – now that they had gone – to fire with an accuracy that suggested the Lord himself was aiming each stone. In truth, this was the Lord's doing and was marvellous in our eyes.[111]

[189] After our men had spent some time working on the machines and had succeeded in weakening a large section of the keep, one day, the feast of St Cecilia,[112] the Count had a trench carefully dug out and covered with hurdles, which would allow sappers to approach the wall and dig under it. The Count spent the whole day on the preparation of the trench without breaking off to eat, and as night approached – it was the eve of the feast of St Clement[113] – he returned to his tent. The enemy in Termes, with the intervention of Divine clemency and the help of the Blessed Clement, were seized with fear to the point of utter desperation.[114] They at once ran out, seeking to escape. The men of our army saw what was happening, raised a great shout, and began to run hither and thither in order to capture the fugitives. I need delay no longer – many escaped, some were captured alive, even more were slain. A crusader from Chartres, a poor man and a commoner, had joined his comrades in pursuit of the fleeing enemy. By a Divine judgment, he captured Raymond, the lord of Termes, who had found a hiding place, and handed him over to the Count. The Count treated his capture as an unexpected gift; he did not kill him but had him confined to a dungeon in the keep at Carcassonne where for many years he paid a wretched penalty worthy of his crimes.[115]

[190] *A miracle.* There was one event at the siege of Termes which I must not pass over. One day the Count arranged for a small siege-engine, commonly

---

110 Latin 'a Lothoringia pedites peregrini'. They probably arrived in the second half of October, and spent some time at the siege before the collapse of resistance on 22/23 November (see §189 below).
111 Psalm 118, v. 23.
112 'In festo sancte Cecilie', 22 November 1210.
113 'In vigilia . . . sancti Clementis', the night of 22–23 November 1210.
114 In the *Chanson* (I, 57, p. 138) William of Tudela says the decision to abandon Termes was prompted by a severe epidemic of dysentery. Clearly referring to the storm described by Peter in §183, he says: 'There came a great rain . . . which changed into a great deluge, and it was this that caused their distress; for from this water they made a great store in casks and vessels, and used it to make bread and put it in their food. Then a great dysentery attacked them . . .'.
115 E. Martin-Chabot notes that the two prose versions of the *Chanson* suggest that Raymond was captured because he went back to the castle having forgotten something (*Chanson* I, p. 139 n. 3). He died at Carcassonne some three years later. His sons Oliver and Bernard became *faidits* and fought the crusaders for many years. Oliver finally submitted in 1240 and went to the Holy Land. Termes was later in 1213 given by Simon de Montfort to Alan de Roucy (Molinier 181 and 185), on whom see n. 58 to §279.

known as a 'cat',[116] to be brought up to help in undermining the wall. The Count was standing near the engine and speaking with a knight. As a gesture of familiarity he placed his arm on the knight's shoulder, when a huge stone, thrown down from the enemy's mangonel and falling from a height with great force, struck the knight on the head. Through God's wonderful power the Count, though he had been embracing the knight, escaped unharmed. The knight received a mortal blow and died.

[191] *Another matter worthy of note.* Another time, on a Sunday, the Count was in his tent celebrating Mass. An incident occurred which demonstrated God's provident mercy. The Count was standing to hear the Mass, and by Divine intervention a sergeant was standing right behind him. Suddenly a bolt from the enemy ballista[117] struck the sergeant and killed him. No one should doubt that this was the result of Divine goodness; clearly in arranging that the sergeant should stand behind the Count and take the force of the missile, God's intention was to preserve the vigorous athlete of His Holy Church. [192] After the capture of Termes, on the eve of the feast of St Clement, and its occupation by our troops, the Count led his forces to a *castrum* named Coustaussa.[118] Finding it deserted he went on to another *castrum* named Puivert, which surrendered within three days.[119]

---

[116] Latin '*machinam . . . que lingua vulgari "catus" dicitur*'. See n. 47 to §96.

[117] A military engine resembling a large crossbow. See Bradbury, *The Medieval Siege*, pp. 250–2.

[118] Coustaussa lies on the south-western edge of the Razès, about 25km west of Termes, not far from Couiza where the River Sais joins the Aude. William of Tudela also says that the fall of Termes provoked the abandonment of 'all the better castles' ('*tuit li melhor castel*') (*Chanson*, I, 58, p. 140). See §280 for Coustaussa's later secession.

[119] Puivert (or Puy-Verd) is sited on top of a knoll which overlooks the valley of the Blau. It lay at the southern edge of an area known as the Kercorb (also spelt Quercorb or Chercorb). In the early 13th century it was occupied by Bernard de Congost, whose family had strong associations with Catharism. A later Inquisition deposition by Bernard's daughter Gallard de Congost in the Doat collection reveals that Bernard's wife Alpais (who was the daughter of William-Roger of Mirepoix and Fournier de Péreille) received the *consolamentum* in 1208 when she fell seriously ill. See Griffe, *LC*, p. 151; Roquebert I, pp. 365–6; and for a summary of the history of Puivert, Jean Tisseyre, *Le Château de Puivert*, Revue annuelle du CAML, Supplément au tome 1, 1982. No details are known about the siege of 1210, but Puivert was by 1213 in the hands of Lambert of Thury, on whom see n. 48 to §248.

[VIII. §§193–212, winter 1210 – spring 1211: *Simon de Montfort in the Albigeois, reoccupies many* castra *– meeting of the King of Aragon, Simon de Montfort, Count Raymond VI of Toulouse and the papal legates at Narbonne, January 1211 – discussion of the position of Raymond VI and of Raymond-Roger of Foix – iniquities of the Count of Foix – Peter of Aragon accepts de Montfort's homage – further meeting at Montpellier to discuss the position of Raymond VI.*]

[193] The Count now determined to advance into the diocese of Albi, to recover the *castra* which had seceded from his lordship.[1] He reached the *castrum* known as Castres, whose inhabitants handed the place over to him and submitted to his will. He then went to Lombers, which I have referred to previously.[2] He found this *castrum* empty of men but full of supplies; the knights and inhabitants of the place had taken flight in fear of the Count, since they had betrayed him. The Count at once garrisoned the place, and retains[3] control of it until this day. I need say little more – almost all the *castra* in the territory of Albi to the south of the River Tarn were recovered by the noble Count of Christ in this same period.[4]

[194] *Treachery of the Count of Toulouse towards the Count of Montfort.* During this period the Count of Toulouse came to a *castrum* near Albi to hold a meeting with our Count.[5] When our Count arrived he found his enemies ready to seize him; the Count of Toulouse had brought with him some traitors of the worst sort who made no secret of their hostility to our Count. Our Count said to the Count of Toulouse: 'What is the meaning of this? You have called me to a meeting and brought with you men who have betrayed me.' The Count of Toulouse replied: 'I did not bring them.' Hearing this, our Count wanted to take the traitors captive, but the Count of Toulouse pleaded with him on their behalf and would not let them be taken. It was from this time that the Count's hostility to the Church and our Count began to be rather more openly displayed.

[195] *Conference at Narbonne.* A few days later the King of Aragon, the Count of Montfort and the Count of Toulouse met at Narbonne for a conference.[6] Also

---

1   Castres and Lombers had rebelled late in 1209: see §§132–3 above. The march northwards into the southern Albigeois probably took place in December 1210.
2   §§112, 117, 133.
3   The use of the present tense clearly implies that this section was written before the death of Simon de Montfort and not revised subsequently. (See Introduction p. xxv for comment on date of composition.)
4   The *Chanson* (I, 58, p. 140), which makes it clear that the fall of Termes had a serious effect on the morale of the southerners, also mentions the retaking of the Albigeois without any sieges, and adds that an unusually clement winter favoured this campaign. The Albigeois north of the Tarn remained largely under the control of Raymond VI; cf. above, §118. It was not occupied by the crusaders until the middle of 1211: see §237 below.
5   The meeting may have been at Ambialet on the Tarn, early in 1211 (G&L I, p. 195 n. 2). Peter now resumes his narrative of diplomatic events concerning Raymond VI, last discussed in §164, when Raymond VI's renewed excommunication by the legates at Saint-Gilles in July 1210 was recorded. This meeting with Simon de Montfort probably indicates that Raymond was trying to reach an understanding with him, prior to the meeting at Narbonne with the legates, described in the next section.
6   The *Chanson* (I, 59, p. 144) dates this to 'about the time of the feast of St Vincent', 22 January 1211.

attending were the Bishop of Uzès and the venerable Abbot of Cîteaux, who, after God, was foremost in promoting the business of Jesus Christ. The Bishop of Uzès, who was named Raymond, had long devoted himself to the business of the faith and done everything in his power to help it; at this time he shared with the Abbot of Cîteaux the office of papal legate in charge of that business.[7] Also at the meeting were Master Thedisius, mentioned above,[8] and many other wise and virtuous men. At the conference discussions took place on the position of the Count of Toulouse – who might have enjoyed extremely favourable and merciful treatment had he been willing to listen to wise counsel. The Abbot of Cîteaux proposed that, provided he expelled the heretics from his territories, the Count of Toulouse should retain all his demesnes and properties whole and unimpaired; he should also keep the feudal rights he enjoyed in the *castra* of other heretics subject to his lordship; finally that these rights in a quarter or even a third of the *castra* of heretics who were not under the Count's lordship should be transferred to his control – the Count himself estimated that there were at least five hundred of these. But God was concerned for the future of His Church; the Count rejected this most generous offer and so made himself unworthy of any favour or kindness.[9]

The conference was called to discuss three main items of business: the position of Raymond VI (this section), that of Raymond-Roger of Foix (§196), and the relationship of Simon de Montfort and King Peter of Aragon (§210 below). Raymond's position after the council of Saint-Gilles in July 1210 was probably still ambiguous (see n. 62 to §164) and the meeting at Narbonne was arranged as yet another attempt to settle it. It is clear that both Raymond VI and Peter of Aragon still believed that a settlement was possible. Innocent had prepared the way by writing to Raymond and the Counts of Foix and Béarn on 17 December 1210 urging them to support de Montfort or risk being counted as supporters of heretics (*HGL* VIII, 601); and seperately to Raymond on the same day ('*Non decet tanti*', *PL* 216, 356) warning him of the consequences of failing to meet the Church's demands and expel the heretics ('*exterminatoribus eorum terras ipsorum noveris esse concessas divino judicio possidendas*', i.e. the heretics' lands will be allowed to fall into the possession of the crusaders, under the doctrine of *exposition en proie*).

[7]   On Raymond of Uzès and his position as a legate, cf. §§160 above and 212 and 285 below.

[8]   §§70, 137, 154, 160, 164, etc.

[9]   William of Tudela gives no details of these terms in his account of the meeting at Narbonne (*Chanson* I, 59, p. 144), simply saying that nothing was achieved worth even a wild rose bush ('*aiguilent*'). Superficially and as related by Peter the terms offerred to Raymond seem attractive, but this raises two questions: why, if they were so generous, did Raymond reject them, bearing in mind all the attempts made in the previous year to reach a settlement and that de Montfort's position was now clearly much stronger; and why were the terms then offerred at Montpellier a few weeks later so much worse (see §§210–12 and notes)? It may be that Peter's account of the terms is incomplete and that there were elements in them which made them less attractive than they appear, although Griffe, *Croisade*, p. 51, argues that there is no reason to doubt their accuracy. However, careful consideration suggests that even as presented by Peter they were probably unacceptable to Raymond. They would have required him to do what he had always been unable and unwilling to do, namely to attack his own vassals, and to persecute heretics, and he probably saw that it would have been impossible to meet these terms without support from the crusaders, which would require him to allow crusading forces into his territories and seriously weaken his independence, as well as undermining his relationships with his vassals; considerations of loyalty and honour may also have counted heavily with him. Roquebert (I, pp. 374–5) also argues that Arnold Amalric would not seriously have expected Raymond to accept the terms; on the contrary he was seeking to manoeuvre Raymond into a position where he, rather than the legates, appeared to be in the wrong. This interpretation is perhaps borne out by what happened when the next attempt at negotiation took place very shortly afterwards at Montpellier: see §211. Cf. also §163, and the attitude of the legates at the time of the Council of Saint-Gilles the previous summer.

[196] The conference also discussed the restoration of peace between the Church and its most monstrous persecutor, the Count of Foix.[10] At the request of the King of Aragon it was agreed that if the Count swore to abide by the instructions of the Church and not to attack the crusaders, especially the Count of Montfort, in future, then the latter would give back all the territories of the Count of Foix which he was then holding with the sole exception of a *castrum* named Pamiers.[11] There were a number of arguments against allowing the Count to regain control of this place, which I will record later.[12] But the eternal God, from whom nothing is hidden and who knows all that the future holds, did not wish the many exceedingly barbarous actions of this, His most monstrous enemy, to go unavenged; knowing what future ills would come from the proposed agreement, in His great and unsearchable judgment,[13] He hardened the heart of the Count of Foix so that he rejected the proposals for peace. Assuredly God was exercising His deep concern for His Church, for in rejecting the treaty Her enemy was, by his own actions, providing justification in advance for the punishment he was to suffer for the mischief he later caused. I must add that the King of Aragon (who was overlord of most of the territories held by the Count of Foix) sent knights to guard in the *castrum* of Foix and promised in the presence of the Bishop of Uzès and the Abbot of Cîteaux that no harm would come to Christianity in the territory of Foix; also in their presence he swore that if ever the Count of Foix chose to abandon the communion of the Holy Church and his friendship with the Count of Montfort and the service he owed him, he would personally hand the *castrum* of Foix itself over to our Count immediately the legates and our Count requested him to do so.[14] Furthermore, he gave our Count a letter-patent setting out the details of this undertaking. I myself saw this document, held it and examined it carefully, so I can bear witness to the truth.[15] It will, however, become clearer than daylight how poorly the King kept his promise and so lost his reputation with our side.[16]

[197] *On the barbarity and malice of the Count of Foix.* The context demands,

---

[10] I.e. the conversion into a permanent peace of the truce agreed the previous summer, on which see §150.
[11] Pamiers had been handed over to de Montfort by the Abbot of Saint-Antonin at Pamiers: cf. §§116–20 above. Simon de Montfort had also taken Saverdun, Mirepoix and Preixan from Raymond-Roger in the autumn of 1209; Preixan was recovered later (§134).
[12] See §198 et seq. below.
[13] Romans 12, v. 33.
[14] King Peter of Aragon was clearly very keen that an agreement should be reached in order to prevent a further attack on one of his vassals, the Count of Foix, by the crusaders. His determination to secure a peace between de Montfort and Raymond-Roger of Foix at this time may have been in part because, along with other Christian rulers in Spain and urged on by Innocent III, he was beginning preparations to campaign against the Islamic Almohades and wanted to settle affairs in the Midi. The campaign against the Almohades was to culminate in the battle of Las Navas de Tolosa the following year (1212), a campaign in which Arnold Amalric and the Archbishop of Bordeaux were also closely involved. Simon de Montfort sent Guy de Lucy with 50 knights to support Peter in Spain in 1211 (see §255 below). See also below, §373, for King Peter's later efforts to secure the reconciliation of Raymond-Roger at the time of the Council of Lavaur in January 1213.
[15] This letter was later referred to at the Council of Lavaur in January 1213; see §381 where an excerpt is quoted.
[16] See §367 et seq. below for details.

and opportunity allows, that I should now say a little about the barbarity and malignity[17] of the Count of Foix, although I could not possibly deal adequately with a hundredth part of it. It should first be stated that he allowed heretics and their supporters to stay in his territories, and helped and encouraged them as much as he could.

[198] In Pamiers, which belonged to the Abbot and canons of St Anthony, he kept his wife and her two sisters (who were heretics), along with a crowd of other heretics.[18] These sowed their evil poison publicly and privately – against the wishes of the canons who did all they could to oppose them – and deceived the hearts of the simple.[19] He had a house built for his wife and his sisters on the canons' own property; indeed, as I have said, the canons enjoyed the overlordship of Pamiers, but the Count held it under them for life and had sworn on the Holy Eucharist not to do any violent act to the Abbot or to Pamiers itself.[20] The monastery itself is about half a mile outside Pamiers.

[199] At one time two knights, kinsmen and intimates of the Count, manifest heretics of the worst sort, whose promptings the Count followed in all matters, brought into Pamiers their mother, who was a leading heresiarch and the Count's aunt, hoping that by living there she would spread the poison of heretical superstition. The Abbot and the canons could not endure seeing such a wrong done to Christ and the Church, and had her thrown out of the place. News of this sent the Count into a frenzied rage. One of the knights who were the sons of the heresiarch came to Pamiers and in hatred of the canons took on the role of most cruel executioner; he dismembered one of them, a priest celebrating mass, on the altar of a church near Pamiers. To this day the altar is still red with the blood of the slaughtered priest. Even this did not exhaust the executioner's fury; he seized a brother from the monastery at Pamiers and tore out his eyes to show his hatred of the Christian religion and his contempt of the canons.

[200] A little later the Count went into the monastery with a crowd of mercenaries, actors and harlots.[21] He summoned the Abbot (to whom he had sworn on Christ's body that he would do him no harm, as related above) and ordered him to hand over the keys of the monastery immediately. The Abbot refused, but since he was afraid that the tyrant would take the keys by force he went into the church and placed the keys over the body of St Anthony the Martyr. It was in honour of St Anthony that the church had been founded, and his remains lay above the altar along with numerous other relics of the saints. The Count

---

[17] Latin *'crudeli malignitate et maligna crudelitate'*, literally 'cruel malignity and malign cruelty', a typical example of Peter's liking for word play.
[18] Raymond-Roger's wife was Philippa, and the best known of his sisters was Esclarmonde. For details of their heretical sympathies see §48 above, and Griffe, *LC*, pp. 152–5. At the Council of Lavaur in 1213, Peter of Aragon denied that Raymond-Roger of Foix had ever himself been a heretic, but the Council accused him of long having been a protector of heretics: see §373 and §381 below.
[19] Romans 16, v. 18.
[20] For the dispute between the Abbots of Pamiers and the Count of Foix over lordship over Pamiers referred to here, cf. §48 and §116 above.
[21] Latin *'ruptarios, mimos, et meretrices'*.

followed the Abbot; showing no respect for the church and quite disregarding the saints' relics, he shamelessly snatched the keys from above the holy martyr's remains. What more? He shut the Abbot and all the canons in the church, barred the doors and kept them there for three days, during which they had nothing to eat or drink and could not even go out to attend to the calls of nature. The tyrant meanwhile pillaged the wealth of the monastery, and to show his contempt for religion slept in the infirmary with his harlots. Finally, after three days, he led the Abbot and canons out of the church and drove them almost naked from the monastery; after which he had a herald deliver a proclamation throughout Pamiers (which, as I said, was the property of the canons) forbidding anyone to give the Abbot or the canons shelter, on pain of a most severe penalty. Surely a new kind of barbarity! A church is usually a refuge for those condemned to imprisonment or death; this author of evil had made the church a prison for the innocent! The tyrant now even pulled down a substantial part of the church of St Anthony itself; he demolished the canons' dormitory and the refectory – as I saw myself at a later date[22] – and used the stones to build a castle in Pamiers.

[201] To add to the list of evils done by this traitor let me record a further incident, well worth relating. There is a church[23] on the summit of a hill near the monastery. One day the canons were visiting the church – as it was their custom to do once a year – and carrying in solemn procession the body of their patron the venerable martyr Anthony, when the Count, who happened to be out riding, chanced to come across them. Showing no proper regard for God or the holy martyr or the religious procession, the Count refused to display even the outward signs of respect and did not trouble to dismount; instead he passed ostentatiously by with his head held high in his customary arrogant manner. The venerable Abbot of Mont Sainte-Marie, of the Cistercian order (one of the twelve preachers mentioned earlier in this history),[24] had come to the ceremony to preach and had joined in the procession. Seeing the Count's behaviour he called out after him and said: 'Count! Count! You show no respect to your overlord, the holy martyr. Know that you will lose the lordship of this town which you hold merely as his vassal, and that you will live to see yourself dispossessed of it by his power.' The holy man's prophecy was to come true, as the history of later events will very clearly show.[25] The Abbot of Pamiers – a man whose account could be trusted, a man of great piety and conspicuous virtue – personally told me of these barbarous actions of the Count, and those that now follow.

[202] *Another example of the Count's malice.* On another occasion the Count went with a crowd of mercenaries to the monastery of Sainte-Marie in the

---

22 Probably in November 1212 when Peter was apparently with the crusaders at the time of the drafting of the Statutes of Pamiers: see §362.
23 The church of St Raymond, about 2km to the south of the town, now a ruin. According to G&L (I, p. 203 n. 1), the procession referred to in this paragraph continued until towards the end of the 19th century.
24 In §47; the abbot (Henry) had come south in 1207 to support the Cistercian preaching campaign.
25 Peter is probably referring to later campaigns against the county of Foix described below, §§354–8.

territory of the Count of Urgel, which was also the seat of the Bishop of Urgel.[26] The canons took fright at the sight of the Count and retreated into the church. Here they were besieged by the Count for so long that they were driven by thirst to drink their own urine. When eventually they gave themselves up, this most cruel enemy of the Church went into the church, took out all the furniture, crosses and sacred vessels, smashed the bells and, in a word, left nothing but the walls. Even more, he extracted a ransom of fifty thousand sous for the church. This done, one of his knights, a very base fellow, said to him: 'We have destroyed St Anthony and St Mary; it only remains for us to destroy God.'

[203] *An unheard-of atrocity.* On another occasion when the Count and his mercenaries were pillaging this church, they descended to such depths of insane barbarity that they cut off the arms and legs of the images of Christ crucified and used them to grind pepper and herbs for flavouring their food, as a gesture to show their contempt for the Passion of Our Lord. Most cruel executioners! Most base scoffers, more cruel than they who crucified Christ, more harsh than they who spat on Him! The Evangelist tells us that when the servants of Herod saw Jesus dead, they did not break his legs.[27] What new depths of enormity, what unheard-of savagery! Surely this man, the Count of Foix, is to be counted a wretch among wretches, a beast more cruel than any wild animal! His mercenaries even led their horses into the church and had them fed by the holy altars.

[204] *An instance of amazing barbarity.* One day the tyrant was in a church with a large body of armed men. His squire set his helmet on the head of the Crucifix and armed the holy image with his shield and spurs; then, seizing his lance, he struck the image repeatedly and said: 'Redeem thyself!' What new depths of wickedness!

[205] On another occasion the Count summoned the Bishops of Toulouse and Couserans to a meeting, naming the time and place; when the Bishops presented themselves for the meeting, the Count spent the whole day attacking a *castrum* belonging to the Abbot and canons of St Anthony at Pamiers. What an evil and perverse betrayal![28]

[206] Another evil deed perpetrated by this tyrant should be recorded. He made a treaty with the Count of Montfort (as I recorded much earlier in this narrative)[29] and handed over his son as a guarantee that it would be kept. The Abbot of Pamiers had already handed over his *castrum* to the Count of Montfort.[30] So, one day the Count of Foix came to Pamiers with his mercenaries, whom he set in ambush nearby. Approaching the walls he ordered the townsmen to come out to hold parley with him, promising on oath that it would be safe for

---

[26] La Seu d'Urgel, on the southern side of the Pyrenees in Aragon. G&L I, p. 205 n. 1, quote testimony of the Bishop and chapter of Urgel which corroborates Peter's account of the following incident.

[27] St John 19, v. 33.

[28] This probably refers to events at the time of the colloquium at Pamiers in 1207, described in §48 above, at which Bishops Fulk of Toulouse and Navarre of Couserans were present.

[29] This refers to Raymond-Roger's submission to Simon in the autumn of 1209, described in §120.

[30] As described in §116.

them to do so, since he would do them no harm. However, as soon as the townsmen came out to him he called secretly to the mercenaries, who were lurking in the ambush. They came up and seized many of the townsmen before they could get back to safety and carried them off as captives. What depraved treachery!

[207] The Count also used to say that if he were to kill, with his own hands, all present and future crusaders opposing the heretics and everyone else labouring on behalf of the business of the faith or favouring that business, he would regard himself as having rendered service to God.

[208] It should also be known that the Count often swore to the papal legates that he would expel the heretics from his territories, which he had no intention of doing.

[209] This most cruel dog committed many other crimes[31] against the Church and God. Even if I wished to record them all I would not be equal to the task, nor would any reader easily believe me. His wickedness exceeded all bounds. He pillaged monasteries, destroyed churches, excelled all others in cruelty. Always he panted after the death of Christians and never lost his thirst for blood. He disavowed humankind, copied the savagery of beasts, and became the worst of wild animals, a man no longer. After this brief account of his wickedness, let us return to our main narrative.

[210] *Resumption of the narrative.* At the meeting at Narbonne referred to above[32] the Bishop of Uzès and the Abbot of Cîteaux begged the King of Aragon to accept the Count of Montfort as his vassal, since Carcassonne was a fief of the King of Aragon. He refused, so the next day they went to the King again, taking the Count with them, prostrated themselves at his feet and implored him humbly and earnestly to deign to accept homage from the Count. The Count himself kneeled before the King and humbly offered homage. At length the King yielded to their entreaties and accepted the Count as his vassal in regard to Carcassonne, so that the latter now held the city from the King.[33]

[211] After this the King, our Count, the Count of Toulouse and the Bishop of Uzès left Narbonne and went to Montpellier.[34] While they were there the question of arranging a marriage between the King's eldest son and the Count of Montfort's daughter was discussed. What more? The proposed marriage was agreed by both sides, on the basis of sworn oaths; additionally the King handed over his son into the Count's custody.[35] However, despite having given his son

---

31 See for example §§130, 218 and 381.
32 §§195–6.
33 See §121 for the King's earlier refusal to accept Simon de Montfort's homage. His change of heart was perhaps due partly to the much stronger position of the crusaders, who now had possession of almost all the former Trencavel lands and had reduced all its strongholds save for Cabaret, and partly to the need to promote a stable situation north of the Pyrenees whilst he turned his attention to the forthcoming campaign against the Almohades in Spain (see n. 14 to §196 above). See also n. 38 to next section.
34 For King Peter's tenure of Montpellier as a fief of the Bishop of Maguelonne see n. 4 to §121.
35 The acts recording this agreement give a date of 27 January 1211 (see G&L I, p. 209 n. 1). The King's

into the Count's hands the King shortly afterwards gave his sister[36] in marriage to the Count of Toulouse's son, and in so doing earned himself considerable – and deserved – disfavour and suspicion amongst our people, since at the time the marriage was made the Count of Toulouse was already openly persecuting the Holy Church of God.

[212] I must also record that whilst the above-mentioned leaders together with numerous other bishops and prelates of the Church were at Montpellier, discussions again took place about the position of the Count of Toulouse. As I indicated earlier[37] the papal legates, the Bishop of Uzès and the Abbot of Cîteaux, wished to treat the Count with as much favour and mercy as possible, but after promising to implement all the legates' demands the next day, the Count in fact left Montpellier very early on the following morning without even bidding the legates farewell.[38] He had seen a bird of the kind local

son James (Jaime) was only three years old and Simon's daughter Amicia presumably about the same. The betrothal was broken off after the King's death at the battle of Muret in 1213. Cf. also the account in the *Llibre dels feyts*, trans. Forster, VIII, pp. 14–16. Amicia was later betrothed for a time to William of Poitiers (see §599). James remained with the crusaders until 1214: see §506.

[36] His sister was Sancia (or Sancha). William of Puylaurens (XVII) refers to the marriage as taking place before the start of the siege of Toulouse (3 April 1211), and Peter suggests below that it took place after hostilities had broken out between Raymond VI and the crusaders, which was around mid-March. The marriage thus probably took place in the second half of March. King Peter was thus pursuing an even-handed policy, concluding agreements both with de Montfort, his new vassal, and with Raymond VI, whose position, notwithstanding his excommunication, he wished to help secure. See also n. 3 to §367 below for the possibility that an attempt may have been made at this time to recognise Peter of Aragon as overlord of Toulouse.

[37] §195.

[38] Peter gives no indication of the terms offerred at Montpellier to Raymond, but William of Tudela (*Chanson* I, 59–60, pp. 144–6) refers in great detail to a meeting which he says took place 'so far as I know' at Arles. Since there are no other reliable references to a meeting at Arles, it is usually thought that his account relates to the meeting at Montpellier. He describes the legates keeping King Peter and Count Raymond waiting outside in the cold wind, and then presenting a written list of demands, effectively an ultimatum. Their terms included demands that the Count and his vassals observe the peace, cease to protect Jews and heretics, and demolish all their castles and other fortifications. They were to allow Simon de Montfort unopposed access to their lands, tolls were to be restricted, and usury was to be forbidden. Furthermore they 'should not eat more than two meats' (taken to mean that they should eat meat only twice a week), and wear only coarse brown capes; and the Count himself should go to the Holy Land and stay there as long as the legates required, and then on his return join the order of the Temple or the order of St John of Jerusalem. Belperron (pp. 216–17) doubted the accuracy of William of Tudela's account, but this seems unnecessary. While the demands were harsh, involving a severe penance on Raymond VI, they were wholly consistent with many of the demands already made and they reflect the aims of the *negotium pacis et fidei*. Even if William of Tudela had indulged in some poetic licence and had exaggerated, his account seems to confirm the determination of the legates not to compromise with Raymond VI. The failure of the meeting led to the promulgation on 6 February 1211 of a new sentence of excommunication against Raymond (not mentioned by Peter) and the placing of an interdict on Toulouse. The act recording the sentence gives as being present Archbishops Berengar of Narbonne and Michael of Arles, and Bishops William of Avignon, William of Maguelonne, Fulk of Toulouse, William of Orange, as well as Thedisius: see G&L I, p. 211 n. 1. On being informed of these decisions, Innocent confirmed them immediately by writing to the Archbishop of Arles and Arnold Amalric on 15 April asking them to publish the sentence on Raymond VI and forbidding the return to him of his *castra* in Provence; Innocent also wrote to Raymond of Uzès, probably on the same day, ordering him to take possession of the county of Melgueil, a fief of Raymond VI's near Montpellier: see *PL* 216, 410–11, for both letters, and cf. above §75 on Melgueil. As for Raymond VI himself, the *Chanson* (I, 60–1, pp. 148–54) says he visited Agen and Moissac, showed the

people call St Martin's bird[39] flying to the left, and the sight had terrified him. Like the Saracens he put great faith in the flight and song of birds and other auguries.[40]

citizens the terms offered, which they rejected outright, and generally publicised the conditions laid down by the legates in order to rally support.

[39] The name seems to have been applied to birds of several different species (see the notes to this paragraph by G&L I, p. 211 and G&M, p. 87). It was said to pass through France around St Martin's day, 11 November.

[40] Cf. §449.

[IX. §§213–230, spring 1211: *Arrival of new crusaders (March 1211) – surrender of Cabaret and release of Bouchard de Marly – siege of Lavaur by de Montfort – attack on crusaders by the Count of Foix – Raymond VI gives covert help to the defenders of Lavaur – Bishop Fulk leaves Toulouse (2 April 1211) – Lavaur falls (3 May 1211) – Roger of Comminges submits to de Montfort – Puylaurens occupied by the crusaders.*]

[213] *Arrival of the Bishop of Paris and many nobles from France.* In the year 1211[1] of the Incarnation of the Word, about the middle of Lent,[2] some noble and powerful crusaders arrived from France, including Peter the Bishop of Paris, Enguerrand de Coucy, Robert de Courtenay, Juhel de Mayenne[3] and numerous others. These noble men conducted themselves nobly in Christ's business.

[214] When they reached Carcassonne discussions were held, and the Count and all the newly-arrived crusaders agreed to proceed to put Cabaret under siege.[4] Already some knights from the diocese of Carcassonne, in fear of our people, had left their fortresses and fled to Cabaret; amongst them were two brothers, Peter Mir and Peter of Saint-Michel, who had taken part in the capture of Bouchard de Marly which I described earlier.[5] These two knights with numerous other individuals had left Cabaret, come to the Count and agreed to surrender to him on the promise that he would restore their lands to them.[6] Peter-Roger, the lord of Cabaret, seeing that the Count and the crusaders intended to besiege Cabaret and realising that the desertion of the two knights had greatly weakened him, was prompted by his fears to come to terms with the Count and the barons on the following basis: he gave up Cabaret and handed over Bouchard de Marly,[7] and the Count gave him other lands in

---

[1]   Given as 1210 in the text, since at this time the New Year was regarded as beginning in spring, usually on 25 March, Lady Day. Here as elsewhere modernised to 1211.

[2]   About mid-March; the Sunday in the middle of Lent was 13 March. William of Tudela (*Chanson* I, 62, p. 154) says that these crusaders began their journey southwards at the beginning of Lent ('*a l'intrat de caresma*').

[3]   Peter of Nemours was Bishop of Paris 1208–18: see G&M, p. 88 n. 2. Robert de Courtenay was the brother of Peter de Courtenay, Count of Auxerre, who had taken part in the campaign of 1209 and who arrived again in the south a little later in 1211 (see §216); the *Chanson* I, 63, p. 154 also mentions his presence at this time, and see also §217 below for the brothers' relationship with Raymond VI. Juhel de Mayenne came from western Normandy; see also G&L I, p. 212 n. 3 for contemporary confirmation of his presence. All of these crusaders left after the fall of Lavaur: see §230 below.

[4]   For Cabaret see n. 103 to §114 above. It was the principal remaining point of resistance in the former Trencavel lands, and had been a centre for attacks on the crusaders during the second half of 1210; see §169 above. The crusaders' strategy was to overcome remaining points of opposition within the Trencavel lands, so as to be in a position to mount a direct attack on Raymond VI. This aim was successfully achieved by early May 1211, with the fall of Lavaur and surrender of Puylaurens, on which see §§226–30.

[5]   §123 above.

[6]   The two brothers belonged to a noble family from Fanjeaux and had a long association with the Cathars, their mother Raymonde having received the *consolamentum* in 1204 at the same ceremony as Esclarmonde of Foix: see *HGL*, VIII, 1150, Roquebert I, p. 304 and G&L I, p. 213 n. 1.

[7]   William of Tudela makes it clear that the freeing of Bouchard de Marly took place before the crusading army had marched north to Cabaret; his release and the celebrations which followed when he arrived at

compensation.[8] Shortly after the surrender of Cabaret the Count and the barons directed their forces to besieging Lavaur.

[215] *Seige of Lavaur.* Lavaur was a very noteworthy and extensive *castrum*, situated by the River Agout and about five leagues from Toulouse.[9] In Lavaur were the traitor Aimeric, who had been the lord of Montréal,[10] and numerous other knights, enemies of the cross, up to eighty in number, who had entered the place and fortified it against us. The Dame of Lavaur was a widow named Giraude, a heretic of the worst sort and sister to Aimeric.[11]

[216] On their arrival, our soldiers laid siege to the *castrum* on one side only, since they had insufficient strength to surround it entirely. After a few days

Carcassonne early in March are described at length in the *Chanson*, I, 63–6. (For dating see *Chanson* I, p. 159 n. 2.)

[8] This was a similar settlement to that made with William of Minerve, §157 above, and Peter-Roger likewise received lands near Béziers. He was to retake Cabaret some 10 years later. The surrender of Cabaret without the need for a long and expensive siege now left Simon de Montfort free to begin the attack on Raymond VI.

[9] Lavaur lay about 35km to the north-east of Toulouse on the west bank of the Agout, close to where the Trencavel lands met those of the Counts of Toulouse. It was an early centre of Catharism and in 1181 during the mission against heresy in the Toulousain led by Abbot Henry of Clairvaux (see n. 24 to §9) it had been briefly besieged and forced to submit: see Griffe, *Débuts*, pp. 124–7, and William of Puylaurens II (who incorrectly dates the episode to 1170). In the later 12th century Lavaur's seigneurs rendered homage to the Trencavels (cf. *HGL* VI, 95), and Adelaide, wife of Roger II Trencavel, had been instrumental in securing the opening of the gates of Lavaur to the force led by Henry of Clairvaux. However, the local seigneurs had long enjoyed considerable independence; Trencavel overlordship of the town had become increasingly weak, and by the time of the Crusade there seems to have been some ambiguity about its overlordship, with indications that Raymond VI of Toulouse, no doubt taking advantage of the weakness of the young Viscount Raymond-Roger Trencavel, had been seeking to establish an interest in the town. In particular in 1203 he had reached an accord with Giraude Dame of Lavaur and Lavaur's other co-seigneurs. G&L, p. 219 n. 1, regard this as showing simply that Giraude and her co-seigneurs were dealing with Raymond on equal terms, although Roquebert I, p. 387 argues that the accord recognised Raymond as principal coseigneur. William of Tudela (*Chanson* I, 67, p. 162) says that Lavaur lay in the Toulousain ('*que lai en Tolza fu*'), and William of Puylaurens (XVI), having noted that it lay in the diocese of Toulouse, goes on to blame the 'negligence of the said Count of Toulouse [Raymond VI]' for the strength of heresy there. However, no doubt reflecting the crusaders' view, Peter in §220 below says that Lavaur was not in the county of Toulouse, clearly implying that he regarded it as part of the former Trencavel lands. Thus whether or not de Montfort was aware of Raymond's interest in Lavaur at the time he attacked it, he would certainly have maintained that Lavaur was part of the former Trencavel territories and justified the attack as part of a move to establish control over remaining points of resistance in those territories. Raymond's attempts now to provide some direct support to the defenders may have reflected a realisation that an attack on the county of Toulouse by the crusaders was becoming increasingly probable, and that it would be very much in his interest to prevent them occupying Lavaur, given its strategic importance on the plain to the south-east of Toulouse itself. Presumably he gave support covertly rather than openly because he wanted to avoid an open breach with the crusaders; here as often he failed to come down decisively in favour of strong action – William of Tudela for example says (*Chanson*, I, 67, p. 162) that Lavaur would have held out longer if Raymond had provided its defenders with better support. For a discussion see Roquebert I, pp. 386–8, and see also §220.

[10] See §135 and §167 above for Aimeric of Montréal. He had agreed peace with Simon de Montfort in the previous year after the fall of Minerve, but was unhappy with the lands offered in return for Montréal and his other fiefs; see *Chanson*, I, 68, p. 164. He thus now rebelled again and went to join his sister at Lavaur; cf. William of Puylaurens, XVI.

[11] Giraude was the daughter of Sicard and Blanche de Laurac (cf. n. 37 to §135). She had married the principal seigneur of Lavaur but by this time was a widow. Later Inquisition records provide many details of the close involvement of her family (especially her mother and sisters) with Catharism: see Griffe, *LC*, pp. 81 and 109–11. Many Cathars had taken refuge in the town at this point: cf. William of Puylaurens (XVI) who says that a substantial number of heretics had come to Lavaur.

siege-engines were erected and our men began to attack the *castrum* in the usual manner, whilst the enemy defended as best they could. Indeed the place contained a huge force and was excellently equipped for defence; in fact the defenders almost outnumbered the attackers.[12] I should add that when our army first arrived the enemy made a sortie and captured one of our knights, whom they took inside and killed instantly. Even though we were laying siege on one side only, the army was split into two parts and so disposed that if the need arose neither division could help the other without hazard. However, not long afterwards the Bishop of Lisieux,[13] the Bishop of Bayeux[14] and the Count of Auxerre[15] arrived from France with a large force of crusaders, and the siege was then extended to another side of the *castrum*; further, a wooden bridge was built across the River Agout which our men crossed so that they now completely surrounded the *castrum*.

[217] However, the Count of Toulouse continued to do all he could to injure the Church of God and our Count, but not openly; for provisions were still reaching our army from Toulouse.[16] At this juncture the Count of Toulouse came to the army, and the Count of Auxerre and Robert de Courtenay, who were his first cousins,[17] set about urging him to come to his senses and obey the commands of the Church. Their efforts came to nothing, and the Count of Toulouse left the Count of Montfort with a show of temper and indignation. The Toulousains who were taking part in the siege of Lavaur left the army, and the Count ordered the citizens of Toulouse to supply no more provisions to the besiegers at Lavaur. I must now record a most depraved crime committed by the Counts of Foix and Toulouse; an unheard-of act of treachery.

[218] *The Count of Foix murders crusaders.* Whilst the discussions at Lavaur on restoring peace between the Count of Toulouse and the Holy Church were in progress, a group of crusaders was making its way from Carcassonne to the army.[18] However, those ministers of deceit, those artificers of betrayal, the Count of Foix, his son Roger-Bernard, and Giraud de Pépieux,[19] together with numerous followers of the Count of Toulouse, set up an ambush at a *castrum* known as Montgey[20] near Puylaurens with the assistance of a huge force of mercenaries.

---

12 Lavaur was also on a naturally strong site on an escarpment of rock overlooking the Agout, and the *Chanson* (I, 68, p. 164) comments on the strength of its fortifications, mentioning its walls and deep ditches.
13 Bishop Jordan (Jourdain), 1201–18.
14 Bishop Robert, 1206–31.
15 Peter II de Courtenay, brother of Robert de Courtenay (see §213). William of Tudela (*Chanson* I, 12, p. 34) and William of Puylaurens (XIII) both mention his presence in the campaign of 1209.
16 Confirmed by William of Puylaurens and the consuls of Toulouse – for details see n. 26 to §220.
17 Raymond VI's mother Constance, a daughter of Louis VI of France, was the sister of Peter I de Courtenay, the father of Peter II (the Count of Auxerre) and Robert.
18 The *Chanson* (I, 69–70, pp. 168–72) also narrates this incident in detail. There were said to be five thousand crusaders in the force, including Germans and Frisians. Cf. §224 below where Peter mentions the presence of Germans.
19 On Giraud, see above §§125–6.
20 Montgey is about 10km south-west of Puylaurens, in a region known as the Vielmorès, just to the north of the Lauragais. It lay at the heart of an area where Catharism had much support amongst the local

They attacked the crusaders as they arrived, killing large numbers since they were not wearing their armour and were unaware that they had been betrayed.[21] The attackers took the belongings of the slain to Toulouse and divided them among themselves. What harsh treachery! What evil madness! How blessed the ranks of the slain, how precious in the sight of the Lord is the death of his saints![22]

[219] It must also be recorded that whilst these executioners were engaged in the slaughter of the crusaders, one crusader who was a priest took refuge in a nearby church, intending, since he was dying for the Church, to meet his death in a church. However, that most evil betrayer Roger-Bernard, the son of the Count of Foix, whose depravity in no way fell short of his father's, followed the priest, insolently entered the church, approached him and asked him what sort of man he was. He replied: 'I am a crusader and a priest.' Said the executioner: 'Prove to me that you are a priest.' The priest removed his cowl from his head (he was wearing his cloak) and showed him his clerical tonsure. His cruel attacker showed no respect for the holy place or the holy man; he raised the sharp lancet which he held and struck a fierce blow through the centre of the priest's tonsure, murdering the Church's minister in the church. Let us now return to where we left off.

[220] *The perfidy of the Count of Toulouse.* I have to record another example of the behaviour of the Count of Toulouse, for which Lavaur provided the scene. This place was the source and origin of the every form of heresy. (It was not part of the Count's territories and indeed had for a long time been engaged in attacking the people of Toulouse.)[23] Here the Count demonstrated his hatred of the Christian religion by secretly sending a seneschal and several knights to help in the defence against our men.[24] After Lavaur was captured, our Count found them and held them chained in prison for a long period. What a new form of treachery! The Count of Toulouse had deployed his men inside Lavaur, in its defence; outside, to make a show of helping us in attacking it, he permitted supplies to be brought from Toulouse. Indeed, as mentioned earlier, when the siege of Lavaur

---

nobility, and where hostility to the Crusade was strong. For details see Griffe, *LC*, pp. 78–80 and 90–102, and Roquebert I, pp. 390–2.

21 William of Puylaurens (XVI) also says that they were caught unawares, but William of Tudela (*Chanson* I, 69, p. 168) says on the contrary that they were armed and fought well to defend themselves.

22 Psalm 116, v.15. De Montfort razed Montgey in retaliation for this attack a few months later: see §232 below.

23 See n. 9 to §215 above on the overlordship of Lavaur.

24 Again, see n. 9 to §215. Testimony given to the Inquisition in February 1245 by Pons Carbonel, an inhabitant of Le Faget (about 15km south of Lavaur), may relate to this covert support given by Raymond to the defenders of Lavaur: see *HGL* VIII, 1147–8. Pons stated that Raymond arrived at his house one day with some knights, including Raymond de Ricaud, his Seneschal (*'bajulus'*), having made prior arrangements for Pons to provide them with food. Two perfected heretics had arrived the previous day and also been given food. When Pons was asked if the Count saw the heretics in his house or ate with them or reverenced them, Pons replied 'not that he saw' (*'Inde interrogatus, si comes Tolosanus vidit tunc ipsos hereticos in domo ipsius testis, vel comedit cum eis, vel adoravit eos, dixit quod non, ipso teste [Pons] videnteʼ*). Later the Count's Seneschal provided horses for the heretics and the Count's party and the heretics left for Lavaur *'quod erat tunc temporis obsessumʼ*, 'which was then under siege'. (Raymond de Ricaud was the son-in-law of one of the co-seigneurs of Lavaur, William Saisset: see G&L I, p. 219 n. 2; he is also mentioned by William of Puylaurens, XXIII.)

started supplies were being brought to the army from Toulouse, although in modest amounts;[25] despite this, the Count strictly refused to allow the transport of siege-engines. However, about five thousand men from Toulouse had been persuaded by their venerable Bishop Fulk to come to help us in the siege.[26] The Bishop himself came, exiled for his Catholic faith. It will not be out of place to relate how he left Toulouse.

[221] *Exile of Fulk, Bishop of Toulouse.* One day – it was the Sunday after mid-Lent[27] – the Bishop was in Toulouse intending to perform ordinations in the manner usual in episcopal churches. However, the Count was present in the city, and under the terms of the sentence of excommunication passed on the Count for his many excesses by the Apostolic See no-one was allowed to celebrate divine services in any town where the Count was.[28] The Bishop accordingly sent to the Count, humbly beseeching him to take a walk outside the city, just as he might do for relaxation, only until ordinations had been celebrated. The tyrant became furious; he sent a knight to the Bishop, ordering him on pain of death to leave the city and all the Count's domains. It is said that on hearing this the Bishop, speaking fervently and fearlessly and with a joyous countenance, answered the knight thus: 'The Count of Toulouse did not make me Bishop, nor was I ordained by his hands or on his behalf.[29] It was the humility of the Church that brought about my election, not the power of princes. I will not go on his account. Let him come if he dares. I am ready to embrace the sword if I can attain glory by drinking the cup of suffering. Let the tyrant come, surrounded by knights and armed; he will find me alone and unarmed. I await my reward. I have no fear of what man may do unto me.'[30] What firmness of heart, what marvellous strength of mind! So the fearless servant of God stayed his ground, expecting each day to meet the tyrant's sword; but the Count dared not kill him – he had already done so many great wrongs to God's Church and was, as the common people say,

---

25 Cf. §217 above.

26 These men belonged to the *confratria candida*, for which see n. 57 to §162. Their presence at the siege of Lavaur is related by William of Puylaurens XVI, where the members are referred to as the '*confratres Tholosani*' and where he describes Raymond VI's unsuccessful attempts to prevent the force from leaving Toulouse. This was an early sign that Raymond was at last preparing himself to abandon his attempts to negotiate and to make an open break with the legates and the crusaders; the expulsion of Fulk described below was a further step. The account of the consuls of Toulouse in their letter of July 1211 to King Peter of Aragon (*HGL* VIII 612–19, see notes to §137, §162 et al. and especially n. 11 to §234 below) says the Toulousains gave help to the crusaders at Lavaur by providing supplies and armed support ('*consilium et auxilium tam in victualibus quam in armis*'), and that 'a great part of the leading citizens (*nobilioribus hominibus*), on the instructions of their Bishop, remained in arms until Lavaur was taken; they then returned to Toulouse with the consent (*cum assensu et voluntate*) of our Bishop Fulk and the Abbot of La Cour-Dieu, who, was then acting as vice-legate'; (see §226 below for the Abbot).

27 20 March 1211.

28 One of the terms of the sentence of excommunication passed on Raymond VI at Montpellier on 6 February 1211 (on which see §212 above and notes) had forbidden the celebration of divine services in any place where Raymond was present: '*Precipimus civitates, castra, villas et loca ad que dictus comes Tolosanus ... devenerit ... a divinis officiis abstinere*', quoted by G&L I, p. 221 n. 3.

29 G&L note (I, p. 221 n. 4) that Raymond VI had earlier renounced intervention in the election of the Bishop of Toulouse, for which see *Layettes* I, 876. For the subsequent exodus of the clergy see §234.

30 Psalm 118, v. 6.

'afraid for his skin' – and after the Bishop had passed fifteen days expecting to meet his end he decided to quit Toulouse.

[222] So on the eve[31] of Easter Day he left the city and went to our Count at the siege of Lavaur, where our men were labouring without respite in their efforts to take the place. Our opponents, as befitted their arrogance, defended themselves vigorously. I must mention that they rode along the walls on horses fully protected by armour, to show their contempt for our side and demonstrate that the walls were substantial and well fortified. What arrogance!

[223] *A matter worthy of record.* One day our men had built a wooden fortification[32] near the walls of the *castrum*, and on top of it Christ's knights had placed the sign of the Cross. Our opponents concentrated fire from their engines on the Cross and broke one of the arms, whereupon the shameless dogs started howling and cheering as if breaking the cross was a famous victory. But He who sanctified the cross avenged this wrong miraculously and for all to see: soon afterwards (most marvellous to relate) it came about that the enemies of the cross, who had rejoiced in destroying the Cross, were captured on the day of the feast of the Cross.[33] So the Cross avenged the injuries it had suffered – as will be shown later in my narrative.

[224] Whilst this was happening our men built a siege-engine of the type commonly called a 'cat'.[34] When it was ready they dragged it to the ditch surrounding Lavaur. Then with a great effort they brought up wood and branches which they tied into bundles and threw into the ditch to fill it. Our enemies, with their usual cunning, dug an underground passage reaching as far as our engine; they went along the passage by night, took the bundles which our men had thrown into the ditch and carried them into the *castrum*. Moreover some of them got close to the cat and under cover of silence made treacherous efforts to drag our men to them by catching them with iron hooks as they strove unceasingly to fill the ditch under the protection of the engine. Also, one night they came out by the underground passage and tried to set fire to the cat by hurling large quantities of lighted darts, fire, tow, fat and anything else that would burn. However, two German counts who were with our army were keeping guard round the cat that night. The alarm was raised amongst our soldiers who hurriedly armed themselves and rushed to protect the siege-engine.[35] The two German counts and the other Germans with them[36] saw that they could not reach the enemy in the ditch from where they were, courageously and at great risk threw themselves into the

---

[31] 2 April 1211.

[32] Latin '*castellum quoddam de lignis*'. Presumably a tower-like structure similar to a cat but not moveable.

[33] I.e. on the day of the Feast of the Invention of the Holy Cross, 3 May: see below §226.

[34] See n. 47 to §96.

[35] An example of word play; '*curritur ad arma machineque succurritur*'.

[36] The counts are described as '*Alemanni*', their companions as '*Teutonici*'. William of Tudela (*Chanson* I, 69, p. 168) also mentions the presence of Germans and Frisians ('*Alaman el Frizon*') in the south at this time, but identifies them as a separate force which fought the Count of Foix in the skirmish at Montgey, on which see above §218.

ditch, and attacked the enemy boldly; they thrust them back into the *castrum*, having first killed some of them and wounded many more.

[225] Meanwhile our men became seriously concerned and began to despair of taking the *castrum*, because whatever materials they were able to throw into the ditch by day were taken out at night by our enemies and carried inside. However, despite the worries of the majority, a few of our men gave deeper thought to the problem and devised a useful counter to the enemy's plan. They had green wood and branches thrown in front of the entrance to the underground passage used by the enemy; next they threw on small dry pieces of wood, together with fat and tow and other inflammable material, right at the exit from the passage; this they set alight, and then piled on more wood and unripe corn and grass in large quantities. Smoke from the fire so filled the passage that our enemies could no longer get out through it; indeed the smoke could not rise through the wood and green corn on top so that it filled the whole passage. Seeing this our men were able to fill up the ditch more easily than before, and once it was filled our knights and their armed sergeants with much effort dragged the siege-engine up to the wall and set sappers to work on it. The defenders kept on hurling fire, wood, tow, stones and heavy sharpened stakes onto the engine, but our men defended it with marvellous courage and the enemy could neither set fire to the engine nor drive the sappers away.

[226] Whilst out men were thus devoting their every effort to the siege, the bishops present and the venerable Abbot of the Cistercian monastery of La Cour-Dieu,[37] who were with the army and had been instructed by the papal legates to act in their stead,[38] gathered together with all the other clergy and with the utmost fervour began to sing the *Veni Creator Spiritus*.[39] When they saw and heard this, our enemies – so God disposed – became stupefied and almost lost their powers of resistance; to the extent that – as they later admitted – they feared those who sang more than those who fought, those who recited the psalms more than those who attacked them, those who prayed more than those who sought to wound. So the wall was penetrated, our men entered Lavaur and our adversaries, no longer able to resist, gave themselves up. Through the will of God, who came in His mercy to our aid, Lavaur was taken on the feast of the Invention of the Holy Cross.[40]

---

[37] La Cour-Dieu lay near Ingrannes, about 20km east of Orléans. The presence of its Abbot, Hugh, with the crusaders in 1211 is attested by other sources: see G&L I, p. 226 n. 2. The Bishops were Peter of Paris, Jordan of Lisieux, Robert of Bayeux and Fulk of Toulouse (§§213, 216, 221 above and 230 below).

[38] The other legates, Arnold Amalric and Raymond of Uzès, were apparently absent from the siege attending to other business in the Midi, including administration of the county of Melgueil and arrangements for the election of a new Bishop of Carcassonne: Innocent III's letters to them of April 1211, asking them to undertake this and a range of other business at this time, are in *PL* 216, 409–11.

[39] This was also sung at Moissac in 1212: see §351.

[40] 3 May 1211, a date confirmed in the *Chanson*, I, 68, p. 166. The siege of Lavaur, which began in the second half of March, must therefore have lasted about five or six weeks, and was shorter than the one month and five weeks given by William of Tudela (*Chanson* I, 67, p. 162). The booty taken after the siege was considerable, and was handed over to Simon de Montfort's banker Raymond de Salvanhac (see *Chanson* I, 72, p. 174; and on Raymond see for example *Cahiers de Fanjeaux*, vol. 4, pp. 289–90).

[227] Soon Aimeric, the former lord of Montréal, of whom we spoke above,[41] was led out of Lavaur with up to eighty other knights.[42] The noble Count proposed that they should all be hanged from fork-shaped gibbets. However, after Aimeric, who was taller then the others, had been hanged, the gibbets started to fall down, since through excessive haste they had not been properly fixed in the ground. The Count realised that to continue would cause a long delay and ordered the rest to be put to the sword. The crusaders fell to this task with great enthusiasm and quickly slew them on the spot. The Count had the Dame of Lavaur, sister of Aimeric and a heretic of the worst sort, thrown into a pit and stones heaped on her.[43] Our crusaders burnt innumerable[44] heretics, with great rejoicing.

[228] *Roger of Comminges joins the Count.* It should be recorded that whilst our Count was at the siege of Lavaur a noble from Gascony, Roger de Comminges, a kinsman of the Count of Foix, came to him to offer his submission.[45] Whilst he was with our Count on Good Friday[46] for the purpose of doing homage to him, the Count chanced to sneeze. On seeing the Count sneeze once Roger called his companions to him to seek their advice, since he was unwilling to carry out his business with the Count at that moment. This was because the foolish natives of the whole of this area are so observant of omens that they genuinely believe that if they, or anyone dealing with them, should sneeze once, then no good can come to them on that day. However, Roger realised that our people were ridiculing him for this and was concerned that the Count would censure him for his perverse superstition, so that in the end he reluctantly did homage to the Count and formally accepted from him the right to his lands. He remained loyal to the Count for some time but later[47] wretchedly withdrew from his allegiance.

[229] I must not pass over a miracle at Lavaur which I heard about from a reliable source. By some mischance the cloak of a crusader knight caught fire; by God's miraculous judgment it came about that it was all burnt except the part

[41] §215.
[42] Both the *Chanson* (I, 68, p. 164) and William of Puylaurens (XVI) give the same figure. The latter says some of the eighty were townspeople who had joined the knights thinking that they would be spared.
[43] William of Tudela (*Chanson* I, 68, p. 166) confirms her fate and adds that this was an unhappy event and a crime, because of her charity and generosity.
[44] William of Puylaurens (XVI) says three hundred were burnt. William of Tudela (*Chanson* I, 68, p. 164) says up to four hundred townspeople ('*sels de la vila*') were collected in a meadow and burnt, and later in laisse 71 he says that at least four hundred ('*ben quatre cens*') perished. Unlike at Minerve the previous year (see §156), and at Les Cassés a short time later (see below §233), no attempt appears to have been made to convert any heretics before the burnings.
[45] Roger of Comminges was Viscount of Couserans, a region to the west of Foix. Through his mother he was a nephew of the Count of Foix, and through his father a nephew of Bernard IV, Count of Comminges. He became Count of Pallars (which lay on the southern side of the Pyrenees) through his marriage to Guillerma, heiress to the county. He was a vassal of the Counts of Toulouse in respect of his castle at Quié, near Tarascon sur Ariège. Roger's submission, which is given in *HGL* VIII, 608–9, took place on 3 April 1211, and was witnessed by (amongst others) Guy de Lucy and Guy de Lévis. It was to be shortlived (see later in this §) and his viscounty was invaded by de Montfort in the autumn of 1212 (§358).
[46] 1 April 1211.
[47] See §358 below.

where the cross was stitched on, which survived without being touched by the flames.

[230] *The Count occupies Puylaurens.*[48] On hearing that Lavaur had been taken Sicard,[49] the lord of Puylaurens, who at one time had sided with our Count but later deserted him, was seized with fear; he left Puylaurens and hurried off to Toulouse with his knights. Puylaurens was a notable *castrum* about three leagues from Lavaur in the diocese of Toulouse.[50] After taking the place the Count gave it to Guy de Lucy, a noble and loyal man who at once entered Puylaurens and fortified it.[51] Meanwhile after the fall of Lavaur the Bishop of Paris, Enguerrand de Coucy, Robert de Courtenay and Juhel de Mayenne left the army and went home.[52]

---

[48] Puylaurens, about 25km south-east of Lavaur, and likewise on the edge of the former Trencavel domains where they bordered the county of Toulouse.

[49] Sicard belonged to an important noble family in the Toulousain. Charter evidence shows that he possessed rights throughout the surrounding area, including at Dourgne to the south-east, Cuq-Toulza to the west, and Saint-Paul-Cap-de-Joux to the north. He also had rights at Saissac further south towards Carcassonne, acquired through marriage to the daughter of the local seigneurial family there. He had submitted to de Montfort in 1209, but quickly reneged on this. Catharism was firmly implanted amongst the rural nobility of this area, and for instance Sicard's mother Ermessende was a Cathar *perfecta.* See Griffe, *LC,* pp. 94–6, and Roquebert, I, p. 399. See also *Chanson,* III, p. 120 n. 1; and for Sicard at the siege of Toulouse in 1218 ibid., 197, p. 121, and 214, p. 314.

[50] I.e. like Lavaur, in the ecclesiastical diocese of Toulouse.

[51] On Guy de Lucy, cf. §152 above. For the subsequent rebellion of Puylaurens see §251 below.

[52] They had arrived around mid-March (§213 above) so that their stay in the South lasted about six weeks, or the forty days required of crusaders.

[**X. §§231–250, summer 1211:** *Opening of hostilities with the Count of Toulouse – siege of Les Cassés – the Catholic clergy leave Toulouse – siege of Montferrand – Count Baldwin of Toulouse joins the crusaders – Simon de Montfort occupies the northern Albigeois – arrival of the Count of Bar – first siege of Toulouse, June 1211 – departure of the Count of Bar – abandonment of the siege – raid on the county of Foix – de Montfort in Quercy – submission of the Bishop of Cahors and lords of Quercy – capture of Lambert de Thury and Walter Langton by the Count of Foix – de Montfort returns to Pamiers.*]

[231] *Malice of the Count of Toulouse displayed for all to see.* After the capture of Lavaur, our men discovered the followers of the Count of Toulouse who had been deployed by him in the *castrum*.[1] They recalled the Count's rancorous departure from our Count, his refusal to allow siege-engines and supplies to be transported from Toulouse[2] and most important of all the fact that for his many excesses he had been excommunicated by the papal legates, and his lands declared liable to seizure.[3] Careful consideration of all these points prompted them to conclude that they should now treat the Count as a man manifestly condemned, and start to take action against him quite openly. [232] Our Count therefore broke camp and set out for Montgey, where the Count of Foix had slaughtered some crusaders.[4] It happened, however, that whilst the army was still some distance from Montgey, a column of fire was seen by our men at the place where the crusaders had been killed, shining and descending down towards the bodies of the slain. When our men reached the place they saw all the bodies lying face upwards, with arms extended to form the cross. What a miracle! I was told of it by Fulk the venerable Bishop of Toulouse, who was present. The Count went on to Montgey and destroyed it utterly; its occupants had fled in terror.

[233] *Siege of Les Cassés.* From there our Count went on to another *castrum* called Les Cassés[5] which belonged to the Count of Toulouse, who had meanwhile gone to Castelnaudary (a notable *castrum*) which he set on fire – since he was

---

[1] Raymond de Ricaud and others: see §220 above, and notes.
[2] See above, §217.
[3] This refers to the sentence of excommunication passed on Raymond on 6 February 1211, after the failure of negotiations with the legates at Narbonne and Montpellier early in 1211 – see §212. One outcome of this was that Raymond's lands again became liable to seizure by others. (Innocent's letter of 15 April 1211, *PL* 216, 410–11, confirming the sentence, would probably have reached the crusaders about this time.)
[4] See above, §218. Montgey was the first *castrum* to be occupied by the crusaders which was indisputably within Raymond VI's lordship.
[5] Les Cassés is about 40km south-east of Toulouse, just south of Saint-Félix, close to the ancient Roman road from Carcassonne to Toulouse. Its castle, overlooking the town, was on a naturally strong site. Its overlord was Raymond VI, but its principal immediate seigneurs were a family from Roqueville, a *castrum* about 20km to the south, two brothers from which family (Raymond and Bernard) held les Cassés at this time. The family, and the other seigneurs of les Cassés, were deeply involved with heresy, and according to William of Tudela (*Chanson* I, 84, p. 200) they 'gave refuge to many heretics'. For further details of heresy in this area see Griffe, *LC*, pp. 137–42 and *Chanson* I, p. 201 n. 5.

afraid that we might take it – and left empty.[6] Our Count reached Les Cassés and laid siege to it. The Count of Toulouse's knights inside the *castrum* saw that despite its strength they would not be able to hold it for very long and surrendered it to our Count on the condition that they would hand over all the heretics in the place but would themselves be allowed to go free. This duly happened. There were in fact a great many 'perfected' heretics in les Cassés and the bishops with the army went in and began to preach to the heretics in the hope of recalling them from error. However, they failed to convert even one and left. The crusaders seized nearly sixty heretics and burnt them with great rejoicing.[7] This was a clear demonstration of the love of the Count of Toulouse for heretics – in this insignificant *castrum* of his there were found more than fifty perfected heretics.[8]

[234] *Clerics exiled from Toulouse.* After this the Bishop of Toulouse, who was with the army,[9] ordered the provost of the cathedral of Toulouse[10] and the other clergy to quit the city. They obeyed and left barefoot taking with them the Holy Sacrament.[11]

---

[6] Castelnaudary occupied an important strategic point on the approaches to Toulouse from the southeast; cf. §170 above.

[7] William of Puylaurens (XVII) also gives a figure of 60 for the number burnt. William of Tudela says that 94 heretics were discovered hiding in a tower in the castle (*Chanson* I, 84, p. 200).

[8] William of Tudela, *Chanson* I, 84, p. 200, says on the contrary that the Roquevilles of les Cassés gave refuge to Cathars against the will of their lord (i.e. Raymond VI), and he cites as his authority one Izarn, archdeacon of the Vielmorès at this time.

[9] He had left Toulouse to join the crusaders on 2 April 1211: see §§221–2 above.

[10] The provost was Mascaron, 1205–16. In July 1205 Innocent III had ordered his deposition but he was allowed to retain his functions (see *PL* 215, 682–3). His account of the battle of Muret in 1213 is printed in G&L III, pp. 200–205.

[11] In ordering this exodus, Bishop Fulk was carrying out part of the sentence passed at Montpellier on 6 February 1211: '*clerici omnes, tam religiosi quam alii, induti sacris vestibus, cum corpore Jhesu Christi egrediantur*' (see G&L I, p. 233 n. 2). This marked a serious worsening of the situation for the inhabitants of Toulouse, forcing them to choose between obedience to the legates and their bishop, and loyalty to Raymond their count. Both Raymond VI and the consuls of Toulouse continued to seek to negotiate with the legates and with de Montfort, and it was at about this time, between the fall of Lavaur in early May and the arrival of de Montfort at Toulouse in the middle of June 1211 (see §239), that three initiatives were taken to try and put an end to hostilities, two by Raymond, and a third by the consuls themselves. These initiatives are known only from the letter of July 1211 from the consuls to King Peter of Aragon (*HGL* VIII, 612–19, and *Layettes*, I, 968, see also notes to §§137, 162 etc.), and no mention is made in any of the narrative sources. This letter begins by giving details of the dealings between the consuls and the legates dating back over at least eight years, and protesting their innocence in the face of charges of protecting heretics and failing to co-operate with the legates. Although giving no firm dates the letter (written in indifferent Latin) then states that after the siege of Lavaur Raymond made two further attempts to come to terms with the crusaders. His first offer was to place himself and his possessions, save Toulouse itself, under the crusaders' control and follow their instructions in regard to the faith. This offer, they said, was rejected even though it seemed acceptable to some of the barons with the army; it apparently foundered because the crusaders refused to guarantee that Raymond and his heirs could retain their domains. Raymond then attempted to meet the legates in response to a summons from them and a promise of safe conduct, but was attacked by de Montfort and numerous knights who 'set on him without warning hoping to capture or kill him, and pursued him for a league'. The consuls themselves then sent a deputation to the crusaders offering co-operation, but the legates and Bishop Fulk responded that they must repudiate Raymond and accept a new lord to be imposed by the crusaders; otherwise they would be treated as heretics and receivers of heretics. The consuls say at this point that they felt compelled to maintain their loyalty to their Count, and it was then that the clerics were ordered to leave the city; they then settled all differences within their city and achieved a degree of unity never previously known (this is confirmed by William of Puylaurens,

[235] *Siege of Montferrand.* After the capture of les Cassés our Count proceeded to another *castrum* belonging to the Count of Toulouse, Montferrand.[12] In command was Baldwin the brother of the Count of Toulouse, who had sent him to defend it.[13] On reaching the place our Count laid siege to it. A few days later our men launched an attack; 'Count' Baldwin (he was called by this title) saw that he was not strong enough to hold out for long and handed over the *castrum* on the basis of an agreement that he and his men should come out free. He also swore an oath that for the future he would offer no opposition either to the Church or to our Count, and further promised that if our Count so desired he would help him in all things against all comers.[14]

[236] *Count Baldwin joins our Count.* Accordingly Count Baldwin left Montferrand and went to his brother, the Count of Toulouse, but after a few days he returned to the Count of Montfort.[15] He approached him, and asked him to consent to accept him as a vassal, promising to serve him faithfully in all matters against all men. What more? The Count assented, Count Baldwin was reconciled to the Church, a servant of the Devil became a soldier of Christ; he kept faith, and from that day forward devoted his every effort to fighting the enemies of the faith. Such is the grace of God, the mercy of the Redeemer! Here were two brothers, sons of the same father, but utterly unlike. Through the mouth of the

XVII). Both Peter and the *Chanson* are silent on all this. See also notes to §§163 and 212 for examples of the legates' intransigence in dealing with Raymond, and for later references to the consuls' letter see notes to §§239 and 241.

[12] About 10km north-west of Castelnaudary in the direction of Toulouse. Its castle occupied a good defensive position overlooking the Col de Naurouze and the main road to Toulouse, although William of Tudela thought it weak and badly fortified (*Chanson* I, 73, p. 178). Having abandoned Castelnaudary, Raymond VI had made Montferrand the key to his defence of the southern approaches to Toulouse. The siege will have taken place in the second half of May 1211.

[13] Baldwin of Toulouse was Raymond VI's younger brother, but he had been born and brought up in northern France. Their father, Raymond V, had married their mother Constance, daughter of Louis VI of France, in 1154, but repudiated her for diplomatic reasons in 1165. She returned north before she gave birth to Baldwin. Baldwin had come to Toulouse in 1194 on the death of his father, but according to William of Puylaurens (XII), Raymond at first refused to recognise him; subsequently Baldwin returned with written confirmation from churchmen and nobles at the French court that he was indeed Raymond's brother, and he was accepted fully, but was denied any fiefs or titles ('*comes . . . bono modo retinuit sed privatum benificio et honore*'). William of Tudela (*Chanson* I, 77, p. 184) also says that Raymond had never liked Baldwin or treated him honourably. Even so, Raymond had recognised Baldwin in the will he made in September 1209 before setting out for France and Rome, giving him part responsibility for the care of his son and an annual income (*HGL* VIII, 573), and Raymond had clearly trusted him enough to give him the task of defending Montferrand. After defecting to the crusaders Baldwin remained loyal to them, being given Montcuq by de Montfort in 1212 (see §318), and taking part in the siege of Puycelsi in 1213 (§426), but he came to be detested as a traitor by the southerners and was murdered in February 1214 (§§495–500).

[14] William of Tudela, whose benefactor Baldwin was, gives more details of the siege. He says that Baldwin fought bravely to defend Montferrand but that eventually he capitulated because he could resist no further; the terms of his surrender are similar to those given by Peter (*Chanson* I, 72–4, pp. 174–8). William of Puylaurens (XVII) simply says that Baldwin was forced to surrender because Raymond failed to send the help he had promised.

[15] William of Tudela, *Chanson* I, 77, pp. 184–6, may refer to this visit when he says that about this time Baldwin went to Toulouse to negotiate with his brother and sought unsuccessfully to persuade him to join the crusaders.

prophet He said: 'Jacob I loved but Esau I hated.'[16] One of these brothers He left mired in the filth of unbelief; the other He rescued marvellously and mercifully, following His secret plan, known only to Himself. I must also record the following; after Count Baldwin left Montferrand and before he returned to our Count, some mercenaries – to show their hatred for the crusaders – robbed some pilgrims returning from a pilgrimage to St James.[17] When Baldwin heard of this he asked who was responsible and saw to it that they restored intact everything they had taken from the pilgrims. Thus the noble Count Baldwin set out on his future path of righteousness and fidelity.

[237] *The Count seizes a number of castra.* After the capture of Montferrand and some other *castra* in the same area, our men fortified Castelnaudary (which, as recorded earlier, had been put to the torch by the Count of Toulouse).[18] Our Count then crossed the River Tarn[19] and reached a *castrum* named Rabastens in the Albigeois, which was handed over to him by the inhabitants.[20] Leaving this place he went from success to success and took six other notable *castra* without opposition. These were Montégut, Gaillac, Cahuzac, Saint-Marcel, Laguépie and Saint-Antonin. These places, all close neighbours, had been taken by the Count of Toulouse from the Viscount of Béziers.[21]

[238] *Arrival of the Count of Bar.* It was now reported to our Count that the Count of Bar[22] was at Carcassonne, making haste to join the army of Christ. Our Count was elated at the news, since the Count of Bar enjoyed a high reputation

16 Malachi 1, vv. 2–3.
17 I.e. to the tomb of St James (Santiago) at Compostela in Galicia in north-west Spain. One of the main routes to and from Santiago went through the county of Toulouse, and many pilgrims passed through the city of Toulouse attracted by the tomb of St Saturninus (Sernin), housed in the great basilica of Saint-Sernin in the bourg there.
18 See above, §233.
19 This was on or about 5 June 1211, since on that date a charter was witnessed on the banks of the Tarn (perhaps near Rabastens) whereby Raymond Trencavel, uncle of the dead Viscount Raymond-Roger, confirmed that he ceded all his rights to Simon de Montfort (*HGL* VIII, 609, and *Layettes*, V, 185).
20 Rabastens lay on the north bank of the Tarn, and its seigneurs had strong associations with heresy: see Griffe, *LC*, pp. 65–8. Early in 1211 its co-seigneurs had made an accord with Raymond VI (see G&L I, p. 236 n. 3), but they now capitulated, and those Cathars who had taken refuge there fled.
21 The Albigeois north of the Tarn had formerly been controlled by the Trencavels, and several charters of the mid-12th century show that Montégut, Gaillac and Cahuzac were Trencavel fiefs (for examples see *HGL* V, 1066 and 1220). However, the Counts of Toulouse had gained control of the region during the later 12th century (cf. above, §118). De Montfort now intended to take possession of this area, both to reclaim a former part of the Trencavel viscounty of Albi, and to weaken Raymond VI by denying him control of the area. Such were the successes of the crusaders at Lavaur, les Cassés and Montferrand that this campaign north of the Tarn was now unopposed. It took de Montfort as far north as the river Aveyron (on the south bank of which, at its confluence with the Viaur, lay Laguépie), and on to the southern borders of Quercy and the Rouergue on the other side of the rivers Aveyron and Viaur (Saint-Antonin lay on the Aveyron's northern bank, just within Quercy). William of Tudela also mentions the occupation of Rabastens, Gaillac and Montégut, 'which were given up through fear', and adds that La Garde-Viaur and Puycelsi were also occupied, as well as Bruniquel which was secured by Baldwin (*Chanson* I, 75–7, pp. 180–4),
22 Theobald, Count of Bar (now Bar-le-Duc in eastern Champagne); he was also Count of Luxembourg. His arrival, along with a substantial number of knights, is also mentioned in the *Chanson* (I, 77, p. 186), and enabled de Montfort to go on the offensive. It was the result of a preaching campaign organised by Arnold Amalric in the region around Verdun and Metz: cf. G&L I, p. 237 n. 7; G&M, p. 98 n. 9; and Roquebert I, p. 408.

and our people expected great results from his coming. His conduct turned out to be much different from what we had hoped, since the Lord, to give glory to His name, wished to show that our trust should be placed in Himself and not in man.[23] Our Count sent knights to the Count of Bar to conduct him towards Toulouse to the banks of a river[24] where our Count and the army would meet him. This plan was duly carried out, but the Counts of Toulouse and Foix and a large force of Christ's enemies[25] on hearing that the army was approaching Toulouse went to the river, which was not more than half a league from Toulouse. Here our men and the enemy faced each other on opposite sides of the river. Our opponents, afraid that our men would cross, had hurriedly demolished a bridge across the river. Our men made a detour in the hope of finding a ford and came across another bridge, but this too the enemy were now busy demolishing.[26] With great courage our men crossed the river, some climbing over the super-structure of the bridge and some swimming, and pursued the enemy to the very gates of Toulouse. Thence they returned to the river and spent the night there. Here the Count was advised to lay siege to Toulouse.

[239] Accordingly our men moved camp the following day, went to Toulouse and pitched their tents before the gates of the city. The Count of Bar and a number of nobles from Germany took part in the siege. The city was besieged on one side only, since our forces were too small to extend the siege to the other side.[27] In the city were the Count of Toulouse and his cousin the Count of Comminges[28] who was giving him all the help he could; also the Count of Foix, a countless number of knights and the citizens of Toulouse, an enormous crowd. What more? The besiegers seemed very few compared with the besieged. It would be too long a task to describe all the attacks mounted during the siege; to be brief, as often as our opponents came out to harass us we resisted valiantly and com-pelled them to withdraw to the city in confusion.[29]

---

[23] Cf. Psalms 96, v. 8, and 118, v. 8.

[24] The River Hers, according to William of Tudela (*Chanson* I, 77, p. 186), who also describes the skirmish which follows.

[25] The *Chanson* (loc. cit.) says five hundred knights and countless footsoldiers and, as well as Raymond VI and the Count of Foix, mentions Count Bernard of Comminges and mercenaries ('*rotier*') from Navarre.

[26] William of Tudela (*Chanson*, loc. cit.) relates this to a Thursday, which was presumably 16 June, since later (*Chanson* I, 83) he says the siege lasted a fortnight and the letter of July 1211 from the consuls of Toulouse to King Peter of Aragon (*HGL* VIII, 612–19, see note to §§137, 234 et al.) gives the feast of St Peter ('*in festo . . . beati Petri*'), 29 June, as the date the siege was lifted.

[27] William of Tudela states (*Chanson* I, 79, p. 190) that the crusaders attacked the best fortified side of Toulouse, which at this time would have been along the southern and eastern walls, between the Porte Narbonnaise in the south (next to which was the comital castle, the Château Narbonnais) and the Porte de Villeneuve. The consuls' letter of July 1211 to Peter of Aragon (see n. 11 to §234 et al.), says that only two gates were attacked, perhaps the Porte Montgaillard and the Porte Montoulieu: see map 4. This side was chosen in part because it was best placed for maintaining communications with Carcassonne, and no doubt obtaining supplies therefrom (G&L I, p. 239 n. 5).

[28] Bernard IV, Count of Comminges, whose mother was a sister of Raymond V of Toulouse, Raymond VI's father. In the will Raymond VI had made in 1209, Bernard (along with Baldwin) had been named as a guardian of the young Raymond of Toulouse (*HGL* VIII, 573–5).

[29] The *Chanson* (I, 79–83, pp. 190–8) gives a detailed account of the siege, and the consuls' letter (see n. 11 to §234) also covers it. Both describe the pillaging of the surrounding countryside by the crusaders, and the

[240] One day, when the enemy had come out and our men had courageously forced them to retire into the city, in the course of the skirmish our soldiers killed a kinsman of the Count of Comminges, and William of Roquefort, a man of the worst sort, brother of Bernard Bishop of Carcassonne whom we mentioned earlier.[30]

[241] On another occasion our men were taking their customary afternoon rest after dining (it was summer); realising that we were resting the enemy came out of the city by a hidden path[31] and made an onslaught on the army.[32] Our men rose up, fought back bravely and forced the enemy to retreat into the city. It so happened that two nobles, Eustace of Cayeux[33] and Simon the Castellan of Neauphle,[34] were away from the camp escorting a convoy of supplies on its way to the army. At the moment of the attack they were just at the entrance to the camp; the enemy who had come out of the city met them and tried to capture them. They put up a brave resistance but one of the enemy threw a javelin (as was their practice) and hit Eustace in the side and killed him. The Castellan of Neauphle, with a mighty effort and a splendid display of courage, escaped alive and unharmed.

[242] The shortage of supplies pushed up the cost of provisions in the army.[35] Moreover, no good was spoken about the Count of Bar, since everyone in the army held a poor opinion of him. What a just judgment of God! It had been hoped that he would do great things; men had expected more than was reasonable from another mortal, but the Lord, who said through the mouth of his

---

destruction of vines and crops; the consuls say men, women and children working in the fields were slaughtered.

[30] See §130.

[31] '*Occultam viam*', presumably one of four new exits which the consuls say in their letter to King Peter, loc. cit., were made in the walls to to facilitate sorties against the besiegers.

[32] The *Chanson* I, 81–3, pp. 194–8, describes this sortie in more detail, saying that Raymond VI opposed it, preferring to remain on the defensive within Toulouse, but that his leading barons (the Navarese Hugh d'Alfaro, Raymond's Seneschal of the Agenais (see §319 below), and his brother Peter Arcès are mentioned by name) disagreed and went on the offensive. Both Toulousain and Navarese soldiers are identified amongst those attacking the crusaders, and no doubt Hugh, who was a former mercenary captain now in Raymond's service, had brought Navarese soldiers to defend the city. See also Roquebert I, pp. 417–19. William of Tudela relates the sortie to a Wednesday, but both G&L I, p. 241 n. 3 and Martin-Chabot, *Chanson* I, p. 196, identify it with the attack described by the consuls, loc. cit., as taking place on Monday 27 June. The consuls claimed a great victory, saying that their forces killed numerous enemy knights and footsoldiers, captured much booty and recovered prisoners; they say the crusaders then retired on the feast day of St Peter, 29 June, leaving behind many of their wounded, arms and other material.

[33] In Latin '*Eustachius de Queu*', who is identified by G&L (I, p. 242 n. 1) as Eustace of Cayeux in Ponthieu, and who is undoubtedly the same individual as the '*Estaci de Caus*' mentioned twice by William of Tudela (*Chanson* I, 82–3, pp. 196–8). He was the son of William of Cayeux who took part in the Crusade in 1210 (see above §168 and *Layettes* I, 888).

[34] Simon was lord of Neauphle, which lay just east of Montfort l'Amaury in the Ile de France. He and his family were benefactors of the abbey of les Vaux-de-Cernay (cf. n. 2 to §1 above), and had been with Simon de Montfort at Zara on the Fourth Crusade (see §106 above, and G&L I, p. 242 n. 2). See also §284 for Simon of Neauphle and his brother Geoffrey, and also §268.

[35] The *Chanson* (I, 83, p. 198) confirms that lack of supplies caused the crusaders to abandon the siege. It says that bread cost two sous (24 deniers) a loaf; in contrast at Carcassonne (see §97 and n. 50) 30 loaves could be had for one denier.

prophet: 'My glory will I not give to another',[36] knew that if our side achieved great success in the siege it would be attributed entirely to man and not to God, and for this reason did not wish great things to be done there.

[243] *The Count abandons the siege of Toulouse.* Our Count now saw that he was achieving nothing, but rather that the siege was very costly and that the progress of Christ's business was thereby being obstructed; accordingly he abandoned the siege of Toulouse[37] and went to a *castrum* known as Auterive[38] in the direction of the territory of the Count of Foix. He garrisoned the place with sergeants and went on to Pamiers.

[244] Suddenly some mercenaries[39] came to Auterive. The men of the *castrum* were for seizing the sergeants the Count had left there and handing them over to the mercenaries, but the sergeants withdrew into the castle, which was quite strong, and set about defending themselves. What deranged treason, what an evil crime! Realising that they would not be able to hold out the sergeants told the mercenaries they would surrender the castle to them so long as they allowed them to leave alive and unharmed. This proposal was duly carried out. However, not much later our Count passed by the place and burnt it to the ground.

[245] The Count now left Pamiers and went to a *castrum* named Varilhes, near Foix, which he found deserted and burnt; he garrisoned it with his own men. He then entered the territory of the Count of Foix, and laid waste numerous fortresses and destroyed the bourg of Foix itself by fire. He then spent eight days round Foix destroying woods and uprooting vines and then returned to Pamiers.[40]

[246] Meanwhile the Bishop of Cahors[41] had been sent to the Count by the nobles of the territory of Quercy,[42] to put to the Count their request that he should go to them so that they could recognise him as their overlord and hold their lands as his vassals.[43] (The Count of Toulouse had so far held the position

---

[36] Isaiah 42, v. 8.

[37] On 29 June 1211 (see note to §238). Apart from the fact that the siege was unlikely to succeed with the number of troops available, de Montfort evidently wanted to take advantage of the presence of Raymond-Roger of Foix in Toulouse to attack his domains to the south: the *Chanson*, I, 83, p. 198, makes this clear.

[38] A possession of the Counts of Toulouse, on the River Ariège, about 25km south of Toulouse.

[39] Presumably troops sent by the Count of Foix from Toulouse.

[40] William of Tudela confirms (*Chanson* I, 84, p. 202) that the crusaders followed this scorched earth policy in the county of Foix, destroying foodstuffs and grain, and laying waste to the fields, adding that they 'caused as much damage as they could'.

[41] William of Cardaillac, who like his brother Bertrand (see next section) had taken part in the crusading campaign in Quercy in the summer of 1209 which is described only by William of Tudela (*Chanson* I, 13–14, pp. 36–44). He had been present at the siege of Toulouse (see note below in this section). See also §272 below for his presence at the siege of Castelnaudary.

[42] The four principal lords were Raymond Viscount of Turenne, Bertrand de Cardaillac (nephew of the Bishop of Cahors), Bertrand de Gourdon and Ratier lord of Castelnau-de-Montratier. They had all taken part in the *Croisade Quercynoise* in 1209: see *Chanson* I, 13, pp. 36–40 and G&L I, p. 245 n. 3. On Ratier de Castelnau see also §495.

[43] According to William of Tudela, it was Arnold Amalric who urged the principal lords of Quercy to do homage to de Montfort, rather than they who sought out the legate (*Chanson* I, 85, p. 202). Whatever the case, an act dated 20 June 1211 records that the Bishop of Cahors, present at the siege of Toulouse with the crusaders, paid homage to de Montfort in respect of the county of Cahors, on the same terms as he had held it 'from Raymond former Count of Toulouse' ('*ab R. quondam comite Tolosano*'); the witnesses

of overlord throughout Quercy.) The noble Count asked the Count of Bar and the nobles from Germany to go with him. They all agreed, promised to go and actually started on the way. However, when they approached Castelnaudary, the Count of Bar went back on his promise to our Count; paying no regard to his reputation or his honour he declared that he would not go with him on any account. Everyone was astounded, our Count was extremely disturbed; he himself begged him to continue, all present joined in, but they could achieve nothing.[44] Our Count now asked the other German nobles whether they wished to accompany him; they all promised most willingly to do so. Accordingly our Count started out in the direction of Cahors, whilst the Count of Bar took another road and set out towards Carcassonne. On his departure he was the target of abuse to an extent that cannot easily be described; everyone in the army, from the lowest to the highest, pursued him with insults such as I would be ashamed to set down. So was it brought about by the just judgment of God that this man, who on his arrival in the Albigensian area had been honoured and feared by everyone throughout the cities and towns of the region, now departed universally derided, and despicable in everyone's eyes.

[247] *The Count returns to Cahors.* On his way to Cahors the Count came to a *castrum* named Caylus,[45] in the territory of Cahors and under the lordship of the Count of Toulouse. He attacked it and burnt the bourg of the *castrum* to the ground. Proceeding to Cahors he was received with honour. After spending a few days there he left with the German nobles and conducted them as far as the town of Rocamadour.[46] From there they went back to their own country, whilst the Count returned to Cahors with a very small force.[47]

---

included the legates Raymond of Uzès and Arnold Amalric, Bishop Fulk of Toulouse, the Abbot of Pamiers, Thedisius, 'brother Dominic, preacher' and Simon de Montfort's banker Raymond de Salvanhac (see *HGL* VIII, 611, and *Layettes* V, 186). Thus de Montfort was now proceeding into Quercy to demonstrate the new position.

[44] William of Tudela (*Chanson* I, 84, p. 200) mentions a dispute within the crusading army at about this time, when an otherwise unknown 'Count of Alos' ('*coms d'Alo*') wanted to make peace with Raymond VI. It is conceivable that this was the Count of Bar, and that his desire to reach an accord with Raymond VI was the reason for his departure from the crusaders and de Montfort. (In the later prose versions of the *Chanson* the 'Count of Alos' becomes the 'Count of Chalon'.) Whatever the case, these divisions within the crusading army may signal that some at least of those who had come from the north to help the campaign believed that de Montfort and the legates were being unreasonable in refusing to entertain Raymond VI's offers to negotiate at this time.

[45] Caylus on the River Bonnette, 12km north of Saint-Antonin-Noble-Val, a possession of the Counts of Toulouse since the 12th century. See also §318 below.

[46] Rocamadour lies in northern Quercy, about 40km north of Cahors. It became a popular place of pilgrimage in the second half of the 12th century, after a tomb was found there in 1166, supposedly that of a hermit, St Amadour. A cult of the Virgin, Our Lady of Rocamadour, was also associated with the site. One tradition is that a standard of Our Lady of Rocamadour was carried by Christian forces at the battle of Las Navas de Tolosa in Spain in 1212, and Roquebert (I, pp. 430–2) speculates that de Montfort's journey to Rocamadour may have been connected with the blessing of the standard, bearing in mind that some of his own knights under Guy de Lucy, accompanied by Arnold Amalric, were to be present at Las Navas de Tolosa the following year (see §255). This visit to Rocamadour is mentioned in the *Chanson*, I, 84–5, p. 202, which states that de Montfort had promised to go there (presumably on pilgrimage) and also adds somewhat enigmatically that Arnold Amalric was present at Cahors at this time, in hiding.

[47] Once again the departure of crusaders from the north after their forty days' service left de Montfort's forces very seriously depleted. William of Tudela (*Chanson* I, 87, pp. 204–6) says that as soon as these forces

[248] *Some of our knights are captured.* At Cahors it was reported to him that two of his knights, Lambert de Thury[48] and the Englishman Walter Langton, brother of the Archbishop of Canterbury,[49] had been captured by knights of the Count of Foix. I can give a brief account of how they were captured, based on what they themselves told me. One day the two were riding near the territory of the Count of Foix with a large group of local men. On hearing of this the Count pursued them with a very large force. The local men with our knights (who, it is said, had previously arranged to betray them) fled instantly when they saw the Count's force approaching, and only six of our people were left. Most of the enemy surrounded the six (the Count himself had set off in pursuit of the local men) and killed all their horses. Thus deprived, our men, surrounded by a host of enemies, defended themselves valiantly. Then one of the enemy, of higher rank than the rest, a cousin of the Count of Foix, told Lambert (whom he knew) to surrender. Thereupon this man of great honour said: 'Mine hour is not yet come.'[50] However, realising that he could not escape, he said: 'We will surrender on condition that you promise us five things; that you will not kill us or cut off our limbs; that you will keep us in honourable custody; that you will not separate us; that you will release us against a reasonable ransom; and that you will not place us under the control of any other person. If you give us your firm undertaking on all these points, we will give ourselves up. If you refuse, we are prepared to die; but we trust in the Lord that we will not die alone, but will sell our lives dearly and, with Christ's help, will first kill many of you. Our hands are not yet bound, you will not take us easily or with impunity.' When the knight heard these words of Lambert he promised that he would gladly do all that was asked. 'Come then,' said Lambert, 'give me your hand to show your good faith.' The other did not dare come near him without further assurances from our men; Lambert and the other five duly gave these assurances. The knight then went up to them and took them prisoner on the agreed conditions, but soon failed to live up to his promises, and handed them over to the Count of Foix. He kept them heavily chained in a foul dungeon, so tiny that they could neither stand nor lie at full stretch. They had no light save only a candle – and that only when they were eating. There was only one tiny opening in that cell, through which food was passed to them. The Count of Foix kept them there for a long time until they were ransomed for a large sum. Let us now return to where we began this digression.

---

left de Montfort, Raymond VI began to rally his forces for a counter-attack. Cf. below, §258 for Peter's summary of de Montfort's position at this time.

[48] Lambert de Thury or de Crécy. He may well have been amongst the crusaders in 1209: see §82 and n. He had been given Limoux by de Montfort in 1209 (see n. 91 to §110), and was thus sometimes called Lambert de Limoux. See also §414. He was later granted Puivert, and in an act of 1213 styled himself lord of Puivert (G&L II, p. 107 n. 2). He was Seneschal of Beaucaire in 1216 (see §575).

[49] Brother of Stephen Langton, Archbishop of Canterbury 1207–28, in whose disputed election Innocent III had intervened: see W. L. Warren, *King John*, ch. 5. Walter Langton was still with the crusaders seven years later (*HGL* VIII, 579).

[50] St John 2, v. 4.

[249] *The Count returns from Cahors.* Having now fulfilled the purpose of his visit to Cahors, the Count decided to return to the Albigensian area. He therefore left Cahors and returned to Pamiers, passing through his fortresses and inspecting the boundaries of his territory on his way.[51]

[250] He came to a castle near Pamiers and found it defended against him. It held six knights and a large supporting force. The Count could not capture the place on the day he reached it, but early next day he initiated an attack, set fire to the gates, undermined the wall and took the castle by force and destroyed it. Three of the knights and all the other soldiers were killed, but on the advice of his followers the Count spared the other three knights since they had promised that they could be exchanged for Lambert de Thury and the Englishman Walter Langton, whom the Count of Foix was holding captive.

[51] The *Chanson* (I, 85–6, pp. 202–4) mentions that de Montfort passed through Saint-Antonin, Lavaur, Gaillac and thence to Carcassonne, where he must have arrived at some point in September 1211. Arnold Amalric was with him, but then left for Albi and Saissac. The castle near Pamiers (next section) may have been Bonnac.

[**XI. §§251–285, autumn 1211:** *Puylaurens defects from the crusaders – gathering of southern forces under Raymond VI, Raymond-Roger of Foix and Gaston de Béarn – siege of Castelnaudary by Raymond VI and his allies – defections from de Montfort – battle of Castelnaudary/Saint-Martin – the crusaders victorious but the southerners claim victory – further defections from the crusaders – Simon de Montfort at Pamiers and Fanjeaux – recruiting campaign of William, Archdeacon of Paris and Jacques de Vitry in northern France and Germany.*]

[251] The Count then proceeded to Pamiers.[1] Whilst he was there it was reported to him that in an act of betrayal the men of Puylaurens had handed their town[2] over to Sicard, who had been its lord;[3] and that Sicard and his knights, together with the townsmen, were besieging the knights whom Guy de Lucy had left as a garrison and were now defending themselves in the castle; as I recorded earlier, our Count had handed Puylaurens to Guy.[4] Much disturbed by this report our Count at once set off to help his knights. When he reached Castelnaudary a messenger told him that Guy's knights had surrendered the keep at Puylaurens to the enemy; the reports were true, and indeed the knight whom Guy had set in charge of the garrison had been responsible for the surrender, motivated, it was said, by a bribe. Some days later when the knight was arraigned for treason in the Count's court and refused the opportunity to defend himself in a judicial duel Guy had him hanged. [252] The Count left some of his knights to garrison Castelnaudary and himself went on to Carcassonne, but before doing so sent some knights and crossbowmen[5] to guard Montferrand; for by now the Count of Toulouse and his fellow enemies of the faith, realising that our Count was almost alone, had recovered their ability to oppose him, and were on the move throughout the area in the hope of regaining, by treason, the *castra* they had lost.[6] Whilst our Count was at Carcassonne it was reported to him that his enemies were coming in force to besiege Castelnaudary, and that the men he had sent to guard Montferrand had left there in fear of the enemy and gone to Castelnaudary. This news greatly disturbed the Count; he at once sent to his knights in Castelnaudary and urged them not to give way to fear in face of the enemy because he would himself come to their aid.

[253] *Siege of Castelnaudary.*[7] One Sunday whilst the Count was at Carcassonne

---

1   Probably during September 1211, but no contemporary source gives a firm dating.
2   'Villa', here apparently with the unusual meaning of the inhabited part of the *castrum* outside the castle.
3   See above, §230.
4   §230. Guy de Lucy himself was in Spain to help the Christian forces against the Muslim Almohades. For his return see §255 below.
5   Latin 'balistarios'. On *balista* see §191 n. 117.
6   See also *Chanson* I, 87–9, pp. 204–10, for this mobilisation of the southern forces in the autumn of 1211.
7   This took place in September or early October 1211; the only explicit indication of date is Peter's remark in §258 below that the siege took place at harvest time. The *Chanson* (I, 92–102, pp. 214–32) also

he had heard Mass and celebrated holy communion and was preparing to leave at once for Castlenaudary, when a Cistercian lay brother[8] who was present began to offer him comfort and encouragement. The Count, putting all his faith in God, said to the lay brother: 'Do you think that I am afraid? We are about Christ's business. The whole Church is praying for me. I know that we cannot be over-come.' This said, this most noble man hastened to Castelnaudary. Several for-tresses near Castelnaudary had already seceded from the Count and many of the men he had placed in them had been betrayed, and slaughtered by the enemy.[9]

[254] Whilst the Count was at Castelnaudary, the Count of Toulouse, the Count of Foix, and a Gascon noble named Gaston de Béarn,[10] with a huge force of followers,[11] left Toulouse and rushed to lay siege to Castelnaudary. With our enemies came that most depraved apostate, that iniquitous transgressor, son of the Devil, servant of the Antichrist, Savary de Mauléon;[12] more evil than any heretic, worse then any infidel, assailant of the Church, the enemy of Christ. O most corrupt of mortals – or should I say himself a mortal infection[13] – I speak of Savary, who, villain unredeemed, shameless and senseless, rushed against God with neck down[14] and dared to assault the Holy Church of God! Prime mover of heresy, architect of cruelty, agent of perversity, comrade of sinners, accomplice of the perverted, a disgrace to mankind, a man unacquainted with manly virtues, devilish – himself the devil incarnate! When our men heard that such a huge enemy force was on its way, some of them urged the Count to leave a part of the

devotes great attention to the siege (about three hundred lines); William of Puylaurens provides a brief summary (XVIII).

8 Latin '*conversus quidam Cisterciensis*'.

9 De Montfort was now left with only his core of knights, as the southerners rebelled against him and sought to undo the conquests of the spring and summer. The *Chanson* (I, 88–92, pp. 208–14) underlines the extent of the rising against de Montfort, and his position was perhaps worse than in the previous winters because now both Raymond VI and Raymond-Roger of Foix were openly fighting against him.

10 Béarn lies in southern Gascony, and its Viscount Gaston VI had not hitherto played any part in the war against the crusaders. He was a vassal of King Peter of Aragon. See especially §§367–98 below for his position at the time of the Council of Lavaur in January 1213.

11 William of Tudela also mentions Raymond VI's Seneschal of the Agenais, Hugh of Alfaro (on whom see n. 32 to §241, n. 72 to §319 and *Chanson* I, p. 194 n. 1), and a multitude of others from Gascony, Quercy, the Agenais, and elsewhere (*Chanson* I, 89, p. 210).

12 Savary was from Poitou, and inherited lordships there and in the Saintonge. He was King John of England's seneschal of Aquitaine, and according to William of Tudela (*Chanson* I, 86, p. 204) he arrived from Bergerac to help Raymond VI. A 13th century source (the anonymous History of the Dukes of Normandy and Kings of England) suggests that it was on King John's initiative that Savary came south, but otherwise there is no evidence to show that his intervention was initiated by King John (to whose sister Joan Raymond VI had been married 1196–9, Joan being the mother of the future Raymond VII). His presence during the Castelnaudary campaign is also covered in the *Chanson* (I, 86–8, pp. 204–8, and 103, p. 234), but his intervention was to be shortlived: because he had not been paid he took Raymond's son to Bordeaux and ransomed him. He was later (in 1219) to go on crusade to the Holy Land (see S. Runciman, *A History of the Crusades*, III (Cambridge, 1950), p. 161), and fought with Louis VIII in Languedoc when he intervened in 1226 (see Roquebert III, p. 299, and Belperron p. 370). He is recorded as having written a poem to Eleanor, Countess of Toulouse, promising to support her with 500 knights (Basques and Bra-bançons) against the invaders of her domains. See also Roquebert I, p. 438, and G&M, p. 105 n. 3, and §394 below.

13 Word play: '*O virum, immo virus, pessimum*'. Just below 'shameless and senseless' is '*impudens et imprudens*'.

14 From Job 15, v. 26.

army to defend the *castrum* and himself retreat to Fanjeaux or even Carcassonne, but through God's grace wiser counsels prevailed and the Count determined to await the onset of the enemy at Castelnaudary.[15]

[255] I must record that whilst the Count was at Castelnaudary and the enemy almost at the gates, suddenly, sent by God, Guy de Lucy arrived with almost fifty knights. These had been sent by the Count to help the King of Aragon against the Turks,[16] and their return greatly cheered the Count and raised the spirits of all our men. However, the King – as was to be expected of so vicious a man, who never favoured either the business of the faith or our Count – behaved in a most disagreeable manner to the knights whom the Count had sent to help him. Indeed when the knights were on their way back to the Count on his written instructions, the King laid an ambush with a view to seizing them. However, the knights found out about this betrayal and made a detour away from the public road. What a cruel return for a pious act, what a harsh reward for such service rendered![17] Let us return to our main theme.

[256] The Count was confidently awaiting the approach of his adversaries in Castelnaudary, when suddenly one day the enemy arrived with a huge force; they covered the whole ground like locusts, and began to run about in every direction. As they approached the *castrum*, the inhabitants of the outer bourg at once climbed over the walls, crossed over to the enemy and abandoned the bourg; our opponents entered it and began to run hither and thither in great glee.[18] Our Count was at this moment at table; when the meal was finished our men armed themselves, left the *castrum*, quickly put to flight any of the enemy they found in the bourg and drove them out trembling with fear as they fled before us. [257] After this, the Count of Toulouse and those with him pitched their tents on a hill near to the *castrum*;[19] they then surrounded themselves with ditches, fences and barriers to the extent that they seemed more besieged than besieging, and their position more strongly defended and more difficult to approach than the *castrum* which was the object of their attack. Late in the day our adversaries re-entered the bourg, which was now empty of men since our forces were too small

---

[15] William of Tudela (*Chanson* I, 90–1, pp. 210–14) gives a reconstruction of the debate over what to do in response to Raymond VI's initiative, crediting Hugh de Lacy with having successfully made the argument that Castelnaudary should be defended.
[16] 'Turcos', i.e. the Moors. Guy had been helping King Peter of Aragon, whose vassal de Montfort was and to whom he hence owed service, against the Almohades: cf. §251 n. 4 and §196 n. 14.
[17] King Peter may have felt that the recall by de Montfort of Guy's detachment was a severe setback, possibly contributing to his defeat, in September 1211, by the Muslims at Salvatierra; this may explain his attitude. (Cf. G&L I, p. 255 n. 1, and Roquebert I, pp. 439–40.)
[18] Castelnaudary lies to the south of the River Fresquel, on a raised spur of land overlooking the plain around it. The castle was at the south-eastern end of the site, at its highest point. Around the castle at this time was a small settlement, the '*burgum exterius*' mentioned here by Peter. For consistency we have followed our usual practice of retaining *castrum* in the translation and rendering '*burgum*' as 'bourg' (see Appendix A), although at Castelnaudary the *castrum* seems to have consisted of the castle and little else, with all the 'civilian' inhabitants residing in the bourg. (They must have returned after the destruction wrought by Raymond VI's forces when they withdrew in May 1211 (cf. above §233), and now they again abandoned the settlement and joined the besiegers.)
[19] Just to the north of the town, on a hill known as Le Pech.

to defend it. (In the *castrum*, knights and sergeants numbered less than five hundred, whereas the enemy forces were believed to amount to almost a hundred thousand.)[20] However, the enemy who had entered the bourg were afraid that our men might drive them out as they had done previously, and fortified the bourg on the side facing us with wooden fences and whatever else they could find so as to prevent us coming out to attack them. They even made numerous holes in the outside wall between the bourg and their camp, to ensure an easy escape route should the need arise. Next morning our men made a sortie from the *castrum*, destroyed the defences erected by the enemy, drove them from the bourg (as they had done previously), and pursued them to their tents.[21]

[258] I must not fail to record the noble Count's difficulties at this time. His Countess was at Lavaur; their eldest son, Amaury, was ill at Fanjeaux; a daughter,[22] born in the area, was being nursed at Montréal. None of them could see each other or give each other any support. I should also record that despite being so greatly outnumbered our men came out every day and made frequent and courageous attacks on the enemy – as I said before, our men seemed to be besiegers rather than besieged, since the enemy had surrounded themselves with so many barriers that our men could not get near them however vigorously they tried. I may add that every day our sergeants took our horses to water a distance of half a league[23] in full view of the enemy, and our footsoldiers daily harvested the vineyards near the enemy encampment with their adversaries looking on and envying them. It was in fact harvest time.

[259] One day that worst of traitors, the Count of Foix, and his son Roger-Bernard – his equal in evil – approached Castelnaudary with a large detachment of their army, intending to attack our men standing at arms at the gates. Seeing their approach our men threw themselves into the attack with great enthusiasm, unhorsed Roger-Bernard and many others and forced them to withdraw in shame to their tents. It would be impossible to record every attack and incident of the siege; I will simply say that whenever our adversaries dared to approach us to mount an attack, our men – who waited each day outside the entrance to the *castrum*, eager for battle – drove them back to their tents to their great shame.

[260] Meanwhile the neighbouring *castra* all around seceded from our Count's lordship and went over to the Count of Toulouse.[24] One day the townsmen of Cabaret sent a message to the Count of Toulouse to tell him that if he would go to them or send his representatives they would hand Cabaret over to him. Accordingly one night a large body of the enemy was sent from their camp

---

[20] The *Chanson* (I, 88 and 90, pp. 208 and 212) refers to a host of two hundred thousand. G&M say 'cinq mille' – evidently an error since they make no comment and G&L record no variants in the manuscripts.

[21] See Roquebert I, pp. 440–1 and 446–8, and Belperron pp. 230–1 for dicussions of Raymond VI's excessively cautious tactics at Castelnaudary.

[22] Apparently Petronilla, who is recorded as having joined the nuns of Saint-Antonin in Paris in 1222 (see G&L I, p. 257 n. 4; and Vicaire, ch. IX, n. 58).

[23] Presumably to the River Fresquel, about 3km to the north.

[24] As well as Puylaurens, these included Les Cassés and Montferrand: see below, §281, where Peter gives details of the widespread defections at this time.

by the Count and set off for Cabaret to take it into their possession. However, Cabaret is five leagues[25] from Castelnaudary, and through Divine clemency the enemy lost the road to Cabaret and despite a long detour through impenetrable country failed to reach it; after wandering about for a long time they returned to their camp.

[261] Meanwhile the Count of Toulouse erected a siege-engine of the type known as 'mangonel'. The enemy began to bombard the *castrum* with the mangonel, but it caused us little or no trouble. After a few days the Count of Toulouse had an enormous siege-engine[26] made ready which was to be used to knock down the walls; it fired huge stones which destroyed whatever they landed on. After the bombardment had continued for a few days one of the Count's jesters came to him and said: 'Why are you expending so much effort on this engine? Why are you trying to break down the walls of this place? Do you not see that every day your enemies are coming right up to your tents, yet you dare not go out to meet them? You ought to be wishing the walls were made of iron, so that they could not reach you.'

[262] It was indeed a most remarkable feature of the siege that whereas it is usual for the besiegers to attack the besieged, here our besieged army more frequently attacked their besiegers, quite contrary to what one would expect. Our men kept mocking their adversaries to this effect: 'Why are you spending so much time and effort on your siege-engine, and trying so hard to knock down our walls? We will save you all this expense, we will release you from your labours. Only give us twenty silver marks and we will totally destroy one hundred cubits of the wall and level off the ground, so that – if you dare – you will be able to come across to us unhindered by the wall.' What spirited courage, what singular strength of purpose! [263] One day our Count came out of the *castrum*, with the intention of demolishing the siege-engine. However, our adversaries had so surrounded it with barriers and ditches that our men could not reach it. Displaying his usual courage our Count, who was mounted, was all for crossing a particularly wide and deep ditch and boldly attacking his foes; however, some of our people saw what he was attempting and thought that disaster would inevitably follow if he went on. They seized his horse by the bridle and restrained him from exposing himself to imminent death. All our men then went back to the *castrum*, having themselves lost no-one but leaving many of the enemy dead.

[264] At this juncture the Count sent his Marshal, Guy de Lévis,[27] a loyal supporter and a fine soldier, to arrange for supplies to be brought from Fanjeaux and Carcassonne and to instruct the citizens of Carcassonne and Béziers to send help without delay.[28] The Marshal could achieve nothing, since the whole of that

---

25 About 35km due east.
26 The *Chanson* (I, 92, p. 216) refers to a trebuchet being set up (on which see n. 45 to §96). Some destruction was wrought, but the machine made relatively little impact because the attackers could find so few stones to throw from it of sufficient quality that they did not shatter when fired.
27 See n. 104 to §185.
28 William of Tudela (*Chanson* I, 93, p. 216) refers to supplies of wine, wheat, bread and oats being brought from Carcassonne to Castelnaudary.

area had corrupted its way;[29] he returned to the Count, who sent him back accompanied by Matthew de Marly, a noble, brother to Bouchard. They came to the Count's vassals and begged them again and again to come to the Count, adding threats to their prayers. These latter, now subverted and wavering in their loyalty, would not listen to them, and they went on to Aimeric, the lord of Narbonne and his fellow citizens, begging and urging them to come at once to the Count's aid. The citizens replied to the Marshal that if Aimeric, their lord, would go with them they would follow him; he – as was to be expected of this most unworthy of nobles – could in no way be persuaded to this. Our knights then left Narbonne; from so populous a city they took barely three hundred men. When they reached Carcassonne they could get together no more than five hundred men from the whole area, and when they tried to take them to the Count they refused to go and immediately fled to their own homes. [265] Meanwhile that most treacherous of men the Count of Foix had occupied Saint-Martin, a *castrum* belonging to Bouchard de Marly, which is near Castelnaudary to the east towards Carcassonne,[30] together with some other castles round about, and fortified them against us. Our Count now ordered Bouchard de Marly and Martin Algai,[31] who were with the Countess at Lavaur, to come to Castelnaudary. This Martin was a Spanish knight and at that time with us; later he was to conduct himself most despicably, as will be shown below.

[266] Amongst the Count's followers there was a knight of the Carcassès, from Montréal, named William Cat,[32] who had received land from the Count and had been knighted by him; indeed the Count had treated him as a close friend, to the extent that he had made him godfather to his daughter.[33] The Count and Countess and all our people placed more trust in him than in any other native of the

---

29 Cf. Genesis 6, v. 12. The failure of these attempts to raise troops locally illustrates de Montfort's lack of support amongst the southern nobility. The defection at Castelnaudary of William Cat, whom de Montfort had apparently trusted (§§266–9 below), further underlines the difficulty of winning over the lesser and middling nobility of the region, and hence the crusaders' reliance on forces from elsewhere.

30 Saint-Martin-la-Lande, 5km due east from Castelnaudary.

31 Martin Algai, a mercenary commander who had previously served the English Kings Richard the Lionheart and John, and who had acted for the latter as seneschal in Gascony and the Périgord from 1203 to 1206. He became lord of Biron in the Périgord through marriage (see Roquebert I, p. 442). His involvement at the siege of Castelnaudary is also mentioned by William of Tudela (*Chanson* I, 89, 93, 95 and 98, pp. 210–26, and see esp. n. 3 on p. 210). He is sometimes identified with the Martin of Olite mentioned later in the *Chanson*, on which see n. 67 to §282. He was fighting with de Montfort at this stage, but apparently sought to defect to Raymond VI shortly after this (see §274) and was later hanged by de Montfort after the siege of Biron (§337).

32 William Cat of Arzens had abandoned his lands after the invasion of 1209, and had become a *faidit* opposing the crusaders. He had taken refuge at Cabaret, and is mentioned in the *Chanson* (I, 54, p. 126) as having been amongst those who came down from Cabaret to attack the crusaders' siege engines at Carcassonne in August 1210 at the beginning of the siege of Termes. He must have become reconciled to de Montfort at some point over the winter of 1210–11, certainly by the time of the surrender of Montréal in March 1211. He may be the same William Cat who is mentioned in Inquisition records in the Doat Collection as having been a Cathar believer (see G&L p. 264 n. 1). William of Puylaurens (XVIII and p. 75 n. 2) also mentions his defection at Castelnaudary, adding that his behaviour caused de Montfort increasingly to eschew association with 'knights of our tongue' ('*fortius abhorrere cepit consortia militum nostre lingue*').

33 Presumably Petronilla, whose birth is mentioned in §258 above.

region, and the Count had once given his eldest son[34] to him to keep safe. The Count sent him from Castelnaudary to Fanjeaux to fetch men from the neighbouring *castra* to come to his aid. But William now began to behave more basely than any enemy, more treacherously than any traitor. He showed no gratitude for the favours done to him, he forgot his friendship with the Count. He joined with others from the area, who shared with him the barbarity needed to concoct a villainous plot – to capture the Marshal[35] and his companions as they returned from Carcassonne and hand them over to the Count of Foix. What an iniquitous kind of treason, what harsh villainy, what barbarous scheming, what devilish contrivance! However, this betrayal become known to the Marshal and he avoided the ambush.

[267] I must record that at this time numerous nobles, who held a large number of strong *castra*, seceded from our Count and secretly swore loyalty to the Count of Toulouse.[36] What a detestable oath to take, what faithless loyalty!

[268] Meanwhile Bouchard de Marly and Martin Algai and others of the Count's knights,[37] who were hurrying from Lavaur to the Count's aid, arrived at Saissac,[38] a *castrum* held by Bouchard, since they did not dare take the direct route from Lavaur to Castelnaudary.[39] On the day before their arrival at Castelnaudary the Count of Foix, who had been forewarned of their approach, left his camp and went to Saint-Martin[40] – which our knights had to pass through – intending to attack them. When he heard of this our Count sent Guy de Lucy, Simon the Castellan of Neauphle,[41] the Viscount of Donges[42] and some other knights, up to about forty in all, to help them. He instructed them to join battle with the Count of Foix on the following day without fail. After their departure the Count was left with barely sixty mounted men, including both knights and squires. When the Count of Foix saw that our Count had sent this help to his beleaguered knights, he left Saint-Martin and returned to the besieging army intending to add to his forces and return to attack the Marshal and those with him.[43] [269] Meanwhile our Count spoke as follows to William Cat and the other local knights who were with him at Castelnaudary: 'My friends, you see that

---

[34] Amaury de Montfort.

[35] Guy de Lévis: see §185 and §264 above.

[36] Further details are given in §281 below.

[37] William of Tudela also describes these events (*Chanson* I, 93, p. 216), mentioning about a hundred knights with Bouchard and twenty with Martin Algai.

[38] For Saissac see n. 41 to §15 n. 91 to §110 (for its occupation by Bouchard), and §123.

[39] The *Chanson* (I, 93) mentions that their route also took in Castres. A detour in order to get from Lavaur to Castelnaudary was necessary because, as mentioned below in §281, places such as Saint-Félix, Cuq-Toulza and Puylaurens, which lay on a more direct route, had defected from de Montfort.

[40] Saint-Martin-la-Lande; cf. above §265. The encounter which followed, one of the very few pitched battles in open country which took place during the Crusade, is known as the battle of Saint-Martin or Castelnaudary (although Wakefield, *Heresy, Crusade and Inquisition*, p. 106, refers to it as 'a skirmish').

[41] See §241 above.

[42] Roard (or Rouaud or Rouaut) Viscount of Donges near Nantes. He had been with de Montfort since the first campaign in 1209; he was for example at the siege of Lavaur (*HGL* VIII, 581) and appears as a witness to various acts in 1211 including the submission of Roger of Comminges on 3 April (*HGL* VIII, 608). He was one of Simon's most trusted companions (Belperron's '*équipe*'); cf. *Chanson* I, 36, p. 92.

[43] Raymond-Roger of Foix's desire to take the initiative and join battle is in stark contrast to Raymond

those powerful nobles, the Count of Toulouse and the Count of Foix, are seeking my blood with a huge force. I am almost alone in the midst of my enemies. In the name of God I ask you that if, swayed by fear or affection, you wish to go to them and leave me, you should not hide your intentions and I will see that you are given safe conduct to join them.' What nobility, what princely conduct! William Cat, that second Judas, replied: 'My lord, may the day never come when we will desert you! If all others leave you, yet I will stay with you to the death!' Those with him all echoed his words; yet shortly afterwards, whilst others remained steadfast, this traitor with some of his allies deserted the Count and from being a close friend became a cruel persecutor.

[270] After this, early in the morning, the Marshal and Bouchard de Marly and those with them[44] heard Mass, made confession and celebrated holy communion, and then took to their horses and set out to join our Count. The Count of Foix was aware of their approach; taking with him a huge force of armed cavalry chosen from the best in his army, and an even larger number of picked footsoldiers, he hurried out to intercept them.[45] His forces were divided into three groups.[46] [271] Our Count was at that moment outside the gates of Castelnaudary anxiously awaiting the arrival of the Marshal and those with him. Seeing the Count of Foix hurrying to attack them he took counsel with his companions as to what action he should take. Various opinions were expressed: some said he should stay in the *castrum* to guard it, others on the contrary urged him to rush to the aid of his knights. This man of unwearying courage and unvanquished honour is reported to have said: 'There are very few of us left in this place, and the whole of Christ's business depends on this fight. Heaven forbid that my knights should die gloriously in battle and that I should escape alive and in shame. I will either conquer with my friends or fall with them. Let us too join the fight and if needs must die with them.' Who hearing these words could hold back his tears? The Count was in tears as he spoke them. At once he set off to help his comrades.[47]

[272] As he drew near the Marshal and his companions, the Count of Foix reunited the three detachments into which he had divided his forces into a single group. Here I must add that the Bishop of Cahors[48] and a Cistercian monk who was attending to Christ's business on the orders of the Abbot of Cîteaux had

---

VI's inertia. Compare the position at the first siege of Toulouse, when according to William of Tudela Raymond had also opposed aggressive tactics (see §241 above).

[44] The Marshal Guy de Lévis and Matthew de Marly were coming from Carcassonne (§264); Bouchard de Marly and Martin Algai were coming from Saissac (§268). They were gathered near Saint-Martin-la-Lande, intending to enter Castelnaudary, when the Count of Foix intervened to stop them.

[45] The battle of Saint-Martin which now ensued is described in detail by the *Chanson*, I, 93–103, pp. 216–32.

[46] Cf. the same formation at Muret in 1213, §454 and §462.

[47] William of Tudela's account (*Chanson* I, 100, p. 228) states that de Montfort decided to intervene when it became clear that the convoy of supplies being brought up to Castelnaudary by Bouchard de Marly had been captured and looted; he therefore came out of Castelnaudary with all his men (i.e. presumably taking all the 60 mounted men referred to in §268), leaving only some footsoldiers in the *castrum*.

[48] Bishop William of Cardaillac, whose presence at the battle is also mentioned by the *Chanson* (I, 98, p. 226), and on whom see §246 above. He is recorded as being in Paris in October 1211, when he paid homage

accompanied the Marshal; when they saw the enemy approaching and realised that battle was about to be joined they began to encourage our men to conduct themselves courageously. They promised them that if they were to fall in this glorious struggle on behalf of the Christian faith they would be given remission for all their sins, would be instantly crowned with glory and honour and would thus receive a reward for their labours. Our soldiers, sure of their reward but also confident of victory, met the enemy vigorously, enthusiastically and without fear. The enemy were approaching in a single group, and had organised their line thus: the mounted men whose horses were protected with armour were in the centre, the remaining cavalry on one flank and the footsoldiers, well equipped with lances, were on the other. Our men therefore held a discussion to decide their tactics, and proposed to direct their first assault at the cavalry with armoured horses. [273] Even as their meeting was taking place they saw from afar our Count leaving Castelnaudary and hurrying to their aid. The immediate effect was as if to redouble their daring; their spirits rose, and calling Christ's name they flung themselves into the midst of the enemy and – quicker than it takes to tell – penetrated their line. The enemy, beaten in an instant and in confusion, sought safety in flight. As they saw this our men at once turned on the footsoldiers stationed on one flank and slew countless of their number. I cannot fail to record that – as the Marshal reliably informed me – the enemy outnumbered us by more than thirty to one.[49] We must recognise the operation of Divine intervention; our Count could not become involved in the battle, despite the great haste with which he arrived on the scene, since Christ the Victor had already awarded the victory to His knights.[50]

[274] Our men pursued the fleeing enemy and killed the stragglers, so that there was an enormous slaughter of our adversaries; no more than thirty of our side fell, whereas vast numbers of the enemy were slain.[51] I must add that Martin

to King Philip Augustus, which was presumably after the end of the siege of Castelnaudary (G&L I, p. 268 n. 2).

49 William of Tudela gives a figure of ten to one (*Chanson* I, 104, p. 234), which may be more plausible. On the French side were the hundred knights with Bouchard de Marly, twenty with Martin Algai, and forty who had been sent to support them by de Montfort (§268 and n. 37). They cannot have had many supporting infantry. William of Tudela (*Chanson* I, 93, p. 218) gives both four hundred and two thousand as numbers on the southern side, and refers also to the Count of Foix taking all his mercenaries (*rotier*), later referring to crossbowmen (ibid. 96, p. 222); he says only Savary de Mauléon remained encamped on Le Pech outside Castelnaudary with Raymond VI's forces.

50 William of Tudela (*Chanson* I, 102, p. 230) and William of Puylaurens (XVIII) both say on the contrary that Simon de Montfort did join in the fighting. The *Chanson* (loc. cit.) also says that the sight of de Montfort coming to support his men made the forces of the Count of Foix (most of whom were mercenaries) lose confidence. But while the sources are not agreed as to the precise timing of de Montfort's own intervention, it does seem clear that after their initial attack the southern forces lost the initiative and their troops became distracted by looting the crusader convoy of supplies and presumably making off with the horses and weapons of those French knights who had fallen; as described in the next section, this enabled Bouchard de Marly and then de Montfort to pursue them and inflict much slaughter. The indiscipline of the southern forces, which was a serious problem in a pitched battle, thus combined with the confidence and sense of purpose of the French forces, and the inaction of Raymond VI, to produce a victory to the crusaders. For a discussion see Roquebert, I, pp. 444–8.

51 William of Tudela's account suggests that this slaughter began before de Montfort arrived on the scene (*Chanson* I, 97, p. 224) and he mentions a hundred routiers being killed by Bouchard de Marly's forces.

Algai (mentioned above) withdrew from the battle during the first attack and started to run off; the Bishop of Cahors who was nearby saw him and asked what he was doing. He replied: 'We are all dead.' The holy man did not believe him, but rebuked him severely and compelled him to rejoin the fight.[52] Again, I must add that in their fear of imminent death the enemy called out 'Montfort! Montfort!' so pretending to be on our side and hoping by this artifice to escape the hands of their pursuers. Our men countered this trick with a trick of their own; when any of them heard an enemy soldier cry out in fear 'Montfort! Montfort!' he would say: 'If you are one of us, kill that fugitive,' pointing to one of the fleeing enemy. In fear, he slew his comrade, but reaped the reward of his deceitful crime and was at once killed by our men. What a wretched and unheard-of happening! Those who had gone to war to kill us came through God's just judgment to kill their own comrades and, however unwillingly, to serve our cause. So after our men had pursued the enemy for a long time and slain a huge number, the Count took his station in the middle of the battlefield so that he could regroup his men who had become widely dispersed in their pursuit of the enemy.

[275] Meanwhile that most notable apostate Savary de Mauléon and a huge force of armed men had left their camp[53] and come to the gates of Castelnaudary. There they stood with standards raised arrogantly awaiting the outcome of the battle; indeed a large number of them went into the lower bourg and began violently to attack those of our men who were still in the *castrum* – no more than five knights and a few sergeants. Few though they were they drove the innumerable enemy host (heavily armed with crossbows and other weapons) from the bourg and defended themselves vigorously. When the traitor Savary saw that our side had gained the victory on the field of battle and that his men would not have been able to take Castelnaudary he gathered his forces together and retired to his tents in shame. [276] Our Count and his companions, returning from the battlefield after their victory, determined to attack the enemy's tents. Knights invincible, truly recruits to Christ's army! However, as I said above,[54] our enemies had so surrounded themselves with barriers and ditches that our men could not get near them without dismounting from their horses. Our Count was for doing this at once, but some of his colleagues advised him to wait till the next day, since the enemy were fresh whereas our men were weary from the battle. The Count agreed and returned to the *castrum*; he always took advice and was willing to go along with the views of his companions in such matters. This noble man knew that it was God's valour, God's victory; so he dismounted at the very gates of

Subsequently, after de Montfort arrived, there was more slaughter, even though the Count of Foix, his son Roger-Bernard, Isarn de Puylaurens, and many other *faidits* lords who were with the Count of Foix fought bravely (ibid., 102, pp. 230–2).

[52] William of Tudela says that Martin Algai and his men fled at the first attack by the Count of Foix, pretending to pursue southern routiers (*Chanson* I, 98, p. 226). He also says that the Bishop of Cahors fled south to Fanjeaux.

[53] At Le Pech, immediately to the north of Castelnaudary: see n. 19 to §257 above.

[54] See §257. The *Chanson* (I, 105, p. 236) confirms that the ditches and defences around the Toulousain camp saved it from a direct attack.

Castelnaudary, and went straight to the church with feet unshod to give thanks to the Almighty for the favours he had received. In the church our soldiers sang '*Te Deum laudamus*' with great devotion and joy. In hymns and prayers they blessed the Lord who had wrought great wonders through His people and brought about victory over His enemies.

[277] I must now include an account of a miracle that occurred at this time at the Cistercian monastery of Grandselve in the territory of Toulouse.[55] The monks of this monastery were in great distress, since if the Count of Montfort were to be captured in Castelnaudary or to fall in battle, they would be threatened with death by the sword. The Count of Toulouse and his accomplices hated the monks of this order above all others, and especially this monastery, because the Abbot of Cîteaux, the papal legate, on whom chiefly they blamed the loss of their territories, had once been its Abbot.[56] One day one of the monks, a pious and holy man, was celebrating divine service. At the moment of consecrating the host he offered prayers with sincere devotion for the Count of Montfort who was at the time besieged in Castelnaudary. A voice from heaven called to him: 'Why do you pray for him? There are so many praying for him that there is no need of your prayers.'

[278] *A cunning ruse of the Count of Foix.* Meanwhile the Count of Foix contrived a new form of treachery, in imitation of his father the Devil who, when defeated on one front, turns to other means of evil-doing. He sent messengers to fortresses over a wide area to report that the Count of Montfort had been defeated, some even saying that he had been 'flayed' and 'hanged'. As a result of these reports a number of fortresses then went over to our adversaries.[57]

[279] The day after our glorious victory the Count's knights advised him to leave Castelnaudary (leaving a few men there) and march through his territories with the objective of persuading as many men as he could to join him. He therefore left Castelnaudary for Narbonne. At this point some crusaders arrived from France; Alan de Roucy,[58] a man of great probity, and a very few others. The

---

55 Grandselve, which lay about 40km north-west of Toulouse (near Verdun-sur-Garonne), was founded in 1114 as a Benedictine house, and joined the Cistercian order in the mid-1140s. It quickly became one of the most influential and wealthy Cistercian houses in the south. For an account see the article by Mireille Mousnier, 'Grandselve et la société de son temps', in *Cahiers de Fanjeaux*, vol. 21 pp. 107–26.

56 He was Abbot of Grandselve between 1198 and his election as Abbot of Cîteaux in 1201: cf. n. 4 to §20 above. An act in *Layettes*, V, 186 records the presence of a monk (Aimeric) of Grandselve with the crusaders in 1211.

57 It is clear from William of Tudela (*Chanson* I, 93ff) and William of Puylaurens (XVIII), as well as from Peter's account, that the crusaders won a significant victory at Saint-Martin, and that the failure of the siege of Castelnaudary was a blow to the southerners. Hence it is perhaps surprising that the Count of Foix was able to claim a victory, and that a number of *castra* seceded from the crusaders soon afterwards (see §§280–1 below and also *Chanson* I, 108, p. 240). A possible explanation is that the false reports were rendered plausible by the fact that the crusaders did not immediately take the enemy camp at Castelnaudary (§276) but instead marched to Narbonne (§279), which might have been interpreted as a retreat. The *Chanson* (loc. cit.) says it was the Toulousains, rather than the Count of Foix, who put out false reports that the French had been defeated.

58 Alan de Roucy (near Reims) was a renowned knight and a vassal of the Count of Champagne and also held fiefs of King Philip Augustus. His arrival, albeit with only a small number of troops, was especially helpful since it was outside the main campaigning season, and winter was approaching. It may have been

Count of Toulouse and his companions now realised that they were making no progress in the siege of Castelnaudary and a few days later burnt their siege-engines and went back to their homes in great shame.[59] I should add that they did not dare leave their camp until they were certain our Count had left.

[280] Whilst the Count was at Narbonne in company with the newly arrived crusaders, he had assembled a large force from the local population with the intention of returning to attack the Count of Toulouse and his allies, but he then received reports that the Count of Toulouse and his men had abandoned the siege of Castelnaudary. Our Count then dismissed the local troops[60] he had assembled and returned to Castelnaudary taking only the crusaders. He now proposed to destroy all the castles in the area which had seceded from him. At this moment it was reported to him that a *castrum* named Coustaussa near Termes had abandoned its allegiance to him and deserted to the enemies of the faith.[61] He at once hurried off to besiege the place. After he had attacked it for a few days the defenders realised that they could not hold out and surrendered to the Count promising to abide by his will in all matters. Thereupon the Count returned to Castelnaudary. [281] He was met with the news that the inhabitants of the *castrum* known as Montégut[62] in the diocese of Albi had joined the Count of Toulouse and were attacking the castle there and the troops our Count had left to garrison it. Our Count set off to help at once, but before he could reach the place the garrison had surrendered the castle to the enemy. What more? All the most notable and strongest *castra* in the area deserted to the Count of Toulouse almost in a single day; two very small places remained. The names of the more notable *castra* lost at this time are: in the diocese of Albi; Rabastens, Montégut, Gaillac, Lagrave,[63] Cahusac, Saint-Marcel, Laguépie and Saint-Antonin; places in the diocese of Toulouse which defected before and during the siege of Castelnaudary were Puylaurens, Les Cassés, Saint-Félix, Montferrand, Avignon, Saint-Michel, Cuq-Toulza and even Saverdun.[64] Many lesser *castra* were lost which it would be impossible to name individually – it is said that there were more than fifty.[65]

---

one of the first fruits of the recruiting campaign in the north mentioned in §§285–6 below. Alan de Roucy's presence in the Midi at this time is also recorded in the *Chanson*, I, 111, p. 246. He was to remain with the crusaders for ten years, and was granted the lordships of Termes in 1213 (see n. 115 to §189), and (by 1214) Bram and Montréal. See G&L I, p. 274 n. 1. He was killed defending Montréal in 1221 (William of Puylaurens, XXXI).

[59] William of Tudela says that the Toulousain army left noiselessly, abandoning their trebuchet to the rain and the wind (*Chanson* I, 106, p. 238).

[60] Latin '*indigene*', as opposed to the crusaders, *peregrini*, (cf. Appendix A(ii)).

[61] Coustaussa had been taken in late November 1210, in the aftermath of the fall of Termes: see §192 above.

[62] It had been occupied in June 1211: see above, §237.

[63] Lagrave lies on the south bank of the Tarn, overlooking a bend in the river, between Gaillac and Albi.

[64] For the original occupation by the crusaders of Rabastens, Montégut, Gaillac, Cahusac, Saint-Marcel, Laguépie, Saint-Antonin and Montferrand see §237; for Puylaurens §230; for Les Cassés §233; for Saverdun §116. The defections of Puylaurens, Rabastens, Gaillac, Salvagnac, Puycelsi, Saint-Marcel, Saint-Antonin, Lagrave and other places during this time are also described by William of Tudela (*Chanson*, I, 104–10, pp. 234–46).

[65] The outcome was that by late 1211 de Montfort had lost most of his gains in Quercy and the northern

[282] I must, however, record a particularly vile and unprecedented example of treachery at Lagrave in the diocese of Albi. Our Count had given this *castrum* to a French knight;[66] this unfortunate man was more trusting of the inhabitants of the place than he should have been – they for their part were plotting his death. One day the knight was having his wine casks repaired by a local carpenter; after repairing one cask the carpenter asked the knight to look inside the cask to see if the repair was satisfactory, but when the knight put his head inside the cask the carpenter raised his axe and cut it off. What unheard-of barbarity! The inhabitants at once rose up and killed the few French soldiers who were there. Count Baldwin, brother of the Count of Toulouse (whom I have previously mentioned),[67] heard of this event and went to the place one day at first light. The inhabitants came out to meet him, thinking he was the Count of Toulouse since the brothers had similar coats of arms, and led him inside. With great glee they told the tale of the atrocity they had committed. Baldwin attacked them with a crowd of armed men and slew almost all of them from the youngest to the oldest.

[283] Faced with the loss of so many important *castra* our Count went to Pamiers to fortify it. Whilst he was there the Count of Foix sent him a message to the effect that provided he were willing to wait for just four days at Pamiers then he, the Count of Foix, would come and fight him. Our Count replied that he would wait there not just for four days, but ten days or more. In fact the Count of Foix did not dare go; but our knights, even without our Count, entered the territory of Foix and destroyed a *castrum* belonging to the Count.

[284] After this our Count returned to Fanjeaux and sent Simon, Castellan of Neauphle,[68] and his brother Geoffrey,[69] valiant knights both, and a few others to a certain *castrum* to fetch wheat to Fanjeaux to strengthen its powers of resistance. As they were on their way back the son of the Count of Foix – not a whit behind his father in villainy – laid an ambush on the road our knights had to pass through. The traitor had with him a large force of armed men. As our men came by the enemy rose up from the ambush and attacked them. They surrounded Geoffrey and set on him from all sides. Like the fine knight he was he defended himself courageously. He had very few men with him to support him, and when at last he had lost his horse and was in desperate straits his enemies called on him to surrender. This man of marvellous courage replied, we are told, to this effect: 'I have given myself to Christ; far be it from me to give myself to His enemies.' Thus, struck down by his adversaries, he gave up his spirit, in glory, we may be

Albigeois, and in the Toulousain, thus repeating the patterns of 1209–10 when many of the conquests of the campaigning season were lost in the winter.

66 Pons de Beaumont, whose name is given in William of Tudela's account of the following episode (*Chanson* I, 108–9, pp. 240–4).

67 See §235 above. Baldwin's role is described in the *Chanson* (I, 109, p. 242), which adds that a Navarrese knight Martin d'Olite was with him; this Martin is sometimes identified with the Martin Algai who was at Castelnaudary (see §265), but the identification is not certain. The *Chanson* also mentions that the inhabitants of Lagrave mistook Baldwin's banner for that of Raymond VI, since both contained a *crotz ramondenca*, a Raymondine cross, the emblem of the family of the Counts of Toulouse.

68 See above, §241.

69 Geoffrey is recorded as a benefactor of the abbey of les Vaux-de-Cernay: see G&L I, p. 279 n. 3.

sure. Alongside him fell a brave youth who was a kinsman of his, and a few others. One knight, Dreux de Compans,[70] gave himself up and was imprisoned by the Count of Foix for a long period. The Castellan escaped alive and returned to the *castrum* from which he had set out, weeping for the loss of his brother and his kinsman. Later our men returned to recover the bodies of the dead, which they buried in the Cistercian abbey of Boulbonne.[71]

[285] At this time William, the venerable Archdeacon of Paris, and another cleric, Master Jacques de Vitry, assumed the duty of preaching the Crusade[72] on the orders of the Bishop of Uzès (whom the Pope had appointed legate[73] to act in the business of the faith – he was devoted to his task and most effective in carrying it out). Fired with zeal for the faith they toured France and Germany, and through that winter[74] recruited an incredible number of the faithful to the army of Christ, placing the sign of the cross on their breasts. After God they were foremost in promoting the business of the faith in those two areas.

---

[70] From the Ile de France (Compans lies east of Paris, about 15km west of Meaux). He was a cousin of Robert Mauvoisin (see §291 below).

[71] It lay east of Saverdun, at Mazères on the River Hers; having been founded c.1129 as a Benedictine house it joined the Cistercian order in 1150. It was destroyed in the 16th century but rebuilt in 1652–70 on a site near Cintegabelle, about 10 km north of Saverdun. See *Cahiers de Fanjeaux*, vol. 19, p. 27.

[72] On William, see §175 above for his presence at the siege of Termes in 1210, and his subsequent career. Jacques de Vitry was a regular canon at the church of Saint-Nicolas d'Oignies in the diocese of Liège. As well as preaching the Albigensian Crusade in 1211–13, he became famous for his enthusiastic preaching of the Fifth Crusade. He became Bishop of Acre in 1216, and took part in the Damietta campaign in Egypt. He returned to Europe in 1225, later resigned the see of Acre, and became cardinal bishop of Tusculum (Frascati). He died in 1240. See for example his letters, in *Lettres de Jacques de Vitry*, ed. R. B. C. Huygens (Leiden, 1960); *The Exempla or Illustrative Stories from the Sermones Vulgares of Jacques de Vitry*, ed. T. F. Crane (London, 1890); and the note on Jacques de Vitry and his preaching campaign in 1213 by G&L (I, p. 281 n. 1). For further references to William and Jacques de Vitry and their recruitment of crusaders in France see §§306, 310, and 508.

[73] Probably late in 1210, and certainly by April 1211 (see *PL* 216, 410, and n. 51 to §160).

[74] I.e. the winter of 1211–1212. After the arrival of Alan de Roucy in (probably) October at Narbonne (see §279), the next arrival was Robert Mauvoisin, reported below.

[XII. §§286–366, December 1211 – December 1212: *Arrival of Robert Mauvoisin with reinforcements for the crusaders – campaign in the Toulousain – Guy de Montfort joins his brother at Christmas 1211 – sieges of Les Touelles, Cahuzac, Saint-Marcel, January–March 1212 – arrival of Guy of les Vaux-de-Cernay, accompanied by his nephew Peter – siege of Hautpoul, April 1212 – consecrations of Guy as Bishop of Carcassonne and Arnold Amalric as Archbishop of Narbonne – recapture of Puylaurens – arrival of more crusaders – campaigns in the Albigeois – siege of Saint-Antonin, May 1212 – campaigns in the Agenais – Simon de Montfort assumes lordship of many places – siege of Penne d'Agenais, June–July 1212 – campaigns in the county of Foix under Guy de Montfort – more crusaders continue to arrive – Martin Algai captured and hanged at Biron – invasion of Quercy and siege of Moissac – Simon de Montfort goes south and reoccupies Saverdun – campaigns in the county of Comminges and in Gascony – Toulouse virtually surrounded – Council and Statutes of Pamiers, December 1212.*]

[286] *Arrival of Robert Mauvoisin with a force of knights from France.* At this point that most noble of knights, Robert Mauvoisin,[1] servant of Christ, foremost in dedication to Jesus' business and in furthering His work, who had gone to France the previous summer, returned with more than a hundred chosen French knights, who to a man had made him their leader and master. Inspired by two venerable men, the Bishop of Toulouse and the Abbot of les Vaux-de-Cernay, they had taken the cross and joined the army of Jesus Christ. The whole of that winter they remained in Christ's service[2] and nobly revived His business which at that time had reached a low ebb.[3]

[287] *The Count goes to meet Robert.* When he heard of their approach, our Count went to Carcassonne to meet these knights. When they arrived, there was great exultation and joy in our army. The Count then went on with the knights to Fanjeaux.

[288] At this time the Count of Foix had laid siege to a *castrum* belonging to a

---

1 See §§129, 154 and 336 for this knight, one of de Montfort's closest associates. He had been sent north during the summer of 1211 with Fulk of Toulouse and Guy of les Vaux-de-Cernay to recruit crusaders, a recruitment campaign which as mentioned in the previous section was to continue all winter. His return south with reinforcements, probably at the beginning of December 1211, meant that de Montfort would be able to go on the offensive during the winter.
2 They left in April 1212 after the siege of Hautpoul: see §304 below.
3 Peter is referring to the uprisings of autumn 1211 against de Montfort in the Lauragais and the Tarn valley, summarised above in §281. The arrival of fresh troops rapidly changed the position, and during the period from December 1211 to December 1212 (now recounted in §§286–366), there was virtually unbroken military success for the crusaders in the Lauragais, the Albigeois, the Agenais, Quercy and later in the territories of the Counts of Foix and Comminges. The outcome was that by the autumn of 1212 Raymond VI controlled little save Toulouse itself and Montauban, and he was effectively encircled (see §359). Except for the Council of Pamiers (see §§362–4), Peter's account of this period contains little reference to diplomatic developments, although as will be seen in §367 et seq. much activity was put in motion by Innocent's letters of May 1212, and by the approach to Peter of Aragon by Raymond VI in the autumn of 1212 (on all of which see also Appendix G).

local knight, William of Aura, an adherent of our Count, whom he had aided to the full extent of his powers. This place, named Quié,[4] was near to the territory of the Count of Foix, who had by now been besieging it for fifteen days. Our forces therefore left Fanjeaux and hurried off to drive the Count of Foix from the siege. When he heard we were coming he raised the siege, leaving his siege-engines, and fled in great shame. Our men laid waste his lands for several days and pulled down four of his fortresses. [289] Our men then returned to Fanjeaux and immediately set off to besiege a *castrum* named La Pomarède[5] in the diocese of Toulouse. After the siege had continued for several days an attack was mounted and the ditch surrounding the *castrum* was filled up, but with darkness intervening the place could not be taken on that day. However, the defenders realised that they were as good as captured and during the night breached the wall and fled in secret. Immediately afterwards our Count heard that Albedun[6] in the diocese of Narbonne had seceded from his lordship; he made his way there and as he did so the lord of the Albedun came to meet him and surrendered himself and his *castrum* to the Count.

[290] *Arrival of the Count's brother from overseas.* After this the Count went to the notable *castrum* named Castres[7] in the diocese of Albi. Whilst he was staying there and celebrating Christmas, his brother Guy, returning from overseas, came to join him. Guy had accompanied Simon to Outremer[8] but had stayed there when his brother came back, having married a noble wife of royal blood who was mistress of Sidon. She also now returned with him and with the sons she had borne Guy. I must add that whilst Guy was on his way to join Simon, some fortresses in the Albigeois which had seceded from the Count gave themselves up to him. The delight of the Count and his men at his brother's arrival is beyond description.

[291] After a few days our men set off to besiege the *castrum* known as Les

---

4   Latin '*Carum*', on the west bank of the Ariège, opposite Tarascon sur Ariège. Roquebert (I, p. 454) suggests that as a fief held by Roger of Comminges, Quié may have come into the crusaders' hands, and been granted to William of Aura, when Roger of Comminges submitted to de Montfort at the siege of Lavaur in April 1211.
5   A fortified village about 10km north of Castelnaudary.
6   Latin '*Albedunum*', in the southern Razès. Its lord was Bernard-Simon, whose family were Cathar sympathisers; he had abandoned the place after the fall of Termes in late November 1210, and become a *faidit* (cf. Roquebert I, p. 365). The circumstances in which he subsequently submitted to de Montfort are unknown, as are his reasons for making this brief rebellion. The site of the castle is at modern le Bézu, now a tiny place near Saint-Just, about 10km to the east of Quillan; it was then a substantial and thoroughly inaccessible fortress (cf. G&L I, p. 285 n. 1).
7   See note to §36.
8   Latin '*ultra mare*', meaning the crusader states in Palestine (see n. 75 to §106). Along with his brother Simon, Guy had joined the Fourth Crusade in 1202, and had gone to the Holy Land with Simon after leaving Zara in 1203, on which see §106. He had remained there and had married Héloïse (Helvis) of Ibelin (daughter of Balian II of Ibelin and Maria Comnena, widow of King Amalric I of Jerusalem), who was mistress of Sidon by virtue of her first marriage to Reynald Garnier of Sidon. As a result of his marriage Guy became lord of Sidon. Their son Philip de Montfort was brought up in the west after Guy and Héloïse's return in 1211, but he went to Outremer in 1239 (cf. J. S. C. Riley-Smith, *The Feudal Nobility and the Kingdom of Jerusalem, 1174–1277* (London, 1973), p. 23). Guy de Montfort was to be present at the Lateran Council in 1215 (see §571), and continued to play an important role in the Albigensian Crusade until his death in 1228.

Touelles[9] in the diocese of Albi, which belonged to the father of that base traitor Giraud de Pépieux.[10] They attacked the place and took it after a few days, putting almost all the inhabitants to the sword. Only the father of Giraud was spared; he was exchanged for a knight whom the Count of Foix was holding in chains, Dreux de Compans,[11] a kinsman of Robert Mauvoisin.

[292] *Siege of Cahuzac.* The Count now set off to lay siege to a *castrum* named Cahuzac[12] in the Albigeois. Since it was not usual to engage in a siege in the middle of winter and he had very few men with him, he took the place by force with great effort after many difficulties.[13]

[293] Meanwhile the Counts of Toulouse, Comminges and Foix had come together with a huge force at a nearby *castrum* named Gaillac.[14] They sent a messenger to our Count to say that they were coming to attack him, hoping thus to frighten him into raising the siege of Cahuzac. The messenger was sent again but even so they did not dare to come. Seeing this our Count said to his men: 'Since they will not come here, I will go and visit them.' Taking some of his armed troops, although not a large force, he hurried off to Gaillac breathing threats to do battle. The Count of Toulouse and his companions thereupon fled to a *castrum* nearby named Montégut.[15] Our Count followed them there – they again fled, this time to another *castrum* named Rabastens. The Count again pursued them, and they now left Rabastens and fled towards Toulouse.[16] The Count now realised that they would not dare to stand and face him and went back to the *castrum* from which he had originally set out.[17]

[294] After this the Count sent to the Abbot of Cîteaux, who was at Albi, to seek his advice as to his next action. The Abbot recommended that he should lay siege to the *castrum* of Saint-Marcel,[18] about three leagues from Albi, which the Count of Toulouse had entrusted to the base traitor, Giraud de Pépieux.

---

9   Latin '*Tudelle*', also mentioned in *Chanson* I, 110, p. 244, as '*las Toellas*'. It lay on the site of modern Briatexte, about 10km north-east of Lavaur.

10   On Giraud, see §125 above and note. His father was Fredolius (or Frézoul or Freso or Frédelon) de Lautrec, one of whose sisters may have become a *perfecta* (Inquisition records from the Doat collection quoted by Griffe, *LC*, p. 65, and cited in Roquebert I, p. 457). See also *Chanson* I, p. 245 and n. 5.

11   See above, §284, for him and his capture.

12   See above, §§237 and 281. The *Chanson* (I, 110–11, pp. 244–9) adds some detail on this siege, saying that after the fall of Les Touelles, the crusaders crossed the Tarn at Albi, presumably to avoid the area further west around Rabastens and Gaillac which was in hostile hands.

13   Cahuzac was besieged early in January 1212. Raymond VI's forces, as recounted in the next section, clearly made an attempt to force de Montfort to raise the siege, but the latter saw them off, and on returning to Cahuzac brought the siege to a successful conclusion quickly (*Chanson* I, 110, p. 246 mentions two days, and adds that after occupying Cahuzac, the crusaders spent eight days there, because it was full of supplies; they were there for the feast of the Epiphany, 6 January 1212, and then went on to meet Arnold Amalric at Albi – see next section).

14   Gaillac, Rabastens, Montégut and Saint-Marcel (mentioned in this and the next section), had submitted to de Montfort in June 1211 and were lost in September 1211: see §§237 and 281 above.

15   Cf. §237 above.

16   The *Chanson* (I, 111, p. 244) also comments on Raymond VI's weakness at this time, saying he feared the crusaders and dared not attack. The outcome of his tactics was the loss of Rabastens and Montégut without any resistance.

17   I.e. to Cahuzac.

18   The *Chanson* (I, 111, p. 246) briefly mentions this siege, saying that it was folly ('*gran folia*') to attack

[295] Our men went to the place and besieged it,[19] but on one side only since they were few in number and it was a large and strong *castrum*. They at once erected a siege-engine and mounted a vigorous attack. After a few days the Counts of Toulouse, Comminges and Foix arrived with a massive force and entered the place to defend it against us. Large though it was, it could not hold such a large body of men, so most of the enemy pitched their tents outside, on the opposite side from our own camp. Our men kept up their assault on the place, and our opponents defended as best they could. What an extraordinary and amazing situation! Besiegers are usually superior to the besieged in numbers and courage; here the besieged outnumbered our besieging force almost ten to one. Our knights did not exceed one hundred – the enemy had more then five hundred, and whereas the three Counts opposing us had a huge contingent of footsoldiers as well, our side had few if any. Surely a remarkable and singular situation! I must add that as often as the enemy dared to come out to confront us, our men at once repelled them most valiantly. At last one day the Count of Foix came out with a large detachment to disable our petrary; when our sergeants saw this they bravely drove back the enemy simply by a bombardment of stones, and confined them to the *castrum* before our knights had time to arm themselves.

[296] *The Count quits Saint-Marcel.* The army was now beset by a great shortage of provisions. Our men could obtain supplies only from Albi, and our opponents were keeping such a close watch on the roads, making sorties in large numbers, that our people in Albi did not dare come to the army unless the Count sent half his forces to conduct them. So, after spending a month on the siege the Count realised that if he were to split his small force of knights into two parts, keeping one with him and sending the other off to protect the supplies, the enemy – whose strength was enormous – would attack one or the other; under such clear constraints, and after the army had had no bread for several days, he raised the siege.

[297] I must add that on Good Friday[20] our Count – as well became a man totally dedicated to the Catholic religion and to serving God – arranged for the Passion service to be conducted with due solemnity in his tent. When our adversaries heard our clerics singing they climbed the walls, making insulting and derisive gestures, and began to howl in a disgusting manner. What perverted want of faith, what faithless perversion![21] If one considers the matter carefully, it is clear that our Count won greater honour and glory in that siege than ever previously in the capture of any fortress, however strong, and from that time on his qualities shone ever brighter, his constancy blazed ever stronger. I must also mention that when our Count left Saint-Marcel the enemy, despite their

---

Saint-Marcel and that it resulted only in great expense to the crusaders. This is consistent with the initially unsuccessful outcome recounted by Peter in §296 below, but Saint-Marcel was later successfully occupied: see §312.

19 About 24 February, since the siege lasted a month (see §296) and ended on 24 March (§299).
20 23 March, 1212.
21 Word play: '*O perversa infidelitas, o infidelis perversitas*'.

enormous strength, did not dare mount even the slightest attack on our men as they retired.

[298] *A Miracle.* I must not pass over a miracle that occurred at that time. One Sunday an Abbot of the Cistercian order from Bonneval[22] was preaching in a certain *castrum*. The church was of moderate size and could not hold all the people attending, so they had all gone outside and were listening to the preacher at the entrance to the church. At the end of his sermon the venerable Abbot was exhorting his audience to take the cross against the Albigensian heretics when suddenly for all to see a cross appeared in the air, seeming to be turned towards Toulouse. I heard about this miracle from the Abbot himself – a devoted man of great authority.

[299] On the day he raised the siege of Saint-Marcel, which was the eve of Easter Day,[23] the Count arrived at Albi to celebrate the feast of the Resurrection. The venerable Abbot of les Vaux-de-Cernay, whom I have often mentioned, had arrived there from France following his election as Bishop of Carcassonne.[24] When the Count and our knights found him there they were quite elated, since they all held him in great esteem and affection. Indeed he had for many years been a close friend of the Count, who had listened to his advice and followed his wishes ever since childhood. At the same time Arnold, the venerable Abbot of Cîteaux, often referred to in my history, had been elected Archbishop of Narbonne.[25]

---

[22] '*Bona Valle*', a Cistercian house in the diocese of Rodez, lying in the valley of the little river Boralde, a few kilometres north of Espalion, north-east of Rodez. It was founded in 1147 by William of Chaumont, Bishop of Cahors. See *Cahiers de Fanjeaux*, vol. 21, p. 26.

[23] 24 March 1212.

[24] Innocent had written to the legate Raymond of Uzès on 15 April 1211 (*PL* 216, 409–10) asking him to find a replacement for Bishop Bernard-Raymond de Roquefort of Carcassonne, on whom see §130. Guy's election to the see must have post-dated this letter. He was consecrated at Narbonne in May 1212 (§307 below). At the time of his election Guy had been involved in the fight against heresy in the Midi for some five years, an involvement which had begun with his participation in the preaching campaign of 1207 (for details see §§51–2, 103, 128, 155, 286). During 1212 he was taking an increasingly active part in the affairs of the Crusade, and when, on 22 May, Arnold Amalric left for Spain to join the Christian forces in their 'crusade' against the Almohades, it was Guy who assumed in his absence the functions of vice-legate (see §324 below), and he is also said to have been vice-legate in 1214 (see §520). See also n. 109 to §342.

[25] Arnold Amalric was elected Archbishop of Narbonne on 12 March 1212: see G&L I, p. 293 n. 1, for dating. He replaced Archbishop Berengar, a member of the family of King Peter of Aragon, and on whom see Griffe, *LC*, pp. 196–200, and Roquebert I, pp. 151–4. Berengar's relations with the legates had been poor from the beginning and Arnold Amalric's success in ousting him was the culmination of a long campaign against him: see for instance letters from Innocent III of 30 May 1203 (*PL* 215, 83–4); 28 May 1204 (*PL* 215, 355–7); 26 June 1205 (*PL* 215, 674–5); 29 May 1207 (*PL* 215, 1164–5); and 28 June 1210 (*PL* 216, 283). Arnold Amalric was confirmed as Archbishop by the legate Raymond of Uzès, and he was to be consecrated in Narbonne at the beginning of May (see §307 below). At the same time he also took the title of Duke of Narbonne, but without any legitimacy. The title belonged to Raymond VI as Count of Toulouse, and insofar as anyone else might claim it, it was Simon de Montfort, who regarded himself as successor to Raymond. In due course this would lead to serious conflict between Arnold Amalric and Simon de Montfort since while the Counts of Toulouse had for long been no more than titular dukes, de Montfort was keen to assert his claim to the title. For later developments in the dispute see §560 and note. By this time, spring 1212, Innocent was becoming increasingly suspicious about the conduct of the legates. He had given some indication of these doubts in his letter to Philip Augustus in August 1211 (*PL* 216, 524), when he had defended the efforts to conquer Raymond VI's lands, but added that he was unsure whether Raymond's failure to purge himself of the charges laid against him was his fault or not (cf. n. 62 to §162).

[300] On Easter Day[26] the Count of Toulouse and his associates left Saint-Marcel and went to Gaillac, three leagues from Albi. Our Count felt that his enemies might perhaps boast that they had beaten our men, and wished to make a public demonstration that he was not afraid to face them; accordingly on Easter Monday he left Albi with his men and placed himself outside Gaillac, offering battle to his opponents. Since they did not dare come out to meet him he returned to Albi. The Bishop-elect of Carcassonne was in Albi, and I myself was with him;[27] he had taken me with him from France to support him in his journey to a foreign land,[28] since I was a monk and his nephew.

[301] *Siege of Hautpoul.* The Count and his men spent some days at Albi[29] and went on to Castres where we stayed for a few days more. After taking counsel the Count decided to besiege a *castrum* between Castres and Cabaret known as Hautpoul,[30] which had crossed over to the enemy at the time of the siege of Castelnaudary.[31] [302] We left Castres on the Sunday two weeks after Easter[32] and came to Hautpoul. The enemy, who had positioned themselves inside Hautpoul for its defence, came out arrogantly to meet our men and began to harass them vigorously. They were at once forced back by our men, who then pitched their tents on one side only of the *castrum*, since they were few in number. Hautpoul is situated on the slope of a very high and steep hill, over huge crags which are virtually inaccessible. Its natural defences are so strong – as I learnt from my own experience as an eyewitness – that even if the gates were opened and no resistance offered from inside, it would be impossible without the greatest difficulty to walk through the *castrum* and climb up to the keep. Our men therefore made ready a petrary, which they set up on the third day after their arrival, and started to fire at the keep. The same day our knights put on their armour, went down into the valley at the foot of the *castrum* and tried to climb up in the hope that they might take it by a direct attack. However, when they had penetrated the first bourg the defenders climbed on to the walls and buildings and began to throw huge quantities of large stones down on to us; others started a large fire at the place where

These suspicions surface again in an important letter he wrote to Arnold Amalric and Bishop Raymond of Uzéz in May 1212 (*PL* 216, 613–14), for which see n. 4 to §368. Innocent's doubts were to be further fuelled by the subsequent approaches made by Peter of Aragon at the end of 1212, on which see §367 below, and Appendix G.

[26] 25 March 1212.

[27] Peter now begins to speak as an eye-witness. He remained with the army until the Council of Lavaur in January 1213 (apart from a three-week visit to Narbonne in late April/May 1212: see §307 below). He was also in the Midi for some months in 1214 and most of the period from June 1216 until the second siege of Toulouse in 1218: see Introduction, pp. xxiv–v.

[28] Latin '*in terra aliena*'.

[29] He was there on 3 April since an act of that date records the granting by de Montfort of the castles of Rouffiac and Marsac as fiefs to the Bishop of Albi, William Peyre (see G&L II, p. 1).

[30] Hautpoul (Latin *Altus Pullus*) is 20km south-east of Castres and 15km north of Cabaret, on the very northern edge of the Montagne Noire, overlooking the valley of the Thoré and the modern town of Mazamet far below. Lying within former Trencavel territory it had nonetheless escaped earlier attack. The *castrum* is sited on a rocky ridge above the River Arnette, and was very difficult of access except from the south. Dwellings were huddled on the craggy slopes around it.

[31] About six months previously in September 1211: see §281.

[32] 8 April 1212.

our men had broken in. Our men saw they were making no progress, since the place was almost inaccessible to human footsteps and they could not stand up to the barrage of stones, and retired in great peril through the fire.

[303] *A case of treachery.* I feel I must record a vile and cruel act of treachery perpetrated by the defenders. Our Count had with him a knight of local origin, a kinsman of a certain traitor in the *castrum* who had been joint lord of Cabaret. The defenders of Hautpoul asked our Count to send this knight to them so that they could discuss terms with him and through him relay their own requirements to the Count. With the Count's permission he had approached them and was talking with them at the gate of the *castrum* when one of them fired at him with a crossbow and wounded him severely. What a savage betrayal! However, soon afterwards, on that very day or the next, it came about by God's just judgment that the traitor who had called the knight his kinsman to the meeting was himself seriously wounded by our men; our knight was struck in the leg, so also was the traitor. A just measure of Divine vengeance!

[304] Meanwhile our petrary maintained an unceasing bombardment of the keep. However, on the fourth day of the siege,[33] after sunset, a dense mist formed. The defenders, seized with God-sent fear, took this opportunity to leave the *castrum* and take to flight. Our men saw this, raised the alarm, burst into the *castrum* and slew any of the enemy they found; others followed the fugitives through the intense darkness and caught some of them. Next day the Count ordered the place to be razed to the ground and burnt. After this the knights who had come from France with Robert Mauvoisin (as related above)[34] and had stayed with the Count throughout the winter almost all left him and returned home.

[305] *An atrocity committed by the citizens of Narbonne.* Here I must include an account of an atrocity perpetrated at this time by the citizens of Narbonne, who were evil men and had never favoured Jesus Christ's business despite the enormous benefits they had derived from it. Guy, the Count's brother, and Amaury, the Count's eldest son, had come to Narbonne and were staying in the city.[35] One day Amaury was wandering around, as any boy might, and went into the palace of Aimeric the lord of Narbonne.[36] The palace was old and had become virtually deserted. Amaury touched a window and tried to open it; it was so rotten with age that it fell out, whereupon Amaury went back to the residence of the Knights Templar where he was lodging.[37] At the time Guy was in the

---

[33] 11 April 1212.

[34] See §286.

[35] They had presumably gone to Narbonne to attend the installation of Arnold Amalric as Archbishop, which took place on 2 May 1212, and at which Guy and Peter of les Vaux-de-Cernay were also present. The incident now related was symptomatic of the distrust in which Guy de Montfort and the crusaders were held by the Narbonnais. See also §488 below, when de Montfort was refused entry to Narbonne after the battle of Muret, and see §§503 and 560 for further developments.

[36] The vicecomital palace lay to the east of the present Place de l'Hotel de Ville and the Archbishop's palace (G&L II, p. 5 n. 2).

[37] The Templar House at Narbonne probably lay outside the city walls, as was the case at Montpellier (see

residence of the Archbishop of Narbonne.[38] At once the citizens of Narbonne, looking for an excuse to commit mischief, accused this boy, the son of our Count, of trying to break into Aimeric's palace by force! A slim excuse for committing a crime, indeed no excuse at all! They armed themselves, rushed to where the boy was and set about breaking into the Templars' residence. The boy realised that they were intending to kill him; he put on armour, retreated to a tower in the residence and hid from the sight of his enemies. They continued to attack the residence vigorously, whilst others seized any Frenchmen they could and killed many of them. The madness of evil men! They even killed two of the Count's armour-bearers. Guy did not dare leave the residence of the Archbishop. The citizens kept up their attack on the house where Amaury had taken refuge for a long time, until on the advice of one of their number they at last desisted. The boy, released from his grave peril, through God's grace escaped alive and well.[39] I shall now return to the thread of my main narrative.

[306] *The Count leaves Hautpoul.* The Count now left Hautpoul with a small force of knights and entered the territory of the Count of Toulouse. A few days later a large group of crusaders arrived from the Auvergne; indeed each day now saw the arrival of crusaders who had been inspired to take the cross by the preaching of William, the venerable Archdeacon of Paris, and Master Jacques de Vitry, which I referred to earlier.[40] I cannot set out every detail of how from that time onwards God in His mercy began wondrously to advance His business; instead I will summarise by recording that our Count captured a large number of *castra* and found many more deserted by the enemy. The list of places recovered by the noble Count within three weeks is: Cuq, Montmaur, Saint-Félix, Les Cassès, Montferrand, Avignonet, Saint-Michel,[41] and many others.

[307] Whilst the army was at the *castrum* known as Saint-Michel, which is about one league from Castelnaudary, Guy, former Abbot of les Vaux-de-Cernay and now Bishop of Carcassonne, arrived and I accompanied him. He had left the army whilst still Bishop-elect after the capture of Hautpoul and gone to Narbonne to be consecrated along with the Abbot of Cîteaux who was Archbishop-elect of Narbonne.[42]

[308] After the total destruction of Saint-Michel the Count decided to lay siege to the notable *castrum* of Puylaurens which, as mentioned above, had

---

G&L II, p. 5 n. 4, and §544 below). Guy was staying there apparently because the Narbonnais did not wish the crusaders to lodge in their city.

[38] The archiepiscopal palace lay on the north side of the modern Passage de l'Ancre, immediately south-east of the site of the cathedral; of 12th century date, it is now called the Palais Vieux, to distinguish it from later buildings on the south side of the passage.

[39] De Montfort did not retaliate for this incident, but G&L (II, p. 7 n. 1) note that he did not formally pardon the Narbonnais until three years later.

[40] See §285 above. William of Tudela (*Chanson* I, 111, p. 248) also refers to the arrival of troops from the Auvergne, Italy, Germany and 'Esclavonia' (which covered roughly the same area as the former Yugoslavia).

[41] Saint-Michel-de-Lanès. See also §281, which recounts the loss of these places by de Montfort in the latter half of 1211.

[42] Guy was at Narbonne on 30 April (*HGL* VIII, 619–20, which records a Council held at Narbonne by Arnold Amalric). Arnold was consecrated Archbishop on 2 May (G&L II, p. 9 n. 1).

seceded from his lordship the previous year.[43] We therefore set out in that direction and encamped about two leagues from the place. Some crusaders arrived that very day – the Provost of the cathedral of Cologne, a powerful and famous churchman, and several German nobles.[44]

[309] *Recapture of Puylaurens.* The Count of Toulouse was at Puylaurens with a huge force of mercenaries; however, when he heard of our approach he did not dare wait for us but swiftly left the place, taking all the men of the *castrum* with him and leaving it deserted, and fled to Toulouse. What folly, what contemptible stupidity he showed! Next day at first light we went to Puylaurens and, finding it empty, marched further on until we pitched camp in a valley. Guy de Lucy, who had been given the lordship of Puylaurens by our Count some time previously,[45] entered it and fortified it with his own people.

[310] The army stayed in the valley near Puylaurens for two days. Here it was reported to our Count that a large group of powerful crusaders were on their way to Carcassonne from France; they included Robert, Archbishop of Rouen, Robert, Bishop-elect of Laon, William the venerable Archdeacon of Paris, and many other nobles and commoners.[46] Realising that he already had a large army the Count took counsel with his colleagues and sent his brother Guy and his Marshal Guy to meet the crusaders at Carcassonne so that they could form another army and move into other areas[47] to further Christ's business. [311] The Count raised camp and marched towards Rabastens. If I may omit trivial details and concentrate on more important matters, I will record briefly that three notable places I have often mentioned, Rabastens, Montégut and Gaillac, surrendered to the Count virtually on the same day without being besieged and without causing him any difficulties.

[312] When the townsmen of Saint-Marcel[48] heard that the Count had recovered so many places and was on his way to besiege them, they became afraid; they sent messengers to him begging him to make peace with them and offering to submit the *castrum* to his will. The Count recalled their crimes and exceptional depravity;[49] he was in no way prepared to treat with them and instead sent messengers to tell them there was no prayer or payment[50] that would suffice to win his agreement to make peace with them. On this they fled from their

---

43 §281.
44 Engelbert, Provost of Cologne, was later Archbishop. The others were Adolf III, Count of Berg; William III, Count of Juliers in the Rhineland; and Leopold VI, Duke of Austria (G&L II, p. 9 nn. 3 and 4).
45 In May 1211: see §230.
46 Robert, Archbishop of Rouen 1208–21; Robert, Bishop of Laon 1210–16; and on Archdeacon William, see above, §175. For details of others with them see §326 below. They remained until about the end of June: see §329.
47 The county of Foix and the Ariège valley: see §326. The arrival of these additional forces thus allowed the crusaders to operate on two fronts, with Simon de Montfort himself going north across the Tarn and the Aveyron into Quercy and then into the Agenais, and Guy de Montfort and Guy de Lévis southwards.
48 See above, §§237 and 294 on Saint-Marcel, which lies on the River Cerou, north of Cordes. The *Chanson* (I, 112, p. 250) records that Lagarde and Puycelsi, west of Cordes, were also taken again at this time.
49 See §297 above.
50 Word play: '*prece vel pretio*'.

castrum, leaving it empty. When we got to it, the Count had the place burnt and the keep and all the walls levelled to the ground.[51] From there we went to the nearby *castrum* of Saint-Martin Laguépie;[52] finding it empty the Count ordered it to be pulled down and burnt.

[313] From here the Count pressed on to lay siege to Saint-Antonin,[53] which the Count of Toulouse had given to an evil and depraved knight.[54] Whilst we were on our way there, the Bishop of Albi[55] went ahead to offer peace and urge this knight to hand the *castrum* over to our Count. With great arrogance and disdain the knight replied: 'Let the Count of Montfort know that a crowd of stick-carriers[56] will never take my *castrum*.' (He called them 'stick-carriers' because of the staves they carried which in common speech are called 'sticks'.) On hearing this the Count made haste to start the siege.

[314] *Siege of Saint-Antonin*. One Sunday, during the eight days of the feast of the Pentecost,[57] we arrived at Saint-Antonin to initiate the siege, and made our camp on one side of the place in front of the gates. This most notable *castrum* occupied a very pleasant site in a valley at the foot of a hill. A clear stream flowed between the hill and the *castrum*, close to the walls.[58] On the other side there was a welcome area of level ground which our besieging forces had occupied. [315] Our adversaries came out of the *castrum* and harassed our men all day long from a distance with bowshot. As evening began the enemy came out and began to come forward a little; they attacked us, still from a distance, and fired their arrows at our tents. The sergeants in the army were not able to put up with this humiliating treatment for long; they set on the enemy and started to drive them back into the *castrum*. What more? A great clamour arose in the army, unarmed crusaders

---

51 See also *Chanson*, I, 113, p. 252, which confirms it was razed.

52 About 8km north of Saint-Marcel, where the Averyon and Viaur meet. See also §§237, 281.

53 See §§237 and 281 above.

54 Peter is presumably referring to Adhémar-Jourdain, Viscount of Saint-Antonin, whose family had held the town for generations. He is also mentioned in the *Chanson* (I, 112 and 114, pp. 250 and 252) as '*Azemar Jorda*'. Lordship was shared between him and a relative, named as 'Viscount Pons' ('*Pons lo vescomte*') in the *Chanson*. See G&L II, p. 13 n. 1; Roquebert I, pp. 467–8, and *Chanson* I, p. 251 n. 3. Apparently he was still alive in 1230.

55 William Peyre, on whom see §118 above. He was giving active support to the crusaders at this time, and the *Chanson* (I, 112, p. 250) mentions Albi as a base for the arrival of new crusaders during the same period. Cf. the grant to him on 3 April of the castles of Rouffiac and Marsac (see §301).

56 Latin '*burdonarius*', equivalent to French *bourdonnier* related to medieval Latin *burdo*, a wand, and French *bourdon*, a (pilgrim's) staff. The *Chanson* twice uses *bordon(i)er* to refer to the crusaders in ordinary narrative and twice has the Toulousains using the word pejoratively (III, 198, p. 136; 201, p. 162; 205, p. 204; and 213, p. 296). The Latin word translated as 'staves' is *baculos*, and 'sticks' is *burdones*. Pilgrims traditionally carried a staff as a symbol of their purpose, and the use of the word as a derogatory term for the crusaders reflects the very close link between the idea of the crusader and the pilgrim during the 12th and 13th centuries, a link which was so close that the same word (*peregrinus*) was commonly used both in the present work and elsewhere to describe both (see e.g. §315 below where it is used three times, and see also n. 78 to §80).

57 20 May 1212.

58 Saint-Antonin lies on the River Bonnette, at the point where it flows from the north into the larger River Aveyron. The hill mentioned here, lying to the south of the town, is Le Roc d'Anglars, a sheer cliff rising from the southern bank of the Aveyron.

of low rank[59] ran to join the fray; without the knowledge or approval of the Count and his knights they began to attack the *castrum*; they set about the enemy with such incredible and unheard-of courage that they reduced them to fear and stupefaction by a continuous heavy bombardment of stones and in the space of one hour captured three strong barbicans.[60] A fight without swords, a glorious victory! I invoke God as my witness that after Saint-Antonin surrendered I myself went into it and saw the walls of houses virtually eaten away by the stones hurled by our crusaders. The defenders, seeing they had lost the barbicans, left the *castrum* on the other side[61] and sought flight through the river; our crusaders saw them, crossed the river and put to the sword those they could capture.

[316] After the capture of the barbicans our crusaders withdrew from the attack: daylight was fading and night imminent. The lord of Saint-Antonin[62] realised that the loss of the barbicans meant that the *castrum* was as good as captured, and about midnight sent to the Count to say he was ready to surrender the place provided he himself could go free. The Count refused these terms; the lord sent again to say he would surrender himself and the *castrum* uncondition-ally. At first light the Count ordered all the inhabitants to be brought out; a consultation with his comrades led to the conclusion that if he ordered the defenders, who were mere untutored countrymen, to be killed, the *castrum* would be devoid of inhabitants and become desolate, so wiser counsels prevailed and he released them.[63] The lord of the place, the cause of all the trouble, he ordered to be shut up in the depths of the keep at Carcassonne, where he was kept in chains for some time; the few knights with him were committed to prison.

[317] *The Count marches towards Agen.*[64] There were present in the camp at this time the Bishops of Uzès and Toulouse and also Guy, Bishop of Carcassonne, who stayed with the army throughout. After taking their advice the Count and his knights decided to march into the Agenais. The Bishop of Agen[65] had pre-

---

[59] Latin 'peregrini pauperes et inermes'. The *Chanson* (I, 113, p. 252) also refers to 'Li ribaut els garson', 'the ribauds and servants'. This attack by the menial poor who were with the crusaders is reminiscent of Béziers in July 1209 (§90 above, and Appendix B). Roquebert (I, p. 469) again suggests that these 'poor' were in essence mercenaries.

[60] These three barbicans defended gates on the east, north-east and north of the town, and were later known as the Porte des Carmes, Porte Rodanèse (or des Cordeliers) and Porte du Pré du Roi (cf. G&L II, p. 15 n. 1). A fourth gate lay on the western side of Saint-Antonin, the Porte de la Condamine.

[61] I.e. the south side, bounded by the River Aveyron.

[62] See §313 above.

[63] The *Chanson* adds that the ribauds had already despoiled the women and men, including clergy, who had taken refuge in the church. Presumably de Montfort realised that massacring the inhabitants would reduce the economic value of the town and the surrounding countryside, and he wished to avoid this. (Cf. the position after the massacre at Béziers, on which see Appendix B.) The town was handed over to Baldwin of Toulouse (*Chanson* I, 113, p. 252).

[64] The account which follows shows that the crusaders did not follow the most direct route, which would have taken them due west along the valleys of the Aveyron, Tarn and Garonne. This route would have taken them close to Montauban, Castelsarrasin and Moissac, all of which were still in Raymond VI's hands, and instead they went first northwards and then west through Quercy towards Agen.

[65] The Bishop of Agen was Arnold de Revignan, who occupied the see from 1209 to 1228. He had been in dispute with Raymond VI, who at the time of the Council of Lavaur in 1213 was accused of having expelled

viously told the Count that if he were to move personally into the area he and his kinsmen,[66] who were influential in the territory, would give him all help within their power. Agen was a notable city, pleasantly situated on the River Garonne between Toulouse and Bordeaux. The city and its territories had long been held by the King of England, but when King Richard gave his sister Joan in marriage to Count Raymond of Toulouse, they were ceded to the Count as a dowry. However, the Pope had given authority to our Count in papal letters to attack all heretics and their supporters with the help of the crusaders.[67]

[318] We therefore left Saint-Antonin and marched directly to Montcuq,[68] a *castrum* belonging to the Count of Toulouse. I must here record that the fortified places we passed had been deserted by their occupants in fear of our army. The Count had them pulled down or burnt, as they might be a source of harm to Christian believers. One notable *castrum* near Saint-Antonin under the lordship of the Count of Toulouse, Caylus,[69] was now handed over to our Count through the efforts of that noble and faithful man, Count Baldwin. Our Count had once held the place but the inhabitants had seceded from him the previous year and handed it over to the Count of Toulouse. Hearing of our approach the defenders of Montcuq all fled in fear, leaving the place empty. It was a notable *castrum* on a

him (see §394). Thus the Bishop no doubt welcomed the opportunity of siding with the crusaders and removing himself from under Raymond VI's lordship. De Montfort's motive in advancing through Quercy and the Agenais will have been to take these areas and their resources from Raymond, thus isolating him in the Toulousain. The diocese of Agen had apparently been an important early centre of Catharism in the 12th century, and at the Cathar Council of Saint-Félix in 1167/72 it is probable that a new Cathar diocese based on Agen was established (cf. Griffe, *Débuts*, pp. 72–4). Heretics were burned at Casseneuil in 1209 by the crusaders who campaigned in Quercy (see *Chanson* I, 14, p. 42), and in §519 below Peter says that Casseneuil was a longstanding centre of heresy. There is very little other direct evidence of heresy in the Agenais, and Catharism appears to have declined there in the early 13th century. Innocent III wrote that '... manifest heretics have, by Divine providence, been driven from the diocese of Agen, but some believers and supporters of heretics lurk there, causing trouble for the churches and churchmen' (Potthast, 3890, and G&L II, p. 17).

66 Including the Bishop's brother Hugh de Revignan, lord of Casseneuil (on whom see §519 below).

67 When the marriage between Raymond and Joan (or Jeanne) took place in 1196 (see William of Puylaurens, V) the gift by King Richard of England of Agen and the Agenais as a dowry was conditional upon Raymond and his heirs holding it as a fief of the kings of England (as dukes of Aquitaine), who would thus retain ultimate overlordship. By invading the Agenais de Montfort was thus arguably infringing the rights of its overlord, King John of England. A complaint about this by Peter of Aragon is recorded in Innocent's letter of 18 January 1213 to the legates (*PL* 216, 739, and see Appendix F(iv)(c) and n. 137 to §358). The argument that de Montfort's occupation of the territory should not override the rights of Raymond VI's son was also deployed at the Lateran Council in November 1215 (see *Chanson* II, 149–50, pp. 72–6). In arguing that it was perfectly legitimate for the crusaders to invade the Agenais, Peter is here invoking as justification the general authority of Innocent III's letters of November 1209 (*PL* 216, 151–3) and June 1210 (*PL* 216, 282), which acknowledged his possession of lands formerly possessed by heretics, and (for instance) Innocent's letter of December 1210 to Raymond (*Non decet tanti*: *PL* 216, 356) in which he warned him that his lands would be liable to seizure if he did not drive out heretics, a reflection of the general doctrine of *exposition en proie* (cf. §62 above). See, however, notes to §299 and especially §§367–8 for Innocent's increasing concern about the actions of Simon de Montfort and the legates at this time, mid-1212; and see also §§505 and 522 below for later intervention in the area against de Montfort by King John, in 1214.

68 About 55km north-west of Saint-Antonin. Cf. also *Chanson* I, 114, p. 254.

69 See §247.

favourable and very fertile site. The Count gave it to Count Baldwin, the brother of the Count of Toulouse.[70]

[319] Leaving Montcuq we came to a *castrum* two leagues distant in the Agenais, known as Penne.[71] The Count of Toulouse had entrusted this place to his Seneschal, a knight called Hugh d'Alfaro from Navarre to whom he had given an illegitimate daughter in marriage.[72] When Hugh heard of our Count's approach he gathered together a body of about four hundred strong and well-armed mercenaries[73] (he had driven out all the inhabitants, from the youngest to the oldest). He retired with the mercenaries to the castle, which he had strengthened and stocked with copious provisions and everything else needed for its defence, and prepared to withstand our attack. When this was reported to our Count he proposed to besiege the place.

[320] However, after taking advice from his companions he decided first to go to Agen to take that city under his command. Leaving the main body of the army to await his return, he went with a selected body of knights to Agen where he was received with honour. The citizens appointed him their lord, swore an oath of fealty and handed the city to him.[74] After this process had been duly completed, the Count returned to the army, to besiege Penne.

[321] *Siege of Penne d'Agenais.* At first light on Sunday 3 June in the year 1212 of the Incarnation, we arrived at Penne, resolved to besiege it with the Lord's help. Seeing the army of crusaders approach, Hugh d'Alfaro, the guardian of the place, mentioned above, retired to the castle with his mercenaries and set fire to the entire lower bourg.[75] Penne was the most notable *castrum* in the Agenais. It was situated on a pleasant hillside, surrounded on all sides by broad and fertile valleys.[76] On one side it was graced by rich and productive farmland, on another by charming flat meadows, on another by delightful woodlands, on another by fertile vineyards, a source of joy. It was moreover blessed by pleasant and healthy

---

[70] For Baldwin see §§235–6 above.

[71] Penne d'Agenais, on the River Lot, to be distinguished from Penne d'Albigeois overlooking the gorge of the River Tarn, see §327 below. The crusaders arrived at Penne on 3 June 1212 (see §321 below).

[72] Hugh d'Alfaro, Raymond's Seneschal of the Agenais, had been present at the first siege of Toulouse in June 1211 (see §241 above, and *Chanson* I, 81, p. 194 and n. 1). He came from Alfaro, near Tudela in southern Navarre. His wife was probably Guillemette, illegitimate daughter of Raymond VI (*HGL* VII, p. 27 n. 10). His brother, Peter Arces, had been with Raymond during the first siege of Toulouse (see *Chanson*, loc. cit.). His defence of Penne on behalf of Raymond is also recounted by William of Tudela (*Chanson*, I, 115, p. 256). Hugh's son Raymond later served Raymond VII, and he is commemorated in the name of the Rue Pharaon in Toulouse.

[73] Amongst them William of Tudela mentions one '*Bausas lo mainaders*', 'Bausas the leader of a (mercenary) band' (*Chanson* I, 114, p. 256).

[74] Simon de Montfort now shared the lordship with the Bishop (G&L II, p. 21 n. 1, citing Rhein 154) noting that an act was witnessed by the two of them on 4 June 1212.

[75] The *burgum inferius*, to the south-west of the castle. Peter's account uses three terms to describe different parts of Penne: first was the castle (*castri munitio*); second was the fortified town as a whole (*castrum*); and thirdly there was the lower suburb (*burgum inferius*) probably unfortified or only partially fortified. G&L (II, p. 19 n. 2) translate '*munitio*' here as '*donjon*' or keep, and G&M as usual translate it as such: see Appendix A (iv) for our reasons for disagreeing with this rendering.

[76] The River Lot was on the northern side of the town. A tributary, the Boudouyssou, flowed along the west and south sides, itself joined by the Lartigue flowing from the south. Penne occupied a naturally strong site on an outcrop overlooking the valleys.

air, and surrounded by a wealth of beautiful streams. The castle itself, built on a huge natural crag and protected by very strong walls, seemed to be almost impregnable. King Richard of England (who as mentioned above had been overlord of Penne) had made the castle very strong and had a well dug, because Penne was in effect the principal place in the whole of the Agenais and the key to controlling it.[77] The knight Hugh, entrusted with the *castrum* by the Count of Toulouse, had so filled the castle with well-armed chosen warriors, with supplies and petraries, with wood and iron and all else needed for its defence, that one could scarcely believe it would yield even after many years. Finally, Hugh had built inside the castle two smithies, a furnace and a mill. So plentifully equipped he awaited the siege without anxiety.

[322] Our men arrived before the *castrum* and set up their tents on all sides. Even as they were doing so some of the defenders came out and harassed us with heavy volleys of arrows. After a few days our men set up petraries inside the bourg which had been burnt, so as to fire at the castle; seeing this the defenders themselves erected petraries to disconcert and impede us, and caused us considerable problems by firing large quantities of heavy stones. Our men set up more petraries, but although our engines kept up a constant fire and knocked down the houses inside the castle they had little or no effect in weakening the walls themselves. It was summer and very hot, about the time of the feast of St John the Baptist.[78] [323] I must add that although our Count had a great many crusaders on foot, he had few knights, with the result that whenever our men approached the castle to attack it they made little or no headway against our adversaries, who were well armed and well trained and resisted bravely. One day whilst they were attacking the castle our men captured a wooden barrier near the wall, but the enemy hurled down an immense barrage of stones from the wall and at once drove our men back. When our men retired to their tents the enemy, despite the midday heat, made a sortie with the objective of setting fire to our siege-engines, bringing with them fire and straw and everything else needed to set them alight; however, our men resisted strongly so that far from setting the petraries on fire the enemy failed even to reach them. This was not the only sortie made by the enemy – on many days subsequently they came out and harassed our men to the best of their ability.

[324] The venerable Bishop of Carcassonne, often mentioned, was present at the siege, and I was with him. Here in the army of the Lord, by the authority of the Archbishop of Narbonne (a papal legate, and previously Abbot of Cîteaux), he was performing the duties of vice-legate.[79] With indefatigable spirit and incredible physical energy he devoted himself to preaching and other duties connected with the siege. To put matters briefly, we were weighed down by such an

---

[77] The castle was built by King Richard of England in the 1180s, and is known in modern times as *le château du roi*.

[78] 24 June 1212.

[79] Arnold Amalric was in Spain, where he took part in the Las Navas de Tolosa campaign in July 1212, when the Kings of Castile, Aragon and Navarre defeated the Almohades. For Guy as vice-legate see §520 below, and also n. 109 to §342.

insupportable burden of cares, one succeeding another, that we scarcely had time to eat or rest, even for a moment.

[325] Nor must I omit to say that whilst the Count was engaged on the siege of Penne all the nobles in the area came to pay him homage and acknowledge him as their overlord.[80]

[326] Whilst this was happening Guy de Montfort, the Count's brother, Robert the Archbishop of Rouen, Robert the Bishop-elect of Laon, William the Archdeacon of Paris,[81] the vice-lord of Picquigny[82] and Enguerrand de Boves[83] (to whom the Count had previously given lordship over part of the domains of the Count of Foix), all accompanied by numerous other crusaders, had left Carcassonne and marched to the territories of the Count of Foix. They reached a *castrum* named Lavelanet,[84] took it by force and slaughtered the occupants. When this became known the inhabitants of the neighbouring *castra* burnt down their fortresses and fled before us. Our men demolished these places as they came to them. From there they turned towards Toulouse and completely destroyed numerous strong *castra* which had been left empty; indeed from the time they took Lavelanet they found no-one prepared to await their arrival in any *castrum*, however strong, since all the inhabitants of the area had been quite overcome by fear.

[327] Whilst these crusaders were conducting themselves with such courage, the Count sent orders to them to join him at Penne, since the crusaders who were with him almost all wished to return home after having performed their forty days service. The others hastened to obey his orders, but on their way came to a very strong *castrum* known as Penne d'Albigeois.[85] This place had so far opposed Christianity and the Count, and was always full of mercenaries. When the crusaders arrived outside, the mercenaries came out against them and slew one of our knights. However, our men did not wish to delay long enough to capture the place, since the Count had called on them to join him with all speed; instead they destroyed the crops and vineyards round about and hurried off to meet the Count. After the departure of our soldiers (who had spent some days at the

---

[80] One of them being Hugh de Revignan: see §§317 and 519.

[81] See §310 above for their arrival at Carcassonne in late April, or early May 1212.

[82] Enguerrand, also vice-lord (*vidame*) of Amiens. His son apparently married a daughter of Simon de Montfort, Laure: see G&L II, p. 26 n. 1.

[83] Enguerrand de Boves had joined the Fourth Crusade in 1202 but like Simon de Montfort had left at Zara (on which see §106 above). He is mentioned again in §354 below, and like a number of other crusaders he is known to have donated property to (St) Dominic's monastery of Prouille near Fanjeaux (G&L II, p. 26 n. 2).

[84] Lavelanet, in the valley of the River Touyre, about 15km south of Mirepoix, in the Pays d'Olmes. One of the most important local lords was Raymond de Péreille, whose family was closely involved with Catharism, and was instrumental in establishing the Cathar stronghold at Montségur, in the mountains to the south of Lavelanet (see Roquebert, IV, chs. 2 and 3).

[85] Penne d'Albigeois lies about 5km east of Bruniquel, overlooking the southern side of the gorge cut by the River Aveyron. The ruins of its castle are on an overhanging outcrop of rock high above the gorge. It was one of Raymond VI's strongholds in the northern Albigeois, and despite its proximity to Bruniquel (held by Baldwin of Toulouse) it had escaped earlier attention. Penne was still resisting the crusaders in 1213 (§428), and Bernard de Penne is mentioned in the *Chanson* (III, 214, p. 306) as supporting Raymond VI at the siege of Toulouse in June 1218.

place) the defenders went to the place where our men had buried the knight who had been killed and tore the body from its tomb; they dragged it through the streets and exposed it to the beasts and birds. What impious madness, what unheard-of barbarity!

[328] The arrival of the crusaders to join the Count, still engaged on the siege of Penne d'Agenais, was greeted by him with great delight. They were split into groups to join the various lines and pitched their tents nearby. The Count and his knights were established on the western side of the place and our siege-engines were set up on this side. The Count's brother Guy pitched his camp on the opposite, eastern side where he now erected a siege-engine and himself mounted a strong attack on the *castrum*. What more? By now a great many engines were in place, and our men were pressing home their attack – indeed there were about nine engines set up around the place. Since I cannot set down everything that happened during the siege I will now summarise. Our Count saw that our existing siege-engines were not adequate to break down the walls, and had another engine built that was much larger than the others. [329] Whilst this engine was being made ready, the Archbishop of Rouen, the Bishop-elect of Laon and their followers were anxious to return home on completion of their forty days service.[86] Indeed, each day saw the departure of crusaders who had completed their forty days service, whilst there were few if any new arrivals. The Count could see that he was about to be left almost unsupported, and was in a position of great difficulty; he approached the leaders of the army and begged them not to desert Christ's business in the hour of need but to stay a little longer. It was reported that a large body of crusaders coming from France was at Carcassonne; this was indeed true. I must add that the Provost of Cologne and the many German nobles who had arrived with him or after him had already left the army.[87] The Bishop-elect of Laon heard but did not heed the Count's entreaties; he offered the excuse of some illness and could in no way be prevailed upon to stay. Almost all the others behaved in similar fashion; only the Archbishop of Rouen (who had shown exemplary devotion to the service of God, maintaining numerous knights and a large household[88] at his own expense) generously acceded to the Count's wishes; he stayed with the Count until new groups of crusaders arrived and he was then able to go home with the Count's willing permission and with honour.

[330] After the departure of the Bishop-elect of Laon and the greater part of the army, William the venerable Archdeacon of Paris,[89] a man of steadfast purpose and admirable integrity, began to devote himself most energetically to all matters pertaining to the siege; the Bishop of Carcassonne, however, had

---

[86] These crusaders had arrived about the middle of May 1212, just before the siege of Saint-Antonin which began on 20 May (see §§310 and 314 above), so their departure will have been about the end of June 1212.

[87] Engelbert of Cologne had left about the end of June; at about the same time Leopold of Austria had gone south into Spain to support Peter of Aragon against the Almohades (G&L II, p. 30 n. 1).

[88] Latin *'familiam multam'*, translated by G&M as *'une grande domesticité'*.

[89] See §175.

returned to that city to attend to some matters of business.[90] Meanwhile the siege-engine of superior size referred to above was being made ready. When it was finished the Archdeacon had it set up near the *castrum*. It was able to fire large stones in keeping with its size, and began gradually to weaken the wall.

[331] After a few days the crusaders mentioned earlier arrived. They included the Abbot of St Remigius at Reims, an abbot from Soissons, the Dean of the cathedral of Auxerre (who later died at Penne), and the Archdeacon of Châlons, all men of importance and learning,[91] as well as large numbers of knights and footsoldiers. After their arrival the Archbishop of Rouen left the army with the Count's willing approval and returned home. The new arrivals set to work on the siege with great energy. [332] One day our opponents drove out the poor and the women in the *castrum*, as they did not want them to consume their supplies,[92] and thus exposed them to the threat of death. The Count, however, refused to kill them but instead forced them to return. What noble and princely conduct! He did not deign to kill those he had not captured and believed he would win no glory from the death of those whose capture would not help him to victory.

[333] So, after a prolonged attack by our siege-engines on the castle had succeeded in breaking up all the dwellings and shelters inside, and the newly-constructed large engine had begun to weaken the wall, the defenders realised that they could not hold out much longer and that if they were captured they would all be put to the sword. Seeing moreover that they were not going to receive any help from the Count of Toulouse, they sought to make terms with us on the basis that they would surrender the *castrum* to our Count so long as they were allowed to go free with their arms. [334] When this was reported to the Count he consulted his companions as to whether he should accept the terms offered by his adversaries. Our men took into account that almost all the crusaders were due to leave after completing their forty days service, so that the Count would be almost alone; they also considered that the enemy would be able to hold out for some time, and believed that the Count had numerous other more important tasks to perform (winter was approaching, and he would not then be able to maintain the siege). After carefully considering all these factors they advised the Count to accept the enemy's proposals, and on the feast of St James[93] in July in the year 1212 of the incarnation of the Word the enemy were expelled from Penne, and the noble Count took possession of this notable place.

[335] The next day saw the arrival of Alberic, the venerable Archbishop of Reims,[94] a man of great piety who had devoted himself most sincerely to Christ's business. He was accompanied by the Cantor of Reims and some other crusaders.

[336] I must record that whilst the Count was engaged on the siege of Penne

---

90 Evidently taking our author with him: see §339.
91 The Abbot of St Remigius at Reims was Guy, 1206–12; the Dean of Auxerre was Renaud who apparently died on 1 July; and the Archdeacon of Châlons was Ralph or Raoul (G&L II, p. 31 nn. 3–7 give details).
92 The *Chanson* (I, 115, pp. 256–8) mentions that the defenders were sufferring from lack of food and drink, that their wells were dry, and that in the heat of the summer they were sufferring from disease.
93 25 July 1212.
94 Archbishop 1207–18 (G&L II, p. 33 n. 3); he was accompanied by his nephew (see §343).

he asked Robert Mauvoisin[95] to go to the very notable town of Marmande, previously held by the Count of Toulouse, and to take control of it and garrison it on his behalf.[96] This most noble man was suffering from a very severe illness, but he did not refuse the task or offer his debilitating complaint as an excuse; instead he acceded willingly and graciously to the Count's request. It was on Robert's wise foresight and salutary advice that the Count, and indeed the whole of Christ's business, chiefly depended. On his arrival at Marmande Robert was honourably received by the townsfolk but some sergeants of the Count of Toulouse who were guarding the castle in the *castrum*, and did not wish to surrender, began to resist and defend the castle. With typical energy Robert at once had a mangonel set up in front of the castle, and after a few missiles had been fired the sergeants gave in. Robert stayed at Marmande for a few days and then returned to the Count at Penne.

[337] *Capture of Biron: hanging of Martin Algai.* After capturing and fortifying Penne the Count decided to lay siege to the neighbouring *castrum* named Biron.[97] This place had been given by the Count of Toulouse to the traitor Martin Algai who (as recorded earlier) had at one time sided with our Count but later deserted him in an act of treason.[98] He was staying in Biron and decided to await our forces' arrival there; what happened subsequently showed that his decision was ordained by a just judgment of God. Our men reached the place and started to besiege it. They then mounted an attack and after great efforts and a remarkable display of courage climbed the walls and seized the bourg. Their opponents at once retired to the castle, but realised they would not be able to hold out and sought to make peace, on the basis that they would hand over the castle so long as they themselves were allowed to escape with their lives. In no way did the Count wish this to happen. Indeed, he feared that the traitor Martin Algai might escape in secret, and since his main objective in starting the siege had been to secure Martin's capture he offered to free his adversaries from the threat of death if they would surrender the traitor to him. They eagerly assented to this proposal, seized Martin and handed him over to the Count. On taking him the Count offered him the opportunity to confess his sins – such had been his practice, as a good Catholic, in dealing with other condemned men. He then had him tied to a horse and dragged through the army and finally hanged from a gibbet – a fate in keeping with his crimes.[99]

---

[95] On Robert see above, §§129, 154 and 286. A donation to the monastery of Prouille by Robert was confirmed by Simon at this time ('*in obsidione Penne in Agennensi*'); the act is dated 17 July and was confirmed '*apud Pennam in Agennensi*' on 5 August (Rhein 99 and 100). Robert died two years later. For details see G&L II, p. 34 n. 4 and p. 35 n. 2 (citing Rhein 100), and Roquebert I, p. 475.

[96] Marmande, on the River Garonne about 50km north-west of Agen, lay at the western edge of the Agenais and thus of Raymond VI's dominions. It had been founded by King Richard of England in the 1180s. See also §518 below.

[97] 25km north of Penne, in the southern Périgord, on the summit of a steep-sided hill.

[98] Martin Algai had acquired Biron by marriage to a daughter of Henry of Gontaud: see n. 3 by E. Martin-Chabot, *Chanson* I, p. 210. He had deserted the crusaders at Castelnaudary in 1211 (see §§265 and 274 above) and Simon de Montfort now sought his revenge.

[99] His fate is confirmed by William of Tudela, *Chanson* I, 115–16, pp. 258–60. He adds that Biron was

[338] After this the Count returned to Penne. Here the leading noble in Gascony, Gaston de Béarn, an evil man who had throughout supported the Count of Toulouse, came to see him to discuss terms.[100] They were unable to reach agreement on that day, and the Count offered to meet him at a later date in Agen; but this enemy of peace drew back from the attempt to make terms and refused to come on the day proposed.

[339] Whilst these events were taking place, the noble Countess of Montfort and the venerable Bishop of Carcassonne, and I myself, were on our way from the Carcassonne area to join the Count, bringing with us a few unmounted crusaders.[101] I must mention that whilst we were on our way many of our crusaders found it impossible to keep going because of the extreme heat and the difficulties of the route. The Bishop and the Countess took pity on their condition and allowed them to ride behind them on their own horses all day; indeed from time to time they each allowed two crusaders to ride on their horses and themselves proceeded on foot. What pious compassion on the part of the Bishop, what noble humility shown by the Countess! As we hurried on our way to joint the Count and reached Cahors it was reported to us that there were some fortresses nearby which were held by mercenaries and enemies of the faith. As we approached these places Divine clemency intervened, so that even though there were so few of us the enemy were terrified and fled before us leaving many strong *castra* empty. We destroyed these, and then went on to meet the Count at Penne.[102]

[340] *Siege of Moissac.* After this the Count took counsel with his companions and decided to lay siege to a *castrum* named Moissac which was under the control of the Count of Toulouse.[103] We arrived before the place on the eve of the feast of the assumption of the Blessed Virgin Mary[104] and started to besiege it.

handed over to Arnaud de Montaigu, a lord from Quercy who had sided with the crusaders. For King John of England's high regard for Martin Algai see W. L. Warren, *King John*, p. 91.

100   Gaston de Béarn had been with the Count of Foix at Castelnaudary in 1211 (see §254 above). See also below, §§367–98, for his position at the time of the Council of Lavaur early in 1213.

101   William of Tudela (*Chanson* I, p. 260) says that the Countess had fifteen thousand troops with her, no doubt a great exaggeration. He adds that amongst the places they passed through was Catus, north-west of Cahors.

102   De Montfort was still at Penne on 6 August 1212, since on that day he wrote from Penne to his mother Amicia of Leicester on business concerning his estates in the Ile de France: see G&L II, p. 38 n. 2. The crusaders apparently left Penne for Moissac on 12 August since they arrived on 14 August (next section) and the *Chanson* (I, 116, pp. 260–2) says they took two days to reach Moissac, going via Montcuq.

103   Lordship over Moissac was shared between the Counts of Toulouse and the Abbots of the Cluniac monastery of St Peter in the town, which was a stopping point for pilgrims on their way to Santiago de Compostela. In the early 13th century relationships between the Abbot and the townsfolk were poor: Peter below (§353) records that the Abbot (Raymond du Proet) had fled the town because the inhabitants would not obey him, and he had gone to join the crusaders. Relations between the Abbot and Raymond VI were also poor, made worse when earlier in 1212 Raymond had occupied Moissac and taken possession of neighbouring places held by the abbey. Moissac lies on the north bank of the Tarn, just before it joins the Garonne, and it covered the approach to Toulouse from the north, which will in part explain the Toulousains' decision to help its defence. At about the same time the Count of Foix's son Roger-Bernard also occupied Montauban (*Chanson* I, 125, p. 276), and Giraud de Pépieux was at Castelsarrasin (*Chanson* I, 117, p. 264), both presumably as part of the attempt to secure the approaches to Toulouse, although Giraud did not stay long. See also Roquebert I, pp. 477–8.

104   14 August 1212.

[341] Moissac was situated at the foot of a hill on level ground near the River Tarn.[105] The site was very fertile and pleasant. Its name is derived from the word 'moys' which means 'water', since there is an abundance of clear springs inside the walls. The men of the *castrum* on hearing of our approach summoned mercenaries and a large force of Toulousains, hoping to rely on their aid to withstand our soldiers.[106] These mercenaries were evil and perverted men; Moissac had long since been placed under an interdict by the papal legates because it had supported the heretics and joined the Count of Toulouse in attacking the Church, but despite this, to show their contempt for God and our army, they rang the bells in the church (which was a large and very fine building) every hour of every day as if celebrating a festival.[107] It is said that Pepin King of the French had founded a monastery for a thousand monks in the place.[108]

[342] After a few days the Count had siege-engines made ready and set up near the *castrum*. They were set to work and had some effect in weakening the walls. However, the enemy set up their own engines and fired against ours. The directors and leaders of this work, the venerable Bishop of Carcassonne and William, Archdeacon of Paris, laboured enthusiastically on everything required for the siege.[109] The Archbishop of Reims,[110] who was present, visited the crusaders, frequently and with a will, to preach to them and give them encouragement; he showed great humility in becoming personally involved in whatever was needed for the success of the siege as well as spending freely from his own resources; he was truly indispensible to Jesus Christ's business.

[343] One day the enemy made a sortie and approached our siege-engines with a view to destroying them, but the Count and some of our armed men rushed to the spot and forced our opponents back into the castle.[111] In this skirmish one of the enemy wounded the Count in the foot with an arrow. They captured a young soldier from our side, the nephew of the Archbishop of Reims,

[105] This hill rises to the west of the town. The crusaders will have camped on the southern side, on the north bank of the Tarn between the river and the southern wall of the town.

[106] William of Tudela (*Chanson* I, 124, p. 276) says that more than 300 mercenaries were slaughtered after Moissac was captured; and also (I, 117, p. 262) that the inhabitants did not wish to resist the crusaders and would have capitulated had it not been for the mercenaries. Moissac was not on a naturally strong site, and its defences relied on its walls, which incorporated the abbey church on their northern side (and whose crenellated 12th century tower still survives), and on the ditches and palisades around them (on the ditches, see §348 below). There were two gates fortified with barbicans (see §350).

[107] The point being made is that ringing church bells was forbidden when a place was under an interdict. The interdict on Raymond's domains (including Moissac) had been imposed in February 1211 after the Council of Montpellier (see §212 n. 38), and had been communicated to the Abbot of Moissac by the Bishop of Cahors, along with an order to quit the town: see G&L II, p. 40 n. 2.

[108] Presumably Pepin (or Pippin) III, son of Charles Martel and father of Charlemagne, who deposed Childeric III, the last of the Merovingians, in 751; but the legend was based on a falsification (see G&L II, p. 40 n. 4). Another legend has the abbey founded in 506 by Clovis, but its foundation is more commonly attributed to two monks from Saint-Wandrille in Normandy between 628 and 648 (cf. note by M. Vidal in *Quercy Roman*, pp. 43–5 (éditions Zodiaque, 3rd ed. 1979)).

[109] G&L (II, p. 41 n. 2) note that Guy of les Vaux-de-Cernay and Archdeacon William of Paris were described as vice-legates in letters written by de Montfort to the Abbot of Moissac after the siege.

[110] Alberic: see above §335.

[111] This lay in the south-west corner of the town, and was held on behalf of Raymond VI by one Durand Mercier (*Layettes*, V, 194, and see also G&L II, p. 198 n. 2).

and dragged him off.[112] They slew him and shamefully dismembered him and threw the remains to us. The Archbishop, the young man's uncle, had loved him dearly, but for the sake of his duty to Jesus Christ he bore his nephew's death with equanimity and concealed his grief courageously, so providing a marvellous example of forbearance and high-mindedness for everyone in the army.

[344] I must also record that in the early days of the siege, since there were too few crusaders for us to surround Moissac completely, our opponents came out each day, climbed the hill which overlooked the *castrum*[113] and attacked us arrogantly; our crusaders climbed up to them and fought them all day long. Whenever they killed a crusader they would surround the corpse to show their contempt for us and attack it with their swords. Such was their barbarity that it was not enough for them to see one of our number killed; they must each and every one add fresh wounds and transfix the body with their swords. A despicable form of battle, the madness of evil men!

[345] Whilst these and similar events were taking place crusaders began to arrive daily from France.[114] One day Reginald, Bishop of Toul,[115] came with some crusaders. As the number of crusaders grew our men occupied the hill I referred to above, and as further bands of supporters arrived they besieged Moissac virtually on all sides.[116] When they saw this the enemy no longer dared to come out so freely as before.

[346] I must record that before Moissac was surrounded the mercenaries used to come out and climb the hill, and when they saw the Bishop of Carcassonne preaching to the army they would fire bolts from their crossbows into the crowded audience; but by God's grace they did not succeed in harming anyone. [347] On another day I myself, a mere monk of the Cistercian order, went quite close to the *castrum* to encourage the crusaders who were supplying the petraries; one of the mercenaries in Moissac, showing no respect for my calling, fired an extremely sharp bolt from his crossbow at maximum power and tried to hit me; I was on my horse at the time – the bolt pierced my robe, missed my flesh by a finger's width or less, and fixed itself in my saddle. Through God's grace neither I nor my horse was harmed; this I do not attribute to my own merit – rather it seems that Divine clemency ensured that the enemies of religion would not be able to rejoice in striking a monk as if this were a significant victory, and thus justify continuing their attacks on our men.

[348] Since I cannot record in detail everything that happened at the siege I will now summarise. After our siege-engines had kept up their fire for a long period and weakened the walls, the Count had an engine built of the type known

---

112 His death is also mentioned by William of Tudela, *Chanson* I, 121, p. 270.
113 Known as the hill of Calvary, on the western side of the town.
114 William of Tudela says that one group of crusaders, coming from Cahors, was attacked by the defenders of Montauban, but was saved by the intervention of Baldwin of Toulouse (*Chanson* I, 122, p. 272).
115 Bishop 1210–17 (G&L II, p. 43 n. 2).
116 William of Tudela says that it was at the beginning of September that the crusaders surrounded Moissac (*Chanson* I, 119).

in the common tongue as a 'cat'.[117] When it was completed the Count had it dragged to the ditch surrounding the *castrum*, which was very wide and deep and full of water. Our opponents erected wooden barriers outside the ditch and dug another ditch beyond the barriers. They then positioned themselves between the two ditches, and made frequent excursions to attack us. In addition they erected a mangonel between the two ditches and used it to fire at our petraries. Meanwhile our new engine was hauled to the ditch. It was covered with fresh cow-hides to prevent its being set on fire by the enemy, but they in turn used a huge petrary to attack it, hoping to destroy it. [349] Our cat had reached the first ditch and it remained only for us to fill the ditch under the cover it provided, when one day after sunset our adversaries came out of the *castrum* bringing fire, dry wood, straw, tow, salted meat, fat, oil and other combustible materials, which they hurled at our cat with the idea of setting it alight.[118] They also had crossbowmen, who caused severe casualties amongst those defending the cat. What more? The flames leapt higher, we were all in disarray. The Count and his brother Guy were inside the cat; the enemy kept on throwing the inflammable material, whilst our men, without a pause and with great effort, threw wine, water and earth on to the flames, others tried to pull the lumps of meat and vessels of oil from the fire with iron hooks. The anguish caused to them by the heat and their exertions was beyond belief and could scarcely be witnessed without tears; but in the end our men dragged the cat from the flames.

[350] Next day our crusaders put on their armour and mounted an attack from all sides; with great daring they went into the first ditch, and with great effort and numerous acts of courage broke down the wooden barriers. Our adversaries, who were stationed behind the barriers and in the barbicans,[119] defended the barbicans to the best of their ability.

[351] *A miracle.* While this battle was going on, the Bishop of Carcassonne and I were passing amongst the army encouraging our men to fight. The Archbishop of Reims, the Bishops of Toul and Albi, William the Archdeacon of Paris, also the Abbot of Moissac with some monks and the other clergy attached to the army stood on the slopes of the hill overlooking Moissac, clad in white robes, unshod, holding before them the cross and relics of the saints. Loudly and devoutly they sang the *Veni Creator Spiritus*, imploring the Lord to help.[120] The Comforter was not deaf to their prayers, but when they came to the verse 'Drive forth our enemy', which they repeated three times, the enemy were filled with divinely inspired fear and driven back; they quitted the barbicans, fled to the *castrum* and shut themselves up inside the walls.

[352] Meanwhile the townsmen of a nearby *castrum* belonging to the Count

---

117 See note to §96 above, and compare the use of the cat at Lavaur (§224). The use of the cat at Moissac, and the attempts of the defenders to burn it, is also recounted in the *Chanson* I, 121.

118 Compare the tactics adopted by the defenders of Minerve in 1210 (§153) and at the siege of Lavaur in 1211 (§224).

119 There were at least two: one protected the Porte Saint-Jacques at the south-east corner of the town, close to the church of the same name; the other was at the Porte Maraveille in the east of the town.

120 This was also sung at the siege of Lavaur: see §226.

of Toulouse, called Castelsarrasin,[121] came to our Count and surrendered to him. The Count also sent his brother Guy and Count Baldwin, brother of the Count of Toulouse, and some other knights to a notable *castrum* named Verdun on the River Garonne, which also belonged to the Count of Toulouse and was five leagues from Toulouse itself.[122] The townsmen surrendered to our Count without opposition. All the *castra* in the neighbourhood did the same, with the sole exception of Montauban.[123]

[353] When the townsfolk of Moissac heard that all the fortresses in the neighbourhood had surrendered to the Count and saw that they themselves would not be able to hold out, they sent to the Count to ask for peace. He took various points into account: Moissac was strongly defended and could not be taken by force without the loss of many of our men; if it were taken by force, the town would be destroyed, although it was a fine place and belonged to the monks; moreover in those circumstances all those in the place would perish alike. He therefore agreed to accept their surrender on condition that they hand over to him the mercenaries and the soldiers who had come from Toulouse to join in the defence of the place, and that they themselves swear on the Holy Gospels not to fight Christians in future.[124] The agreement was duly concluded, the mercenaries and the men from Toulouse were handed over; the Count received Moissac into his control and restored it to the Abbot, although reserving to himself the rights enjoyed by the Counts of Toulouse.[125] (The Abbot had left the place long before the siege because the townsmen refused to obey him in any matter.) Our crusaders took charge of the mercenaries and killed them with great enthusiasm. I feel it should be pointed out that Moissac, which was first laid under siege on the eve of the feast of the Assumption of the Blessed Virgin Mary, was captured on the day of her birth.[126] Thus, one can recognise the intercession of the Blessed Virgin.

[354] The Count then left Moissac and determined to besiege a *castrum*

---

[121] 8km south of Moissac. Raymond VI's garrison was commanded by Giraud de Pépieux (see *Chanson* I, 117, p. 264), who had fled. It was entrusted by Simon de Montfort to William of Contres (*Chanson* I, 124, p. 276, and see §496 below).

[122] Verdun-sur-Garonne lies about 40km north of Toulouse, on the western bank of the river. William of Tudela (*Chanson* I, 124, p. 276) says it was given by Simon de Montfort to a knight called Perrin de Sissy (from Picardy); he had been with de Montfort from the beginning of the Crusade (see *Chanson* I, 36, pp. 88/9 n. 3) and is referred to as Peter de Sissy in §§424 and 434 below. See also §359 below for attacks from Verdun on the Toulousain hinterland.

[123] William of Tudela mentions (*Chanson*, loc. cit.) that Montech, south of Castelsarrasin, was also taken and given to Baldwin of Toulouse. Montauban, defended by Roger-Bernard of Foix (*Chanson* I, 125, p. 276), was not attacked, presumably because it was so well defended, enjoying a strong natural position on the eastern bank of the Tarn.

[124] The inhabitants of Moissac also had to pay a ransom of 500 gold marks (see *Chanson* I, 124, p. 276).

[125] The agreement was witnessed on 14 September, one copy being made for de Montfort and one for the Abbot. De Montfort was careful to specify his rights over justice and taxation both in Moissac and surrounding villages: see *HGL* VIII, 621–5 for details, and Roquebert I, pp. 482–3, where the terms are summarised. But the crusaders nonetheless pillaged the abbey, and at the end of the year Abbot Raymond was writing to Philip Augustus and to the Abbot of Cluny to complain about their behaviour, saying that they had destroyed everything, both in the abbey and elsewhere (*HGL* VIII, 635–6, and G&L II, p. 50 n. 3).

[126] 8 September 1212.

named Saverdun in the diocese of Toulouse, near Foix.[127] This place had defected from its allegiance to our Count,[128] and the Count of Foix was holding it and using it as a base to mount strong attacks on Pamiers. Meanwhile some crusaders of noble rank from Germany had arrived at Carcassonne. Enguerrand de Boves, to whom our Count had given the greater part of the county of Foix, as recorded earlier,[129] and other of our knights who were guarding the Carcassonne area, conducted the Germans to Pamiers. The Counts of Toulouse and Foix were at Saverdun. The knights and the Germans then left Pamiers and hurried to Saverdun; when they heard of this the Counts of Toulouse and Foix fled from Saverdun, whereupon Enguerrand recovered Saverdun without opposition or any fighting.

[355] While these events were taking place our Count was on his way from Moissac with his army. As he approached Saverdun he himself went to Pamiers where the Germans were, whilst the army went on to Saverdun. The Count took the Germans under his command and rode out before Foix; from there he returned to the army, which had left Saverdun and gone on to Auterive. The men of Auterive fled before us and left it empty. The Count left a garrison in Auterive, since its position between Toulouse and Foix meant that it was a good base from which to keep the enemy in check.

[356] The Count now decided to invade the territory of the Count of Comminges,[130] and went to Muret,[131] near Toulouse, a very pleasant *castrum* on the River Garonne. As we approached, the men of the place fled in fear before us and took refuge in Toulouse; some of them set fire to the bridge in the *castrum* over the Garonne, which was of wood and very long and which we needed as a crossing point.[132] So when we reached the place we were unable to cross with the bridge in flames, but the Count and a large number of our men plunged into the river, which was very deep and flowing fast, and succeeded in crossing not without great danger to themselves. The main army, however, pitched camp on the nearer side of the river, whilst the Count and some of his companions rushed to

---

[127] To the north of Toulouse, only Montauban now remained outside the crusaders' control. They decided, however, not to besiege it, partly because it was so strongly defended and would probably have required a long siege, and partly because it was now isolated, with both Montech and Verdun further south towards Toulouse already having been taken. Instead, for several reasons, they decided to go south: according to William of Tudela (*Chanson* I, 125, p. 278) the Abbot of Pamiers was urging de Montfort to come to his aid because Pamiers was in danger of falling, and its supplies had been cut off by the men of Saverdun. Securing the Ariège valley was also a priority because of its importance as a line of communication between Toulouse and Foix, and beyond into Aragon. If the crusaders could recover control of the area, Toulouse would be more isolated than ever.

[128] In the autumn of 1211, at the time of the battle of Castelnaudary: see §281.

[129] See above, §326.

[130] Bernard IV, Count of Comminges, on whom see n. 28 to §239 above. There is little evidence for heresy in his county, but he was a firm supporter of Raymond VI. As stated below in §358, de Montfort had been asked to enter Comminges by the Bishops of Comminges and Couserans.

[131] Muret lies on the west bank of the Garonne, about 20km south-west of Toulouse. For details of its layout and site see map 5 on p. xv, and §447 et seq. on the battle of Muret.

[132] Building of the bridge had been authorised by the Count of Comminges on 2 June 1203, so it was of recent construction (see G&L II, p. 52 n. 5).

the bridge and with great efforts put out the fire.[133] Soon afterwards rain fell very heavily and the river rose so high that no one could cross without seriously endangering his life.

[357] As evening came on the Count realised that almost all his knights and the stronger members of the army had crossed the river with him and entered Muret, whilst those on foot and the weaker members had been unable to cross and had stayed on the other side. He summoned his Marshal[134] and said: 'I wish to go back to the army.' The Marshal replied: 'What are you saying? The strongest part of the army is here inside Muret – only crusaders on foot are left on the other side of the river, which is now running so strongly that no one will be able to cross. If you were to go back the Toulousains would be able to come and slaughter you and the crusaders over there.' (It would indeed have been possible for the large and well-armed enemy forces in Toulouse to come and attack the crusader army, since our knights inside Muret could not have gone across to them or given them any help.) The Count replied to his Marshal: 'Far be it from me to follow your advice: these poor men of Christ are threatened with death by the sword; would you have me shelter in this castle? With me, let God's will be done; I will go and keep them company.' He at once left the *castrum*, crossed the river and returned to the footsoldiers' camp, where he stayed for several days with very few knights – only four or five – until the bridge was rebuilt and the rest of the army crossed over. What princely virtue, what invincible courage! He did not wish to stay with his knights in the *castrum*, whilst the crusaders of the poorer sort were unprotected in the open.

[358] *The Count goes to Gascony.* Whilst the Count was at Muret he was approached by the Bishops of Comminges and Couserans,[135] venerable and pious men who were singularly dedicated to Christ's business and sought to promote its success by their actions. It was through their advice and help that the Count had come to this region. They now urged the Count to advance further, and take control of most of Gascony without having to engage in fighting. The Count therefore hurried forward and reached a *castrum* known as Saint-Gaudens,[136] which had belonged to the Count of Comminges. The inhabitants handed the place over to him and received him with enthusiasm. The nobles of the area also came to him, did homage to him and recognised him as their overlord. What more? The Count gained control of the whole territory of the Count of Comminges in a very few days without striking a blow. He also went into the high country towards Foix, lands belonging to Roger de Comminges the nephew of the Count of Foix, and laid waste the greater part of it. As recorded

---

133 Coming from Auterive, the crusaders had arrived on the east bank of the river, opposite Muret itself which lay on the west bank. De Montfort and a detachment of his knights had crossed to the west side, and entered Muret, but leaving the main body of the army, including the infantry, on the east bank where, since they were unable to cross, they pitched camp.

134 Guy de Lévis, on whom see n. 104 to §185.

135 The Bishop of Comminges was Garsia, 1210–13, on whom see also §398 below. Bishop Navarre of Couserans had been an active supporter of the legates and the Crusade from the beginning: cf. §48 above.

136 In the Garonne valley, some 80km west of Pamiers.

above, Roger had done homage to our Count at Lavaur, but later showed himself to be a wretched and faithless man and abandoned his loyalty to the Count.[137]

[359] Meanwhile the Bishop of Carcassonne, who had remained at Muret with some crusaders, worked assiduously on preparing the defences. After achieving his objectives in Gascony the Count returned to Muret. He had a few knights with him; there were no crusader knights, except the Count of Toul and a very few others.[138] Even with such limited support he frequently rode up to the very gates of Toulouse; the enemy in Toulouse were very numerous and well-armed, but did not dare come out against him. He laid waste to the lands all round, and destroyed their castles before their eyes. The city of Toulouse was at this time unusually full; heretics from Béziers, Carcassonne and Toulouse, with the supporters of heretics and mercenaries, who had by God's judgment lost their lands, had gone into the city and so crowded it that the canons had been driven from the monasteries and the cloisters turned into sheepfolds and stables. I must not omit to record how Toulouse – a nest of heretics, the tabernacles of robbers![139] – was beset and virtually under siege. Our Count was on one side at Muret, some of our knights on another side at Verdun, Count Baldwin on another and Guy the Count's brother on another.[140] So they were putting considerable pressure on the city from all sides, making frequent excursions on horseback right up to the gates. The Count of Toulouse, deprived by his sins of his heritage, had lost all his lands except Toulouse itself and Montauban, and had fled to the King of Aragon to seek his advice and his help in recovering his domains.[141]

[360] O just judgment of God, most just of judges! What a true prophecy of that most holy man, Peter of Castelnau! This blessed man said – as I have heard from those who themselves heard it often from his lips: 'There will never be a prosperous outcome for Christ's business in the South until one of us, the preachers in defence of the faith, shall meet his death. May I be the first to suffer

---

[137] Roger was Viscount of Couserans: see above, §228 for him and his submission to de Montfort in May 1211. In describing this campaign, William of Tudela (*Chanson* I, 126, pp. 278–80) also mentions the capture of Muret and Saint-Gaudens, and mentions that Samatan and l'Isle Jourdain to the west of Muret were taken, adding that de Montfort occupied the lands of Gaston de Béarn, and went as far west as Oloron (which is perhaps unlikely given the distance). As well as Comminges and Couserans, his influence now extended to the counties of Bigorre, Armagnac, and Astarac and to the viscounty of Lomagne (see G&L II, p. 56 n. 1). The counties of Comminges and Bigorre and the viscounties of Couserans and Béarn were, like Foix, subject to the overlordship of Peter of Aragon (see Roquebert II, pp. 65–6), and de Montfort's intervention there alarmed the King, as is revealed in Innocent's letter to the legates of 18 January 1213 (*PL* 216, 739, see n. 141 to this section, §399 and Appendix F(iv)(c)).

[138] Frederick V, Count of Toul. William of Tudela says (*Chanson* I, 126, p. 280) that most of the crusaders had returned home, their forty days' service completed.

[139] Job 12, v. 6.

[140] William of Tudela (*Chanson* I, 127–9, pp. 280–6) recounts various episodes which took place during October 1212, involving skirmishes between Toulousain troops and William of Contres and Perrin de Sissy, around Castelsarrasin and Verdun.

[141] That Raymond VI visited Peter of Aragon in the early autumn of 1212, perhaps in September, is confirmed in a letter of 18 January 1213 from Innocent III to Arnold Amalric and his fellow legates (*PL* 216, 739, see notes to §§367–8 and 399 below and Appendix F(iv)(c) for translation). In the letter reference is made to a meeting between King Peter and Raymond which marked the beginning of renewed intervention by the King in the Crusade, made possible by the end of the campaign against the Almohades in Spain.

the sword of the persecutor!' See how this wretch, the Count of Toulouse, brought about the death of this holy man because he had shown him guilty of his crimes, publicly and to his face; and thought by this means to escape and recover his domains. But the Lord brought retribution and avenged the blood of his martyr – from which the Count had hoped to achieve gain, but instead won only the heaviest of penalties and irreparable loss. Let it be noted that this wretch, the Count of Toulouse, received the murderer of the man of God with love and friendship;[142] he led him through cities and towns, as if exhibiting him, and declared to everyone: 'This man alone loves me, he alone truly obeys my wishes, he has saved me from my enemies, he has avenged me against my foes, he has won victory for me, he has restored my lands to me.' Although the Count thus lauded this most cruel murderer, even dumb animals shunned him; many canons of the church at Toulouse – worthy men whose account can be trusted – told me that from the day the assassin slew the man of God never did a dog deign to take food from his hands, thus to show contempt for the foul deed. What a marvel, unheard of through the ages! I have included this digression to show how deservedly the Count of Toulouse was deprived of his inheritance.

[361] *The son of the Count of Foix murders crusaders.* During the events related above, Roger-Bernard, son of the Count of Foix, was passing with some mercenaries near Carcassonne and was riding one day towards Narbonne hoping to find some crusaders and take them back to Foix as prisoners or condemn them to a cruel death.[143] On his way he came across a small group of crusaders who were on their way from France to join the Count. The crusaders saw the enemy coming but thought they were from our side and went unafraid to meet them; indeed the traitors had planned their crime in advance and were walking slowly on the public road, so that the crusaders could not easily see they were not from our side. As the two parties drew near each other the cruel executioners suddenly set on our crusaders, who were few in number and unarmed because they were unaware of the enemy's treachery; most of them they killed and tore limb from limb, the rest they took to Foix. Here they kept them in chains and tore them to pieces with the most monstrous tortures. Each day they applied themselves diligently to thinking up new and original torments with which to afflict their prisoners; as I heard from a knight who was imprisoned there and an eye-witness, they subjected the captives daily to so many tortures, and of such severity, that they could claim equality in their iniquity with Diocletian and Domitian – or even surpass them. Not to mention all they did, they made a frequent practice of suspending priests and other servants of the Lord's ministry, and on occasion, most dreadful to relate, tied cords to their genitals and pulled them violently. What cruel barbarity, what unheard-of madness!

[362] *A General Council is held at Pamiers.* In the year 1212 of the Incarnation

---

142   Cf. §62, where a similar accusation is recorded.
143   He must have managed to leave Montauban (which he had been defending: see n. 103 to §340 above) without the crusaders' knowledge, and was able to operate further east because de Montfort was in Gascony and had presumably left only the smallest garrisons in the area mentioned here.

of the Lord in the month of November, the noble Count of Montfort summoned the bishops and nobles in his territories to Pamiers to hold a general council. The purpose of the council was this: our Count wished to develop good customs[144] in the territories he had won and brought under the Holy Roman Church;[145] and, now that the heretical filth which had corrupted all those territories had been driven out, to ensure the establishment of a sound set of customs[146] to promote both the observation of the Christian religion and the maintenance of peace and order in civil life. The area had indeed long been exposed to plunder and rapine; the powerful oppressed the powerless, the strong the weak. Accordingly the Count wished to impose a definite set of customs on his vassals and to set boundaries on their holdings of land, which it would be forbidden to transgress, so that his knights would be able to live honourably from sure and legitimate revenues whilst the ordinary people would be able to live under the protection of their lords unencumbered by immoderate exactions.

[363] To establish these customs twelve men were chosen, who swore on the Holy Gospels that they would, to the best of their knowledge and ability, establish customs that would allow the Church to enjoy its proper freedom and would improve and strengthen the condition of the whole area. Of these twelve four were men of the Church (two Bishops, of Toulouse and Couserans,[147] one knight Templar and one knight Hospitaller), four French knights and four men of local origin[148] (two knights and two townsmen). A set of customs adequate to protect

---

[144] Latin '*bonos mores*', translated here as good customs, in the sense of customary and established rules of conduct, and implying much the same as *consuetudines*, on which see below, n. 146.

[145] At this time the conquered lands comprised the viscounties of Béziers and Carcassonne, and the southern Albigeois and the Razès (§§101, 108); the northern Albigeois (§237); the Agenais (§§317ff); Quercy except Montauban (§§246, 359); most of the Toulousain (§§231ff); part of the county of Foix (§354); and parts of Gascony (§358). However, in the Statutes themselves de Montfort refers to himself first as '*comes Leycestrie, dominus Montisfortis*' and then only as '*Bitterrensis et Karcassonensis vicecomes et Albiensis et Reddensis dominus*', i.e. Viscount of Béziers and Carcassonne and lord of the Albigeois and the Razès, which were the titles inherited from the Trencavels, and he was not yet formally claiming the title of Count of Toulouse. See also Appendix C.

[146] Latin '*consuetudines*', the term used in the rest of Peter's account to refer to what are now known as the Statutes of Pamiers; the term *consuetudines* is also used in the statutes themselves. The basic meaning is 'customs, rules, established usages,' often with quasi-legal force. (The *Revised Medieval Latin Wordlist*, ed. R. F. Latham (Oxford, 1965) gives *consuetudines regni* as meaning 'the common law'.) There are forty-six articles or *consuetudines generales* in the Statutes of Pamiers, effectively a code of rules and practice to control the government of the occupied territories, and appended to which are three more articles representing an agreement on specific points between de Montfort and his vassals. The Statutes cover the position of the Church, relationships between de Montfort and his vassals (including liability to military service), the government and administration of the common people, the law of succession (where French practice was introduced to supersede southern custom), the position of heretics and Jews, economic affairs, and other matters. Strongly influenced by the ecclesiastical representatives at Pamiers, and reflecting their ideas on the orderly governance of Christian society, they also represent the imposition of feudal practice from the Ile de France into the conquered lands. In this they are reminiscent of the introduction of such laws into the crusader kingdoms in the Holy Land. The Statutes were promulgated on 1 December 1212. A full translation of their text is given in Appendix H; they are discussed at length, and largely (and sometimes loosely) translated into French, in Roquebert I, ch. 35; see also Belperron pp. 244–51.

[147] On Fulk of Toulouse see §33; and on Navarre of Couserans see §48.

[148] Latin '*indigenae*', on which see Appendix A(ii). The word translated as 'townsmen' in the next phrase is '*burgenses*'.

the interests of the Church, the rich and the poor was now established and confirmed by this group of churchmen, knights and townsmen. The choice of a body comprising both French and local men to establish the customs was deliberate; the intention was to remove all suspicion from the hearts of men, since both sides had representatives amongst those responsible for what was decided.

[364] So these twelve, after much deliberation and discussion, established the best possible code to ensure the safety and protect the interests of the Church and indeed the whole body politic. To guarantee that the new customs would be kept inviolate, before they were made public the Count and all his knights swore on the four Gospels that they would never presume to violate them. To give them even greater force they were put into writing and the seals of the Count and the numerous bishops present were affixed.

[365] Whilst the council at Pamiers was taking place, the enemies of the faith came out of Toulouse and made excursions into Gascony, doing whatever mischief they could. The Bishop of Comminges led some of our knights into Gascony and defended it valiantly against the enemies of the faith.

[366] Our Count went to Carcassonne and thence to Béziers to hold a discussion with the Archbishop of Narbonne on matters concerned with Christ's business.[149] The see of Béziers was vacant and whilst we were there the canons of the church unanimously elected William the venerable Archdeacon of Paris[150] as their Bishop and pastor; however, nothing could induce him to accept their decision.

---

[149] De Montfort and Arnold Amalric had, it appears, not met since before the latter's election as Archbishop of Narbonne in April 1212, and his departure in May to fight the Almohades in Spain.
[150] See above, §175.

[**XIII. §§367–398, January 1213:** *King Peter of Aragon goes to Toulouse – Council of Lavaur – exchange of letters between the King and the legates – the legates reject the King's demands – the King takes the Counts of Toulouse, Foix and Comminges and Gaston de Béarn under his protection – report of the legates to Innocent III.*]

[367][1] *The King of Aragon enters Toulouse.* About the time of the feast of the Epiphany[2] King Peter of Aragon, who was extremely hostile to the business of the faith, went to Toulouse, where he spent a considerable period associating with excommunicants and with heretics.[3] He indicated to the Archbishop of

---

[1] The chronology of §§367–421 is again confusing; in this case the slow speed of communications between the Curia and the South of France adds to the problems caused by Peter's tendency to relate groups of events out of order. The following is a summary in approximate chronological order; details will be found in the relevant text and notes.

  (i) In May 1212 Pope Innocent had instructed his legates to arrange a council to re-examine the position of Count Raymond of Toulouse (see n. 5 to §368).

  (ii) Towards the end of 1212 Innocent was successfully lobbied by King Peter's envoys (n. 3 to §367 and nn. 1 and 2 to §399; Peter records this *after* his record of the events of January 1213).

  (iii) Meanwhile the legates reacted slowly to Innocent's instruction of May 1212 and arranged a Council of prelates, to take place at Lavaur in January 1213 (§368).

  (iv) King Peter, apparently aware of the success of his envoys, came to Toulouse early in January 1213 and asked to hold discussions with the prelates (§367). The discussions, fully documented by Peter in §§369–388, were held between 14 and 21 January.

  (v) Whilst the Council of Lavaur was in session, and unaware of it, Innocent now reacted to the lobbying of the King's envoys by issuing the important letters of 15–18 January 1213 to the legates and Simon de Montfort (§399 and notes) which inter alia ordered the suspension of the Crusade but would not have reached the crusaders until sometime in February (see n. 3 below).

  (vi) The events related by Peter in §§389–398 (the oaths of allegiance to King Peter, §389, the despatch of the legates' envoys to Rome §391), took place about the end of January; those related in §§412–21 (the breach between de Montfort and the King, Prince Louis' assumption of the cross and King Peter's embassy to Paris) took place between January and May 1213.

  (vii) Meanwhile there was intense lobbying of Innocent by Arnold Amalric and his allies (n. 42 to §392 and n. 4 to §400), which resulted in Innocent's volte-face set out in his letter recorded in §§400–411, see below; this is dated 21 May, i.e. *after* the events recorded by Peter in §§412–21.

[2] 6 January 1213.

[3] This fresh intervention by King Peter of Aragon marked an important new phase in the Crusade. Following his failure to secure the reconciliation of Raymond VI and Raymond-Roger of Foix at Narbonne and Montpellier in January and early February 1211, the King had cemented his alliance with Raymond VI in spring 1211 by the marriage of his sister Sancia to Raymond VI's son (see §§195–6 and 211 above). His immediate attention then turned to the war against the Moors in Spain, and urged on by Innocent III he played an important part in organising the force which secured victory at the battle of Las Navas de Tolosa in July 1212. However, after the battle, King Peter was once again able to turn his attention to the position north of the Pyrenees. He was evidently increasingly alarmed at de Montfort's sweeping successes in 1212, which culminated not only in the conquest of most of Raymond's lands, but in campaigns against the Counts of Foix and Comminges, the Viscount of Couserans and Gaston de Béarn (§358), all of whom were Peter's vassals. There is also a possibility that an attempt had been made in 1211 to make Toulouse a fiefdom of the Kingdom of Aragon. William of Puylaurens (XVII) says that, at the time of his son's marriage to Sancia, Raymond made a pretence of handing suzerainty of Toulouse to the King ('*ficte donavit*'), to give him just cause for taking the county under his protection. Lack of direct confirmation and the confused chronology of this chapter of William's account has led to the suspicion that he has transferred the oath of allegiance taken after the Council of Lavaur (§389) back to 1211; however, the editor of William, J. Duvernoy, points out (p. 73 n. 5) that in their appeal of July 1211 to the King (*HGL* VIII, 612–19, see also notes to §§137, 162 and 234) the consuls of Toulouse address him as 'their most

Narbonne, the papal legate, and our Count that he wished to hold discussions with them and negotiate a truce and an agreement between our Count and the enemies of the faith.[4]

[368] A date was agreed for a meeting, to be held at a place between Toulouse and Lavaur.[5] The Archbishop of Narbonne summoned a council of bishops to attend the meeting; about twenty archbishops and bishops were present.[6] After we had assembled at the place agreed for the meeting, the King began to put demands to the Archbishop and the bishops for the restoration of the occupied territories to the Counts of Toulouse, Comminges and Foix, and to Gaston de Béarn. In reply, the Archbishop told the King to put all his requests in writing and send them duly sealed to the bishops at Lavaur.

[369] The King, after a great show of praising our Count and his brother and

excellent lord' ('*Excellentissimo suo domino*'), rather than, say, 'illustrious King', thus possibly implying that they then regarded him as their suzerain. However that may be, after having been approached by Raymond in the autumn of 1212 (§359), the King now resolved to intervene. He began by sending two envoys to Innocent, who probably arrived in Rome in November or December 1212. They were clearly successful in their mission, and the outcome was the series of important letters from Innocent to de Montfort and the legates in mid-January 1213, calling a halt to the Crusade; these will not, however, have reached their destined recipients until some time after the events about to be related in §367 onwards: for details see below, §399, where the Aragonese mission and Innocent's letters are mentioned by Peter and discussed in notes. By early January 1213 King Peter was himself at Toulouse, where he had arrived with a large entourage, whose membership is reconstructed by Roquebert II, pp. 90–1. He spent about a month there (*Itinerario*, pp. 92–4), and whilst at Toulouse his receipt of homage from William of Montpellier was witnessed by Raymond VI, Raymond-Roger of Foix, and Bernard of Comminges, all of whom were excommunicated at the time (see also G&L II, p. 66 n. 2).

4   Thus as well as the mission to Rome, Peter made a direct attempt to negotiate with the leaders of the Crusade; it is conceivable that he already had an early indication that his envoys to Innocent had been successful, and that this now encouraged him to approach Arnold Amalric and de Montfort directly.

5   By early January 1213 a council of prelates was in session at Lavaur, having been convened by the legate Thedisius to deal once more with the position of Raymond VI. This council was the eventual outcome of an initiative taken by Innocent III in the previous May, when he had revived the issue of the purification of the Count of Toulouse. By then Innocent seems to have been harbouring increasing doubts about the justice of the campaign against Raymond VI. In an important letter of May 1212 (probably May 25th, *PL* 216, 613–14) addressed to Arnold Amalric and Bishop Raymond of Uzès, he reminded the legates that Raymond had never been formally convicted of the two major crimes of heresy and complicity in the murder of Peter of Castelnau, and indeed that the procedure laid down in his letter of 25 January 1210, with its requirement that he Innocent should have the final say (n. 49 to §137 and Appendix F(iii)) had not been carried out; in consequence his consent could not be given to transferring Raymond's possessions to some other party ('*non intelligimus qua ratione possumus adhuc alii concedere terram ejus*'). He proposed therefore to instruct Thedisius and Bishop Hugh of Riez again to deal with the accusations against Raymond in the manner previously laid down. He wrote similarly to Thedisius and Hugh (*PL* 216, 614) adding '. . . taking care not to be cool and remiss (*tepidi et remissi*) in carrying out our instruction, as you are said to have been so far'. In response to these letters, Bishop Hugh and Thedisius later said (in a letter written after the Council of Lavaur: see *PL* 216, 833, and n. to §401) that they convened a conference at Avignon 'immediately', but in fact it was not due to meet until the end of 1212; however, they added that it had to be postponed because Thedisius was ill and 'many of us could not take part in a conference because of the general bad state of the air'. Instead they called a conference at Lavaur in January 1213. Thus the Council which met at Lavaur was originally intended to deal with the matter of the Count of Toulouse, but became concerned mainly with negotiations with King Peter of Aragon as a result of the latter's decision to intervene directly.

6   The meeting took place on 14 January, somewhere between Lavaur and Toulouse. Those present included Archbishops Arnold Amalric of Narbonne and William of Bordeaux, and Bishops William Peyre of Albi, Fulk of Toulouse, Garsia of Comminges and Hugh of Riez (all mentioned in *PL* 216, 833–4), and Guy of Carcassonne.

his sons,[7] asked the Count to desist from harming his enemies for the period of eight days[8] during which the meeting was to take place. With characteristic nobility and courtesy the Count replied: 'I will not desist from harming them, but out of respect for yourself I will for these eight days desist from helping them; since I believe that to attack the enemies of Christ is not to harm them, but to help them.' The King made similar promises on behalf of our enemies that they would do our side no harm during the meeting; but with typical faithlessness, and despite the guarantees of our safety given by the King, when they knew we had assembled for the meeting they began to run through our territory towards Carcassonne and did a great deal of damage, killing many of our people. What despicable deceit! On the third day after he had left the meeting place[9] and arrived at Toulouse the King sent his requests to the archbishops and bishops in these words:

[370] *The King's requests.* 'The requests of the King of Aragon at the Council of Lavaur.[10] Since it is held that the Holy Mother Church not only wields the rod of chastisement, but also displays the loving kindness of a mother,[11] Peter, by God's grace King of Aragon and a devoted son of the Church, [371] humbly petitions and earnestly begs of your holinesses as follows on behalf of the Count of Toulouse, who wishes to return to the bosom of the Church. If he will give personal satisfaction, as may seem fitting to the Church herself, for the excesses he has committed, and make reparation, such as the Mother Church in her clemency may determine for the wrongs and injuries he has done to various churches and churchmen, then may he be restored by your clemency and grace to the possessions and other advantages he has lost. Should the Church not wish to hear the King's petition on behalf of the Count himself, the King repeats the petition on behalf of the Count's son;[12] although in that case the Count will still give personal satisfaction for his excesses, by going with his knights either to the frontier against the Saracens[13] to help the Christians there, or overseas, as the Church may require. In that event the son is to be faithfully and diligently

---

7   His brother Guy, and (presumably) his elder sons Amaury and Guy. G&L II, p. 67 n. 3, suggest that the third son, Simon, who can only have been four or five at this time, may also have been present.
8   14–21 January 1213.
9   On 16 January 1213.
10 The text which follows is also given in *PL* 216, 839–40. The King was probably aware of the success of his lobbying of Innocent (see n. 4 to §368), and this seems to be confirmed by his approach to the current negotiations. His letter closely reflects the case made by his envoys, which is set out in Innocent's letter of 18 January 1213 to Arnold Amalric and his fellow legates (see n. 2 to §399 and for a translation Appendix F(iv)). We may note especially the references in §371 to the young Raymond and to the elder Raymond's willingness to go to Spain or overseas. In contrast, to judge from their handling of the discussions, the legates seem either to have been unaware of the lobbying or not to have realised how successful it had been, and were probably taken by surprise when the letter of 18 January and the associated letters from Innocent reached them some time later. At this period the King seemed generally confident that he enjoyed Innocent's support; see also his actions after the failure of the negotiations as described in §386 and §389.
11 Literally 'has not only blows but breasts', '*non solum verbera sed ubera quoque docetur habere*'.
12 Raymond, later Raymond VII, who was fifteen years old by January 1213.
13 Latin '*in frontaria Sarracenorum*', meaning the frontier in Spain. For a similar use of *frontaria* see Innocent's letter of 18 January 1213 to Arnold Amalric and others (Appendix F(iv)(c) and n. 2 to §399).

protected in his own lands, to the honour of God and the Holy Mother Church, until such time as he can himself provide clear proofs of his good character.

[372] 'And since the Count of Comminges[14] has never been a heretic or a supporter of heretics, but rather their opponent, and is said to owe the loss of his territories to his support for his cousin and overlord the Count of Toulouse, the King therefore requests on his behalf (since he is the King's vassal) that he be restored to his lands, on the understanding that he will give satisfaction as demanded by the Church if he appears to have given any offence. [373] Since the Count of Foix[15] never has been and is not now a heretic, the King requests on his behalf (as it is appropriate for him to do, since the Count is his dear kinsman and vassal, whose interests it would be shameful for him to ignore) that he be restored to his possessions – this request to be granted out of respect for the King and as a favour to him; on the understanding that the Count will none the less give satisfaction as demanded by the Church in any matters where it appears to the merciful Mother Church that he has erred. [374] Next, the King earnestly petitions and requests on behalf of his vassal Gaston de Béarn[16] that he be restored to his territories and that the fealty owed to him by his vassals be reinstated; especially since he is ready to obey the law and give satisfaction as demanded by the Holy Mother Church; his case to be heard by trustworthy judges if you yourselves are unable to hear and judge it.

[375] 'In all these matters the King has preferred to invoke your mercy rather than look for judgment, and has sent his bishops, clerics and barons to seek your clemency.[17] He is ready to accept whatever may be decided between you and them and begs you to employ careful consideration in this situation, so that he will be able to call on the help of the nobles mentioned above and the Count of Montfort in the business of Christianity in Spain,[18] to the honour of God and the advancement of the Holy Church. [376] Given at Toulouse, 16 January.'

[377] *Response of the prelates.*[19] "To the illustrious Peter, beloved in Christ, by God's grace King of Aragon and Count of Barcelona, greetings and sincere love in the Lord from the Council at Lavaur. [378] We have seen the petitions and prayers which your Royal Serenity has sent to us on behalf of the Count of

---

14 Bernard of Comminges, on whom see §239 and §§293–6 above; and §§356–8 for the invasion of his lands by de Montfort.

15 Raymond-Roger, on whom see e.g. §§48 and 197–209 above. King Peter had several times intervened on behalf of Raymond-Roger: see §§150 and 196 above. By early 1213 his effective lordship was confined to the southern part of his county.

16 Gaston IV of Béarn; see above §254 for his support for Raymond VI and Raymond-Roger of Foix at Castelnaudary in the autumn of 1211; and §338 for his attempt to make peace with de Montfort after Biron was taken in 1212.

17 Amongst them Bishops Berengar of Barcelona, Garcia of Tarragona and William of Vich; Nuno Sanç, the son of Peter's brother, Count Sancho of Provence; William-Raymond of Montcada, Seneschal of Catalonia and a relative of Gaston de Béarn; and Michael of Luesia, high steward of Aragon. Bernard de Portella was also present (on whom see §500). The presence of these and others is attested by their having witnessed various acts made whilst King Peter was at Toulouse at this time: see G&L II, p. 72 n. 1, and Roquebert II, p. 91.

18 Latin '*negotio christianitatis in partibus Hispanis*', meaning the war against the Moors.

19 Also given in *PL* 216, 840–2.

Toulouse (and his son), and the Counts of Foix and Comminges and the noble-man Gaston de Béarn. In your letter, amongst other things you refer to yourself as "a devoted son of the Church". In this connection we recall to the notice of the Lord Jesus Christ and your Royal Highness many instances of favourable treat-ment,[20] and in view of the mutual love in which, as we believe, the Holy Roman Church has embraced you and you Her, and in view also of our respect for your Royal Excellency, we are glad to accede to your requests, in all matters where our duty to God allows us to do so. [379] In regard to your requests on behalf of the Count of Toulouse and his son, we consider our reply to your Royal Serenity should be this. We are prevented by higher authority from dealing with the Count's case (and likewise his son's, which depends on the Count's), since the Count obtained from the Pope a decision that all negotiations concerning his affairs should be conducted with our venerable brother the Bishop of Riez and Master Thedisius, on conditions already determined.[21] You will surely recall the numerous occasions on which the Pope has shown great consideration to the Count, after his many excesses; equally the consideration shown to him in re-sponse to your intercession and prayers by the venerable father the Archbishop of Narbonne, papal legate (then Abbot of Cîteaux) at Narbonne and Montpellier, two years ago if our memory serves us well.[22] The legate was willing for the Count to retain all his dominions and property whole and intact, and also to retain the rights (whether *alberga, quista* or *cavalgata*),[23] which he enjoyed in other heretical *castra* under his lordship; as to the heretical *castra* which did not fall under his lordship (of which there were at least five hundred, according to the Count's own reckoning) the legate was prepared to transfer a quarter or even a third to the Count's control. However, the Count spurned this generous offer of the Pope, the legate and the Church of God; instead, in direct violation of every oath he had sworn to the legates he piled iniquity on iniquity, crime on crime, evil on evil, and in alliance with heretics, mercenaries and other evil men he attacked and subverted the Church of God and Christianity, the faith, and peace, so violently as to render himself unworthy of any consideration or favour.

---

[20] Latin '*multiplices ... gratiarum ... actiones*'. The writers appear to be looking forward to the *gratiam* (favourable treatment or consideration) and *gratias* (individual examples of this) referred to in the follow-ing section (said to have been granted by Innocent and Arnold Amalric to the Count of Toulouse), and in §381 (granted by Arnold to the Count of Foix); Christ seems to be brought in as a witness or arbiter.

[21] This refers to the instructions for dealing with Raymond VI given by Innocent to Hugh of Riez and Thedisius in his letter of May 1212 (*PL* 216, 613–14); see n. 5 to §368.

[22] A reference to events of January 1211: see §195 and §212 above. The terms offered to Raymond which are now described (including the references to *castra* under Raymond's control ('*que de feudo ejus erant*'), and those not under his control), were also summarised in similar terms in §195.

[23] *Alberga*, French *droit de gîte*, or *albergue*, and *cavalgata*, French *chevauchée*, were respectively the rights of a lord to require lodging and mounted service from a vassal; they also refer to payments in lieu thereof, effectively a form of taxation. *Quista*, French *quête*, appears to cover various forms of exaction; see an example from Provence dated 1235 in Du Cange, *Glossarium*, which allows the Count to make a *quista* in several circumstances including making a journey to the Emperor, embarking on a sea journey '*cum armis*', or the marriage of his daughters. All three words occur in various forms: Du Cange, *Glossarium*, and *Lexicon* also give numerous examples of usage. See also article by A. Molinier in *HGL* VII, pp. 155–67, on feudal rights in Languedoc ('*cette masse confuse de droits et de redevances*') in the 12th and 13th centuries.

[380] 'As to your requests on behalf of the Count of Comminges, we consider our reply should be as follows. We know for sure that after committing innumerable excesses and violating his sworn oath he allied himself with the heretics and their supporters and joined with these pestilential men in attacking the Church as if he had sustained some personal injury from her; although he was then earnestly counselled to abandon these ways, to return to his true self and become reconciled with the unity of the Church, he nevertheless persisted in and still persists in his evil ways, tied by the chain of excommunication and anathematisation. It is said that the Count of Toulouse is wont to declare that it was the Count of Comminges who drove and induced him to go to war; so he was and still is to be regarded as the originator of the war (and the many ills the Church has suffered from it). However, if he shows himself deserving of absolution, then, after he has received absolution and is then competent to appear in court, the Church will not deny him justice if he has any grievance. [381] Your Royal Highness then puts forward requests on behalf of the Count of Foix, to which our answer is this. It is well known that he has for a long time been a receiver of heretics and remains to this day their receiver and defender, especially since there is no doubt that heretical believers must be counted as heretics.[24] He committed numerous grave excesses; he destroyed and despoiled churches; he personally swore oaths and gave undertakings, in regard to people and things, but went on to lay his hands on clerics and cast them into prison (for which offences, and many others,[25] he was struck with the sword of excommunication and anathematisation). After all this, and even after the consideration given to him by the papal legate in response to your intervention and prayers,[26] he was responsible for the bloody slaughter of crusaders, both clerics and laymen, who in their humility and simplicity were on their way to enter God's service against the heretics of Lavaur.[27] Your Royal Highness will, we believe, well remember the nature and extent of that consideration, since it was in response to your intercession that the legate reached an agreement with the Count. The failure to carry this agreement into effect is to be attributed to the Count himself; there is even a letter[28] written by you to the Count of Montfort, sealed with the royal seal, which contains the following sentence concerning this matter: "We say to you also that if the Count shows himself unwilling to stand by this agreement and you then do not wish to countenance any requests we may put forward on his behalf, we will feel no resentment." Even so, if he is prepared to do what he must to secure the benefit of absolution, and if subsequently, when he has gained the grace of absolution, he has any grievance, the Church will not deny him justice.

[382] 'You further request that Gaston de Béarn be restored to his lands and to the rights of fealty due to him from his vassals. To this request our reply is this.

---

[24] On the distinction between believers, *credentes*, and full heretics, *perfecti(ae)*, see §13 above.
[25] See §§197–209 for example.
[26] At Narbonne in January 1211: §196 above.
[27] A reference to the attack on crusaders at Montgey, at the time of the siege of Lavaur in 1211: see §§218–19 above.
[28] Peter earlier said that he himself saw this letter: see §196 above.

We will for the present say nothing of the numerous – indeed innumerable – other allegations made against Gaston, and mention only his alliance with heretics, and their receivers and defenders, against the Church and the crusaders; he is a most manifest and pernicious persecutor of churches and clergy; at the siege of Castlenaudary he came to help the Counts of Toulouse and Foix against those who were following the instructions of the Pope to go against the heretics and their supporters;[29] he kept in his company the murderer of Brother Peter of Castelnau, of blessed memory; he has maintained and continues to maintain mercenaries; last year he introduced his mercenaries into the cathedral church of Oloron, where they cut the rope from which the casket containing the sacred host was suspended, so that it fell to the ground and – dreadful to tell – the host itself was scattered over the earth; one of the mercenaries, by way of mocking and insulting the clergy, put on the Bishop's ornaments to imitate the Bishop saying Mass – he is even said to have preached and received obeisance from the other mercenaries. Gaston forswore his oaths, laid violent hands on priests.[30] For these and many other crimes – about which we will say nothing for the moment – Gaston was marked with excommunication and anathematisation. Even so, if he gives due satisfaction to the Church and obtains the benefit of absolution, and subsequently after receiving absolution has any grievance, he will be heard in accordance with his legal rights.

[383] 'Renowned prince, since these men have been excommunicated, it would be improper for your Royal Highness to intercede for them in any other way than you have done, and we would not dare make any other response in regard to such men and such matters. We now strongly urge you in the Lord's name to recall to memory how the Apostolic See has honoured you[31] and is even now honouring your brother-in-law, the illustrious King of Sicily;[32] also the promises you made to the lord Pope when you were annointed king, and the

---

29 See above, §254, for Gaston de Béarn's intervention at Castelnaudary in 1211.

30 G&L II, p. 79 n. 3, note that Gaston later made due apology to the Bishop admitting that '*multas feci injurias tam in ipsa cathedrali ecclesia quam in suis hominibus et pertinentiis dampna multiplicia inferendo*', 'I have committed many wrongs both against the cathedral church and its servants and belongings.'

31 A reference amongst other things to Innocent's crowning of Peter in Rome in November 1204, when Peter had sworn fealty to the Pope (see e.g. T. N. Bisson, *The Medieval Crown of Aragon* (1986), pp. 38–9). *PL* 215, 503–4, gives details of his oath: '*Ego Petrus, rex Aragonum . . . semper ero fidelis et obediens domino meo pape Innocentio . . . defendens fidem catholicam et persequens hereticam pravitatem*', 'I Peter, King of Aragon, . . . will always be faithful and obedient to my lord Pope Innocent . . . and defend the Catholic faith and pursue heresy.'

32 A reference to Innocent III's support for Peter's brother-in-law, the young King Frederick II of Sicily, who had married one of Peter's sisters, Constance, widow of the King of Hungary, in August 1209. Frederick was a vassal of Innocent, who also regarded himself as ultimate suzerain of Sicily. Frederick was also, however, head of the Staufen family, which had strong German interests and claims to the throne of the Holy Roman Empire. In late 1211, Frederick had accepted the offer of the Imperial Crown made by the enemies of the rival claimant Otto of Bruswick, and was strongly supported in his claim by Innocent who had by now broken with Otto (see n. 66 to §72), and by Philip Augustus of France. In the following year Frederick left Sicily to be ruled by Constance in the name of their new born son Henry, and after being acclaimed Emperor at Rome, was crowned in Mainz on 9 December 1212, shortly before the Council of Lavaur. The legates' comment here reflects Innocent's close involvement in all these arrangements. (For further details see, for example, D. Abulafia, *Frederick II* (London, 1988), ch. 3, and D. Matthew, *The Norman Kingdom of Sicily* (Cambridge, 1992), pp. 298–314.)

instructions the Apostolic See then gave you. We pray that God may long preserve you, to His own honour and the honour of the Holy Roman Church. If,
however, our answer is not satisfactory to your Royal Majesty, we will in view of
our regard and respect for you ensure that the lord Pope is speedily informed.
[384] Given at Lavaur, 18 January.'

[385] On hearing the reply he had received from our prelates, the King of
Aragon saw that it amounted to a complete rejection of his requests and that he
was not going to achieve his objectives; he therefore thought of another way
round his difficulties. He sent again to the prelates, urgently begging them to
persuade the Count of Montfort to grant a truce to the Count of Toulouse and
the other enemies of the Christian faith until Pentecost or at least until Easter.[33]
Our prelates realised that the King was making this request merely in the hope
that the existence of a truce would become known in France and lead to a
diminution in enthusiasm amongst crusaders.[34] They therefore firmly rejected
this request, as they had the earlier ones. [386] It would take too long to set down
in order all the King's demands and the answers decided on by our side.[35] I will
therefore say in brief that the King's whole objective was to work for the restitution of the Count of Toulouse and the other enemies of the Christian religion to
their territories, or at least to arrange a truce for the purpose mentioned above;
whilst our side, as ever prudent and firm of purpose, did not wish either to
restore the territories or allow a truce. The King saw that he was making no
progress and decided – at great cost to his reputation and honour – to take the
excommunicated nobles and the territories they still held under his own protection.[36] In the hope of somewhat mitigating his crime he also appealed to the
Apostolic See.[37] Our prelates paid little heed to this appeal, which was for many
reasons worthless and invalid, but the Archbishop of Narbonne, as papal legate,
wrote to the King to the following effect.

[387] *Letter of the Archbishop of Narbonne to the King.*[38] 'To the most serene
and Christian prince Peter, by God's grace most illustrious King of Aragon,

---

[33] Easter Day was 14 April, and Pentecost 2 June, 1213. It seems likely that Peter of Aragon had also made
such a request for a truce directly to Innocent III, since Innocent was to refer to this in his letter of 15
January 1213 to Arnold Amalric instructing him to stop the Crusade (*PL* 216, 744; see n. 2 to §399 and
Appendix F(iv)).

[34] There was indeed a diversion of effort away from the Albigensian Crusade when, in the spring of 1213,
Robert de Courçon preached in northern France in favour of Innocent's projected Crusade to the Holy
Land. For details see below, §439, where Peter is giving his recapitulation of the events of winter and spring
1212–13.

[35] Peter does not for example record that at some point during the Council of Lavaur Raymond himself
also made a direct approach to Hugh of Riez and Thedisius, seeking reconciliation to the Church; his letter
does not survive, but the reply to him from Hugh and Thedisius, in which they flatly refuse absolution, is
given in *PL* 216, 844–5.

[36] Thus he unilaterally adopted the proposals he had put to this effect to Innocent, as reflected in
Innocent's letter of 18 January 1213, on which see n. 10 to §370. For further comment and details of the
arrangments made, see §389 below.

[37] This probably refers to his envoys' second visit to Rome in the spring of 1213 (§404), rather than the
visit late in 1212 (see §399).

[38] This letter is also given in *PL* 216, 842–3.

greetings in the charity of the spirit and flesh of Jesus Christ from Brother Arnold, by God's mercy Archbishop of Narbonne and legate of the Apostolic See.

[388] 'We have heard, not without great concern and bitter sorrow, that you propose to take under your protection and guardianship the city of Toulouse, the *castrum* of Montauban and other places which for the crime of heresy and many other evil acts have been surrendered to Satan, and have by the authority of God (whose name is gravely blasphemed in those places) been cut off from all communion with the Holy Mother Church and exposed to seizure by the crusaders;[39] further that you mean to defend them against the army of Christ and the Church. If this is true (which God forbid) it must not only affect your hopes of attaining salvation but also do harm to your honour as a king and your reputation and renown. For this reason we – who are earnestly concerned for your salvation and honour with the full force of our charity – beseech, urge and exhort your Royal Highness, in the name of the Lord and in the power of His virtue and on behalf of God and our Saviour Jesus Christ, and His most blessed Vicar, our lord the Supreme Pontiff, not to take these territories under your protection or defend them either in person or through the agency of others; indeed by the authority vested in us as papal legate we forbid you so to do, and conjure you by all the means in our power to refrain from this course. We also hope that you will take care – on behalf of your followers as well as yourself – not to risk incurring the stigma of excommunication by communing with excommunicants and accursed heretics and their supporters. We wish your Serene Majesty to be fully aware that if you leave any of your followers to defend these territories, they will stand as justly excommunicated, and we will ensure that the fact of their excommunication as defenders of heretics will be publicly proclaimed.'

[389] The King of Aragon gave no sign of coming to his senses, but made his evil intentions worse by proceeding to implement them. He took under his protection, and accepted oaths of allegiance from, all the heretics and excommunicants – the Counts of Toulouse, Comminges and Foix, Gaston de Béarn, all the knights of Toulouse and Carcassonne who had fled to Toulouse after being deprived of their possessions for heresy, and the citizens of Toulouse. He also presumed to take under his guardianship the city of Toulouse, which in truth is part of the domains of the King of France, and all the territories previously held by the nobles named above.[40] [390] I must not omit to record the behaviour of

---

[39] '*Crucesignatis . . . expositas*', a reference to the doctrine that their lands were liable to seizure by the crusaders, on which see n. 34 to §62.

[40] The oaths of allegiance (including those of the consuls of Toulouse) were sworn on 27 January 1213 and are given in *PL* 216, 845–9. The first oath was sworn by both Raymond VI and his son Raymond, in which they pledged fealty to King Peter and handed themselves and all their rights and possessions to him, and said they were asking the city of Toulouse to do likewise; a translation into French is given in Roquebert II, pp. 99–100. The second oath was sworn by the twenty-four consuls of Toulouse in which they likewise placed their city under the lordship of the King. Finally, similar oaths were sworn by Raymond-Roger of Foix and his son, Roger-Bernard; by Bernard of Comminges and his son Bernard; and by Gaston de Béarn. Each of the oaths gives details of the rights and territories which were being placed under Peter's lordship. Faced with the intransigence of the legates (who, as related in §385, refused even to grant a truce), and – we have suggested – still confident of support from the Pope, the King now showed

our enemies whilst our men were at Lavaur for the purpose of the meeting; the Count of Montfort had granted them a truce during the period of the meeting, out of respect for the King, and the King had confirmed the truce on behalf of our adversaries,[41] but despite this, whilst the meeting was still going on and with the truce still in force so that our men were not on their guard, the enemy cavalry made frequent excursions into our territory where they seized much booty, killed many men and took many others prisoner, and generally did us much harm. Frequent requests were made to the King, but he took no steps to see that we were compensated for these losses. It was for this reason that the Archbishop wrote the letter quoted above.

[391] Our people could now see that the King was simply making use of envoys, letters and pointless requests to restrain us from taking action, and indeed that during the meeting and the truce he was allowing us to be openly and frequently set upon by the excommunicants, whose cause he favoured. They accordingly left Lavaur, but before doing so wrote to the Pope concerning the affairs of the Church in general and the Council in particular, in the following terms.

[392] *Letter of the prelates to the Pope.*[42] 'To their most holy father in Christ and most blessed lord Innocent, by God's grace Supreme Pontiff; his devoted and humble servants, the archbishops, bishops and other prelates of the Church gathered at the Council of Lavaur to further the business of the holy faith send affectionate greetings and their wishes for a long life and salvation. [393] Since neither tongue nor pen are sufficient for us to thank you suitably for your fatherly care, we pray to the Rewarder of all good deeds to remedy our inadequacy in this respect and recompense you in good measure for every benefit you have provided, to us and our churches and other churches in this region. Here, the plague of heresy, its seed sown long ago, has in our times so flourished that the worship of God has become entirely a target for derision and insult. Heretics and mercenaries have each in turn violently assaulted the clergy and the property

---

willingness to take a more clearly defined and determined stance. His decision to take these territories under his protection was clearly of great significance. As Peter notes, the county of Toulouse was held by its counts from the French Crown (as Philip Augustus himself reminded Innocent in his letter of April 1208, see n. 65 to §72), and even though the French kings had had no real influence in the area for centuries, Raymond was in effect replacing the French King with the King of Aragon as his overlord. The outcome was that as well as being overlord of the former Trencavel lands, which de Montfort held as fiefs of him, King Peter had assumed overlordship of virtually all the other territories occupied by or threatened by the crusaders. This was an ambitious move, but his defeat and death at Muret was to see it come to nothing. See also n. 3 to §367, which discusses a possible earlier attempt to recognise King Peter as suzerain of Toulouse.

41 See §369 above.

42 This letter, dated 21 January 1213, is also given in *PL* 216, 836–9. It is undeniably a powerful piece of propaganda. Letters strongly urging continuation of the Crusade, and probably reflecting an orchestrated campaign by Arnold Amalric, were sent to Innocent at about the same time by Archbishop William of Bordeaux, writing with the Bishops of Bazas and Périgueux (*PL* 216, 839); by Bishop Bertrand of Béziers (*PL* 216, 843–4); and by Archbishop Bertrand of Aix (*PL* 216, 844). See also the summaries of these letters in Griffe, *Croisade*, pp. 91–2, and Roquebert II, pp. 128–30, and see below, §398 and §400, for the further letter to Innocent from the Council of Orange, 20 February 1213.

of the Church. The people and their prince are given over to a reprobate mind[43] and have left the true path of faith. At last, prompted by your watchful care, the tender mercy which comes from on high has visited us, and through the agency of the blessed crusaders (whom you have in your great wisdom appointed to wipe out the filth of this plague) and of their most Christian leader the Count of Montfort (that intrepid athlete of Christ and invincible warrior of the Lord) – through them the Church, which had so miserably come to ruin in this land, has begun to raise its head; and the land itself, so long crushed underfoot by the cultivators of false dogmas, has now at last become reaccustomed to the worship of God, in a manner most worthy of congratulation, now that opposition and errors of all kinds have been almost completely overcome. [394] There still remain traces of this plague, the city of Toulouse and a few *castra*,[44] where – like filth sinking into a bilge-hold – the residue of the evil of heresy has collected. Their leader the Count of Toulouse (for so long the supporter and defender of heretics, as you have already heard so often) continues to attack the Church with such resources as remain to him and so far as he is able sets himself against the supporters of the faith on behalf of its enemies. Since he returned from your Holiness's presence, with your decrees[45] in which you displayed forgiveness far beyond his deserts, clearly the angel of Satan has entered into his heart. Ungrateful for the benefits bestowed on him by your grace he has kept none of the promises he made in your presence – on the contrary he has grossly increased the tolls he frequently swore to abandon,[46] and as if deliberately intending to renounce the benefit of your decrees he has turned to all those he knows to be your adversaries and the Church's. With the approval of Otto that enemy of God and the Church,[47] he decided to join battle with the Church herself, and – so it is said – relying on Otto's support threatened to uproot the Church and the clergy from his territories. Although he had so often sworn to have no more to do with mercenaries and heretics he now began to cultivate them and consort with them more eagerly than ever. When the Catholic army besieged Lavaur, the seat of Satan and a prime source of heresy, he sent his knights and followers to help the faithless.[48] Moreover, in Les Cassés, which is part of his domain, the crusaders discovered and burnt more than fifty perfected heretics and a large crowed of heretical believers.[49] He called Savary, Seneschal of that enemy of the Church the King of England, to join him in his fight against the Church and with his aid

---

43 Romans I, v. 28.

44 In particular Montauban: see §359 above.

45 Presumably a reference to Innocent's letter of 23 January 1210, issued after Raymond VI's visit to Rome in the winter of 1209–10: see *PL* 216, 173–4 (Appendix F(iii)), and §137 and §162 above, and notes.

46 On the charge that Raymond VI increased tolls unjustly, see §137 above.

47 For Otto see n. 66 to §72 and n. 32 to §383. Raymond VI held the marquisate of Provence as a fief of the Holy Roman Emperor, and he had visited Otto seeking support in the winter of 1209–10 (see §139 above). By referring to this connection now, the legates were no doubt trying to associate the two men in Innocent's mind, just as a few lines later they also invoke links between King John of England and Raymond.

48 See above, §220 for Raymond VI's covert support of the defenders of Lavaur in spring 1211.

49 See §233 for the siege of Les Cassés, also in 1211.

dared to besiege the Count of Montfort, Christ's champion, at Castelnaudary;[50] but Christ's right hand came to our aid and his presumption was soon turned to confusion, so that a few Catholics routed an infinite multitude of Arians.[51] Deceived in his trust in Otto and the English King – as one who trusts in the staff of a broken reed[52] – he thought up a scheme of abominable wickedness, quite detestable to Catholic ears; he sent his emissaries to the King of Morocco to beg his aid in destroying not only our land but the whole of Christianity, but Heavenly goodness obstructed his efforts and his damnable intentions.[53] He drove the Bishop of Agen from his see and robbed him of all his possessions.[54] He took prisoner the Abbot of Moissac[55] and held the Abbot of Montauban in captivity for almost a year.[56] His mercenaries and accomplices condemned innumerable crusaders, both clergy and laymen, to all kinds of martyrdom – others they have held captive for long periods.

[395] 'For all this his anger is not turned away, but his hand is stretched out still.[57] Each day his perversity increases, and every possible evil is being done to the Church of God by the Count himself, by his son, and by his criminal and evil accomplices the Counts of Foix and Comminges, and Gaston de Béarn. Aided, however, by Divine vengeance and the censure of the Church, the most Christian athlete of the faith, the Count of Montfort, has occupied almost all their territories, treating them as enemies of God and the Church in a holy and just war. But they themselves have persisted in their evil ways and refused to humble themselves beneath the Lord's mighty hand; they have now run to the King of Aragon, hoping to make use of him to take advantage of your clemency and flout the Church. They invited him to Toulouse to hold a meeting with us, after we had gathered at Lavaur for a council on the instructions of your legate and your envoys.[58] You will be fully apprised of the proposals he made to us and of our

---

[50] For Savary de Mauléon and his role at the siege of Castelnaudary in autumn 1211, see §254. At this time King John was still excommunicate and the kingdom of England was under interdict: Innocent had imposed these penalties in March 1208 over John's refusal to accept Stephen Langton as Archbishop of Canterbury, and as with Otto above, the legates are trying to associate Raymond with him. The excommunication and interdict were lifted in May 1213 when John accepted Langton and placed himself under Innocent's protection by becoming (like Peter of Aragon) a papal vassal.

[51] I.e. the heretics. The term Arian (Latin *Arriani*) was commonly used to describe all heretics, and is chosen here to provide a word-play with *castrum Novum Arrii*, the Latin name of Castelnaudary.

[52] Isaiah 36, v. 6.

[53] The 'king of Morocco' referred to here is Abu Abdallah Mohammed Al-Nasir, caliph of the Almohades, the rulers of Moorish Spain at this time. They had originated in Morocco in the 12th century, and their army under Al-Nasir was defeated by the combined forces of the Christian kings of Spain at Las Navas de Tolosa in July 1212. G&L II, p. 91 n. 2, note that there were rumours reported by Caesar of Heisterbach and in the Annals of Cologne about links between the Almohades and the Cathars, and Arnold Amalric, who had of course taken part in the Las Navas de Tolosa campaign, may have wished to encourage such ideas. But the story seems highly improbable: see discussion in Roquebert II, pp. 122–3.

[54] See above, §317.

[55] See n. 103 to §340 and §353 above.

[56] Abbot Raymond of the abbey of Saint-Théodard at Montauban; see also *Chanson* I, 33, pp. 98–9.

[57] Isaiah 9, v. 12.

[58] The envoys ('*delegati*') were Thedisius and Bishop Hugh of Riez. See above, §§367–8, and notes, for King Peter's proposal for a meeting, and for the background to the Council of Lavaur.

replies by the accounts being sent to your holiness under seal.[59] We have also sent to you a record of the advice given at their request to your envoys in the matter of the Count of Toulouse.[60] [396] We are all unanimous in our decision to make your Holiness aware of the foregoing, since we wish to satisfy our consciences that nothing should be overlooked that touches on the business of the faith through any failure of ours to make matters clear. Lastly, for the sake of our souls and the protection of the churches entrusted to us, we earnestly beg your merciful self, through the tender mercy of our God,[61] to bring to a happy conclusion the business of liberation and peace which involves our very lives – that business which you have already happily advanced, since the power of justice is now plain to see amongst us. We beg you to lay the axe to the root of the accursed tree[62] and destroy it forever so that it can do no further harm. For you must surely know that if these lands which have been wrested from these tyrants, justly and with much effusion of Christian blood, are restored to them or their heirs, this would cause enormous offence to the faithful who have fought this fight; and beyond that it will not only give rise to a new error worse than the first[63] but will be a source of incalculable disaster to the clergy and the Church. [397] Since we do not wish to list in this letter all the enormities committed by these men, their blasphemies, outrages and other crimes, lest we seem to be writing a book, some parts of what we have to tell have been entrusted to envoys who will be able to relate them to your blessed ears by word of mouth.'

[398] The envoys who delivered the letter to the Pope were: the venerable Bishop of Comminges, the Abbot of Clairac, William Archdeacon of Paris, Master Thedisius and a cleric named Peter Marc who had for a long time been *Corrector Litterarum* at the Papal Curia.[64]

---

[59] I.e. King Peter's demands, given in §§370–6, and the response of the prelates, §§377–84.

[60] The '*consilium*' or 'advice' referred to here was given to Hugh and Thedisius by the Council of Lavaur. It is recorded in the letter from Hugh and Thedisius to Innocent, written after the Council of Lavaur, for which see n. 4 to §400 below (and see also n. 5 to §367). The advice covers much the same ground as the letter printed here.

[61] Luke 1, v. 78.

[62] Matthew 3, v. 10.

[63] Matthew 27, v. 64.

[64] The Bishop of Comminges was Garsia (see §358 above for his first appearance). The Abbot of Clairac (on the River Lot north-west of Agen) was Peter, who also appears in §470 below; see also G&L II, p. 95 n. 3. On William Archdeacon of Paris see §175 above. Peter Marc (Petrus Marci) was for some time a draughtsman (*scriptor*) in the Papal Chancellery, and then became *corrector litterarum*. He had been sent to the Midi by Innocent the previous year to supervise the collection and distribution of the various taxes which de Montfort had agreed to collect for the Church from the lands taken over from the Trencavels: see G&M, pp. 142–3 n. 3, and G&L II, p. 95 n. 6. He is mentioned again in §440 below, where he is said to be a native of Nîmes. These envoys, with Thedisius, passed through Orange in February 1213 on their way to Rome, where they met the prelates of Provence then assembled there in council. The outcome was a letter to Innocent of 20 February, for which see n. 4 to §400.

[**XIV. §§399–445, January–August 1213:** *Innocent III orders the suspension of the Crusade (letters of January 1213) – envoys from the legates go to Rome – Innocent III's volte-face – he withdraws his support for King Peter (letter of 21 May) – King Peter repudiates his ties of allegiance with de Montfort – Prince Louis of France takes the cross – King Peter sends envoys to Paris – the crusaders are reinforced – campaigns near Toulouse – siege of Puycelsi by Guy de Montfort – Amaury de Montfort knighted – Simon de Montfort in Gascony – recapitulation of earlier events.*]

[**399**] Before these wise and experienced envoys arrived at the Curia, the King of Aragon had sent his own envoys there with the intention of taking advantage of the open-mindedness of the Apostolic See.[1] By false suggestion and by suppressing the truth he had succeeded in obtaining a letter in which the Pope instructed the Count of Montfort to give back to the Counts of Comminges and Foix, and Gaston de Béarn, the territories taken from them. He also sent a letter to the Archbishop of Narbonne in which he appeared to be revoking the indulgence he had granted to those proceeding against the Albigensian heretics.[2]

[**400**] So when our envoys reached the Curia[3] they found the Pope somewhat hard since he had been too ready to believe the false accounts of the King's envoys. Later when he had heard the truth from our envoys he declared his response to the King's envoys invalid and wrote to the King himself in the following terms.[4]

---

[1] King Peter's envoys had been sent to Rome late in 1212, and probably arrived there in December; cf. above, n. 3 to §367. They were Hispan, Bishop of Segorbe (north of Valencia) and Albarracin (west of Teruel), both sees in the kingdom of Aragon; and one Master Colomb, the King's secretary: see G&L II, p. 100 n. 5, and p. 101 n. 1 for details. This visit and its outcome are recapitulated below in §§437–9, and discussed in Griffe, *Croisade*, pp. 84–8, and Roquebert II, ch. 2. See also §404, when their presence in Rome in the spring of 1213 on a second visit is recorded.

[2] Peter correctly places receipt of these letters (and the two associated letters – see below) after the conclusion of the Council of Lavaur, but does not make it clear that they were written whilst the Council was in session. The letter to de Montfort, dated 17 January 1213 is strongly worded; it sets out and by implication accepts the accusations of King Peter's envoys that Simon de Montfort had used the Crusade as a pretext for occupying the territories of the King's vassals (which the envoys claimed were untainted by heresy) and instructs Simon to restore them. The letter to Arnold Amalric calling a halt to the Crusade was dated 15 January; there was a second letter to him, of 18 January, addressed also to Hugh of Riez and Thedisius, again in strong terms and implying acceptance of King Peter's allegations that Arnold and Simon had 'stretched out greedy hands' to territories untainted by heresy, and ridden roughshod over the established feudal order; Count Raymond is said to be ready to offer satisfaction and the King puts in a plea for the county of Toulouse to be reserved for the younger Raymond, whom he promises to take under his tutelage together with Toulouse itself; the prelates are ordered to summon a council of churchmen and others to hear King Peter's pleas. Translations of these three letters are given in Appendix F(iv), together with references. Innocent had also written another letter to de Montfort dated 15 January in which he urged him to fulfil his duties as a vassal of King Peter. All four letters are in *PL* 216, 739–45. The letters suggest strongly that Innocent had come to realize that the Crusade he had initiated had run out of his control, but as the next section relates, his attitude was soon to change dramatically.

[3] Probably some time in March 1213. These events are recapitulated in §§440–1 below.

[4] The letter which follows represents an almost complete reversal by Innocent of the stance he had taken in the letters referred to in the preceding section; it was written some four months later, on 21 May 1213, and several months after the arrival in Rome of Thedisius and the other envoys sent by Arnold Amalric

[401] *Letter from the Lord Pope to the King of Aragon.*[5] 'From Bishop Innocent, servant of the servants of God, to Peter, illustrious King of Aragon. [402] May He in whose hands are the hearts of all kings[6] listen to your humble prayers and inspire you wisely to reflect that our duty, as laid down by the apostle,[7] is to reprove, rebuke and exhort; and may He inspire you also to receive with filial devotion those exhortations, which we address to you with paternal affection, and to listen well to our salutary advice; so that by dutifully accepting apostolic correction you will show that you have sincere intentions even in those matters where your actions have undoubtedly been wrong.[8] By now almost all the world is aware that of all Christian princes we honour you especially, nor do we think that your Serene Highness is unaware of this, or disbelieves it. This has led to the growth of your power and reputation – would that your wisdom and piety had increased in proportion, since this would have been helpful to us, but of even greater value to yourself. [403] In fact, in this matter you have neither looked to your own interests nor deferred to us as you should. The citizens of Toulouse

after the Council of Lavaur. For letters of the same date to Simon de Montfort and others see n. 18 to §405. The period between January and May must have seen considerable diplomatic activity at the Curia, by Thedisius and his fellow envoys (§398) as well as King Peter's representatives (§404). Innocent will have had before him the report on the Council of Lavaur recorded by Peter in §§392–7 above, and the letters referred to in n. 42 to §392; as well as the letter from Thedisius and Bishop Hugh of Riez in which they take the same stance as they had at Saint-Gilles in July 1210 (§164), reiterating the charges against Count Raymond and recording the decision of the Council of Lavaur in his regard (*PL* 216, 833; Mansi XXII, 880; January 1213): 'They [the Council] have decided that they should not allow the Count of Toulouse to receive purification for very many reasons in addition to the crime of heresy and the murder of the legate; since it is agreed and well known that he has on numerous occasions given sworn oaths to the legates to expel heretics and mercenaries from his territories, and on many other matters, but kept none of them ...'. The meeting at Orange in February 1213 between Thedisius and the prelates of Provence (see n. 64 to §398) produced a letter of 20 February addressed to Innocent from the Archbishop of Arles, ten bishops (including Raymond of Uzès) and the Abbot of Saint-Gilles, denouncing Raymond in the strongest terms and urging Innocent to continue the Crusade: see *PL* 216, 835–6. (The tone of this letter suggests that the legates had by this time received Innocent's letters of January 1213: see Roquebert II, p. 130.)

The result of this activity and pressure now emerges in the Pope's letter, in a volte-face which was typical of him. However, even though Innocent dramatically changed his views of the participants, his basic stance as set out in §§405–7, first given in his letter of 25 January 1210 (n. 49 to §137) and confirmed in his letter of 25 May 1212 (n. 5 to §367), had not changed. He still believed that reconciliation between the southerners and the Church was possible and that efforts to reach it should continue; meanwhile no final decision to dispossess the Southern lords could be taken. This stance was to be maintained until the Fourth Lateran Council in November 1215: see e.g. notes to §§503, 547, 556 and 570–2, and Appendix G.

As pointed out in n. 1 to §367, the events recorded in §§412–21 also took place between the Council of Lavaur and the issue of this letter. These included King Peter's attempt to replace Maria of Montpellier as his wife by Philip Augustus' daughter (§419) which may have adversely affected his standing with the Church at this time.

5   Dated 21 May 1213: see §411 below. The letter is also in *PL* 216, 849.
6   Cf. Proverbs 21, v. 1.
7   Timothy 4, v. 2.
8   In this and succeeding passages, in which Innocent tells King Peter that it is his duty to be corrected by the Pope, Innocent is reflecting not just the fact that Peter was his vassal, but also (as suggested by the phrase '*correctionem apostolicam*') his view that as a secular ruler, Peter was ultimately subject to Papal authority. This reflects Innocent's overall view of himself, as Pope, as being God's vicar on Earth, responsible for the orderly government of the Christian commonwealth. These responsibilities gave him complete power ('*plenitudo potestatis*') over all Christians and set him above all other authority, with ultimate power not just over the Church but over secular rulers as well. For a succinct discussion of these ideas as developed by Innocent, see Ullmann, *A Short History of the Medieval Papacy*, ch. 9.

have been cut off from the body of the Church by the sword of excommunication, and the city itself placed under papal interdict.[9] The grounds for this are that some of them are declared heretics, many more are believers, or the supporters, receivers and defenders of heretics. Indeed, others from outside the city, driven from their tents by the army of Christ (nay, by Christ himself, whom they had provoked by their contriving), have fled for refuge to Toulouse, as to the bilge-hold of error.[10] There they wait for an opportunity when, like locusts coming forth from the bottom of a pit,[11] they may extirpate the true faith which has been newly planted in these lands. But you have forgotten that you should fear God, instead you have taken these people and their accomplices under your protection, as if you had the power to prevail against God or turn aside His hand which is held out against them as their crimes demand; in doing so you have practised impiety under the guise of piety, so causing great offence to Christians and grave damage to your own reputation. This you have done despite the strict orders given to you by our legate[12] in God's name and ours, so incurring great dishonour and the danger of even graver suspicion.

[404] 'We have recently listened to the points put forward in our presence by our venerable brother, the Bishop of Segorbe, by our beloved son Master Colomb, your envoys,[13] and by the envoys of our legate and of Simon Count of Montfort.[14] We have also taken full note of the letters exchanged between the various parties,[15] and held full discussions and taken counsel with our brothers. The object of our paternal care is to provide for the protection of your reputation, the salvation of your soul and the preservation of the land.[16] We have therefore decided formally to instruct your Serenity, in the name of the Holy Spirit and under the mantle of divine and apostolic grace, to abandon the Toulousains and their accomplices without delay. Any promises or undertakings given by them or received from them[17] which are derogatory to the teachings of the Church must not stand in the way. They and their allies must receive no advice, help or favour from you or anyone else so long as they remain in their present state.

[405] 'If they truly wish to become reunited with the Church, as was suggested by your envoys in our presence, we have given written instructions to our venerable brother Fulk, Bishop of Toulouse[18] (a man unsullied in his beliefs and in his

---

9 The citizens had been excommunicated in September 1209 (see §138). The city had in 1207 apparently been included in an interdict laid on Raymond's territories (n. 35 to §27, and see *PL* 215, 1165–8 translated in Appendix F(i)); and was also placed under an interdict in 1211 (n. 38 to §212).

10 Compare the language in the prelates' letter to Innocent, above §394.

11 Cf. Revelations 9, vv. 2–3. G&M, p. 157, identify four other biblical echoes in this section.

12 A reference to Arnold Amalric's letter to King Peter of January 1213, given in §§387–8 above.

13 See above, §399 for Hispan and Colomb. Colomb was an experienced diplomat and had known Innocent since 1200: cf. G&L II, p. 101 n. 1.

14 Thedisius and his four colleagues: see above §398.

15 I.e. at the Council of Lavaur: see §§370ff.

16 Simply '*terram*', presumably the territory under consideration – the area infected by heresy.

17 A clear reference to the oaths of allegiance to King Peter of 27 January 1213: see §389.

18 These instructions and those to Arnold Amalric, §407 below, and to Simon de Montfort, §408, are all recorded in *PL* 216, 852, where it is stated that for most of their length the letters are virtually the same as

way of life, who has a good report not merely of them which are within but also of them which are without),[19] that he should choose two other wise and upright men, and reconcile to the Church any who wish to return to her out of a pure heart and of a good conscience and of faith unfeigned.[20] Sufficient guarantees must be exacted from them. As to those, however, who remain in the shadows of error and who may therefore come to be stigmatised by the Bishop for heresy – these we have decided shall be driven from Toulouse and their possessions confiscated; never to return unless perhaps, through some divine inspiration, they show by their deeds that they have become true followers of the orthodox faith. Thus the city itself may become reconciled and purged and may rest under the protection of the Apostolic See; no longer to be troubled by the Count of Montfort or others of the Catholic faith, but rather to be defended and cherished by them.

[406] 'We are amazed and disturbed that, by using your envoys to suppress the truth and give a false account of matters, you have extorted from us a papal letter[21] ordering the restitution of their territories to the Counts of Comminges and Foix and Gaston de Béarn, bearing in mind that – to pass over their many other monstrous misdeeds – they have been bound with the chain of excommunication for their support of the heretics, whom they openly defend. Since a decree obtained by such means for such men is not valid, we have treated it as if it had been stolen and cancelled it in its entirety. [407] If these three truly wish to be reconciled to communion with the Church, as they claim, we have given written instructions to our venerable brother the Archbishop of Narbonne, legate of the Apostolic See, to accord them the benefit of absolution after accepting from them not only the security of a sworn oath, but also (since they have previously violated such undertakings) any other security which he considers appropriate. After these procedures have been duly carried out (as signs of true devotion), we will in accordance with your wishes despatch to these territories a legate *a latere*.[22] He will be a cardinal, an honourable, wise and faithful man who will not turn aside either to the right hand or to the left[23] but will always go along by the King's high way;[24] he will approve and confirm whatever he finds to have been done rightly, will correct and rectify errors, and ensure that justice is done to the nobles named above and any other complainants equally. [408] Meanwhile we wish and enjoin that a firm truce should be agreed and maintained between you and your territories, and the Count of Montfort and his territories. From this

---

the letter to King Peter reproduced here. The date of all these letters is almost certainly 21 May 1213: see G&L, II, p. 105, note t.

[19] Taken in part from I Timothy 3, v. 7, and meaning that he has a good reputation not merely in the Church but also in the world at large.

[20] I Timothy 1, v. 5.

[21] I.e. the letter from Innocent to de Montfort, 17 January 1213, on which see §399 above and Appendix F(iv).

[22] Eventually a new legate was sent, in the person of Peter of Benevento, appointed early in 1214 in the aftermath of the battle of Muret: see §503 below.

[23] Deuteronomy 5, v. 32.

[24] Numbers 21, v. 22.

the heretics must be excluded; it is not fitting that those who profess the true faith should make a truce or make peace with them (since light has no communion with darkness, and Christ has no concord with Belial, and he that believes has no part with an infidel).[25] Nevertheless we instruct the Count to perform with due respect all the duties which he owes to you in regard to the territories which he holds as your vassal.

[409] 'We wish Your Excellency to be fully aware that if the Toulousains and the nobles named above persist in their error, we intend to renew our promises of indulgence and call out a fresh force of crusaders and the faithful who with God's help will rise up to eliminate this plague and go forth in the name of the Lord God of Hosts to fight not only the heretics themselves but also those others, their protectors and defenders, who are more dangerous than the heretics themselves.

[410] 'So we ask, beg and beseech Your Serenity, in the Lord's name, to do what we have requested, in so far as it concerns you, with a willing heart, in the sure knowledge that if you were to do otherwise (which we do not think possible), you would not only incur Divine displeasure (which such a course would be sure to provoke), but would be likely to suffer serious and irreparable harm. Whatever affection we have for you, we could not spare you or give way to you if you go against the business of the Christian faith. There are recent as well as ancient examples to teach you what danger would threaten you if you were to oppose God and the Church, especially in a matter that concerns the faith, and in doing so stood in the way of the accomplishment of our sacred work.

[411] 'Given at the Lateran, 21 May, in the sixteenth year of our pontificate.'

[412] After the conclusion of the Council of prelates at Lavaur[26] the King of Aragon, showing complete lack of faith, had left Toulouse after sending a substantial force of knights to the city to defend it and to give aid to Christ's enemies.[27] A few days later he told our Count that he would like to hold a meeting with him near Narbonne. Our Count wished to defer to the King, his suzerain, and to obey him – so far as his duty to God allowed – in all matters, and replied that he would be happy to attend the meeting. However, the King did not go to the rendezvous, and indeed had no intention of ever going. A great many heretics and mercenaries from Aragon and Toulouse did come, and this produced concern that if the Count of Jesus Christ were to go to the meeting-place with a small force, he would be taken prisoner in treacherous fashion. The Count was made aware of what was happening and kept away from the meeting place.

[413] *The King repudiates the Count.* A few days later the King sent envoys to

---

25 II Corinthians 6, vv. 14–15.

26 For the chronology of events now covered in §§412–21 (which occurred before the issue of the Pope's letter just recorded), see n. 1 to §367.

27 King Peter left Toulouse during February 1213. He is recorded as being at Toulouse on 7th, Perpignan on 21 February and Collioure on 27th (G&L II, p. 106 n. 1, citing *Itinerario*). As well as leaving knights in Toulouse, Peter later suggests (§427) that mercenaries were also present. The *Chanson* (II, 133, p. 6), mentions 'Catalans' as having been left by the King. These Aragonese forces were commanded by William-Raymond of Montcada, King Peter's seneschal (again see §427). According to William of Puylaurens (XIX), a knight called William of Alcala was also installed at Toulouse as the King's '*vicarius*' (French *viguier*), meaning a deputy able to act on his behalf: see William of Puylaurens, ed. Duvernoy, p. 76 n. 1.

the Count with a letter in which he repudiated the allegiance owed to him by the Count[28] and threatened to do his utmost to injure him. Despite the King's high-handed renunciation of their connection, the Count had no wish to harm the King's territory, even though he was himself constantly subjected to serious injury from that direction; not only were Catalans[29] entering our territory and themselves doing their utmost to cause damage there, but they were providing safe entry and exit for mercenaries who were devastating the area. [414] After a few days the Count sent Lambert de Thury,[30] an honourable and prudent knight, to the King to ask whether the King's decision to renounce his ties of allegiance with the Count, as reported by the King's envoys, was truly meant; he was to point out that the Count had never failed to carry out his obligations to the King and indeed was ready to go on performing every duty he owed to him as his lord; moreover, if the King had any case to make concerning the Count's behaviour in regard to the heretics' lands which he had acquired on the authority of the Supreme Pontiff with the crusaders' help, then he was ready to stand before the law in the Curia or the court of the Archbishop of Narbonne, legate of the Apostolic See. He also gave a letter to Lambert with instructions to hand it to the King if he persisted in his obstinate behaviour. The contents of the letter were as follows. The Count wrote to the King without a formal greeting, as a sign[31] that since he was persisting in renouncing his relationship with the Count and in his obstinate behaviour even after the many offers of a just peace that had been made to him, then the Count similarly was renouncing his allegiance to the King; and saying that from now on he would no longer regard himself as bound to render any service to the King, but would defend himself with God's help against the King as against any other enemies of the Church. [415] Accordingly Lambert went to the King and with great care and thoroughness reported everything the Count had instructed him to say, in the presence of the King and a number of his barons.[32] However, the King remained obstinate and rejected every proposal for

---

28 Latin '*diffidabat*', from *diffidare*, literally meaning 'to break faith with'. Here it refers to the semi-formal procedure whereby the ties between a vassal and lord could be broken, and homage renounced, known in French as a *défi*, or 'defiance' in the sense of a renunciation of faith. When it happened, the procedure was more usually followed by a vassal when renouncing homage to a lord, but it was sometimes, as here, followed when a lord wished to renounce his ties with a vassal. The usual practice was to make the act of 'defiance' either through a messenger or in writing. (See for example M. Bloch, *Feudal Society*, trans. L. A. Manyon (London, 2nd ed. 1962), p. 228.) In this case, King Peter's 'defiance' of de Montfort meant that he now regarded their relationship as lord and vassal (established early in 1211 when he accepted de Montfort's homage in respect of the former Trencavel lands: see §210) as being at an end, leaving the King free to make war on de Montfort without breaking his obligations to a vassal.

29 Catalonia made up the eastern portion of Peter's kingdom, and included Perpignan and those parts of Roussillon and the Cerdagne in northern Catalonia which were to be ceded to the French in 1659. The attacks on the crusaders were presumably coming from northern Catalonia.

30 See n. 48 to §248 on Lambert.

31 '*Significans*'; the sense seems to be that de Montfort's renunciation of his ties to the King was implicit in the failure to address him as his overlord, rather than being made explicit. For a similar example, see also G&L II, p. 98 n. f. Immediately below 'saying' ('*dicens*') etc. presumably reports what was said explicitly in the letter.

32 This meeting took place at some point during Peter's stay in Roussillon in February 1213. About 15 of his barons were recorded as being with him witnessing acts made by him during this period (*Itinerario*, pp. 94–5, cited in G&L II, p. 108 n. 2).

peace and refused to withdraw his renunciation of his lordship over the Count. Thereupon Lambert presented the Count's letter on this subject, which was read by a bishop to the King and his barons. After having heard and thoroughly understood the letter, the King and his entourage became furiously angry. The envoy was then sent from the royal court and put under close guard, and the King asked his followers what he should do with him. Some of the barons advised him to send to the Count with orders to come to the royal court and render due homage to the King as his overlord; if the Count refused to come, the envoy should be condemned to death. [416] Next morning the envoy returned to the court and repeated his message of the previous day from the Count, with even greater care. With great courage he declared that if any of the King's knights were willing to accuse our Count of having dealt unjustly with the King or having been disloyal to him in any way, then he was ready to defend his lord against such charges of disloyalty in a duel in the King's own court. No one dared accept his challenge, but a general clamour was raised against him. At length the King released him in response to requests from some knights of Aragon who had some acquaintance with him, and he returned to the Count after surviving numerous threats to his life. From now on the King, who had this far been the secret adversary of Christ's Count, began to attack and oppose him openly in all manner of ways.

[417] *Louis, son of the King of France takes the cross.* In February in the year of our Lord 1213,[33] Louis, eldest son of the King of France, the most gentle of young men, of excellent disposition, took the cross against the pestilential heretics.[34] When they heard of this a large number of knights from France were prompted by affection for him and by his example to take the cross themselves. The King himself was very sad to hear that his son had joined the Crusade, but it is not for me to explain the reasons for his grief.[35]

[418] On the first Sunday of Lent[36] the King held a general assembly of barons at Paris to make arrangements for his son's departure and to determine how many were to accompany him, and their names and rank. In Paris that day were the Bishops of Toulouse and Carcassonne,[37] who had come to France to promote the Crusade against the heretics.

---

[33] The Latin gives 1212 (MCCXII) but here as elsewhere dates are modernised in respect of the start of the year: see Introduction p. xxi.

[34] It is clear that at this stage the news of Innocent's letters of 15–18 January calling a halt to the Crusade would not have reached the French court; Philip Augustus may therefore also not have heard of Raymond VI's decision to transfer his allegiance to King Peter (see §389). Prince Louis was at this time aged twenty-five (G&L II, p. 109 n. 1) and had formally been made a knight by his father several years earlier. He was presumably persuaded to take the cross by Fulk of Toulouse and Guy of les Vaux-de-Cernay, who were present at the French court at this time to argue the case for the Crusade (see §418). Louis later joined the Crusade in 1215: see §550 below.

[35] For Philip Augustus' persistently lukewarm support for the Crusade, especially against Raymond VI see nn. 65 and 67 to §72. Peter may perhaps be referring in part to this – if so 'grief' ('*dolor*') is an odd word to choose. Whatever the case, although Louis' preparations became quite advanced, Philip prevented him from joining the Crusade and instead planned an invasion of England for May 1213: see below, §421.

[36] 3 March 1213.

[37] See also §439 for Guy's activities in the North.

[419] *The King of Aragon sends envoys to the King of France.* The King of Aragon, doing his utmost to impede the business of the faith, now sent envoys to the King of France: the Bishop of Barcelona[38] accompanied by several knights. His object in sending the envoys was twofold. Firstly, he wished to ask the King of France to give his daughter to him in marriage, since he wished to repudiate his legitimate wife, the daughter of William of Montpellier[39] (and indeed had already repudiated her in so far as he could do so unilaterally); however, she had gone to the Pope to complain that her husband's repudiation of her was unjust, and the Pope, after investigating the facts, had pronounced against the King and confirmed the validity of the marriage.[40] King Peter was hoping to marry the King of France's daughter,[41] since he thought by such an alliance to draw the King over to his side and deflect him from supporting the business of the faith and helping the Count of Montfort. However, when the envoys realised that the Pope's decision

---

[38]   Bishop Berengar de Palou. His embassy to the French court, for which Peter is the principal source, is discussed in Roquebert II, pp. 133–6.

[39]   For Montpellier see also §121 and note. King Peter's wife was Maria, daughter of William VIII, lord of Montpellier, and Eudocia, daughter of the Byzantine Emperor Manuel I Comnenus. A condition of Eudocia's marriage to William was that a child of the union should inherit Montpellier, whatever other children William might have. Maria was born in 1183 and thus became heiress to the lordship of Montpellier, but William VIII soon divorced Eudicia and in subsequent years Maria suffered repeatedly from the efforts of her father and husbands to deprive her of her rights. In June 1204 she married King Peter as her third husband, after which he persuaded or cajoled her into ceding her possessions to him (William of Puylaurens says (XI) that he married her out of his desire to gain control over Montpellier, '*ambitione dominandi in Montepesulano*'). In August 1205 she bore his daughter Sancia, who whilst still a baby was betrothed to the seven year old son of the Count of Toulouse, Raymond the younger, and the seigneury was promised as a dowry; Sancia died, however, not long afterwards. Having obtained control of Montpellier, Peter then had no further use for Maria and he sought to have the marriage annulled by Pope Innocent, even though subsequently (February 1208) Maria bore the future King James of Aragon. (William of Puylaurens, loc. cit., says there was a brief reconciliation instigated by the prelates, although according to some Catalan sources the consuls of Montpellier, anxious for a legitimate heir, engineered James's conception by substituting Maria for the King's mistress one night when he was staying in the city. In the *Llibre dels feyts*, V (trans. Forster, pp. 9–11) James himself says the reconciliation was arranged by the knight William of Alcala (Dalcala), for whom see n. 27 to §412.) In January 1211, at the time the young James of Aragon was betrothed to Simon de Montfort's daughter and handed over to Simon (§211), King Peter also handed the seigneury of Montpellier to him to hold safe until James should reach age eighteen and be able to rule the city. In January 1213, having broken with de Montfort, the King then by a *fait accompli* transferred the rights to Montpellier to Maria's half brother, William IX, on condition that William promised to be his vassal, and undertook to help William recover the city from the crusaders. Since this had the effect of depriving Peter's own son of the seigneury, he appears to have made the donation in order to nullify the agreement made two years earlier with Simon de Montfort, in the light of the deterioration in relations between the two since then; however, the young James was to remain in de Montfort's custody until April 1214 (see §§503 and 506). For further details and references, see J. Rouquette, *Marie de Montpellier, reine d'Aragon, 1181(?)–1213* (Montpellier, 1914); *HGL* VII, pp. 38–42, note XIV; Roquebert II, pp. 113–18, and William of Puylaurens, ed. J. Duvernoy, n. 1 on pp. 56–7. See also §544 and note for later developments.

[40]   Maria had appealed to Innocent in 1206 and he ordered the legates Peter of Castelnau and Ralph of Fontfroide to examine the case. Their deaths in 1207 and 1208 (see §50 and §55 above) delayed further consideration of Maria's appeal, but Innocent took it up in 1212, and summoned Maria to Rome, while King Peter's envoys repeated the demand for a divorce. Eventually, on 19 January 1213 (*PL* 216, 749) Innocent wrote to Maria and Peter refusing the King's request for an annulment, and confirming Maria in her inheritance. He also notified the Bishops of Carcassonne, Orange and Avignon in the same terms (*PL* 216, 749; *RHGF* XIX, 563 and 565). Maria thereafter continued to protest over Peter's grant of Montpellier as a fief to William IX, but she died in Rome in April 1213.

[41]   Marie, widow of Philip of Namur, who was later betrothed to Henry of Brabant (G&L II, p. 110 n. 4).

to confirm the marriage between the King of Aragon and his queen was public knowledge in the French court,[42] they did not dare bring up the question of arranging the marriage, which was the original purpose of their visit. [420] The second objective of their visit to France was this. The King of Aragon had taken under his guardianship and protection the city of Toulouse (from of old the reservoir and bilge-hold of heretics), together with the heretics themselves and their supporters and defenders. He was communing fully and openly with ex-communicants and heretics; practising impiety under the guise of piety, he was doing his utmost to ensure that the dedication of the crusaders should wane and their ardour cool, and he wanted Toulouse and certain *castra* nearby which were still attacking Christianity to remain unharmed. In this way he hoped presently to undermine and utterly demolish the whole business of the holy faith. At this time he also sent letters to the King of France and the Countess of Champagne[43] sealed by numerous bishops in his realm, in which the Pope was represented as revoking the indulgence he had granted to anyone proceeding against the here-tics; he also arranged the publication of these letters throughout France, hoping to turn the minds of all and sundry away from the Crusade against the heretics.[44] After these brief comments concerning the King's evil intentions, let us return to our main subject. When the Bishop of Barcelona and the King's other envoys (who had come to try and divert the crusaders from proceeding against the heretics) realised that Louis, the King of France's son, and many other nobles with him had taken the cross against the heretics, they did not dare breathe a word with the idea of diverting our people from their commitment to the Crusade, and returned to the King of Aragon without achieving any of the objectives of their visit.

[421] As mentioned above,[45] the King of France had called his barons to a general assembly at Paris. He now made arrangements for the participation in the Crusade of his son and the others who had taken the sign of the cross, and arranged for them to depart one week after the feast of the Resurrection.[46] What more? There was immense joy and rejoicing amongst Christians, great grief and fear amongst the heretics. Alas! Soon our harp is turned to mourning[47] the mourning of our enemies is turned into joy![48] That ancient enemy of mankind, the Devil, saw that Christ's business was on the point of success, through the great labour of the crusaders, and found a new device for causing hurt, so that he

---

[42] One of those charged with ensuring the implementation of Innocent's ruling over Maria's case was Bishop Guy of Carcassonne, who was then present at the French court.

[43] Blanche of Navarre, widow of Count Theobald III of Champagne, and regent on behalf of her young son Theobald IV.

[44] These copies of Innocent's letters of January 1213 (see §399 and n. 2) were probably made at Perpignan by Raymond, Archbishop of Tarragona, and were authenticated with the seals of other Aragonese bishops present there at the time. Copies (*PL* 216, 845–9) were also made there of the oaths of allegiance sworn to King Peter in January – see §389 and note.

[45] See §418.

[46] 21 April 1213.

[47] Job 30, v. 31.

[48] Jeremiah 31, v. 13.

might hinder what he grieved to see succeed. He involved the King of France in wars and undertakings so numerous and so great that he had to delay the proposed departure of his son and the other crusaders.[49]

[422] *Arrival of the Bishops of Orleans and Auxerre from France.* At this time Manasses, Bishop of Orleans,[50] and William, Bishop of Auxerre,[51] took the cross against the heretics; men steadfast and admirable in every respect, at that time great, indeed leading luminaries of the Church in France and in fact brothers by birth. They observed that a large body of crusaders had delayed their departure, and realised that the business of the faith was now in a critical phase, since this delay was prompting the enemies of the faith to vaunt their strength with more then their usual ferocity. They therefore gathered a force of as many knights as they could muster,[52] and with marvellous enthusiasm and courage set out against the heretics – ready not only to sacrifice their possessions but, if need be, to risk danger and death for themselves in the service of Jesus Christ. These men of God hastened directly to Carcassonne. On their arrival the Count of Montfort and his few companions rejoiced with exceeding great joy.[53] [423] The Bishops found the Count and our men at Fanjeaux,[54] near Carcassonne. Here they stayed a few days, after which the Count and the Bishops went to Muret near Carcassonne, which I have referred to previously.[55] From this base our men rode about before Toulouse, with the object of closely containing Christ's enemies. One knight, Alard de Strépy, and a few others, showing poor commitment to Christ's work, refused to accompany the Count.[56] Indeed his forces were inadequate to allow him to put Toulouse or any other well-defended place completely under siege, and he therefore decided to make frequent sorties around Toulouse with such forces as he had, with the object of destroying the numerous strong castles round Toulouse,

---

[49] More specifically, Philip Augustus decided during April 1213 to organise an expedition against King John of England, with an invasion scheduled for May. This was backed by Innocent III, who had excommunicated John in 1209 and declared the throne of England vacant, and Philip hoped to install his own son in John's place. In the event, on 13 May, John submitted to the Pope (see n. 50 to §394 above), and the invasion came to nothing. There are records of the presence at the English court of ambassadors from both Raymond of Toulouse and King Peter of Aragon at about this time (April/May 1213, details and sources given by G&L II, p. 113 n. 5), but there is no evidence either way to show whether or not John contemplated becoming actively involved against the crusaders. For Philip Augustus' general attitude to the Crusade see n. 65 to §72.

[50] Manasses de Seignelay, Bishop 1207–21; for corroboration of his presence on the Crusade see G&L II, p. 114 n. 1.

[51] William de Seignelay, Bishop 1207–20 (G&L II, p. 115 n. 1). The dean of his cathedral had been present with the crusaders at the siege of Penne the previous year, and had died there (see §331 above).

[52] Including Peter de Savary and Evrard de Brienne (G&L II, notes to pp. 114–15, cited above).

[53] Matthew 2, v. 10.

[54] De Montfort had been at Béziers on 1 May 1213, when he made an agreement with Bishop Bertrand (see *HGL* VIII, 637–8).

[55] See §356 above. Despite the arrival of some reinforcements, the crusaders still had insufficient strength to mount any serious attack on Toulouse, and hence chose to base themselves at Muret which was well fortified and provided a good base from which to harass the enemy and conduct raids against them, as described below.

[56] Alard de Strépy (from near Mons) was a vassal of the English king, who on 27 April sent a messenger to him, which may explain his want of enthusiasm; he returned home in the summer. See G&L II, p. 116 n. 3 for details.

cutting down the fruit trees and laying waste the crops and vineyards (harvest time was approaching). His campaign successfully achieved its objectives. The two Bishops constantly accompanied the Count, and exposed themselves to danger every day in the service of Christ. To the knights who accompanied them in the Lord's service they gave freely of their possessions; they ransomed captives and diligently performed their duties in the generous and pious spirit to be expected of such holy men. Since I cannot record every detail, I will summarise by recording that within a few days our men destroyed seventeen castles, laid waste the crops round Toulouse and cut down most of the vines and trees. I must also record that when our men were making their sorties before Toulouse, the men of Toulouse and their mercenaries, who outnumbered us two to one, frequently came out and harassed us from a distance, but fled at once whenever our men made to attack them.

[424] Among the castles destroyed by our people there was one near Toulouse which was weak and poorly fortified;[57] nevertheless three very worthy knights, Peter de Sissy, Simon the Saxon and Roger des Essarts[58] – who from the first had shared with the Count the burden of the war – asked the Count to hand the place over to them so that they might use it as a base to make sorties before Toulouse and harass the men of that city. The Count eventually yielded to their request, albeit with reluctance.

[425] About the time of the feast of the nativity of John the Baptist[59] the Count decided that his elder son Amaury should be created a knight. After consulting his followers he arranged for the ceremony to take place on the day of the feast at Castelnaudary between Toulouse and Carcassonne.

[426] Whilst the Count and his companions were so employed his brother Guy de Montfort was engaged in the siege of a *castrum* named Puycelsi in the diocese of Albi.[60] With him were the Abbot of Saint-Hubert in the diocese of Liège,[61] Count Baldwin (brother of the Count of Toulouse),[62] a few knights and

---

57 Pujol (mentioned in the *Chanson* II, 132 as Pujols), a small fortress about 13km south-east of Toulouse near Sainte-Foy-d'Aigrefeuille.
58 On Peter de Sissy, who had been granted Verdun-sur-Garonne by de Montfort in 1212, see n. 122 to §352 and n. 140 to §359 above. Simon the Saxon was from Normandy and had likewise been with the crusaders from 1209: see *Chanson* I, 52, p. 124, and 55, p. 130 for his presence at Carcassonne that year. Roger des Essarts, from the same area as his two companions, was similarly a crusader in 1209 (*Chanson* I, 36, p. 93). (See also G&L II, notes on pp. 118–19 for detailed references on these three.)
59 The feast day was 24 June 1213.
60 Puycelsi occupies a hilltop site high above the valley of the Vère on the south-western edge of the Grésigne plateau in the northern Albigeois. In 1180 it had passed under the control of Raymond V of Toulouse, becoming one of his strongholds in the Albigeois north of the Tarn. In June 1211 Puycelsi opened its gates to de Montfort, who left a token garrison there (*Chanson* I, 75, p. 182), but in the autumn of that year, after the battle of Castelnaudary, it was one of many places repossessed by Raymond VI (*Chanson* I, 110, p. 244). De Montfort retook Puycelsi in early May 1212, a few weeks before the siege of Saint-Antonin (*Chanson* I, 112, p. 250), its inhabitants having fled, but at some point later that year it was reoccupied by its inhabitants and again rebelled against the crusaders. By early 1213, together with nearby Penne d'Albigeois (see §428) and Montauban (§§352 and 359), it was one of very few places still in Raymond VI's hands apart from Toulouse itself.
61 Abbot Theodoric, 1212–42 (G&L II, p. 120 n. 4).
62 Baldwin (on whom see above §§235–6) was based at Bruniquel, which lies about 10km north of Puycelsi, at the point where the Vère joins the Aveyron.

numerous crusaders on foot. They erected siege-engines and mounted strong attacks on the *castrum*. Our adversaries inside, who were numerous and well protected by fortifications, defended to their utmost. The huge force of mercenaries from Toulouse made frequent attacks against our army outside the fortress and did all they could to harm us. [427] One day the Counts of Toulouse, Comminges and Foix, and a seneschal of the King of Aragon,[63] also a huge body of mercenaries, operating under a common plan, came to the besieged *castrum* to attack our men. When they approached the place and came near our army, the King's seneschal went inside with the idea of joining with the defenders to attack our petraries. A large body of knights went into the *castrum* with him. The three Counts and their companions now proposed to mount an attack on the army from within the *castrum*. Here I should mention that because of their small numbers our men had laid siege to the place from one side only. At first light the seneschal and the defenders came out and rushed towards our siege-engines to destroy them. Seeing what was happening William of Ecureuil,[64] a knight of great courage who was with the army, mounted his horse, attacked the enemy and valiantly defended our siege-engines. Guy de Montfort, Count Baldwin and some other knights, few in number, now arrived to join in defending the petraries, showing great determination. What more? The enemy at once returned to the fortress, leaving the petraries unharmed. When they saw what had happened, the Counts of Toulouse, Comminges and Foix withdrew without making an attack. [428] After Guy had kept up the siege for some considerable time, the crusaders with him, having completed the period of service decreed by the papal legates (forty days), left the siege and returned home. Left almost alone, Guy was compelled to abandon the siege, but not before the enemy had reached an agreement with him; they would not attack the Christian faith, and if Penne d'Albigeois[65] (which was hostile to us) were to surrender or be captured, they would themselves surrender to the Count of Montfort without further argument.

[429] Having raised the siege of Puycelsi, Guy of Montfort went off to join his brother the Count, who for his part was hurrying to Castelnaudary for the induction of his son Amaury into the knighthood (which I mentioned earlier), since the feast of the nativity of John the Baptist was now approaching. Barons and knights had also arrived from the Count's domains for the ceremony. I will describe in detail the procedure used for the Count's son's installation as a knight of Christ, since it was new and without precedent.[66]

---

[63] William-Raymond of Montcada, Seneschal of Catalonia (see G&L II, p. 121 n. 1, and cf. n. 27 to §412 above).

[64] See also §179 for this knight at the siege of Termes in 1210.

[65] Penne d'Albigeois, about 12km north of Puycelsi, had been unsuccessfully attacked by a force led by Guy de Montfort in 1212 (§327 above).

[66] Peter himself was not present, being with his uncle Guy in northern France, but he was clearly struck by the ceremony. The practice of dubbing to knighthood, in which a young man became a knight, involved the ceremonial handing over of a sword and belt to the new knight and the girding on of the sword. Religious elements in the ceremony were not new: it was for instance common by this time for a knight's sword to be blessed before girding on, while there were already precedents for ecclesiastical involvement in the ceremony itself. But the unusual feature here seems to have been the high degree of ecclesiastical

[430] *The Count's eldest son becomes a knight.* In the year of the Incarnation of the Word 1213, the noble Count of Montfort and numerous of his barons and knights gathered together at Castelnaudary on the feast of the nativity of John the Baptist. The Count was accompanied by the two venerable Bishops already mentioned,[67] and some crusader knights. Our most Christian Count wished the Bishop of Orleans to appoint his son a knight of Christ and personally hand him the belt of knighthood. The Bishop for some time resisted this request but was at length vanquished by the prayers of the Count and our people, and yielded to their request. As it was summertime and Castelnaudary was too small to hold the huge crowd in attendance (not least because it had previously been destroyed once or even twice) the Count had a number of pavilions erected on a pleasant level place nearby. [431] On the day of the feast the Bishop of Orleans donned his robes of office to celebrate a solemn Mass in one of the pavilions. Everyone, knights as well as clergy, gathered to hear the Mass. As the Bishop stood at the altar performing the Mass, the Count took Amaury, his eldest son, by his right hand, and the Countess by his left hand; they approached the altar and offered him to the Lord, requesting the Bishop to appoint him a knight in the service of Christ. The Bishops of Orleans and Auxerre, bowing before the altar, put the belt of knighthood round the youth, and with great devotion led the *Veni Creator Spiritus.* Indeed a novel and unprecedented form of induction into knighthood! Who that was present could refrain from tears? In this way, with great ceremony, Amaury became a knight.

[432] A few days after the ceremony the Count left Castelnaudary with the Bishops and his son and made a mounted sortie near Toulouse. After capturing a few men from the city they went to Muret. There the Count was joined by some nobles he had summoned from Gascony; the Count desired them all to render homage to his son, which they did.

[433] *The Count in Gascony.* A few days later the Count left Muret for Gascony. He took his son with him to hand over to him those parts of Gascony which had already been taken,[68] hoping also that he would with God's help gain control of the rest of the area. [434] The Bishops remained at Muret, intending to return home two days later; they had now completed their forty days service on the Crusade, in admirable fashion – as was to be expected of men so admirable in every respect – and had made a great contribution in terms of effort and expenditure. So on the third day they left Muret and went to Carcassonne. The Toulousains and their fellow enemies of the faith saw that our Count was on his way to Gascony with his son, and that the Bishops and the crusaders with them were on their way home. Now that they could safely do so, they came out of Toulouse with a large army and laid siege to certain of our knights – Peter de Sissy, Simon

---

ceremonial introduced by de Montfort, no doubt intended to emphasise the sacred character of his and his son's role as warriors in Christ's cause. For a discussion, see M. Bloch, *Feudal Society*, pp. 312–16, and M. H. Keen, *Chivalry* (New Haven and London, 1989), pp. 74–6.

67 The Bishops of Auxerre and Orleans: see §422.
68 In the autumn of 1212, after the siege of Moissac: see §358 above.

the Saxon and Roger des Essarts – who, as I have recorded, were holding a weakly defended castle near Toulouse.[69] Our adversaries went to the place and attacked our forces vigorously; the defenders did all they could to ward off the attacks. After a few days they realised they would not be able to withstand the siege for long, and that they could not expect prompt relief with the Count having gone to Gascony and the Bishops and their fellow crusaders on their way home. After great tribulations they surrendered to the enemy, having established the condition – with firm guarantees – that their adversaries would preserve their lives and limbs. [435] Here I must record that when the Bishops of Orleans and Auxerre (already at Carcassonne) heard that our knights were under siege near Toulouse, they used all their powers to persuade the crusaders with them to turn back and help the beleaguered knights. Such praiseworthy and valiant men in every respect! All agreed; they left Carcassonne and rushed to give aid to the besieged. As they approached Castelnaudary, they were met with a report, which was true, that our men had already been taken by the forces from Toulouse, and they returned sadly to Carcassonne. Our enemies took the captured knights to Toulouse; at once showing themselves worse than infidels[70] and without any regard for their sworn undertakings to preserve their lives and limbs, they had our knights dragged by horses about the city streets and then hanged from gibbets. What treachery, what cruelty![71]

[436] The Count of Montfort (who, as previously recorded, had taken his son to Gascony and with God's help had already captured numerous strong *castra*) also heard that the forces from Toulouse and their supporters had laid siege to his knights near Toulouse. Leaving his son in Gascony[72] with a few knights he also rushed to their aid. Before he could reach them they had been captured and taken to Toulouse. Meanwhile his son Amaury with his small force applied himself vigorously to attacking and capturing *castra* in Gascony. Several bishops and some Gascon nobles, supporters of their lord the Count and Christianity, came to help him.

[437] I think it will now be well worthwhile to say a little about the general

[69] Le Pujol: see above, §424. The siege, which took place in July 1213, is also recounted in some detail in the *Chanson* (II, 132–4, pp. 4–10), and by William of Puylaurens (XIX). It is at this point that the authorship of the *Chanson* changes, becoming now the work of an anonymous poet, probably originating in or around Toulouse. His account makes clear the concern of the Toulousains (amongst whom there were now great expectations of deliverance from their troubles by King Peter of Aragon) at the threat to their harvest posed by the crusaders in Pujol, only 13km from the city, especially given the depredations already inflicted by de Montfort and described by Peter in §423 above.

[70] Cf. I Timothy 5, v. 8.

[71] The accounts by the *Chanson* and William of Puylaurens differ in describing the outcome of the siege. The *Chanson* says Pujol was taken by assault and that the whole garrison was either put to the sword or hanged. William of Puylaurens says that Roger des Essarts was killed during the fighting; he then agrees with Peter that the garrison surrendered on a promise of safety, although Simon the Saxon was at this point killed by the 'crowd' ('*a vulgo subito interfectus*') – probably indicating the rank and file, as opposed to the knights and their attendants, but perhaps including camp followers. Again he agrees with Peter that the survivors of the garrison were taken as captives to Toulouse, but says that a mob ('*populari concursu*') came to slaughter them; they were then dragged like carrion outside the city.

[72] He recalled him later, probably around the end of July: see §443.

situation in France at this time, and also about the conduct of the French in relation to the holy business of the faith. It will help in this if I recapitulate my account of earlier events.[73]

[438] *Recapitulation of earlier events.* In the previous winter King Peter of Aragon sent his envoys to Rome,[74] falsely insinuating to the Pope that the Count of Montfort had unjustly robbed the Counts of Foix and Comminges and Gaston de Béarn of their territories. Through the same envoys he stated that these three nobles had never been heretics – even though it was abundantly clear that they had always supported heretics and had opposed the Holy Church with all their might. He also suggested to the Supreme Pontiff that the business of the faith had been successfully concluded, with the heretics utterly put to flight and all driven out from the whole Albigensian area;[75] so that the Pope would need to withdraw completely the indulgence he had granted to the crusaders who had gone to fight the heretics, and employ it instead against the pagans in Spain, or as a means of bringing aid to the Holy Land. What unheard-of impiety, masquerading as piety! The King argued in this way not out of concern for the problems and difficulties of the Holy Church, but because – as his subsequent actions showed so clearly – he wished to stifle and bring to a speedy end Christ's business, the Crusade against the heretics, which had been marvellously advanced for so many years, with immense labour and much effusion of blood. [439] The Supreme Pontiff was too ready to believe the King's false representations, and too easily yielded to his requests; he wrote to the Count of Montfort, instructing him immediately to hand back to that villainous and damned trio, the Counts of Foix and Comminges and Gaston de Béarn, the territories he had seized from them by God's just judgment, with the help of the crusaders. He also revoked the indulgence he had granted to crusaders proceeding against the heretics.[76] He also sent Robert de Courçon, an Englishman,[77] as his legate to France, with letters and indulgences,[78] with the object of advocating help for the Kingdom of Jerusalem,[79] personally and through the agency of other clerics. On his arrival in France the legate began to perform his allotted task with great energy. He toured the country,[80] held meetings of archbishops and bishops, instructed preachers and advanced the

---

[73] Effectively, those covered in §§398–421 above. This recapitulation adds some details.

[74] See §399.

[75] I.e. as elsewhere and several times in the next few sections, the whole territory pervaded by heresy and involved in the Crusade, and not just the Albigeois (see Appendix A (iii)).

[76] I.e. Innocent's letters of 15–18 January 1213: see n. 2 to §399 and Appendix F(iv).

[77] Often called Robert Curzon in English, he was a native of Kedleston, Derbyshire. He became a canon of Noyon, then of Paris and finally a Cardinal-preacher with the title 'of St Stephen of the Coelian Hill'. His vigorous preaching in the spring of 1213 was instigated by Innocent, who by this time was intent on organising a new Crusade to the Holy Land. Robert was later, in 1214, to play an important role in the Albigensian Crusade: see §§494, 508, 513 and 523. In 1218, as a Cardinal Legate, he was sent by Pope Honorius III to take part in the Crusade against Damietta, but he died soon after arriving. See also G&L II, p. 129 n. 1, and G&M, p. 169 n. 5.

[78] These letters are summarised in Potthast, 4710–12, 4725 and 4727.

[79] Latin 'terre Jerosolimitane'.

[80] For details of his preaching see G&L II, p. 130 n. 2 and p. 131 notes.

cause of a Crusade to the Holy Land[81] by every means available to him. He withdrew the preachers working for the Crusade against the heretics[82] from that task, and instead instructed them to preach the Crusade to the Holy Land. It thus seemed to human eyes that the Crusade against the pestilential heretics had been almost abandoned. In the whole of France there was no one save the Bishop of Carcassonne, a man most distinguished for his piety, who was still working for the business of the faith; he toured France unceasingly and did everything in his powers to advance that business and ensure that it was not forgotten.[83]

After this discussion of the state of affairs in France, let us return to the main thread of our recapitulation of events.

[440] After the issue of the letter in which the Pope instructed the Count of Montfort to restore the occupied territories to the three nobles referred to above, our most Christian Count and the bishops of the Albigensian area sent their own envoys to the Pope – the Bishop of Comminges, the Archdeacon of Paris and an Abbot from Clairac, all prudent and steadfast men; also two clerics whom the Pope had earlier sent to the Count as legates *a latere*, Master Thedisius from Pisa (who was supporting the business of the faith with marvellous enthusiasm), and Peter Marc,[84] who had been one of the Pope's secretaries and came originally from the diocese of Nîmes. On their arrival at Rome they found the attitude of the Curia difficult and somewhat hostile, since the King's envoys, some of whom were still present, had succeeded in gaining the support of almost everyone in the Curia by their false representations. [441] At last, after great efforts by our envoys and numerous audiences,[85] the Pope learnt the true state of affairs from his own appointed messengers. He issued a letter[86] to the King in which he reproved him sternly for taking the people of Toulouse and other heretics under his protection; he strictly enjoined him in the name of the Holy Spirit to break with them without delay and to afford them no counsel, help or favours for the future. He further complained that the King had used misrepresentation of the facts to

---

[81] Latin '*terrae sanctae negotium*', 'the business of the Holy Land'; so also in the next sentence.
[82] '*Negotium fidei contra hereticos*'; similarly in the next sentence.
[83] Guy remained in France for a year (see §508 below). It is clear that the drying up of new recruitment to support de Montfort during 1213 caused him very serious problems: see below, §442. During 1213 Innocent III himself became increasingly preoccupied with his plans for a new Lateran Council, and on 11 April he issued bulls calling the Council to meet on 1 November 1215 (*PL* 216, 823–7, '*Vineam Domini*'). His other preoccupation was his plan for a new Crusade to the Holy Land, which he set in motion through his bulls of April 1213 (*PL* 216, 817–22, '*Quia Major*') which were issued throughout Christendom. He cancelled future remissions in regard to the Midi and Spain on the grounds that the need for them was no longer pressing, but said he would reinstate them should the need arise in future and allowed those applying to crusaders in the South and in Spain to remain in force ('*remissiones et indulgentias hactenus a nobis concessas procedentibus in Hispaniam contra Mauros vel contra haereticos in Provinciam revocamus . . . Concedimus tamen ut hujusmodi remissiones et indulgentiae apud provinciales remaneant et Hispanos*'). Some months after he had rescinded the suspension of the Albigensian Crusade we find him instructing the Dean of Speyer to divert to the East crusaders who had taken the cross against the heretics of the Midi (9 September 1213, Potthast, 4807).
[84] For the envoys and Peter Marc see §398 and §400 above.
[85] The envoys from the crusaders probably arrived in Rome in March 1213, so their lobbying of Innocent must have gone on over several months if the resulting letters were not issued until 21 May.
[86] I.e. the letter of 21 May 1213, recorded in §§401–411 above. For the chronology see n. 1 to §367.

secure the papal letter ordering the restitution of territories to the Counts of Comminges and Foix and to Gaston de Béarn. He went on to revoke this letter on the grounds that it had been obtained falsely; and to instruct the aforesaid nobles and the citizens of Toulouse to render satisfaction to God and be reunited with the Church in line with the advice and wishes of the Archbishop of Narbonne, legate of the Holy See, and the Bishop of Toulouse; should they be unwilling to do so, the Pope intended to renew his indulgences and arouse the peoples against the men of Toulouse, their supporters and defenders. After procuring the letter our envoys left the Curia.

[442] The noble Count of Montfort and his companions were now faced with a serious crisis. They were virtually alone and deserted,[87] for few if any crusaders were now coming to their aid from France; as I have recorded, the business of the faith had been almost forgotten because of the new preaching campaign undertaken by the legate the Pope had sent to promote the Crusade to the Holy Land, which meant that hardly any crusaders were taking the cross against the pestilential heretics. Besides this the King of France was involved in internal wars,[88] and on this account would not allow those knights who had earlier taken the cross against the heretics to make their preparations to fulfil their vows. To cap all this, reports were current throughout the Albigensian area that the King of Aragon was gathering his army together with the arrogant intention of invading our territory and driving out the knights of Christ.

[443] In this crisis our Count sent to his son, who was in Gascony engaged on the siege of a *castrum* named Roquefort,[89] to instruct him to abandon the siege and join him with all speed; he was indeed afraid that if the King invaded Gascony with his army he might be able to seize his son, who had very few Frenchmen with him. But the Lord Jesus, our ever-present helper in times of trouble, so ordained matters that the Count's son was able to obey his father's orders and yet avoid the shame of raising the siege, for on the very evening that the Count's letter arrived the enemy besieged in Roquefort asked for peace. They were ready to hand over the *castrum* and their prisoners (almost sixty in number) on condition that they themselves should be allowed to leave unharmed. Under the pressure of necessity, the terms were agreed by Amaury, who left a few knights to garrison the place and hastened to join his father. [444] The whole of the Albigensian area was now in a confused and unstable state. The enemies of the faith and the King of Aragon's knights, who by now had spent a considerable time at Toulouse, were visiting our fortresses and inviting the inhabitants to desert and surrender. Most of them did go over to our adversaries because of the promise of protection offered by the King of Aragon, whose arrival they eagerly awaited. In this way we lost numerous large and strong *castra*.

---

[87] Latin '*quasi soli et pene penitus desolati*'; cf. the position after the departure of the Duke of Burgundy in 1209, '*solus et quasi desolatus*' (§115 above), and the use of a similar phrase in §187.

[88] The Count of Flanders (Ferrand of Portugal) and the Count of Boulogne (Renaud of Dammartin), alarmed at French expansion, had allied with King John of England. In the second half of 1213, after the abandonment of his plans to invade England, Philip Augustus mounted a campaign against Flanders.

[89] Roquefort-sur-Garonne, about 20km east of Saint-Gaudens.

[445] At this time the noble Count of Montfort and the bishops of the Albigensian area sent two abbots to the King;[90] they took with them the letter issued by the Pope and his instructions.[91] They begged him to stop helping the heretics and attacking Christianity, as the Pope had ordered. The King, deceitful as ever, gave the false reply that he would gladly fulfil all the Supreme Pontiff's instructions;[92] but despite his constant assurances to this effect he had no intention of recalling the knights he had sent to Toulouse the previous winter, whom he was employing together with the Toulousains and other heretics to attack Christianity. Instead he sent many more knights to Toulouse, and summoned all the knights he could muster from his own country. What is more, we have heard that he pledged a large part of his lands as security for funds to pay mercenaries to help the heretics and to join his attack on the Christian faith. What deceitful cruelty! What cruel treachery! Whilst he was using all his resources to gather an army against us, he was promising willingly to obey the Pope's orders to abandon the excommunicants and heretics, so as to ensure our safety and security. The later tide of events proved that there is no wisdom nor counsel against the Lord.[93]

[90] This attempt to negotiate with King Peter suggests that the legates now regarded de Montfort's position as critical. The embassy is described in the report to the Pope written immediately after the battle of Muret by Mascaron, the Provost of Toulouse (see n. 28 to §456 below). The report confirms Peter's account, but in more detail. The two abbots sent to King Peter were William, Abbot of Lagrasse, and Gerald, Abbot of Caunes. They left for Spain on 24 July, met the King at Lérida and returned to Fanjeaux on 16 August.
[91] Presumably the copies of Innocent's letter of 21 May to King Peter, reproduced in §§401–11 above, and on which see n. 18 to §405.
[92] King Peter clearly had no intention of treating with the legates, but his response to the embassy to the effect that he would obey Innocent may also in part reflect the contents of a letter from Innocent to Peter which had probably reached him by the time the embassy did. The letter, dated 4 July 1213 (*PL* 216, 888), confirmed a bull of March 1095 issued by Urban II which provided that the Kings of Aragon could only be excommunicated by the Pope himself, and not by any legate or other prelate. At the same time Innocent firmly reminded Peter of his obligations to the Pope and his duties as a vassal of the Holy See. Whilst the King was clearly failing to act as instructed by Innocent in his letters of 21 May 1213, he no doubt thought that he could safely ignore the legates and that by the time any further approach to Innocent could be made, he would have defeated the crusaders and be able to present the Pope with a *fait accompli*.
[93] Proverbs 21, v. 30.

[XV. §§446–486, August–September 1213: *Campaign and battle of Muret –
Peter's account (§§446–466) – the prelates' account (§§468–483) – negotiations with the Toulousains after the battle.*]

[446] *The King of Aragon enters Gascony.* At this time[1] the King of Aragon
determined to bring to birth the mischief he had long ago conceived against
Christ and His followers. He left his territory with an enormous crowd of cavalry[2] and entered Gascony – hoping to hand back to the heretics and bring under
his own lordship all the lands which had been gained by God's grace and the help
of the crusaders. Having crossed the Gascon boundary he made towards Toulouse. Numerous fortresses in Gascony which were on his route surrendered to
him in fear. What more? Reports of the King's approach spread throughout the
whole area. The local inhabitants rejoice, many defect, the rest prepare to defect.

[447] After passing several *castra* the ungodly King reached Muret,[3] a notable
but somewhat poorly fortified *castrum* about three leagues from Toulouse. Although the walls and ditches were inadequate, the place was defended by about
thirty knights and a few footsoldiers, left there by the Count of Montfort as a
garrison – this because the Toulousains were intent on attacking the place more
than any other of our strongholds; and indeed the garrison was more effective
than any others in harassing the Toulousains. On his arrival at Toulouse[4] the
King mustered the citizens, and the other heretics, with a view to laying siege to
Muret.

[448] *Siege and glorious battle of Muret.*[5] In the year 1213 of the Incarnation of

---

[1] August 1213. The King was at Huesca on 22–23 August, and at Lascuarre (just north of Benabarre) on
25 August: *Itinerario*, 103–4, cited by G&L II, p. 138 n. 1. The most direct route to Toulouse from Lascuarre
would have taken him across the Benasque pass (Col de Vénasque), and then down the valley of the
Garonne. However, this was a difficult crossing of the Pyrenees, and it is therefore often assumed that if he
did take this route, the bulk of his troops must have taken easier routes, with forces from Aragon perhaps
going by way of the Col du Somport, and those from Catalonia across the Col de Puymorens. See the
discussions in Roquebert II, pp. 170–1, and E. Martin-Chabot, *Chanson* II, p. 12 n. 1.

[2] The *Chanson* confirms the substantial scale of the King's expedition, saying (II, 132, p. 2) that he and
his vassals had had to borrow money to equip themselves, and describing the force as comprising 'the elite
of Catalonia and the best warriors in Aragon' (II, 135, p. 12). On the question of the size of the armies at
Muret, see below, §460.

[3] On Muret, see n. 131 to §356 above. As Peter says below, it was being used by the crusaders as a base
from which to harass the Toulousains: see §423 above, and cf. William of Puylaurens (XX), who says that
the crusader garrison at Muret was causing Toulouse considerable trouble ('*civitatem Tholose plurimum
infestabat*'). King Peter arrived there by 8 September.

[4] William of Puylaurens, XX, also says that the King went to Toulouse, where he took counsel with the
counts and leading citizens. However, according to the *Chanson* (II, 135, p. 12) he simply pitched camp at
Muret and asked Raymond VI to come from Toulouse and join him there. Whatever the case, the forces of
the Counts of Toulouse, Comminges and Foix, and the militia of Toulouse, had joined King Peter's army at
Muret by 10 September.

[5] For the campaign and battle of Muret the main sources are as follows. (1) The account of the prelates,
written on 13 September 1213, the day after the battle, which Peter reproduces in §§468–483 below. (2)
Peter's own account in §§456–466. He himself was not present at Muret but was with his uncle Guy in
northern France (§508). Hence his account was probably written soon after his return to the army in May
1214 and is no doubt based partly on the prelates' account and partly on the eye-witness testimony of

our Lord Jesus Christ, on 10 September, the third feast day after the nativity of the Blessed Virgin Mary,[6] King Peter of Aragon joined with the Counts of Toulouse, Comminges and Foix and laid siege to Muret with a large army drawn from Aragon and Toulouse. Muret was situated on the River Garonne, three leagues from Toulouse in the direction of Gascony.[7] With their first assault after reaching the *castrum* our opponents captured the first bourg – our men were too few in numbers to defend it and had retired to the other rather stronger bourg.[8] However, the enemy soon quitted the first bourg.[9] Our knights in Muret now sent to the Count of Montfort to tell him that they were besieged and asking him to come to their aid, since they had few if any supplies and did not dare leave the place. [449] The Count was at Fanjeaux, about eight leagues[10] from Muret; he had already decided to go to Muret and take men and supplies to strengthen the

prominent crusaders, including, as he mentions in §452, Simon de Montfort himself. (3) The account in the *Chanson* (II, 135–41, pp. 12–36), believed to have been written about fifteen years after the event, but not by an eye-witness, although it seems clear that the author will have talked to eye-witnesses, especially amongst the Toulousains and King Peter's troops. (4) The account of William of Puylaurens (XX–XXI), written probably fifty or sixty years after the event. It is inaccurate at least in placing Guy of les Vaux-de-Cernay in Muret at this time, but like the *Chanson* it gives more attention to events involving the southern-ers than the first two accounts, and more detail than is usual for this author. Moreover, in describing the battle William mentions as a source the younger Raymond of Toulouse (later Count Raymond VII – see n. to §463), who was an eye-witness, and his account is therefore important; a full translation is given in Appendix I. (5) Finally there is the *Llibre dels feyts* of King Peter's son, James I of Aragon, ch. 9 of which briefly recounts the battle. James was only five at the time of the battle of Muret, and while he will have heard of the battle from surviving members of his father's retinue, his account adds little except for its explanation of the reasons for the defeat. His account is translated in J. Forster, as *The Chronicle of James I king of Aragon, surnamed the Conqueror (written by himself)* (London, 1883), and is printed in J. Anglade, *La bataille de Muret d'après la Chanson de la Croisade* (Toulouse, 1913); for references to it see notes to §§459, 460 and 466. Only these accounts seem genuinely to derive directly from contemporary eye-witness evidence; by contrast the contemporary account of William the Breton seems to rely on second or third hand sources and to owe much to his imagination (see e.g. n. 38 to §460 and n. 46 to §463). For a discussion of these sources see Roquebert II, pp. 195–8. Despite differences in detail the principal accounts are broadly consistent, and indeed the overall picture of what took place is reasonably clear. However, none of these accounts have much to say on the topography of the battle, and there remain particular uncertainties about precisely where the various southern forces had encamped, and where exactly the battle between the crusaders and King Peter was fought. Although many attempts have been made to analyse events in detail, in the end reconstructions must at best be tentative given the absence of clear and detailed information in the primary sources. The reliability of any secondary accounts adding to or differing from the principal sources must be suspect. For accounts of the battle see Belperron, pp. 267–82, and Roquebert II, ch. 9, and the bibliography in his notes to that chapter; see also bibliography in G&L II, p. 139 n. 3. Some comments on certain aspects of the battle will be found in footnotes to the following sections.
[6] The dates of the Muret campaign and the battle (Tuesday 10 to Thursday 12 September 1213) are clearly indicated at various points by Peter and by the prelates' letter, §§468–483 below (see n. 58 to §469).
[7] About 20km south-west of Toulouse.
[8] For the layout of Muret at this time see map 5 on p. xx. The outer town is called the '*primum castri burgum*' by Peter; this was the 'new town', on the western side of Muret. It was called '*castrum novum*' in a document of 1165, and is described as the '*vila nova*' (French *Villeneuve*) in the *Chanson* (II, 137). To its east was the 'old town' (the *vetus castrum*, or bourg, here called the '*aliud burgum*', literally 'other bourg', by Peter) which contained at its north-eastern corner the castle. In later sections Peter does not clearly distinguish between the two. For discussion and bibliography, see Roquebert II, ch. 9, and notes.
[9] According to the *Chanson* (II, 137, p. 18), this withdrawal was on the orders of King Peter, who did not want Muret and its small garrison to be taken yet. He had news that de Montfort was on his way, and he wanted to let him enter Muret and thus, as he hoped, trap him and all his forces and then destroy them altogether.
[10] About 65km south-east of Muret

defences of the *castrum*, since it was suspected that the King would come to besiege it. On the night before he had decided to leave Fanjeaux, our Countess (who was with him) had a dream which terrified her; it seemed to her that blood flowed in great quantities from both her arms. In the morning she related the dream to the Count and told him it had disturbed her deeply. The Count replied: 'You speak as one of the foolish women.[11] Do you think I am going to rely on dreams and auguries like a Spaniard? To be sure, even if I had dreamt last night that I was going to be killed in this battle I am setting out for, I would go all the more confidently and gladly, so as to refute utterly the stupidity of the Spaniards and the people of this land, who set such store on dreams and auguries.'[12] So saying the Count left Fanjeaux and hastened with his men to Saverdun.[13] [450] Whilst he was on his way a messenger from the knights besieged in Muret met him with a letter reporting that the King of Aragon had strengthened the siege; whereupon all on our side were quite delighted since they could scent the prospect of victory. The Count at once ordered his Countess, who had left Fanjeaux and was on her way to Carcassonne, to send as many knights as she could to help him. On her arrival at Carcassonne the Countess mustered as many knights as she was able and also asked a noble from France, the Viscount of Corbeil,[14] who was starting on his way home after completing his forty days' service on the Crusade, to return and go to help our Count. He gladly agreed and said he would willingly go back. Accordingly the Viscount and the few knights sent by the Countess to help the Count went to Fanjeaux. Our Count and his companions made for Saverdun and found themselves near a Cistercian abbey at Boulbonne; the Count made a diversion to the abbey and entered the church to pray and to commend himself and his soldiers to the prayers of the monks.[15] After prolonged and devoted prayer he drew the sword he was wearing and placed it on the altar, saying: 'Loving Lord, Bountiful Jesus! You have chosen me, unworthy as I am, to fight your battles. Today I take my arms from your altar, so that as I prepare to fight your battles, I receive from you the instruments of battle.' He then left and went with his comrades to Saverdun.

[451] The Count was accompanied by seven bishops and three abbots, whom the Archbishop of Narbonne, legate of the Apostolic See, had gathered together to discuss terms for peace with the King of Aragon.[16] Also with him were about

---

[11] Job 2, v. 10.

[12] Cf. above, §212, for Raymond VI's alleged belief in auguries.

[13] On Tuesday 10 September.

[14] Payen (G&L II, p. 142 n. 1).

[15] On Boulbonne, which lay about 8km east of Saverdun, see n. 71 to §284 above. For an account by William of Puylaurens (XX) of a meeting between Simon and Maurin, the Sacrist of Pamiers, see Appendix I. The incident is discussed in Roquebert II, pp. 178–80.

[16] These prelates are listed in §470 below. The bishops were Fulk of Toulouse, Arnold of Nîmes, Raymond of Uzès, Peter-Raymond of Lodève, Raymond of Agde, Bertrand of Béziers, and Garsia of Comminges; the abbots were Berengar of Saint-Thibery, Peter of Clairac, and Raymond of Villemagne. According to the account written by Mascaron the Provost of Toulouse (for which see n. 28 to §456) Arnold Amalric was not able to accompany them because he fell ill. Peter refers only briefly here to the attempts by Arnold Amalric and Fulk to negotiate with King Peter at this time, but it is clear that the prelates made a number of attempts to do so. After the embassy of the Abbots of Caunes and Lagrasse to Aragon in July (see §445

thirty knights, lately arrived from France to fulfil their vows as crusaders. Amongst these was a young knight who was the Count's half-brother on his mother's side, William of Barres.[17] Truly this was the Lord's work! [452] When he reached Saverdun the Count summoned the knights who had accompanied him and sought their advice as to his course of action. He himself was extremely keen (as I heard later from his own lips) to go into Muret that very night – he was, as befitted so faithful a leader, very anxious about the well-being of his men be-sieged in the *castrum*. However, the others were for staying that night in Saver-dun, since their horses were hungry and weary; in particular they pointed out that they might have to fight the enemy on their way to Muret. Somewhat unwillingly the Count agreed – it was his way always to act in accordance with any advice he received.

[453] Next day[18] at dawn the Count summoned his chaplain,[19] made his confession and drew up his will, which he signed and sealed and sent to the monastery at Boulbonne, with instructions that if he were to meet his death in battle the will should be sent to Rome to be confirmed by the Pope. As full daylight arrived, the bishops in Saverdun and the Count and his men gathered at the church. One of the bishops put on his sacred robes to celebrate Mass in honour of the Blessed Virgin Mary. During the Mass, by candlelight, the bishops united in excommunicating the Count of Toulouse and his son; the Count of Foix and his son; the Count of Comminges; and all their supporters, helpers and defenders. Beyond doubt the King of Aragon was included in this sentence; although the bishops deliberately avoided referring to him by name[20] he was in fact excommunicated not merely because he was a helper and defender of the three Counts, but also because he was the head and originator of all evil being done at Muret.

[454] After the celebration of Mass, the Count and his men made their confes-sions, armed themselves and left Saverdun. They drew up their forces in three lines on level ground[21] nearby, in the name of the Holy and Indivisible Trinity.[22] They then moved forward to a *castrum* named Auterive, midway between

---

above), Bishop Fulk wrote directly to the Toulousains on 1 September from Fanjeaux, urging them to submit, but received no reply (see *Chanson* II, pp. 22–3 n. 1). He is also said to have written other letters which do not survive, and with de Montfort's army at Saverdun on 10 September, Fulk tried again to negotiate, and wrote both to King Peter and the Toulousains: details of these attempted negotiations are given in the prelates' letter, §§471–2 below. See also §456 and §§473–5 for negotiations when de Montfort arrived at Muret.

[17] William IV of Barres. His mother Amicia of Leicester first married Simon de Montfort, father of our Simon, but on becoming a widow she then married William III of Barres, some time before 13 January 1188 (see Cokayne, *Complete Peerage*, vol. VII, pp. 537–40, and see also Appendix C). His presence at Muret is also mentioned by the *Chanson* (II, 139, p. 26) and William of Puylaurens (XX).

[18] I.e. Wednesday 11 September 1213.

[19] Clarin or Clairin, chaplain and later chancellor of Simon de Montfort, appears in numerous contem-porary documents: G&L II, p. 144 n. 3 give details. He later became Bishop of Carcassonne (1226–48).

[20] This may have been because the bishops were aware that in July 1213 Innocent III had confirmed a privilege whereby the Kings of Aragon could only be excommunicated by the Pope himself: see *Pl.* 216, 888 and n. 92 to §445 above.

[21] '*Planicie*'; see n. 44 to §462.

[22] This tactic of using three formations was to be used in the battle of Muret itself (see §462 below).

Saverdun and Muret.[23] Thence they proceeded to a place[24] between Auterive and Muret which was difficult to go through. They expected the enemy to confront them here because the place was marshy and the road narrow and waterlogged. There was a church nearby, and the Count, as was his custom, went into the church to pray. It was raining heavily at the time, much to the distress of our troops, but as our Count, the knight of Jesus Christ, began to pray, the rain stopped and the clouds gave way to clear skies. Boundless bounty of the Creator! The Count rose from his prayers and our men passed through the difficult terrain without any impediment from the enemy.

[455] Our forces marched on until they approached Muret from the nearer side of the River Garonne.[25] The King of Aragon and his forces were besieging the *castrum* from the opposite side of the river, increased in numbers above the sand of the sea.[26] Our knights, ever eager for the fray, urged the Count to enter the *castrum* and join battle with the enemy that day; the Count, however, did not wish to do so, since evening was approaching and our knights, as well as their mounts, were weary whereas the enemy were fresh. Moreover, the Count wished to display humility and to talk peace with the King and beg him not to go against the Church and join with Christ's enemies. For these reasons the Count did not wish battle to be joined that day.

[456] *The Count enters Muret.* Accordingly, our men crossed over a bridge[27] and entered Muret. At once our bishops sent numerous envoys, several times, to the King, begging him to take pity on God's Holy Church. Displaying great obstinacy the King would not listen to their pleas or respond in conciliatory terms, as will be shown later.[28] During the night the Viscount of Corbeil and the small body of French knights, whom I referred to above,[29] arrived at Muret from Carcassonne, to the great delight of our Count and his comrades. I should make the point that there was only one day's supply of provisions in Muret for our forces. So matters stood on this night.

[457] Early next day[30] the Count went into his chapel in the castle[31] to hear

[23] Auterive, on the River Ariège, about 20km south-east of Muret. According to the prelates' account they halted here: see §472.
[24] Identified by G&L II, p. 146 n. 3 as Lagardelle, on the east bank of the River Lèze, about mid-way between Auterive and Muret.
[25] The crusaders approached from the south-east, and Muret lay on the opposite side of the Garonne. The Aragonese and Toulousain forces were encamped on the other side of the river, probably to the west of Muret. See map 5 on p. xx.
[26] Jeremiah 15, v. 8.
[27] The bridge over the Garonne, which gave entry to Muret at the eastern end of the Villeneuve, at the market place or *mercadal;* cf. *Chanson* II, 138, p. 22, which says that de Montfort entered '*per lo mercadal* '.
[28] For details see the account in the prelates' letter below, §§473–5, and G&L II, p. 148 n. 1. The bishops' efforts continued during the following morning: see §457. The attempted negotiations are also mentioned by William of Puylaurens (XX), see Appendix I, who says the King was unwilling to agree to a peace except on conditions which were unacceptable to the crusaders. Some details are also to be found in the report to the Pope, written on the day after the battle, by Mascaron the Provost of Toulouse which survived in incomplete form in the town library of Carpentras and is printed in G&L III, pp. 200–205.
[29] See §450.
[30] I.e. Thursday 12 September 1213.
[31] Latin '*basilicam suam que erat in munitione castri* '. It seems clear that this is a chapel within the castle at

Mass; the bishops and our knights went to the church in the bourg[32] so that they too could hear Mass. The Count afterwards left the castle and went to the bourg to consult with and take advice from his followers. During this time they were unarmed, since negotiations with the King for a truce were so to say still being carried on through the bishops. With the unanimous agreement of everyone on our side, the bishops decided to go to the King, barefoot, to beg him not to attack the Church. Then, after the bishops had despatched an envoy to announce their coming, a large detachment of the enemy, armed and mounted, arrived in the bourg where our men were;[33] the gates were open, since the Count had forbidden them to be closed. [458] Our Count then addressed the bishops in the following words: 'You see you are achieving nothing; rather, a tumult is made.[34] We have endured enough, more then enough. The time has come for you to allow us to fight.'[35] The circumstances compelled the bishops to heed his words and agree. Our men left the meeting place and went to their several lodgings to put on their armour. As the Count was going into the castle to put on his armour and passing in front of his chapel, he looked inside and saw the Bishop of Uzès[36] celebrating Mass and reciting the *Dominus vobiscum*, after the Gospel reading and before the offertory. Our most Christian Count ran inside, knelt before the Bishop, took his hands and said: 'Today I offer my soul and body to God and to you.' What princely devotion! He then entered the castle and put on his armour; he then returned to the Bishop in the chapel and again offered himself and his arms. As he knelt before the altar, the girdle from which his metal hose were suspended broke across; as a true Catholic he did not let this happening frighten or disturb him, but merely ordered another girdle to be fetched.

[459] The Count now left the chapel, whereupon his horse was led to him. As he tried to mount he happened to be on slightly raised ground, so that the men of Toulouse, who had left their camp, were able to see him. His horse raised its head

---

the north-eastern corner of Muret (for *munitio* meaning castle see Appendix A (vi)); so Roquebert II, p. 201, who refers to it as '*la chapelle du château*'. (G&L identify this as the church of Saint-Sernin in the bourg, but this is surely incorrect.) Here and again in the next section Peter calls this chapel '*suam*', Simon's own chapel; perhaps this implies that the chapel had been reserved for Simon de Montfort and his entourage.

[32] Latin '*ecclesiam que erat in burgo*'. While it is not entirely clear whether this means the church of Saint-Sernin in the inner bourg, or the church of St James in the Villeneuve, the description of the attack which follows in §457 seems to imply the church of St James.

[33] This assault, apparently by the militia of Toulouse, is mentioned in the account of the prelates in §475 below, where it is said that the attack was on the '*vicum*', which must refer to the Villeneuve rather than the bourg. The *Chanson* (II, 139, pp. 24–6) also relates the episode as a major assault, which it appears was made on the Porte de Toulouse at the north-western corner of the Villeneuve.

[34] St Matthew 27, v. 24.

[35] Each of the main accounts is clear that the result of the assault on the morning of 12 September was that Simon de Montfort now intervened to argue that further negotiations were pointless, and taking the initiative he sought to leave Muret and enter battle with King Peter's forces. See the prelates' account in §476 below; de Montfort's 'speech' in the *Chanson* II, 139, p. 26; and William of Puylaurens (XX), who says de Montfort saw the dangers of allowing Muret to fall and decided it was better to risk all in a single day than prolong matters and allow the enemy's confidence to grow.

[36] Bishop Raymond; cf. n. 51 to §160 above.

and knocked against the Count making him jump back a little.[37] Seeing this the enemy raised loud shouts of derision. The Count said to them: 'You mock me now by shouting, but I have faith in the Lord that today I shall pursue you with shouts of victory to the gates of Toulouse.' This said the Count mounted his horse and went to join his knights in the bourg, where he found them armed and ready for battle. [460] A certain knight suggested the he should have a count made of his knights to ascertain their number. The Count replied: 'There is no need. We are enough, with God's help, to vanquish our enemies.' On our side, the knights and mounted sergeants numbered no more than eight hundred, whilst there were thought to be almost a hundred thousand men on the other side. We had few, hardly any, footsoldiers, and in any case the Count had forbidden anyone on foot to join the battle.[38]

[461] Whilst the Count and our knights were gathered to discuss their plan of battle, the Bishop of Toulouse arrived on the scene, his mitre on his head and a wooden crucifix in his hands. Thereupon our knights began to dismount and reverence the cross, one by one. However, the Bishop of Comminges,[39] a man of admirable piety, realised that if our men were to continue in this way, an excessive delay would result. He seized the crucifix from the Bishop of Toulouse, climbed to a higher piece of ground, and gave his blessing with the sign of the cross to them all, saying: 'Go forth in the name of Jesus Christ! I am your witness, and will stand as surety on the Day of Judgment, that whosoever shall fall in this glorious battle will instantly gain his eternal reward and the glory of martyrdom, free of the punishment of purgatory, so long as he is repentant and has made confession, or at least has the firm intention of presenting himself to a priest as soon as the battle is over for absolution from any sins he has not yet confessed.'

---

[37] William of Puylaurens (XX) also relates this incident; see Appendix I. (Cf. §463 where Peter says Simon broke a stirrup whilst fighting.)

[38] Apart from these figures, there is little precise information on the size of the two armies in the main sources. On the crusaders' side, William of Puylaurens (XX) mentions 'Guy de Montfort, Baldwin of Toulouse, William of Barres and Alain de Roucy, together with many others numbering a thousand armed men' ('*et alii multi ad mille numerum armatorum*'), a total referring both to mounted knights and sergeants, and footsoldiers, which is thus not inconsistent with our author's figure of eight hundred mounted men and a small number of footsoldiers, and with the statement of King James of Aragon in his *Llibre dels feyts*, section IX, that Simon had from eight hundred to a thousand horsemen. (The note on p. 16 of the *Chanson* wrongly relates this to the King's forces.) On the southern side, it is likely that there were about a thousand knights from Aragon and Catalonia, since the *Chanson* (I, 130, p. 288) says King Peter promised to come with a thousand knights. There would then have been additional knights in the retinues of the Counts of Toulouse, Foix and Comminges. If mounted sergeants and squires are added, plausible estimates might be a total of between two thousand and four thousand mounted men on the southern side, but the evidence for these calculations is thin. Nevertheless, it seems clear that the overall mounted strength of the southern army will have significantly outnumbered that of the crusaders. As to numbers of footsoldiers and total strength on the southern side, the figure given by Peter of a hundred thousand (which William the Breton doubles to two hundred thousand) is clearly a way of saying 'a large number'. Modern estimates range from twenty thousand to more than forty thousand, but these figures are high and it is impossible to make close estimates with confidence. However, the main sources as far as they go and tradition as represented by later chroniclers do imply that the crusaders were vastly outnumbered in total strength.

[39] Garsia; see §358 above.

[462] *The Count sets out for the battle.*[40] At the earnest request of our knights, this promise was repeated again and again by the bishops, whereupon our men left Muret,[41] cleansed of their sins by the contrition of their hearts and their confessions, granting each other forgiveness for any grievances that might exist between them. They were drawn up in three lines in the name of the Trinity,[42] and set out fearlessly against the enemy. The bishops and the clergy went into the church to offer prayers to the Lord on behalf of His servants, who were now exposing themselves to the threat of death in His name. As they prayed and cried out to heaven, they produced a deep roaring sound, in the face of the danger confronting them, such that they might be said to be 'howling' rather than praying. So the knights of Christ went joyously to the place of battle, ready to suffer not merely shame for his name[43] but even death. As they left they saw the enemy nearby on the level ground of the plain, ready to fight, so many that the whole world seemed drawn up against them.[44]

[463] Our first line at once boldly attacked the enemy and plunged into their

---

[40] William of Puylaurens (XXI) also reports a discussion on strategy between King Peter and the other Southern leaders on the morning of the battle. Count Raymond was for staying in the camp to await the onset of the crusaders and attack their horses with missiles, but the King ascribed this counsel to 'fear and cowardice'. The *Chanson* (II, 139, pp. 22–4) reports the discussion in broadly similar terms, saying that the Count recommended erecting a barricade; an Aragonese baron, Michael of Luesia, made the accusation of cowardice, which Raymond repudiated.

[41] The question of how the crusaders left Muret has caused some difficulty in attempted reconstructions. The *Chanson* (II, 139, p. 26) says they left by the Porte de Salles at the southern corner of the town. William of Puylaurens might appear to contradict this, saying (XX) that 'they decided not to go out directly against the enemy, since that would expose their horses to showers of missiles from the Toulousains [i.e. the mainly infantry force attacking the town from the west]; they left by a gate which looks east [implying the gate opening onto the Pont Saint-Sernin], whereas the camp [of the southerners] was on the west, so that the enemy, not knowing their purpose, would think they were fleeing; they then went forward a little, crossed a river and turned back to the level ground to face the [enemy] army'. It has, however, been argued that the Porte de Salles could provide an exit either to the south-west or the south-east (see M. Dieulafoy, 'La Bataille de Muret', *Institut de France, Mémoires de l'Académie des Inscriptions et Belles-Lettres* XXXVI, pt. 2 (1901), cited in Roquebert II, p. 208 and p. 429 n. 4), thus enabling a reconciliation of the two accounts. If so, the crusaders would then have moved between the eastern wall of the town and the Garonne, till they crossed the River Louge by the Pont Saint-Sernin, and then turned towards the southern army.

[42] Cf. above §454, and William of Puylaurens XXI in Appendix I. The prose version of the *Chanson* states that William of Contres commanded the first line, Bouchard de Marly the second, and de Montfort himself the third (*HGL* VIII, 96).

[43] Cf. Acts 5, v. 41.

[44] This account agrees with that of the prelates (see §476) and William of Puylaurens (XXI) that King Peter's forces were already drawn up when the crusaders attacked. (Thus the story in the London (British Library, Cotton) manuscript of Matthew Paris that the King was surprised while at his dinner is certainly inaccurate: it is printed in G&L II, p. 171 n. l.) However, exactly where the Southern forces were drawn up is not certain, because the main sources give only vague topographical information. The phrase used by Peter to describe the location of the Aragonese (*'in campi planicie juxta castrum'*, 'nearby on the level ground of the plain next to the *castrum*') could refer to anywhere to the immediate north or west of Muret. (The basic meaning of both *campus* and *planities* is 'level ground'; either might mean 'a plain'.) The *Chanson* simply says that the crusaders rode to the attack across a marsh; this may well point to the area west of Muret at the foot of the Perramon hill where the Saudrune runs (see E. Martin-Chabot's n. 1 in *Chanson* II, p. 28), but has also been interpreted as the area a little further to the north, near where the Pesquiès flows into the Garonne (cf. G&L II, p. 153 n. 3).

midst.[45] The second line followed close behind and penetrated the enemy ranks as had the first line. In this assault, the King of Aragon fell, and many Aragonese with him. In his arrogance he had taken his station in the second line – although it is the universal practice of kings to stand in the rear line. Moreover, he had exchanged his own armour for that of another.[46] Our Count now saw that his two leading lines had been submerged by the enemy, and had virtually disappeared from view; he therefore mounted an attack from the left[47] against the enemy standing opposite him, drawn up for battle in countless numbers along a ditch which lay between them and him.[48] As he started his attack he could see no way of reaching the enemy, but then found an insignificant path in the ditch (provided, we believe, by Divine providence), which enabled him to cross and reach his adversaries, whose line he now penetrated most courageously, like the courageous knight of Christ he was. I must add that as the Count was attacking them, they struck him from the right with such violent blows from their swords that his left stirrup broke. He tried to fix his left spur in the horse-blanket, but the spur itself broke and fell away. The Count, who was a very strong knight, kept his seat and struck back against his foes vigorously. An enemy knight struck him violently on the head, but the Count hit him under the chin with his fist and forced him off his horse. Immediately they saw this, the knights' companions (a huge crowd) and the rest of the enemy, defeated and in confusion, sought safety in flight. Thereupon our men in the first and second lines pursued the fugitives closely and harassed them severely. They set upon the hindmost and slew many

---

[45] William of Puylaurens says that this first attack was against the forces commanded by Count Raymond-Roger of Foix, who had with him Catalans and a great mass of warriors ('*Catalanis et copiosa multitudine bellatorum*'); for the rest of his account see Appendix I.

[46] This was not uncommon practice: cf. article cited by G&L II, p. 154 n. 2: M. Prinet, 'Changement et partage d'armoiries', in *Bulletin de la Société nationale des Antiquaires de France* (1909), pp. 363–9. The objective was not so much to save a leader's life as to prevent him from being captured and held to ransom, which could be costly both financially and in terms of other concessions which might be needed to secure his release. The outcome in this case seems to have been that King Peter was killed in the general fighting rather than deliberately. De Montfort's decision to honour the King's body (§465), and the restrained comments of the prelates on the death of King Peter (§478), are indications that the anonymous death in battle of a King of such eminence was not what the crusaders had been seeking. See also the general discussion of the King's death in Roquebert II, ch. 10 (where he refers to '*les morts imaginaires de Pierre II*' including William le Breton's description of a personal combat between de Montfort and the King). King Peter's death at Muret left the Crown of Aragon in considerable difficulty. His heir, James, was only five, and was in the custody of the crusaders (see §211 above, and n. 39 to §419), while the monarchy's fiscal resources were exhausted by wars. Appointed as regent for the young King James was his great uncle Sanç (or Sancho), who was titular Count of Roussillon and the Cerdagne, and had been Count of Provence in 1181–5. He was chosen in part because King Peter's younger brother Alfonso, who had been Count of Provence from 1196, had died in 1209, leaving an infant son, Ramon-Berengar. The first task was to secure the release of King James, and negotiations involving Innocent III soon began, to bear fruit with the legation of Peter of Benevento (see §506 below).

[47] Whether this means from the crusaders' left (so that de Montfort went south or west) or the Aragonese left (in which case north or east) has been much discussed. See the discussion in Roquebert II, n. 16 to ch. 9, on pp. 433–4.

[48] The location of this 'ditch' ('*fossatum quoddam*') is uncertain. It has been identified as the bed of the River Pesquiès, that of the River Aoussaou or that of the Louge, but there is no firm evidence. The *Chanson* also mentions fighting continuing 'up to a little river' (II, 140, pp. 28–30), which could be either the Saudrune or the Pesquiès.

thousands of them. Our Count and his companions followed our pursuing forces at a slow pace – deliberately, so that if the enemy were to regroup and recover the will to resist, our men, who were split into separate groups as they followed the enemy, would be able to withdraw to the Count. I must record that the Count never thought it fitting to strike anyone in battle whom he might see in flight and with his back towards him.[49]

[464] Meanwhile the multitude of citizens of Toulouse who had remained fully armed and ready for battle at their camp were exerting every effort to capture Muret.[50] The Bishop of Toulouse, a man of piety and compassion, who was in Muret, took pity on them and sent a priest to urge them to turn to the Lord God even at this late stage, and to lay down their arms; he hoped by doing this he might snatch them from imminent death. As a sign of guarantee, he sent his monk's cowl (he was a monk as well as a bishop).[51] But they were obstinate and blinded by the Lord's will; they replied that the King of Aragon had vanquished all our army, and that the Bishop wished to deliver them to death, not save them. For this reason, they seized the cowl from the messenger, and struck the messenger himself violently with their spears. Meanwhile our knights were returning from the slaughter and their glorious victory. They turned their attention to the Toulousains, and slew many thousands.[52]

[465] After this the Count instructed some of his followers to take him to the place where the King of Aragon had been killed – he had no knowledge of the place, or indeed of the time, of the King's death. He went to the spot and found the body of the King, lying naked in the middle of the battlefield; he had been stripped by some of our footsoldiers who had come out of Muret when they saw we were victorious, and finished off any of the enemy they found still alive. Ever a man of great piety, the Count dismounted and mourned over the body – a second David over a second Saul.[53]

[49] For William of Puylaurens' account of this part of the battle (XXI) see Appendix I. It is broadly consistent with the other accounts, as is the less explicit account of the *Chanson* which says 'the King cried out "I am the King", but he was not heard'.
[50] The Toulousains were attacking Muret from its western side whilst the cavalry battle between the crusaders and the Aragonese was taking place. This was a second attack, following the earlier one described in §457, and was likewise being undertaken by the militias of Toulouse.
[51] Fulk had been a monk at the Cistercian abbey of Thoronet in Provence, and was its abbot from 1199 until his election to the see of Toulouse in 1205; see n. 43 to §33 above. This incident is also referred to in the prelates' letter: see §479 below.
[52] See also the figure of twenty thousand in §466 below. William of Puylaurens gives a figure of fifteen thousand, and says 'it was not found that even one man on the Church side fell in the battle'. The prelates' account (§480) says that the number was impossible to estimate, and that the crusaders lost one knight and a few sergeants. The slaughter arose in particular when the victorious crusader cavalry turned on the Toulousan infantry, some of whom were attacking Muret whilst others had remained in their camp. When they realised that King Peter was dead the Toulousains began to flee, many making for the Garonne, seeking either to cross or gain the barges moored there, and many were either killed or drowned. Details are given in William of Puylaurens XXI (see Appendix I), and *Chanson* II, 140, pp. 30–2. In 1850 and 1875 quantities of human bones were unearthed at a place called Le Petit Joffrey on the west bank of the Garonne north of Muret, and this may be the site of a mass grave for the slain: see Roquebert II, pp. 222–3.
[53] See §463 above on the circumstances of the King's death and de Montfort's wish to honour his body. William of Puylaurens (XXI) says the body was removed from the battlefield by the Hospitallers of St John of Jerusalem, at their request; it was taken to their House in Toulouse. In a bull of February 1217 Pope

[466] After this – and the death of about twenty thousand of the enemies of the faith, some by drowning, some by the sword – our most Christian Count walked barefoot from the place where he had dismounted to the church, to render thanks to Almighty God for the victory He had granted, since he recognised that this miracle had been wrought by God's grace and not the efforts of men.[54] His horse and his armour he gave as alms for the poor. [467] So that the true nature of this marvellous battle and glorious victory may be more firmly fixed in the hearts of my readers, I think it will be well worth quoting a letter which the bishops and abbots present at the scene despatched to all believers in Christ.[55]

[468] *The prelates' report of the victory*.[56] 'Glory to God in the highest and peace on earth to all men of good will who love the Church.[57]

[469] 'On the fifth feast day preceding the octave of the nativity of the Blessed Virgin Mary,[58] the Lord strong and mighty, the Lord mighty in battle, did miraculously cast down the enemies of the Christian faith and grant to the Holy Church a glorious victory and a glorious triumph, as we shall now describe.[59]

'The Supreme Pontiff, inspired by paternal piety, had given firm instructions to the King of Aragon, in firm but friendly terms, to cease from giving help,

Honorius III agreed to a formal request from the young King James and the Hospitallers of Aragon for the body to be transferred to the abbey for women at Sigena in Aragon, which had been founded by King Peter's mother in 1183: see *Chanson* II, p. 32 n. 2, and G&L II, p. 157 n. 1.

[54] Much has been written about the reasons for the crusaders' victory, heavily outnumbered as they undoubtedly were. Some indications are given in the main sources. The *Llibre dels feyts* which King James of Aragon had written under his own name contains the observation (doubtless gained from eye-witnesses) that those on his father's side did not know how to dispose themselves for battle or how to work together, but each knight fought on his own accord, as if at a tourney (quoted by Roquebert, II, p. 232). This confirms the impression gained from other sources that the King's cavalry were poorly organised and simply collapsed in face of a disciplined and determined attack, and that all else followed from this. Once again therefore de Montfort's decisive leadership, and firm command of strategy and tactics, had brought victory despite the odds. Peter's criticism of the King's decision to stand in the second line (§463) implies that it was seen by contemporaries as a blunder which contributed to the disaster. There is also an anecdote in the *Llibre dels feyts* that King Peter spent the night before the battle with a mistress and was too exhausted to stand to hear Mass. The discussions in the King's camp before the battle, as related in the *Chanson* (II, 139, pp. 22–4) and by William of Puylaurens (XXI) suggest that he and his knights were over-confident, and indeed in describing the run-up to the battle the sources in general indicate that everyone in Toulouse expected the King to win; this helps to explain the Toulousain army's reluctance to believe that his forces had been overcome, and the subsequent slaughter. There is no reference in our sources to active involvement of the Counts of Toulouse and Comminges and their troops. Some commentators have suggested that their non-appearance may have contributed to the defeat and that Count Raymond, having disagreed with the King on tactics (see William of Puylaurens XXI) deliberately held back, but there is no direct evidence for this in the main sources. It may also be noted that Gaston de Béarn was wholly absent from the Muret campaign.

[55] This letter was widely reproduced in manuscript and early printed sources: see G&L II, p. 158 n. d.

[56] It will be seen that the account covers broadly the same ground as Peter's and is consistent with it. We have noted only points not mentioned by Peter or not covered in our notes to his account.

[57] The phrase '*Gloria in Excelis Deo*' was also used by Arnold Amalric in his letter to Innocent III describing the victory at Las Navas de Tolosa, and there are other parallels with the present letter: see *RHGF* XIX, 250–4.

[58] Thursday 12 September 1213. Latin '*quinta feria infra octobas beate Marie Virginis*'; similarly we have 'sixth feast day' in §483. Elsewhere the Latin name for the day is used (*dies Jovis* etc.).

[59] The letter now refers to events in the first half of 1213, on which see §§399–447.

advice or favour to the enemies of the true faith; instead he was to break with them at once and conclude a firm agreement with the Count of Montfort.[60] The papal letter ordering the restitution of territories to the Count of Foix, the Count of Comminges and Gaston de Béarn, which the King's envoys had obtained against the Count of Montfort by false representations, was annulled by the Pope and declared utterly void, once he had come to know the truth.[61] The King did not accept the Holy Father's admonition with filial devotion, but arrogantly rebelled against the Pope's instructions as if still further hardening his heart. Although the Archbishop of Narbonne (legate of the Apostolic See) and the Bishop of Toulouse transmitted the Pope's instructions in writing,[62] the King wished to bring to birth the evils which he had long since conceived; he now invaded the lands which had been won from the heretics and their defenders by the Lord's might and with the help of the crusaders, and sought to bring them under his control and return them to our enemies, quite against the Pope's orders. He succeeded in subduing a small part of the area;[63] much of the rest, trusting in his protection, decided to secede and now prepared to do so; whereupon the King joined with the Counts of Toulouse, Foix and Comminges and a large army from Toulouse and laid siege to Muret on the third feast day after the nativity of the Blessed Mary.[64]

[470] 'The Archbishop of Narbonne, as papal legate, had summoned the Bishops of Toulouse, Nîmes, Uzès, Lodève, Agde, Béziers and Comminges, and the Abbots of Clairac, Villemagne and Saint-Thibéry to join him for the further-ance of Christ's holy business;[65] they had come united in their enthusiasm and devotion to Christ, to concern themselves with that business and with the attain-ment of peace. Escorted by these venerable men, Simon the Count of Montfort now set out in haste to give valiant aid to the besieged *castrum*. Already with him were some noble and powerful crusaders from France who had lately come to aid Christ's business, and his own followers who had long toiled with him to further that business.

[471] 'On the Tuesday before the octave of the festival Christ's army had reached Saverdun.[66] The venerable Bishop of Toulouse, who had been commis-sioned by the Pope to arrange to reconcile the Toulousains,[67] had already written to them three or four times to urge reconciliation, but they had put off comply-ing with his advice, salutary though it was, replying merely that they had no reply

---

[60] A reference to Innocent's letter of 21 May 1213: see §§401–11.

[61] See §399 and notes for this letter of 17 January 1213.

[62] See §445 and n. 91.

[63] In Gascony: see §446.

[64] Tuesday 10 September 1213: see §448.

[65] See §451 and n. 16 for these prelates, and for the absence through illness of Arnold Amalric himself. Instead, he appointed Bishop Fulk of Toulouse as his vice-legate: see §476.

[66] On Tuesday 10 September. The account which follows of the negotiations with King Peter is more detailed than that given in Peter's own account above.

[67] Fulk of Toulouse was commissioned to reconcile the Toulousains in Innocent's letter of 21 May 1213: see §405 above.

whatever to give. Nevertheless, the Bishop now wrote again[68] to the King and the Toulousains engaged on the siege of Muret, indicating that he and the other bishops were on their way to negotiate a peaceful settlement and asking for a safe conduct. [472] However, on the next day, Wednesday, as the need for action was now urgent, the army left Saverdun, intent on bringing help to Muret with all possible speed. The bishops proposed that a halt should be made at Auterive (which is midway between Saverdun and Muret and two leagues from each) to await the return of their envoy. When he arrived, he passed on the King's response, which was that since the bishops were coming with the army he would not promise them a safe conduct. There was in truth no other way they could proceed without manifest danger because of the fighting. [473] As the bishops and Christ's army approached Muret, the Prior of the Hospitallers at Toulouse[69] came to them. He had been sent to the Bishop of Toulouse on behalf of the citizens and brought with him a letter which stated their readiness to obey the Pope and the Bishop in all matters; which would have been greatly to their benefit had their deeds matched their words. The Bishop immediately sent the Prior back to the King, who now answered that he was not prepared to offer a safe conduct to the Bishop; if, however, the Bishop wished to go to Toulouse to negotiate with the citizens, then he, the King, would grant him permission. His words were derisory.[70] The Bishop replied: "It is not fitting for a servant to enter a city from which his master has been ejected and exiled.[71] Therefore, since the body of Christ has been ejected from that city, I will not return there until my God and Master returns there." [474] However, the bishops and the army entered Muret on the Wednesday. Ever mindful of their responsibilities they sent two priests to the King and the citizens of Toulouse. The King replied that it was on account of four vagabonds[72] in their company that the bishops wished to hold a meeting with him (he said this to deride the crusaders and show his contempt for them). The citizens told the envoys they would give them their reply the next day, and on these grounds detained them overnight. [475] Next day, the Thursday, they gave as their reply that they were joined in alliance with the King of Aragon and would act only in accordance with his wishes.[73] On the return of our envoys with this message early on Thursday the bishops and abbots proposed to go unshod to the King. A priest was sent to the King to announce their coming; the gates of Muret had been left open, and the Count of Montfort and the

---

[68] This and the other letters mentioned do not survive, but are also mentioned in Mascaron's report to the Pope (n. 28 to §456).

[69] Bernard de Capoulet (G&L II, p. 166 n. 3, give detailed references).

[70] Mascaron, in his report to the Pope, explained why: 'since the Toulousains were not at Toulouse but in the army and at the siege' (*'derisorie fuit dictum, cum Tolosani non Tolose set in exercitu essent et in obsidione'*).

[71] One of the terms of the sentence passed on Raymond VI in February 1211 at Montpellier (§212) was that divine offices could not be celebrated anywhere he was present. The result was that Fulk had left Toulouse early in April 1211 and joined the crusaders, and his fellow clergy soon followed (see §221 and §234) and an interdict was placed on Toulouse (§403).

[72] '*Ribaldi*', the term also used for the attackers at Béziers in 1209 (see Appendix B).

[73] A reference to the oath of allegiance sworn by the consuls of Toulouse to King Peter on 27 January 1213 (*PL* 216, 846–7, and see n. 40 to §389 above).

crusaders had not yet put on their armour since the bishops and abbots were at that time still engaged in negotiations for a peace. Taking advantage of the situation, the enemies of God arrogantly and deceitfully attempted to make an armed foray into the bourg; but through God's grace their wishes were frustrated.

[476] 'When the Count and the crusaders witnessed this arrogant behaviour, it became clear to them that it would be dangerous and damaging to delay any longer.[74] As true followers of the Christian faith they cleansed themselves of their sins by the contrition of their hearts and by confession. Courageously they put on their armour, and went to the Bishop of Toulouse (who was acting as papal legate by delegation from the Archbishop of Narbonne, legate of the Apostolic See),[75] humbly to seek permission to go forth against the enemy. Since Christ's business was now in a critical situation, the bishops granted this permission; the pressing need for them to do so was further increased by the fact that the enemy were now making urgent preparations to mount an attack, insolently, on the very building occupied by the bishops. Siege-engines and other instruments of war had already been set up for this purpose, and the enemy were firing bolts from crossbows and hurling javelins and spears from all directions. The knights of Christ now marched out, after receiving a blessing from the bishops with a crucifix adorned with priestly insignia, and were drawn up in three ranks in the name of the Holy Trinity. The enemy had already put on their arms and left their tents – they were drawn up in numerous ranks and great numbers. On their side were many knights and a vast crowd of ordinary soldiers, but the followers of Christ were trusting in His help; despite their much smaller numbers they felt no fear of the host opposing them but attacked them valiantly, endued with power from on high.[76]

[477] 'The might of the Highest at once shattered His enemies through the hands of His servants, and brought them to nought in an instant. They turned their backs in flight, and became as chaff before the wind, and the Angel of the Lord chased them.[77] Some, fleeing shamefully, escaped the threat of death by shameful flight. Others escaped the sword but perished by water. Very many were devoured by the mouth of the sword.

[478] 'As to the King of Aragon, who fell among the slain, it is greatly to be regretted that so powerful and noble a prince (who, had he but so wished, could and should have been of great service to the Church) had now joined with Christ's enemies and had wickedly troubled Christ's friends and the Holy Church. [479] When the victors returned in glorious triumph from the slaughter and pursuit of the enemy, the Bishop of Toulouse, showing the charity and compassion of a noble heart, took pity on the slaughter and wretchedness of the

[74] For de Montfort's decision to attack, the bishops' agreement, and preparations for battle, see also §§458–61 above.
[75] Because Arnold Amalric was unwell: see notes to §§451 and 470.
[76] Luke 24, v. 49. The prelates give little information for the numbers of troops on each side or the battle itself, for which see §460 and n. and §§462–6.
[77] Psalm 35, vv. 5–6. In the next sentence there is an example of word play '*turpi . . . turpiter*'.

men of Toulouse. He wished to save from death those who had stayed in their tents and escaped the slaughter, and hoped that after suffering such mighty blows and escaping from such perils they might be brought back to the Lord and live for the future in the Catholic faith. He sent his cowl to them in the hands of a priest, through whom he ordered them to lay down their arms and abandon their hostility, and come to him unarmed so that he might save them from death. But they persisted in their wickedness, believing they had defeated Christ's people although they themselves were already defeated; not only did they disdain to obey the counsel of their own Bishop, they even seized the cowl and showered the messenger with blows. The army of Christ returned to attack them and slew them as they took flight amongst their tents. [480] So great was the number of the enemy slain – nobles and others – that it cannot be told with certainty. Only one of Christ's knights was lost in the struggle, and a few sergeants.[78]

[481] 'Let all Christendom give thanks to Christ for the victory of the Christians with sincere and heartfelt devotion; for He, through a few of the faithful, has overcome an innumerable multitude of the faithless and granted His Holy Church a happy triumph over His enemies. Honour and glory be His to all eternity, amen.

[482] 'We, the Bishops of Toulouse, Nîmes, Uzès, Lodève, Béziers, Agde and Comminges, and we the Abbots of Clairac, Villemagne and Saint-Thibéry, who came together by order of our venerable and beloved father the Archbishop of Narbonne,[79] legate of the Apostolic See, and strove with every effort to bring about peace and concord, hereby in God's name affirm the truth of this account, having ourselves seen and heard the matter described; we accordingly affix our seals hereto, since what is set down is worthy to be preserved for all time in human memory.

[483] 'Given at Muret, on the morrow of our glorious victory, on the sixth feast day preceding the octave of the nativity of the Blessed Virgin Mary,[80] in the year of our Lord 1213.'

[484] After this glorious and unprecedented victory, the seven bishops and three abbots, who were still at Muret, believed the surviving citizens of Toulouse would be so intimidated by God's great miracle and His scourge that it would be easier than previously to recall them from error into the bosom of the Mother Church.[81] Accordingly, following the charitable course of action laid down in the

---

[78] On the numbers slain, see §§464–6.
[79] See above, §470.
[80] 13 September 1213.
[81] The bishops thus chose to continue to try to negotiate a reconciliation of the city, as Innocent III had instructed (the letter referred to in the next sentence was from Innocent to Fulk, 21 May 1213, see §405 and note and another reference in §471). It is perhaps surprising that de Montfort did not now seek to take Toulouse by force, particularly given that the heavy losses which the Toulousain militias sufferred at Muret must have weakened the city's ability to resist. He seems, however, to have decided to allow the process of reconciliation to continue, rather than attack Toulouse without express permission from Innocent himself. The point is considered by G&M, p. 186 n. 2, by Roquebert II, pp. 242–4, and by Belperron, pp. 283–4.

Pope's letter,[82] they sought to reunite them with the Church by a combination of persuasion, exhortation and threats. The citizens promised to implement the Pope's instructions. The bishops met them face to face and demanded adequate guarantees of their intentions – specifically, two hundred hostages; they could not be satisfied simply with a sworn oath, since the citizens had so often broken similar promises in the past.[83] After much argument they promised to provide just sixty hostages from the citizen body. The bishops felt they needed as many as two hundred hostages to ensure that any promises made would be kept, bearing in mind the city's size and the deceitful[84] and uncontrollable nature of its numerous people – who had, moreover, on a previous occasion, failed to redeem some of their richer citizens given as hostages on the same account.[85] The citizens, merely looking for a subterfuge, promised to give sixty and no more. The bishops were keen to ensure that the citizens should have no excuse, no opportunity for deceit and no means of cloaking their errors; without further delay they replied that they would be content to take the promised sixty hostages, and would on that basis reconcile the people of Toulouse and protect them in the peace of the Church and the unity of the Catholic faith. The citizens, abandoning any further efforts to conceal their evil intentions, now said they would give no hostages at all, thus clearly revealing that their earlier promise to give sixty hostages had been made only to defraud and deceive.[86]

[485] Here I will record that the inhabitants of a notable *castrum* known as Rabastens, which had deserted God and our side some time previously and joined Toulouse, fled their *castrum* in fear and left it empty when they heard of the victory at Muret.[87] The town had been given as a fief to Guy of Montfort (brother of our Count), who now sent his people there to occupy and fortify it.

[486] A few days later[88] a small group of crusaders arrived from France – Ralph, Bishop of Arras,[89] with a few knights and a small band of footsoldiers.

---

82 Innocent had written to Fulk on 21 May 1213 with instructions about the reconciliation of Toulouse: see §405 and §471.

83 See §7 for their oath of 1203 to the legates Peter of Castelnau and Ralph of Fontfroide.

84 '*Dolosam*', another example of the *Tolosa/dolosa* pun; cf. §§8, 68, 600 etc.

85 A reference to the reconciliation of Toulouse by Fulk in March 1210, when ten hostages had been handed over to the crusaders: see §162.

86 The *Chanson* (II, 141, p. 32) relates that after Muret Raymond VI secretly told the consuls of Toulouse to secure the best terms they could from the crusaders; he himself would personally lay a complaint against de Montfort before the Pope. The *Chanson* says he then left the country with his son. In fact they went to the English court (King John was of course brother of Joan, Raymond's second wife and the mother of the younger Raymond), where their presence is attested by two records of expenses at the court, a payment for maintenance on 15 December 1213 and one on 16 January 1214 for Raymond VI's return journey. The Chronicle of Ralph of Coggeshall and the Annals of Dunstable and Waverley record a report current in England that Raymond secured a payment of 10,000 marks from John in return for doing homage to him for Toulouse; and that King John recovered 10,000 livres by a levy on the Cistercians in England in retaliation for their support of the crusaders against Raymond. (For sources see n. 1 in *Chanson* II, pp. 34–5. For later developments in relations between Toulouse and the Church see §507 and n. 55.)

87 For Rabastens see §237 above. It had surrendered to de Montfort in June 1211 (§237), but rebelled later that year (§281).

88 Probably towards the end of September, since they had left (presumably after completing their forty days' service) by early November (§489).

89 Bishop 1204–21 (G&L II, p. 178 n. 4).

Our Count and his companions rode into the territory of the Count of Foix, and set fire to the lower bourg of Foix itself. They rode further into the area and destroyed everything they came across outside that was not protected by fortifications.[90]

---

[90] On 17 October de Montfort was at Carla-de-Roquefort, about 15km east of Foix, where he witnessed a charter in favour of the abbey of Fontfroide, confirming grazing rights and guaranteeing its safety from attacks (Rhein 116, Molinier 72).

[**XVI. §§487–549, September 1213 – January 1215:** *Simon de Montfort in Provence – Count Baldwin hanged (February 1214) – breach between Narbonne and the crusaders – Peter of Benevento, the Pope's new legate, reconciles the Narbonnese, the counts of Comminges and Foix and the Count and consuls of Toulouse (April 1214) – marriage of Amaury de Montfort – reinforcements join the crusaders, including the legate Robert de Courçon (April 1214) – activity in Quercy and the Agenais – siege of Casseneuil (June–August 1214) and campaigns in the Périgord and Rouergue (autumn 1214) – the Council of Montpellier (January 1215) recommends to the Pope that Simon de Montfort should be declared Count of Toulouse.*].[1]

[487] *The Count goes to Provence.*[2] After this the Count was told that some Provençal nobles had broken their agreement to maintain peace,[3] and were harassing God's holy Church; in addition they were occupying the public roads and doing all they could to harm the crusaders making their way from France.[4] After taking advice from his comrades the Count decided to go to the area to suppress the insurgents and make the public roads safe from the attacks of the hostile elements.

[488] He accordingly made for Narbonne, accompanied by the crusaders who had joined him. The citizens of Narbonne had always been hostile to Christ's business, and opposed its prosecution on many occasions, albeit in an underhand fashion.[5] They could not be persuaded to allow entry into the city for the Count and the crusaders, or even the crusaders without the Count, so that they were compelled to pass the night of their arrival in the fruit-gardens and woods outside the walls. Next day they proceeded to Béziers,[6] and two days later reached Montpellier,[7] whose inhabitants, rivalling those of Narbonne in hostility, also

---

[1]   The defeat at Muret did not produce a collapse of resistance to the crusaders; on the contrary it provoked a substantial revolt against them – cf. Roquebert II, p. 252. As will be seen, de Montfort's main concern in the autumn of 1213 was to subdue opposition in the east, whilst from spring to autumn 1214 he was mostly involved in Quercy and the Agenais.
[2]   Latin '*provincia*', here meaning the Rhône valley in general: see Appendix A(i).
[3]   A reference to the oaths sworn in the spring of 1207 by many of the lords of Provence (§27 above), and to the oaths of June 1209 (see §§75–7).
[4]   The Rhône valley was the main route south for crusaders coming from northern France and the Rhineland. The disorder is also mentioned in Innocent III's letter of 17 January 1214 announcing the arrival of the new legate Peter of Benevento (*PL* 216, 955, see n. 44 to §503). The motives for the attacks on crusaders at this time are unclear, but presumably the aim was to prevent further reinforcements reaching de Montfort after Muret. The crusaders mentioned at the beginning of the next section are presumably those referred to in §486.
[5]   Although Viscount Aimeric of Narbonne and the Narbonnais had earlier given some active support to de Montfort (see e.g. §125 and their involvement in the siege of Minerve in 1210, §§151–2 above), there had been previous suggestions of their hostility to the crusaders, see e.g. §264 and the incident involving Amaury de Montfort recounted in §305. Narbonne openly broke with de Montfort in the spring of 1214 (see §501); for later developments in relations between Narbonne and de Montfort see §§560–1 below.
[6]   De Montfort was there on 30 October 1213 (G&L II, p. 180 n. 2).
[7]   Montpellier had been a possession of King Peter of Aragon, who had granted it as a fief to William IX of Montpellier in January 1213: see n. 39 to §419 above for details.

refused to allow the Count and his men into the city to spend the night. Indeed
Montpellier followed the behaviour of Narbonne in every respect. Leaving
Montpellier the crusaders came to Nîmes.[8] At first the citizens refused to allow
the Count into the town, but when they saw what anger and indignation this
attitude provoked they admitted the Count and everyone with him and received
them with all proper hospitality. From there our Count went to the *castrum* of
Bagnols[9] where he was honourably received by the lords of the place.

[489] The Count then proceeded to a town named Largentière,[10] in view of
the presence in that area of a noble named Pons de Montlaur,[11] who was doing
everything in his power to hinder the Church and the bishops and the promotion
of peace in the area. By this time all the crusaders[12] had left the Count, and he
had with him only a few paid soldiers,[13] and the Archbishop of Narbonne. When
Pons heard of the Count's approach he became afraid and submitted himself and
his possessions to the Count's will. [490] There was another powerful and hostile
noble in the area, Adhémar of Poitiers,[14] who had always been hostile to Christ's
business and was a keen sympathiser with the Count of Toulouse. When news
reached him of our Count's advance, he put his *castra* in a state of readiness and
gathered as many knights as he could into one particular *castrum*[15] with the idea
that if our Count passed close to it he would go out and attack him. In the event
when the Count did approach the place Adhémar did not dare go out even
though his forces outnumbered the Count's small party.

[491] Whilst the Count was in this area he was joined by Odo, Duke of
Burgundy,[16] a powerful and well-disposed noble and a very keen supporter of the
Crusade against the heretics[17] and of our Count. The Duke was accompanied by
the Archbishops of Lyon and Vienne.[18] Whilst the Count and the Duke were at
Romans, near Valence, they summoned that enemy of the Church, Adhémar, to a
parley. He came, but refused to agree to the terms for peace proposed by the
Duke and the Count. They called Adhémar to a second meeting, but again could
make no progress. This failure roused the Duke's anger and indignation against

8 On 20 January 1214 Innocent instructed Peter of Benevento to investigate the position of the viscounty
of Nîmes: *PL* 216, 958, again see n. 44 to §503.
9 Bagnols-sur-Cèze, west of the Rhône.
10 He was there on 5 November, when he granted the castle of Berriac in the Carcassès to the abbey of
Cîteaux (Rhein 117, Molinier 73). As Peter mentions below, Arnold Amalric was also present.
11 Pons III, on whom see G&L II, p. 181 n. 4.
12 I.e. those who had come with the Bishop of Arras: see §486 above.
13 'Stipendiarios'; see Appendix D on mercenaries.
14 Adhémar II, Count of the Valentinois. He had initially joined the crusaders in 1209 (*Chanson* I, 12, p.
36 and n. 2 on p. 37), but did not remain with them long, presumably leaving after the fall of Carcassonne.
In 1216 he supported the young Raymond of Toulouse (*Chanson* II, 154, p. 100), and continued to do so
(below, §§596–8), but then made peace with de Montfort (§599).
15 Probably Cruas, to the west of the Rhône, about 12km north of Montélimar (see G&L II, p. 182 n. 2).
16 Odo had taken part in the campaign of 1209 (see §82) and had remained with de Montfort for some
time after the fall of Carcassonne (§§108–115) before returning north probably in early September 1209.
He had now been called south by Arnold Amalric: see §492 below.
17 'Negotium fidei contra hereticos', literally 'the business of the faith against the heretics', so also in §494
and elsewhere.
18 Renaud of Lyon, 1193–1226, and Humbert of Vienne (G&L II, p. 183 nn. 2–3).

Adhémar, and he promised firmly that he would join the Count in attacking Adhémar unless he showed himself willing to abide by the Church's instructions, to follow the Count's wishes, and to provide firm guarantees of his intentions. The Duke at once summoned a substantial number of knights to enable him to carry out this proposal. When Adhémar heard of this, he at last found himself compelled to come to the Duke and the Count and undertake to obey them in all matters. He handed over several *castra* as a guarantee; these the Count entrusted to the Duke to garrison.

[492] Meanwhile the Archbishop of Narbonne – a man wise in counsel and of valiant spirit, at whose special request the Duke of Burgundy had come to Vienne – discussed with the Duke the business for which he had been summoned. This was the arrangement of a marriage between Amaury, our Count's eldest son, and the daughter of Dauphin,[19] a powerful prince and the Duke's brother. The Duke was ready to follow the Archbishop's advice and wishes, and at the latter's request gave undertakings to him and the Count to follow their requirements with a will.

[493] Whilst these events were taking place,[20] mercenaries from Aragon and other enemies of the faith began to make incursions into our Count's territory. They penetrated as far as Béziers, and did whatever harm was in their power. Many knights in the Count's territory now seceded from God, the Church and our Count, breaking their oath of fealty and revealing their true evil nature. After achieving the objectives for which he had gone to Provence, the noble Count returned to his own territory[21] and at once made an excursion into the areas controlled by the enemy. He rode out before Toulouse and stayed in the district for a fortnight, destroying numerous castles.

[494] It will be recalled that Master Robert de Courçon, a Cardinal and legate of the Apostolic See, had been energetically engaged in France in promoting the Crusade to the Holy Land, and had withdrawn from us the preachers who had been preaching the Crusade against the heretics, arranging for them to devote their efforts to preaching help for the Holy Land instead.[22] Now, in response to the promptings of certain well-disposed and wise advisers he returned some of the preachers to us to preach for the business of the faith, and himself took the cross against the heretics of Toulouse. What more? The preaching campaign in France to promote the business of the faith revived, and large numbers of the faithful took the cross – to the great joy of the Count and our army.[23]

[495] *Capture of Count Baldwin.*[24] There occurred at this time an act of brutal betrayal involving Count Baldwin, which I do not wish to pass over – nor indeed

---

[19] The Dauphin of Burgundy was André-Dauphin, Count of the Viennois. His daughter was Béatrice. The marriage took place the following year: see §511.

[20] I.e. during November and December 1213.

[21] De Montfort was still at Valence early in December 1213, and seems to have made his way back to Languedoc only slowly. He is recorded as being at Caux, near Pézenas, on 13 February 1214, and at Béziers during that month (Rhein 128, and G&L II, p. 185 n. 1).

[22] For Robert and his preaching in 1213 in support of a Crusade to the Holy Land, see above, §439. See also §513 and §523 for his presence in the South with the crusaders.

[23] See §508 below for the arrival of the new crusaders.

[24] On Baldwin, see §§235–6 and notes. Since coming over to the crusaders' side in 1211, he had remained

should I do so. Count Baldwin was the brother of the Count of Toulouse and cousin of the King of France. His character was far different from his brother's; he put all his energies into fighting for Christ and did everything in his power to help the Count of Montfort and the forces of Christianity against his brother and the other enemies of the faith. On the Monday following the first Sunday in Lent[25] the Count went to a *castrum* known as Lolmie in the diocese of Cahors.[26] The knights in this place (who were actually the Count's vassals) sent a messenger to some mercenaries and knights of local origin – traitors of the worst sort – who were in the neighbouring *castrum* of Mondenard.[27] They reported that the Count was in Lolmie and told them to come over from Mondenard; they would then be able to hand over Count Baldwin without any difficulty. A similar message was delivered to Ratier of Castelnau,[28] who was, covertly, a most villainous traitor. This man had long previously entered into a treaty with the Count of Montfort and sworn fealty to him, and Baldwin trusted him as a friend.

[496] What more? As night fell Baldwin, unconcerned for his safety since he felt he was among friends, went peacefully to sleep. With him in Lolmie were a French knight named William of Contres,[29] to whom the Count of Montfort had given a *castrum* named Castelsarrasin, and a French sergeant who was guarding the *castrum* of Moissac.[30] As the Count and his companions slept, separated from each other in different houses, the lord of Lolmie seized the key of the room in which Baldwin was sleeping and locked the door. He then left Lolmie and rushed off to Ratier and the mercenaries. He showed them the key and said: 'Why are you waiting? Your enemy is in my hands. Make haste, and I will deliver him[31] to you asleep and unarmed. Indeed I will deliver not just him but more of our enemies.' Hearing this the mercenaries hurried to the gates of Lolmie in great delight.

[497] The lord of Lolmie, the leader of those plotting to capture the Count – a second Judas! – secretly summoned the townspeople and carefully ascertained from each of them how many of the Count's entourage were quartered with

steadfastly loyal to de Montfort, and had campaigned with him and his brother Guy (see §§282, 318, 352, 426–7). His capture and murder are also recounted by William of Puylaurens, XXII.

[25] 17 February 1214.

[26] Lolmie lies about 8km south of Montcuq in western Quercy. After de Montfort's campaigns there in 1212, Baldwin had been given extensive possessions in the area, including Montcuq itself (§498).

[27] Mondenard lies about 7km further south from Montcuq.

[28] Ratier, lord of Castelnau-de-Montratier in Quercy, about 20km south-east of Montcuq, and the same distance north-west of Caussade. He had taken part in the Crusade in Quercy in 1209: see *Chanson* I, 13, p. 40, and also n. 43 to §246 above for the settlement of June 1212 when Ratier and others swore allegiance to Simon de Montfort. For de Montfort's revenge on Ratier for his part in Baldwin's murder see §514 below.

[29] He had been a crusader since 1209, and was one of de Montfort's most faithful companions. He is mentioned frequently by William of Tudela in the first part of the *Chanson*. He was left to defend Carcassonne in 1210 when de Montfort went to lay siege to Termes and defended the crusaders' siege engines when they were attacked there (*Chanson* I, 51–6, pp. 120–36), and played an important part in the siege of Moissac, at which time he was given Castelsarrasin (*Chanson* I, 118–30, pp. 264–88, several references). See also notes to §§168–9 and §352 above.

[30] The serjeant was named as Simon in an act of 1213: G&L II, p. 188 n. 2.

[31] Cf. Matthew 26, v. 15, 'I will deliver him unto you', said by Judas, and cf. the reference to Judas in the next section.

them. This done, he stationed at the entrance to each house more than twice as many armed mercenaries as there were of our men sleeping and unarmed. Large numbers of candles were lit, and to the accompaniment of a loud clamour the enemy rushed against our people who were taken completely by surprise. Ratier of Castelnau and the lord of Lolmie went to the room where Baldwin was sleeping, opened the door and seized him, asleep, unarmed and indeed quite naked. Some of our men in Lolmie were killed, others captured, some fled to safety. I must record that they took one of our men alive and after promising on oath to preserve his life and limbs, subsequently killed him as he sought refuge in the church. [498] After seizing Count Baldwin our enemies took him to the *castrum* of Montcuq, which belonged to the Count himself, in the Cahors area.[32] The townsfolk, thoroughly evil men, welcomed the mercenaries who were bringing their lord as a captive. Some French soldiers were guarding the keep in the *castrum* on the Count's instructions, and the mercenaries now told Baldwin to order the garrison to surrender it to them. He strictly forbade them to do so, even if they were to see him hanging from a gibbet; instead they should defend themselves with all their might until help could arrive from the noble Count of Montfort. What princely courage, what marvellous strength of mind! Quite incensed by this the mercenaries starved the Count for two whole days.

[499] The Count now summoned a chaplain and made his confession most meticulously. He then asked to be allowed holy communion, but as the chaplain was bringing the sacraments a particularly vicious mercenary came along and declared on oath that the Count would not be allowed to eat or drink until he released another mercenary whom Baldwin had captured and was holding in chains.[33] The Count said: 'What cruelty! I am not asking for a feast of bread or wine, or a portion of meat. I have not asked for bodily sustenance, but for holy communion for the salvation of my soul.' The executioner again swore that the Count would neither eat nor drink unless he did as he was asked. Showing true nobility, the Count replied: 'If I am not to be permitted communion and the holy sacraments, at least let the Eucharist, my salvation, be shown to me, so that in the life to come I may look upon my Saviour.' The Eucharist was raised high by the chaplain and shown to the Count, who worshipped it reverently. Whilst this was happening, the garrison in the keep, afraid for their lives, surrendered it to the mercenaries, after receiving from them a promise that they would be allowed to leave alive and unharmed; but these evil betrayers, breaking their sworn oath, immediately condemned them to a shameful death by hanging.

[500] *Count Baldwin hanged.* This done they seized the Count and led him off to Montauban,[34] a *castrum* in the territory of the Count of Toulouse, where they imprisoned him in chains to await that Count's arrival.[35] After a few days the

---

32 Montcuq had been given as a fief to Baldwin by de Montfort in 1212: see §318 above.

33 He was being held in the prison which was inside the keep.

34 About 40km south of Montcuq; it was one of the few places which had never been taken by the crusaders (see §352).

35 Raymond had returned from England in February 1214 (G&L II, p. 191 n. 3; see also n. 86 to §484 above).

latter duly came, accompanied by those vile traitors the Count of Foix, his son Roger-Bernard and a knight from Aragon named Bernard de Portella.[36] On the orders of the Count of Toulouse the noble Count Baldwin was led out from Montauban. Who will ever be able to read or hear of what followed without tears? The Count of Foix and his son – fully his father's equal in villainy – and Bertrand attached the rope round the neck of the noble Count, ready to follow the wishes, indeed the orders, of the Count of Toulouse, and hang him. Baldwin, a most devout Christian, thereupon humbly and resolutely asked to make confession and receive the viaticum. The cruel dogs vehemently refused both requests. Christ's knight then said to them: 'Since I am not allowed to see a priest, God will be my witness that I have always served Christianity and my lord the Count of Montfort with a ready will and an eager heart, and that I am willing to die for this and for the defence of the faith.' Scarcely had he finished speaking when the three traitors raised him aloft and hanged him from a walnut tree.[37] What unheard-of brutality! A second Cain, a brother worse than Cain – I name the Count of Toulouse, for whom it was not enough to slay his brother (and such a brother!) but he must condemn him to a form of death of unprecedented barbarity.

[501] *The Narbonnais break with the Count.* About this time Aimeric, the lord of Narbonne, and the citizens of that city, who had never favoured Christ's business, brought forth the mischief they had long ago conceived;[38] they openly broke with God and received into their midst some mercenaries and men from Aragon and Catalonia,[39] hoping that through them they might drive the Count of Montfort from their lands. The men of Aragon and Catalonia were attacking the Count to avenge their King, but the men of Narbonne committed their crime not because the Count was injuring them, or had done them any injury in the past, but because they believed no more crusaders would come. But He who taketh the wise in their own craftiness[40] disposed matters otherwise; whilst our enemies were all gathered together at Narbonne intending to run upon the

---

[36] Bernard de Portella (near Lérida in Catalonia) had been one of those accompanying King Peter of Aragon during his stay in Toulouse in January 1213 (see n. to §375 above). For details of Bernard see also G&L II, p. 192 n. 1. His and Roger-Bernard of Foix's role in the murder of Baldwin is confirmed in William of Puylaurens' account (XXII), which says that Baldwin was hanged on their advice; the purpose was 'to avenge the King of Aragon, because he had been at the battle [of Muret]', '*in ultionem regis Aragonum, quia in campo illo fuerat*'.

[37] William of Puylaurens adds that he was buried in the Templar house at Lavilledieu.

[38] On Viscount Aimeric see §125. For earlier relations between Narbonne and the crusaders see n. 5 to §488, and for later developments §560.

[39] Present at Narbonne at this time were numerous prominent Aragonese, including Hispan Bishop of Segorbe, William of Montredon, Master of the Templars of Aragon, the Archdeacon of Huesca, Berengar the Master of the Hospitallers of Aragon, William of Montcada, Count Hugh of Ampurias, and the young King James's great uncle and regent Count Sanç of Roussillon and his son Nunyo Sanç, together with other nobles and knights (see G&L II, p. 194 n. 2, and King James's own account in the *Llibre dels feyts*, ch. X). He makes it clear that the presence of the Aragonese was connected with attempts to secure his release from the crusaders' custody (he reached the age of six in February 1214 – see also notes to §§463, 503 and 506); his account adds that the Aragonese 'made war on the French, and on the lands they occupied . . . carrying on war from Narbonne and other places' (trans. Forster, p. 18).

[40] Job 5, v. 13.

Count and his few companions with one accord,[41] a group of crusaders suddenly arrived from France – William of Barres,[42] a man of proven prowess in war, and a large number of knights with him. Our Count joined forces with them, and with their help went almost as far as Narbonne,[43] laying waste the lands of Aimeric, lord of Narbonne, and seizing nearly all his *castra*.

[502] One day the Count decided to make a mounted excursion to the neighbourhood of Narbonne. He had all his men arm themselves and drew them up in three lines. The Count himself took his place at the forefront of his troops and approached the city gate, but the enemy had come out of the city and were positioned at the gate. That invincible knight, our Count, wished to attack them by surprise by a difficult and inaccessible path, but the enemy, who were on higher ground, repelled him with so many lances that his saddle was broken and he fell from his horse. The enemy rushed in from all sides to capture or kill him – our men likewise to protect him. By God's grace, after mighty and courageous efforts, they were at last able to lift him up. William of Barres, who was in the last line, and the rest of our troops then attacked the enemy and quickly forced them to retire into the city. Thereupon the Count and his men returned to the position they had left earlier in the day.

[503] *Arrival of a papal legate in the Narbonne region.* Whilst these events were taking place Master Peter of Benevento, a Cardinal-deacon and legate of the Apostolic See, was on his way to the Narbonne region on the instructions of the Pope to order matters relating to peace and the faith.[44] When he heard of the

---

41 Cf. Acts 7, v. 57.

42 G&L II, p. 195 n. 3, cite Alberic de Trois-Fontaines who confirms that this was William III, father of William IV who led the attack at Muret (see n. 17 to §451).

43 De Montfort came from the Toulousain (§493), and passed Carcassonne on 28 March (G&L II, p. 195 n. 4, quoting Rhein, 121).

44 Peter of Benevento's arrival is also mentioned in William of Puylaurens, XXIII. He was chaplain to Innocent III in 1205, later papal notary and by 1214 Cardinal-deacon of Santa Maria in Aquiro: see G&L II, p. 196 n. 4. Innocent equipped him with three letters of instruction before his departure from Rome, dated 20, 22, and 25 January 1214 (*PL* 216, 958–60). The appointment of Peter of Benevento seems in effect to have been Innocent's response to Muret, and it may be noted that Innocent had not reacted directly in any recorded correspondence to the crusaders' victory at Muret; indeed the tone and content of his letters to Peter of Benevento suggest that he greatly regretted the death of King Peter. (Belperron's view (p. 284 n. 1) that the absence of a letter of congratulation on the victory 'could be explained by gaps in the papal registers (*peut s'expliquer par les lacunes des registres pontificaux*)' is wishful thinking on his part.) In his letter of 20 January to the new legate, Innocent required him to investigate the legal position of the viscounty of Nîmes, possession of which (along with the viscounty of Agde) de Montfort was seeking to obtain from their Viscount Bernard-Aton, although nominally at least the viscounties were under the suzerainty of the counts of Toulouse. The letter of 22 January instructs Peter of Benevento to seek to reconcile the Count of Comminges and the Viscount of Béarn to the Church; and that of 25 January similarly to seek to reconcile Toulouse. On 17 January Innocent addressed a general letter to the prelates and clergy of the provinces of Embrun, Arles, Aix and Narbonne announcing Peter's mission (*PL* 216, 955); in this he was at pains to emphasise his personal attachment to Peter of Benevento ('*quem inter caeteros fratres nostros specialis charitatis brachiis amplexamur*', literally 'whom amongst our other brothers we embrace with the arms of special affection') and the extent of his authority, urging the recipients to 'receive him as if he were our own person, indeed as if we were present in him'. On 23 January he also wrote to de Montfort (*PL* 216, 959) in a letter which for most of its length repeats the letter to the prelates but which goes on to instruct him specifically to hand over King James of Aragon to the new legate: 'we have sent . . . Peter . . . with instructions [inter alia] to arrange the return of the son of King Peter of Aragon, of renowned memory, to his kingdom, where he will make provision for him to be cared for. We therefore

conduct of the citizens of Narbonne he gave them strict instructions to arrange a firm truce with the Count, until he himself could arrive on the scene. He even instructed our Count to do no harm to the men of Narbonne. He arrived a few days later and entered Narbonne, having first met and conferred with our Count. The enemies of the faith, the Counts of Foix and Comminges and numerous others, at once went to the legate and begged him to restore the possessions they had so deservedly forfeited. The legate, a man of wisdom and discretion, reconciled them all with the Church, after receiving from then not only sworn guarantees that they would obey the orders of the Church but also certain very strong *castra* which they still controlled.[45]

[504] So matters stood when in an act of treachery the men of Moissac handed their *castrum* over to the Count of Toulouse.[46] Our Count's supporters in Moissac retired to the castle, which was only weakly fortified. The Count of Toulouse, with a large force of mercenaries, laid siege to the castle for three weeks,[47] but the besieged, though few in numbers, defended themselves valiantly.

---

earnestly enjoin you . . . to give heed to his instructions, humbly and devoutly. And, since it is not fitting (*indecens*) that you should any longer hold the King's son, for whatever reason (*occasio*, perhaps with the connotation 'pretext'), you must hand him over to the legate who may then make arrangements for him as he thinks fit. Otherwise (*alioquin*) he will proceed in this matter according to the instructions I have given him verbally.' (It should be noted that 'otherwise' is the usual meaning of *alioquin* in papal correspondence of the period, and if it carries that meaning here the implication is that Innocent accepts the possibility that de Montfort will disobey him and that Peter of Benevento will have other sanctions at his disposal to coerce him. However, the primary meaning of *alioquin* in classical Latin is 'for the rest' and it might possibly have this meaning here; in that case the implication would be that Innocent is simply referring to the return of King James to the Aragonese court.) The despatch of Peter of Benevento as legate ('*a latere*') effectively with authority over the other legates, and the fact that the purposes of his visit were confided to him privately rather than being announced generally, suggest that the Pope's reservations about the crusaders' objectives (see notes to §367 and §399) persisted. His concern is perhaps further evidenced by the tone of his instruction to de Montfort about the young King, and by passages in the instructions to the legate to seek the reconciliation of the southern counts and the city of Toulouse: 'Even though their excesses are considerable and serious, entry to the Church should not be denied to those who knock on her doors with humility' and 'once reconciled she [Toulouse] will live under the protection of the Holy See without concern at the prospect of entry by the Count of Montfort or the other Catholics, so long as the inhabitants continue to adhere to the faith and to peace'. Although he does not specifically mention Raymond VI in these letters, it seems probable from later developments (§§507, 547, 553–6 and notes) that he had him in mind as well; see also William of Puylaurens XXIII.

45 Oaths were sworn to the legate on 18 April 1214 by the Counts of Comminges and Foix in the archiepiscopal palace at Narbonne (see *HGL* VIII, 643–6, and *Layettes* I, 1068–9). They are for most of their length identical, each declaring that they would not in future help heretics or their supporters or other enemies of the Church to recover lands taken by the crusaders; specifically they would give no help openly or secretly to Toulouse until the city was reconciled to the Church. The Count of Foix undertook to hand over Foix itself to the Church as a guarantee (see also below, §564, and William of Puylaurens XXIII); the Count of Comminges similarly to hand over the fortress of Salies-du-Salat, and one of his sons. Viscount Aimeric and the citizens of Narbonne also swore an oath in April (*HGL* VIII, 646–7), giving similar general undertakings not to support heresy but more specifically to help the Crusade, but not if this involved taking up arms outside the diocese of Narbonne 'unless neighbouring bishoprics similarly wish to make war against violators [of the peace]'; they also promised not to take over the fortresses given as a guarantee by Sanç (who was acting as regent in Aragon), or seek to remove the young King James from the authority of the legate or of anyone to whom he might wish to commit the King. For settlement of the position of Toulouse and of Raymond VI see §507 and note.
46 For Moissac, besieged and captured by the crusaders in 1212, see §§340–53 above.
47 This period of three weeks was probably in late March and early April 1214.

Our Count rushed to help them when he heard of their plight, but the Count of Toulouse and his troops, with most of the men of Moissac, the principal authors of the treason, fled hurriedly as soon as they knew our Count was on his way, and raised the siege which they had maintained for so long.

[505] When they heard of the enemy's flight our Count and his companions set out for the Agenais,[48] in the hope of seizing a *castrum* named Le Mas d'Agenais on the boundary of the diocese of Agen, which had defected earlier that year.[49] This had happened because King John of England – who had always opposed Christ's business and the Count of Montfort – had come to the area that year, and most of the local nobles had defected from God and the Count's overlordship in the hope of receiving help from the King;[50] but through God's grace they were disappointed of their hopes, like men leaning on a staff of reeds,[51] and soon paid the penalty for their treason. Our Count hastened to Le Mas and came to a place where he needed to cross the River Garonne. He himself had only a few ill-defended boats, but the inhabitants of La Réole, a *castrum* belonging to the King of England, came up with a large force of armed ships to prevent his crossing. However, our men went into the water and crossed easily despite the enemy's opposition. They then went on to Le Mas and attacked the place for three days. However, without siege-engines the Count could not mount a strong siege and left for the Narbonne area, as he had been instructed to do by the papal legate.

[506] When the legate heard that the Count was coming to meet him, he instructed the Count to bring with him the King of Aragon's son, who was at Carcassonne. (As I recorded much earlier in this history,[52] the King had handed his son over to the Count so that he could be married to the Count's daughter.) The Count then held a meeting with the Cardinal at Capestang, a *castrum* near Narbonne;[53] the Cardinal wished the King's son to be handed over to him, and this was done.[54] [507] A few days later the legate went to Castelnaudary in the

---

[48]   De Montfort was at Penne d'Agenais on 13 April, where he received the homage of a local lord Pons Amanieu (G&L II, p. 199 n. 1, citing Molinier, 78).

[49]   Le Mas d'Agenais lies on the Garonne about 50km north-west of Agen.

[50]   King John had landed at La Rochelle in February 1214. His arrival in western France was part of an attempt to wrest control from Philip Augustus of his lost domains in Anjou, Poitou, Maine and Normandy, through an alliance with Otto of Brunswick and others. Otto was to attack the French King from Flanders, and John to do so from the west. For details and a summary of his itinerary see W. L. Warren, *King John*, pp. 217–21. After spending March further north, John went south to Gascony and advanced as far as la Réole where he stayed from 13 to 15 April 1214, and while there received forty-three oaths of allegiance (G&L II, p. 199 n. 3). In making this journey and receiving the oaths John was asserting his claim to overlordship of the Agenais, which had been held by Raymond VI as a fief of the kings of England (see §317 above). Raymond will have had the opportunity to remind John of these points (if that were needed) when he went to the English court after Muret, and John was of course no friend to Simon de Montfort, who had chosen allegiance to Philip Augustus rather than John when the latter lost Normandy in 1204. John would thus not wish to see the Agenais fall under de Montfort's control. See also §518 below for the presence of John's chamberlain, Geoffrey de Neville, at Marmande in the western Agenais; and §522 for John in the Périgord in August 1214.

[51]   Isaiah 36, v. 6.

[52]   §211.

[53]   Capestang is about 18km north of Narbonne; cf. §125.

[54]   For Innocent's instruction to de Montfort to release the young King see n. 44 to ch. 503. King James's

Toulouse region. Here he was approached by large numbers of the citizens of Toulouse begging him to reconcile the city with the Church. To summarise the results of these negotiations, the Cardinal, after taking advice with due care, reconciled the city; in addition to receiving sworn undertakings he took a hundred and twenty of the more important citizens as hostages.[55]

[508] *Arrival of the Bishop of Carcassonne from France with a large body of crusaders.* About the time of the octave of the feast of the Resurrection[56] in the year 1214 of the Incarnation the venerable Bishop of Carcassonne (who had spent the whole of the previous year travelling and preaching in France on behalf of the Crusade against the heretics)[57] set out for the Albigensian area. He had arranged a day for the departure of all the crusaders on whom he himself had bestowed the cross, as well as those who had received the cross from Master Jacques de Vitry[58] (a man worthy of praise in every respect) and other prelates. Accordingly all the different groups assembled at Nevers fifteen days after Easter, ready to travel with the Bishop through the Lyon area to confront the pestilential heretics. Master Robert de Courçon,[59] legate of the Apostolic See, and William, Archdeacon of Paris,[60] had also arranged for their crusaders to assemble fifteen days after Easter at Bourges, ready to march against the heretics by a different

---

own account of his release is in ch. X of his *Llibre dels feyts* (trans. Forster, pp. 18–19), in which he says that he was six years and four months old at the time; he adds that he was sent to the castle of Monzon, mid-way between Lérida and Huesca, where his education was supervised by William of Montredon, grand master of the Templars of Aragon and Catalonia.

55 Oaths were sworn by the consuls on behalf of the city on 25 April 1214 (*HGL* VIII, 647–51). They are to the same general effect as the oaths sworn by the Counts of Foix and Comminges (see §503). In particular, the consuls swore not to give aid to the Count of Toulouse and his son 'notwithstanding the loyalty we and the citizens owe to them', and promised to give hostages. Peter fails to mention that Raymond VI also gave sworn undertakings to the legate 'on a Friday in April' (*RHGF* XIX, 210). In two separate oaths, Raymond avowed total submission to the will of the Curia, offering in the first oath to place himself in the hands of the Church and the legate and to obey all instructions of the Pope and the legate, and to ensure his son also would place himself and his domains at their disposal. In the second, he undertakes to place in the legate's hands his domains (which he declares have passed to his son), and to go to the English King or anywhere else the legate wishes until such time as he can go to the Pope to plead for mercy and grace. He further places his son and his son's domains in the legate's hands, and promises to ensure that his son's advisers will abide by these conditions. Thus by the end of April 1214 Peter of Benevento had achieved the reconciliation of all parties, as Innocent had instructed in his letters of January, and he then left for Aragon. Innocent confirmed this on 4 February 1215: see *Layettes* I, 1099, and G&M, pp. 193/4 n. 4. In §509 our author says that the legate accepted the submission of the Toulousains and the others as a trick to divert them whilst the crusaders proceeded to attack the Agenais and Quercy. However, this seems most unlikely, since Innocent's sincerity in seeking a peace seems beyond doubt (see Appendix G), and it is hardly likely that this trusted legate would so blatantly seek to thwart his master's intentions. The truth was probably that the crusaders had no real justification for continuing the war, but nonetheless chose to circumvent the legate's achievement, using the standard pretext that there were still some heretics to be found in the area they proposed to invade. In the event the only heretics they found were the seven Waldenses burnt at Morlhon, §513. It may also be noted that on 3 May 1214, Bernard-Aton, Viscount of Nîmes and Agde, formally ceded his rights to de Montfort (*HGL* VIII, 651–3), despite Innocent having ordered Peter of Benevento to investigate the matter.

56 6 April 1214. 'Fifteen days after Easter', below, is 13 April.

57 See §418 and §439 above for Guy's preaching.

58 See §285 above on Jacques de Vitry.

59 See §439 and n. 77, and for his later activities §522, §523.

60 See above §175 for William.

route. The Bishop and the crusaders with him left Nevers and after an easy journey reached Montpellier; I myself accompanied the Bishop.[61] There we found the Archdeacon of Paris and the crusaders who had travelled with him from France. Cardinal Robert had stayed behind in the region of Puy to attend to certain business. We left Montpellier and went to the *castrum* named Saint-Thibéry, near Béziers, where the Count of Montfort met us.[62] There were about a hundred thousand of us, taking mounted men and footsoldiers together. Amongst the nobles present were the Viscount of Châteaudun[63] and numerous knights whom I need not name individually. We now left the Béziers area and went to Carcassonne where we stayed for a few days.

[509] The whole succession of events in that year is worth careful study – indeed there is a strong element of the miraculous in the way matters turned out. As recorded above, when the papal legate Master Peter of Benevento arrived in the Albigensian area, the men from Aragon and Catalonia had assembled at Narbonne to oppose Christianity and the Count of Montfort; for this reason the Count was positioned near Narbonne and unable to withdraw, since the enemy would immediately have set about ravaging the country round about. Moreover, the men of Toulouse, Agen and Quercy were mounting frequent heavy attacks against him from more distant parts. Whilst the athlete of Christ was in this difficult situation he was not without a helper in his hour of need; at one and the same time came a legate from the Curia and a host of crusaders from France! How great is God's mercy! As was widely realised, the legate would not have been so successful without the crusaders, and the crusaders would have achieved little without the legate; for, if the enemies of the faith had not been in fear of the crusaders they would not have obeyed the legate, and again if the legate had not come the crusaders (who subsequently came to face such large numbers of our enemies) could have made but little progress. Thus, Divine intervention mercifully brought it about that whilst the legate, by pious deception, diverted the attention of the enemies of the faith assembled at Narbonne and held them in check, the Count and the crusaders arriving from France were able to cross to Quercy and the Agenais and attack their enemies – Christ's enemies. Such the pious deceit, the deceitful piety, of the legate![64]

[510] *The Count goes to the Viennois.* After the crusaders had spent a few days at Carcassonne the Count of Montfort asked them to accompany the Bishop of Carcassonne and Guy de Montfort, the Count's brother, to Rouergue and Quercy[65] to lay waste the territories of Ratier de Castelnau (who had so brutally

---

[61] Thus began our author's second journey to the Midi.

[62] Saint-Thibéry lies about 18km north of Béziers; de Montfort is recorded at Béziers on 3 May 1214, when Bernard-Aton ceded to him the viscounties of Nîmes and Agde (*HGL* VIII, 651–3), so that the arrival of the crusaders there was probably at about the same time. They were to leave around the middle of June: see §516.

[63] Geoffrey IV (G&L II, p. 204 n. 3).

[64] Another word play: Latin '*O legati fraus pia, o pietas fraudulenta!*'

[65] Both the Rouergue and Quercy had been under the immediate lordship of Raymond VI. The campaign in these regions in the summer of 1214 by the crusaders was no doubt intended to reassert and demonstrate de Montfort's authority there at a time when the murder of Baldwin of Toulouse and the defection of

betrayed the most noble and Christian Count Baldwin),[66] and other enemies of Christ.

[511] The Count himself and Amaury, his eldest son, went to Valence for the marriage of Amaury to the daughter[67] of Dauphin de Viennois, brother of the Duke of Burgundy. At Valence the Count met the Duke and Dauphin, discussed the proposed marriage and reached an agreement; as, however, it was not a suitable time for the wedding and the Count could not stay long because of the various exigencies of the war, he took the girl to Carcassonne where the marriage ceremony was performed.[68]

[512] The crusaders, who had some time previously left Carcassonne and entered the diocese of Quercy, laid waste the territories of the enemies of the faith, who had left them undefended in their fear of the crusaders.

[513] *Siege of Morlhon.* I must record that whilst we were passing through the diocese of Rodez we came to a *castrum* named Morlhon.[69] The inhabitants determined to oppose us, since the place was incredibly strong and virtually inaccessible. Master Robert de Courçon, legate of the Apostolic See, mentioned earlier, was with our army, having recently arrived from France. Immediately after his arrival our men went to Morlhon and attacked it fiercely. The defenders realised they could not hold out any longer and on that very day surrendered to the legate and agreed to follow his wishes in every respect. On his instructions our men completely destroyed the place.[70] I must record that we found seven heretics of the Waldensian[71] sect; they were at once led to the legate and confessed their unbelief freely and fully. The crusaders seized them and burnt them with great rejoicing.

[514] We left Morlhon and set about laying waste the territories of that most evil traitor, Ratier of Castelnau, and others who that year had treacherously deserted God and the Church. We destroyed Castelnau and razed to the ground numerous strong castles in the area, after which we came to a *castrum* named

many local lords must have been felt to threaten it. While de Montfort at first went east to the Viennois to conclude the arrangement of his son's marriage (§511), leaving his brother Guy to begin the campaign in the Rouergue, he rejoined the main force as soon as he could in June (§515) in order to take the campaign west into Quercy and the Agenais.

[66] See §§495–500 above.
[67] Béatrice de Viennois, daughter of André-Dauphin, Count of the Viennois. See §492 above for the earlier arrangement of this marriage.
[68] De Montfort is recorded as being at Carcassonne on 4 June when he gave Verfeil to Bishop Fulk of Toulouse (Rhein 122, and *HGL* VIII, 653). The future St Dominic blessed the marriage (see Vicaire, p. 145 and n. 59).
[69] Morlhon lies just south of Villefranche-de-Rouergue.
[70] Throughout the campaign of 1214 in the Rouergue, Quercy, the Agenais and Périgord, now described in §§514–41, de Montfort's policy was to destroy most of the fortifications he took, in order to make it much more difficult for the local lords to resume their resistance to him once he had left the area. The policy is stated clearly by our author in §517, when he notes that only the strongest places were left intact and garrisoned with crusader troops.
[71] Apart from the references in §§18 and 48 this is the only appearance of the Waldensians in the History. For a discussion of the Waldensians in the Midi at this time see Roquebert II pp. 269–74 and Lambert, *Medieval Heresy*, pp. 160–2, where he comments that the Crusade whilst creating the conditions for their persecution did not have a major impact on them.

Mondenard. The lord of this place, Bertrand,[72] had been the principal author of the betrayal of Count Baldwin. We found the place empty and destroyed it.

[515] The Count of Montfort joined us here.[73] His brother Guy had left the army and gone to the Albigeois[74] to deal with certain matters needing his attention.

[516] After the destruction of Mondenard the Count was informed that some knights from the Agenais who in the previous year had treacherously rejected his overlordship, had fortified a notable *castrum* named Montpezat[75] in the diocese of Agen. We therefore set off for this place with a view to besieging it, despite the small number of crusaders with us – those who had come from France with the Bishop of Carcassonne had completed their forty days' service and returned home.[76] However, the knights in Montpezat fled in fear when they heard we were coming and left the place empty. Our men then destroyed it completely.

[517] Our Count then left Montpezat and marched into the diocese of Agen intending to occupy the *castra* which had treacherously deserted him in the previous year. All his adversaries, fearful of his approach, surrendered to him before he actually reached them, with the exception of a notable *castrum* known as Marmande.[77] The Count had the keeps and walls of almost all these places torn down, to improve his security and to ensure that they would not revolt again, as they had been wont to do. He followed this practice in regard to the fortifications of captured places not only in the diocese of Agen, but in all the territories he captured, except for a few of the stronger *castra* which he decided to fortify and hold for the benefit of himself or of the French.

[518] The Count now set off to lay siege to Marmande and found it strongly defended. A certain knight,[78] a chamberlain of the English King, had brought some sergeants into the *castrum* and fixed his standard on top of the keep, intending to defend the place against us. As our men approached and reached the walls the inhabitants, after a modest show of resistance, began to flee; they took refuge in some boats on the Garonne and quickly went downstream to a *castrum* named La Réole,[79] which belonged to the English King. The King's sergeants who

---

72 Bertrand is not mentioned by name in Peter's account of Baldwin's death in §§495–500 above; he is recorded as an ally of Raymond the Younger of Toulouse when he retook Moissac in 1222 (see G&L II, p. 209 n. 1). A relative who had sided with the crusaders, one Armand, is mentioned in the *Chanson* (I, 122, p. 272, and II, 185, p. 296).

73 He is recorded as being at Montcuq, 12km from Mondenard, on 12 June when he received the homage of Déodat de Barasc, who held Béduer, Montbrun and Lissac, near Figeac in Quercy (Molinier 81). Déodat undertook to destroy his castles or pay a large fine.

74 '*Partes Albienses*', as opposed to '*partes Albigenses*' in §508 etc. See n. 10 to §4, and Appendix A(iii).

75 Montpezat-d'Agenais, about 18km north of Agen.

76 This force of crusaders had arrived at Béziers during the first week of May 1214 (see §508 above), so that their forty days' service will have come to an end about the time that de Montfort rejoined the force in the middle of June.

77 Marmande, in the western Agenais and at almost the westernmost point of Raymond VI's lands, was held by Raymond VI of the English Kings. It had been taken by Robert Mauvoisin in July 1212 at the time of the siege of Penne d'Agenais (see §336 above). It had probably been occupied by forces of King John at the time he was present in the area earlier in 1214 (see §505).

78 Geoffrey de Neville (G&L II, p. 211).

79 Cf. above, §505, for La Réole.

had come to defend Marmande retreated into the keep. Our men now entered the *castrum* and pillaged it, but the Count allowed the sergeants to leave alive and unharmed. After this the Count was advised by his companions not to destroy the place completely, in view of its importance and its location at the boundaries of his territories; instead he should leave a garrison in the keep and pull down the other towers and part of the walls. This was done, and the Count resumed his march towards Agen with the object of laying siege to Casseneuil.

[519] *Siege of Casseneuil.*[80] Casseneuil was a noteworthy and very strong *castrum* in the Agenais.[81] It stood on pleasant level ground, at the foot of a hill. It was surrounded by streams which were overlooked by rocky outcrops. It was one of the most important and long-established seats of heresy.[82] Most of its inhabitants were heretics, thieves and perjurers, full of iniquity and sins of every description. Twice they had been reconciled with Christianity;[83] now they intended for the third time to oppose Christianity and our Count. The lord of the place was Hugh of Revignan, brother of the Bishop of Agen. He had been a close friend of our Count, but that year he had renounced his oath of fealty and in an act of treachery seceded from God and the Count. Numerous other traitors, including those who had taken part in the betrayal of Count Baldwin,[84] had assembled in the *castrum* since it was very strong and was the only remaining refuge in the area for the enemies of the Christian faith.

[520] The Count arrived before Casseneuil with his army on the eve of the festival of the Apostles St Peter and St Paul. He established the siege on one side of the place only, on the hill,[85] since his forces were not adequate to make a complete circle. After a few days he had siege-engines set up to break down the walls; by constant firing both against the walls and inside the *castrum* they very soon destroyed numerous dwellings. The arrival of some crusaders a few days later prompted the Count to come down from the hill and pitch his camp on level ground near the *castrum*.[86] He took part of the army with him, but left part on the hill with that noble and gallant youth Amaury, his son, and Guy the Bishop of Carcassonne, who was performing the functions of papal legate[87] and

---

[80] The siege lasted from 28 June (the feast of St Peter and St Paul, see §520) until 18 August 1214 (§527).
[81] Casseneuil lies about 25km north of Agen. The River Lot runs along its south-western side, with smaller tributaries (the Lède and the Saoune) flowing from the north-east and north-west. On its north-western side in particular it was overlooked by limestone outcrops. A deep ditch protected its south-eastern side. It was thus a naturally well protected site.
[82] See n. 65 to §317 for heresy in the Agenais, and discussions in Griffe, *Débuts*, pp. 72–83, and Duvernoy, *Histoire des Cathares*, pp. 215–19. But apart from the burnings of 1209 (see next note) there is little direct evidence that by the early 13th century the Agenais was a major centre of Catharism.
[83] In July 1209, Casseneuil had been besieged by those crusaders who entered Quercy in the *Croisade Quercynoise* (see n. to §83), and it was the scene of the first burnings of heretics when it was taken: see *Chanson* I, 13–14, pp. 40–4. Its lord, Hugh of Revignan (see below), had submitted to de Montfort in July 1212 at Agen, when de Montfort first entered the Agenais (see §317 and §325 above). For his brother, Bishop Arnold of Revignan, see §317 above.
[84] See above, §§495–500 and §514.
[85] To the north-west of Casseneuil.
[86] To the south-east of the *castrum*, known as the plaine du Magiscat (G&L II, p. 214 n. 4).
[87] For an earlier reference to Guy's acting as vice-legate see §324.

was working hard and to great effect to assist in the seizure of the *castrum*. The Count now had siege-engines of the type known as 'petraries' erected on the level ground where he had positioned himself. These kept up a constant fire by night and by day and severely damaged the walls.

[521] One night as dawn approached a large contingent of our adversaries left the *castrum*, climbed the hill, and mounted a concerted attack against our army. They went to the tent where the Count's son Amaury was sleeping and rushed in hoping to capture or kill him. Our men ran to the spot and attacked the enemy valiantly, compelling them to retire.

[522] Whilst these events were taking place at the siege, John, King of England (who was much disturbed that his nephew the son of the Count of Toulouse[88] had been dispossessed of his territories, and was envious of our successes), advanced towards the area, specifically to the city of Périgueux, with a large army.[89] He had been joined by large numbers of the enemies of Christ and of ourselves, whose sins had by a just judgment of God led to their losing their possessions. The King took them under his wing and kept them with him for some time, which was the subject of wide-spread scandal and gravely injured his reputation. The enemy besieged in Casseneuil kept sending envoys to the King begging him to help them; the King for his part kept sending messengers and making promises and thus inciting them to resist. What more? Our army was alive with rumours that the King was going to attack us, and indeed he would have done so had he dared. As it was the courageous Count of Montfort was not in the least frightened by these reports, but resolutely determined that if the King did attack the army he would not raise the siege but would fight him in defence of his men and himself. The King followed wiser counsels, and made no attempt to carry out any of the actions which were the subject of these rumours – and which he may well have been considering.[90]

[523] I must add that Master Robert de Courçon, Cardinal and legate of the Apostolic See, mentioned above, had joined the army at the siege of Casseneuil; there he remained for a few days, exerting every effort to help in the attack on the

---

[88] Raymond the younger's mother was John's sister Joan, who had been Raymond VI's third wife: see n. 49 to §38, n. 67 to §317 and n. 86 to §484.

[89] See above, §505 and n. 50, for John's presence in Gascony and Aquitaine in 1214. He had remained there after the disastrous defeat of his allies by Philip Augustus at Bouvines on 27 July 1214. For details of his movements in Périgord in August see G&L II, p. 215 n. 4. The sources for John's dealings with Raymond VI in 1214 are helpfully summarised in J. Sumption, *The Albigensian Crusade* (London, 1978), p. 255 n. 23.

[90] Despite John's interest in recovering the Agenais for Raymond VI, and his poor relationship with Simon de Montfort, it is unlikely that he had any serious intention of military confrontation with the crusaders at this time. During June the legate Robert de Courçon was also active in Aquitaine negotiating a peace between John and the French King and at a council in Bordeaux on 26 June he had declared that John was 'prepared to stand by the orders of the Pope and the advice of the Church in all matters in regard to all *castra* and towns belonging to him in the dioceses of Agen and Cahors'; in another letter written in August John instructs the mayor and leading citizens of La Réole to reimburse the Archbishop of Bordeaux with 20,000 *solidi* which he had advanced to de Montfort as guarantor for John, and to arrange to recover the money from the town: for sources see G&L II, pp. 216–17 n. 1. Moreover, John's main interests lay in the north, where early in July he had suffered a severe setback when, besieging Roche-au-Moine in Anjou, his Poitevin allies had melted away at the approach of Prince Louis of France. Opening a campaign against the crusaders was unlikely to have been a priority for him.

castrum, as was to be expected of so well-disposed a man. However, pressing business connected with his duties took him away and he did not stay to see Casseneuil taken.[91]

[524] So we continued to press on with the siege, and had succeeded through our siege-engines in weakening the walls at many points. One day the Count summoned some of the leaders of the army and a master carpenter[92] and asked the latter to suggest some means of enabling our men to get close to the walls and take the *castrum* by an assault, bearing in mind that there was deep water between our forces and the *castrum*, which our men would have to cross to reach the walls. There was no bridge, since the existing bridge had been destroyed by the enemy from the other side before we arrived. At the meeting there was much discussion, but at length it was agreed to follow the advice of the master carpenter to construct a bridge of wood and hurdles, which could by an ingenious arrangement be driven across on large casks and thus serve to carry our men over the water. At once the venerable Bishop of Carcassonne (who was labouring to an incredible extent night and day on anything that might help the siege) summoned a crowd of crusaders and had them gather large quantities of wood to build the bridge. As soon as the bridge was completed our men put on their armour ready to attack, and rolled the bridge up to the water's edge. However, as soon as the bridge reached the water, its own weight and the fact that the bank at that point was high and not level enough caused it to plunge under the surface of the water with such force that it could not be drawn back or lifted up. So all our work on the bridge came to nothing in a single moment. After a few days our men constructed another bridge of a different kind, in the hope that it would enable them to cross the water, and also made ready a few small boats which would allow part of our force to cross, albeit at great risk. When all was ready our men put on their armour and dragged the bridge to the water, whilst some of them boarded the boats. The defenders, who had a large number of petraries, kept up a constant heavy bombardment. What more? Our men pushed the bridge across the water but achieved nothing, since the bridge proved to be too short and quite inadequate. Our men were greatly dejected, the enemy quite delighted.

---

91 In July, while at Sainte-Livrade near Casseneuil, Robert de Courçon issued a general letter (*HGL* VIII, 653–5) confirming Simon and his heirs in possession of all conquests, past and future, in the dioceses of Cahors, Agen, Rodez and Albi, '*in perpetuum*'. The justification advanced was based on the doctrine of *exposition en proie* (on which see n. 34 to §62), to which his letter refers specifically ('*precipue quia terre hereticorum, defensorum, receptatorum and fautorum eorum a sede Apostolica erant expositae*' 'chiefly because the territories of the heretics, their defenders, receivers amd supporters had been exposed by the Apostolic See'). Robert's letter makes no direct reference to the current involvement of other legates, but he claimed to have the authority to act as he did ('*auctoritate qua fungimur*'). However, Innocent III had never abandoned his basic position that no final decision regarding possible dispossession of Count Raymond could yet be reached (see Appendix G) and continued to maintain it until the Fourth Lateran Council: see notes to §547, §§571–3. Thus Robert seems to have exceeded his authority. How his brief from the Pope interacted with that of Peter of Benevento is unclear.

92 '*Artifex carpentarius*'. He is referred to below as '*artifex*' and '*magister artificum*', and his subordinates as '*artifices*' which we translate as 'carpenters'. These craftsmen, highly skilled in constructing siege engines, might perhaps deserve the title of 'engineers'.

[525] Our Count, steadfast as ever, was not in the least disheartened by this setback. Instead he summoned his carpenters, consoled them and ordered them to make fresh efforts to construct engines which might provide a means of crossing the water. The master carpenter thereupon devised a marvellous and novel engine. He had some large timbers brought up and first, using the most substantial timbers as a foundation, built a sort of large house of wood, with a roof of hurdles which was flat rather than pitched. Then on the roof he erected a sort of high tower of hurdles, with five storeys to act as platforms for crossbow-men. Round the tower, on the roof of the 'house' he built a sort of wall of hurdles, on which a substantial number of our men would be able to stand to defend the tower; they would be supplied with copious quantities of water in large bowls to put out any fires the enemy might start. In addition, to prevent the enemy setting the construction on fire the master carpenter had the front covered with ox-hides. When all was ready our men began to drag and push the engine towards the water. The enemy kept up a heavy fire of large stones from the petraries, but by God's grace did little or no damage. When our men had man-aged to drag the engine up to the water, they brought up earth, wood and other materials in baskets and deposited them in the water; the men who were pro-tected by the lower roof, and unarmed, filled the moat, whilst the crossbowmen and others on the higher parts of the fortified engine contained the enemy's attacks. One night the enemy filled a small boat with dry wood, salted meat, fat and other inflammable material, hoping to propel it against our engine and set it alight; they failed, because our sergeants burnt the boat.

[526] What else? Our men continued to work on filling the moat and our engine was gradually moved across dry and unharmed, since each day they filled up a little more of the moat and moved the engine forward by the same amount. One Sunday[93] our adversaries realised that with the advance of the engine they were in imminent danger of being captured; they hurled fire against the engine but achieved nothing since our men were able to extinguish the flames with water, for by now the two sides were so close together that they could attack each other with lances. This led the Count to think the enemy might succeed in setting fire to the engine at night, and accordingly on that same Sunday, towards evening, he ordered his men to put on their armour and had them summoned by trumpet to assemble, ready to attack. The Bishop of Carcassonne and the numerous other priests with the army gathered on raised ground near the *castrum*, to cry out to heaven and pray for our men as they fought. Our armed men entered the engine, broke down the front wall of hurdles and with great courage crossed the moat. Meanwhile the priests sang the *Veni Creator Spiritus*[94] with great devotion. As we attacked, the enemy retired inside the walls and began to counter-attack us fiercely by hurling rocks down from the top of the walls. Night was approaching and our men had no ladders, so they could not scale the walls, but they were able to take up positions on a small level area between the walls and the moat, and

---

[93] 17 August (see §527, where 18 August is '*[a.d.] XV kalendas septembris*').
[94] As was done at the sieges of Lavaur (§226) and Moissac (see §351).

during the night destroyed several barbicans which the enemy had erected outside the walls.

[527] Our carpenters worked all next day to construct ladders and other equipment in the hope that an assault on the *castrum* on the following day would succeed in capturing it. The mercenaries inside saw this and were fearful of the outcome, and during the night they came out of the *castrum*, mounted and armed, as if to attack us, but in fact they all fled. Most of our troops pursued them for some time, but failed to capture them; the rest approached the *castrum* in the middle of the night, forced an entry, and set the place on fire. They burnt it, and put to the sword anyone they came across. Blessed is God in all things! He gave the wicked into our hands, even though not them all. After this the Count had the walls razed to the ground. In this way Casseneuil was taken and destroyed, on 18 August, in praise of our Lord Jesus Christ, to whom be glory and honour, with the Father and Holy Spirit, for ever and ever, Amen.[95]

[528] *The Count enters the Périgord region.* After these events, our Count was informed that certain *castra* in the diocese of Périgueux were harbouring enemies of peace and the faith; the reports were true. The Count therefore decided to march against these *castra* and occupy them. Thus, through God's grace and with the help of the crusaders, he might drive out the mercenaries and brigands and leave the churches of Périgord – indeed the whole territory – to enjoy peace. All the enemies of Christ and our Count were so seized with fear when they heard of the fall of Casseneuil that they did not dare wait for his arrival, even in the most strongly fortified places.

[529] The Count thus led the army from Casseneuil and reached one of these *castra*, Domme,[96] and found it empty and without a single defender. It was a noteworthy place, strongly fortified and pleasantly situated above the River Dordogne. The Count had the keep, which was very high and most attractively constructed, made of stone almost to the top, undermined and pulled down.

[530] About half-a-league further on there was a remarkably strong *castrum* named Montfort.[97] Bernard de Cazenac,[98] the lord of the place, a most cruel and

---

95 St Dominic's biographer Jordan of Saxony says (37) that after the siege de Montfort 'who was especially devoted to [Dominic], granted him, with his consent, the important *castrum* which is called Casseneuil, to support him and his colleagues in their ministry of salvation'. Jordan of Saxony also makes it clear (40) that it was the revenues of Casseneuil which Dominic received. The donation came at the time Dominic was moving his base from Fanjeaux to Toulouse. For details and references see Vicaire, ch. IX, p. 162, with full discussion given in n. 248; a French translation of Jordan's text is given in Vicaire, ed., *Saint Dominique et ses Frères: Evangile ou Croisade?* (Paris, 1967), pp. 81–4.

96 Domme lies on the southern bank of the River Dordogne, not far from Sarlat. The *castrum* at this time was sited a little to the west of the modern town, on a spur overlooking the river.

97 Montfort lies about 5km north-east of Domme, overlooking the north bank of the Dordogne.

98 Our author here portrays Bernard as an odious tyrant, but for the author of the *Chanson*, writing of his entry into Toulouse in 1218, he was the perfect knight, the personification of noble qualities (see *Chanson* III, 199, pp. 138–9). He was subsequently given Castelsarrasin by Raymond VII, and is known from later Inquisition depositions taken there to have received Cathars in the town. His relationships with the Church were very poor, and the abbot of the nearby monastery of Sarlat welcomed the crusaders and was instrumental in securing the submission to them of the knights and townsmen of La Roque-Gageac on 12 September 1214 (Molinier 87). He was deprived of his lands by de Montfort in September 1214, and they

evil man, fled in fear before our Count leaving the town empty. So numerous were the cruelties, the rapines, the enormities, perpetrated by this vicious criminal, that they can scarcely be believed or even imagined. Perverted though he was, the Devil had procured for him a helper like himself, his wife,[99] sister of the Viscount of Turenne.[100] This second Jezebel – rather, far more beastly and cruel than Jezebel, more evil than any woman ever – was no whit behind her husband in brutality and evil-doing. These two, in the depths of their criminality, despoiled and even destroyed churches. They attacked crusaders, they persecuted widows and the poor. They cut off the limbs of the innocent; in a single Benedictine monastery, at Sarlat,[101] our men found a hundred and fifty men and women whose hands or feet had been amputated, or who had their eyes torn out, or suffered other mutilations inflicted by this tyrant or his wife. She indeed, utterly without pity, had the nipples of women of the poorer sort torn out, or their thumbs cut off so that they would be useless for any labour. What unheard-of cruelty! Since I cannot describe even one thousandth part of the evil crimes committed by this tyrant and his wife, let us leave this topic and return to my main theme.

[531] *Destruction of Montfort and other castra.* After destroying Domme the Count decided to destroy Montfort, the seat of this tyrant. At once the Bishop of Carcassonne, who was devoting himself unstintingly to advancing Christ's business, took with him a section of the army of crusaders and set about destroying the place. The walls were, however, so strong (since the cement had become as hard as stone) that it proved barely possible to pull them down, and our men had to spend several days on the task. The crusaders set out to their work early each morning and returned to their tents each evening; the army had not moved from Domme, which was larger and more suitable for an encampment.

[532] There was another fortress near Montfort named Castelnaud,[102] which was just as perverted as its neighbours. It had been deserted by its inhabitants in fear of our army. The Count decided to occupy it to help him to keep in check those who were working against peace. He now carried out this intention.

[533] There was a fourth *castrum* nearby, named Beynac.[103] Its lord[104] was an evil man, a cruel robber and a violent oppressor of churches. Our Count gave him a choice of alternatives; either he must restore everything he had stolen by a

---

were granted instead to his brother-in-law Raymond of Turenne (see n. 100 below). Bernard recovered his lands in 1215 (§569) and appears as helping Raymond of Toulouse in §606; see *Chanson* III, p. 60 and n. 4 on p. 61 which gives details on Bernard.

99   Elise or (Hélis) of Montfort, for whom see G&L II, p. 225 n. 2.

100   Raymond of Turenne had joined the crusaders in Quercy in 1209 (*Chanson* I, 13, p. 40). At the end of June 1214 he paid homage to de Montfort (Molinier 82) and as noted above he was granted Bernard de Cazenac's lands in September (Molinier 88). For further details see G&L II, p. 225 n. 3.

101   The abbey lay about 6km north-west of Montfort. Its abbot was with the crusaders in September (G&L II, p. 226 n. 3, citing Molinier 87).

102   About 8km west of Montfort, on the south bank of the Dordogne, at the point where it is joined by the River Céou. It was recovered by Bernard de Cazenac the following year (§569 below).

103   Beynac lies about 3km north of Castelnaud, on the north bank of the Dordogne, on an outcrop overlooking the river.

104   Gaillard de Beynac (G&L II, p. 228 n. 2).

date to be fixed by the Count and the bishops present, or see the walls of his *castrum* torn down. He was granted a truce for several days to reach his decision. As he failed to make restitution of the stolen property within the period allowed the Count decided to pull down the castle of the *castrum*. Accordingly, much against the wishes of this tyrant and to his great distress, the Count had the keep and the walls levelled. The perverted lord of Beynac pleaded that his *castrum* should be spared this fate on the grounds that he alone in that area had helped the King of France against the King of England.[105] The Count knew these claims were empty and frivolous, and did not turn from his purpose. The tyrant had previously laid these claims before the King of France but had gained nothing.

[534] In this way we achieved the subjugation of four *castra*, Domme, Montfort, Castelnaud and Beynac. For a hundred years and more Satan's seat[106] had been in these four places, from them iniquity had gone forth on the face of the earth. After their subjugation by the toil of the crusaders and the valour and skill of the noble Count of Montfort peace and tranquillity were restored not only to the inhabitants of Périgord, but also to the people of Quercy, the Agenais and most of the Limousin.

[535] After these triumphs had been accomplished, to the glory of Christ's name, our Count and the army returned to the Agenais.[107] Now that the opportunity had arisen he arranged for the demolition of all the fortified places in the diocese of Agen.

[536] The Count then went to Figeac[108] to sit in judgment in the King's stead on lawsuits and prosecutions involving the local inhabitants, since the King had appointed him as his representative in the area for many purposes.[109] He heard many cases, and set right numerous wrongs. He could have dealt with many more had he not been reluctant to exceed the authority given him by the King.

[537] *The Count goes to Rodez.* The Count then proceeded to the diocese of Rodez, and took possession of a very strong *castrum* near Figeac named Capdenac,[110] which had from of old been a nest and refuge for mercenaries. The Count and the army then went to the city of Rodez. Our Count had numerous causes of complaint against Henry, Count of Rodez, who was our Count's liegeman; however, by way of excuse Henry argued that he held the greater part of his lands as a

---

[105] This was because some twenty years earlier, when campaigning in Aquitaine, Richard of England had granted Beynac to one of his most favoured mercenary captains, Mercadier: see G&L II, p. 228 n. 5.

[106] Cf. Revelations 2, v. 13.

[107] He was at Penne d'Agenais towards the end of September when he received the homage there of a local seigneur Raymond de Montaut (Molinier 89).

[108] Figeac lies in north-eastern Quercy. Having left the Agenais at the end of September (see preceding §) de Montfort and his army crossed Quercy and passing through Cahors reached Figeac in October 1214. During that month the Abbot of Figeac granted him as a fief the castle of Peyrusse, south of Capendac, and associated rights in the area formerly belonging to Raymond VI (Molinier 91, Rhein 124).

[109] Thus Philip Augustus was apparently recognising Simon as de facto Count of Toulouse, since in February 1195 he had delegated all his rights over Figeac to Raymond VI (*HGL* VIII, 432, and G&L II, p. 230 n. 2).

[110] The submission of the lords of Capdenac to de Montfort took place during October 1214 (Molinier 90, Rhein 123), and was witnessed by the Bishops of Rodez, Cahors and Mende, and Guy de Montfort.

vassal of the King of England.[111] After numerous arguments Count Henry agreed that he held all his lands as our Count's vassal and did homage to him in respect of the whole. In this way the two became friends and allies.[112]

[538] *Siege and capture of Séverac-le-Château.* Near Rodez there was a strong *castrum* known as Séverac-le-Château,[113] the haunt of mercenaries, disturbers of the peace and of the faith. It is not easy to describe the number and gravity of the ills originating in this place; its inhabitants were not only molesting the diocese of Rodez, but were inciting disorder in the whole surrounding area as far as Puy. Whilst our Count was at Rodez he ordered the lord of Séverac[114] to surrender it; the latter refused, since he had great faith in the strength of the castle and believed the Count would not be able to maintain a siege, bearing in mind that it was winter and that Séverac was in a mountainous region exposed to the cold weather.

[539] One night Guy de Montfort, the Count's brother, left Rodez taking with him some knights and sergeants. During the night he rode to Séverac and at first light, just as dawn arrived, he rushed into the lower bourg[115] and at once seized and occupied it. The enemy retreated into the castle, which was higher up on the summit of a hill; the bourg extended from outside the castle down the slope to the bottom of the hill. Guy installed himself in the bourg to prevent the enemy from setting it on fire when our army approached.

[540] Accordingly, when the Count with his army reached Séverac[116] he found the bourg unharmed and an ample number of houses suitable for lodging his troops. After occupying these our men strengthened the siege. This was indeed the doing of the Lord, a true support in times of trouble and a goodly helper in the hour of need. After a few days our men erected a siege-engine of the type

---

111   The county of Rodez (the Rouergue) was a fief of the Counts of Toulouse, and Henry Count of Rodez was thus a vassal of Raymond VI. Henry was the illegitimate brother of William of Rodez, who on his death in 1208 had left the county to Count Guy of the Auvergne. However, Raymond VI had managed to recover the fief and had granted it to Henry in 1210 (see Roquebert II, p. 291). Any claim that Henry was a vassal of Simon de Montfort could be based only on the latter's as yet unconfirmed tenure of the county of Toulouse following the charter issued by Robert de Courçon in June 1214, on which see n. 91 to §523. During the siege of Casseneuil (§§519–27) Bishop Peter of Rodez had pressed Simon to take control of Rodez, and on 11 September promised in writing that he and his chapter would conform to Simon's wishes (see Molinier 86). Peter seems to be correct in saying that Henry's claim to hold part of his fiefdom from the King of England was an excuse; there is no direct evidence of this, although his neighbours the Count of Auvergne and the Viscount of Limoges were the King's vassals (G&L II, p. 231 n. 4).

112   Pressure from the Bishop of Rodez and other prelates persuaded Henry to yield. The act of homage to Simon, dated to 7 November 1214, is in *HGL* VIII, 655, Molinier 93, and Rhein 125. It was witnessed by the Bishops of Rodez, Mende, Cahors, Carcassonne, Albi and Uzès, and by a number of crusader knights: for further details see Roquebert II, pp. 291–2. William de Beynes, from near Montfort l'Amaury, became de Montfort's seneschal of the Rouergue (G&L II, p. 231 n. 6).

113   Séverac-le-Château is about 40km east of Rodez, at the eastern extremity of the Rouergue, on the border with the Gévaudan.

114   Déodat III of Séverac (G&L II, p. 232 n. 3).

115   The '*burgum inferius*', which lay on the south-east side of the hill, below the castle (the '*munitionem superiorem*' of the next sentence).

116   Simon arrived before 16 November since he is recorded as being at Séverac on that date, when the Bishops of Mende and Rodez granted him (in return for payment) control of two castles they held on behalf of the Church (*HGL* VIII, 657; Molinier 94; Rhein 126; and see G&M, p. 206 n. 2).

known as a petrary and began to bombard the *castrum*. The enemy set up a similar engine and used it to harass us as best they could. I must not pass over the point that the Lord had so reduced the enemy's supplies that they were in extreme want. Moreover, they had only thin clothing of poor quality, so that the bitter cold of winter was severely affecting them and they did not know which way to turn. If anyone is surprised at their wretched condition, he should realise that our forces had beset them so suddenly that they had no time to collect supplies of arms or provisions; as I said, they did not expect us to be able to mount a siege in the middle of winter in such a cold place.

[541] After only a few days, overcome by hunger and thirst, by cold and their nakedness, they asked for a truce. What more? Discussions about terms were long and complex, but at last wise counsels were followed both by our side and by the lord of Séverac, and accord was reached[117] on the following terms: the lord was to surrender Séverac to the Count, who in turn would hand it to the Bishop of Rodez[118] and a powerful local noble named Peter Bermond[119] for garrisoning. The agreement was duly carried out. At once the noble Count, with true generosity, restored to the lord of Séverac all the rest of his territories which had been occupied by Guy of Montfort, but before doing so he exacted from him a promise that he would not take reprisals against his vassals for having surrendered to Guy. Later, again demonstrating his generosity, the Count even restored Séverac to its former lord, having received from him homage and an oath of fealty. Thus the Count granted him pardon and accepted him as a friend. I must add that the surrender of Séverac led to the restoration of peace and stability to the whole area. For all this, praise be to the Lord and gratitude to his most faithful athlete, our most Christian Count of Montfort.[120]

[542] After this, Master Peter of Benevento, legate of the Apostolic See, whom I mentioned above,[121] returned from Aragon, where he had for some time been engaged on important business.[122] He now summoned a Council, with a very

---

117 On 30 November 1214 (G&L II, p. 234 n. 3).

118 Bishop Peter, 1211–34: G&L II, p. 234 n. 4.

119 Peter-Bermond, lord of Sauve, Sommières and Anduze, and married to Constance, daughter of Raymond VI of Toulouse by his second wife, Béatrice de Béziers. He had earlier taken part in the Fourth Crusade, and had joined the Albigensian Crusade in 1209 (*Chanson* I, 12, p. 36) and was amongst the oath-takers at Saint-Gilles in June that year (cf. §77 and see *PL* 216, 96). He claimed to be entitled to be recognised as heir to the county of Toulouse on the grounds that Count Raymond's marriage to Joan of England was illegal so that Raymond the Younger was a bastard. This claim was set out in a letter he wrote to Pope Innocent on 20 December 1212 (*PL* 216, 754–5), in which incidentally he recorded a long-standing friendship with Simon de Montfort. There is no record of a response from Innocent. He attended the Fourth Lateran Council to restate his claim (see William of Puylaurens XXIV), and died there. For a full account of the claims of the House of Anduze to the county of Toulouse see Roquebert II, pp. 75–9.

120 Thus the campaigns of 1214 had seen Simon de Montfort traverse the Périgord, the Agenais, Quercy, and the Rouergue, reducing all opposition and taking control of strong points. He had received the submission of many local lords, and with the active support of local bishops he had made himself master of the whole of the northern portion of Raymond VI's possessions.

121 See §§503–7 above.

122 After the oath taking of April 1214 (§§503–7), Peter of Benevento had gone to Aragon where he was involved in establishing a regency to cover the minority of King James I. During his absence de Montfort and the crusaders, supported by Robert de Courçon and the southern prelates (cf. §523 n. 91), had in effect ignored the settlement he had reached with Raymond VI and had continued with the conquests of

large attendance, representing many interests, to meet at Montpellier fifteen days after Christmas 1214.[123]

[543] *Council of Montpellier.* Accordingly on the fifteenth day after Christmas in the year 1214 of the Incarnation, in response to the summons issued by Master Peter, the papal legate, a Council of archbishops and bishops gathered at Montpellier.[124] Their purpose was to enable the legate to make arrangements relating to peace and the faith, in line with the advice of the prelates. Amongst those present were five archbishops (those of Narbonne, Auch, Embrun, Arles and Aix),[125] twenty-eight bishops and numerous local barons and nobles.

[544] The Count of Montfort did not enter Montpellier with the others, but spent the period of the Council at a nearby *castrum*[126] under the lordship of the Bishop of Maguelonne; the inhabitants of Montpellier – evil and arrogant men – nourished a deep hatred of the Count and the French, and refused him entry into their town.[127] Accordingly, as mentioned, he stayed in the *castrum* and each day went to the hospice of the Knights Templar outside the walls of Montpellier,[128] where the archbishops and bishops came to him whenever the need arose.

[545] So, after the legate, the archbishops, bishops, abbots and other church-men had gathered at Montpellier, the legate delivered a sermon in the church of

---

Raymond's lands described in §§508–41 above. Thus by the end of 1214 Peter of Benevento was presented with something of a *fait accompli.*

[123]   The summons to the Council was issued on 7 December 1214, so that it was due to convene on 8 January 1215 (for the summons see Mansi, XXII 950–1). Peter of les Vaux-de-Cernay here (and in the next chapter) states that the Council of Montpellier was summoned by Peter of Benevento, and this is accepted by some modern authorities (see e.g. Griffe, *Croisade*, pp. 101–2). On this view the legate's motive may have been to seek to review and clarify the Church's attitude to de Montfort's conquests of 1214, bearing in mind Innocent III's instructions to him (see §503 above). But if so he was in a weak position given that all the southern prelates strongly supported de Montfort, and wanted to see him formally recognised as Count of Toulouse. However, the copy of the summons noted above is in Robert de Courçon's name, and Roquebert II, pp. 297–8 argues that this shows that it was de Courçon, an active promoter of de Montfort's interests since coming south with new crusaders in April 1214 (see §508), who was the driving force behind the Council. If so, then de Courçon's aim in calling the Council would have been to ensure formal recognition by the prelates of the southern churches for de Montfort's conquest of Raymond VI's lands, and help put pressure on Innocent to accept the position.

[124]   On 8 January 1215 (G&L II, p. 236 n. 5).

[125]   Arnold Amalric of Narbonne, Garsia of Auch, Bernard of Embrun, Michael of Arles and Bermond of Aix (see G&L II, p. 237 nn. 1–5).

[126]   At le Terral, south-west of Montpellier (see G&L II, p. 238 n. 1).

[127]   The attitude of the citizens of Montpellier to Simon de Montfort at this time is discussed in Roquebert II, pp. 298–301; cf. also A. Fliche, 'La vie religieuse à Montpellier sous le pontificat d'Innocent III 1198–1216', in *Mélanges d'Histoire du Moyen Age dédiés à la mémoire de Louis Halphen* (Paris, 1951), pp. 215–24. Montpellier had never been regarded as anything but loyal to the Catholic Church, but the attempts by King Peter of Aragon to secure control of the lordship after the death of William VIII (see n. 39 to §419) and his inability to enforce its donation to William IX had resulted in the consuls and the citizens gaining effective control of the city's administration. The consuls of Montpellier were now anxious to preserve their position and prevent any incursion by the crusaders. This was especially so bearing in mind that in 1211 King Peter had nominally given charge of the city to de Montfort as part of the arrangements governing the betrothal of his young son James and de Montfort's daughter (again see n. 39 to §419); given his successful conquests and by now unconcealed ambitions the citizens of Montpellier would have been anxious to exclude him from their city and discourage him from seeking to reassert his claims. See also n. 10 to §552, on the attempts at this time by the consuls of Montpellier to secure the protection of Philip Augustus, and for their approach to Innocent himself.

[128]   To the south of the town (see sources cited in G&L II, p. 238 n. 2)

the Blessed Virgin Mary.[129] Then he summoned the five archbishops, the twenty-eight bishops, the abbots and numerous other prelates to the house where he was lodging. When they had gathered together he first addressed them thus: 'I ask and require you – calling to witness Divine Judgment and reminding you of your duty of obedience to the Church – to cast aside all prejudice, hatred or fear, and advise me faithfully and to the best of your ability on these questions. To whom would it be best and most useful to grant and assign the city of Toulouse, for the honour of God and the Holy Church, for the sake of peace in these lands, and to help to eliminate the filth of heresy? The same, in regard to all the territories formerly held by the Count of Toulouse? And the same in regard to the other territories which the army of the crusaders has occupied?'[130]

[546] The archbishops and bishops deliberated long and conscientiously, each consulting the abbots in his diocese and the clergy in his entourage. They then set down in writing the advice they considered to be right and just. In the end they agreed on one choice and one recommendation – that the Count of Montfort should be chosen as chief and sole ruler[131] in the whole territory. What a wondrous outcome! When a bishop or an abbot has to be appointed, even a few electors can hardly agree on one candidate; here in selecting a ruler for such a large territory, the votes of so many important men were unanimously in favour of this great champion of Christ. Without doubt this was the Lord's doing and it is marvellous in our eyes.[132]

[547] Having thus chosen the Count, the archbishops and bishops pressed the legate to hand the territories over to him immediately, but after re-reading the letters the Pope had sent him the legate found he could not do this without consulting the Pope.[133] By common consent, of the legate as well as the prelates, Bernard, Archbishop of Embrun,[134] a man of great learning and the utmost probity, was then sent to Rome, accompanied by some clerics, with letters from

---

129 The church of Nôtre Dame des Tables. The medieval church was largely destroyed in the 16th century wars of religion, and the church now bearing the name is on a different site.
130 This threefold distinction between Toulouse, held under the personal authority of Peter of Benevento, the other possessions of Raymond VI, and other lands conquered by the crusaders, is echoed in Innocent III's letter of 2 April 1215, in §556 below.
131 Latin '*principem et monarcham*'. The meaning of *monarcha* here is not that of monarch in the modern sense, and it simply carries the literal meaning of sole ruler; for discussion see P. Guébin, 'Sur le sens du mot "monarcha" au concile de Montpellier', in *Revue historique de droit français et étranger* (1931), pp. 417–18, and Roquebert II, pp. 301–2.
132 Psalm 118, v. 23. Our author's views on the unanimity of the prelates' choice seem an example of his naivety rather than any cynicism.
133 The letters referred to here are those of 20–25 January 1214 from Innocent to Peter of Benevento, giving the legate his initial instructions, for details of which see n. 44 to §503 above. In pressing for recognition of de Montfort as ruler of the possessions of the Counts of Toulouse and all the other lands conquered by the crusaders, the prelates seem to have been ignoring the rights of the ultimate suzerains of those territories, namely the kings of France, Aragon and England, and (in respect of the marquisate of Provence) the Emperor. Their aim was apparently to put pressure on Peter of Benevento to install de Montfort as ruler of all the conquered territories (as a papal vassal?), but the legate stuck steadfastly to the line that only Innocent III himself could deal with the matter. This line was maintained by Innocent in his further letter to the legate of 4 February 1215 (*Layettes* I, 1099, and see n. 135 below for details).
134 One of those present at the Council: see §543 above.

the legate and the prelates in which they urgently requested the Pope to grant them the appointment of the Count of Montfort, their unanimous choice, as lord and sole ruler of the territories.[135]

[548] I must record that one day whilst the Council of Montpellier was in session the legate summoned our Count (who was of course at the hospice of the Knights Templar outside the walls) to come inside the town to meet himself and the prelates. The Count at once did so, accompanied by a few of his knights who proceeded to stroll through the town whilst the Count, with his brother and his two sons, was with the legate and the prelates. A large group of the townsmen, inspired by their malignity, secretly armed themselves; some went into the church of the Blessed Mary, whilst others watched the gate by which the Count had entered and the road by which they expected him to return. There they awaited his return, hoping to murder him. The good Lord provided a different and far better outcome. The Count became aware of what was going on; he left by a different route from the one he had used to go in, and escaped the ambush.

[549] The Council continued to meet for several days and duly completed its business, after which the prelates in attendance returned home.[136] The legate and the Count went to Carcassonne.[137] Meanwhile the legate had dispatched the Bishop of Toulouse to that city with instructions to occupy and fortify on his behalf the Château Narbonnais (which was the name given to the fortified castle and palace of the Count of Toulouse).[138] Following the legate's orders – but

---

[135] At about this time (presumably at some point in January 1215) Raymond VI was in Rome to press his case with Innocent III directly. His meeting with the Pope is recorded in a letter from Innocent to Peter of Benevento of 4 February 1215 (Potthast, 4950; *Layettes* I, 1099); since the Council of Montpellier probably lasted well into the second half of January, this was presumably written before the arrival in Rome of Archbishop Bernard. In this letter Innocent still maintains the basic stance he had adopted when briefing the legate a year earlier (see §503), namely that reconciliation was still possible; he says that in view of Raymond's manifest contrition, and the fact that he had by a public act submitted his lands and his rights to Innocent as a guarantee, he had granted the Count absolution, and affirms, very emphatically, that great care is needed in dealing with the Raymond's position and that the final decision on the Count's possessions will depend on deliberations at the forthcoming Lateran Council. For the next developments see §§553–6 and notes.

[136] The council probably dispersed towards the end of January (see G&L II, p. 241 n. 4).

[137] After leaving Montpellier de Montfort went to Beaucaire on the Rhône, where on 30 January 1215 Archbishop Michael of Arles granted him as a fief Beaucaire and its dependencies and the Terre d'Argence, which had previously been held of the Archbishop by Raymond VI (Molinier 95, Rhein 127). On 7 February he was at Pont-Saint-Esprit, where he granted to the Bishop of Nîmes the castle of Milhaud, which he was claiming as successor to Raymond VI (Molinier 96, Rhein 129, and *HGL* VIII, 658). Thus de Montfort's assumption of Raymond VI's rights and titles continued. He had probably arrived at Carcassonne by early March: an act made there dated 6 March records his grant to the Bishop and chapter of Uzès of all the lands and rights possessed by Raymond VI in that diocese (Molinier 98, Rhein 130, *HGL* VIII, 660). G&L II, p. 241 n. 5, give grounds for thinking that the act may not be genuine, but its authenticity is defended in detail by Roquebert II, pp. 308–12.

[138] Latin 'castrum Narbonense: sic enim vocabatur municio et palacium comitis Tolosani'. The Château Narbonnais was the fortified residence of the counts of Toulouse in the city. It was integrated into the southern walls of Toulouse, and commanded the Porte Narbonnaise (Narbonne Gate) at the southern point of the city walls, and through which the ancient road from Carcassonne and Narbonne (the *Via Domitia*) entered Toulouse. William of Puylaurens (XXIV) described it as 'solidum . . . usque altum', massive to its top. It was demolished in the 1550s, and the Palais de Justice now stands on the site, next to the modern Place du Parlement.

perhaps motivated more by fear of him than by willingness to obey him – the citizens of Toulouse drove out the Count's son, who had been occupying the Château, and handed it over to the Bishop, who took possession of it in the legate's name and garrisoned it with knights and sergeants, at the citizens' expense.[139]

[139] Bishop Fulk had left Toulouse in the spring of 1211 (see §221 above) and now returned in effect as its master. William of Puylaurens (XXIII) also says that hostages were taken as a guarantee and sent to join the 120 already being held at Arles (see §507). The records of the proceedings of the consuls of Toulouse of 20 February (Catel, *Comtes*, p. 302) also refer to twelve hostages, chosen from amongst them, being taken. William of Puylaurens (XXIII) also records that Count Raymond and his son went to stay with one David of Rouaix, a leading citizen of Toulouse; that Foix was surrendered by its Count to the legate Peter, who in turn handed it to the Abbot of Saint-Thibéry (this would have been in consequence of the oath of April 1214, see n. to §503, and see §564 for next developments); and that Count Raymond then went to visit those he thought might help him (his movements at this time are not known), whilst the younger Raymond went to the English court (although this may be a confused reference to the earlier visit of the two Raymonds to England in the winter of 1213–14; see n. 86 to §484).

[XVII. §§550–573, April 1215 – April 1216: *Prince Louis joins the crusaders – the Pope confirms de Montfort's provisional tenure of the county of Toulouse and other conquered territories – breach between Arnold Amalric and de Montfort – activity of Prince Louis – Fourth Lateran Council, resulting in de Montfort taking over the county of Toulouse – de Montfort does homage in Paris to King Philip Augustus.*]

[550] *Louis, son of the King of France, arrives in the Albigensian area.* In the year 1215 Louis, eldest son of the King of France (who had taken the cross against the heretics two years previously but had been prevented from joining the Crusade by numerous burdensome wars),[1] now took advantage of the fact that these numerous burdensome wars undertaken by himself and his father had for the most part been brought to a conclusion,[2] and set out for the Albigensian area to fulfil his vow and take part in the Crusade. He was accompanied by a number of powerful nobles, who assembled at Lyon on the agreed day, Easter Sunday.[3] They included Philip Bishop of Beauvais, Gaucher the Count of Saint-Pol, the Count of Ponthieu, Count Robert of Sées and Alençon, Guichard de Beaujeu, Matthew of Montmorency and the Viscount of Melun, and many other noble and powerful knights.[4] Also with him was Guy, the venerable Bishop of Carcassonne, who some time previously had gone to France at the Count of Montfort's request to further the business of the faith.[5] Louis and those with him held him in the highest regard and followed his wishes and advice in all matters. [551] On Easter Monday Louis and his companions left Lyon and marched to Vienne.[6] Much cheered by their arrival, the Count of Montfort went to meet Louis, his overlord,[7] and advanced as far as Vienne. It is not easy to describe the enthusiasm with which they greeted each other when they met.

[552] Louis and his men left Vienne for Valence. The legate Peter of

---

[1] See §§417–21.

[2] A reference to Philip Augustus' victory over the Emperor Otto and his allies at Bouvines in July 1214, and the failure of King John of England's intervention in western France in the same year (see §505 and §522 above, and notes).

[3] 19 April 1215.

[4] A number of these knights had earlier joined the Crusade and this was their second journey south: Bishop Philip of Beauvais had been with the Crusade in 1210, as had Count William of Ponthieu (see §174); Gaucher de Châtillon, Count of Saint-Pol, and Guichard de Beaujeu had joined the Crusade in 1209: see above, §72 and §82. For Robert of Sées and Alencon and Adam of Melun this was their first time with the Crusade. Matthew of Montmorency was the brother of de Montfort's wife Alice, and later Constable of King Philip Augustus (G&L II, p. 241 n. 1). Many of them had fought for Philip Augustus at Bouvines the previous year.

[5] For Guy of les Vaux-de-Cernay's preaching see §§418, 439 and 508.

[6] Vienne is 25km south of Lyon in the Rhône valley.

[7] Latin '*dominus*'; in §552 he is called '*dominus principalis*'. Whilst the King of France was ultimate overlord of many of Raymond VI's possessions (see n. 65 to §72 and n. 10 below), as yet Simon de Montfort had not been recognised by Innocent as Count of Toulouse, and held Raymond's fiefs as a guardian on behalf of the Church. Thus (unless Peter is thinking merely of de Montfort's possessions in northern France), his claim here is somewhat anticipatory. It also ignores the position of the Count of Toulouse's other suzerains: compare n. 123 to §542 and nn. 133 and 135 to §547.

Benevento, referred to above, went to Valence to meet him. As I recorded earlier in my history,[8] the legate had granted absolution to the citizens of Toulouse and Narbonne and other enemies of Christianity and our Count, following a secret and resourceful plan known only to himself. He now controlled and held under his protection the cities of Toulouse and Narbonne and certain *castra* belonging to Christ's enemies in the Albigensian area, and he was concerned that Louis, as eldest son of the King of France and supreme suzerain of all the lands concerned, might use his authority to act against his, the legate's, advice and dispositions, by occupying or even destroying those cities and fortressess. Thus it was being rumoured – it seemed quite credibly – that Louis' arrival and continued presence were not welcome to the legate. This is not to be wondered at; the whole territory had been infected with the evil poison of heresy for many years, and the King, as supreme overlord, had time and time again been urged and begged to join in driving out this great sickness and to set about purging his realm of the filth of heresy, yet he had given neither counsel nor support as he should.[9] So, now that the territory had been secured by the Pope with the crusaders' help, the legate felt that Louis should not act contrary to his dispositions and was hardly in a position to do so. Indeed, he considered that having taken the cross and come in effect as a crusader Louis ought not to go against the arrangements he had made in any particular. Louis, a man of kindly and benevolent disposition, responded to the legate that he would go along with his wishes and decisions.[10]

[553] Louis now left Valence for Saint-Gilles.[11] Whilst he was there, and the

---

[8] See §503 and §507 above.

[9] Innocent had urged Philip Augustus to intervene on a number of occasions, beginning in 1204: for details see n. 65 to §72.

[10] For Philip Augustus's generally wary attitude to the Crusade and his reservations about the possible extension of papal influence in the south of his kingdom again see n. 65 to §72. The fear of de Montfort and the legate was that Prince Louis, with more or less encouragement from Philip Augustus, might now assert his father's rights over the county of Toulouse and in effect reap the benefits of the Crusade and claim control of the region. Ultimately of course the Crusade did lead to the absorption of the lands of the house of Toulouse into the French royal demesne, but at this stage Louis' interest seems mainly to have been to make a demonstration of royal presence in the South. The *Chanson*, which briefly mentions Louis' crusade (II, 141–2, pp. 34–5), says that when Louis returned north and told his father how de Montfort had enriched himself, the King said nothing and kept his silence, indicating his displeasure at de Montfort's successes. A further indication of Philip Augustus's attitude at this time may be gleaned from his action in response to an embassy from the consuls of Montpellier, presumably despatched at the time of the Council of Montpellier (see §544). The consuls asked the King to take their city under his protection; he agreed to do so for five years, but said that if at any time the Pope's legate asked Louis to take the city in the name of the Crusade his obligation to the city would be overruled. He also undertook to maintain his protection if the Pope were to designate King James of Aragon as heir to the lordship (charter in *HGL* VIII, 642, probably dated to the first half of April 1215: for date see Roquebert II, n. 3 to ch. 15). This seems to confirm that whilst Philip Augustus was keen to 'register his interest' in the southern territories, especially now that the influence of the Aragonese crown had been drastically weakened, he had no wish to enter into a direct dispute with the Holy See as to who had supreme authority over them. To make doubly sure of their position the consuls also approached the Pope, who on 10 April agreed effectively to take the city under his protection and on 15 April wrote to Louis commending the city and the protection of James's interest to him (Roquebert II, p. 317, and G&L II, p. 246 n. 2). In 1217 Philip Augustus sent 100 knights to help de Montfort (§598) but his next major intervention in the Midi was in 1219 (§619).

[11] Louis would have been at Saint-Gilles at about the beginning of May 1215.

Count of Montfort with him, the envoys who as recorded above[12] had been sent by the legate and the archbishops and bishops of the South to ask the Pope to appoint the noble and Christian Count of Montfort as their lord and sole ruler now returned from the Curia. The Pope sent letters of identical content to the legate and the prelates and also to the Count,[13] in which he ordered that all the lands previously held by the Count of Toulouse, together with those won by the crusaders and those now controlled by the legate either through hostages or by garrisons,[14] should be entrusted to the Count to be held secure until he, the Pope, could make more complete arrangements at an Ecumenical Council which he had summoned to meet in Rome later that year on 1 November.[15] Louis and the Count accordingly told the legate of the envoys' arrival – he was at that time at the city of Arles near Saint-Gilles, accompanied by several bishops. The text of the letter sent to the Count of Montfort is as follows.

[554] *Letter from the lord Pope to the Count of Montfort.* 'Bishop Innocent, servant of the servants of God, sends greetings and his apostolic blessing to his beloved son, Simon Count of Montfort.

[555] 'We commend that you be praised in the Lord's name, as is your due for fighting His battles in so praiseworthy a manner, with unsullied devotion, a pure heart and tireless energy, as a true and valiant soldier of Christ and invincible champion of the Catholic faith. Because of these achievements the report of your righteousness and faith has spread over almost all the earth; the blessings of many are continually heaped on your head, to gain you a larger share of Christ's favour; and the whole Church is united in prayer to intercede for you, so that a crown of righteousness[16] will be reserved for you, to be delivered to you by the Just Judge hereafter – a crown which we believe is already laid up for you in heaven, as you have well deserved. So forward, knight of Christ! Make full proof of your ministry,[17] run the race that has been ordained for you until you receive the prize,[18] faint not in your tribulations[19] in the knowledge that the Lord God Sabaoth, the Lord of Hosts and leader of the army of Christ, will be at your side to help you. Do not think to wipe away the sweat of battle until you have won the palm of victory. Rather, since you have started so well, see to it that this good

---

[12] The envoys were Bernard of Embrun and others: see §547.

[13] These letters are dated 2 April 1215. For the letters to the legate and the prelates see *Layettes* I, 1113 and 1116; also *Layettes* I, 1115, for a similar letter of the same date to the barons and consuls in territories previously held by the Count of Toulouse. The first and third of these are referred to in §558 and §557 below; Peter reproduces the text of the letter to de Montfort below.

[14] The 'other lands won by the crusaders' were presumably those parts of the counties of Foix and Comminges and of the viscounty of Béarn occupied by de Montfort mainly in 1214 (see §§514–41). The places held by the legate were Foix, Toulouse and Salies-du-Salat (see n. 45 to §503). This threefold description of the lands handed over to de Montfort is repeated in Innocent's letter, §556 below. Of Raymond's former possessions, only the county of Melgueil was not entrusted to de Montfort, remaining under papal administration.

[15] The Fourth Lateran Council, arrangements for which were by this time well advanced. See §570 below.

[16] II Timothy 4, v. 8.

[17] II Timothy 4, v. 5.

[18] I Corinthians 9, v. 24.

[19] Ephesians 3, v. 13.

beginning (and the subsequent progress you have so commendably worked to achieve) will lead on to the desired conclusion. Put your faith in patience and the perseverance which deservedly brings the crown of success, and remember always that, in the words of the Apostle, no one is crowned except he strive lawfully.[20]

[556] 'Now, we have decided that all the territories previously held by the Count of Toulouse, together with those won by the crusaders and those controlled by our beloved son Peter, Cardinal-Deacon of Santa Maria in Aquiro and papal legate, either through hostages or by garrisons, shall be entrusted to your wise governance, until the meeting of the Ecumenical Council (whose members we shall consult with a view to making sound and more complete arrangements).[21] It will be your task to preserve, guard and defend these territories. With the exception of the expenses incurred in maintaining garrisons in the castles held in my name you will be granted the revenues and produce of these territories and the exercise of judicial authority and all matters pertaining thereto, since you cannot maintain the war from your private resources nor should you be expected to do so. We now earnestly charge your grace, we entreat you in God's name; do not refuse to undertake this mission on Christ's behalf, since Christ himself accepted a mission from His Father on your behalf, and ran like a giant along the way of the commandments to death on the gibbet of the cross. We require that you regard it as your duty to accept this charge, we beg you to do so in the name of Divine Justice, promising in return remission of your sins. Since you will have devoted yourself totally to the service of Christ, do not falter in fighting for Him through weariness or want of purpose before a successful outcome is achieved, nor let it enter into your heart to oppose these my gentle and paternal counsels and commands; rather, strive to follow them with all your heart and strength, so that you may be cherished eternally in Christ's embrace, to which He invited you as He stretched out His arms unwearyingly on the cross. Take every care, every precaution, to ensure that you do not prove to have run in vain, neither laboured in vain[22] if, through your negligence, the hordes of locusts which emerged from the bottomless pit,[23] but have been driven by your forceful

---

[20] II Timothy 2, v. 5.
[21] Latin '*plenius . . . ordinare*'. Cf. also Innocent's letter of 4 February 1215 to Peter of Benevento (see n. 135 to §547) in which he had also reserved final judgment until the Lateran Council. Between the Council of Montpellier in January 1215 (§§542–9) and the issue of this letter of 2 April, de Montfort had continued to act as de facto Count of Toulouse, as indeed he had done at least since the charter of Robert de Courçon of June 1214 (see n. 91 to §523). He had systematically made a series of acts and donations settling the disposition of his new lands, and received acts of homage (see n. 137 to §549, and the summary list of acts in Roquebert II, pp. 454–7). It seems abundantly clear that by now Innocent was no longer able to control the Crusade. It was inconceivable that Simon de Montfort would in future ever voluntarily give up any substantial part of his gains. Nevertheless, Innocent's conduct of the debate at the Lateran Council as described in the *Chanson* (see §§570–2 and notes) suggests that at this time he still believed that if rational discussion at the Council had led to a decision to restore Raymond VI to his possessions, then the decision would have been accepted.
[22] Philippians 2, v. 16.
[23] Revelations 9, vv. 2–3.

ministry from the lands they seized, should again seize those lands (which Heaven forbid!) and drive out God's people.

[557] 'It is our firm expectation that in concern for your salvation you will never stand opposed to our apostolic instructions. We have therefore commanded the barons, consuls, rulers and other believers in Christ in the territories named above, and firmly charged them in the name of the Holy Spirit, to give full heed to your authority and obey without exception your instructions in regard to peace and the faith and other matters referred to above.[24] They must furnish you with help and advice, generously and in full measure, in your struggle against the enemies of the Catholic faith and disturbers of the peace, so that with their help you will be able to bring the business of peace and the faith to a successful end.

[558] 'We are also instructing our legate to take whatever measures he considers necessary for that business, and to provide you with appropriate advice and assistance. He must take every care to ensure that his decisions are implemented, and if any one should offer resistance or open rebellion he must use whatever means he deems expedient to coerce them to comply with his wishes, allowing neither opposition to nor appeal against his decisions to stand in the way.

[559] 'Given at the Lateran, 2 April, in the eighteenth year of our Pontificate.'

[560] *Return to the main narrative.* Leaving Saint-Gilles,[25] Louis went to Montpellier and thence to Béziers. Béziers is only four leagues[26] from Narbonne, whose citizens, driven by fear, sent to Louis indicating their willingness to follow his wishes in all matters.[27] [561] I should add that Arnold, the Archbishop of Narbonne, was doing everything in his power to prevent the walls of the city being pulled down, and with this objective in mind he went to meet Louis at Vienne. He maintained that Narbonne was his, and that was indeed true in part.[28] Moreover, he had usurped and was still claiming the title of Duke of Narbonne, which had from ancient times been held by the Counts of Toulouse.[29]

---

[24] See n. 13 to §553 for the letter containing these instructions, and for the letter to the legate referred to in the next section.

[25] Probably early in May 1215.

[26] 25km.

[27] For the earlier history of relations between the crusaders and the citizens and Viscount Aimeric of Narbonne see §§488, 501 and 503. The reconciliation achieved by Peter of Benevento, §503, had clearly failed to achieve lasting results and relations now became further complicated as a result of the dispute between Arnold Amalric and de Montfort over the title of Duke of Narbonne (see next section). By taking the initiative and sending a delegation to meet Prince Louis the Narbonnais presumably hoped to head off open conflict with the crusaders.

[28] In the early 13th century lordship over Narbonne was shared between the Archbishop and the Viscount. Broadly speaking Narbonne was divided into two parts, the northern part comprising the *Cité* and the southern part the *Bourg*, divided by a tributary of the Aude, now the canal de la Robine. The city also contained a large and important Jewish community, and there were Jewish quarters in both the *Cité* and the *Bourg*. Each part of Narbonne had its own consulate responsible for controlling taxation, public order and the maintenance of the city walls. Administration of justice was also shared by the Archbishop and the Viscount in the *Cité* and the Viscount and the Abbot of the Monastery of Saint-Paul in the *Bourg*.

[29] After his appointment as Archbishop in March 1212 in place of Berengar (see §299) Arnold Amalric continued to play a major part in the leadership of the Crusade, especially at the Council of Lavaur in January 1213 (§§367ff). He was still involved at the time of the Muret campaign in August–September 1213 (see §451), but as time went by his involvement diminished especially after the appointment of Peter of Benevento as legate in January 1214. Narbonne is recorded as a fief of the Counts of Toulouse in the

However, even though the men of Narbonne were in part subject to the Archbishop, they had set themselves up as opponents of God, Christianity and the Count of Montfort, and had fought against him with all their strength. In their hostility they had admitted Christ's enemies into their town and given them shelter there for a long period;[30] the previous year, they had even threatened the Archbishop himself with death, despite his strenuous efforts to preserve their walls intact. It thus seemed to our people that the Archbishop was acting against the interests of the Church, and indeed his own, in opposing the destruction of the city walls. For this reason (and others which I need not enumerate) a degree of discord had arisen between the Archbishop and the Count, and there was a widespread – indeed unanimous – view that in these matters there must be some doubt about the Archbishop's future commitment to serving the business of the Christian faith.

[562] Whilst the legate, Louis, the Count of Montfort and the crusaders were at Béziers, the legate (supported by the advice of the numerous prelates who were present) issued a mandate to the effect that Louis should have his full authority to demolish the walls of Narbonne, Toulouse and certain *castra*, on the grounds that these fortified places had done much damage to the Christian cause; however, Louis was to do no harm to the inhabitants of these cities apart from destroying the walls. To ensure that this requirement would be met Louis ordered the citizens of Narbonne to demolish their walls themselves within three weeks, under the supervision of two knights whom he sent to the city for this purpose; if

---

11th century (see *HGL* V, 542, 743), and the Counts took the ancient title of dukes of Narbonne. This continued into the 13th century, and in 1205 Viscount Aimeric had rendered homage to Raymond VI for the viscounty of Narbonne, although this was largely nominal and at the time the influence of King Peter of Aragon over Aimeric was stronger. However, despite the very clear position of the Counts of Toulouse, on his appointment as Archbishop Arnold claimed the dukedom and – importantly – lordship over the viscounty, and received homage from Viscount Aimeric. De Montfort, clearly regarding himself as by now de facto Count of Toulouse, claimed the duchy for himself. The dispute resulted in appeals to Pope Innocent as well as to Prince Louis. On 22 May 1215, as a step towards gaining his ambition, de Montfort made an agreement with Aimeric (*HGL* VIII, 659), promising to protect him and the citizens of Narbonne, and Aimeric paid conditional homage to him. Although on 2 July Innocent wrote to de Montfort (*RHGF* XIX, 596; Molinier 106) urging him to cease persecuting Arnold Amalric, he persisted in his claim. At the Fourth Lateran Council Arnold avoided giving support to de Montfort (see n. 49 to §571). Attempted mediation by other clergy early in 1216 was ineffectual, and there was even a minor skirmish as de Montfort sought to force his way into the city, and an episode where paving stones were hurled against the Archbishop's quarters. (Details of these and other incidents were given in a letter written later by Arnold Amalric (11 September 1216, *RHGF* XIX, 620; Molinier 133) to Innocent's successor Honorius III.) In February 1216 Arnold Amalric pronounced a provisional sentence of excommunication on de Montfort, although in the event this had little effect. In April 1216 de Montfort, always a master of the art of *fait accompli*, was able to gain recognition as Duke by Philip Augustus when he rendered homage to him for his new possessions and the duchy was one of the those covered (see §573). An appeal by Arnold Amalric to Honorius III in September 1216 had no immediate result, and although the latter continued to be involved intermittently, in the end Simon de Montfort's heir Amaury was saluted as Duke of Narbonne. For detailed treatment of the affairs of Narbonne at this time and of the long-running dispute between Arnold Amalric and Simon de Montfort see Y. Dossat, 'Simon de Montfort', in *Cahiers de Fanjeaux* vol. 4, pp. 293–8, and Roquebert II, pp. 320–1, 327–31 and 389–93, and III, pp. 72–3.

[30] Probably a reference to the presence of Aragonese at Narbonne after the battle of Muret in 1213: see §501 above.

they failed, they would suffer severe penalties. Accordingly the citizens set about pulling down the walls of Jericho – the walls of Narbonne.[31]

[563] Louis now left Béziers and went with his men to Carcassonne, where the legate joined him a few days later. On a certain day the legate summoned the bishops present, together with Louis, the Count of Montfort and the nobles in Louis' entourage[32] to join him at the residence of the Bishop of Carcassonne. When they were assembled the legate, following the Pope's instructions, placed the whole territory in the Count's charge, until the Ecumenical Council.[33] [564] Louis then left Carcassonne[34] for the nearby *castrum* of Fanjeaux, where he stayed for a few days. Meanwhile the legate and the Count of Montfort went to Pamiers. That vicious man, the Count of Foix, arrived there to see the legate, but our Count refused to meet him. At the same time the legate transferred the *castrum* of Foix, which he himself had held for some time,[35] to our Count, who at once sent some knights to the place to garrison it.

[565] I must also record that before the legate and Louis left Carcassonne the Count sent his brother Guy with some knights to take possession of Toulouse in his name.[36] When they reached the city they occupied the fortified castle which is known as the Château Narbonnais.[37] They then took oaths of fealty from the citizens on the Count's behalf and ordered them to demolish the walls without delay. Though unhappy and unwilling to do so, the citizens agreed and – inspired by fear rather than by any feelings of goodwill – set about the process of demolition.[38] From this time forward the pride of the city of Toulouse was utterly humbled.

[566] After the legate had handed Foix over to our Count, he himself entered Toulouse, accompanied by Louis, the Count and the whole body of crusaders. Louis and the crusaders then returned to France, having completed their period of forty days service on the Crusade.[39]

---

[31] The Chronicle of the Abbey of Saint-Paul in Narbonne records that the dismantling of the walls took place in May 1215 (G&L II, p. 255 n. 1, quoting *HGL* V, 39).

[32] See §550 for those in Louis' entourage.

[33] The instructions were those in Innocent's letters of 2 April 1215, on which see §§553–9 above.

[34] He was still there on 22 May (Rhein 131, *HGL* VIII, 660).

[35] After taking charge of Foix following the oaths at Narbonne in April 1214 (see §§503 and 549 and notes), Peter of Benevento in turn gave it in charge to Abbot Berengar of Saint-Thibéry, who installed his nephew, also Berengar, as castellan (William of Puylaurens XXIII). De Montfort now took over Foix by virtue of Innocent's mandate (§556 above) that he should hold all places controlled by the legate pending the decision of the Lateran Council. For subsequent developments see §§570–2, 588, 606D and notes.

[36] The *Chanson*, the first part of which, written by William of Tudela, ended after the battle of Muret, now resumes under anonymous authorship, and reports (II, 141, pp. 34–6) an alleged discussion between Louis, Simon de Montfort, the legate Peter and Bishop Fulk; they are said to have agreed to abandon Toulouse to pillage and fire, but Simon, 'evil and cruel', reflected that this would not be to his advantage and it was decided instead to pull down the walls and fortifications.

[37] See above, §549. One of these knights, Gervais de Chamigny, became Castellan and later Seneschal of Toulouse (G&L II, p. 256 n. 3, and *Chanson* II, p. 282 n. 2).

[38] Details of the demolition are given in the *Chanson* II, 141, p. 36, and, apparently referring to further demolitions after the Lateran Council, in William of Puylaurens XXIV, on which see n. 54 to §573 below. In addition de Montfort also received 3,000 silver marks from the citizens (Roquebert II, p. 334).

[39] They left early in June 1215 (G&L II, p. 257 n. 4).

[567] The legate then left Toulouse for Carcassonne and awaited the arrival of the Count of Montfort, who joined him after spending a few more days in Toulouse.[40] The legate had thus spent many days in the Albigensian area, and had performed his duties in a truly praiseworthy manner, as became a man of his wisdom and judgment, and had entrusted all the conquered territories to the Count as commanded by the Pope. He now went to Provence, and then returned to the Pope. The Count accompanied him from Carcassonne as far as Saint-Antonin near Vienne, whence the legate departed for Rome.[41]

[568] After staying a few days in Provence the Count returned to Carcassonne. A few days later he went to the area of Toulouse and the Agenais to visit the territories he now controlled and set to right any matters needing his attention.[42] By this time the walls of Toulouse had mostly been pulled down.

[569] Some days later Bernard of Cazenac, an evil and cruel man whom I have mentioned above,[43] recovered by treachery Castelnaud,[44] a *castrum* in the diocese of Périgueux, which had previously been in his possession. The French knight who had been appointed by the Count to garrison the place had failed to fortify it adequately and left it almost empty of defenders. When the Count heard what had happened he laid siege to the place and quickly captured it. He condemned the knights he found to be put to death by hanging.[45]

[570] In November in the year 1215 of the Incarnation, Pope Innocent III held a solemn General Council of patriarchs, archbishops, bishops, abbots and other prelates in the Lateran Church in Rome.[46] The business of the faith in regard to the Albigensian heretics was one of the matters discussed and decided on. [571] Raymond, the former Count of Toulouse, with his son Raymond and the Count

---

[40] De Montfort was still at Toulouse on 6 June (Molinier 103) but by 8 June he was at Montauban where he received the homage of Géraud, Count of Fézensac and Armagnac (Molinier 105), and which he now occupied for the first time. He must then have proceeded to Carcassonne.

[41] Having completed his mission Peter of Benevento thus returned to Rome in the second half of June 1215, to prepare for the forthcoming Lateran Council.

[42] De Montfort was at Loriol-sur-Drôme, south of Valence, on 4 July (*HGL* VIII, 665), at Beaucaire on 12 July (*HGL* VIII, 667) and by 6 August he was at Béziers (*HGL* VIII, 668). He had arrived at Carcassonne by 20 August and was still there on 25 August (*HGL* VIII, 670). He is then recorded as being at Lavaur on 31 August (Molinier 114 and Rhein 138), and at Condom near Agen on 25 September (Molinier 115). These dates all come from acts which settled various arrangements covering rights and lands formerly held by Raymond VI and now held by de Montfort. For further references see G&L II, p. 258 nn. 2–5, and for discussion see Roquebert II, pp. 339–44, with detailed source references given on pp. 459–60.

[43] See §530.

[44] See §532.

[45] After this incursion into the Périgord, probably in late September 1215, de Montfort's movements are unknown until February 1216. He did not attend the Lateran Council, and presumably spent the winter at Carcassonne.

[46] For a concise general view of the Council see W. Ullmann, *A Short History of the Papacy*, pp. 221–3; Roquebert II, chs. 17–19 gives a detailed account. The canons are in Mansi XXII, 979–1058. Over four hundred archbishops and bishops and eight hundred abbots and priors attended; the main sessions were held on 11, 20 and 30 November (G&L note to this section). Peter's uncle Guy of les Vaux-de-Cernay is amongst the many prelates whose presence is recorded (see G&L II, p. 262 n. 2, for an extensive list); there is no direct evidence that Peter accompanied him to Rome.

of Foix – manifest disturbers of peace and the faith – had also come to the Council;[47] their purpose was to plead before the Council for the restoration of their lands, which they had lost by God's will and through the intervention of the crusaders. The Count of Montfort sent his brother Guy[48] and other trusted and experienced envoys. Some of those present (including, more regrettably, some priests) were obstructing the business of the faith by working for the restoration of the Counts of Toulouse and Foix to their former position.[49]

[572] However, the counsel of Ahithophel[50] did not prevail; the wishes of the malignant were confounded. The Pope followed the views of the larger and wiser party in the holy Council, and decided that the city of Toulouse and the other territories won by the crusaders should be committed to the Count of Montfort, who had struggled courageously and faithfully above all others in the fight for the faith.[51] However the Supreme Pontiff wished the territory in Provence previously

[47] Raymond VI had also been in Rome early in 1215 (see n. 135 to §547), and his hope was clearly that despite de Montfort's occupation of almost all his possessions, Innocent III and the Council might rule in his or at least his son's favour. William of Puylaurens (XXIV) says the younger Raymond 'came from England with a certain merchant, masquerading as a retainer' ('*servientis*', which may have its usual meaning of an armed sergeant, or could in this context indicate any class of attendant). The *Chanson* (II, 143, p. 40) also says he came from England secretly, after a dangerous journey through France, accompanied by a merchant, and names him as Arnaut Topina; for possible identification of him see *Chanson* II, p. 41 n. 3.

[48] His presence is also mentioned by William of Puylaurens (XXIV) and the *Chanson* (II, 150, p. 74).

[49] The debates are recorded in great detail in the *Chanson* (II, 143–50, pp. 40–76; see also n. 53 below), in over four hundred lines, and are discussed by Roquebert II, ch. 18. The account in the *Chanson* is generally regarded as broadly authentic. According to the poet the Pope began by declaring to the Council that there was no accusation against Count Raymond sufficient to justify his being dispossessed, and no proof that he was a heretic; rather Innocent considered him to be a good Catholic. He also produced a written act (probably the '*instrumentum publicum*' mentioned in his letter of 4 February 1215 to Peter of Benevento, on which see n. 135 to §547) in which Raymond had placed his domains under the Pope's control, after which he had been given absolution. At one stage (149, p. 68) the poet quotes Innocent as saying that 'to counterbalance Simon's merits is the fact that he has ruined Catholics equally with heretics – each month grave and bitter complaints reach me, such that the good grows less and the bad increases'. Throughout the debate the Pope is represented as giving strong support to Count Raymond and – even more – to the younger Raymond; and in the end as being driven reluctantly to accept the majority decision. The protagonists in the debate were the Count of Foix for the southerners, arguing the case of the two Raymonds as well as his own, and Bishop Fulk of Toulouse for the crusaders. Amongst other speakers Raymond of Roquefeuil argued on behalf of the young Raymond Trencavel, son of the dispossessed Raymond-Roger who died in 1209 (§124); Arnold Amalric sat on the fence, thus in effect opposing Simon; of the prelates from the South only the (unnamed) Archdeacon of Lyon took the part of Raymond – apparently he was the priest excommunicated by Pope Honorius III in 1217 and deposed the following year 'for having dared to defend heretics' (*Chanson* II, n. 5 on p. 65). There was an intervention from England on behalf of King John's nephew, the younger Raymond, by the Archbishop of York (for amendment of corrupt name see G&L II, p. 261 n. 2, and *Chanson* II, p. 72 n. e) and the Abbot of the Cistercian Abbey of Beaulieu (Hants).

[50] II Samuel 17, v. 14.

[51] The judgment (here correctly summarised by Peter) is set out in the Pope's letter of 14 December 1215 (*RHGF* XIX, 598–9; *HGL* VIII, 681), of which a full translation appears in Appendix F(v), with notes on some of the detail. Although compelled to give way on the main issue Innocent had avoided complete abandonment of his position. Simon de Montfort now formally acquired a huge fiefdom, but was doubtless disappointed that he had not been given the marquisate of Provence; probably he had also hoped that the Council might have transferred to him the possessions of the Count of Foix (on whom Innocent temporarily deferred his decision – see n. 46 to §588) and the Count of Comminges and the Viscount of

held by the Count of Toulouse[52] to be sequestered so that it might later be used, in whole or in part, for the benefit of the Count of Toulouse's son – although if this were to happen he would have to give clear proof, through his commitment to the true faith and his conduct, that he was genuinely entitled to forgiveness. I shall show later how badly he conducted himself and how in place of mercy he came to deserve a severe judgment.[53]

[573] After the return of his envoys from the Council[54] the Count of Montfort followed the advice of the prelates of the Albigensian area and of his own barons and went to France to his lord the King so that he could receive from him those territories of which the King was the overlord.[55] I cannot easily describe the honour shown to him in France, nor would the reader readily believe me. Wherever he went, be it city, fortress or town, the clergy and the people came in procession to meet him, crying: 'Blessed is he that cometh in the name of the Lord.'[56] Such was the piety and devotion of the people that any man who could but touch the hem of the Count's garment[57] proclaimed himself blessed. The Count went to the King and was received by him graciously and with honour. After a pleasant and very friendly conversation the King invested the Count and

Béarn, although in November 1216 he gained control of the county of Bigorre through the marriage of his son Guy to the Countess (§§587–8 and notes).

52 The marquisate of Provence; see also n. 6 to §575.

53 The *Chanson* records audiences granted by the Pope to Count Raymond (II, 151, pp. 78–82) and to his son (II, 152, pp. 82–8), in which Innocent's attitude to the two as represented by the poet seems much more favourable than could be expected from his formal judgment, even if his wishes had been as opposed to the majority view as the *Chanson* earlier suggests. The *Chanson* also says that the elder Raymond left Rome at once for northern Italy, arriving at Genoa to await his son (having gone via Venice and Ravenna, reaching Genoa about mid-January 1216: *Chanson* II, 151, p. 83 nn. 4 and 5), and that the younger Raymond stayed in Rome for forty days before leaving for Genoa, which he would then reach early in February. Reunited, the two then went to Marseille (see n. 3 to §574).

54 Guy de Montfort probably arrived back from Rome during January 1216, bearing news of the outcome of the Council. However, de Montfort did not start styling himself Duke of Narbonne and Count of Toulouse until March 1216, when he formally assumed these titles (see G&L II, p. 264 n. 1). This is not mentioned by Peter, but took place in ceremonies held at Toulouse on 7 and 8 March, when oaths were sworn by the citizens to de Montfort, and in return by him to them: see Rhein 143, Molinier 120, and Roquebert II, p. 394. William of Puylaurens (XXIV) also gives the following account: 'The Château Narbonnais was then handed over to Count Simon, and the citizens and burgers of Toulouse swore to accept his lordship, and he was called and held to be the Count of Toulouse; and he was named Count by the notaries in public acts. He had the walls of the city and the internal walls of the bourg pulled down, and the ditches and towers of fortified houses in the town levelled, so that they [the citizens] would not in future think to rise up against him; and he had the chains at the crossroads removed. Also . . . he had a gate made in the walls of the Château Narbonnais on the eastern side, so that he could enter the town at will without the citizens knowing, even if they did not wish it . . . The hostages handed to the legate [see §507 above] were given permission to return to their homes.'

55 The prelates with de Montfort at this time included the Bishops of Embrun, Gap, Toulouse, Tarbes and Comminges: they witnessed Simon de Montfort's oath of 8 March mentioned in the previous note. Three of them went to France with de Montfort: see G&L II, p. 264 n. 2. In paying homage to Philip Augustus and receiving the conquered lands from him as fiefs de Montfort set the final seals on his formal assumption of his new titles and rights, as well as giving Philip Augustus the opportunity of demonstrating the ultimate rights of the Kings of France over the lands now held by de Montfort.

56 Matthew 21, v. 9.

57 Matthew 9, v. 20.

his heirs with the duchy of Narbonne, the city of Toulouse and all those territories within his domains which had been won by the crusaders from the heretics and their supporters.[58]

---

[58] Precise dating of the journey to Paris is lacking. The act recording the King's investiture of de Montfort with his new titles, which survives in various forms (see Roquebert II, p. 463), is dated to April 1216. As well as investing him with the county of Toulouse, King Philip also granted him the former Trencavel viscounties of Béziers and Carcassonne, which of course Raymond VI had never held and over which the Crown of Aragon had claimed suzerainty. He also recognised de Montfort as Duke of Narbonne, thus legitimising de Montfort's claims to the title against Arnold Amalric, the dispute over which was at its height following Arnold Amalric's excommunication of de Montfort in February (on which see n. 29 to §561). De Montfort remained with the King until the end of April, and is recorded as still being in Paris on 30 April (G&L II, p. 266 n. 1). He returned south in May 1216.

[XVIII. §§574–620, April 1216 – December 1218: *Major uprising of the southerners – siege of Beaucaire, summer 1216 – partial sack of Toulouse by de Montfort, September 1216 – marriage of de Montfort's second son, Guy, to the Countess of Bigorre – siege of Montgrenier in the county of Foix, February–March 1217 – campaign of Simon de Montfort in the Rhône area, summer 1217 – Count Raymond returns to Toulouse, September 1217 – prolonged siege of Toulouse, autumn 1217 – summer 1218 – death of Simon de Montfort, 25 June 1218 – his son Amaury takes his place as leader of the Crusade – Prince Louis and others join the Crusade, winter 1218 – military activity in the areas of Foix and Comminges.*]

[574][1] Whilst the noble Count was in France, Raymond, the son of the former Count of Toulouse (still a youth,[2] but acting more out of stupidity than youthful immaturity), went to the area of Provence[3] in total opposition to the Pope's orders – thus showing contempt for the generous and merciful treatment he had received, however undeservedly, from the Holy See. Relying on the support of certain nobles in Provence, he occupied all the territories there which the lord Pope had entrusted to the safe keeping of the Count of Montfort.[4]

[575] After occupying the territory to the east of the Rhône he crossed the river to a very notable *castrum* named Beaucaire, which is in the territory of the

---

[1]   Peter's narrative of events between the spring of 1216 and October 1217, when the siege of Toulouse began, is very condensed (see comments in the Introduction, pp. xxv–vi). It consists of only twenty-seven sections, of which almost half relate to the two sieges of Montgrenier and Beaucaire. For this period the most detailed narrative is in the *Chanson* (II, 153–82, some 2,000 lines). There is a more laconic contribution from William of Puylaurens, XXV–XXVII, which adds some important information. A full modern account is given in Roquebert III, chs. 1–6.

[2]   Now aged nineteen (see §29).

[3]   Having reunited at Genoa in February 1216 (see n. 53 to §572) Raymond VI and his son arrived in Marseille in February 1216 where, according to the the *Chanson* (II, 153, p. 90), they received a warm welcome. This was the beginning of a major revival of the fortunes of the southerners, which culminated in the crusaders losing all their conquests by 1226. The revival accelerated after the death of Simon de Montfort in June 1218 (see §612), after which Peter's narrative soon comes to an abrupt halt (see Introduction, pp. xix and xxv).

[4]   There was in effect a general uprising in the Rhône valley, involving towns both in the marquisate and the county of Provence and in adjacent areas. The *Chanson* (II, 153–4, pp. 90–104) paints a vivid picture of the enthusiastic support given to the Raymondine cause, and lists its supporters, with the city of Avignon in the lead, and its opponents (see Roquebert III, ch. 1, for an analysis). Especially noteworthy on the Raymondine side were Adhémar of Poitiers, Count of the Valentinois, and his son William, and Guy de Cavaillon, a troubadour as well as a knight. The elder Raymond soon left for Aragon (*Chanson* II, 155, p. 108, and William of Puylaurens XXV; see also §583 below) hoping to rally support, although nothing substantial was to emerge. Except for a possible attempt to enter Toulouse in August 1216 (see §585) he remained in Spain until he returned to lay siege to the crusaders in Toulouse in September 1217 (§600). The younger Raymond was thus left in charge of the campaign in Provence, albeit well supported by numerous knights and nobles, and was destined to prove himself a capable leader, militarily and otherwise.
   At this point William of Puylaurens (XXV), in an extended and highly rhetorical passage, draws the attention of his readers to the operation of Divine judgment, as manifested in the renewal of hostilities. He says, inter alia, that after Simon, a man worthy of praise in every respect, had conquered the South and divided it amongst his followers, they occupied it for their own selfish purposes, 'not for the purposes for which it had been acquired, or in Christ's interests, but for their own ends, slaves to lusts and pleasures'.

Kingdom of France.[5] This place had at one time been held by the Count of Toulouse, but the Church of Rome had granted it to the Count of Montfort and the grant had been confirmed by the King of France.[6] When he reached Beaucaire Raymond was welcomed by the inhabitants – who had indeed invited him to come.[7] He was at once joined by several Provençal nobles, by the citizens of Avignon and Marseille and by the townsmen of Tarascon and Vallabrègues – all men of treacherous and evil intent.[8] He now besieged the Count of Montfort's Seneschal[9] and the knights[10] and sergeants who were with him guarding the castle of the *castrum*, and set about attacking them vigorously.[11]

---

[5] Beaucaire lies on the west bank of the Rhône, opposite Tarascon on the east bank. The Rhône here formed the boundary between Provence on its eastern side, which lay within the Holy Roman Empire, and the viscounty of Nîmes on the west bank which was nominally part of the Kingdom of France. Beaucaire comprised a castle, built on an imposing outcrop of rock overlooking the river, and the approach to which from the west was protected by an outlying tower known as the Redoubt; the main town or bourg immediately to the south, separated from the castle by ditches and defended by its own walls; and the new suburb of La Condamine to the west of the main town, outside its walls: see map in Roquebert III, p. 18. Beaucaire and Tarascon were important commercial towns, and powerful corporations of boatmen in each town controlled the crossing of the Rhône here, there being no bridge at this time.

[6] Beaucaire was a possession of the Archbishops of Arles, and was held of them by the Counts of Toulouse (see *HGL* VIII, 333, for homage in respect of Arles by Raymond V in 1178). After the Council of Montpellier in January 1215 (see §§542–9 above) it had formally been granted as a fief to Simon de Montfort by Archbishop Michael of Arles, along with its dependencies and the Terre d'Argence, all previously held of the Archbishop by Raymond VI (30 January 1215: *HGL* VIII, 667, and Molinier 95). However, Innocent III's letter of 14 December 1215 announcing the decisions of the Lateran Council (see n. 51 to §572 and Appendix F(v)) had ordered that the possessions which Raymond VI's fifth wife Eleanor of Aragon had brought as a dowry should remain nominally in her possession. The *Chanson* II, 152, p. 86, reports Innocent III as explicitly including Beaucaire, the Terre d'Argence and the Venaissin as amongst the lands to be reserved for the younger Raymond. Taking these points together, it has been suggested (*Chanson* II, p. 86 n. 2) that Beaucaire was part of the dowry settled on Eleanor of Aragon, having originally been part of the dowry of Joan of England, Raymond VI's fourth wife and mother of the younger Raymond (who was born in Beaucaire). Roquebert II, p. 380 follows this suggestion, which gains support from the fact that at the end of December 1215, just after the Fourth Lateran Conference, Innocent wrote to Arnold Amalric and de Montfort (letters summarized in *RHGF* XIX, 606) ordering that Eleanor should receive an allowance of 150 marks from Beaucaire. However, Belperron p. 309 argues against the idea, on the basis that Beaucaire was occupied by the crusaders and thus covered by Innocent's ruling that lands so occupied should be granted to de Montfort, while Griffe, *Croisade*, pp. 111–12, also dismisses the *Chanson*'s evidence; their views are supported by a letter from Honorius III to the younger Raymond of 29 December 1217 (*RHGF* XIX, p. 643) which refers only to lands to the east of the Rhône having been reserved for him after the Lateran Council, which would exclude Beaucaire. Beaucaire is not mentioned in the documents recording Philip Augustus' recognition of de Montfort as his vassal (see §573), so Peter's statement here is not confirmed.

[7] The young Raymond first entered the suburb of La Condamine, and the town's council then opened their gates to him and handed him the keys (*Chanson* II, 156, p. 108).

[8] Details of those coming to support the Raymondine cause are given in the *Chanson*'s account, especially II, 154, pp. 100–5, and notes. The role of the men of Vallabrègues is also mentioned in the *Chanson* (II, 158, p. 118), and for their blockading of the Rhône with their boats see ibid., 162, pp. 146–8. There is a full analysis in Roquebert III, ch. 1.

[9] This was Lambert de Thury (or Limoux) (*Chanson* II, 156, p. 110), on whom see n. 118 to §119.

[10] Including William de la Motte, nephew of Lambert de Thury (or Limoux), Bernard Adalbert (*Chanson* II, 156, p. 110), and Rainier de Chauderon (ibid., 158, p. 120), who had been with de Montfort since the seige of Carcassonne in 1209 (*Chanson* I, p. 90). See Roquebert III, p. 14 for further details.

[11] Peter's account of the important siege of Beaucaire is very condensed (see Introduction pp. xxv–vi on the probably incomplete state of the second half of the History). Consequently, although it appears to be factually correct as far as it goes, it hardly gives an adequate impression of what was an intense and prolonged struggle, lasting from early June to 24 August 1216. The success of the younger Raymond in

[576] When they heard what was happening Guy, the Count of Montfort's brother, and Amaury, his eldest son, supported by the other barons and knights in the Count's following who were in the Toulouse area, rushed to Beaucaire with the object of helping the beleaguered garrison if they could do so.[12] With them went Guy, the venerable Bishop of Carcassonne who was, as I have often recorded, totally dedicated to supporting the business of the faith.[13] Meanwhile the Count himself journeyed hurriedly from France, leading a force of knights whom he had recruited there with the promise of high rates of pay. Making rapid progress towards Beaucaire, Guy and Amaury reached the city of Nîmes,[14] about four leagues from Beaucaire, where they camped for one night. [577] Next morning they heard Mass, made their confessions and celebrated holy communion; they then took to their horses, left Nîmes and rode quickly to Beaucaire. They were fully prepared for battle, and it was their dearest and indeed their only wish to meet the enemy in open country. However, whilst we were making our way, information reached us that there was a *castrum* near the public road named Bellegarde[15] which had crossed over to the enemy and would be able to threaten our passage along the road. On the advice of the nobles with us we made a diversion to this place; we captured it immediately and passed the night there.

[578] The following day,[16] at first light, we heard Mass, left Bellegarde and made for Beaucaire. Our men were ready for the fight, drawn up in three lines in the name of the Trinity.[17] When we arrived before Beaucaire, we found a huge multitude of the enemy besieging our knights and sergeants in the castle. Their vast numbers were in contrast with our much smaller forces, but even so they did not venture to come outside the lower walls of the *castrum*, despite the fact that

repelling the crusaders' attacks on the town and forcing the surrender of the castle was a setback for de Montfort, although it was not decisive and he was able to recover much ground in the Rhône area between May and September 1217 (see §§592–9). However, it was the worst military reverse he had suffered to date. He had devoted great effort and resources to the campaign, and in addition the crusaders' failure provided a great and lasting boost to the morale of the southerners, especially since it was the first time their new leader, the young Raymond, had been involved. This is clear from the *Chanson*, which in contrast to Peter's account devotes much space (about 1100 lines, II, 155–171) to the siege, and makes clear the high morale of the southerners, confirmed by Peter's own comment at the end of §581. The crusaders' primary objective, to relieve the garrison penned in the castle, could only be achieved by capturing the main part of the town; to this end they launched four major attacks which all failed, the last on 15 August. Peter draws attention to the problems created for the crusaders by difficulties of supply; in contrast the Southern forces controlled the Rhône, and could thus rely on supplies and reinforcements reaching them both from the north (especially Avignon) and the south (especially Marseille). For a full analysis of the campaign see Roquebert III, ch. 2.

12 Guy was at Lavaur on 1 June, where he made a donation to Dominic's house at Prouille (G&L II, p. 269 n. 5, and Roquebert III, p. 20 and note). He must then have immediately set off for Beaucaire.
13 Guy of les Vaux-de-Cernay's presence is confirmed by his witnessing two acts at this time (Rhein 148 and 150). His nephew Peter was with him (hence the phrase 'while we were making our way' in the next section).
14 On the evening of 3 June 1216. Dates in this and the next two sections are calculated by reference to the arrival of Simon at Nîmes, §578, which is given as 6 June by the chronicler Alberic de Trois Fontaines (see Roquebert III, p. 456 n. 4, and G&L II, p. 272 n. 3).
15 About 12km south-west of Beaucaire.
16 5 June.
17 On this formation, see also §454 and §462 above.

our men stood close to the walls for a long time and kept inviting them to join battle. After waiting for the enemy for a long time and repeatedly challenging them to come out, our men realised that they had no intention of fighting; accordingly they returned to Bellegarde, intending to go back to Beaucaire the next day. Whilst we were at Bellegarde the Count of Montfort reached Nîmes on his way from France to Beaucaire.[18]

[579] Very early next day[19] the Count left Nîmes and we left Bellegarde. Our forces thus approached Beaucaire from two directions and set about besieging the besiegers.[20] When the son of the former Count of Toulouse realised that the Count of Montfort had laid siege to Beaucaire, he set about collecting as many men as he could, from Avignon, Marseille, Tarascon and Vallabrègues,[21] as well as from numerous other fortresses and towns in the neighbourhood – a faithless and rebellious nation![22] Gathered together to oppose God and His athlete, the Count of Montfort, they set about attacking ourselves and our beleaguered troops inside the castle, with all their might. Indeed, we were so to speak besieging not only Beaucaire but the cities and fortresses I named above, in fact almost the whole of Provence.[23]

[580] The enemy had constructed a wall and ditch outside the castle to prevent our men from reaching it,[24] and were bombarding it fiercely with siege-engines of the type known as 'petraries'. They mounted frequent heavy attacks on our men inside, but they resisted their attackers in a valiant and admirable fashion and killed very many of them. The enemy also built a battering-ram[25] of enormous size; this they brought to bear on the wall of the castle, shaking it severely. However, our men used devices of great effectiveness and ingenuity to lessen the impact of the ram, so that the wall suffered little damage. The enemy constructed numerous other engines of various kinds, but our besieged men destroyed them all by fire.

[581] Outside the walls, the Count of Montfort kept up the siege, not without considerable risks and at great cost, since all the neighbouring land had

---

[18] Simon de Montfort had presumably come down the Rhône valley and arrived at Nîmes on 5 June 1216.
[19] The morning of 6 June.
[20] Thus the southerners were inside the town, laying siege to the crusaders under Lambert de Thury/Limoux within the castle, while de Montfort was outside the town besieging it in an effort to relieve the castle.
[21] G&M, p. 219, render this as 'Villabergues', but this is an error since the Latin name (*Volobricenses*) is the same as the '*Volobricensibus*' of §575, which is clearly Vallabrègues, on the east bank of the Rhône, north of Tarascon. G&L II, p. 272 n. 4, agree.
[22] Cf. Ezekiel 2, v. 3.
[23] Peter means that so many southerners were in Beaucaire that it seemed as if de Montfort was besieging the whole of Provence there.
[24] For the construction of these walls and ditches at the beginning of the siege see also *Chanson* II, 158, p. 118. Built on the northern side of the town (called '*bourg*' in §581), they blockaded the castle and made the town secure against attack. The north and east sides of the castle were also cut off by the steep banks of the Rhône, access from the river being controlled by water craft under the command of southerners (on which see for example *Chanson* II, 156, p. 112). The church of Sainte-Pâque in the north-west corner of the town was also fortified, and the early fall of the outlying tower (the Redoubt) to the southerners (*Chanson* II, 157, pp. 112–14) ensured the southerners' command of the western approaches to the castle.
[25] Also described in the *Chanson* II, 158, p. 118.

corrupted its way.²⁶ We were able to obtain supplies for the army only from the town of Saint-Gilles and from Nîmes,²⁷ and even when we wanted to fetch provisions from these two towns we had to send a force of knights to provide an armed guard for the supply trains. We also had to keep one-third of our knights in a permanent state of armed readiness, by day and by night, partly because of fears that the enemy might launch a sudden attack (although they never dared to do so), and partly to guard our siege-engines.²⁸ The Count had ordered the construction of a petrary, which bombarded the outer wall of the bourg – he could not erect more engines, since he did not have the footsoldiers needed to haul them into position. Indeed, he had very few footsoldiers recruited from the local inhabitants; those he had were unenthusiastic and fearful, and of little if any use to Christ's army. By contrast, those on the other side were keen and courageous.

[582] I must also record that whenever the enemy made captives of any of our side, whether priests or laymen, they murdered them in a most abhorrent fashion. After slaughtering them, they hanged some of them, and dismembered others. A shameful mode of warfare, a victory without honour! Moreover, one day they captured one of our knights; first they killed him, then they hanged him, then they cut off his hands and feet. Unheard-of barbarity! They then used a mangonel to hurl his feet into the castle, to inspire terror amongst our besieged troops and put pressure on them.

[583] Meanwhile Raymond, the former Count of Toulouse, rode through Catalonia and Aragon recruiting as many knights as he was able, hoping with their help to invade our territory and take possession of Toulouse.²⁹ The citizens of that city, vile and faithless as ever, were ready to receive him if he should come.

[584] Our besieged garrison in Beaucaire now began to run out of supplies; it was indeed clear that the enemy would not have been able to overcome them so long as they had enough food to keep them going.³⁰ Their lack of victuals was

---

²⁶ Genesis 6, v. 12.
²⁷ Both towns remained loyal to the crusaders at this time. On 19 July, during the siege of Beaucaire, de Montfort had confirmed the position of the consulate at Nîmes (Molinier 130, Rhein 148), perhaps as a reward for loyalty hitherto and as an incentive to continue it. Later, on 25 August, while at Nîmes, de Montfort exempted the citizens from taxes and tolls (Molinier 131, Rhein 150). Saint-Gilles on the other hand had seen its consulate abolished in March 1215 by the Archbishop of Arles and the Bishop of Nîmes on the instructions of the legate Peter of Benevento, and all jurisdiction over the town was vested in the Abbot, whose loyalty was thus not surprising. (Since its establishment in or before 1195 the consulate had come to control most activities in the town although the Abbot was recognised as having seigneurial rights over jurisdiction.) The townsmen were, however, soon to reinstate the consulate (see §586 and n. 41). For the history of Saint-Gilles at this time see Roquebert II, pp. 322–3 and III, pp. 75–6.
²⁸ For de Montfort's siege engines see also *Chanson* II, 162, p. 148.
²⁹ Raymond VI had gone to Aragon in the spring of 1216 leaving his son to lead the siege of Beaucaire (*Chanson* II, 155, pp. 104–8).
³⁰ By early August the lack of supplies within the castle had become critical. The *Chanson* (II, 166, p. 170) relates that the members of the garrison, having eaten their mules and found them palatable, discussed eating their horses and that one of them, William de la Motte, proposed cannibalism as a last resort. William of Puylaurens (XXVI) also says that they had eaten their horses. On 15 August de Montfort began a final attempt to relieve the castle in an assault described in detail by the *Chanson* (II, 168–9, pp. 178–92),

made known to the Count.[31] He was very concerned about the situation, and did not know what action to take; he was unable to rescue the garrison, but totally against leaving them exposed to certain death. Apart from this, there was the ever-present danger that the city of Toulouse, and the territories he was holding, would desert him.[32] After carefully considering all these factors, the Count set to work to find some way of relieving and recovering his besieged men. What more? Discussions took place with the enemy through intermediaries.[33] An arrangement – it could hardly be called a settlement – was agreed as follows: our men under siege in Beaucaire were to surrender the castle, on condition that they would be allowed to leave with all their equipment.[34] And it was so! Anyone who carefully considers the circumstances of this siege must agree that whilst the Count, having failed to take Beaucaire, could not claim a victory, nevertheless he did secure in full measure the honour merited by his noble and faithful conduct.

[585] So the Count and his troops left the siege of Beaucaire and went to Nîmes.[35] There he left some knights to guard the city and make sorties through the surrounding territories. He himself hastened to Toulouse.[36] Hearing of his approach Raymond, the former Count of Toulouse, who was himself on his way to the city with the intention of occupying it,[37] fled in shame. As he neared Toulouse our Count sent some of his knights ahead. The citizens – disloyal and ready to defect – seized them and kept them shut up in a house.[38] Our Count was angry and astonished to hear this; realising that the citizens were minded to oppose him, he had part of the city set on fire. The citizens fled to the bourg,[39]

---

but this was repulsed, and thereafter the decision was made to abandon the siege. Innocent III died while the siege was in progress, on 16 July 1216, aged fifty-five.

[31] See also *Chanson* II, 170, p. 194.

[32] For the position at Toulouse at this time see §585 and note.

[33] The main intermediary was Dragonet de Mondragon, who had hitherto not opposed the crusaders but was now supporting the younger Raymond: see *Chanson* II, p. 105 n. 7, and 170, p. 196. He possessed lands around Vaison, Bollène and Saint-Paul-Trois-Châteaux, for details on which see *Chanson* II, p. 103 n. 5. He also appears in §599 below.

[34] The siege was raised on 24 August (G&L II, p. 277 n. 2, dating based on Alberic de Trois-Fontaines). The *Chanson* (II, 170, p. 197) gives a different account of the terms of surrender, saying that the crusaders were in fact forced to abandon their equipment and their horses and pack animals; there is also a reference to the terms in the tenson attributed to Bertrand d'Avignon, on which see *Chanson* II, p. 137 n. 4, and p. 196 n. 3. William of Puylaurens (XXVI) simply says that the garrison in the castle was allowed out alive and that de Montfort lifted the siege.

[35] He was there on 25 August when he issued an act exempting the citizens from tolls: *HGL* VIII, 694; Molinier 131; Rhein 150.

[36] The speed with which de Montfort made the journey to Toulouse is confirmed by the *Chanson* (II, 171, p. 198), which says he took only three days to make the journey from Nîmes to Montgiscard, about 20km south-east of Toulouse. He will thus have arrived there in the last few days of August 1216.

[37] In a speech attributed to him in the *Chanson* (II, 171, pp. 200–202), de Montfort says that he had received over 20 reports that the Toulousains had written to Raymond VI in Aragon asking him to return, and William of Puylaurens XXVII also says that they were negotiating with him in secret at this time. Peter is the only source to state that Raymond was actually on his way to Toulouse in September 1216, his statement no doubt based on the reports which had reached the crusaders. That de Montfort took them seriously is confirmed by his abandonment of the siege of Beaucaire and the speed of his journey to Toulouse. In the event Raymond did not return until September 1217.

[38] The Count of Comminges' house, according to the *Chanson* (II, 173, p. 214).

[39] The Bourg, to the north of the Cité.

still intending to resist, but when they saw that the Count was planning to mount an attack they were seized with fright and surrendered themselves and the city to him. The Count ordered the destruction of part of the walls and fortified towers, and took hostages whom he placed under guard in the *castra* which he control-led.[40]

[586] At this time the inhabitants of Saint-Gilles[41] – treacherous and faithless – received into their town the son of the former Count of Toulouse. This they did against the wishes of the Abbot and the monks, who thereupon left the town, barefoot and carrying the Holy Sacrament. They pronounced an interdict and anathema on the town and its inhabitants.

[587] After staying at Toulouse for a few days the Count went to Gascony where his second son Guy was married to the Countess of Bigorre.[42] A few days later he returned to Toulouse.[43]

---

[40] Peter's account of these events is very compressed, whereas the *Chanson* (III, 171–9, pp. 198–254) gives much more detail. The poet represents Simon de Montfort as furiously angry after his reverse at Beaucaire, for which he blamed the Toulousains, and determined to exact vengeance. He also complained that the siege had used up all his funds, and threatened to replenish them from Toulouse. His brother Guy and others are said to have tried to restrain him from ruining the city. A deputation of leading citizens met Simon on his way to the city, promising that he would be allowed to enter without opposition. They were promptly taken as hostages. News of this caused panic in Toulouse, where some crusaders were already despoiling the city, and the citizens took up arms. Street fighting ensued; Simon therefore ordered the city to be set on fire; the Jewish quarter, the Joutxaigues, was especially affected. After more fighting a deputa-tion of citizens met Bishop Fulk and other clergy, to discuss coming to terms. They promised that Simon would be lenient. This promise was, however, not kept; more hostages were taken, Simon ordered the complete destruction of the fortifications and the houses of leading citizens. At Fulk's suggestion a sum of 30,000 marks was ordered to be levied on the city, and de Montfort's troops set about collecting this in what amounted to a sack of the city. William of Puylaurens (XXVII) gives a less detailed account which broadly agrees with that of the *Chanson*. He emphasises de Montfort's shortage of funds; says that he ignored counsels of moderation which pointed out that a severe exaction would give rise to injustice and compel the citizens to recall their former master; instead 'blinded by money, he did not foresee the danger'. Roquebert (III, ch. 5) argues that after this de Montfort effectively, if not formally, abolished the consulate of Toulouse.

[41] For the position at Saint-Gilles see n. 27 to §581. The Raymondine success at Beaucaire now clearly prompted the consuls to recover control of the town.

[42] De Montfort was in Toulouse on 13 September 1216, and probably remained there until towards the end of October, when he began the journey into Gascony, passing through Saint-Gaudens. The wedding between his younger son Guy and Petronilla, widow of Gaston VI of Béarn and heiress to the viscounty, took place at Tarbes on 6 and 7 November, 1216 (G&L II, p. 279, and see *Chanson* II, 180, pp. 256–7). As William of Puylaurens says (XXIV), it was arranged by Simon 'to strengthen the boundaries of his county on the Gascon side' ('*ut latera comitatus a parte Vasconie roboraret*'). Guy was fifteen or sixteen years old at the time and his bride Petronilla thirty-two or thirty-three. She was the daughter of Bernard IV Count of Comminges and had inherited the county of Bigorre from her mother Stephanie. She was first married in 1196 to Gaston VI, Viscount of Béarn, on whose death in 1214 she recovered the county which had been her dowry. She was then married to Nunyo-Sanç, cousin of Peter II of Aragon and son of the Regent then governing for James I of Aragon. However, de Montfort, whose ambitions to expand in the south-west had been partially thwarted by the decisions of the Fourth Lateran Council, persuaded the Gascon clergy to annul the marriage to Nunyo-Sanç so that his own son could marry Petronilla and gain control of Bigorre. Petronilla was to bear Guy two daughters and after he died of wounds in 1220 the county reverted to her and she married twice again. For a full account of the background see Roquebert III, pp. 49–51.

[43] After the marriage of Guy and Petronilla had been celebrated, de Montfort sought to take possession of the whole county (*Chanson*, loc. cit.), but later in November 1216 he was unable to take Lourdes and was opposed by William-Raymond of Montcada (the new Viscount of Béarn) who had formed a defensive alliance with Sanç and Nunyo-Sanç. From Lourdes de Montfort went to Saint-Lizier in Couserans,

[588] At this time the Count of Foix, that inveterate enemy and untiring persecutor of Christ's business, built a castle at Montgrenier[44] near Foix, in opposition to the mandates which the Pope and the Second Lateran Council[45] had issued and which were intended to secure peace or at least a four-year truce. The castle was built on the summit of a very high hill, and by human reckoning seemed impregnable and indeed almost inaccessible. Here dwelt disturbers of the peace and subverters of the faith, here the enemies of the Church had their refuge and retreat. The Count of Montfort was advised that this castle could be the source of much serious harm, and realised that unless he could counter the imminent threat without delay Christ's business might suffer unparalleled damage. He therefore decided to lay siege to it.[46]

[589] The siege of Montgrenier was accordingly put in train on 6 February, 1217. Those besieged in the castle included Roger-Bernard, son of the Count of Foix and a true inheritor of his father's iniquity, as well as a substantial force of knights and sergeants.[47] He thought it impossible that any mere mortal could capture Montgrenier or even dare to lay siege to it at that time of year; as I

---

accompanied by the Bishop of Couserans, where he was on 22 December. On 23 December at Aspet he received the homage of a local lord Terren de Castillon, and then returned to Toulouse (see Roquebert III, pp. 50–3).

[44] Overlooking Montgaillard, about 5km south of Foix. The castle was built on a hill now known as the Pain de Sucre, or sugarloaf.

[45] So most manuscripts, and see §600 below where the Fourth is again called the Second Lateran.

[46] In continuing his hostility against the Count of Foix de Montfort was ignoring the efforts of the Church to establish a peace between them. After his oath at Narbonne in April 1214, Raymond-Roger of Foix had handed over the castle at Foix to Peter of Benevento to hold on behalf of the Church and as a guarantee of good faith. He had in turn handed it to the Abbot of Saint-Thibéry. However, in May 1215 de Montfort had occupied Foix, and Raymond-Roger had complained bitterly about this breach of the agreement at the Lateran Council. (See §§503, 549, 564, 570–2 and notes thereto; Roquebert II, pp. 382–3, III, pp. 54–8; *Chanson*, notes to vol. II pp. 47–9, III, pp. 63–4.) Raymond-Roger's case was accepted by the Council and on 21 December 1215 (*HGL* VIII, 682) Innocent III, having now reached the decision he had previously deferred, wrote to the Bishop of Nîmes and the Archdeacon of Conflent, instructing them to return the castle to the Abbot of Saint-Thibéry with a view to its later return to the Count of Foix. He wrote that 'in the meantime there must be no hostile action taken (*nulla penitus guerra fiat*) by the Count of Montfort or his men against the Count [of Foix] and his nephew Roger of Comminges or their territories; instead they should be left in peace and security, so long as they themselves keep the peace'. In December he wrote to Simon himself (*RHGF* XIX, 607A) instructing him to hand the castle to the Abbot, to be held on behalf of Raymond-Roger until other arrangements could be made. The death of the Archdeacon interrupted this process, but on 26 May 1216 Innocent appointed the Bishop of Gerona in his place. No progress was made during the summer, largely as a result of delaying tactics on de Montfort's part. On 27 November 1216 Pope Honorius instructed the Abbot to arrange to return Foix to its Count, and wrote to him again on 8 December saying he had arranged for the Bishop of Maguelonne and the Prior of Fontfroide to obtain guarantees from Raymond-Roger, his son and Roger of Comminges; he wrote to Raymond-Roger on the same day confirming that subject to the provision of these guarantees Foix would be returned to him (*HGL* VI, p. 500; Potthast, 5383/4). These letters produced no immediate result, and de Montfort seems to have used the building of the castle at Montgrenier as an excuse for reopening hostilities with Raymond-Roger. Having thus far succeeded in circumventing the wishes of both Innocent and Honorius, he continued to hold Foix until the following year: see also n. 51 to §590 and §606D.

[47] The garrison at Montgrenier was commanded by Roger-Bernard of Foix, and included Roger of Comminges, Viscount of Couserans, Peter-Roger of Mirepoix, and Baset de Montpezat (see *Chanson* II, 180, p. 258).

mentioned, it was situated amongst high mountains which were very exposed to cold weather. It was still winter, which is usually very harsh in that area. However, our courageous Count trusted in Him who commands even the winds and the waters,[48] and with temptation gives also a way to escape.[49] He had no fear of the stormy winds and the bitter snows, nor of the torrential rains which caused such difficulties for the besiegers. Instead, despite the mud and the frost he strengthened the siege and mounted a vigorous assault on the *castrum* – and indeed the defenders resisted with all their might. I can hardly list in detail all the difficulties involved in conducting the siege; suffice it to say that it deserved to be called not a task but a martyrdom.

[590] After many days had passed the defenders ran out of water and their supplies also began to run out,[50] and as these diminished so did their will to resist. Despite the problems facing them our men had succeeded in blocking all the approaches to the *castrum*, by night as well as by day, so that the enemy could not bring in supplies of food and did not dare come down to draw water. In this critical situation the enemy opened negotiations for surrender.[51] Our army did not know the full extent of the enemy's difficulties and were thus the more ready to listen to their request. The terms the enemy offered were that they would surrender the *castrum* provided they were allowed to leave with their arms. The Count agreed, and Roger-Bernard left with his men. He promised the Count to keep the peace for a whole year – it will be clear from later events[52] how little regard he paid to this promise. Montgrenier was surrendered to the Count on the eve of Easter Day.[53] The Count left a force of sergeants to garrison the place and afterwards went on to Carcassonne.[54]

---

[48] Luke 8, v. 25.

[49] I Corinthians 10, v. 13.

[50] This will have been by the third or fourth week of March. The siege is also mentioned in the *Chanson* (II, 180, p. 258), which confirms that a lack of water forced the capitulation of the defenders.

[51] Peter fails to mention any of the negotiations which Raymond-Roger of Foix and the defenders of Montgrenier were undertaking with the Abbot of Saint-Thibéry and the Prior of Fontfroide in the second half of February 1217 (following Honorius' intervention – see n. 46 to §588) in an attempt to force de Montfort to abandon the siege and abide by the Church's rulings that Foix should be returned to its Count. For details see Roquebert III, pp. 56–8, and Belperron, p. 324.

[52] See §600.

[53] 25 March 1217. De Montfort thus occupied both Foix and Montgrenier in defiance of the orders of the Church.

[54] De Montfort's movements between the end of March 1217 and the end of May, when he went east to Provence, are not well documented. He was apparently based at Carcassonne, but was at Agen on 18 April, where he confirmed an agreement with the Bishop about the administration of the city (*Layettes* V, 232). He had returned to Carcassonne by 7 May when he recorded an agreement with the Abbot of Lagrasse (Molinier 142). See also G&L II, p. 282 n. 4.

[591] There were some *castra* in the diocese of Narbonne, near Termes, occupied by mercenaries who for their crimes had been expelled from their own country.[55] The Count went to the area and took some of the *castra* by force; others surrendered to him without opposition.[56]

[*In §§592–597 there are six passages which occur only in some of the manuscripts and are printed by G&L, not in the main text but in the notes. A translation is given in square brackets. Some aspects of the writing suggest they are not by Peter.* See Introduction, p. xx.]

[592] After this the noble Count went to the diocese of Nîmes in Provence, since the town of Saint-Gilles[57] (which had made a death-pact with the inhabitants of Avignon and Beaucaire) and several *castra* in the diocese had that year deserted God and the Church and joined Raymond, the son of Raymond the former Count of Toulouse. [When the Count of Montfort went to Saint-Gilles to perform a pilgrimage at the request of the Abbot, who had full lordship over the town, he was refused entry by the townsmen; instead they appealed to the Cardinal lord Bertrand and closed the town gates. Our Count, humble and devout as ever, gave proper regard to this appeal and left.][58] [593] At this time Master Bertrand, Cardinal priest of St John and St Paul and legate of the Apostolic See, a man of great learning and integrity, had arrived in the South.[59] He had been commissioned by the Pope to administer the affairs of peace and the faith in the province of Narbonne and neighbouring areas. He established himself across the Rhône at Orange.[60] The citizens of Avignon and Marseille and the inhabitants of

---

[55] The area to which de Montfort now went was the southern part of the Corbières, to the east and south of Termes. This is a rugged and at times mountainous area. It lay outside the former Trencavel lands and its principal lordship was that of the Perapertusès, centred on Peyrepertuse, a near impregnable fortress on a precipitous ridge high above the villages of Duilhac and Cucugnan. This area, and the Fenouillèdes to its south, had since the early 12th century owed allegiance to the Counts of Barcelona and thence to the Crown of Aragon. Under them, however, the area was immediately subject to the Viscounts of Narbonne, following the grant of the lordship of Peyrepertuse and of the Fenouillèdes in 1112 by Count Raymond Berengar of Barcelona to his half brother Aimeric of Narbonne. At the time of the Crusade William of Peyrepertuse held the lordship. For details and bibliography see M. and F. Burjade, *Le Château de Peyrepertuse*, Revue annuelle du CAML, Supplément au tome 1 (1983); and R. Quehen, *La Seigneurie de Peyrepertuse* (Montesquieu-Volvestre, 1975). As Peter says, many of the *faidits* from the southern Trencavel lands had taken refuge here.

[56] This brief campaign in the Corbières took place in May 1217. Details are few, but Montgaillard near Tuchan was one of those places taken by force, and on 22 May William of Peyrepertuse made a formal submission acknowledging Aimeric of Narbonne as his immediate lord, and through him de Montfort as his overlord (see G&L II, p. 283 n. 1).

[57] For Saint-Gilles at this time see n. 27 to §581 and n. 41 to §586.

[58] The passage translated in brackets describes an attempt by de Montfort to regain control of Saint-Gilles which was thwarted by the townsmen's appeal to the new legate Bertrand, for whom see next section. If the content of the additional passage is accepted, the assumption must be that Simon felt that the disadvantages of appearing to ignore the legate Bertrand outweighed any benefit he might have gained from taking control of the town.

[59] He remained in the South for three years and was to be a strong supporter of Simon de Montfort and the Crusade: see *Chanson* II, 186, p. 306 n. 3. Innocent recorded his appointment in a letter of 19 January 1217 (Pressutti 265).

[60] William of Baux, the Prince of Orange, was one of the very few southern lords who had remained

the town of Saint-Gilles and of Beaucaire and Tarascon, given over to a reprobate mind[61] and turning to treason, refused to obey him. [When the legate summoned them, they sent their consuls to Châteauneuf, a *castrum* belonging to the Bishop of Avignon. There, as well as making other demands, the legate urged them to restore the possessions of the Roman Church,[62] which they had despoiled by seizing Beaucaire. A man from Avignon, Audebert of Morières, raising his face towards heaven, gave this arrogant reply: 'If we have despoiled the Roman Church, we will invest her with a robe of scarlet, decked with various furs, and we will make for her a shirt and breeches.' It is thought that he said this because, infected with the poison of heresy, they intended to crucify the Lord a second time and sow heresy by propagating a variety of beliefs. The legate saw he was making no progress with them and returned to Orange where he excommunicated all those mentioned above and excluded them from the peace.]

[594] Meanwhile the Count of Montfort was mounting a strong campaign against the *castra* in the diocese of Nîmes which (as I recorded above) had defected earlier that year. He was supported by Girard the Archbishop of Bourges and Roger the Bishop of Clermont;[63] powerful men both, who had taken the cross against the disturbers of the peace and subverters of the faith in the previous year.[64] They were accompanied by a substantial force of knights and sergeants. With these reinforcements the Count laid siege to a *castrum* near Saint-Gilles known as Posquières.[65] This was soon taken, and he then besieged another *castrum* named Bernis.[66] He attacked it courageously and captured it by force. He hanged many of the inhabitants – as they richly deserved. This inspired such terror in all rebels in the area that they became dumbfounded; they fled

largely loyal to the Crusade from the beginning. He and the consuls of Orange had submitted to the legate Milo in 1209 (*PL* 216, 128–31, and see §77). On 14 July 1210 he had made an agreement with Raymond VI (*HGL* VIII, 590), which was part of Raymond's attempts to secure at least his neutrality. In April 1214 he had been given charge of the marquisate of Provence by Peter of Benevento after the oath sworn by Raymond VI (see §507 and n. 55), and this was confirmed by Innocent in February 1215 (*Layettes* I, 1099). The *Chanson* (II, 154, p. 98) says that in the spring of 1216 Raymond VI made a further treaty with William of Baux, but details are unknown and eight lines later the author of the *Chanson* cites William of Baux as one of Raymond's enemies (ibid., p. 100). In the end he was killed fighting the younger Raymond (*Layettes* I, 1301).

61 Romans 1, v. 28. Honorius III later wrote to the consuls and inhabitants of the five places named by Peter referring to a sentence of excommunication pronounced on them by Bertrand (Pressutti 946).

62 Latin '*ut ecclesiam . . . reinvestirent*'; compare 'invest' ('*vestiemus*') in Adhémar's reply below.

63 Girard Archbishop of Bourges 1209–18, and Bishop Robert of Clermont; the latter had joined the Crusade in 1209 (see §82). They probably arrived in the second half of June since they left (§595) forty days later, about the middle of July.

64 At the time of the appointment of Cardinal Bertrand as legate in January 1217, Honorius had also launched another appeal in the north of France for new crusaders to support de Montfort: see Pressutti 264 for an appeal to the masters and scholars of the University of Paris. The new arrivals were presumably the result.

65 The *castrum* lay about 15km west of Saint-Gilles. The castle at Posquières overlooked the town of Vauvert. Its lord was Rostang (or Rostand), who had submitted to the Church in 1209 (*PL* 216, 96, §77), but who had now defected. For further details see G&L II, p. 286 n. 3, and *Chanson* II, 180, p. 258.

66 About 8km north of Vauvert, it was subject to several co-seigneurs at this time. Its capture is also mentioned in the *Chanson* (II, 180, p. 260), which confirms that many of the inhabitants were slaughtered, but adds that they were all good people who gave alms, sowed corn, and had never been condemned.

before the Count and left empty all the *castra* in which they dwelt. In all the territory to the west of the Rhône there was now hardly any resistance to the Count, except from the town of Saint-Gilles and Beaucaire [and a few other fortified places].[67]

[595] The Count now[68] went to a town called Port-Saint-Saturnin on the Rhône.[69] The Cardinal crossed the Rhône at Viviers intending to meet the Count for a discussion on the progress of Christ's business. (He could not cross the Rhône at any nearer point because the men of Avignon and other enemies of the faith could easily impede any attempt he might make to do so; indeed as he himself complained they had for some time virtually besieged him in Orange.) [When he reached Saint-Saturnin he suffered several injuries at the hands of the enemies of the faith and peace, not least when he was sitting with a large group of clerics and laymen at a place overlooking the Rhône; the enemies of the faith, who had fortified the port, suddenly fired seven or eight bow-shot against him. God saved him from harm, but the Pope's courier, who was present, was severely injured.] The Count rushed to meet him with great enthusiasm. It would be hard to describe the great honour shown by our most Christian Count to the Cardinal! About this time the Archbishop of Bourges and the Bishop of Clermont returned home after completing their forty days as crusaders. [Our Count then besieged the very strong tower of Dragonet, which is situated in a very well defended position a league from Saint-Saturnin. He took it and destroyed it and captured all the occupants, whom he threw into chains. This tower had been built to serve as a den of thieves who were despoiling crusaders and others passing by on land or crossing the Rhône.]

[596] After this the Cardinal proposed that the Count should cross the Rhône to suppress the disturbers of the peace in Provence, where Raymond (son of the former Count of Toulouse) and Adhémar of Poitiers[70] and their accomplices were exerting every effort to confound the progress of the business of peace and the faith. The Count fell in with the Cardinal's wishes and arranged for boats to be got ready at Viviers so that he could cross the river.[71] When they heard of this our opponents joined forces to impede his crossing, and the inhabitants of Avignon came down the Rhône by boat with the same object. However, when they saw that a few of the Count's knights had succeeded in crossing the Rhône they became afraid and sought safety in flight. Indeed all our opponents' supporters in the area were so affected by fear of the Count that they left many strong *castra* quite deserted.

---

[67] Thus in a characteristically determined and ruthless campaign de Montfort had now restored his authority in almost all his territories west of the Rhône.

[68] Mid-July 1217. On 14 July, near Pont-Saint-Esprit, de Montfort received the homage of Raymond Pelet, lord of Alès and a former vassal of Raymond VI, who had also originally submitted in 1209 (*PL* 216, 96, §77). See also G&L II, p. 287; Molinier 145; *Layettes* V, 234; and Roquebert III, pp. 77–9.

[69] Port-Saint-Saturnin, on the west side of the Rhône, is now known as Pont-Saint-Esprit.

[70] See §490 and n. 14 above. William of Puylaurens (XXVIII) mentions Adhémar as the particular target of the campaign east of the Rhône in the summer of 1217.

[71] The *Chanson* (II, 180, p. 260) says that de Montfort asked the Bishop of Viviers secretly to send boats to help the crossing.

[597] Thus the Count and his men crossed the Rhône and reached a *castrum* named Montélimar.[72] The Cardinal, whose every wish and instruction the Count was ready to obey, crossed with him. Giraud Adhémar, lord of most of Montélimar, was with the Count's opponents. [Although he was a liege-man of the Pope, when he was required to hand over Montélimar (which he had turned into a refuge for heretics) to the Cardinal, he refused.] Even so the men of the *castrum* welcomed the Count. One knight, Lambert of Montélimar, a kinsman of Giraud, who was the other lord of the place, was and always had been a supporter of the Count.[73]

[598] After spending a few days at Montélimar the Count left to lay siege to a *castrum* in the diocese of Valence known as Crest,[74] which was held by Adhémar of Poitiers. As I have previously recorded,[75] Adhémar was an enemy of our Count and had for a long time been persecuting the Bishop of Valence; in contrast the city of Valence itself was and always had been on the Count's side. The Count reached Crest and laid siege to it. It was a notable and very strong *castrum*, defended by a large force of knights and sergeants. Once the siege was established, the Count set about attacking the place vigorously, whilst the besieged enemy resisted with all their might. The Count was supported by several bishops from the area[76] and by a force of almost a hundred French knights whom King Philip of France had sent to aid the Count for a six months' period. [599] During the siege discussions were initiated about the possibility of a settlement between Adhémar and the Count, and after protracted negotiations peace was arranged,[77] with a firm commitment from both parties that Adhémar's son should marry one of the Count's daughters.[78] Adhémar handed over several *castra*[79] as a guarantee that he would not oppose the Count in future. Another noble from the

---

72 Montélimar, on the east side of the Rhône, about 35km north of Pont-Saint-Esprit. Its Latin name is Montilium, whence Monteil-Adhémar now contracted to Montélimar.

73 Lordship over Montélimar was divided between Giraud-Adhémar who held the larger part, and Lambert of Montélimar. In 1209 they had both sworn the oath to uphold the peace to the legate Milo (*PL* 216, 132–3, and see §75 above). But Adhémar had not supported the crusaders (see G&L II, p. 290 n. 3) while Lambert apparently had (see *Chanson* II, 154, p. 100, where he is mentioned as amongst those hostile to the younger Raymond in 1216). The *Chanson* (II, 180, p. 260) also confirms that Lambert now helped secure de Montfort's entry to Montélimar.

74 Crest, on the River Drôme, about 25km east of the Rhône valley. Adhémar of Poitiers held one of the two castles there and part of the the town; the rest, and the second castle, was held by a local lord Silvion de Crest, who in turn held it of the Bishop of Die. En route to Crest the crusaders devastated a number of places. See G&L II, p. 291 n. 2 and *Chanson* II, p. 261 n. 7 and p. 262 n. 1.

75 §490.

76 Amongst them the Bishop of Die, who according to the *Chanson* (II, 180, p. 262) was instrumental in securing that part of Crest held by his vassal Silvion for the crusaders.

77 The *Chanson* (II, 186, pp. 300–304) makes it clear that the peace with Adhémar of Poitiers was prompted by the arrival at de Montfort's camp of messengers from Toulouse, bearing news of the rising there against the crusaders and the arrival of Raymond VI, on which see next section.

78 Adhémar's son was William of Poitiers, who was amongst those supporting Raymond VI the previous year (see n. 4 to §574). The proposed marriage was to Simon's daughter (Amicia) who had earlier (in 1211) been betrothed to James of Aragon (see §211). This proposed marriage to William of Poitiers did not take place either (G&L II, p. 292).

79 Including Etoile near Valence, Pontaix near Die, and la Voulte-sur-Rhône (G&L II, p. 293 n. 1).

area, Dragonet,[80] who had seceded from the Count in the previous year, now rejoined him. Peace was also established between Adhémar and the Bishop of Valence. Then, when the Lord Jesus Christ was thus marvellously ensuring the success of His business in these parts, the Ancient Enemy, witnessing and envious of this progress, wished to hinder what he grieved to see succeed.

[600] For at this time[81] the citizens of Toulouse – perhaps we should say 'the deceivers'[82] – were inspired by the Devil to secede from God and the Church and revolt against the Count of Montfort. They welcomed into their city Raymond,[83] their erstwhile Count and lord, who had been deservedly deprived of his possessions and exiled on the authority of the Pope and the Second[84] Lateran Council. The noble Countess, wife of the Count of Montfort, and the wives of his brother Guy and his sons Amaury and Guy, and other sons and daughters of the Count and his brother were living in the castle of Toulouse called the Château Narbonnais.[85] Raymond and Roger-Bernard, son of the Count of Foix, together with various supporters who had accompanied them and helped by the citizens of Toulouse, at once set about fortifying Toulouse by constructing barricades and ditches. As soon as they heard of the city's treachery the Count's brother Guy and his son Guy, supported by some knights whom the Count had sent to garrison the Carcassonne area, rushed to Toulouse and took up positions in the Château and neighbouring houses, to prevent the Toulousains from besieging the Château.

[601] As soon as he heard of the revolt of Toulouse the Count crossed the Rhône and returned hurriedly.[86] The Cardinal crossed with him. Together they marched to Toulouse and laid siege to the city.[87]

---

80 See §584 above.
81 Mid-September 1217.
82 Once more the pun on '*Tolosani/dolosani*': cf., for example, §§8 and 68.
83 Raymond VI reached Toulouse on 13 September (*HGL* V, 2211). He had journeyed from Spain through Couserans where he was welcomed by Viscount Roger de Comminges and others and discussed with them his strategy (*Chanson* II, 180–1, pp. 262–70, and G&L II, p. 293 n. 4). William of Puylaurens (XXVIII) confirms this and says that Raymond was taking advantage of de Montfort's absence in the Rhône valley. On their approach to Toulouse they encountered resistance at la Salvetat, on the Garonne north-east of Cazères, described by the *Chanson* at II, 181–2, pp. 270–2. Raymond had been in Spain for most of the time since the spring of 1216 (see §574 above), but may have attempted to return to Toulouse in August 1216 (see §585). He was apparently in Provence between the end of March and early May 1217 (see Roquebert III, pp. 74–5) but if so he must then have returned to Spain again.
84 I.e. the Fourth Lateran: see also §588 above.
85 See §549 above.
86 The *Chanson* recounts that de Montfort's wife Alice had sent a messenger ('a squire fluent in many dialects') to her husband in the Rhône valley as soon as Raymond VI arrived and the uprising of Toulouse took place (*Chanson* II, 183, pp. 282–4). De Montfort's reaction and his decision to leave Provence for Toulouse immediately is described in the *Chanson* at II, 186, pp. 300–308.
87 There now occurs an apparent break in the text, and one of the main manuscripts (A in G&L's edition) stops completely. (Another manuscript (C) ends just before the end of §606D.) The remaining sections of the *Historia*, called the *continuatio secunda* by G&L, are clearly in a less developed state than much of the rest of the work, and for a discussion of possible reasons see Introduction, pp. xxv–vi. They cover the siege of Toulouse, which began early in October 1217 and lasted over nine months; Simon de Montfort's death in June 1218 at the siege; and his succession by his son Amaury. The coverage of the siege in the *Historia* is brief and episodic. A very much fuller account is given in the *Chanson* (II, 182, to III, 207, almost 2,000 lines); William of Puylaurens (XXVIII) gives an extended summary. The three accounts are broadly

[602] . . . [This was on] 1 October in the year of our Lord 1217. At this time Toulouse was a large, heavily populated city in which all the mercenaries, *faidits*[88] and many previously secret enemies of the Count of Montfort had taken refuge in order to defend the city against the Count and the Holy Church, to whose interests the Count was devoting his every effort. Numerous *castra* and nobles in the area round Toulouse had joined in the city's treachery, having promised to give their support if the opportunity presented itself.[89]

[603] The Count arrived at the defences round Toulouse hoping to take the city by force, but he was vigorously driven back by the citizens, and pitched his camp next to the Château Narbonnais.[90] No effective siege could be mounted unless a force could be positioned across the River Garonne (which formed a defence for Toulouse from the direction of Gascony)[91] so as to deny the Toulousains an exit on that side – there was an easy route provided by two bridges[92] across the river. The Count crossed over[93] with a large detachment, and left another large force on the other side under the command of his son Amaury. He stayed for some days in the suburb of Saint-Cyprien[94] (which is joined to the city by the two bridges), but then realised that Amaury's force was too small to resist the enemy. He therefore recrossed the river, thus to combine two weak forces into a single strong one. [604] A miracle which God worked whilst the Count was crossing back must be recorded, so that His name may be glorified for ever and in all things! As the Count, fully armed and mounted on a heavily armoured horse, was trying to climb into a boat, he fell into the river at a point where it was clearly very deep. For some time he did not surface, and our men were seized with terror and began to cry out in grief. Rachel mourns her son! Treacherously the Infernal One[95] howls with joy, calling us 'orphans', although our father still lives. But he who in answer to Elisha's prayers made the axe to swim on the water[96] raised our leader from the depths after a long delay, his hands clasped together and raised to

---

consistent where they overlap – see later notes for some detailed comments. There is a detailed modern account in Roquebert III, chs. 8–10.

[88] On *faidits*, meaning outlawed and dispossessed members of the southern aristocracy, see Introduction p. xlii.

[89] Details of those supporting Raymond VI at Toulouse are given, for example, in the *Chanson* at II, 185, pp. 296–8.

[90] This initial attack, in October 1217, is recounted in detail in the *Chanson* at III, 188, pp. 16–24. The Château Narbonnais was on the southern side of Toulouse: see map 4, and n. 138 to §549. De Montfort encamped on the site of the later *faubourg* Saint-Michel. The position was thus that the crusaders still held the Château Narbonnais, which now had its own entrance (see n. 54 to §573 above), but the Château was being besieged from within Toulouse by the citizens; while they, protected by the newly refortified walls they had built, were themselves being besieged by de Montfort.

[91] From the south-west.

[92] The Pont-Vieux and the Pont-Neuf, respectively a little up-stream and a little down-stream from the later Pont-Neuf

[93] I.e. from the east (right) bank to the west.

[94] See map 4. The assault by de Montfort on Saint-Cyprien is described in the *Chanson* at III, 197, pp. 114–24.

[95] '*Infernus dolose*', but the variant '*Tolose*', 'the Infernal One in Toulouse', is followed by G&M, who translate '*l'Infer Toulousain*'.

[96] II Kings 6, vv. 5–7.

heaven in sincere devotion. Joyfully our men in the boat lift him up and keep him safe for the Holy Mother Church, for whom the Count had offered himself as a rampart. Such the ineffable mercy of God the Saviour!

[605] Meanwhile the Toulousains had erected several siege-engines – petraries and mangonels – to attack the Château Narbonnais,[97] hoping to overwhelm with stones Cardinal Bertrand, legate of the Apostolic See, and his companions[98] – and with them the Church of Rome! How often the Cardinal feared for his life at this time; a man of great resource who never spared himself in devoting his life to the business of Jesus Christ.[99]

[606] At this time[100] the noble Count took hostages from Montauban.[101] It was suspected that its inhabitants were plotting with the Toulousains to subvert the peace; there was honey on their lips, but gall in their hearts,[102] as is clear from subsequent events. For when the Seneschal of the Agenais[103] and the Bishop of Lectoure[104] went to Montauban with a small detachment on the Count of Montfort's behalf, and were peacefully sleeping on the night of their arrival, the inhabitants sent to Toulouse urging Raymond the former Count to come to the *castrum*, when they would deliver the Seneschal into his hands and kill all the latter's companions. Raymond promptly sent a force of five hundred armed men. That night they went into the *castrum*, which was only six leagues from Toulouse. On the advice of the inhabitants, who numbered more than three thousand, they set up barriers in the streets and posted armed guards at the doors of the houses where the Seneschal and his companions were asleep to ensure they could not escape; they then piled firewood at the doors so that if they could not be taken prisoner they would be burnt to death. This done, the enemy calls out: 'Toulouse! Toulouse!' Trumpets are sounded, there is a great commotion and much noise. The French soldiers rise from their beds, heavy and dull with sleep. Placing no

---

97   See *Chanson* III, 192, p. 62, for the construction of these engines.
98   Including Hugh of Miramas, a canon of Arles, and Raymond Escrivan, a canon of Toulouse (*HGL* VIII, 578).
99   For discussions between de Montfort and Cardinal Bertrand at this stage see *Chanson* III, 193–4, pp. 78–88. He proposed that Alice de Montfort and Bishop Fulk of Toulouse should go north to seek reinforcements, while he himself would write to Rome to urge that a new recruitment campaign should begin. (The despatch of the Countess and her party is also mentioned by William of Puylaurens (XXVIII), who adds the name of Jacques de Vitry.) In response, Pope Honorius III wrote at the end of December to the Bishops of France and to Philip Augustus, urging that help be given to de Montfort (cf. *HGL* VI, p. 514, and Pressutti 950, 959). He wrote also (27/29 December) to the inhabitants of Toulouse (Potthast, 5642) and the younger Raymond (Potthast, 5645), urging them to desist from their rebellion, and to the inhabitants of Avignon, Marseilles, Tarascon, Beaucaire and Saint-Gilles (Potthast, 5647, Pressutti 946), King James of Aragon and Sanç (Potthast, 5643/4), and Count Raymond-Roger of Foix (Potthast, 5646), admonishing them all for opposing de Montfort or supporting the Toulousains.
100 Perhaps in December 1217 or January 1218. Honorius III wrote on 13 January 1218 to Raymond of Turenne and other barons of Quercy, instructing them to stop giving help to the enemies of Simon de Montfort (*RHGF* XIX, p. 648), help which might have been connected with a mission to seek support from Quercy which was undertaken by Arnaud de Montégut on behalf of the Toulousains over the winter of 1217–18 (on which see *Chanson* III, 191, p. 60). See also Roquebert III, pp. 111–12.
101 The incident now related occurred during the winter of 1217–18.
102 From Plautus, *Truculentus* I, 2, 76ff.
103 Philip of Landreville; he later served Amaury de Montfort (G&L II, p. 302 n. 1).
104 Bishop Arnold. Lectoure was a see in the viscounty of the Lomagne, south of Agen.

faith in their own strength but relying on God's help they quickly arm themselves. Although they are dispersed through the *castrum*, a single will, a single faith in the Lord, a single hope of success inspires them. Despite the enemy, they escape from the houses where they had been sleeping and rush against their foes with the courage of lions. The enemy flee; some fall into traps they had themselves set, others hurl themselves from the walls – even though there is no one pursuing them. Our men seize almost all the moveable property in the *castrum* and set fire to the rest.

606A At this time[105] Toulousains – footsoldiers as well as mounted men – made a sudden excursion in the hope of capturing our camp, which at the time held only a few men. Peter des Voisins,[106] a valiant knight, stood ready to oppose them with a single companion. He was surrounded by the Toulousains, but the Count of Montfort, determined that none of his followers should perish and ready to lay down his life for his friends, dashed against the enemy to rescue Peter, with only one man to support him. The enemy attack him ferociously, concentrating all their efforts on him; blows are rained on him from every side, but this man of God, fearless among his enemies, continues to assault them with the help of Peter who struggled bravely on his lord's behalf. Meanwhile our men, unaware of what had developed, were arming themselves. As soon as they leave their tents the enemy all flee in terror.

606B The siege of Toulouse had now continued for six months,[107] during which Cardinal Bertrand and the Count had expended enormous efforts and endured great hardships. At this stage the Countess of Montfort – how like her husband! – arrived with the Bishop of Toulouse from France, accompanied by a large group of crusaders including Michael of Harnes[108] and Amaury of Craon,[109] nobles of great influence.[110] The Count led them across the Garonne to ensure the investment of Toulouse on both sides, and they went to the suburb of Saint-Cyprien where they intended to pitch their camp. However, the Toulousains came out in force to prevent our forces from entering the suburb.[111] Our men could not bring up their armoured horse because of the numerous ditches the Toulousains had dug, so despite the large size of our force we had to retire shamefacedly and pitch camp on the banks of the Garonne, some distance from Saint-Cyprien. Our men are sad, the enemy rejoice; our men cry out in anguish,

---

105 The siege continued throughout the winter of 1217–18, but neither Peter nor the *Chanson* give any details. The incident now related took place at about Easter 1218 (*Chanson* III, 195, pp. 94–8).

106 He was a knight from the Ile de France who, with his parents, was a benefactor of the Abbey of Les Vaux-de-Cernay: see G&L II, p. 304 n. 6. He is mentioned several times by the *Chanson* as being at the siege of Toulouse: see esp. *Chanson* III, 193, p. 75 n. 8, and 195, p. 98.

107 This brings us to May 1218.

108 From Artois (Harnes is north-east of Arras).

109 Son-in-law of William des Roches who had been with the crusaders in 1209 (see §82 above).

110 For the Countess Alice's journey north see n. 99 to §605. The *Chanson* (III, 196, pp. 104–12) also describes the arrival and installation of these reinforcements early in May 1218, and specifically mentions both Michael of Harnes and Amaury of Craon (ibid., pp. 106 and 108).

111 The reactions of the Toulousains to the new arrivals, the battle which followed for Saint-Cyprien and the bridges over the Garonne, and the flood described by Peter, are recounted in the *Chanson* (III, 197–8, pp. 114–30).

the enemy shout with joy; our men raise their standards, the enemy display not only their standards but the horns of their insolence as well. Our men are in despair, realizing that they will not be able to enter the suburb – and thus cut off access to the city by the two bridges – without enormous effort and heavy loss of life. This, our failure, was appointed by the All Highest, since He did not intend it to be said that men had accomplished what He wished to bring about by His own merciful grace and without the intervention of material things or human hands. Suddenly a thick cloud appears, although the weather had been calm all day. Heavy rain begins to fall. The enemy is delighted, as they think that faced with such an accumulation of troubles we will flee from our tents. Gradually the level of the Garonne rose and as night approached the right hand of the Lord did valiantly.[112] The unexpected force of the water broke both bridges in the middle; a large part of the suburb's fortifications were knocked down, the ditches and the enemy's equipment were miraculously destroyed. Such the divine power of the Creator! Our men enter the suburb without hindrance or fear, with the Lord preventing the Toulousains from coming out.

606C I cannot be silent about the brutality of the Toulousains at this time, so that those who hear of it may understand how richly deserved was the retribution that awaited men who were not afraid to commit such acts of madness. When they succeeded in capturing any of our men, they would lead them through the streets of Toulouse with bags round their necks and their hands bound, inviting anyone they met to place one or more coins in the bags, so that the captors could make a profit from their captives. Then the executioners put out the eyes of some of their prisoners, and cut out the tongues of others. Others they dragged behind their horses, and left them for the dogs and crows. Others again they cut into pieces, which they catapulted with a trebuchet into our ranks. Others were burnt or hanged.[113] An acolyte from Toulouse named Bernard Escrivan,[114] who was supporting the Holy Church as was his duty, they buried alive up to his shoulders, with his hands bound; they then hurled stones and fired arrows at him, as if he were a target set up for archers, and finally heaped fire on him. His roasted remains were fed to the dogs. Surely he was in every respect a martyr. Others again were stoned to death. Others had mill-stones tied to their necks and were drowned in the river, yet others were thrown from the walls. Whenever they heard Mass being celebrated in the chapel of the Château Narbonnais they would fire huge stones from their trebuchets and mangonels, hoping to destroy the Cardinal and his companions and any others attending with the body of Christ. They succeeded in killing one priest with a shot from a trebuchet. This was the work of the sons of Belial,[115] the sons of Cain, the sons of evil.

606D At this time the *castrum* of Foix was lost through negligence on the part

112 Psalm 118, v. 16.
113 For similar atrocities committed by the southerners see especially §§127, 530; and by the crusaders, §§142, 227.
114 Perhaps a relative of the Raymond Escrivan who was with the crusaders (see n. 98 to §605).
115 I Kings 21, v. 10.

of the Abbot of Saint-Thibéry. The Count of Foix, a second Cain, a second Judas, fortified it and used it as a base from which to attack the Holy Church.[116] The *castrum* of Najac[117] rejected the fealty and allegiance it owed to our Count as its lord and joined Raymond, son of Raymond the former Count of Toulouse, who continued his unwearying efforts to subvert peace, the Church and the Count of Montfort.

[607] The noble Count had now been engaged on the siege of Toulouse for about nine months.[118] One day – it was the day after the feast of John the Baptist[119] – the defenders in Toulouse armed themselves at first light, intending with their usual deceitfulness and inborn maliciousness, to make a sudden attack on our men whilst some were still asleep and others attending divine service.[120] To ensure a more savage attack on an unprepared foe, a more brutal assault on unprepared men, a part of their force was directed against the soldiers deputed to guard our siege-engines, whilst the rest planned to strike our camp from another direction. In this way they hoped that our men, unarmed and attacked on two fronts, would be too disorganised to resist their foes and too weak to withstand a two-fold assault.

[608] The noble Count was told that his enemies had taken up their arms and

---

116   For the position of Foix, and Raymond-Roger's earlier attempts to regain possession of it from the Abbot of Saint-Thibéry who was holding it on behalf of the Church, see §588, §590 and notes. On 29 December 1217 Pope Honorius had written again to the Count of Foix enjoining him to stop helping the Toulousains (*RHGF* XIX, 643; see §600 for his presence in Toulouse). The *Chanson* (III, 192, pp. 62–4, and see n. 5 on p. 93) says that (apparently in late 1217) the Count left Toulouse to take over Foix, and that 'to strengthen and improve the situation and re-establish Parage [the right order of things]' Abbot Bérenger of Saint-Thibéry handed the castle to him. The Abbot apparently assumed that the condition laid down by Honorius was satisfied by the Count of Foix's departure from Toulouse, although the Count's son stayed (*Chanson* III, 193, pp. 76ff). This prompted allegations of treachery against the Abbot, but in a letter of 5 June 1218 to the legate Bertrand (Pressutti 1412, confirmed in a letter to the Abbot of 9 June, Pressutti 1423) Honorius absolved Bérenger of the charge. The Count of Foix himself was to rejoin the Raymondines early in 1219 (*Chanson* III, 210, p. 258). For further comment see Roquebert III, pp. 113–15.
117   Najac, in the Aveyron valley north of Laguépie, on the borders of Quercy and the Rouergue. The castle occupied a commanding site on an outcrop overlooking the steep-sided river valley. It was a possession of the counts of Toulouse, and may have been occupied by de Montfort's forces in the campaigns of 1212–14, although there is no direct evidence. In an act of 1216 (Molinier 122) Bishop Peter of Rodez recognised de Montfort's rights at Najac. An act of the younger Raymond of Toulouse at Najac in January 1219 is recorded in *HGL* VIII, 698.
118   This now brings the narrative to June 1218. The *Chanson* describes events in late May and early June (*Chanson* III, 199–201, pp. 136–66) in some detail. They included an assault on Toulouse by de Montfort on 2–3 June, which was repulsed after much fighting; and the return to Toulouse of the younger Raymond, amidst great rejoicing, a few days later.
119   25 June 1218.
120   The events which follow, and the death of Simon de Montfort, are related in the *Chanson* (III, 205, pp. 196–210) in an account which broadly agrees with Peter's. The prelude to the Toulousains' attack was the construction by the crusaders of an enormous 'cat' to attack the walls of Toulouse between the the Château Narbonnais and the Montoulieu Gate. The decision to make this attack was taken after lengthy discussions amongst the crusaders, which are recorded in the *Chanson* (III, 202–3, pp. 172–8), and which make clear de Montfort's frustration at the continued success of the Toulousains' resistance, and the disagreements amongst the crusaders about what should be done. The decision to use the siege engine represented a change of tactics following the failure of earlier direct attacks. William of Puylaurens (XXVIII) also describes this decision in similar terms. The attack with the cat began on 24 June, and the Toulousains could see that it was essential for them quickly to render the cat ineffective, so they counter-attacked vigorously in the assault now described, on 25 June.

were positioned inside their fortified lines near their defensive ditch.[121] The report reached him as he was attending Matins. He ordered his armour to be got ready, put it on and, true Christian that he was, hurried to the chapel[122] to hear Mass. The Mass had already started and the Count was devoutly at prayer when a huge Toulousain force left their trenches by concealed pathways, raised their standards, and with a great clamour ferociously attacked our men guarding the siege-engines near the ditch. Others leaving by a different route struck at the camp. Shouting broke out amongst our men, who set about preparing their defence as quickly as they could. However, before they were able to arm themselves the small detachment guarding the siege-engines and the camp, struggling against innumerable adversaries, had to endure an uncalculable profusion of blows and wounds.

[609] As the enemy mounted their attack a messenger came to the Count (who was attending Mass, as I recorded above) begging him to come to the aid of his men immediately. This devout man replied : 'First let me hear the divine mysteries and see the holy image of my Saviour.' As he was still speaking another messenger arrived, saying: 'Make haste! The battle grows more intense, and our men can hold out no longer.' To which the most Christian man replied: 'I will not go until I have seen my Redeemer.' As the priest raised the Host in the usual manner the Count, kneeling but with his arms raised to heaven, said most devoutly: 'Lord now lettest thou thy servant depart in peace, according to thy word, for mine eyes have seen thy salvation.'[123] He continued: 'Let us go and if needs must die for Him who deigned to die for us.'[124] So saying, this most invincible of men hurried to the fight.

[610] The battle now grew fiercer, many on both sides were wounded and others were slain, but with the arrival of Jesus Christ's knight our courage and our strength were doubled. All our adversaries were repulsed and bravely driven back to their trenches by our men. The Count and those with him withdrew a little in face of the hail of stones and intolerable storm of arrows. They took their stand in front of the siege-engines, using hurdles to protect themselves from the stones and arrows, for the enemy were firing intense salvoes against us from two trebuchets, a mangonel and numerous sling-staffs.[125]

---

121 At the Montoulieu Gate, which was about 500 metres east of the Château Narbonnais.
122 The chapel in the Château Narbonnais.
123 Luke II, 29–30.
124 Peter may be using dramatic licence in this passage. The *Chanson* (III, 205, pp. 202–4) reports him as saying: 'Most just Jesus Christ, allow me today either to die on this ground or be victorious.' William of Puylaurens (XXVIII), just before reporting Simon's death, says (in typically tortuous Latin): 'At this time the Count was much affected by his labours and by weariness, and weakened and worn out by the drain on his resources (*diminutus sumptibus et exhaustus*); nor did he easily bear the prick of constant accusations by the legate that he was unthinking and remiss. Whence, it is said, he began to pray God to give him peace by the remedy of death.'
125 Latin '*duobus trabuchetis, mangonello et pluribus machafundis*'. The medieval Latin word *machafunda* meaning sling-staffs (alternative spelling *matafunda*, on which see G&L II, p. 314 n. 1, and Du Cange) is equivalent to the classical Latin *fustibalus*, meaning 'an offensive weapon consisting of a staff with a sling attached' (Lewis and Short, *A Latin Dictionary*). For the use of slings ('*frondas*') see also *Chanson* III, 205, p. 204.

[611] Will anyone have the strength to record or listen to the account of what followed? Who will be able to write it down without grief? Who can repeat it without tears? Who can hear it without grieving? Who indeed can fail to dissolve in tears faced with the sorrow of the wretched? With him fallen, all else crumbled. With his death, all else died. He was the comforter of those beset by grief, a tower of strength for the weak, balm for the afflicted, a refuge for the wretched. Therefore must we continue with our lamentable task.

[612] As I recorded above, the Count was courageously standing his ground with his men in front of our siege-engines, near the ditch, to prevent the enemy from renewing their attack on the engines. Suddenly a stone from an enemy mangonel struck Christ's knight on the head. The blow was lethal.[126] Twice beating his breast he commended his soul to God and the Blessed Virgin. Like St Stephen[127] – and stoned to death in that Saint's city – he went to rest in the Lord's keeping. Before he received the fatal wound the Lord's brave knight – say rather, if we are not mistaken, His most glorious martyr – was five times wounded by the enemy archers, like the Saviour for whom he now patiently accepted death, and by whose side he now lives in sublime peace, as we believe.[128]

[613][129] He was succeeded by his eldest son Amaury, a young man of great character and courage, who strove to emulate his father's character and courage in every respect.[130] All the French knights to whom his father had granted lands swore an oath of fealty and homage to him.

---

126 The *Chanson* (III, 205, pp. 206–8) says Simon de Montfort's brother Guy was wounded and that Simon had dismounted to be near him; and that the stone, which was thrown by a petrary operated by ladies, young girls and married women ('*la donas e tozas e mulhers*'), shattered his skull. William of Puylaurens (XXVIII) says 'a stone fired from a mangonel fell on his head and he died at once (*cominus expiravit*)'.

127 Peter likens the death of Simon de Montfort to the martyrdom by stoning of St Stephen. The Cathedral at Toulouse is dedicated to St Stephen, hence the reference to Toulouse being his city.

128 In a fine passage (*Chanson* III, 208, p. 228) the poet of the *Chanson* refers to an epitaph (not extant) which said Simon 'was a saint and a martyr, that he would rise again and enter his inheritance and flourish in marvellous joy, wear the crown [of martyrdom] and sit in the Kingdom of Heaven'. He goes on: 'and I have heard it said that it is so and that it should be so, if, by killing men and shedding blood, by causing the loss of souls, by authorising murders, by following evil counsels, by lighting fires, by ruining barons and dishonouring Parage (*Paratge*), by seizing lands and nourishing arrogance (*Orgolh*), by inflaming evil and smothering good, by massacring women and slaying children, – if by all this a man can, in this life, win over Jesus Christ, then this man has indeed the right to wear the crown and shine in heaven.' William of Puylaurens says: 'So, the man who inspired terror from the Mediterranean to the British sea fell by a blow from a single stone; at his fall those who had previously stood firm fell down. In him, who was a good man, the insolence of his subordinates was thrown down. I affirm that later I heard the Count of Toulouse (the last of his line) generously praise him – even though he was his enemy – for his fidelity, his foresight, his energy and all the qualities which befit a leader. God then gave a signal that those who arrogantly sought to govern unwilling subjects and gave no thought to purging the land of heresy (for which everything had been begun) had departed from His way.'

129 These remaining sections of the *Historia* cover the period from Simon de Montfort's death on 25 June 1218 until the end of that year, at which point it ends abruptly (see Introduction p. xxv). The coverage is very sparse. The *Chanson* provides a fuller narrative, and documentary evidence, some of which is cited below, is also important. A detailed modern account is in Roquebert III, pp. 144–62.

130 On Amaury see Appendix C. He had been dubbed into knighthood at Castelnaudary in June 1213 (see §430), and cannot have been more than about twenty at this time. The *Chanson* (III, 206, p. 16) describes Amaury's succession and the role played by Cardinal Bertrand in it.

[614] After a few days[131] the new Count realised that he could no longer
sustain the siege of Toulouse, partly because when they heard of his father's death
many of the local inhabitants – deserters of the worst sort and evil betrayers –
defected from him and the Church, and indeed from God, and joined the enemy;
and partly because some of the French crusader knights were returning home. So,
sadly and reluctantly he abandoned the siege.

[615] He had his renowned father's body borne to Carcassonne and buried
with honours in the cathedral church of Saint-Nazaire.[132] [616] He then patrolled his own territories, so as to protect his possessions and inflict as much
damage as possible on his adversaries.[133] Amongst the places which betrayed the
Church and crossed over to Christ's enemies at this time were the notable *castra*
of Pamiers[134] in the territory of Toulouse and Lombers[135] in the diocese of Albi.

[617] Immediately after the Count's death the lord Cardinal and the new
Count sent the Bishops of Toulouse, Tarbes and Comminges and the noble
Countess Alice, widow of Simon, to France to plead for help for the Church of
God from the King and his kingdom.[136] When Pope Honorius heard of the
Count's death[137] he wrote to the King urging him in the strongest terms, with the
promise of remission of sins, to bring to a successful conclusion the Crusade
against the heretics of Toulouse, to the honour of God and the glory of the Holy
Church. He granted full indulgences to all those prepared to join in this business,
in the same way as to those who took part in crusades overseas.[138]

[618] About Christmas time the Countess left France and returned to the
Albigensian area, accompanied by the noble Bouchard de Marly[139] and about
sixty other knights.

[619] On 20 November[140] in the year of our Lord 1218 Louis, the illustrious
eldest son of the King of France, took the cross, for the glory of God and the

---

131 The *Chanson* (III, 207, p. 226) says that the siege was not lifted until St James's day, 25 July, a month
after de Montfort's death; and describes fighting which took place during that period.
132 William of Puylaurens (XXIX) says that he was buried '*more gallico*', according to (northern) French
custom, on which see the note by E. Martin-Chabot, *Chanson* III, pp. 226–7 n. 5.
133 He was at Albi on 22 September, at Moissac on 26 September, and at Gontaud in the Agenais on 8
October (Rhein 163–5; G&L II, p. 318 n. 2).
134 On 8 July 1218 Amaury de Montfort had gone to Pamiers and there renewed the agreement over
shared lordship over the town which had been originally made by Simon de Montfort (in September 1209,
§116): see *HGL* VIII, 578–9.
135 Cf. §§112, 117 and 133 above.
136 The discussions between Cardinal Bertrand, Bishop Fulk and the crusaders which led to this mission
are described in the *Chanson* at III, 207, pp. 222–6, and 208, pp. 228–34.
137 Honorius did not hear of Simon de Montfort's death until about a month afterwards, since on 19 July
1218 he wrote a letter encouraging more support for him (Pressutti 1536). The poet of the *Chanson* makes
Cardinal Bertrand say that he would send letters to Rome informing Honorius of Simon's death (*Chanson*
III, 208, p. 230).
138 Honorius issued a number of letters in August and September 1218. They included a general letter to
the bishops of France urging support for the Crusade and renewing promises of indulgences (11 August,
Pressutti 1577); one to Philip Augustus urging him to send his son Louis to support the Crusade (12
August, Pressutti 1578); and one to Louis (12 August, Pressutti 1582). A further letter to both Philip
Augustus and Louis was issued on 5 September (Pressutti 1583).
139 See §123.
140 '*[A.d.] duodecimo kalendas decembris*'.

suppression of heresy in the Toulouse area, with the willing assent of his father. Inspired by his example many powerful French nobles also took the cross.[141] [620] About this time Count Amaury patrolled the boundaries of the territory of the Count of Foix and laid much of it waste. After seizing several castles which had seceded from him he entered the territory of the Count of Comminges in Gascony and laid siege to the *castrum* of Cazères.[142] Within a few days he took it and burnt it, and killed the occupants. Proceeding further he severely harassed the enemy by destroying their *castra* and slaying unbelievers.

[141] Including twenty bishops and numerous nobles: see G&L II, p. 321 n. 2. Louis and his supporters did not reach the South until early summer 1219. For Louis' earlier involvement in the Crusade see §§417, 550–3, and 560–66.
[142] Cazères lies on the Garonne, on the borders of the county of Comminges and the viscounty of Couserans. G&L II, p. 323 n. 1, give other references to this campaign for which the *Historia* is the only narrative source.

APPENDIX A

On the Translation of Certain Terms

The notes which follow explain the approach taken in this edition to the translation of various terms which are used frequently by Peter of les Vaux-de-Cernay in the *Historia*, but whose meaning is either unusual or varies according to context.

(i) *Provincia*

In the *Historia*, Peter uses the word *Provincia* in three distinct senses. Firstly, and especially in the first eighty or so sections, he commonly uses it to denote what is now the South of France. This use ultimately derives from the Latin *Provincia* as applied to the Roman province of *Gallia Narbonensis*, which covered the swathe of territory between the Alps in the east and Aquitania in the west, with its capital at Narbonne. *Provincia* used in this broad sense is also common in papal correspondence of the period. Examples may be found in the letter quoted by Peter in §§57–65; in letters in *PL* 215, cols. 1354, 1360, 1361; *PL* 216, cols. 128, 158, 820; and in the letter of January 1213 (*PL* 216, cols. 744–5) translated in Appendix F(iv). We have throughout translated *Provincia* in this broad sense as 'the South'.

The French now refer to much the same general area as *Le Midi*, the South, and Guébin and Maisonneuve use this term in their translation of the *Historia*. We have also used the term *Midi* in some of our notes to indicate this same area.

Other terms often used to denote roughly the same area are based on its distinctive language. The speech of the southern half of France was the *langue d'oc* (*oc* being the word for 'yes'), in contrast to the *langue d'oil* (or *oui*) of the north. In its various forms (Provençal, Gascon etc.) this was spoken throughout the whole of the South, with the linguistic dividing line in the 13th century being formed by the Massif Central. The term Languedoc, initially coined by French royal officials later in the 13th century, derives from this linguistic division. Strictly speaking Languedoc refers only to part of the South, broadly to the former domains of the counts of Toulouse and of the Trencavels which became part of the French Royal demesne, but it is often used more loosely to refer to the whole of the area affected by the Albigensian Crusade.[1] A related term, which has medieval origins, is 'Occitania', the land where 'Occitan', or the *langue d'oc* in its various forms, was spoken.[2] This included almost the whole of the southern half

---

[1] For example by Belperron (p. 7 n. 1), and by W. L. Wakefield, *Heresy, Crusade and Inquisition in Southern France 1100–1250* (London, 1974), p. 50. We have sometimes used the term with this sense.
[2] See e.g. Linda M. Paterson, *The World of the Troubadours* (Cambridge, 1993), pp. 1–3; and J. R. Strayer, *The Albigensian Crusades* (New York, 1971), ch. 1.

of modern France, and was thus a wider area than that directly affected by the Crusade or the Cathar heresy.

The second use of *Provincia* in the *Historia* has a narrower sense, indicating the lower Rhône valley and the various territories on either side of it. It thus included the viscounty of Nîmes and county of Vivarais on the western side of the Rhône, but also, in particular, the two principalities which lay mainly to the east of the Rhône known as the marquisate of Provence (to the north of the River Durance), and the county of Provence (mostly to the south of the Durance). The marquisate was a possession of the Counts of Toulouse, and the county was held by the Kings of Aragon. This narrower usage is common amongst Peter and his contemporaries and also derives ultimately from *provincia* as applied to the old Roman province. For examples of this usage see §§27, 42, 75–6, 137–8, 487 and 567–96. It partly survives as modern 'Provence', which strictly speaking is confined to lands east of the Rhône, but like Guébin and Maisonneuve, we have translated as 'Provence'.[3]

Finally *provincia* is used to denote an ecclesiastical Province or Archbishopric. Examples are in §5 (Province of Narbonne) and §67 (Provinces of Narbonne, Bourges and Bordeaux), and occur throughout the papal correspondence.

(ii) *Francia* and *Gallia*

In contrast to *Provincia*, the South, northern France is referred to as *Francia*, and crusaders coming from *Francia* are *Francigen(a)e*. The term *Francia* had different connotations at different times. Peter nowhere gives any precise indication of what he meant by the term, but he does at times use it to signify areas other than the Ile de France and its immediate vicinity.[4] For example, Count Baldwin of Flanders (§106), the Duke of Burgundy (§108), William of Cayeux (§168), Juhel of Mayenne (§213), clerics from Laon (§310) and the Bishop of Arras (§486) are referred to as coming from *Francia*. *Gallia* is used as an equivalent (except for the special case in §82). We have throughout translated both *Francia* and *Gallia* as 'France'. Neither ever includes 'the South' or the *Midi*.

Francigene (translated as 'French') excludes the inhabitants of the South, for whom there is no generic term, although they are often referred to by Peter as *indigen(a)e*, literally 'natives'.[5] These terms were commonly so used, as for example in connection with the Statutes of Pamiers of 1212. Peter tells us in §363 that the group set up to draft the Statutes consisted of 'four men of the Church, four *Francigene* knights, and four *indigene* (two knights and two burgers)'. In the Statutes themselves (which are translated in Appendix H), clause XVIII contrasts

---

[3]   In his letter of September 1209 (*PL* 216, 124–5, see n. to §81) the legate Milo appears to use the word in the two senses discussed in this paragraph within a few lines: he says 'After proceeding from Lyon through *Provinciam* as far as Montpellier . . . it seemed fitting . . . that I should go to the territories of the Counts of *Provinciae et Furcalcariensis* . . .'.

[4]   See also R. McKitterick, *The Frankish Kingdoms under the Carolingians* (London, 1983), pp. 18–19, for a discussion of the meaning of the term *Francia* in the ninth century; she notes 'the tendency to understand the name *Francia* as referring to the western [Frankish] kingdom north of the Loire'.

[5]   William of Puylaurens, XIV, uses '*Terrigene*'.

milites Francigene and *milites istius terrae*, and in clause XLVI widows, heiresses etc., are forbidden to marry *indigene istius terrae* without Simon de Montfort's permission for a ten-year period, but marriage to *Francigene* is allowed. Although Peter never refers to the substantial linguistic differences between the two areas, he and his contemporaries may have thought of anyone speaking the *langue d'oil* as *Francigene*. In the Chanson 'French' is virtually a synonym for 'the crusaders'.

(iii) *Partes Albigenses*

The terms *terra Albigensis* or *partes Albigenses* are also sometimes used to denote all the area in the South where the 'Albigensian' heresy was present. (For use of 'Albigensian' in the *Historia* to denote 'heretical' see §4, n. 10.) In §148, the term '*milites Albigenses*' means Albigensian (heretical) knights or lords. We translate *Albigensis* throughout as Albigensian. It should be noted that a separate adjective, *Albiensis*, is used to describe the narrower area known as the Albigeois, or the episcopal see of Albi.

(iv) *Civitas, villa* and *urbs*

For large places, usually those which were the seats of bishoprics, Peter uses the term *civitas*, translated as 'city'. Thus we have *Bitterris civitas* (the city of Béziers), *Valentiam civitatem* (the city of Valence), and so on. Very rarely, our author also uses the word *urbs* to denote a large city, on occasion referring to Toulouse in this way. In §82, Lyon is called '*Lugdunum, urbem Galliae*' which appears to have the very specific sense of 'the ancient capital of Roman Gaul' (see note to that section). *Villa*, translated as 'town', is sometimes used, and is applied for example to Alzonne (§110), Rocamadour (§247), Marmande (§336), Moissac (§§353, 504–5), Saint-Gilles (e.g. §75, several times in §§581–94; Saint-Gilles is also called a *villa* by Pope Innocent III in §57), and Port-Saint-Saturnin (§595). In §251 we also find *villa* used apparently to indicate that part of Puylaurens outside the *munitio*, or castle.

(v) *Castrum*

The word Peter uses to describe most of the places he refers to is *castrum*, plural *castra*. The word is generally used in the same way by his contemporaries. Translating this into English is not straightforward since no single word conveys the full range of its meanings. It can signify a free-standing castle or fortress, and there are a few points in the *Historia* when the translation 'castle' seems appropriate. Examples are in §122, and again in §127 where *plurima castra* belonging to Giraud de Pépieux are razed by de Montfort.[6] But for the most part 'castle' is not a satisfactory translation for *castrum* as used in the *Historia*, and Peter generally uses the separate term *munitio* to mean what we would usually think of as a castle (see discussion below). Most *castra* mentioned were more than castles as the word is usually understood in English; rather they were fortified

---

6 Cf. Innocent III's letter of 14 December 1215, in Appendix F(v), where *castrum* is used to refer to the Castle of Foix.

settlements of one kind or another (towns, villages etc.) in which both seigneurial families and others (often many others) lived. The total number of places described as *castra* was considerable, and many must have been very small. Raymond VI of Toulouse is said to have reckoned that there were at least five hundred heretical *castra* not under his lordship (§379, in the legates' letter of January 1213 to King Peter of Aragon, cf. §195) – no estimate is given for the number he did control; there is also the statement in the legates' letter of August 1209, *PL* 216, 139 (see Appendix B) that the inhabitants of 'over a hundred' notable *castra* between Béziers and Carcassonne fled in terror after the massacre at Béziers.

The lords of most of these *castra* were members of the middling and lesser nobility who were so important in the social structure of the areas ruled by the counts of Toulouse and the Trencavels, and the function of *castra* was social and cultural as well as military. Some *castra* were dominated by a single family, as at Laurac. In others lordship was shared by several families, and multiple lordship was fostered by the practice of partible inheritance which was common amongst the lesser aristocracy of the South. There were for example a number of co-seigneurs at Verfeil and Fanjeaux, while at Mirepoix in the early 13th century there were over thirty co-seigneurs.

Within this broad description *castra* varied considerably in size, shape, physical layout, and in the nature of the sites they occupied. At one end of the spectrum were those *castra* which in themselves were not much more than large fortresses. These included *castra* in mountainous areas, such as Termes in the Razès, or Cabaret in the Montagne Noire north of Carcassonne. In the early 13th century Cabaret comprised the castle of Cabaret itself (described in §149 as '*munitionem castri Cabareti*', the castle of the *castrum* of Cabaret) and two further castles immediately next to it.[7]

But even in such cases there were further dwellings clustered around the fortresses themselves, in associated settlements usually called *burga* in the text, and which were also fortified, although less strongly than the main *castra*. Thus at Termes we are told (§§171–6) of two *burga*, one of which was protected by an outer wall, and there was an outlying fortification called Termenet. At Hautpoul, at a similarly inaccessible site, the *castrum* comprised a 'keep' (*turrem castri*), at least one inhabited area (*burgum*) and other buildings (see §§302–4). Away from the mountains, on the plain of the Lauragais, Castelnaudary was a *castrum* which consisted of little more than the castle, although this was large enough to accommodate five hundred knights and sergeants (§256); however, here too there was an inhabited suburb attached, referred to once as the *burgi exteriori* (§257), and once as the *inferius burgum* (§275), which was outside the main fortified area but was itself also fortified, and which seems to have housed most of the ordinary inhabitants.

Other *castra* occupied naturally strong defensive sites but in less mountainous terrain, and these in particular can be regarded essentially as fortified towns or

---

[7]   See n. 103 to §114 on Cabaret.

villages. Fanjeaux (§110) and Montréal (§116), both near Carcassonne, and Puy-celsi north of Gaillac (§426) were fortified hilltop villages, without a *burgum* attached, and apparently without keeps or castles within them. Lavaur, on the River Agout at the boundary of the county of Toulouse and the Albigeois (§216) had defensive ditches surrounding it (§224). Other *castra* of this sort did, how-ever, have castles within them, which are usually described as *munitiones castri.* This was the case at Minerve, a fortified town occupying a site between the gorges cut by two rivers (see §152). There was a castle (*munitio*) within the *castrum* of Penne d'Agenais (§§319–22; see also under *munitio* below), and at Muret (§§359 and 457–8; Muret also had two *burga*, see under '*Burgum*' below). Castles within a *castrum* are also mentioned at Auterive (§244) and Biron (§337), which also had a *burgum*. When Peter uses *castrum* to refer to places which contain a *munitio* or have a *burgum* attached, he almost always has in mind the whole, not just the heavily fortifed part.

Yet other places described as *castra* had few strong natural defences and had to rely on their walls and surrounding ditches for protection. Most of them are again best thought of as fortified towns or villages. Saint-Antonin (§§314–15), sited at the confluence of two rivers, and Moissac (§341) on the northern side of the River Tarn, were both fortified towns of this sort. On the plain in the Laura-gais without any natural defences was the *castrum* of Bram, which de Montfort captured without the need to use siege engines (§§135 and 142). The inhabitants of *castra* of this kind are sometimes referred to as burghers or townsmen, as at Saint-Marcel (§312) where they are called *burgenses castri*. At Castelsarrasin (§352) the inhabitants are '*burgenses . . . castri comitis Tolose, quod . . . vocabatur castrum Sarracenum*', and those of Moissac are described in §353 as '*burgenses Moysiaci*'. Some urban *castra* of this sort were apparently quite large: the fortified town of Montauban, described as a *castrum*, is said to have had over three thousand inhabitants (§606).

It would of course be possible to translate *castrum* in different ways according to context – as fortress, castle, fortified town or village. However, this would at times be cumbersome, and would not reflect the fact that the *Historia* uses a single word. As a result we have almost always chosen to follow the practice adopted by some modern French historians[8] and have not translated *castrum*, but instead have simply used the Latin word as it stands. (Frequently the word occurs several times in one paragraph in conjunction with the name of a place but adds nothing to the sense, and to avoid excessive repetition we have some-times used 'place' as an alternative or simply given the name alone, so for in-stance *castrum Vauri*, Lavaur, may just be given as Lavaur after its first mention as 'the *castrum* of Lavaur'.)

(vi) *Munitio*
In 'classical' Latin *munitio* means, primarily, '(the process of) fortifying or de-fending'; then, by transference, 'a means of fortification, a rampart etc.' A simple

---

[8]   See for example the discussion of the word *castrum* in Griffe, *Débuts*, pp. 12–14.

extension of the second meaning is 'a fortified place or area', and as indicated above Peter almost always uses *munitio* to refer to the fully fortified part of a *castrum*, in contrast to the *burgum*. 'Castle' seems an appropriate description of such a *munitio*, and our usual practice has therefore been to translate the word as 'castle'. To illustrate further, in §321 the '*munitio*' at Penne d'Agenais is contrasted with the '*burgum inferius*', and in §539, at Sévérac-le-Château, the '*burgum inferius*' is contrasted with the '*superiorem munitionem*'. In §§575ff '*munitio*' is used to describe the elevated castle or citadel at Beaucaire, where the crusader garrison was besieged by the southerners. It is used similarly in §200 (Pamiers) and §244 (Auterive). Sometimes, *munitiones* is also used in isolation to refer to unnamed castles or groups of castles, which might not have had any of the civilian habitations normally to be found at a *castrum*; for examples see §§148, 149, 150, 250, and 359. In §§588–9 the castle built on the hill at Montgrenier south of Foix is a '*munitio*', not a *castrum*.

Another clear indication of Peter's use of *munitio* to mean a 'castle' is to be found in his references to the Château Narbonnais at Toulouse, which was the fortifed residence of the counts of Toulouse, a large imposing castle built into the southern city walls. In Latin it is known as the *castrum Narbonense*, but in his first reference to it (§549) Peter says '*sic enim vocabatur municio et palacium comitis Tolosani*', 'this is what the castle and palace of the Count of Toulouse was called'. Later he calls it simply '*munitio*', and does not use any other term for it.

These examples support the translation of *munitio* as 'castle,' and historians do frequently refer to Peter's *munitiones* as *châteaux* or castles. However, it should be noted that Guébin and Maisonneuve translate *munitio* in most contexts as *donjon*, or keep. We do not agree with this interpretation. Peter's usual word for keep is *turris*,[9] which occurs frequently, and we can find no place where he uses *munitio* and *turris* interchangeably. Moreover, in §§322–3 Peter refers to '*domos quae in municione erant*' at Penne d'Agenais, where to maintain their rendering Guébin and Maisonneuve translate '*domos*' etc. as '*les chambres du donjon*' which, though not impossible, is very strained; this is especially so when one considers that in addition to a well, and large quantities of supplies the *munitio* at Penne contained two smithies, a furnace and a mill, and that the remains of the walls of the *munitio* are, according to Guébin and Lyon (II, p. 22 n. 6) now known as 'le château du roi'. *Donjon* also seems inappropriate as a description of the Château Narbonnais at Toulouse, or the *munitio* at Beaucaire where the besieged crusaders kept horses and mules from early June to late August 1216 (n. 30 to §584).[10]

(Sometimes, but much less frequently, Peter uses *munitio* in other senses; e.g. in §353 where he refers to mercenaries and others who had come to Moissac from Toulouse '*causa munitionis castri*', 'in order to fortify, or garrison, the *castrum*', or in 606B where he says the '*munitiones burgi*', the fortifications of the suburb of Saint-Cyprien at Toulouse, were destroyed by floods.)

---

[9] Cf. also Niermeyer, p. 1049, where *turris* is given as 'keep or *donjon*'.

[10] It may also be noted for instance that in her edition of *The Ecclesiastical History of Orderic Vitalis*, Oxford Medieval Texts (Oxford, 1980), M. Chibnall records numerous examples of *munitio* as meaning castle or fortress, in the *Index Verborum*, vol. I, p. 329.

(vii) *Burgum*

As many of the examples given above show, there was often a *burgum* attached to a *castrum*, which housed at least some of the population of the place. In cases where the context clearly warrants, and where French authors translate as *faubourg*, we have translated *burgum* as 'suburb'. An example is at Toulouse, where the suburb of Saint-Cyprien is called the '*burgum Sancti Subrani*' (§606B). We should also note, however, that occasionally Peter of les Vaux-de-Cernay uses *suburbium* to denote 'suburb', as at Carcassonne in §§94–6. *Burgum* on the other hand is more usually found in references to smaller places to denote an inhabited area which is clearly within the main part of a fortified town, where 'suburb' is not appropriate. At Muret, for example, there were two *burga* (§§447–52), both of which were fortified and which comprised the bulk of the place; while the second of the *burga* can perhaps be regarded as a suburb, the first constituted the main part of the town, and the whole is described by Peter and his contemporaries as a *castrum*. Peter usually refers to the main town of Beaucaire, i.e. excluding the *munitio*, as *castrum*, but once calls it *burgum*. French writers use the term *bourg* in cases of this sort, and we have normally used the same word, which has appeared in English in approximately the same sense (see e.g. the main definition offered in the *Shorter OED* which is 'a town or village under the shadow of a castle').

(viii) *Castellum*

Castellum (plural *castella*) is often used in the *Historia* to refer to fortified places, and several times in the plural to describe groups of them (e.g. §§108, 119, 122, 136, 149, 446 etc.). Peter may have been aware of the derivation of the word *castellum* as a diminutive of *castrum*, but there is little to suggest that he was consciously using the term to signify smaller *castra*. On the contrary, he does not maintain any hard and fast distinction between the two terms. For example in §110 Fanjeaux is referred to both as a '*castellum*' and a '*castrum*' within a few lines, as is Preixan in §120, while in §246 we find 'in the cities and *castellis*' where we might have expected *castra*. Thus, as with *castrum*, there is probably no single satisfactory rendering, but whereas (as noted above) the use of *castrum* untranslated has gained some currency, this is not so with *castellum*. For this reason, and to enable the reader to distinguish between Peter's own use of the various terms, we have thought it reasonable usually to translate *castellum* as 'fortress'.

(ix) Conclusion

For the most part Peter of les Vaux-de-Cernay seems to be careful in his choice of terms. For example, once a place has been identified as a *civitas* or a *villa* he will usually continue to apply the same term to it; and we may note the care with which he uses *cives* for the inhabitants of cities but not for those of other places.[11] However, there are exceptions. As noted above, Marmande in §336 is described as

---

11 Two examples may suffice. In §575 we find '*civibus etiam Avinionensibus et Massiliensibus, burgensibus insuper Taraconensibus et Volobricensibus*' – 'the citizens of Avignon and Marseille, but the burgers or

a '*villa*', but later in the same section its castle is called '*muntionem castri*'; in §353 Moissac, which has regularly been referred to as a *castrum* in the preceding thirteen sections, is called a '*castrum*' and a '*villa*' in a single sentence. We would hardly expect complete consistency in the use of these terms, which – like similar terms in our own times – did not have a precise and rigidly defined meaning. Peter was using the words which most readily came to him in referring to a particular place or set of places. Some of the '*castra* near Minerve' committed by de Montfort to Giraud de Pépieux (§125) or the 'numerous *castra* belonging to Giraud' (§127) may have been mere forts; and we may note in §265 'the Count of Foix had occupied *quoddam castrum* [Saint-Martin] . . . together with some other *munitiones* round about'.

townsmen of Tarascon' etc.; and in §593 '*cives vero Avinionenses et Massilienses et homines villae Sancti Aegidii et Belliquadrenses et Terraconenses*' – the 'citizens' of the two cities as distinct from 'men' of a town, with the inhabitants of two *castra* referred to by the adjectives derived from the place names.

APPENDIX B

The Massacre at Béziers, 22 July 1209

The massacre of the inhabitants of Béziers on 22 July 1209 was the first major incident of the Albigensian Crusade. It apparently involved the slaughter of most of the citizens who, having prepared themselves to resist a siege as the crusaders approached, found their defences suddenly overwhelmed. The mass killing of men, women and children which followed has provoked much discussion. This note concentrates on reviewing the evidence about whether the slaughter was intended, and who actually carried it out. For fuller treatment of the massacre, including the question why the Crusade was directed against Béziers in the first place, see Roquebert I, ch. 17; Belperron pp. 163–9; and H. Vidal, *Episcopatus et pouvoir épiscopal à Béziers à la veille de la croisade des albigeois* (Montpellier, 1951), esp. pp. 75–90.

The main sources for the massacre are the letter written in August 1209, shortly after it occurred, by the legates Arnold Amalric and Milo to Innocent III (*PL* 216, 137–41); the account by William of Tudela in the *Chanson* (I, 16–23, pp. 48–62); the account in the *Historia* (§§84–91); and the much briefer reference in William of Puylaurens' *Chronica* (XIII), written some years later.

When the massacre took place the main crusading army had only just arrived at Béziers and established its camp on the south-western bank of the river Orb outside the city. It appears that the suddenness with which the city was over-whelmed was a surprise to all, and the main sources clearly attribute responsibility for initiating the attack not to the leaders of the Crusade, but to camp-followers. The *Historia* (§90) states that the '*servientes exercitus*', 'the servants of the army',[1] 'commonly called *ribaldi*'[2] carried out the attack. The legates' letter (col. 139) states:

> whilst discussions were still going on with the barons[3] about the release of those in the city who were deemed to be Catholics, the *ribauds* and other persons, of low degree and unarmed ('*ribaldi et alii viles et inermae personae*'),[4] attacked the city without waiting for orders from their leaders. To our amazement, crying 'to arms, to arms!', within the space of two or three hours they crossed the ditches and the walls and Béziers was taken. Our men ('*nostri*') spared no one, irrespective of rank, sex or age, and put to the sword almost

---

[1] *Servientes* normally means 'sergeants' (see n. 53 to §98), but in this case clearly does not.

[2] *Ribaldus* is not a true Latin word but a translation of French *ribau(l)d*, derived from *riber*, a word of Germanic origin meaning 'to pursue licentious pleasures'.

[3] I.e. between the clerical and lay leaders of the army.

[4] I.e. not equipped with proper military weapons or armour. William of Tudela (*Chanson* I, 19, p. 54) says they each seized a club (*masseta*).

20,000 people. After this great slaughter the whole city was despoiled and burnt, as Divine vengeance raged miraculously . . .

A later passage in this letter provides a further pointer in the same direction. Clearly with Béziers in mind, and explaining to the Pope why the crusaders accepted the surrender of Carcassonne, rather than storming it, the legates say that the decision arose:

> because we greatly feared that if the city was captured, then, as had already happened in other places, everything would be destroyed by fire, even against the wishes of the leaders [of the army], either by those who were with us in body but not in spirit, or by the enemy.

William of Tudela's account in the *Chanson* also attributes responsibility for the initiation of the attack solely to the *arlotz*, whom he also calls *ribaut* (ribalds), *truans* (sturdy beggars, vagrants) and *gartz* (churls, boors). He gives their numbers as fifteen thousand (*Chanson* I, 19, p. 54), and assigns an important role to the 'king' of the *arlotz*. He says that after a week of skirmishing as the crusaders approached Béziers, the 'king' became angry when a crusader was killed and mutilated, and then assembled the *arlotz* and urged them to attack the city. Seizing clubs they set about undermining the walls and destroying the gates. Seeing this the citizens were seized with fear; when they saw the crusaders in the army proper ('*los Frances de l'ost*') taking up their arms, they realised resistance would be futile and rushed to take refuge in the cathedral. Once in the town the *ribauds* killed anyone they met and set about collecting booty. This enraged the barons, who set about ejecting the *ribauds* from the houses and depriving them of the booty; it was this treatment that prompted the frustrated *ribauds* to set fire to the city and the cathedral; it was apparently at this time, rather than earlier, that the refugees in the Cathedral died (see p. 62, the beginning of laisse 23).

Finally, there is the much briefer account by William of Puylaurens. This is less definite, but is consistent with the other accounts. He makes no reference to *ribaldi*, but says that 'the citizens were unable to repel the initial attack of the crowd (*vulgi*) which rushed upon them'. *Vulgus* probably implies a mob rather than simply a large group.

If it thus seems clear that the camp-followers started the attack, the extent of the subsequent involvement of the army proper is less clear, although some historians[5] have taken the view that they did join in. The legates' letter and Peter's account say nothing of this, although the reference in the legates' letter to 'our men', '*nostri*', has been taken by some as a hint, on the basis that they would not have used the term to apply to the *ribauds*. The best evidence is to be found in William of Tudela's account; as we have seen, he says the main army went into the city, but seems to imply that the *ribauds'* assault had already succeeded and that they were already engaged in looting and slaughtering the inhabitants. His only

---

5   E.g. J. Sumption, *The Albigensian Crusade* (London, 1978); and Wakefield, *Heresy, Crusade and Inquisition*, p. 102.

specific reference to the army's involvement thereafter is to say that they attacked the *ribauds* and seized the booty which the latter had been collecting. The second extract quoted above from the legates' letter ('because we greatly feared') also suggests that the army proper was not to blame for setting fire to the city (and therefore by extension also not involved in the slaughter in the churches).

Despite this, there is evidence to suggest that as they approached Béziers the leaders of the Crusade were not intending to show any mercy to the inhabitants of captured towns, and that they intended to slaughter those who resisted. Firstly there is the testimony of William of Tudela in the *Chanson*. In describing the discussions at Rome early in 1208 which followed receipt by Innocent III of the news of Peter of Castelnau's murder he says (I, 5, p. 18) that 'it was determined to destroy all who resisted, from Montpellier to Bordeaux'. He goes on to specify as his source one Pons de Mela, a Navarrese ambassador in Rome at the time. Whilst taken in isolation this might be dismissed as a poet's exaggeration, his account of the massacre itself makes the same point in more detail. He says (I, 21, pp. 56–8):

> The barons of France and from around Paris, clergy and laymen, princes and the marquises, all agreed that at every castle [*castel*] the army approached, which refused to surrender, all the inhabitants should be put to the sword, once the castle had been taken by assault. They would then find no one daring to resist them, so great would be the terror produced by such examples. That is how they took Montréal and Fanjeaux and the rest of that country; without this, I swear, they could never have conquered them by force. That is why the inhabitants of Béziers were massacred; they were all killed, it was the worst they could do to them.[6]

Next is the threat contained in the message conveyed to the inhabitants of Béziers by their Bishop, Renaud of Montpeyroux, as the crusading army arrived before the city. This is referred to in §89 of the *Historia*, in the legates' letter, and in the *Chanson*. The Bishop urged the inhabitants not to resist, and warned them of the dire consequences of doing so. The legates' letter states:

> Although the citizens [of Béziers] were given clear warnings by ourselves and their Bishop [Renaud], and we gave them strict instructions, on pain of excommunication, either to hand over the heretics in the city and their belongings to the crusaders, or, if they were unable to do this, to come out from amongst them, otherwise their blood would be on their own heads, they paid no heed
> . . .

The same threat is found in the *Chanson*'s account (I, 16–17, pp. 48–50):

---

[6] Perhaps because it occurs part-way through William of Tudela's description of the massacre rather than before it, this passage has sometimes been interpreted as indicating that a policy of slaughter was decided on *after* events at Béziers (see e.g. J. Sumption, *The Albigensian Crusade* (London, 1978), p. 94). However, if this was so then the phrase 'that is why' seems not to make sense; nor does this interpretation fit well with the other evidence we cite in this Appendix.

He [the Bishop] advised them [apparent lacuna in text, assumed to say, to surrender to the legate] without waiting to be conquered, being made prisoners or killed, or losing all their goods and money. He added that what they might lose would shortly be restored to them [i.e. presumably if they surrendered peacefully], and if they refused to follow this counsel they risked losing everything and being put to the sword.

Peter of les Vaux-de-Cernay's own account (*Historia*, §89) is very much to the same effect, but may well have used the legates' letter as a source.

These accounts suggest that at this stage the crusaders did not intend to spare those who resisted them, and the slaughter at Béziers was consistent with this. Such a policy would also have reflected awareness by the leaders of the Crusade of the need to make rapid progress before crusaders started to return home as their forty days' period of service ended. Indeed in this respect the massacre was a success, since its immediate consequence as related by the legates, and confirmed, in less detail, by Peter (§92) and by William of Tudela, was that the inhabitants of 'over a hundred notable fortresses between Béziers and Carcassonne' fled in terror. (We may note also William's reference to Fanjeaux and Montréal in the extract quoted above.) Finally, there is the phrase famously attributed to Arnold Amalric in regard to the massacre: 'Kill them all, God will know his own!' This is first reported in the *Dialogue concerning miracles* of the Cistercian monk, Caesar of Heisterbach in the diocese of Cologne, written about forty years after the event.[7] The interlocutor describes how some '*satellites*' (presumably his word for the camp-followers), fired with zeal, placed ladders against the walls and climbed up; the heretics were terrified, those who had climbed the ladders opened the gates to the others and they took the city. He goes on to say (evidently now referring to priests at the scene or others on the crusader side):

> Knowing from their confessions that Catholics were mingled together with heretics they asked the Abbot [of Cîteaux] "What shall we do, lord? We cannot tell the good men from the bad." It is said that the Abbot, fearing – as did the others – that some might pretend to be Catholics through fear of dying but would return to their error after the crusaders had gone, replied: "Kill them. The Lord knows who are his own." (*"Caedite eos. Novit enim Dominus qui sunt eius."*) Thus it was that an innumerable host of people were killed in this city.

This story sounds apocryphal, although Roquebert (I, pp. 258–61) argues that it may be reliable, bearing in mind that monks from any of the Cistercian foundations might have been with the army at this time. However, even if we accept it, it is not inconsistent with the main conclusion that, as Arnold himself and Milo said, the attack took place 'without orders from the leaders'. There is certainly no reason to suppose that the leaders instigated the massacre but then sought to conceal their responsibility for it from the Pope; on the contrary, the legates' delight at the result (which they describe as a 'miracle') is clear, and Arnold

---

[7] *Caesarii Heisterbacensis Monachi . . . Dialogus Miraculorum*, ed. J. Strange (Cologne, Bonn and Brussels, 1851), vol. 1, p. 302.

Amalric's attitude to shedding the blood of opponents is also clear from his machinations to ensure the burning of heretics at Minerve (see *Historia* §154).

The evidence thus points to the *ribauds* as being largely if not solely responsible for carrying out the massacre, but also suggests that this was consistent with the intentions of the leaders of the Crusade at this stage. Whether this was accidental and unwitting, or whether the *ribauds* knew what was in the minds of the leaders of the Crusade, is impossible to tell. Otherwise, although the evidence is thin, part at least of the army proper may have joined in the attack when it was well advanced, but may not have taken part in the wholesale slaughter since their main concern was apparently to make sure that they, rather than the *ribauds*, secured the booty. In the event the sack of Béziers was not repeated at Carcassonne, for the reasons set out by Peter in §98 of the *Historia*.

As to the numbers killed, the only figure given in the primary sources is the 'almost (*fere*) 20,000' in the legates' letter. This is clearly an approximation and is much more likely to have been an exaggeration than the reverse. Peter of les Vaux-de-Cernay says (§91) that up to 7,000 were killed in the church of La Madeleine, but it could not have held so great a number. For a discussion see Roquebert I, p. 262, who mentions figures given by other sources ranging from 17,000 to the 100,000 given by Caesar of Heisterbach as the population of the city.

There is perhaps one further question: how did an untrained mob (albeit a large one), without proper weapons, so easily overcome a well defended city? Roquebert (I, pp. 254–8) argues that the attackers must have included armed mercenaries, and that both the legates and Peter concealed their presence because of the known strong hostility of the Curia to the use of mercenaries in wars within Christendom (see Appendix D). The primary sources give no direct evidence to support Roquebert's view. On the contrary the legates' letter refers specifically to 'the *ribaldi* and other *unarmed* persons', and William of Tudela's account states that the *ribauds* armed themselves with clubs. The straightforward explanation suggested by William of Tudela – that the defenders panicked when they saw the *ribauds* beginning to destroy the walls and the gates, and then the crusaders themselves taking up their arms – seems much to be preferred.

APPENDIX C
Simon de Montfort, his Family and Background[1]

The Simon de Montfort of the Albigensian Crusade[2] (henceforth 'our Simon') was born about 1165, and was killed during the siege of Toulouse on 25 June 1218, as described in §612 of the *Historia*. His family came from the Ile de France, and their seat was at Montfort (later known as Montfort l'Amaury), about 40km west of Paris. He was the second son of another Simon de Montfort and became seigneur of Montfort l'Amaury on the death of his father in a July some time before 1188. His grandfather was also named Simon, and died in 1181.[3]

The family was descended from William of Hainaut who married the heiress of Montfort early in the 11th century; they produced a son Amaury I. Thereafter the family gradually acquired more possessions around Montfort (largely through marriage) and by the second half of the 12th century they also held the county of Evreux in eastern Normandy as a fief of the kings of England. Their lands thus straddled the border between Normandy (held by the kings of England until 1204) and the royal demesne of the French kings.

When our Simon's grandfather died in 1181, his elder son Amaury inherited the county of Evreux; his younger son, our Simon's father, became seigneur of Montfort and several neighbouring fiefs including Ferté-Alais and Brethencourt (respectively about 40km south and 50km south-west of Paris). This Simon married Amicia, daughter of Robert de Beaumont III, Earl of Leicester, and the marriage produced two sons (our Simon, and his younger brother Guy) and a daughter, Petronilla.

Our Simon's father had died by 1188, and Simon succeeded him as lord of Montfort. His brother Guy received the fiefs of Ferté-Alais and Brethencourt. Guy was present with his brother Simon at Zara during the early stages of Fourth Crusade in 1202–1203 (see §106) and thereafter went with him to the Holy Land. He remained there and married Heloise, heiress of Ibelin, but returned west and joined his brother at Christmas 1211 (see §290), and thereafter was to remain

[1] For further comment see: Belperron, pp. 181–5; A. Rhein, *La Seigneurie de Montfort en Yveline* (Versailles, 1910); Y. Dossat, 'Simon de Montfort', in *Cahiers de Fanjeaux*, vol. 4, pp. 281–302; and the biography of the 'English' Simon de Montfort, our Simon's son, on which this note is partly based, J. R. Maddicott, *Simon de Montfort* (Cambridge, 1994), pp. 1–6.

[2] Sometimes referred to as Simon III (e.g. by Maddicott), but more commonly he is counted as Simon IV.

[3] Our Simon's father and grandfather are often conflated into a single Simon said to have died in 1181 (see e.g. the genealogical table in Roquebert III, p. 444; Dossat, op. cit., p. 282; and Belperron, p. 181). However, Maddicott (op. cit.) draws attention to evidence which clearly shows the separate existence of the two in G. E. Cokayne, *Complete Peerage of England, Scotland, Ireland, Great Britain and the United Kingdom*, ed. V. Gibbs et al. (1912 onwards), vol. VII, Appendix D, with table on p. 709.

with his brother, appearing frequently in the second half of the *Historia*.The marriage of our Simon's father to Amicia of Leicester also brought with it a family claim to the earldom of Leicester in England. Amicia's father died in 1190, leaving the earldom to his son, Robert de Beaumont IV. However, Robert IV died without issue in 1204, whereupon our Simon inherited through his mother Amicia a claim to the earldom, and became titular Count of Leicester. After his return from the Fourth Crusade in 1206,[4] Simon visited England,[5] when King John seems to have acknowledged his claim to the earldom. However, Simon had little prospect of taking up the title. Since the loss of Normandy to Philip Augustus in 1204, John would not allow vassals who remained loyal to the King of France also to occupy their English fiefs. Simon retained Montfort, and thus could not take up his English claims. Instead in 1207 the inheritance was divided between Simon, as Amicia's heir, and her sister Margaret, who had married Saer de Quincy, Earl of Winchester; Simon's portion was given in charge to a succession of keepers. Our Simon's third (or perhaps fourth) son Simon, who was to play such a prominent part in English affairs in the reign of Henry III, came to England in about 1230 and was later able to recover the Leicester domains and was invested with the title of Count of Leicester in 1239.

After 1204 Simon usually styled himself 'Count of Leicester and lord of Montfort' and he used this formula in most of his correspondence and in records of his numerous donations and other acts which survive. After August 1209 he generally adds the former Trencavel titles; see for example his letter of that month to Innocent III, where he announces himself as '*Simon Comes Leicestriae, dominus Montis Fortis, Biterriensis et Carcassonnensis Vicecomis*' (Count of Leicester, lord of Montfort, and Viscount of Béziers and Carcassonne).[6] He often adds also the titles of lord of Albi and the Razès (see e.g. the Statutes of Pamiers, Appendix H). In papal correspondence we usually find the simpler reference '*nobilis vir Simon de Montforti*'.[7] From March 1216 the basic formula in documents is changed to '*Dux Narbone, comes Tholose et Leicestrie*' etc., with the lesser titles tending to be omitted.

However, because of Simon's claim to be Count of Leicester, the practice developed amongst his contemporaries of calling him Count of Montfort, which was in effect a courtesy title, and this became well established in ecclesiastical correspondence. Examples are found in §395 of the *Historia* (the prelates writing from Lavaur to Pope Innocent), §404 (the Pope to King Peter of Aragon) and the Pope's letter of 14 December 1215 (Appendix F(v)), and of course we find it

---

[4] See G&L I, p. 111 n. 2.
[5] There is evidence that our Simon acquired a high reputation in England; in particular Maddicott (op. cit., p. 3) draws attention to a monastic record of a rumour circulating in 1210 that King John's enemies had chosen Simon as king (*Annales Prioratus de Dunstaplia A.D.1–1297* in *Annales Monastici*, ed. H. R. Luard (1864–69), vol. III).
[6] *PL* 216, 141.
[7] E.g. *PL* 216, 140 (Arnold Amalric and Milo to Innocent, August 1209); col. 154 and col. 739 (Innocent to the Emperor Otto, November 1209, and to Arnold Amalric, January 1213).

throughout the *Historia*. However Simon never formally claimed the title Count of Montfort or used it in formal documents.

Simon married Alice,[8] a member of the important family of Montmorency, also from the Ile de France. Her brother Matthew joined the Crusade in 1215 (see §550). Alice appears quite frequently in the *Historia*, and Peter of les Vaux-de-Cernay gives his own appreciation of her in §107. From the *Historia* alone it is clear that she was a woman of strong character and a great support to her husband, playing a significant part in events after she came south to join Simon in the early spring of 1210 (see §141). For example she was at the siege of Termes in late 1210 (§181), and came with Peter of les Vaux-de-Cernay and his uncle Guy from Carcassonne to join de Montfort at the siege of Biron in the summer of 1212 (§339). For much of the time she was based at Carcassonne, but in 1216 moved to the Château Narbonnais in Toulouse, where she was living at the start of the siege of Toulouse in 1218 (§600), helping to organise its defences. After her husband's death she went north to recruit support for her son Amaury, and returned south around Christmas 1218 (§618).

Alice and Simon had four sons, two of whom appear in the *Historia*. The eldest was Amaury, on whom see especially §§305, 430–32 (becomes a knight) 492 (marriage) and 613–20 (takes command of the crusaders on his father's death). The second son was Guy, on whom see §§587 and 600. A third son, Simon (the 'English' Simon) who was born c. 1208 is not mentioned but probably spent his early years growing up in the de Montfort household in the South.[9] The fourth son was Robert. They also apparently had three daughters. The eldest, Amicia (Amicie), was betrothed early in 1211 to James, the infant son of King Peter of Aragon (see §211); the engagement was broken off after the battle of Muret, and she was then in 1218 betrothed to William son of Adhémar of Poitiers (§599) before eventually marrying Gaucher de Joigny. Another daughter, Petronilla (Pétronille), was born in 1211 during the Crusade (see §258). The third was Laure (see G&L II, p. 26 n. 1).

It is clear from the *Historia* that Simon de Montfort was a pious and devout man, in general fiercely loyal to the Church. His conduct at Zara in 1202–03 (§106) showed that he was not prepared to join in the assault on a Christian city when Innocent III had forbidden it. During the Albigensian Crusade he clearly won the unwavering support of prelates such as Fulk of Toulouse, Raymond of Uzès, and Navarre of Couserans, as well as of the legates. His alliances with local prelates such as the bishops of Agen (see §317), Cahors (§246), Comminges (§358) and Rodez (see §537 n. 111) were instrumental in his gaining control of their dioceses, while at Pamiers in the autumn of 1209 it was Abbot Vital of Saint-Antonin who invited him into the town (§116).

---

[8]   For an account of Alice de Montmorency see M. Zerner, 'L'épouse de Simon de Montfort et la croisade albigeoise', in *Femmes – Mariages – Lignages, XII–XIV Siècles: Mélanges offerts a Georges Duby*, ed. J. Dufournet, A. Joris and P. Toubert (Brussels, 1992).

[9]   See Maddicott, op. cit., p. 4.

Simon de Montfort and his family had established close links with several religious houses in the neighbourhood of Montfort l'Amaury. One of these was the Cistercian monastery of les Vaux-de-Cernay, which lay south-east of Montfort. Simon's family donated land to the house, and evidently knew it well. Peter of les Vaux-de-Cernay's uncle Guy, who became Abbot in 1181, had accompanied Simon at Zara, and in §299 of the *Historia* we are told that he had been a close friend (*'familiarissimus'*) of Simon for many years. Simon clearly made an enormous impression on Peter of les Vaux-de-Cernay himself, as emerges from the eulogy in §§104–7. Indeed they must have rubbed shoulders frequently (see Introduction, p. xxiv), and thus Peter's *Historia*, despite his partiality, provides an excellent basis on which assessments of Simon de Montfort can be founded.

Simon and Alice also seem to have developed a close relationship with (St) Dominic, who baptised their daughter Petronilla in 1211 and blessed the wedding of their eldest son Amaury in 1214. Dominic's preaching work benefited from donations from Simon de Montfort. On 15 May 1211 he granted to Dominic's house at Prouille some nearby land confiscated from Bertrand de Saissac, and other grants both by him and by other crusaders followed.[10] This support continued once Dominic had moved to Toulouse: on 13 December 1217 Simon ordered his seneschals of Agen and Carcassonne to protect the possessions of Dominic and his colleagues.[11]

But de Montfort's loyalty to the Church and to Innocent III was not unqualified, and when it conflicted with his ambitions or with his own sense of what was his due he was prepared to confront or ignore ecclesiastical authority. His quarrel with Arnold Amalric over the title of Duke of Narbonne (see §560) showed that he was perfectly prepared to challenge the legate when he felt his legitimate rights were threatened. He also persistently flouted the spirit and at times the letter of Innocent's instructions when establishing his control of the lands of Raymond VI of Toulouse and those of the Count of Foix in 1214–15 (see Appendix G). His relations with the Abbey of Moissac after he had gained control of the town in 1212 were apparently not happy (§355 n. 125).

Simon de Montfort was highly ambitious and at times very ruthless. He was intent on expropriating both the Trencavels and the counts of Toulouse and establishing himself as overlord of their lands, and he pursued these aims relentlessly, even when Innocent III tried to restrain him. His ambition was coupled with decisive leadership and great military skill, and it was this combination of qualities that lead to his successes in the Midi from 1209–16. At times during those years his determined leadership, and the sheer force of his will, seem to have prevented the military collapse of the Crusade; and his decisive seizure of the initiative at Castelnaudary, Muret and on other occasions is striking. His vengeance against those who betrayed him was measured but merciless, as the

---

[10] See Vicaire, pp. 125–6 and 129, and n. 95 to §336 for a donation to Prouille by Robert Mauvoisin, and n. 83 to §326 for a similar donation by Enguerrand de Boves. See also Roquebert I, p. 301.
[11] See G&L III, pp. 205–8.

men of Bram were to discover in 1210 (§142), and as Martin Algai did at Biron in 1212 (§337). The judgments of later generations have varied greatly according to the viewpoint of those judging; the verdicts of some of his contemporaries are noted under §612.

APPENDIX D

Mercenaries and the Crusade

Peter of les Vaux-de-Cernay frequently mentions the use of mercenaries by Raymond VI and other southern lords, and the charge that he employed mercenaries was one of the most serious laid against Raymond VI by the Church. This note seeks to set these points in context.

Mercenaries in general in this period are discussed in, for example, P. Contamine, *War in the Middle Ages*, trans. M. Jones (Oxford: Blackwell, 1984), esp. pp. 243–8. They ranged from well-organised, usually small, groups of professionals, who were outside any recognised system of feudal loyalties but otherwise comparable to ordinary knights and sergeants, through specialist engineers who built and operated siege engines, down to opportunist bands who were little better than brigands. Recruited particularly from northern Spain and the Netherlands (whence they were often called 'Aragonais' or 'Flemings' or 'Brabantines'), professional mercenaries serving under their own captains would often be engaged to garrison castles or to serve as auxiliary troops. Their employment was very common in the 12th and 13th centuries in western Europe. They seem to have been less prominent and numerous at the time of the Crusade than they had been a few decades earlier, but about this time King Philip Augustus was employing mercenaries,[1] and King John of England was very reliant on mercenaries for his wars in France, as his brother Richard had been before him.[2]

The use of at least the better classes of mercenaries would thus have been common practice in the South in the later 12th and early 13th centuries. It was especially important for Raymond VI because the relatively loose ties between him and his vassals made it more difficult to obtain troops through feudal service (which was far less developed in the South than in the north of France).

Mercenaries as a whole had acquired a sinister reputation in the 12th century, particularly because they often in effect lived off the land, plundering indiscriminately and causing disruption and insecurity. The Church disliked them not only because of the general disruption they caused, but also because they were not governed by the normal bonds of a hierarchical Christian society, and because of their reputation for despoiling churches and monasteries. They were formally condemned at the Third Lateran Council in 1179 in the same canon (27) which anathematised the Cathars, and Innocent III continued the efforts of his predecessors to curb their use. The suppression of mercenaries was thus a fundamental part of the *pax* element of the *negotium pacis et fidei*, 'the business of peace and the faith' (on which phrase see n. 9 to §3 and Appendix G). Indeed the two

---

[1] See Contamine, op. cit., p. 244.
[2] See W. L. Warren, *King John* (London, 2nd ed., 1978), pp. 30, 60–6 and 91.

elements were very closely linked in ecclesiastical thinking: without the establishment of orderly Christian peace, which required amongst other things the suppression of mercenaries, neither the Church nor lawful secular authority would be able to deal effectively with heresy.

The use of mercenaries was hence treated as a major offence by the Church. The charge that he used them was often laid against Raymond VI, and it was one of the counts on which he was excommunicated in 1207: see e.g. the references to *Aragonenses* in Innocent III's letter to Raymond of 29 May, *PL* 215, 1166–8, in Appendix F(1), and the '*mandata* before absolution' given to Raymond by the legate Milo at Valence (see §77), recorded in the *Processus* (*PL* 216, 91) where Milo says 'I instruct you immediately to expel from your territory and dominions *Aragonenses, Ruptarios, Cotarellos [Cotereaux], Bramenzones [? Brabançons], Blascones, Mainadas* or whatever other names they may be known by.'[3] Harbouring mercenaries was later to be one of the main charges on which Raymond was eventually found guilty by the Fourth Lateran Council (see §572 and Appendix F(v)).

Throughout the *Historia*, Peter himself regularly draws attention to the employment of mercenaries by Raymond VI, Raymond-Roger of Foix, and other opponents of the Crusade, and concerns about mercenaries feature prominently in, for example, the letters from the prelates to King Peter of Aragon and Pope Innocent at the time of the Council of Lavaur (§§377–84 and 392–7); there and in the *Historia* all mercenaries are usually classified together under the pejorative term *ruptarii*. One of the most prominent mercenary captains in the service of Raymond VI was Hugh d'Alfaro from Navarre, who rose to become Raymond's Seneschal of the Agenais: see n. 72 to §319. His career perhaps shows how the distinction between a trusted member of a seigneurial service or household and a mercenary captain could become blurred. Employing mercenaries did, however, also have its disadvantages: they would usually fight only if victory seemed likely, and if not they fled, while obtaining booty was a high priority. At the battle of Castelnaudary in 1211 the mercenaries with the Count of Foix fled as soon as they had secured booty.

Simon de Montfort also employed mercenaries of various kinds during the Crusade. He could not rely simply on the services of those to whom he gave fiefs or on the supply of crusaders from the north, many of whom came only for the forty days required for them to fulfil their vows, and he probably had to use paid troops particularly to garrison the *castra* he conquered. In the *Historia* Peter is careful to avoid drawing attention to this, as were the legates in their correspondence, but there is direct evidence that the crusaders did sometimes employ mercenaries. For example, the 'Aragonese knights' whom Peter describes in §110 as operating for the crusaders at Fanjeaux were mercenaries, since the *Chanson* (I, 34, p. 84) says they were headed by Peire Aragonese, described as '*un mainader ardit*' (see n. 2, loc. cit., by Martin-Chabot, and our note to §100 in the text). He

[3] Cf. in canon 27 of the Third Lateran Council '*de Brabantionibus et Aragonensibus, Navariis, Bascolis, Coterellis et Triaverdinis*'.

witnessed an act of de Montfort's in July 1209 (*HGL* VIII, 601). Martin Algai, who fought with the crusaders in 1211, was another mercenary captain who had also fought for King John of England (see §265 and note, also *Chanson* I, note on p. 242, and Warren, op. cit. p. 91). In a letter to the Pope (see n. 105 to §116) de Montfort also refers to '*soldarii*' in his employ, and in §489 Peter refers to '*stipendiarii*', but these were probably soldiers working for pay as individuals rather than mercenaries working under their own leader in the usual sense – as probably were the knights recruited by Simon de Montfort in France for 'high rates of pay' ('*magnis stipendiis*') to whom Peter refers in §576. Finally, we may also note the use of highly skilled, and apparently highly paid, siege engineers by de Montfort, as for example at Carcassonne (§96), Minerve (§152), Termes (§180) and Casseneuil (§§524–7).

The Chronology of Events in the Autumn of 1209

As indicated in our note to §110, the chronology of the period from the fall of Carcassonne on 15 August 1209 to the end of that year, covered in §§110–36 of the *Historia*, is very uncertain. Peter of les Vaux-de-Cernay gives only one firm date: the Feast of St Michael (29 September) in §134 for the attempt by the Count of Foix to recover Fanjeaux. While his dating of events by reference to religious feast days is sometimes approximate, in this case he is quite precise, using the phrase '*in festo Sancti Michaelis*' ('on the feast of . . .') not, for example, '*circa festum . . .*' ('about the feast of . . .'). He says that this attack on Fanjeaux occurred shortly after ('*non multo post*') the Count of Foix's recovery of Preixan, implying a date of, say, 20–26 September for that event. The only other dating he gives is at the end of §136 when he says 'all this' took place about Christmas time ('*facta sunt autem hec omnia circa festum Dominicae nativitatis*'), which is clearly very approximate. His other indications are also approximate: '*paucis diebus peractis*', '*in ipso tempore*', '*in eodem tempore*' ('after a few days', 'at this time' 'at the same time') and similar phrases.

The only other positive date we have for this period is for the death of Raymond-Roger Trencavel which is given as 10 November 1209 in the death-roll, or necrology, of Carcassonne (*HGL* V, 36); Peter records this in §124, but gives no date. There is also an indication that the death of the Abbot of Eaunes, which Peter records in §130, occurred during November 1209; G&L I, p. 134 n. 1, quote Robert of Auxerre as placing this between 4 October and 25 December, and a date in November seems likely since the Abbot had been visiting the legates in Saint-Gilles, and the legate Milo is known to have been there on 6 November.

The main problem which arises is thus as follows. In §134 Peter places the attack on Fanjeaux by Raymond-Roger of Foix, and by clear implication the recovery of Preixan, almost at the end his account of the period from August to Christmas 1209, ten sections after his record of the death of Viscount Raymond-Roger, which took place on 10 November, and four sections after the death of the Abbot of Eaunes which probably also occurred in November; yet at the same time he dates the attack to 29 September. It seems we must assume *either* that the order in which he narrates events is out of sequence and confused *or* that the date of 29 September is wrong.

Since Peter was recounting events which occurred several years before he wrote, and on the basis of testimony from those who took part but whose own recollections may have been becoming uncertain, mistakes of either kind could easily have been made. However, if we take the first assumption, that the date of 29 September is right and that Peter has simply misplaced the recovery of Preixan in his narrative, a further problem arises, since Peter places the original occupation of Preixan by de Montfort, following the conclusion of his accord with Count Raymond-Roger of Foix, in §120 – at the end of his initial campaign in his newly acquired territories. We do not know how soon after the fall of Carcassonne on 15 August 1209 that campaign started, but if we follow Peter's ordering of events for this earlier period the occupation of Preixan by de Montfort could hardly have taken place earlier than mid-September. If this is so we would then have to assume an interval of only a week or so between the occupation of Preixan by de Montfort on the one hand, and the break-down of his accord with Count Raymond-Roger and the latter's recovery of Preixan on the other, and this seems too short. Apparently for this reason Roquebert (I, pp. 309–10), who accepts the date of 29 September for the attack on Fanjeaux and assumes that Peter's ordering of events is wrong, finds it necessary to make the further assumption that events in the earlier part of the period, mid-August to mid-September, are also related by Peter in the wrong order, and to relocate the original occupation of Preixan to the early stages of de Montfort's campaign – before the occupation of Castres, which Peter describes in §112 (cf. Roquebert I, pp. 309–10).[1] This interpretation would also mean that the whole campaign was over by the end of September, and thus leads Roquebert (I, p. 322) to the unsatisfactory assumption that de Montfort was idle throughout October.

One argument in favour of this first assumption is that Peter does frequently record events out of order; for notable examples see the notes to §§137 and 367. There is, however, usually some reason for this – for example he may pursue a line of narrative to its conclusion and then double back in time as he introduces a new subject. This is not the case in §134, and the simplest answer to the problem may therefore be to adopt the second assumption, namely that the date of 29 September is incorrect. Peter's ordering of events can then be retained throughout, so that the events related in §§110–17 would take place between late August and late September, with Simon's visits to Albi and Limoux (§§118–19) and his seizure of Preixan (§120) taking place in late September to early October.[2] The Count of Foix's recapture of Preixan and his failed attempt to retake Fanjeaux will have been much later than 29 September, quite reasonably where Peter places them after the death of Raymond-Roger Trencavel on 10 November; it does seem more probable that the Count would have taken this action later in the autumn, by which time the crusaders' difficulties would have become clear, rather than at the earlier date. There is no certainty about this and there remains no possibility of even approximately precise dating for the period 15 August to Christmas 1209 as a whole, but the sequence of events suggested here on the basis of this second assumption, that the date of 29 September is wrong, seems more acceptable.

[1]   Roquebert later (I, pp. 321–2) refers to 'la chronologie peu embrouillée du récit de Pierre'. In favour of his view is the point that Preixan is only 10km south of Carcassonne and it would have been good tactics for de Montfort to have tackled Preixan at the same time as he attacked other places in the same area (namely Fanjeaux, Mirepoix, Pamiers and Saverdun) – in late August rather than later. However, this is very hypothetical.
[2]   There is a faint possibility that the original occupation of Fanjeaux took place on 29 September and that Peter mistakenly transferred the date to the attempt to retake it; however, this means taking the occupation much later than Peter's narrative in §110 implies.

Translated Extracts from Papal Correspondence, 1207–1215

(i) 29 May 1207: Innocent III to Count Raymond VI of Toulouse (*PL* 215, 1166–68, *RHGF* XIII, 140)

This letter confirms Raymond VI's excommunication by Peter of Castelnau issued in April 1207 (see Historia, *§27). It is over 13,000 words long and consists of a sustained attack on Raymond, emphasising in particular how he risks incurring the wrath of God if he persists in his evil-doing. We translate (a) the opening few lines of the letter; (b) passages in which Innocent sets out the main charges against Raymond (including especially his failure to join the peace initiative of 1206–07) and confirms the sentence of excommunication pronounced against Raymond and the laying of an interdict on his territories; and (c) the closing section in which Innocent threatens to declare Raymond's lands to be liable to seizure. See also notes to §§24 and 27.*

(a) If with the prophet's help we could pierce the wall of your heart, we would enter it and show you the terrible abominations you have wrought in it. But since it seems to have hardened beyond stone it will be hard to penetrate, although it might perhaps be easy to shake it with the healing blow of speech; so, although we may be able to reproach you, we can hardly hope to correct you. Grief! What pride has swollen your heart, what madness, wretched man, has seized you, that you despise keeping peace with your neighbours, and, departing from the laws of God, ally yourself with the enemies of Catholic truth? Do you think you cannot be sufficiently troublesome to men, unless you are also troublesome to God? . . .

(b) What indeed are you making of yourself, that when our most gracious son in Christ, the illustrious King of Aragon, and almost all the magnates (*magnates*) of the area have responded to the exhortations of the legates of the Apostolic See and joined in swearing treaties of peace, you alone have refused, looking to find gain in acts of war, and feeding on corpses like a crow? Are you not ashamed to have failed to observe the numerous oaths you swore, when you promised to proscribe all the heretics living in your dominions? . . .

We join in your grief – if indeed you do grieve – especially for the fact that, because you cherish heretics, you are yourself strongly suspected of heresy (*suspectus de haeresi vehementer haberis*). So we ask you, what madness has seized you, that you listen to frivolous opinions and favour followers of this path?

. . . you stand convicted as an adversary of the Gospel. For this, and other reasons the legates have pronounced sentences of excommunication against you and of interdict on your territories; namely, you are retaining men from Aragon [i.e. mercenaries], treating them in friendly fashion, and have joined them in devastating the land; you have violated the feast days of Lent and other festivals which ought to rejoice in the security of peace; you have refused to offer justice to your adversaries when they submitted themselves to justice and swore to keep peace; you have entrusted public offices to Jews thus insulting the Christian faith, and you have robbed the Monastery of St William and other churches of property and [dependant] churches; you have fortified churches, and have not hesitated to wage war from them; you have again increased tolls; and you have driven our venerable brother the Bishop of Carpentras from his see. We now ratify these sentences. . . .

(c) . . . we instruct you to give swift and sufficient satisfaction on these matters so that you may earn the benefit of absolution. Otherwise, since we cannot allow such a massive injury to the Church, nay, to God himself, to go unpunished, we shall arrange that the territory which you are recognised as holding from the Roman Church[1] shall be taken from you. And if this threat does not lead you to understanding, we shall enjoin all the princes around you to to rise against you as an enemy of Christ and persecutor of the Church and to keep for themselves whatever parts of your territories they are able to occupy, lest they become even more infected by the stain of heresy under your rule (*universis circumpositis principibus injungemus ut in te velut in hostem Christi . . . insurgant, retinendo sibi quascunque terras de tuis poterunt occupare*). In all this the wrath of the Lord will not be turned from you; rather will His hand stretch out to grasp you, thus to show that it will be hard for you to flee from the face of His anger, which you have gravely provoked.

(ii) April 1208: King Philip Augustus to Innocent III (*HGL* VIII, 558)

The King replies to Innocent's request of 10 March 1208 for support for the Crusade (see Historia, *§72 and note).*

In regard to your instruction[2] in the matter of the death of Peter of Castelnau, who has been killed with the approval of the Count of Saint-Gilles [Raymond VI of Toulouse], be sure that we greatly regret his death since he was a good man engaged on a deserving task. If you have reason to complain about him [the Count], so indeed do we. When we were engaged in a major war against King Richard of England, he went against us by marrying the King's sister, even though our father, of blessed memory, and we ourselves had helped to defend his father and his father's territory at very great cost (*magna constamenta and impensas miserimus ad defendendum*). When we were engaged in

---

[1]   Principally the County of Melgueil, on which see n. 73 to §75.
[2]   '*Quod nobis mandavistis*'. *Mandare* is the word usually employed by Innocent when he is instructing anyone; the meaning can vary in strength from 'request' to 'recommend' to 'order', but although it would be binding for a subordinate clearly it would not be so for the King.

warfare against King John because of the wrong he had done to us, we found some of his men helping in the defence of Falaise against us. We must also tell you that in all the wars we have been engaged in we have never had any help from him or his people, even though he holds one of the largest baronies in our kingdom as our vassal. As to your request for us to provide such help as we consider appropriate in this venture, you should know that when your letter reached us we were en route with our army to engage the army of the King of England, who had broken off our truce and was not prepared to give any compensation to us or to our vassals. The bishops have discussed this matter with us, and we have replied to them that if the clergy and barons are prepared to supply adequate help (such as we might consider to be of use to the land)[3] and we can be satisfied that there is a firmly secured truce in place, then we will gladly send help in men and money. As to the matter of your declaring the Count's territory open to seizure, I must tell you that I have been advised by learned and eminent men that you cannot legally (*de jure*) do this until he is condemned for heresy. When he is so condemned, you should clearly indicate it and request me to declare the territory open to seizure, since it belongs to my domain (*id significare debetis and mandare, ut terram illam exponamus tanquam ad foedum nostrum pertinentem*). So far you have not told us that the Count has been condemned. We say this not to excuse him, since we would rather accuse than excuse him, as we will show by our actions if, with God's will, the opportunity arises.

(iii)   25 January 1210: Innocent III to Bishop Hugh of Riez and Master Thedisius (*PL* 216, 173)[4]

Innocent instructs the legates to give Count Raymond of Toulouse an opportunity to clear himself of the major charges against him (see Historia, *§137 n. 49).*

[The first part of the letter relates that Count Raymond, at an audience with the Pope, complained that he had been wronged by the actions of the legates. He maintained that he had fulfilled most of the requirements laid down by Milo (producing written testimonies from various churches in support of his claim), and was willing to fulfil the rest. It continues:] He therefore humbly asked us that in the matter of the Catholic faith, on which he has long been held to be suspect, albeit unjustly, we should now arrange for him to be purified in our presence, in proper form; and after that to ensure that his *castra* to be restored to him, rather than that they should be retained indefinitely, to his great disadvantage, on the grounds that they were handed over as a guarantee. It is being argued that since he failed to fulfil many of the instructions he had been given, these *castra* have now come under the control of the Roman Church in accordance with the terms of the undertaking he provided; however it is not proper that the Church should

---

3   '*Terre*'; it is not clear whether he means the South or his own kingdom.
4   A similar letter to the archbishops of Narbonne and Arles is in *PL* 216, 171–2.

be enriched at the expense of other parties, and we have therefore thought it appropriate to treat him with apostolic consideration, and after consulting our brothers have decided that he should not be deprived of his rights to the *castra* on these grounds . . . so long as he is truly intending to fulfil the instructions known to have been given to him. For the same reasons we have decided to ensure that his territory will be protected from harm by the Christian army (*curavimus utiliter providere quod terram suam illaesam fecimus conservari ab exercitu Christiano*) which went forth to drive out the heretics, in accordance with our mandate, and has now almost entirely destroyed its adversaries. Accordingly . . . we now instruct you, within three months of receiving this letter, to summon in a suitable place a council of archbishops, bishops, abbots, priors, barons, knights and others whose presence you think will be useful; and if before the conclusion of the council there shall appear against the Count (whom in the meantime we have instructed to carry out the instructions given to him) a lawful accuser on the matters of deviation from the orthodox faith and the murder of Peter of Castelnau (of blessed memory, then papal legate) then you should after hearing arguments from each side proceed to reach a judgment; you should then send us a statement of the case, properly drawn up, and set for the parties a time limit for them to present themselves before us to receive the judgment; if however no accuser appears against him on these matters, then you should carefully consider by what means the Count may legally purify himself so that his ill fame may die where it was born. If the form of purification determined by you with the council's approval is acceptable to him, you should put it into effect, but if he fails to carry it through you should retain the *castra* in your control and send us a full report; the same procedure to be followed if he complains that the form of purification is likely to be unjustly burdensome; and in either case you should await confirmation of your decision from the Apostolic See (*in utroque casu apostolicae responsionis oraculum expectetur*). If he properly purifies himself in accordance with your instructions you should publicly declare him to be a true Catholic, and completely innocent of the murder of the legate, and return the *castra* to him when he has carried out the instructions given to him; however he must provide some other suitable guarantee of his intention to keep the peace, which he should promise to do for the indefinite future, and proper care must be taken to ensure that the process of carrying out our instructions is not impeded by malicious or frivolous complaints. . . .

(iv) Innocent III's letters of January 1213 (see *Historia*, §399)

(a) 15 January 1213: Innocent III to the legate Arnold Amalric (*PL* 216, 744–5)[5]

Innocent orders the suspension of the Crusade.

   In the South, which had been infested with the poison of heresy and oppressed by disastrous war, the little foxes that were spoiling the vines[6] of the
Lord God of Hosts have been taken, so that with God's help the business of the
faith has by now sufficiently prospered. A more urgent cause is now at hand, and
it is right that the hands of Christians should turn to it. We have heard that the
King of the Saracens is preparing everywhere for battle, his resolve to attack
followers of the Christian faith compounded by the severity of his fall at the
hands of Christians – or rather at the hands of Christ who exercised a propi-
tious judgment on our behalf. The Holy Land, which is a portion of our inheritance from the Lord,[7] is greatly in need of help and looks to receive the support
of Christians. Often, very often, efforts concentrated on a single end have led to
success – the opposite, to failure, and the less we are engaged on other matters,
the more we will be able to attend effectively to the general and special business
of Christian believers in opposing the faithless race of Saracens (*Christicolarum
generali ac speciali negotio contra Saracenae gentis perfidiam*). We therefore hereby
enjoin you, our dear brother, to devote your earnest attention to negotiating
treaties for peace and a truce with our dearest son in Christ, Peter the illustrious
King of Aragon, and counts and barons and other men of good sense whom you
think should be involved, so that you may through such treaties provide a secure
and lasting peace for the whole of the South. You should thus cease to call
Christians to arms, or weary them (*non convoces aut fatiges*) through the indulgences granted by the Apostolic See for the fight against the heretics, until or
unless you receive a specific instruction on this matter from the Apostolic
See.

(b) 17 January 1213: Innocent III to Simon de Montfort (*PL* 216, 741–3)

Innocent orders Simon to restore the territories taken from King Peter's vassals.

   Envoys of King Peter, the illustrious King of Aragon, our dearest son in
Christ, have informed us on his behalf that you have turned your hands against
Catholics, when they should have been directed against heretics, and used the

---

5   Also *RHGF* XIX, 566; Mansi XXII, 873.
6   Cf. Song of Solomon 4, v. 15.
7   Cf. Psalms 16, v. 5.

army of the crusaders, which you have induced to spill the blood of the just and injure the innocent, to occupy the territories of the King's vassals, the Count of Foix, the Count of Comminges and Gaston de Béarn, in so doing greatly wronging the King himself; this even though no heretics live in those territories and no ill report of contamination by the evil of heresy has involved the people living there. The King's envoys maintained that by taking oaths of fealty from the occupants of those territories and allowing them to continue to live there, you are tacitly admitting that they are Catholics, since you deny that you are a supporter of heretics; alternatively you must admit that you are in some way supporting heretics, if you claim that you were acting legitimately in occupying their territories. The envoys then put forward the particular complaint that when the King was engaged in the service of Jesus Christ against the Saracens, and was exposing himself and his people to the risk of shedding their blood because of their reverence for the Christian faith, you appropriated the possessions of his vassals, and found it easier to subdue them because the King's ability to protect them was restricted by his having devoted his resources to helping Christians against the faithless race of Saracens. He intends to resume his war against the Saracens and would be the better able – under God's leadership – to fight them if he were enjoying a stable peace with other parties; he therefore requested the Apostolic See to bring about the peaceful restitution of the territories of his vassals. Since we do not wish the King to be defrauded of his rights or to be hindered in his purpose [of fighting the Moors] we hereby instruct you to restore these territories to the King and his vassals, lest by retaining them illegally you appear to have worked for your own personal advantage rather than the general advantage of the Catholic faith.

(c) 18 January 1213: Innocent III to Arnold Amalric, Hugh Bishop of Riez and Thedisius (*PL* 216, 739–40)

Innocent accepts the representations of King Peter of Aragon and censures Arnold and Simon de Montfort.

Although it is necessary to cut off putrid flesh, lest the contagion of corruption spread to healthy parts, the hand of the surgeon must be applied cautiously so that the corrupt parts are removed with sufficient care to ensure that the healthy parts are not harmed through carelessness. We have now received reports, by letters and through envoys, from Peter, the illustrious King of Aragon. They referred to the time when the crusaders invaded the territory of the Viscount of Béziers, after the issue of the mandate from the Apostolic See against the heretics in the South; the Viscount appealed to the King as his overlord for help, but the King gave him no help and denied him the remedy of counsel; and to ensure that the Church's purpose should not be hindered decided to refuse help to some Catholics, rather than appear to be helping heretics who were mingled with them. As a result the Viscount lost his territory and in the end was wretchedly killed. You, however, brother Archbishop, and Simon de Monfort have led the crusaders into the territory of the Count of Toulouse and thus not only occupied places inhabited by heretics but have equally extended greedy hands (*manus avidas extendistis*) into lands which had no ill reputation for heresy; and since you have exacted oaths of fealty from men in those lands and allowed them to continue to live there, it does not seem credible that there are heretics in those places. The King's messengers have added that you have usurped the possessions of others indiscriminately, unjustly and without proper care, to the extent that only the *castrum* of Montauban and the city of Toulouse remain in the Count's hands.

Amongst the places which the King asserts to have been occupied he mentions especially the territories which Richard of England, of illustrious memory, gave to the Count as a dowry for his sister; also the territories of the Count of Foix, the Count of Comminges and Gaston de Béarn. He has complained especially that although these three Counts are still his own vassals you, brother Archbishop, and Simon have sought to persuade the men of the territories they have lost to swear an oath of fealty in respect of those territories to another person. The King added that the Count [Raymond] met him as he was returning from his victory over the Saracens, and set out the wrongs he had suffered at the hands of the crusaders. He blamed his own wrongdoing for the Church's failure to allow him absolution, but was ready to do anything we might now order him to do, if it was within his capabilities. So that he should not be alone in bearing the disgrace of such enormous shame, he was committing his territory, his son and his wife, the King's sister, to the King who was free to decide whether to protect them or send them into exile (*ut eos, si vellet, defenderet vel permitteret exulare*). Since punishment should fall on those who have committed the offence, and retribution should not go further than befits the crime, the King humbly requested that the county of Toulouse should be reserved for the Count's son, who had never fallen, and with God's help never would fall, into the error of heresy. He also promised to take charge of the Count's son, as well as the county, ensuring that he would be educated to follow the true faith and conform to proper standards of conduct; and to purge the whole territory of Aragon[8] of the contagion of heresy and return it to the worship of the true faith; he would provide whatever guarantees the Apostolic See might require for the performance of all these promises. He added that Count Raymond was now willing to perform whatever penance we might decree, whether to go overseas or to Spain to the frontier with the faithless race of Saracens (*sive quod in partes adeat transmarinas, sive quod sit in Hispania circa frontariam contra gentis perfidiam Saracenae*).

[The letter concludes by emphasising the need to proceed with all due care in matters of this weight and instructing the recipients of the letter to arrange a council of prelates, barons etc., to examine the King's proposals carefully and

---

8   Clearly referring to the vassal territories.

without prejudice, and report the council's recommendations to himself so that he may reach an appropriate decision, 'since it seems without doubt fitting that a decision should be made concerning a suitable ruler for this territory'.]

(v) 14 December 1215: Innocent III publishes the decision of the Fourth Lateran Council (*RHGF* XIX, 598)[9]

Bishop Innocent sends greetings to all the Christian faithful who may receive this letter.

Almost the whole world knows how hard the Church has laboured, through preachers and crusaders, to drive out heretics and mercenaries from the Province of Narbonne and neighbouring areas. Through God's grace and our care her efforts have met with great success; both have indeed been driven out, and the land itself is now governed soundly in the Catholic faith and fraternal peace. But a new plant still needs to be watered, and after consulting the Holy Council we have decided to make arrangements as now set out.

Since the Count of Toulouse has been found culpable on both charges[10] and his territory will never be able to be kept safe in the true faith under his rule (as has long been clear from sure indications), he is to be excluded forever from his rights of dominion, which he has exercised so badly. He is to stay in some suitable place outside his former territory, there to perform due penitence for his sins. He is however to receive for his maintenance 400 marks annually from the revenues of that territory, so long as he takes care to show humble obedience. His wife, sister of the former King of Aragon, who as all witnesses agree is a virtuous woman and a true Catholic, is to retain the possessions appertaining to her dowry in their entirety and undisturbed;[11] she is however to ensure that they are administered in accordance with the requirements of the Church in such a way that the business of peace and the faith suffers no harm from them; alternatively she may receive on their account adequate compensation as determined by the Holy See. All the territory which the crusaders have won in their fight against the heretics, heretical believers and their supporters and receivers, together with Montauban and Toulouse (of all places the most corrupted by the stigma of heresy), is to be handed and granted to the Count of Montfort (a man of courage and a true Catholic who more than any other has laboured in this business), subject in all things to the rights of Catholics, both men and women, and of the Church. He is to hold this territory from those from whom it should

---

[9] Also *HGL* VIII, 681; *Layettes* I, 1132; Molinier 116b. For a general commentary see Roquebert II, ch. 19; see also *Chanson* II, 151–2, pp. 78–89 and notes.

[10] I.e., presumably, harbouring heretics and mercenaries.

[11] Beaucaire, Vallabrègues, Valliguières, Saint-Saturnin and Bollène. Innocent may initially have overlooked the fact that Beaucaire had been donated to Simon de Montfort by the Archbishop of Arles on 30 January 1215 (Molinier 95); at the end of the month he wrote to Arnold Amalric and Simon (letters summarised in *RHGF* XIX, 606) ordering that she should receive an allowance of 150 marks from Beaucaire; see also n. 6 to §575, Roquebert II, pp. 379–81, and *Chanson* II, n. 3 on p. 75 and n. 1 on p. 76.

rightly be held.[12] The territory not occupied by the crusaders[13] is to be given in charge, as will be laid down by the Church, to persons who will be capable of maintaining and defending the business of peace and the faith, with the intention that it be given over to the young son of the Count of Toulouse after he has reached adulthood, so long as he demonstrates that he deserves to take possession of it, in whole or in part, whichever shall seem to be most appropriate.

As to the matter of the Count of Foix, further enquiries should now be undertaken, after which a fair judgment should be made. Meanwhile the *castrum* of Foix, which has been committed to our care on his behalf, is to be held in accordance with the Church's instructions until this business is concluded.[14]

Finally, the many doubts and difficulties that are likely to arise in these matters must all be referred to the judgment of the Apostolic See, since what has been achieved at great cost and with much toil should not be lost through the arrogance or malice of any person.

Given at the Lateran, 14 December in the eighteenth year of our pontificate.

---

[12] I.e. Innocent again refers to the requirement to preserve the rights of superior lords, first encountered in §62. He has in mind the King of France, since none of the territories held by Raymond VI from the Emperor were transferred to Simon de Montfort.

[13] Chiefly the marquisate of Provence; see again, however, n. 6 to §575.

[14] See §564 and for developments §§588, 606D and notes.

APPENDIX G
Innocent III and the Albigensian Crusade

Pope Innocent III initiated the Albigensian Crusade in 1207–09. Thereafter he sought, with limited success, to control it from the Roman Curia through the use of a succession of legates and through correspondence, until his death in July 1216. Peter of les Vaux-de-Cernay dedicates his work to Innocent III but writes very much from the standpoint of Simon de Montfort and the other leaders of the Crusade; moreover, his understanding of political and diplomatic events was incomplete. He thus gives only a partial picture of the development of Innocent's policies both prior to the Crusade and after it had been launched, and it is not always easy to follow the twists and turns of those policies from the *Historia* alone. Some of the gaps are filled by detailed references to papal letters and other sources in the notes to this translation, and by the extracts from papal correspondence in Appendix F. In this note we summarise (i) the main features of Innocent's policies before the Crusade, and the evolution of the idea of a crusade against heresy and Count Raymond VI of Toulouse; and (ii) the development of Innocent's policies once the Crusade began in 1209, and some of the general themes which emerge.

Innocent's policies towards the Midi, 1198–1208

When he became Pope in 1198 Innocent clearly gave a high priority to dealing with heresy and associated problems in the Midi. His overall aims are reflected in the phrase *negotium pacis et fidei*, the business of peace and the faith, which is used in one form or another throughout the *Historia* and papal correspondence to refer to the campaign against heresy and Raymond VI, and in many cases is synonymous with the Crusade (see n. 9 to §3). The phrase encapsulates Innocent's concept of the orderly governance of Christian society under the ultimate authority of the Pope. It implied a series of linked objectives. One, reflecting the faith element, was the suppression of heresy, the reinvigoration of orthodox religion, and the removal of inadequate prelates. Equally important were elements related to 'peace', such as curbing the use of mercenaries, the establishment of peaceful government (including proper repect for ecclesiastical property and other rights, and support for the church in their maintenance and protection), and the suppression of unjust tolls levied by local rulers. Secular authorities were to carry out their duties properly, with regard both to the Church and those who lived under their rule. Without peace and order, the faith could not be protected and heresy would flourish; disorder and petty warfare would reign, lords would act arbitrarily and without proper reference to law and justice, while the Church and its property would be unprotected.

Innocent's initial approach to prosecuting the *negotium* had several strands. One, which reflected established doctrine, was to call upon appropriate secular authority to support the Church in combating heresy. As early as 1 April 1198 Innocent wrote to the Archbishop of Auch and mentioned at the end of his letter the need for co-operation with secular authority in suppressing heresy (*PL* 214, 71). He also set out his general views on the penalties for heresy in the decretal *Vergentis in senium* issued at Viterbo on 25 March 1199 (*PL* 214, 537–9): in particular, the property of heretics subject to papal lordship was to be confiscated by the Curia, while other property should be confiscated by secular overlords, and without respect for the rights of Catholic heirs. Whilst this provision, which was to remain a standard feature of Innocent's approach for several years, may to an extent foreshadow the idea that the lands of heretics and their supporters were 'liable to seizure', there is an important difference in that at this stage such confiscation is to be undertaken by overlords, not anyone else.

Reflecting this approach, Innocent wrote in November or December 1201 to Raymond VI urging him to expel heretics from his lands and warning him that if he failed to act then the Curia would call upon Philip Augustus, the supreme overlord of Raymond's lands, to intervene directly (Potthast, 1549). In the light of Raymond's perceived failure to respond to this and other demands Innocent began to put this threat into effect in May 1204 (*PL* 215, 361), when he wrote to Philip Augustus urging him, as the secular authority, to give direct support to Arnold Amalric and his fellow legates in fighting heresy, either in person or through his son Louis, and in particular to put pressure on his vassals, clearly with Raymond in mind although he is not mentioned by name. He again emphasises the need for co-operation between the secular powers and the Church, saying that spiritual authority and secular power should join together to defend the Church, 'so that those whom spiritual discipline fails to recall from evil should be curbed by the secular arm' ('*ut, quos a malo ecclesiastica non revocat disciplina, bracchium saeculare compescat*'); if any counts, barons or citizens refuse to expel the heretics from their land, or give them support 'you should confiscate their possessions and not hesitate to bring all their land into the royal domain' ('*ipsorum bona confisces, et totam terram eorum domanio regio non differas applicare*'). Much of the content of this letter is repeated in a letter of February 1205 (*PL* 215, 526–8).

As well as seeking the support of secular authority in suppressing heresy, Innocent was also determined to see that Raymond VI and other lords in the Midi maintained the peace and behaved as good Christian rulers should, reflecting the broader aspects of the 'peace' element in the *negotium*. Thus the diplomatic initiatives undertaken by the legate Peter of Castelnau in 1206–07 (on which see §24 n. 22 and §27 n. 33) had as their objective the establishment of peace amongst the nobles of Provence through the suppression of mercenaries and other measures, and Raymond VI's excommunication in April 1207 was largely due to his refusal to fall in with the legate's intiative. The close relationship between the need to establish peace and the suppression of heresy is also reflected in the diplomacy in Provence undertaken by the legate Milo in 1209. In

September of that year he described his work in a letter to Innocent as being aimed '*contra hereticos et pro pace ac quiete Provinciae stabilitum*', 'against heretics and for the peace and stability of Provence'.[1] Attempts would also be made to curb Raymond VI's alleged raising of unjust tolls (on which see e.g. §137 and §394), and a good idea of the range of these wider objectives of the *negotium* as it affected secular authority can be found in the *Processus* of June 1209, on which see n. 75 to §77.

A second strand in Innocent's policies was the reform and reinvigoration of the southern episcopate so as to make it a more effective agent in countering heresy.[2] In December 1198 Innocent wrote to his legate Rainier and to Archbishop Berengar of Narbonne ordering them to receive the resignation of the Bishop of Carcassonne, Otto, on account of his age and his inability to govern his diocese effectively (he was described as '*inutilis et insufficiens*': PL 214, 457–8). Archbishop Berengar of Narbonne was himself the subject of an investigation by John of St Paul, Cardinal of Santa Prisca, in 1200 (*PL* 214, 903–6), and this was the beginning of a series of moves against him, culminating in his replacement as archbishop by Arnold Amalric in 1211–12 (for details see n. 24 to §299). Action was also taken against a number of other bishops. On 18 February 1204 Innocent confirmed the deposition of the Bishop of Béziers, William of Roquessels, by the legates Peter of Castelnau and Ralph of Fontfroide (*PL* 215, 272); on 8 June 1204 an inquiry was ordered into the Bishop of Vence (*PL* 215, 366–8); and in January 1205 Innocent ordered the deposition of the Bishop of Viviers. An inquiry into the affairs of Bishop Raymond of Agde, who was accused of simony and failure to perform his duties properly, was ordered in May 1205 (*PL* 215, 642–4), while in July that year Innocent confirmed the deposition of Raymond of Rabastens, Bishop of Toulouse (*PL* 215, 682–3). Some of these bishops were sooner or later replaced by Cistercian monks: for example Fulk was elected to Toulouse in 1205 (see n. 43 to §33), while Guy of les Vaux-de-Cernay became Bishop of Carcassonne in succession to Bernard-Raymond of Roquefort in 1211–12 (see n. 24 to §299).

Initially Innocent did seek to work with the local episcopate to achieve his aims: cf. the letter of 1 April 1198 to the Archbishop of Auch noted above. But an important feature of Innocent's approach was the use of legates to represent him directly in the south and to give effect to his policies. The first legates to be appointed were the Cistercians Rainier and Guy in 1198, and the former's powers were extended in 1199 (*PL* 214, 676); they were followed by John of St Paul in 1200 (see n. 5 to §6). There is little evidence of much achievement by these legates, and so Innocent sought to reinvigorate the legatine mission through the appointment of Peter of Castelnau and Ralph of Fontfroide in 1203 (see §6), and of Arnold Amalric in 1204 (see n. 4 to §20). The legates were involved in the moves against some of the southern clergy noted above, and another important aspect of their work was to persuade local lords to swear oaths to uphold the

[1]   See *PL* 216, 124–6, and §§69–81.
[2]   See Maisonneuve, *Etudes sur les Origines de l'Inquisition*, pp. 186–93, for a discussion of this point.

peace, respect the property rights of the Church, avoid employing mercenaries, and co-operate with the Church in suppressing heresy. This, reflecting the *pax* element of the *negotium*, was a particularly important aspect of the work of Peter of Castelnau in 1203–04 (see §§6–7) and in 1206–07 (see §§27–8), and of the legate Milo in 1209 (see §§74–81).

Finally, we may note the development of the preaching campaign against heresy in the South. This began under Peter of Castelnau and Ralph of Font-froide, apparently in 1203–05, but initially enjoyed little or no success (see §20, and the comment by William of Tudela quoted in n. 5 to that section). The campaign was given a vital new direction under the leadership of Bishop Diego of Osma and his sub-prior (St) Dominic in 1206–07, and involved the use of Cistercian monks following the *vita apostolica* (see §§20–6 and 47–51). But by the end of 1207 the future of the Cistercian preaching was in doubt, especially after the deaths of Diego and of the legate Ralph (see §§49–51 and n. 79 to §51).

The idea of a crusade against Raymond VI and the heretics of the South does not seem to have taken shape until 1207–08, when the continued failure of Raymond VI and the other lords in the South to meet Innocent's demands, and of Philip Augustus to respond positively to his requests to intervene (see above and e.g. n. 65 to §72) contributed to a clear and very important shift of emphasis in Innocent's thinking.[3] In his letter of 29 May 1207 following Raymond VI's excommunication by Peter of Castelnau (*PL* 215, 1166–8, discussed in n. 35 to §27, and for extracts see Appendix F(i)), Innocent threatened to call on all good Catholic princes, not just Raymond's overlord, to dispossess him. By this stage

---

[3] It is sometimes pointed out that as early as 1198 Innocent had raised the possibility of granting indulgences similar to those enjoyed by pilgrims to Rome or Compostela to those who were prepared to support the legates Rainier and Guy in their mission against heresy in the South; this was set out towards the end of a letter of 21 April 1198 to the archbishops of the South and their suffragan bishops (*PL* 214, 81–3). The letter also at one point states: '*Scribimus etiam universo populo vestrae provinciae, ut cum ab eisdem fratribus R. et G. fuerint requisiti, sicut ipsi mandaverint, contra haereticos accingantur*', i.e. he is also writing to everyone in their dioceses, enjoining them to 'gird themselves' against the heretics, as and when they may be called upon by brothers Rainier and Guy. Some have interpreted this passage as showing that Innocent was thinking of a crusade against heresy as early as this (see e.g. Belperron, pp. 127–8; the discussions in Roquebert I, pp. 134–5; and Maisonneuve, *Etudes sur les Origines de l'Inquisition*, p. 193; the letters are also discussed in Griffe, *LC*, p. 205). Such an interpretation seems to rest wholly on taking the word *accingantur* in a literal physical sense, as implying 'to gird themselves with weapons'. However, this places considerable weight on a single word, and *accingor* is often used figuratively with the meaning 'to prepare oneself for action' in some respect, and this seems an entirely natural interpretation in this case.

Similarly the reference to the possible use of force in the letter of 1 April 1198 to the Archbishop of Auch (*PL* 214, 71, mentioned above) seems to fall well short of any suggestion of a crusade. It states: '*etiam, si necesse fuerit, per principes et populum eosdem [heretics and their supporters] facias virtute materialis gladii coerceri*', meaning that secular authority could be invoked to apply compulsion, but this was nothing new. It seems that too much may have been read into these letters in the light of later developments, and, especially since there is no other direct evidence that Innocent was thinking of a crusade at this time, there seems no reason to interpret the letters as reflecting anything more than a vigorous expression of the established view that local lords should co-operate with local bishops in driving out heresy.

Innocent's later letters of May 1204 and January/February 1205 to Philip Augustus, referred to in detail above, seem to give support to this interpretation. Despite again using martial rhetoric, he still seems clearly to be thinking of co-operation between the Church and the secular arm and not of a crusade launched by the Church, and of persuading the King to use his authority and influence as suzerain rather than urging him actually to invade his vassals' territories.

Innocent was clearly thinking of a general call to armed intervention against Raymond VI, and he threatened the *exposition en proie* of Raymond's possessions, i.e. that they would be liable to seizure by any good Catholic. The shift in emphasis was confirmed in his letters of November 1207: not only did Innocent then write to Philip Augustus, he also wrote directly to the leading barons of the north of France seeking their armed intervention: see n. 79 to §51. Raymond VI himself was not named, but Toulouse was identified as the centre of heresy. The letter also shows that at this stage at least the main charges against Raymond concerned his failure to keep the peace; suspicion of involvement in heresy was only one of numerous other charges listed.

The development of the idea of a crusade against Raymond VI and against heretics was completed in Innocent's letter of 10 March 1208 following the murder of the legate Peter of Castelnau (recorded by Peter in §§56–65, and discussed in n. 34 to §62).[4] This letter called for a crusade against Raymond VI, promising indulgences to those who took part, and clearly setting out in fully developed form the idea of a crusade against Raymond. At this stage Innocent accepted without question Raymond VI's complicity in the murder of Peter of Castelnau, identified him as the Church's main enemy, and authorised any Catholic to proceed against Raymond in person and sieze his lands.

Innocent III and the Crusade, 1209–16

The terms of Innocent's letter of March 1208 hardly suggested the possibility of a future reconciliation, and preparations for the Crusade continued throughout 1208 and during the first half of 1209 (see n. 46 to §67). Despite this, Raymond VI was able to negotiate a reconciliation with the Church which was formalised at Saint-Gilles in June 1209 (see §§77–80 and notes; again the main emphasis of the *mandata* given to Raymond VI is on the maintenance of peace). The upshot was that Raymond then joined the crusaders, and removed any immediate threat to his own lands and person. As a result the Crusade was turned against Raymond-Roger Trencavel, who had hitherto attracted no attention from the Curia. The outcome was the conquest of the Trencavel viscounties of Béziers and Carcassonne in the summer of 1209 by the crusaders, and the assumption of lordship over them by Simon de Montfort. Raymond VI's reconciliation appears to have satisfied Innocent. On 27 July 1209 he wrote to Raymond (*PL* 216, 100, and n. 79 to §80) in friendly terms, commending the reconciliation.

The legates nonetheless remained determined to pursue Raymond VI, and he was excommunicated again by them at Avignon in September 1209 (see §138). Raymond then appealed directly to Innocent. He went to Rome in person and his reception at the Curia in late 1209 was far from hostile (§§137–9 and notes), and the outcome was the letters of 25 January 1210 to Hugh Bishop of Riez,

---

[4] See also the discussion in Maisonneuve, *Etudes sur les Origines de l'Inquisition*, esp. pp. 199–209, and R. Foreville, 'Innocent III et la croisade des Albigeois', in *Cahiers de Fanjeaux*, vol. 4.

Thedisius and others (*PL* 216, 171–3, see Appendix F(iii) and notes to §137 etc.). They give the first clear statement of what was to become Innocent's basic position in dealing with Raymond VI henceforth until the Fourth Lateran Council. He insisted that Raymond should be given a genuine opportunity to clear himself of the major accusations of heresy and involvement in the murder of the legate (references to these two charges recur constantly in the letters and in the *Historia* in the next four years), emphatically reserving the final judgment to himself, and meanwhile the threat of *exposition en proie* was effectively suspended. These letters also provide the first clear hint that he might have reservations about accepting everything that the leaders of the Crusade put to him. The letter of 19 January 1210 instructing the legates to reconcile Toulouse to the Church (*HGL* VIII, 612ff, also notes to §137 etc.) is also markedly different in tone from earlier references to the city.

The success of the legates in thwarting Innocent's objectives during 1210 is described in §§162–4 and discussed in the notes thereto. Innocent's immediate reaction seems to have been to reserve judgment (see notes to §§164 and 195). However, when the legates again excommunicated Raymond VI in February 1211 and placed an interdict on Toulouse he accepted their decision without demur (see notes to §212). It is thus surprising to find Innocent's comment in his letter to Philip Augustus in August 1211 (*PL* 216, 524, n. 62 to §164), acknowledging that Raymond VI had so far failed to purge himself, but adding that 'we do not know if it is his fault'. No more is heard until May 1212, when, in a letter which again suggests that he was becoming suspicious of the crusaders, he once more instructed the legates to seek to reconcile Raymond VI to the Church (*PL* 216, 613–14, n. 5 to §368), warning them not to be 'cool or remiss' in carrying out his instructions, 'as you are said to have been so far'. This letter refers back to the letter of 19 January 1210 and once more displays a markedly conciliatory attitude to Raymond VI; it was even more specific in stating that as he had not yet been condemned Innocent could not agree to transfer Raymond's possessions to any other person ('*non intelligimus qua ratione possemus adhuc alii concedere terram eius*').

The representations of King Peter of Aragon to Innocent in the autumn of 1212, and Innocent's desire to launch a new Crusade to the Holy Land, then led to his decision to suspend the Crusade (§§367, 399 and notes). This was announced in January 1213 even whilst at the Council of Lavaur the legates were again making certain that there should be no reconciliation between Raymond VI and the Church (see §§368ff). Peter makes it clear that Innocent's decision did lead to problems for the crusaders in that the supply of new recruits from the north largely dried up for a time (see §§442–4), but Guy of les Vaux-de-Cernay continued to preach the Crusade in the north of France throughout 1213, while Simon de Montfort paid no heed to Innocent's instructions and continued his war against Raymond VI. Innocent's suspicion of the crusaders was at this stage very apparent, as is shown especially in the letter of 18 January 1213 to Arnold Amalric, Bishop Hugh of Riez and Thedisius, with its denunciation of Arnold and de Montfort for 'stretching out greedy hands to lands not tainted by heresy'

(*PL* 216, 739–40, for translation see Appendix F(iv)). In this letter Innocent seemed to accept King Peter's representations unhesitatingly.[5] Yet only four months later, responding to strong pressure from the legates and their allies, Innocent reversed his stance almost completely (letter of 21 May, given in full in §§401ff. of the *Historia*); he rejected King Peter's case and again accepted that the Toulousains (and by implication Raymond VI) had persisted in their evil ways. The contrast between his acceptance of the King's views shown in the letter of 18 January, and the letter of 21 May, is remarkable.

Even so, the door to reconciliation was kept open, and this is a notable feature of the instructions given to Peter of Benevento when in January 1214, after an interval of silence on the subject of the Crusade (and the absence of any direct reference to the Battle of Muret and the death of King Peter), Innocent appointed him to renew efforts to establish peace in the Midi (§503). Peter of Benevento was very much Innocent's own man; many of his instructions were given to him by Innocent privately and orally, and the tone of his letter to de Montfort about the new legate (*PL* 216, 959, n. 44 to §503) again indicates Innocent's realization that matters were not firmly under his control. There was further reference in the instructions to the reconciliation of the city of Toulouse, without specific mention of Raymond VI, but bearing in mind that Peter shortly afterwards obtained the submission of Raymond as well as the Toulousains, the Counts of Foix and Comminges, and the Narbonnese (notes to §§503 and 507) it seems likely that Innocent's personal briefing to his new legate also covered Raymond VI.

Peter of Benevento's apparent success in fulfilling his instructions did not prevent the crusaders continuing their campaign against Raymond VI; indeed during 1214–15 Innocent's control of the Crusade remained ineffective (note to §507). However, at no stage did he abandon his basic stance; a meeting with Raymond early in 1215 produced Innocent's letter to Peter of Benevento of 4 February 1215 (*Layettes* 1099, n. 135 to §547), again sympathetic in tone to Raymond and again insistent that since the Count had obtained absolution no decision to dispossess him could be taken before the Fourth Lateran Council.

There was then another pronounced change of emphasis in Innocent's approach. In letters of 2 April 1215 Innocent accepted the recommendations of the Council of Montpellier and wrote to Simon de Montfort in terms which seem markedly different from those used in the February letter and suggest that he might have been ready to accept Simon as Count of Toulouse without further argument (§§542, 547, 554–559 and notes). His statement that a final decision was to await the deliberations of the Fourth Lateran Council might therefore at first sight seem to be merely paying lip service to the need to observe legal forms, but his determined efforts at the Council to ensure a fair hearing for Raymond VI (notes to §571) suggest that this was not so. Indeed his partial success in resisting the demands of the southern prelates, in regard to the Count of Foix as well as

---

[5] Roquebert (I, pp. 520–3) suggests that Innocent was reluctant to risk an open breach with the crusaders before the end of 1212 because up to that time the Curia had not received the revenues earlier promised by de Montfort and his fellow leaders.

the younger Raymond, show beyond reasonable doubt the he had throughout been sincere.

This brief review of Innocent's policy towards the Crusade shows the pronounced variations in his attitude to the Toulousains and especially Raymond VI over the years of the Crusade. His attitude to King Peter of Aragon when he took up the cause of Raymond and the other southern lords in 1212–13 also underwent dramatic change between January and May 1213. Nevertheless there was a consistent thread in Innocent's policy, which was to keep open the possibility of a reconciliation between the Church and Raymond VI and the city of Toulouse, and not to allow Raymond, and indeed the other southern counts, to be formally dispossessed of their territories so long as that possibility existed. In particular, Raymond was to be given every chance to clear himself of the two major charges against him, at first by way of a formal hearing before a council of clerics, and ultimately by formal debate at the Lateran Council.

Some general conclusions are perhaps as follows. Firstly, Innocent attached great importance to observing proper procedural practice, and was determined that Raymond and the other southern counts should receive a demonstrably just hearing. This no doubt reflected his own legal training and his keen sense of justice. Secondly, he thought that he could control events from the Curia through his legates and through diplomacy, but events showed clearly that he was not master of the forces which he had unleashed. His inability to control the Albigensian Crusade parallels the experience of the Fourth Crusade earlier in his pontificate. Thirdly, even when denouncing Raymond VI in the strongest terms, he kept the door open to the possibility of a reconciliation, and his view seems to have been that this rather than the dispossession of Raymond VI was the most desirable outcome. But nonetheless he does not seem to have understood the practical problems of dealing with heresy in the Midi, nor to have appreciated the strength of the personal ambitions of some of those involved – in particular Simon de Montfort and Arnold Amalric (which the latter demonstrated especially by his determination to acquire the dukedom of Narbonne, see §561).[6] Given these circumstances it is easy to see how as time went by events ran increasingly out of Innocent's control. This was not helped by Innocent's apparent tendency to be unduly influenced by the last person to put a case to him. The letters of 25 January 1210 and 4 February 1215, written after meetings with Raymond VI, are markedly more sympathetic to the Count in their tone than letters written at other times, even if the basic stance is unchanged; similarly his letter of 19 January 1210 to the Toulousains shows a sympathetic reaction to his recent reception of their envoys. This tendency must surely have contributed to the volte-face between January and May 1213.

---

[6] Cf. Walter Ullmann's judgment on Innocent III: 'Yet, as is so often the case with men of outstanding intellectual qualities, he had a quite remarkable lack of knowledge of men and a corresponding inability to realise on what base motives men, even if they were archbishops, princes and kings, could be prompted to act' (W. Ullmann, *A Short History of the Papacy in the Middle Ages* (London, 1972), p. 207). Innocent's handling of the Albigensian crusade, and his choice of legates, amply bears out this judgment.

APPENDIX H
The Statutes of Pamiers, December 1212

The Latin text here translated is that printed in Timbal, Un Conflit d'annexion au Moyen-Age: l'application de la coutume de Paris au pays albigeois *(Paris-Toulouse, 1950), Appendix, pp. 177–84. It also appears in HGL VIII, 625–35. The translation given here is quite literal and reflects the legalistic and often cumbersome wording of the original. For the Statutes in general, see §§362–4 and notes. For a general discussion of feudal rights in the Midi in the 12th and 13th centuries, see also the article by A. Molinier in HGL VI, pp. 155–67.*

[*Document of Simon, Count of Montfort, on the government and jurisdiction of the Albigensian territory.*]

It is in the name of our Lord Jesus Christ that we make all our decisions and undertake our every action; for it is through him that we have been appointed to this, no ordinary seat of justice, so that by our wisdom and care we may right the wrongs done to God, the Church of Rome and Justice, and see to it that once made right they will unfailingly remain so. Most of all we are concerned to ensure the removal of the evil of heretics and the elimination of the ill-doing of robbers (*predonum*) and all evil-doers. Accordingly we, Simon, Count of Leicester, Lord of Montfort and by God's grace Viscount of Béziers and Carcassonne and Lord of Albi and the Razès, desiring to achieve these ends and bring peace and order permanently to this land, to the honour of God and the Holy Roman Church and our Lord the King of the French, and the benefit of all our subjects, have taken counsel of our venerable lords, namely the Archbishop of Bordeaux and the Bishops of Toulouse, Carcassonne, Agen, Périgueux, Couserans, Comminges and Bigorre and also wise men and barons and chiefs amongst my followers (*nostrorum*), and now establish the following customs (*consuetudines*) to be followed in all our territory, and order that they shall be held inviolable by everyone. The customs are these.

I. All privileges of the churches and religious houses granted by canon or human [i.e. civil] law, and their liberties, are to be kept and preserved by all men everywhere.

II. We forbid the fortification of churches or their being reduced to subjection by lay persons; further we order that such as have been fortified be demolished, or be maintained at the discretion of the bishops; but the bishops may not retain such fortifications in the *castra* and towns of other lords.

III. All first fruits be given to the churches without obstacle, following established custom in these parts, and all tithes are to be paid as is written and enjoined by the Pope.

IV. No cleric is to be taxed (*talliabitur*),[1] even on the occasion of his inheriting, unless he was a merchant (*mercator*) or had been married; and let poor widows be similarly exempt.

V. On Sundays, let no new public market (*forum venale*) be set up in future, and if it is found that such a market has been established, let it be changed to another day according to the wish of the lord of the territory and the Count.

VI. If anyone should arrest a cleric in the course of a crime or any other circumstance, even if he has only a simple tonsure,[2] he must return him without delay to the bishop or archdeacon or their representative. Anyone who detains him is to be excommunicated forthwith and compelled by his superior lord to return him.

VII. Let any inhabited house in the conquered land held in common[3] pay three Melgorian *denarii* yearly to the Pope and the Holy Roman Church as a sign and perpetual reminder that it was with the help of the Church against the heretics that it was acquired, and has been granted and confirmed in perpetuity to the Count and his successors. This sum is to be collected between the beginning of Lent and Easter.

VIII. Let no barons or knights compel men of the churches or religious houses to pay *tallia*; that is to say, any persons they [the churches and religious houses] have been masters of (*possederunt*) who have previously been free, by the gift or grant of kings and princes (*principum*) and other lords of territories, from all exactions of the lords in whose territories or towns they are living. If the control (*possessio*) of the churches or religious houses over those men has at any time been interrupted by the malice of heretics and other ill-disposed princes, and for this reason any doubt arises, the truth must be sought without delay, or definite proofs established. And if it should be found that violence has been involved, the lords of the *castra* or towns where they live must from now on abstain from making any exactions or levying *tallia* from them.

IX. Let parishioners be made to go to church on Sundays and feast days, on which all work shall cease, and let them hear the mass and the preaching in their entirety; but if on these feast days the master or mistress of any house, being present in the town, fails to come to church and stays at home, then unless they are prevented by illness or any other reasonable cause, let them pay 6 *denarii* of

---

[1] From *tallia*, a very general word for tax nowhere defined in the Statutes.
[2] Latin '*eciam si non haberet nisi coronam*'. The double negative/double conditional is confusing; our interpretation of the Latin is not shared by Roquebert (I, p. 500), who translates in the opposite sense as '*sauf s'il n'a que la simple tonsure*', 'except if he only has a simple tonsure'.
[3] '*Domus inhabitata terre adquisete communis*'; we have taken '*communis*' as genitive with '*terre*' rather than nominative with '*domus*'.

the coinage of Tours, one half to belong to the lord of the town and other half to be equally divided between the priest and the Church.

X.   In all towns where there are no churches and there are houses of heretics, let the most suitable house be made into a church and another be given to the priest to live in. If there should be a church there but the priest has no house, let one which is close to the church be given to him, to serve as a priest's house (*presbitero*) in perpetuity.

XI.   Whoever in future knowingly permits a heretic to stay in his territory, whether for money or any other cause, and confesses to or is convicted of doing so, let him for this single reason lose all his land forever and let his person be handed to the lord, to make amends according to the will of the lord.

XII.   It will be permitted to any knight or peasant (*rusticus*) to make a bequest for alms from his estate to the fifth part, according to the custom and use of France round Paris; except in the case of the baronies and forts (*forciis*), and subject to the rights of others and the preservation of the rights to which any superior lord is entitled in the land which remains to the heirs as their inheritance.[4]

XIII.   In the exercise of justice and the making of judgments let there be no exaction of fees from the parties on the pretext of any custom or request of advocates or assessors, but let justice be exercised without charge to all, and if a poor man has no advocate, let one be provided for him by the court.

XIV.   No heretical believer, even if he has been reconciled, is to be made provost or bailiff or judge or assessor in a judgment or witness or advocate; and the same is to apply to Jews, except that a Jew may be allowed to bear witness against another Jew.

XV.   No robed (*vestitus*, i.e. perfected) heretic, even if reconciled, is to have licence to remain in the town in which he took part in that perverse activity, but he will be allowed to live outside the town, in a place where the Count gives his permission.

XVI.   Clerics and men of religion, pilgrims and knights may pass through the whole of my territory free and free from the exaction of any toll, unless they should be merchants.

XVII.   The barons and knights of France are required to render service to the Count whenever and wherever there is a war against his person, arising in connection with this territory, whether already acquired or to be acquired, [such service to be given] in this territory; the number of knights to be provided is to be that on which the Count's gift to them of lands and revenues was decided. The basis will be that if the revenues assigned to them fully matched what they were

---

4   This appears to be an attempt to prevent estates being passed to the Church in mortmain.

promised, then the baron or knight concerned will be held to provide service with the promised numbers of knights for as long as the lord Count is involved in warfare for the conquered territories stated above; however, a knight who was not given a full assignment according to the previous agreement will not be required to provide service with the full number of knights, but the number of knights will be determined according to the proportion and amount of the assignment made. However, if the Count, not for his own requirements or those of his territory but of his own will volunteers to help any person or persons in a war, whether they are neighbours or distant, his above-mentioned knights are not required to follow him in this or to provide service to him, either personally or through others, unless they do this out of affection and their own goodwill.

XVIII. French knights who owe service to the Count are required to render service to him with French knights, and may not substitute for them local knights (*milites istius terrae*), for a period of twenty years; but thereafter anyone may provide service to him with any suitable knights they may find in the territory.

XIX. Knights who have been given leave by the Count to go to France must not stay there without reasonable cause beyond the time fixed for them by the Count, but the Count is obliged to wait for them after the expiry of the time-limit, without prejudice to the service due to him, for four months; but after that time he will be able without any objection from them to take possession of their land and therein do his will, unless they can show the Count in full a sufficient or unavoidable reason as to why they could not come more quickly.

XX. All barons, knights and other lords in the Count's lands are required to hand over their *castra* and forts (*forcias*) without any delay and protest according to his wishes, whether for reasons of his displeasure or not (*irato vel pacato*), that is, as often as he wishes, the *castra* and forts which they hold from him, and the Count as befits a good lord is required to hand them back in the same state and strength as they were when he received them, without loss or damage, when his business is finished.

XXI. All barons and knights of higher and lower rank, who may be summoned to a land war (whether war has been declared or not) or to help the Count if he is under siege, or in response to a *rereban*[5] are required to respond to such requests. But if a baron or knight or other lord of a territory shall be proved not to have come to help the Count in this his hour of supreme need, then unless he has sufficient reason for his refusal, his movable property, to the extent of one half, shall be placed in the hands of the Count and the lord from whom he holds his lands, for them to deal with as they wish.

XXII. If barons, knights and other lords of territories who owe service to the Count, on being summoned to provide fifteen days' service, fail to come to the

---

5   '*Arrière-ban*' in French or English. *Shorter OED* states the term derives from Frankish **hariban* (OHG *heriban*) and means the order of a (Frankish or French) king summoning his vassals to the military service due by holders of fiefs (or the body of vassals thus summoned).

place set by the Count for [assembling] the army, then, provided he has set out within the period of fifteen days,[6] one fifth of all the revenues for one year, i.e. revenues from the lands they hold from the Count shall in compensation be taken by the Count for him to deal with as he wishes and at the will of the Count [? and] unless he can provide a sufficient reason for his failure, the land he holds from the Count will be taken by the Count for him to deal with as he wishes. If he comes but without the due number of knights he shall pay for each knight missing, a double contribution for so long as the due number of knights is lacking. This same penalty shall apply to local barons and knights if they fail to provide the service they owe to the Count.

XXIII.   Let no one in the Count's territory who is under his jurisdiction and power try to build a new fort, or rebuild one that has been pulled down, without the Count's assent.

XXIV.   Knights of local origin (*indigene*) who are Catholics and have remained so far in the Catholic faith are required to give service to their lords, whether the Count or others, as they were required to give it to their own local lords before the crusaders arrived. Those, however, who were heretical believers will be required to provide service as required by the Count and barons.

XXV.   No men are to be judged to have been heretical believers or to have been heretics, except on the testimony of bishops or priests.[7]

XXVI.   No baron, knight or any other lord to whom the Count has given land in these parts, may make exactions beyond the measure of *tallia* laid down and confirmed in the documents of the same lords and the Count, whether in the name of *tallia* or *questus*[8] or in the name of bounty (*bonitas*) or any other cause, without prejudice to rents (*censibus*) and other revenues from lands, vineyards, houses, and the like, and to sentences of the courts. This *tallia* has been established and is to be counted in place of any other *tallia* or *questus* or demand, and beyond it nothing further may be exacted from anyone. But if anyone is proved to have exacted more than this, and protests have been made on that account, the Count shall be required to send to the town and the lord of the town concerned and the lord is to be compelled to determine and return the amount he has exacted beyond his charter and is to be forced to keep to his charter.

XXVII.   It will be allowed to all men who are liable to *tallia* to move from the jurisdiction (*dominium*) of one lord to that of another at their own wish; on the

---

[6]   The meaning here is not entirely clear, but the implication seems to be that a lesser penalty (loss of one-fifth of revenues) would apply if the offender had made the effort to respond to the summons rather than (as below) forfeiture of land if no excuse could be proferred.

[7]   Thus the Statutes acknowledge that it is for the Church to judge heretics. Cf. Pope Innocent III writing to Raymond VI of Toulouse in January 1209 (*PL* 216, 173), where his definition of 'manifest heretics' includes those who publicly preach against the Catholic faith, or profess or defend error, or have confessed to or been duly condemned for heresy in the presence of their prelates.

[8]   Like *tallia*, *questus* is an exaction which is nowhere defined in the document. For *questus* see also n. 23 to §379. *Quista* in XXVII below is a variant.

basis that those called free may move with their moveable goods, leaving their inheritance [of land] and dwelling (*hostisia*)[9] to their previous lord together with whatever they hold from others. However, others who are called unfree men or serfs (*proprii homines sive servi*) will similarly be able to move to the jurisdiction of another lord but must leave not only their inheritance of land and dwelling, but also their moveable goods to the previous lord. However, once any man who has left his lord is under the dominion of another, the previous lord shall not be able to exact anything further from him wherever he may be, on account of his moveable goods or *quista* or any other cause. However, no persons will be able to move to the dominion of clerics or churches, until they [presumably the clerics etc.] have agreed to this and have written on the matter to the Count and barons.

XXVIII.   No man is to be sent to prison or kept a captive so long as he can give adequate pledges of his intention to comply with the law.

XXIX.   No lord is to take pledges or any other warranty from his men, to prevent them leaving his dominion when they wish under the provisions above [section XXVII].

XXX.   According to the ancient custom of their territories and towns, the lords are to receive day work (*journalia*) from those owing allegiance to them, and are to give them food according to custom.

XXXI.   If the subjects of the princes and lords of local origin in this land become aggrieved about *talliae* and exactions and complain to the Count, then the Count must summon the lords and knights and agree a sufficient and reasonable level of *talliae* and exactions, and will be empowered, if need be, to compel them to keep this agreement, so as to prevent their subjects becoming unduly aggrieved by the undue wrongdoing of their lords.

XXXII.   The men of the towns (*homines villarum*) are to have rights of use in the woods, waters and pastures as they have had for the past thirty years [presumably meaning 'so long as those rights have been in existence for thirty years'], and if disagreement arises from this cause between the people and the lord, whoever is in possession of these rights is to retain them until the position has been established by witness on oath from the elders in the land concerned or by some other means.

XXXIII.   No man is to be imprisoned for the debt of his lord unless he had given surety or was himself a debtor.

XXXIV.   No baron or knight or burger (*burgensis*) or peasant (*ruralis*) is to dare to appropriate or seize the goods of another man by violence, nor is the injured party to dare to avenge himself without permission from his superior, but let them refer the dispute to the superior. But if they are convicted of acting against

---

9   *Hostisia* primarily meant services due to a lord in respect of tenure of a residence, then by transference, as here, the residence itself to which the service applied. See Du Cange, *Glossarium* under *hospitatus* which quotes several examples, including this passage.

this rule, or confess to having done so, he who first took the goods of another shall give in penalty to his superior lord, if a baron 20 livres (*librae*), if a knight 10 livres, if a burgher 100 sous (*solidi*), if a peasant 20 sous, and in addition let him return all that he took to the person suffering the injury as ordered by the lord, and let him give him full satisfaction for any loss inflicted. But anyone who has avenged himself [privately] shall in the same way pay a penalty to his lord and also pay compensation of 60 sous to the man from whom he took vengeance, making restitution of the property taken and making good any loss. However, the exception to this is that it shall be allowed to anyone to repel force with force without restraint.

XXXV.   No barons, knights, burgers or peasants are to dare to join together in consideration of any form of belief or oath or form any union bound by sworn oath (*conjuratio*), even on the pretext of brotherhood or any other good cause, except with the assent and agreement of the lord. If they are proved to have conspired together against their lord, they and their property shall be placed in the hands of their lord and be subject to his will. If they do swear together (albeit not against the lord, but to the detriment of other people), if they are convicted of this or confess to it, each shall give, if barons 10 livres, if ordinary knights 100 sous, if burgers 60 sous, if peasants 20 sous. However, merchants and pilgrims (*negotiatores et peregrini*), who join together under oath for the preservation of their fellowship, are exempted from this penalty.

XXXVI.   Whoever in future transports foodstuffs or any other goods or men without the knowledge of the Count, to Toulouse or any other enemies of Christ or the Count, and are convicted of this or confess to it, are to lose their inheritance [of land] for ever, together with their other goods, for this sole cause. If any sergeant or bailiff does this without the knowledge of his lord, he shall lose all his goods and his person will be subject to the power and mercy of the Count. All men and property taken whilst being so transported shall become the property of those who take them, in their entirety and without appeal.

XXXVII.   If anyone in the territory of the Count has had the opportunity of capturing enemies of the faith or of the Count, but fails to do so, and can be convicted of having so failed, his land shall be occupied and his person shall be in the hands of and at the mercy of the Count. The same penalty shall apply to anyone who has become aware of such enemies and has been unwilling to proclaim the fact and pursue them, according to the custom of the land in good faith.

XXXVIII.   Bakers are to make and sell bread according to the manner and measure or weight laid down for them by their lord; and if they fail to keep to this, whenever they go against this they are to lose all their bread; and the same is to apply to innkeepers.

XXXIX.   Prostitutes are to be placed outside the walls in all towns.

XL.   Tolls (*pedagia*) which have been established by princes and other lords for thirty-four years or less are to be totally abolished without any delay.

XLI.   Possessions subject to quit-rent (*censuales* from *cens*) are not to be given or sold if that involves loss to the superior lord.

XLII.   Quit-rents are to be paid to lords, at the dates determined, in their houses; and if those owing the rents fail to pay them by the date fixed, for each due date passed they are to pay the lord a penalty of 5 sous. But if he [the defaulter] has allowed three years to pass without payment of the rent, the lord may without protest from him give or sell [the property] to another person; but if he [the lord] keeps it in his own hands, he must return it if a payment of 5 sous is made to him for each year or due date passed, as set out above.

XLIII.   Succession to inheritances amongst barons and knights, also burgers and peasants, is to take place according to the custom and usage of France round Paris.

XLIV.   The dowries of women are to revert to their heirs, and they may make wills to cover this if they wish.

XLV.   All the wives of traitors and enemies of the Count, notwithstanding that they may be found to be Catholics, are to quit the territory of the Count to prevent any suspicion arising about them; and they will retain their lands and the revenues from their dowries, provided they swear on oath that they will make over no portion thereof to their husbands so long as they continue in a state of war against Christianity and the Count.

XLVI.   No women of high rank, whether widows or heiresses, who possess castles or *castra*, are to dare to marry, within ten years from now, with men of local origin (*indigenis istius terrae*) without the permission of the Count because of the danger to the territory; but they may marry Frenchmen as they wish, without seeking the permission of the Count or any other. But after the end of the term set they may marry amongst themselves.

I, Simon, Count of Leicester, Lord of Montfort, by the providence of God Viscount of Béziers and Carcassonne, Lord of Albi and the Razès, have affirmed on oath that I will keep the above general customs in good faith. And all my barons have similarly sworn that they will keep them, subject to any improvements or changes that may be made by the Holy Church or my barons and without prejudice to agreements made and privileges granted, oaths sworn in certain places (*aliquibus locis*) and other established customs, so long as they are found not to be in conflict with the above.

Given (*actum*) at Pamiers in our palace, 1 December 1212.

[*The main text ends here, but the Count's seal applied to the document extends to an additional sheet of parchment which contains the following.*]

The following are the customs which the Lord Count wishes to be observed between himself and the barons from France and others to whom he has given land in these parts.

Amongst barons and knights and also amongst burgers and peasants, heirs are to succeed to their inheritances according to the custom and usage (*morem et usum*) of France around Paris.

No baron or knight or other lord in our territory is to allow judicial combat (*duellum*) in his court for any reason, except in the case of treason, theft, robbery or murder.

In pleas (*placitis*), judgments, and matters concerning dowries, fiefs (*feodis*) and the apportionment of land (*particionibus terrarum*) the Count is obliged to guarantee for his barons from France and others to whom he has granted land in these parts the usage and custom observed in France around Paris.

Given at Pamiers in our palace, 1 December 1212.

APPENDIX I

William of Puylaurens' Account of the Battle of Muret, 1213

William of Puylaurens, Chronica, chapters XX and XXI (text from William of Puylaurens, ed. J Duvernoy). This account should be read in conjunction with those given in §§446–83 of the Historia, *and the notes to those sections.*

XX. At the same time the King of Aragon, having enjoyed success against the Saracens, wished to try for success against Christians. He came to Toulouse about the end of summer, took counsel with the counts and magnates and the citizens of Toulouse, went out in great strength and laid siege to the *castrum* of Muret, where Count Simon had installed a garrison which was causing great difficulties for the city of Toulouse. A great many men joined the army from the neighbouring territories.

When the Count of Montfort became aware of this, he at once hurried to help his men. Many years later I heard lord Maury, Abbot of Pamiers, a man praiseworthy in every respect and a reliable witness, who was formerly in charge of the *castrum* of Pamiers as sacristan, relating how he went to Boulbonne to meet the Count as he was on his way [to Muret]. Hearing that he was making his way to help his besieged men, and even prepared to join battle with the besiegers if they decided to wait for him in open ground,[1] the sacristan said to him: 'You have very few allies compared with the number of your adversaries, amongst whom is the King of Aragon, a man experienced and of proven ability in warfare, who has with him the counts and a very large army. It will be an unequal match if you make trial of your strength against the King and such a large force.'

At these words the Count produced a letter from his wallet, and said: 'Read this letter.' He did so, and found that it was addressed by the King of Aragon to a noble lady, the wife of a noble in the diocese of Toulouse, telling her that it was for love of her that he was coming to drive the French from the land, and containing other flattering remarks. After reading the letter the sacristan said to the Count: 'What do you wish to say about this?' He replied: 'What do I wish to say? May God be my helper, that I will have no fear of a King who comes against God's business for a harlot!' This said he carefully replaced the letter in his purse. Perhaps some servant or secretary of the lady had made a copy of this letter for the Count, thinking it a matter worthy of note; and the Count was carrying it with him in witness before God against the King, since trusting in God he had no fears that a man who seemed womanish[2] would be able to stand against him. They [the crusaders] left there and entered Muret. As they crossed the bridge, the

1 Latin '*in campo*'; possibly meaning 'on the plain'.
2 Latin '*effeminatum*'; possibly William means to imply 'under female influence' rather than 'effeminate'.

enemy would easily have been able to estimate their numbers if they wished. After they had entered the town, the venerable fathers who had come with him – Fulk, Bishop of Toulouse, Guy, Bishop of Carcassonne[3] and Thedisius, Bishop of Agde – began to look for ways of making peace or a truce, bearing in mind the uncertainties of warfare. The King would not accept either proposal, except on conditions which were dishonourable and harmful to the Church side.[4] Simon de Montfort thought it likely that if he gave Muret over to his adversaries the whole territory would rise against him and join the other side, which would create a new and dangerous situation; so, considering that he was pursuing the cause of God and the faith, whereas the others were pursuing the opposite cause and were bound with the chains of excommunication, he thought it better to risk all in a single day rather than strengthen the courage of his adversaries by ineffectual temporising. What more? The champions of Christ crucified chose to fight their battle on the eve of the Exaltation of the Holy Cross. They made confession of their sins, heard Divine service in their usual manner; then, re-freshed by the comforting nourishment of the altar and fortified by a modest meal, they took up their arms and prepared for battle. As the Count mounted his horse the stirrup-strap of his saddle broke. He stood down, and his saddle was repaired immediately. As he remounted his horse struck him on the forehead, and for a while he was stunned. Had it been his way to pay attention to portents, as many men do, he would have expected an unfavourable outcome from the battle.

They decided not to go out directly against the enemy, since that would expose their horses to showers of missiles from the Toulousains;[5] they left by a gate which looks east, whereas the camp [of the southerners] was on the west, so that the enemy, not knowing their purpose, would think they were fleeing; then they went forward a little, crossed a river and turned back to the plain to face the [enemy] army.

With the Count were those valiant men his brother Guy, Baldwin the brother of the Count of Toulouse and William of Barres, Alan de Roucy and many other armed men to the number of a thousand.

XXI. The King of Aragon then prepared for battle, but the Count of Toulouse urged instead that they should stay within their camp; they would then be able to weaken the horses of the enemy as they approached with bowshot and javelins, and it would be safer to attack them once so weakened, and easier to turn them back or put them to flight, since shortage of supplies would prevent them remaining in the town. The King refused to listen to this advice, ascribing it to fear and cowardice.

The battle lines were drawn up by the King, and they set out for the battle. The first line was given to the Count of Foix with the Catalans and a large force of

---

3   William is in error here: Peter of les Vaux-de-Cernay tells us (§508, see also §§418 and 439) that Guy returned from (northern) France in April 1214 'having spent the whole of the previous year in France'.

4   Latin '*Rege neutrum acceptante, nisi cum conditionibus indecoris parti Ecclesie et dampnosis*'.

5   I.e. the mainly infantry force attacking Muret from the west.

fighting men. On the other side, as I heard related by the lord Raymond, the last Count of Toulouse, who, being unfitted for fighting because of his age[6] had been led from the camp on an unarmoured horse to high ground from which he could see the contest, Count Simon came with his forces in three lines,[7] following his usual practice in battle. Those behind followed quickly so that they joined those in front as the first assault took place – knowing that it is an attack mounted with a united purpose that leads to victory. With their first onset they threw back the enemy, to the extent that they drove them from the battlefield as the wind drives dust from the ground; and they were unable to regroup in their rear line. Then, when they recognised the King's standard they turned to his part of the line; they rushed on him with such force that the clash of arms and the noise of blows was carried through the air to the place where the person who told me this was standing, as if a large number of axes were cutting down a wood. The King died there and many nobles from Aragon with him. The rest turned in flight and very many were slain as they fled.

The Count of Toulouse and the other Counts fled to safety. But the people of Toulouse did not know who had won the battle until they recognised the standards [of the defeated southern forces] which the crusaders were carrying back as trophies;[8] they ran from their camp where they were entrenched behind their chariots and other equipment to their boats on the Garonne, where those who were able to embark escaped. The rest either drowned or fell to the sword on the plain, to the extent that the number of dead everywhere[9] was said to be fifteen thousand.

The brothers of the Hospital of St John asked for and were granted the body, which they found naked on the field of battle (so it was said at the time) and took it away.

As the people of Toulouse fell everywhere, many were to be found who reproached them for the recent riot at Toulouse when they had killed the prisoners there. Many of those captured in the battle escaped with their lives and either died in prison or obtained their release by paying ransom.

It was not found that even one man on the Church side fell in the battle. Such was the result in this battle of Christians that arrogance and love of pleasure deservedly brought upon a King who had always enjoyed success against the Saracens. Even love for his son did not avail to draw him back from his folly, once he had embarked on it – the son he had given as hostage to his enemy because of the treaty they had made; now that enemy, had he wished, could have taken his life in revenge for the breach of the treaty.

It was pitiful to see and hear the laments of the people of Toulouse as they

---

[6] Sixteen years.

[7] Latin '*Tribus ordinibus usu ut noverat militari*'.

[8] Latin '*donec redeuntium ex tropheo vexilla notantes*'; the usual interpretation of this is as given in the translation.

[9] Latin '*ubique*', i.e. probably including those killed in the cavalry encounter. In 1850 and 1875 quantities of human remains were found at a place known as Le Petit Joffery on the banks of the Garonne, which may thus be the site of a mass grave for the slain (see Roquebert II, p. 223, and map on p. xv).

wept for their dead; indeed there was hardly a single house that did not have someone dead to mourn, or a prisoner they believed to be dead. The cause of this evil was the King. He had lost his senses, and because of his temerity everyone else rushed to behave senselessly, trusting not in the power of the Lord but in the strength of men. Their adversaries, trusting in the Lord, did not hold back because of their inferior numbers. The prayers of bishops and good men, devoutly celebrating the Exaltation of the Holy Cross, were with them on that day, when God's champions overcame the enemies of the Cross. Returning triumphant to their camp from the enemy camp they gave thanks to the Lord Jesus Christ, who had deigned to grant them, few as they were, victory over so numerous an enemy.

INDEX OF PERSONS

*(Entries may refer either to the text or to notes on the given page.
References to the notes, Introduction and Appendices are selective.)*

INDEX OF PLACES